The FAMILY COOKBOOK

in color

Marguerite Patten

HAMLYN
LONDON · NEW YORK · SYDNEY · TORONTO

© Copyright 1968
The Hamlyn Publishing Group Limited
First published 1968
Formerly published under the title
American Every Day Cook Book in 1971
This impression 1973

Published by
THE HAMLYN PUBLISHING GROUP LIMITED
LONDON   NEW YORK · SYDNEY · TORONTO
Hamlyn House, Feltham, Middlesex, England

Photoset by BAS Printers Limited,
Wallop, Hampshire
Printed in Czechoslovakia by TSNP, Martin
ISBN 0 600 33541 0

CONTENTS

FOREWORD

Marguerite Patten is to England what Julia Child, Craig Claiborne, and Erma Raumbauer are to America. She combines the warmth and television talent of Julia with the acumen and skill of Mr. Claiborne and the down-to-earth family economy of Mrs. Raumbauer.

Mrs. Patten's first cookbook, published in 1961, is testimony to her authority and popularity in Britain. It sold over one million copies. Since then she has written many cookbooks, whose combined sales have passed the six million mark, a record to be envied by any cookbook author.

Perhaps the secret of Marguerite Patten's popularity is her flair for simplification and her ability to communicate her enthusiasm for cooking. She has great imagination and ingenuity, and both these qualities were taxed to the full in 1942, when she was a senior demonstrator for the Ministry of Food. During that austere period of severe wartime food rationing she showed what miracles could be done with powdered eggs and potatoes, the weekly ration of a couple of ounces of butter, and a meager cup of milk per day, and created nutritious dishes which not only tasted interesting but looked appealing and attractive too. Through her cooking demonstrations she was a familiar figure to British housewives long before the publication of her first cookbook.

Today Mrs. Patten lives with her husband in Brighton on the south coast of England, where she is always busy writing and creating new recipes. She loves to travel and collect new material, appears frequently on television, and is the most sought-after food consultant in England. It is indeed time that she was introduced to America, for American homemakers will quickly take her into their homes, their kitchens and their hearts.

Her *Family Cookbook* is exactly that – a book for every day and everyone. It contains more than 1,000 tested recipes in all the usual culinary categories as well as invaluable additional sections such as cooking for invalids, for the elderly, for vegetarians, and for children, with a last chapter devoted to suggestions for entertaining and special occasions. The *Family Cookbook* is lavishly illustrated with over 100 of the most appetizing full color photographs ever to grace a cookbook. The pictures of such easy everyday dishes as beef stew with dumplings, spaghetti with meat sauce, Hungarian goulash, and blanquette of veal are all so luscious looking that you can't wait to start cooking. And desserts! Brandy snap cake, sponge pudding, blackberry and apple dumplings, and an apricot tart with a crust so flaky you want to eat it right off the page.

The recipes are concise and straightforward, with dozens of hints, shortcuts, and cooking techniques woven into the text. This is a no-nonsense book for every budget, catering to the novice and the experienced cook alike, and its continuous theme is Mrs. Patten's philosophy that cooking has a perpetual interest and fascination for everyone who is willing to try something new.

If you are willing – and who isn't – this book is for you.

INTRODUCTION

This is a book of cooking for every day throughout the year – meals for all occasions from family snacks to meals when you entertain, and I hope it will give you both pleasure and inspiration. In addition to the recipes, you will find useful information on cooking techniques, hints on buying food and wise shopping, 'emergency' dishes, and helpful suggestions for dealing with minor mishaps in the kitchen.

In planning the book, I have tried to include recipes to suit every budget – they range from ideas for those cooking a meal for a small household on a limited income to lavish suggestions for buffet and dinner parties; and I have included special recipes for weight watchers, invalids, children, and the elderly.

Many of the dishes in this book are illustrated by color photographs which, in addition to being inspiring, will help you to present the finished dish as attractively as possible. I would like to express my thanks to the home economists and firms who contributed these pictures. I hope this book will really help you to enjoy your day to day cooking, as well as enabling you to prepare those more exciting 'special occasion' dishes!

Marguerite Patten

GUIDE TO GOOD COOKING

WEIGHTS AND MEASURES

Frequently used food equivalents

about 3 cups beef suet, chopped ..	1 lb.
6 cups bread crumbs, fine fresh ..	1 lb.
2 cups butter or other fat	1 lb.
4 cups candied peel, chopped mixed	1 lb.
4 cups cheese, grated Cheddar ..	1 lb.
about 2 cups cherries, candied ..	1 lb.
about 1⅓ cups coconut, flaked ..	3½ oz.
3 cups dried fruit (currants, seedless white raisins, and raisins)	1 lb.
4 cups flour	1 lb.
1 tablespoon gelatin, unflavored ..	1 envelope
2 cups meat, finely diced cooked ..	1 lb.
4 cups mushrooms, button	1 lb.

4 cups nuts, chopped	1 lb.
2½ cups rice	1 lb.
2 cups sugar, brown	1 lb.
4 cups sugar, confectioners'	1 lb.
2 cups sugar, granulated ..	1 lb.

SEE AT A GLANCE

dash ..	..	..	..	less than ⅛ teaspoon
3 teaspoons ..	..	..	..	1 tablespoon
4 tablespoons ..	..	..		¼ cup
5⅓ tablespoons ..	..	..		⅓ cup
16 tablespoons ..	..	..		1 cup
2 cups ..	..	..	..	1 pint (16 fl. oz.)
4 cups ..	..	..	..	1 quart
2 pints ..	..	..	..	1 quart
4 quarts ..	..	..	..	1 gallon

OVEN TEMPERATURES

Oven temperature, where necessary, has been given in two ways in this book – at the top of the recipes you will find the approximate cooking time and under this the approximate oven temperature. Different makes of ranges vary slightly, and it is a fact that even the same make of range may give slightly different individual results at the same temperature or setting. If in doubt as to whether the temperature given is EXACTLY right for your particular oven, then do at all times refer to your own manufacturers' temperature chart. Remember the temperature given is for the center of the oven – the temperature above or below the center will vary.

The author's own personal recommendations on temperature head each recipe.

Positions in ovens

The method of heating ovens varies a little from make to make, so always read through the manufacturers' instructions and follow these. As you see, the top of both a gas and an electric oven is the hottest part.

Average gas oven
Hotter zone
Cooler zone
Coolest zone

Average electric oven
Hotter zone
Cooler zone
Hot – or moderately hot zone

The latest electric ranges should have little oven temperature variation.

PLACE NEAR THE TOP OF THE OVEN (gas or electric): small cake, sponge cakes, Yorkshire pudding, shallow tarts, flans, etc. (deeper ones are browned more evenly lower in the oven), dishes that need quick browning, e.g. macaroni and cheese, etc., meat cuts that need quick cooking, etc.

THE CENTER OF MOST ELECTRIC OVENS IS THE COOLEST PART, SO PLACE: large cakes, fruit pies, casserole dishes etc. here, also egg custards or food requiring slower cooking.

THE CENTER OF A GAS OVEN IS COOLER THAN TOWARD THE TOP, BUT HOTTER THAN LOWER DOWN IN THE OVEN, SO YOU MAY COOK: large cakes in the center (or just below the center if very rich), fruit pies, etc.

THE BOTTOM OR NEAR THE BOTTOM OF AN ELECTRIC OVEN IS SOMETIMES THE SAME HEAT AS THE TOP: so the same food may be cooked there – in some ovens, however it is less hot than toward the top, so food that needs a moderately hot position may be put here.

THE BOTTOM OF A GAS OVEN IS THE COOLEST PART, so foods that need slow cooking may be put here – egg custards, casserole dishes, etc.
By considering the approximate temperature in various parts of the oven, it is possible to have the oven filled with a complete meal or various kinds of dishes and have perfect cooking for them all. NEVER PACK THE OVEN SO FULL THAT YOU CANNOT HAVE GOOD HEAT CIRCULATION – AN OVER FILLED OVEN MEANS UNEVEN COOKING.

Choosing cooking utensils, pans, etc.

It is important to choose cooking utensils that allow adequate heat circulation. Never have baking sheets so large or so many that the oven heat cannot circulate easily. Alternate the position of layer cake pans for the maximum heat circulation – one at the top shelf left, and one at the bottom shelf center.

TERMS

In this, as in every cookbook, certain words appear quite often and may be termed 'cookery language'. It is important to understand their correct meaning.

TERMS USED IN PREPARING FOOD

BEAT – brisk movement to lighten or blend using a spoon, whip, or beater.

BIND – to blend ingredients together with an egg or a thick sauce (panada) so they form the desired consistency. The term often used for the binding agent is a 'liaison'.

BLEND – to combine ingredients thoroughly until smooth.

BLANCH – some variety meats, e.g. tripe, sweetbreads, are put into cold water, the water brought to a boil then discarded. The purpose is to whiten or 'blanch'. Almonds are 'blanched' when placed into boiling water for a short time so the skins may be removed.

CHOP – to cut food into small pieces with a sharp knife on a chopping board using a pivoting motion – one hand holds the tip of the knife on the board while the other moves the blade up and down.

CLARIFY – to clean. Generally used in connection with drippings or fat (see page 86).

COAT – to roll food in flour, egg and bread crumbs, sugar, nuts or batter (see pages 54 and 208).

CONSISTENCY OF MIXTURE – this means the appearance and texture of the mixture. It is used a great deal in cake making to describe whether the mixture should be soft, stiff, etc. (see page 256).

CREAM – beat shortening and sugar until smooth and light. Use a wooden spoon or an electric mixer.

CRUSH – to extract juice by pressing with the flat side of a knife, or a juicer, or a garlic press.

CUBE – to cut into even pieces larger than ½ inch.

CUT IN – to mix solid fat with flour using a pastry blender or a fork (see rub in).

DICE – to cut into even pieces less than ½ inch.

DREDGE – to coat liberally with a dry ingredient, generally with seasoned flour or sugar.

DUST – to coat lightly, generally with flour or sugar.

FLAKE – to divide food (fish and poultry in particular) into small pieces by a pulling or breaking motion.

FOLD – to combine an ingredient into others already beaten together, to retain lightness, e.g. flour into eggs and sugar. Use a metal spoon in a combination of a cutting motion and a lifting and turning motion.

GARNISH – to decorate any food to make it look more attractive.

GLAZE – to brush with egg, milk, or liquid and sugar before baking to give a shine *or* cover fruit in a flan (see page 229).

GRATE – to rub food against a grater to obtain small pieces, e.g. cheese, citrus fruit (for peel) etc.

GRIND – to force food through a food chopper or grinder. The size of the holes in the blade will determine the fineness of the food particles.

KNEAD – a word used in making yeast doughs (see page 288), also in handling some biscuit dough. The ingredients are pressed and rolled with the heels of the hands, to give an even texture.

MARINATE – to soak a food in any liquid to absorb flavor, and in the case of meat, to tenderize it.

MASH – to beat food, e.g. potatoes, into a smooth purée. Use a fork or potato masher.

MINCE – to chop or cut very finely.

11

PARE OR PEEL – to remove the outer skin or covering of vegetables or fruit by cutting in the former, or by stripping in the latter.

PIPE – to press a mixture, generally some form of frosting, cream, mashed potatoes, etc. through a nozzle.

PREHEAT – to heat the oven to the required temperature before putting the food in it.

PURÉE – to rub food, e.g. spinach, fruit, etc. through a sieve to obtain a soft consistency. Or in a blender.

RISE – the word used to describe the change that takes place in certain dishes which swell and become light during cooking, e.g. cakes, due to the action of the leavening agent used; or pastry and a beaten sponge cake dough where correct handling incorporates air; and bread, where yeast makes the dough ferment and so rise.

ROLL OUT – dough for pastry etc. is rolled lightly with a rolling pin to the required shape and thickness.

RUB IN – to mix solid fat with flour with your fingertips until the mixture is like fine bread crumbs.

SEASON – to add salt and pepper; in many recipes the word 'seasoning' is used to denote these. Mustard and other flavorings are listed separately. It is also the term for preparing an omelet pan (see page 207).

SCRAPE – to remove peel etc. by a scraping movement with a sharp knife. Use for new potatoes, new carrots, when it would be wasteful to peel.

SIFT – to put one or more dry ingredients, flour, salt, and baking powder usually, through a fine sieve or a sifter to remove any lumps and evenly distribute the ingredients.

STIR – to combine ingredients using a broad circular motion.

STRAIN – a) to remove food from liquid, e.g. vegetables when cooked; b) to remove bones from stock, etc.

TOSS – one method of turning a pancake (see page 208); or vegetables are tossed for a salad using a light motion.

WHIP – to beat rapidly to increase the volume and incorporate air in whipping cream or eggs.

WORK – the method of moving eggs in an omelet (see page 206).

TERMS USED IN COOKING

BAKE – to cook in the oven with dry heat without using additional fat. Custard, cakes, cookies, and pastry are baked. When applied to meats, it is called roasting.

BASTE – to spoon liquid sauce, or fat over meat, poultry or other food while cooking, to keep moist and to add flavor.

BOIL – to cook in water at boiling point – 212°F. Liquid is boiling when it bubbles hard. Many foods are brought just to a boil, and then the heat lowered so the food simmers – see next column.

BRAISE – to brown meats or sometimes vegetables in a small amount of hot fat, then cover tightly, and cook slowly. Wine or other liquids are often added.

BROIL – to cook 2–5 inches under the broiler, generally a quick process.

COOK IN LIQUID – to brown in hot fat, if desired, cover with liquid, cover tightly, then cook below the boiling point.

CURDLE – this means that ingredients separate and look lumpy instead of smooth. This may happen in egg dishes; cheese sauce, or when adding eggs to a creamed mixture.

FRY – to cook in fat; sometimes a very small amount is used for pan-frying or shallow frying, sometimes a larger amount (see page 86). The correct temperature of fat must be used in frying (see page 54 for testing this).

PANBROIL – to cook uncovered in a skillet without adding fat or water. The fat is removed as it accumulates.

PANFRY – to cook uncovered in a skillet in a small amount of fat.

PARBOIL – to partially cook in boiling salted liquid e.g. parsnips before roasting.

POACH – to cook eggs or fish in liquid below the simmering point. Eggs may be cooked in a special pan over water.

ROAST – to cook on a rack in the oven in an open roasting pan with the fat-side up. Do not add water, or cover, or baste.

SAUTÉ – to fry in a small amount of fat, stirring occasionally.

SCALD – to heat almost to the boiling point, or until small bubbles form at the edges of the pan; such as milk.

SIMMER – to cook steadily in liquid. You should see occasional bubbles on the surface. The temperature is 180 to 190°F. Cover pans when simmering food for a long time, otherwise the liquid evaporates. Sometimes the liquid needs to become thicker, in which case remove the cover.

STEAM – to cook in steam rather than liquid. A proper steamer which is put over a pan of water is ideal. Otherwise use a small quantity of water so the food is not immersed (see page 164).

STEW – to cook slowly by simmering in liquid to cover the food in a closed pan or casserole.

USUAL FRENCH TERMS

In cookery certain French words have become an 'everyday language' and the most usual are given below.

AU GRATIN – means browned on top with a crisp bread crumb topping; often cheese is mixed with the crumbs but this is not essential.

BAIN-MARIE – used for caramel custard, etc. – e.g. a container of water, in which dishes are cooked.

BOUQUET GARNI – a selection of fresh herbs tied in a small bunch with white thread. They generally include bay leaf, thyme, parsley, rosemary or tarragon (or marjoram) or other herbs. Sage may be added, but may be omitted in some dishes since it has a very definite flavor.

CROUTON – a small toasted cube of bread.

FLAMBÉ – to sprinkle a food with brandy etc., then ignite, and serve.

GRATINEE – means browned on top – see the French onion soup gratinée on page 45.

MORNAY – means in a rich cheese sauce.

Names of some of the classic garnishes and sauces which give their names to dishes are on pages 87, 88.

SUCCESSFUL HOME COOKING

Success in cooking and catering depends on so many factors. The following pages will, I hope, assist in giving you interesting ideas for good, nourishing and appetizing meals.

Selecting food

FOOD THE FAMILY NEEDS

PROTEIN, the most important body-building food, is found in fish, meat, eggs, cheese, milk, peas, beans, and lentils. It ensures healthy growth in children and teenagers and maintains strength in adults.

FAT is important to create a feeling of warmth – and fats are in butter, margarine, shortening, lard, oil, and fat in meat and oily fish.

CARBOHYDRATES. These foods – both starches and sugars – create energy, so are necessary in the diet of the whole family.

STARCHES are found in flour and everything made with flour, e.g. cakes, cookies, pasta and also in some vegetables, e.g. potatoes.

SUGARS are in anything made with sugar – cakes, candy, jam, marmalade, sugar itself, honey, molasses, corn syrup, etc.

There are minerals essential to health; two of the most important are:

IRON which ensures healthy red blood – is in liver, heart, kidney; in bread and flour, eggs, cocoa, molasses; in dried fruits such as apricots and prunes, and in dark green vegetables, e.g. spinach and water cress.

CALCIUM helps to build healthy teeth and bones and keeps the body strong – the absorption of calcium into the body is helped by Vitamin D. It is in cheese and milk.

VITAMINS

VITAMIN A, promotes healthy growth, a good skin, and good eyesight and is found in oily fish (herrings, for example), in butter, margarine, eggs, liver, carrots, and green vegetables.

VITAMIN B, this group of vitamins is all-important and helps to prevent tiredness – they are found in wheat germ (so are present in flour) and in yeast (that is why bread is an essential food).

VITAMIN C, helps to build up resistance to infection and promotes a healthy skin. It is found in many fruits, particularly citrus fruits, black currants, and strawberries, lightly cooked or raw green vegetables, and to a limited degree in potatoes, particularly when new.

VITAMIN D, which comes from sunlight, as well as food, is another factor in healthy growth and the formation of good teeth and strong bones. This is in oily fish, butter, margarine, eggs, and liver.

Following recipes

In order to have the maximum success with the recipes in this book, read them through quickly before starting to assemble the ingredients, to ensure:—

a) You have sufficient time to cook the dish in the manner described; for if the recipe says 'simmer gently' for 3 hours, you risk spoiling the ingredients if you 'boil steadily' for a shorter period. In this case it would be wiser to choose another recipe, where the cooking time is shorter.

b) You have the ingredients given in the recipe – naturally minor substitutions of vegetables in meat dishes, soups, etc. do not matter, but it is very important to keep to the basic proportions in cakes and puddings.

c) When you have decided you have both the time and ingredients to make the dish. Follow the method of mixing described, i.e. folding, beating, etc. – these terms are described on pages 11–13. The right technique of handling the ingredients can make all the difference between success and failure.

d) Measure carefully; all measures are level – and in standard measuring utensils.

e) The cooking time in the recipes has been tested carefully, but naturally the quality of food varies, also the size into which meat, vegetables, etc. are cut makes a difference, so you may well find that in a few cases the dish cooks in a slightly shorter time – do test early. On the other hand, it could take a little longer. Timing is particularly important in the case of cake making.
The size of the cake pan is given in each recipe, but if this is changed then the cooking time will alter – see page 256. Generally it is not recommended to change pan sizes.

f) The number of servings is given in each recipe; these are for average portions.

Good kitchen tools and gadgets

Good tools make food preparation and cooking easier. There are many labor-saving tools available today and if selected with care they are most helpful. Make certain that the particular pieces of equipment will help you personally, for often when seen in a store they are tempting, but they may be designed to do jobs which have little bearing on your particular needs.

TOOLS FOR CUTTING, ETC.

BLENDER: the rotating blades are used to purée, whip, crumb, grate, chop, or liquefy foods.

CHOPPING BOARD: although most laminated surfaces withstand cutting, they can be harmed by continual chopping, so a wooden board is a great asset.

GRATER: choose one with holes of various sizes. Do wash and dry well, but remove any surplus food with a brush. Always stand the grater on a plate or chopping board to make certain no food is wasted.

GRINDER: make sure you choose a model sufficiently heavy to deal with reasonable quantities of meat, etc., and check that the screw-on attachments are suitable for your particular table. Always wash and dry a grinder very thoroughly.

KITCHEN SCISSORS: these are ideal for cutting chicken into pieces, chopping parsley or cutting dates or marshmallows. If you buy the fairly big ones, they may be used for snipping poultry.

KNIVES: spend as much as possible on these, for they should last a long time. You need one or two small knives for preparing fruit, vegetables, etc.; a cook's knife for slicing and chopping; a bread knife; a filleting and/or boning knife are both also very useful to have. Store knives carefully so the tips are not harmed. Many other shapes are also useful.
For slicing and shredding you can occasionally get attachments for electric mixers, or use a mouli grater or food mill.

POTATO PEELER: for paring vegetables. Remember you can obtain one for left-handed people as well as right-handed.

VEGETABLE SCOOP OR MELON BALLER: for making potatoes, carrots, and melon into small balls before cooking or serving.

TOOLS FOR HANDLING FOOD

A PERFORATED SPOON: this is excellent for lifting poached eggs out of water, etc.

RUBBER SPATULA: ideal for removing the last of the cake batter from bowls.

TONGS: it is a great mistake to pierce meat with a fork while it cooks (because you lose some of the juice and therefore some of the flavor). Tongs are the ideal tool for turning meat, sausages, and bacon.

TOOLS FOR MEASURING

MEASURING CUPS: use a glass cup for liquids, reading the measurement at eye level. Use graduated nested cups for non-liquid measurements. Dry ingredients such as flour, sugar, and confectioners' sugar are spooned lightly into the measure, then the excess scraped off with a knife or spatula. Brown sugar is measured firmly packed into the measure. Grated cheese, coconut, chopped nuts, and bread crumbs are measured lightly packed.

A SET OF MEASURING SPOONS: these are useful to make certain you consistently use the same measure.

TOOLS FOR PREPARING FOOD

ROLLING PIN: for pastry, crushing crackers, or making fine dry or toasted bread crumbs.

BRUSHES: the type known as a pastry brush is used for brushing fat in pans, for glazing the top of pastry, flans, etc. see page 220. It is a good idea to have two of these. You also need a stiff brush for washing vegetables.

COLANDER: this is very necessary for washing fruit, vegetables, and for draining.

CUTTERS: plain and/or fluted and decorated for making cookies, tarts, etc. While plastic ones may be obtained, they are generally of metal, so should be washed and dried well. Flour lightly when using to ensure a good cutting edge.

SIEVE: for making a purée of fruit and vegetables, straining, etc. A nylon mesh is better for all purposes, since it does not affect the flavor of acid fruits.

WOODEN SPOONS: choose them with varying lengths of handle, since most people prefer a short handle when creaming and stirring, but a spoon with a long handle is safer to use when making jam.

UTENSILS FOR COOKING FOOD

CAKE PANS AND PANS FOR BAKING: these are so many and varied and have such a bearing on the cooking time etc. of cakes that a full description will be found on pages 256–257.

CASSEROLES: these are of various types and you will find them described more fully in the section dealing with casserole cooking.

FLAN RINGS: these are the easiest and most efficient way of making a good pastry flan. Choose a plain one for savory flans, a fluted one for sweet flans. They resemble a round layer cake pan with a removable bottom.

PAPER: paper is used both in preparing food and in cooking. There is a considerable range of papers today – parchment paper for cooking, which gives browning; foil, which keeps in the flavor and juices (see page 111), wax paper for wrapping; paper towels for draining food, wiping out pans, etc.

PRESSURE COOKER: a pressure cooker enables food to be cooked in a very short time. You will find notes about cooking food by this method in the book – page numbers are in the index.

ROASTING PANS: these may double for a 9-inch by 13-inch pan used for cakes, or be a larger pan, if desired. A wire rack should fit in the bottom.

SAUCEPANS, SKILLETS, ETC.: saucepans and skillets are made in a wide range of materials. They are obtainable with a plastic resin coating, which means the food does not stick and less fat is required cooking. This finish may be harmed by careless use or cleaning so follow the manufacturers' instructions. Ceramic saucepans and skillets mean the food may be served in the cooking utensil, where suitable.

The metals used include iron, copper, aluminum and stainless steel.

Saucepans should be well soaked if food sticks in them and cleaned gently rather than scratching with knives or harsh cleaners. Choose a good range of sizes in saucepans.

Skillets and omelet pans give better service if they are well seasoned before using. Information about this is on page 208.

STEAMER: a one or two-tier steamer enables a whole meal to be cooked on one gas burner. Make certain you have a steamer that fits securely over the pan.

HORS D'OEUVRES

Although soups are often served as a first course, the hors d'oeuvres in this section may precede the soup at a formal meal or take the place of a soup in a less substantial menu.

Wise choice of hors d'oeuvres

Select a light hors d'oeuvre, such as fruit juice or fruit, if you are having a substantial main course. If the dessert is based on fruit, however, you may not wish to serve this twice. A fish hors d'oeuvre is a wise choice if meat or poultry follow. Pâté, salami or other meats are ideal if fish constitutes the main course.

Ways to serve hors d'oeuvres

Fruit juices – frost the rims of the glasses by dipping them into water or egg white then granulated sugar.
Serve grapefruit, melon balls, etc., in small dishes or glasses and set these in a larger dish filled with crushed ice. Use fresh mint leaves, orange twists, or cherries to garnish.
Form a soft pâté into a round shape with either an ice cream scoop or soup spoon; this looks more interesting than the usual slice.
If you do not have a special hors d'oeuvre dish, serve mixed hors d'oeuvres on individual plates or arrange dishes on a long thin tray.
Canapés should be arranged on flat dishes or trays, so they are easy to handle, and they must be 'bite-sized' and the filling fairly firm, for it is very difficult to stand up, hold a glass, (and maybe a handbag in the case of a woman) and try to eat canapés.

To use leftover hors d'oeuvres

Fruit juices – put in a cool place. Serve again later, mixing with another juice to make a change. Add to fruit salads.
Tomato juice – add to a soup or stew.
Pâté – store carefully, cover well and use for sandwich fillings or as a stuffing for hard-cooked eggs, or tomatoes, (see page 205).
Other hors d'oeuvre ingredients may be used as sandwich fillings.
Canapés do not keep well, so plan quantities carefully.

Easy remedies when things are wrong

PROBLEM – if fresh grapefruit or melon seems dry and tasteless, it is probably unripe.
TO REMEDY – counteract by sprinkling with fresh orange juice and/or sherry.
PROBLEM – if fish or meat pâtés are dry and hard on the outside – the mixture was too dry before cooking, or the pâté was cooked with inadequate protection, (see page 26).
TO REMEDY – remove pâté from the dish, cut away any hard edge, beat cream into the mixture and press back again into the dish to form a neat shape.
PROBLEM – if smoked fish is dry – it has been exposed to the air or is slightly old.
TO REMEDY – *first make certain it is fresh enough to eat.* Sprinkle with a little lemon juice and a few drops of oil; let stand to marinate for a short time.
The type of food served as a canapé varies so much that it is difficult to make general statements – see the various sections on eggs, cheese, pastry, etc. Remember toast will become soft in a short time, so toppings may be put on fried bread, if desired, or on buttered crackers.

FRUIT HORS D'OEUVRES

These will always taste more pleasant if served very cold, so, where possible, chill fruit juices (including tomato juice) and fruit before serving.

Fruit juices

CANNED OR FRESH ORANGE JUICE. To make this mor interesting, blend with a little pineapple juice i desired.

 French onion soup, page 45

Brown vegetable soup with salmon dumplings, page 35

Shellfish, page 51

CANNED GRAPEFRUIT JUICE. This is generally more practical than fresh.

CANNED PINEAPPLE JUICE. This is delicious if poured over one or two bruised fresh mint leaves, then strained into glasses.

CANNED TOMATO JUICE. Add seasoning and lemon juice to taste. Serve with Worcestershire sauce. Allow approximately ⅔ cup per person.

Avocados

These have become extremely popular as an hors d'oeuvre and due to the ready acceptance of them, they are available in shops throughout most of the year. To be palatable an avocado must be ripe, and it is ripe when it yields to very gentle pressure. The most popular way to serve them is with a French or vinaigrette dressing or filled with shellfish.

Avocado vinaigrette

Cooking time   *None*

2 avocados · vinaigrette sauce (see page 186) little lemon juice.

Halve the avocados just before serving. Remove the pits and discard, and fill cavity with vinaigrette sauce. If halving them some little time before the meal, they must be sprinkled with lemon juice to prevent discoloration. Avocados are an acquired taste, so ascertain everyone will like them or serve an alternative.   *Serves 4*

Avocado with shellfish

Cooking time   *None*

2 avocados
either 3–4 tablespoons mayonnaise *or* use the sauce for the shrimp cocktail (see page 24)
approximately ¼ cup shelled cooked shrimp *or* the equivalent in flaked crab *or* lobster meat.

Halve the avocados just before serving. Remove and discard the pits. Blend the mayonnaise or sauce with the fish, pile into the center of the avocados and serve. They may be garnished with wedges of lemon or the fish may be served in a vinaigrette or French dressing, if desired.   *Serves 4*

Grapefruit

If the grapefruit are very small, allow 1 per person and remove from the skin in exactly the same way as a fresh orange, (see page 169). Prepare as grapefruit cocktail. Normally, however, half a grapefruit is allowed per person.
Most grapefruit are golden. But do not discard one if the peel is slightly darker and slightly shrivelled – it will be very ripe and beautifully sweet. Pink grapefruit, the flesh of which is pink, has a particularly fine flavor.

Cold grapefruit

Cooking time   *None*

2 grapefruit · granulated sugar
TO GARNISH: 4 candied *or* maraschino *or* canned cherries.

Halve the grapefruit, loosen each segment from the skin and the center so it is easy to remove. The fruit is more juicy if sprinkled with a little sugar and allowed to stand for awhile. Garnish with cherries and serve with extra sugar.   *Serves 4*

While many people like to remove the center pith from the grapefruit, others find that if the segments are well loosened from the membrane and from the rim of the fruit it is easier to lift out the fruit if the center is left untouched.

Broiled grapefruit

Cooking time   *1–2 minutes*

2 grapefruit · 1–2 tablespoons butter
2–3 tablespoons brown sugar
½ teaspoon cinnamon

Prepare the grapefruit as when serving the fruit cold. Spread with the butter (this is easier if it is slightly softened first). Sprinkle with the sugar mixed with the cinnamon and put under the broiler until the top bubbles. This is a very good way to serve grapefruit which is not very juicy.   *Serves 4*

Grapefruit cocktail

Cooking time   *None*

Fruit from 2 fresh grapefruit *or* medium can of grapefruit · granulated sugar to taste.
TO GARNISH: 4 candied *or* maraschino *or* canned cherries.

Put the grapefruit segments into glasses, sweeten to taste and garnish with cherries.   *Serves 4*

GRAPEFRUIT AND ORANGE COCKTAIL
Use half grapefruit and half can mandarin oranges or fresh orange segments.

MIXED FRUIT COCKTAIL
Melon, orange, and grapefruit make a refreshing blend of flavors. Mix together and serve in glasses garnished with fresh mint leaves or a twist of orange.

Types of melon

There are many types of melon and some of the very best are Cantaloupe, Persian and casaba (these are generally the most expensive), as well as honeydew and watermelons.

To tell that a melon is in perfect condition press gently but firmly at either end and the flesh should yield just a little; do not press too hard otherwise you may bruise the flesh. Melon is improved if chilled lightly before serving but it should never be stored in the refrigerator for any length of time, since when cut it absorbs smells from other food.

Melon with ginger

Cooking time   *None*

1 large melon *or* 2 small melons (1 for each 2 servings)
TO GARNISH: orange slices *or* maraschino cherries
TO SERVE: granulated sugar · ground ginger
little sherry (optional).

Cut the large melon into wedges. Scoop out the center seeds, and serve with a spoon and fork, or knife and fork.

They look more attractive if the flesh is cut into slices down, loosened all around and left in place on the rind, but pulled out, slightly sideways and alternately first to one side and then to the other, to give a serrated effect. Garnish with either a twisted orange slice or maraschino cherry. Serve granulated sugar and the ginger separately. If desired, sprinkle with a little sherry.   *Serves 4*

Melon cocktail

Cooking time   *None*

1 medium melon · granulated sugar to taste
3 tablespoons orange juice *or* 1 tablespoon lemon juice *or* 1 tablespoon sherry.
TO GARNISH: sprigs of mint · maraschino cherries.

This is an excellent way of serving a melon which may have one small blemish. Halve the melon, remove and discard the seeds, then scoop out the flesh with a melon ball cutter or cut it away from the skin and dice neatly. Put into glasses and sprinkle with sugar. Add either a little orange juice, lemon juice or sherry. Serve as cold as possible. Garnish with fresh mint and/or maraschino cherries.
                                                            Serves 4

MELON GINGER COCKTAIL
Prepare the same as for melon cocktail but add finely diced preserved ginger and just a little ginger syrup diluted with orange juice or sherry. Decorate with small pieces of preserved ginger.

VEGETABLE HORS D'OEUVRES

Many vegetable and salad dishes could be served as an hors d'oeuvre – stuffed eggplant (see page 338), asparagus mornay, ratatouille (see page 171), salad niçoise (see page 170) are four well-known examples. They may also form part of a mixed hors d'oeuvre. Some of the most popular, however, are:

Artichokes

Cooking time   *45–60 minutes*

4 globe artichokes · salt · $\frac{1}{3}$ cup butter.

Cut the stem from the bottom of each artichoke, discard the outer bottom leaves and wash well in cold water. Trim the sharp leaf tips if desired or do this when cooked. Simmer steadily in boiling salted water for about 45 minutes until the base of the leaves and the artichoke hearts feel tender when tested with the tip of a knife. Drain well and trim the leaves if you have not already done so. Serve with melted butter, dipping the base of each leaf into the butter and eating the fleshy part. The artichoke heart is eaten with a small knife and fork, the leaves with the fingers, and the hairy choke discarded, so finger bowls should be put on the table, (see asparagus).   *Serves 4*

ARTICHOKES WITH VINAIGRETTE DRESSING
Cook the artichokes as described above, then drain and cool. Remove the sharp leaf tips with kitchen scissors and pull out the center hairy choke, leaving a cavity. Fill this with vinaigrette dressing (see page 186) just before serving.

Corn on the cob

Cooking time   *4–5 minutes*

4 corn ears · $\frac{1}{4}-\frac{1}{3}$ cup melted butter.

Strip off the husks and silks and put into boiling water. Simmer gently 4–5 minutes, or until tender, adding salt toward the end of the cooking time. Do not boil too quickly or over-cook, otherwise the corn becomes tough. Drain and serve with melted butter. There are special holders that can be inserted at either end to make the corn cob easier to hold. If not available put a fork in either end. Have finger bowls on the table, (see asparagus). Frozen corn may be used instead of fresh, if so follow the package directions.   *Serves 4*

Asparagus

Cooking time   *20–30 minutes*

Bunch of asparagus · salt · ⅓ cup butter.

Scrape the bottom of each asparagus stalk, then cut the stalks level – try to have these sufficiently short so they stand upright in the tallest pan available. Wash well in cold water, then tie into one large or four smaller bunches – this allows the steam to penetrate and gives more even cooking. Half fill the pan with water, add salt to taste and bring to a boil. Put in the asparagus and lower the heat so the water boils steadily. If it boils too quickly the bunches will fall over and this will damage the delicate tips. Put a cover on the pan and cook until tender – this will vary with the thickness of the stalks. Remove from the pan, drain well, and carefully put onto heated plates. Serve with melted butter. Since the asparagus is held in the fingers and dipped into the hot butter it is essential to put a small finger bowl of water beside each person so he may dip his fingers into it to remove the butter. Soup cups could be used instead. Heated canned or cooked frozen asparagus may be served instead of fresh.   *Serves 4*

ASPARAGUS AND VINAIGRETTE DRESSING
Cook asparagus as above. Allow to cool and serve with vinaigrette dressing instead of butter.

EGG HORS D'OEUVRES

Egg dishes, because they are light and so do not spoil the appetite for the main course, are ideal to serve as an hors d'oeuvre – choose omelets, stuffed eggs, etc. (see pages 196–209). The following oeufs en cocotte – eggs baked in small individual dishes – are ideal as the start to a meal. The flavoring may be varied according to the ingredients available.

Oeufs en cocotte

Cooking time   *10–15 minutes*
Oven temperature   *350°F.*

2 tablespoons butter · ¼–½ cup cream.*
FLAVORING: about 8 cooked *or* canned asparagus tips *or* some sliced fried mushrooms *or* diced cooked ham, etc. · 4 eggs · seasoning.

* Whipping cream will form a golden crust which looks very attractive but coffee cream may be used.

Put the butter and half the cream in the bottom of 4 small ovenproof dishes and top with flavoring. Break the eggs gently into a cup, so they may be transferred to the dishes without breaking, pour on top of the butter, cream and flavoring. Season lightly. Add the remaining cream. Bake for 10–15 minutes in a 350°F. oven or until the eggs are lightly set. Serve with hot toast and butter.   *Serves 4*

If a light main dish follows it is best to allow 2 eggs per person.

Eggs Florentine

Cooking time   *5–15 minutes plus cooking of spinach and eggs*

1–1½ cups creamed spinach · 4 hard-cooked eggs
1¼ cups white sauce (see page 183)
¼–¾ cup grated cheese.

Arrange the spinach on the bottom of an ovenproof dish. Top with the halved eggs and the sauce. Sprinkle with grated cheese and heat for a few minutes under the broiler or in the oven.
    Serves 4 as hors d'oeuvre or 2 as a main course

Mimosa eggs

Cooking time   *10 minutes*

6 eggs · 3 tablespoons mayonnaise
½ cup shelled cooked shrimp · seasoning.
TO GARNISH: lettuce · cucumber · tomato.

Hard-cook the eggs for 10 minutes, plunge into cold water at once to prevent a dark line forming round the yolk. When cold, remove the shells and halve the eggs lengthwise. Remove the yolks carefully. Blend the mayonnaise with the shrimp, chopping them if large. Season the egg whites lightly, then fill with the shrimp. Arrange on a flat dish and garnish with lettuce, thinly sliced cucumber and tomato. Rub the egg yolks through a coarse sieve so they fall over the top of the egg cases like mimosa flowers.   *Serves 4*

Instead of shrimp, diced ham or salami could be used – or flaked crab or lobster meat or cooked or canned salmon.

FISH HORS D'OEUVRES

Many fish dishes, given in the chapter beginning page 48, are suitable for an hors d'oeuvre – shellfish, shrimp in particular, being extremely popular. Fried shrimp (see page 64) is a good choice to serve at the beginning of a meal since it may be fried then served at once, without having to be kept hot; whereas if fried shrimp is the main dish it needs to be fried before the hors d'oeuvre and kept hot.
Serve smaller portions of all the fish dishes – a dish that serves 4 as a main course will be enough for 6–8 as an hors d'oeuvre.
Other suitable hors d'oeuvres are fish cocktails and smoked fish.

Shrimp cocktail is given below but flaked whitefish, flaked salmon or a mixture of fish may be used instead of *all* shrimp. Try mixing shrimp, mussels, whitefish, and shredded smoked salmon for a very interesting fish cocktail. Allow about 1 oz. PREPARED shrimp per person, and 1½–2 oz. flaked fish per person.

Serve fish cocktails with brown bread and butter. Rollmop herrings (see recipe below and page 65), in various forms are another excellent hors d'oeuvre.

Shrimp cocktail

Cooking time   *None*

FOR THE COCKTAIL SAUCE: ¼ cup stiff mayonnaise (see page 186)
1 tablespoon tomato ketchup, *or* tomato paste, *or* skinned fresh strained tomatoes
1 tablespoon Worcestershire sauce
3 tablespoons whipping cream *or* evaporated milk
seasoning · little celery salt (*or* chopped celery)
little finely chopped onion (optional)
little lemon juice
lettuce · 1 cup shelled cooked shrimp.
TO GARNISH: lemon.

To make the sauce; mix all the sauce ingredients together and taste to check seasoning and lemon juice.
To make cocktail; this may be arranged in glasses or flat small dishes. Shred the lettuce very finely, so it may be eaten with a spoon or small fork. Top with the shrimp and cover with the sauce. Garnish with lemon wedges or slices. Serve as cold as possible.
Serves 4

Chunky herring salad

Cooking time   *None*

6 or 8 rollmop herrings
about 1 lb. small cooked new potatoes
small piece cucumber · few cooked peas
vinaigrette dressing (see page 186).
TO GARNISH: fresh mint or sage · chopped parsley.

Lift the herrings out of the liquid, drain well – some of the strained liquid could be used in the vinaigrette dressing if making this specially. Arrange the herrings on a flat dish. Blend the potatoes, diced cucumber, and peas and toss in a little dressing. Put around the herrings. Garnish with a sprig of mint or sage and chopped parsley. Illustrated on page 39.
Serves 6 as an hors d'oeuvre or 3 as a main course

Smoked fish

Arrange the fish with a garnish of lettuce and lemon and serve with brown bread and butter, and the accompaniments given in the individual instructions.

EEL – make sure the eel flesh is white, not dry looking. This may either be bought in fillets, which are already skinned, or whole. If the latter, then remove the skin before serving. Eel is very satisfying and approximately 1–1½ oz. of eel fillets or 2–2½ oz. of the whole eel should be allowed per person. Serve with horseradish sauce.

MACKEREL – this is less plentiful than some other smoked fish, but it is delicious. Allow approximately 4–6 oz. per person and, since this is very rich, it is excellent with scrambled eggs.

SALMON – make sure the salmon looks moist and pink. It is possible to buy cheaper smoked salmon than the Scotch variety, which is very good although not such a good color. Serve with cayenne pepper or paprika and plenty of lemon. Allow 1½–2 oz. per person. Illustrated on page 125.
A very good hors d'oeuvre is to serve a small quantity of smoked salmon with a few shrimp. Another interesting variation is to serve rolls of smoked salmon with very creamy spinach in tiny pastry shells.

TROUT – make sure the trout look reasonably oily on the outside. These keep well but do dry sometimes. Remove the skin before serving; the head is sometimes left on. Serve with horseradish sauce or cream and lemon. Allow 4–6 oz. per person.

Mock smoked salmon

Cooking time   *None*

frozen kipper fillets · little oil
little vinegar · seasoning.

Let kipper fillets defrost, then put on a flat dish (allowing 1 per person). Cover with a little oil, vinegar and seasoning and particularly a good shaking of pepper. Let stand for several hours, remove from the dressing, and serve in the same way as smoked salmon with lemon and brown bread and butter.

Fresh kippers may be used, but make sure all the bones are removed.

Smoked salmon and shrimp whirls

Cooking time   *None*

Approximately ¼ lb. smoked salmon
¾ cup shelled cooked shrimp
3 tablespoons stiff mayonnaise (see page 186)
squeeze lemon juice · lettuce.
TO GARNISH: lemon.

Lay the slices of smoked salmon flat – try to get these cut in fairly large pieces. Blend the shrimp with the mayonnaise and lemon juice. Arrange lettuce leaves on the serving plates. Put the shrimp mixture onto the smoked salmon and roll firmly. Arrange on the lettuce and garnish with slices of lemon. *Serves 4*

Cod's roe pâté

Cooking time None

¼ lb. smoked cod's roe · ¼ cup cream*
squeeze lemon juice · few drops Tabasco sauce.

TO SERVE: short crust pastry *or* toast.
TO GARNISH: salted almonds · lettuce · lemon.

* Choose whipping cream for a rich pâté or coffee cream for a lighter pâté.

Blend together the cod's roe and cream. Flavor with a little lemon juice and a few drops of Tabasco sauce. Spread on thin strips of crisp short crust pastry and garnish with salted almonds, or serve with hot toast garnished with lettuce and lemon wedges. *Serves 6*

To make a milder pâté, add approximately ¼ cup very fine fresh breadcrumbs and beat well into fish. Continue as above.

Salmon cream

Cooking time 10 minutes

2 tablespoons butter · ¼ cup all-purpose flour
⅔ cup milk · medium can salmon
⅓ cup whipping cream · 3 tablespoons mayonnaise
small piece cucumber
1½ teaspoons lemon juice · seasoning.
TO GARNISH: lettuce · lemon.

Heat the butter, stir in the flour and cook for several minutes, then gradually blend in the milk and cook until a thick smooth sauce (this consistency is a panada or binding sauce). Flake the salmon, remove the skin and bones and put into the sauce with any liquid from the can. Add the lightly whipped cream and mayonnaise, peeled diced cucumber, lemon juice and seasoning to taste. Shred the lettuce finely and put into glasses or on shallow dishes. Pile the cream mixture on top and garnish with wedges or twists of lemon. Serve with brown bread and butter. *Serves 4*

MEAT HORS D'OEUVRES

The most well-known meat hors d'oeuvre is a pâté and there are many recipes which are popular.

Liver pâté

Cooking time 55 minutes
Oven temperature 325°F.

2 tablespoons butter · ¼ cup all-purpose flour
⅔ cup milk · 2 teaspoons finely chopped onion
¼ cup cream* · ½ lb. bacon
1 lb. lamb *or* pork liver · ½ teaspoon granulated sugar · 2 teaspoons salt · pinch black pepper
2 eggs.
TO COVER PÂTÉ WHILE COOKING: 5 slices bacon.
TO GARNISH: gherkin · parsley · lemon
hot toast.

* Choose whipping cream for a rich pâté, coffee cream for a lighter pâté.

Make a thick sauce with the butter, flour, and milk. Stir in the onion and the cream. Chop the bacon and liver coarsely for a less smooth pâté, or put in a blender or through a fine grinder twice for a more creamy pâté. Stir into sauce. Add all other ingredients. Press mixture firmly into a greased shallow ovenproof dish. Partially fry the bacon, then arrange the bacon across the pâté. Stand in a dish, partially filled with cold water and cook for 55 minutes in a preheated 350°F. oven. Let stand until cool, then serve garnished with gherkin, parsley, lemon, and hot toast. *Serves 6–8*

For a pâté with more 'bite', add chopped gherkins, a little extra onion, and 3 tablespoons brandy.

CHICKEN LIVER PÂTÉ
Use half the quantity of bacon to chicken livers, (i.e. ¼ lb. bacon to 1 lb. chicken livers).

Quick pâté in a blender

Cooking time Few minutes

¼ cup butter
½ lb. beef liver *or* the liver from 2 chickens *or* ducks *or* one goose liver · 3 tablespoons stock
3 tablespoons cream* · seasoning
pinch of herbs. TO COAT: 2–3 tablespoons butter.
TO SERVE: toast.

* Choose whipping cream for a rich pâté, coffee cream for a lighter pâté.

Melt the butter and toss the liver in this until just tender. Put into the blender with the hot stock, any butter remaining in the pan and the other ingredients. Blend on medium speed until a smooth pâté is obtained. Remove from the blender, put into a dish and cover with melted butter. Serve with hot toast. This pâté may be varied in a number of ways – a little brandy may be added or a gherkin and small pieces of onion put in while the blender is operating. The secret is to use enough hot stock to make a mixture which is soft enough to allow the blades of the blender to rotate, but which will stiffen as it cools. *Serves 3–4*

Pâté de foie gras

Cooking time   *25 minutes*
Oven temperature   *325°F.*

1 large *or* 2 small goose livers
small piece of a clove of garlic · seasoning
3 tablespoons cream* · 1 tablespoon brandy.
TO COAT: ¼ cup butter. TO GARNISH: lettuce
lemon · gherkin. TO SERVE: toast · butter.

* Choose whipping cream for a rich pâté, coffee
cream for a lighter pâté.

Grind the liver and mix with the other ingredients.
Put into a small well-buttered dish, top with
buttered wax paper or foil. Stand in a dish of cold
water to keep the pâté from drying and cook for
approximately 25 minutes in a preheated 325°F. oven.
Remove from oven. When pâté is cold, cover with a
layer of melted butter. To serve, cut in slices,
arrange on plates and garnish with lettuce, lemon
and gherkin fans. Serve with hot toast and butter.
Serves 4

PIQUANT FLAVORED PÂTÉ
Omit the cream, moisten with a little stock, add 1
teaspoon finely chopped onion, gherkin, plenty of
seasoning and 3 slices finely chopped bacon; cover
with bacon slices.

SAUSAGE
HORS D'OEUVRES

There are many interesting varieties of salami,
garlic and other sausages to be bought in delicates-
sen shops and these make an interesting hors
d'oeuvre, particularly if several kinds of salami and
sausages are used. For a light hors d'oeuvre buy
approximately 2–3 oz. meat per person.
Parma ham, which is raw Italian ham, is a very
expensive but very excellent meat to serve at the
beginning of a meal. It is cut very thinly so allow
approximately 1 oz. per person.
Serve all salami with brown bread and butter or
toast and butter. Parma ham also may be served
with slices of melon and cayenne or paprika, or
other fruit, as below.

PARMA HAM AND FRESH FIGS
Serve slices of Parma ham with well-drained canned
or, preferably, fresh figs. Pears could be served
instead.

PASTA AND RICE
HORS D'OEUVRES

Pasta of various kinds make a good and sustaining
hors d'oeuvre. Spaghetti, with various sauces,
ravioli and cannelloni are three of the most popular
pastas that may be served at the beginning of a
meal as well as for a main dish. Allow approximately half the quantity when serving as an hors
d'oeuvre.

Many rice dishes make excellent hors d'oeuvres. A
small portion of risotto or paella (see pages 192 and
193) could be served. Naturally you will allow
approximately half the normal portion if the first
course is being followed by a fairly substantial main
course.

Salami risotto

This is savory rice and meat hors d'oeuvre.

Cooking time   *None*

Approximately ½ lb. salami cut thinly (use two kinds
if possible) · ¼ lb. liver sausage, garlic sausage
and luncheon meat cut thinly (if possible)
2 green sweet peppers · 1 red sweet pepper
4 large ripe tomatoes
approximately 1 cup cooked green beans
approximately 8 stuffed olives
scant 1 cup cooked, medium *or* long-grain rice
¼–⅓ cup vinaigrette dressing.

Chop some of the meat and roll the remainder. Chop
most of the vegetables, but leave a few large pieces
for garnish. Slice the stuffed olives. Blend the rice
with the dressing, chopped meat, vegetables and
olives and put on the bottom of a shallow dish. Top
with the whole pieces of vegetables and meat rolls.
(Illustrated on page 17).   *Serves 4*

MIXED
HORS D'OEUVRES

A mixed hors d'oeuvre can consist of a large range of
ingredients. It is a good idea, however, to have them
from various groups of food, i.e. fish, meat, etc. The
following gives suggestions:
FISH – sardines, anchovies, rollmop herrings, mus-

sels, shrimp, smoked salmon, fresh salmon, fish salads of any kind, cod's roe, cooked roes. Dress the fish with mayonnaise or oil and vinegar and garnish it with chopped parsley, etc.

SALADS – potato, Russian, tomato, sliced cucumber, corn on the cob, lettuce, water cress, celery, rice mixtures, beet, etc. The salad should be mixed with mayonnaise or French dressing.

MEAT – diced salami, chopped sausages, small cubes or rolls of ham, tongue, chicken; these should be mixed with some dressing.

EGGS – sliced hard-cooked, hard-cooked and stuffed.

In addition the following are generally included in an hors d'oeuvre: gherkins; cocktail onions; pickled walnuts, etc.

Recipes for all the above salads are given in this book.

Antipasto

Cooking time	None or few minutes

$\frac{1}{4}$ cup tuna fish
scant $\frac{1}{2}$ cup boiled rice · oil · vinegar
seasoning · 8 anchovy fillets
8 rolled anchovies · $\frac{1}{2}$–1 cup small mushrooms (washed and raw or cooked in a very little vinegar)
1 pickled beet, cut into tiny shapes
8 pickled onions · 2–3 sliced hard-cooked eggs
1 diced red or green sweet pepper · 2–4 sliced tomatoes · 4–8 sardines · 8–12 olives, black and green · $\frac{1}{4}$–$\frac{1}{2}$ cup diced chicken · sliced fennel

Blend the fish and rice with oil and vinegar. Season. Arrange all the ingredients on individual dishes or one long dish. *Serves 6–8*

'EMERGENCY' HORS D'OEUVRES

These are interesting and quick first courses.

Savoury baked eggs

Cooking time	20 minutes
Oven temperature	375°F.

1 onion · 2 tomatoes · $\frac{1}{4}$ cup butter
seasoning · 4 eggs · 3 tablespoons grated cheese.

Peel and dice onion, skin and slice tomatoes. Heat two-thirds of the butter in 4 small ovenproof dishes. Add onion and tomatoes and season well. Bake in a preheated 375°F. oven for 10 minutes. Add the eggs, a little seasoning, cheese and remaining butter. Bake for a further 10 minutes. Serve with strips of toast. *Serves 4*

Tomato cups

Cooking time	None

8 small or 4 large tomatoes · 2 raw carrots
$\frac{1}{4}$ cup grated cheese · 2 hard-cooked eggs
seasoning · little mayonnaise or oil and vinegar.
TO GARNISH: parsley. TO SERVE: lettuce.

Halve the tomatoes, scoop out the pulp, chop and mix with the grated carrots, cheese and chopped hard-cooked eggs. Season the tomatoes and the filling and flavor this with mayonnaise or oil and vinegar. Pile into the tomatoes, garnish with parsley, and serve on a bed of lettuce. *Serves 4*

HORS D'OEUVRES TO IMPRESS

Try these recipes when something completely original is required. They are expensive, but delicious.

Avocado cream salad

Cooking time	None

2 ripe avocados · lemon juice
3 oz. package cream cheese, softened · 6–8 black olives · $\frac{1}{4}$ cup walnuts · 1 tablespoon chopped chives or 1$\frac{1}{2}$ teaspoons chopped shallot
little mayonnaise or whipping cream · seasoning.
TO GARNISH: 4 black olives · lettuce · lemon.

Cut each avocado in half lengthwise. Remove and discard the pits. Sprinkle with lemon juice to prevent discoloration. Blend the cream cheese with the chopped olives, walnuts and chives or shallot. Moisten with a little mayonnaise or whipped cream and season. Fill the depression in the avocados. Garnish with the olives, small lettuce leaves and lemon wedges. *Serves 4*

Stuffed fennel

Cooking time   *None*

1 large head fennel · can anchovy fillets
⅔ cup cottage cheese. TO GARNISH: parsley · lemon.

Wash the whole fennel then pull apart the stalks –
do this carefully for they are very delicate. Use only
the outer stalks for this dish and cut into 12–16
equal lengths. Wash in very cold water to crisp,
drain well. Remove the anchovies from the can, and
cut 2 or 3 into thin strips for garnish. Pound the
remaining anchovies in a bowl using a wooden spoon.
Add the oil from the can if you like a rich mixture,
but discard it for a less 'oily' filling. Blend the
anchovies with the cottage cheese and pile into the
fennel stalks, arrange on plates and garnish with
the anchovy strips, sprigs of parsley and lemon
twists.   *Serves 4*

Caviar tomatoes

Cooking time   *None*

8 small *or* 4 medium firm tomatoes
2 hard-cooked eggs · lemon juice · seasoning
small jar of caviar (see page 53)
8 slices brown bread · butter.
TO GARNISH: lettuce · lemon.

If desired the tomatoes may be skinned by placing
them in boiling water for *30 seconds*, then into cold
water. Cut a slice from the top of each tomato
(check to see the tomatoes balance well), remove
the pulp and blend with two finely chopped egg
whites and one egg yolk. Add a squeeze of lemon
juice and seasoning. Put in the bottom of the
tomatoes. Top with caviar and a ring of finely
chopped egg white. Cut circles of bread. Butter and
stand the tomatoes on them. Garnish with lettuce
and lemon.   *Serves 4*

CANAPÉS

TO PREPARE COCKTAIL CANAPÉS
Prepare as many of the toppings as possible early in
the day. Make and bake pastry cases or toast. Put
the canapés together as late as possible, and keep
covered with foil to prevent their drying.
With hot canapés such as 'Devils on horseback'
prepare completely, and put in the oven as the first
guests arrive.
A tempting recipe for Cheese straws is found on
page 299.

Bengal canapés

Cooking time   *12 minutes*

FOR THE SAUCE: 1 tablespoon margarine · 3 tablespoons all-purpose flour · ⅔ cup milk
seasoning.

4 slices bread · butter *or* margarine · ½ cup
cooked ham · 1 tablespoon whipping cream
3 tablespoons sweet chutney *or* finely chopped
pickles · 3 tablespoons grated cheese.
TO GARNISH: parsley and tomato.

To make the sauce: heat the margarine, stir in the
flour and cook for 2–3 minutes, then gradually add
the milk, bring to a boil and cook until thickened.
Season well. Toast or fry the bread, remove crusts,
butter and cut into 'bite-size' squares. Chop the ham
finely and heat for several minutes in the sauce,
then add the cream. Spread a little over each toast
square, then add the chutney. Sprinkle with grated
cheese and put under a hot broiler for a few minutes
until crisp and golden brown. Garnish with parsley
and strips of tomato. This does not keep for more
than a few minutes; therefore prepare *just before*
serving.

Angels on horseback

Cooking time   *few minutes*

Seasoning · 4 large *or* 8 small oysters
squeeze lemon juice · 4 slices bacon
4 small slices buttered toast.

Season the oysters and add lemon juice. Lightly fry
or broil the bacon, then drain and wrap a slice
around each oyster, securing with a toothpick (if
using small oysters, cut the slice of bacon in half).
Cook under the broiler until the bacon is crisp and
brown. Do not overcook as this toughens the oysters.
Serve on hot buttered toast.   *Serves 8*

Breton fingers

Cooking time   *few minutes*

1 small can sardines in oil
3 tablespoons bread crumbs · seasoning
1 teaspoon Worcestershire sauce
¾ cup Cheddar cheese, grated
¼ teaspoon prepared mustard
little margarine *or* butter, if necessary
4 slices buttered toast. TO GARNISH: 1 tomato.

Mash the sardines very well and season. Mix the oil from the sardine can with the bread crumbs, seasoning, Worcestershire sauce, cheese, and mustard. If there is not sufficient oil to give a soft mixture, then add a little margarine *or* butter and cream well. Spread the mashed sardines on the slices of toast (cut into strips) and cover with the crumb mixture. Put under a hot broiler for a few minutes until crisp and golden brown. Garnish with small pieces of tomato and serve hot or cold. If serving hot, the fingers may be prepared earlier and just heated in the oven.   *Serves 12–16*

Mussel titbits

Cooking time   *8 minutes*

1½ pints mussels
18 small toast circles or crackers
¼ cup margarine *or* butter
small quantity of finely chopped water cress
few drops lemon juice · anchovy paste
paprika.

Put the mussels into a large saucepan, adding just enough water to cover bottom of pan. Heat gently until mussels open. Remove them from shells, discarding 'beards'. Spread toast or crackers with mixture made by creaming margarine or butter and adding finely chopped water cress and lemon juice. Put a mussel on each, then pipe a ring of anchovy paste round it. Dust with paprika.   *Serves 18*

Devils on horseback

Cooking time   *few minutes*

8 large juicy cooked prunes
4 slices bacon · 8 strips toast
butter · paprika

Pit the prunes, cut each bacon slice in half, crosswise, lightly fry or broil then drain and wrap round a prune, securing with a wooden toothpick. Cook under the broiler until the bacon is crisp and brown. Serve on buttered toast dusted with paprika. If desired, a little liver pâté may be inserted into the center of the prunes.   *Serves 8*

Haddock pyramids

Cooking time   *None*

¼ cup cooked haddock
1 tablespoon mayonnaise (see page 186)
sieved white of 1 hard-cooked egg · seasoning
24 small toast circles or crackers.
TO GARNISH: gherkins *or* stuffed olives.

Chop or flake the fish very finely, mixing with the mayonnaise and egg white. Season well, then form into pyramids on toast or biscuits and garnish with a ring of gherkins or olives.   *Serves 24*

Canapés Diane

Cooking time   *few minutes*

4 chicken livers · seasoning
squeeze lemon juice · 4 slices bacon
8 tiny strips toast.

Cut chicken livers in half. Season and flavor with lemon juice. Cut each bacon slice in half. Wrap each chicken liver in a piece of bacon and secure with a toothpick. Broil until bacon is crisp and brown. Serve on pieces of hot buttered toast.   *Serves 8*

Scotch woodcock

Cooking time   *10–15 minutes*

3 tablespoons butter · 4–6 eggs · seasoning
little milk · 4 slices buttered toast.
TO GARNISH: 8 anchovy fillets · few capers.

Heat the butter. Beat the eggs with seasoning and milk. Scramble slowly and, when set, pile onto buttered toast (cut into strips) and garnish with the anchovy fillets and capers.   *Serves 12–16*

Salmon balls or dumplings

Cooking time   *5 minutes*

Medium can salmon · thick sauce (made from 2 tablespoons butter · ¼ cup all-purpose flour
⅔ cup milk and salmon liquid
seasoning – see white sauce 1, page 183
1½ cups all-purpose flour (approximately)
2¼ teaspoons baking powder.
TO FRY: deep fat *or* oil.

Drain the salmon and flake finely, then measure the liquid from the can and add enough milk to make ⅔ cup, use this with the butter and flour to make a thick white sauce (see page 183). Blend with the salmon and season well, and gradually add enough flour mixed with baking powder to make the consistency of a dumpling. Form into balls with lightly floured hands, then test the temperature of the fat for deep-frying (see page 54). Lower the balls into the fat and fry steadily until crisp and golden brown. Drain well, serve hot.   *Serves 20*

filling g) sliced hard-cooked egg.
filling h) sliced cucumber · sliced tomatoes.
filling i) crab meat · chopped tomatoes.
TOPPING: stuffed olives · gherkins
sliced cucumber.

Butter the white and brown bread and then make a
very tall sandwich of the various fillings. Garnish
with the olives, etc. (see page 295).   *Serves 4*

Welsh rabbit

Cooking time   *5–10 minutes*

2 tablespoons butter · 2 cups grated Cheddar
cheese · dash salt · dash cayenne pepper
dash dry mustard (optional)
⅓ cup milk *or* 3 tablespoons milk and 3 tablespoons
light ale *or* beer
few drops Worcestershire sauce
egg yolk (optional) · 4 slices bread · butter.

Melt the butter, add all the other ingredients and
heat very gently to a smooth thick sauce. Meanwhile, toast and butter the bread. Put the mixture
on top. This is a soft Welsh rabbit or it is also called
a sauce; for a firmer consistency blend 3 tablespoons
flour into the butter, cook for 2–3 minutes, then
add the remaining ingredients and heat gently. This
firmer mixture may be spread on the toast and
browned under a broiler for 2–3 minutes. The dish
at front of picture on page 150 shows this recipe,
which may also be garnished in a variety of ways –
with sardines; sliced mushrooms fried in butter; a
crisp slice of bacon cooked under the broiler; sliced
pickled onions; or grilled tomatoes and parsley.
                                              Serves 8

SANDWICHES

Sandwiches make an easy yet pleasant supper dish.
On the opposite page are many suggestions for open
sandwiches, toasted sandwiches, etc. The fillings
suggested are often suitable for ordinary sandwiches
also. Two very impressive ways to serve sandwiches
are given below; the first recipe is shown in the
picture on page 295, the second on page 274.

Skyscraper sandwiches

Cooking time   *None*

5 slices white bread · 5 slices brown bread
(the same size) · butter
filling a) flaked salmon · mayonnaise
chopped green sweet pepper.
filling b) cooked chicken.
filling c) sliced tomato · lettuce.
filling d) cooked chicken · cooked ham
lettuce.
filling e) cooked ham.
filling f) sliced cheese.

Sandwich gâteau

Cooking time   *None*

1 large loaf unsliced bread · butter
filling a) ½ cup ham · little mayonnaise
filling b) 3 oz. cream cheese · ⅓ cup nuts
filling c) 1 can sardines · 2 hard-cooked eggs.
TO GARNISH: 6 oz. cream cheese
little mayonnaise · few radishes
few stuffed olives.

Cut away the crusts from the bread then cut into 4
long slices. Spread these with butter then with the
various fillings made by blending the ingredients
together. The ham should be chopped in the top
filling and the sardines drained and mashed in the
bottom filling. Blend the cream cheese and mayonnaise and coat the outside of the loaf with it. Garnish
with radish flower shapes on top and sliced olives
around the sides.   *Serves up to 12*

OPEN SANDWICHES

While many of the fillings suggested for ordinary
sandwiches are excellent to use as a topping on open
sandwiches, it is better to keep the ingredients for
a topping rather larger for an attractive arrangement.

Basic open sandwiches

Use white or brown bread – rye bread, often obtainable at large stores or health food stores – crispbread, split rolls, etc. Remember the toppings may
be hot or cold, and you may mix a variety of ingredients together – see the pictures on pages 313
and 274. Butter the bread – which should not be cut
too thickly – lavishly, then arrange the fillings on
top. Hot fillings may be put on bread and butter,
toast, or fried bread.
Open sandwiches may be large enough for a main
meal, or small enough for cocktails (See picture
page 313.)

VEGETABLE TOPPINGS
COLD
Lettuce – topped with potato salad and Russian
salad.
Lettuce – topped with sliced tomatoes and gherkins.
Mustard and cress – topped with beet salad and
apple rings, topped with mayonnaise and chopped
nuts.

Fried sliced mushrooms and fried tomatoes.
Fried sliced mushrooms and tiny fried new potatoes topped with chopped chives.

EGGS and CHEESE
COLD
Lettuce topped with sliced hard-cooked eggs and rolled slices of cheese (cut this with a cheese slicer to get it thin enough).
Cream cheese and rings of fresh or canned pineapple.
Water cress topped with scrambled eggs mixed with grated cheese and topped with mayonnaise and cucumber twists.
Sliced tomatoes topped with curls or triangles of cheese.
Hard-cooked eggs, sliced and topped with shrimp, mayonnaise and parsley.

HOT
Welsh rabbit mixture topped with a poached egg (Buck rabbit).
Toasted cheese topped with scrambled egg and cucumber twists.

FISH
COLD
Lettuce, smoked eel, mackerel or salmon, and scrambled egg.
Cooked fish and canned tuna, blended with mayonnaise, topped with paprika, cucumber twists, and parsley.
Sardines and tomatoes.

HOT
Lettuce, fried fish fillets or fish cakes, tartar sauce, and cucumber and lemon twists.

MEAT
COLD
Salami topped with thin rings of raw onion.
Liver sausage topped with scrambled egg and small twists of crisp bacon.
Mustard and cress topped with thin slices of cooked ham rolled around cream cheese.
Tongue topped with scrambled egg and chopped gherkin, or blend some of the tongue with the egg.

Lettuce, sliced cooked beef, beet salad, and potato salad.
Lettuce, sliced cooked pork, cooked prunes, thick apple sauce and/or red cabbage.
Steak tartar: raw chopped tenderloin steak, topped with an egg yolk, capers, chopped gherkin and

chopped onion . . . this is served with the egg yolk in the half shell – this is then mixed with the steak, etc.

HOT
Hot fried slices of veal and prunes.
Wafer-thin slices of steak and onion rings.

TOASTED AND DOUBLE-DECKER SANDWICHES

Toasted sandwiches are ideal to serve in colder weather and are easily made.
The technique is to broil one side only of two slices of bread, to make the sandwich with the toasted sides inwards, then to put one of the untoasted sides under the broiler until golden brown, turn, and toast the other side. This may be varied by adding more food to the top of the sandwich, see recipes below and the picture on page 294.

TOASTED BACON AND EGG SANDWICHES
Fry or broil two slices of bacon and one egg, toast one side only of the bread. Make the sandwich and toast, topping the finished sandwich with another slice of bacon and sliced tomatoes.

TOASTED CHEESE AND BACON SANDWICH
Fry or broil the bacon, and toast one side only of the bread. Top the toasted side of one slice with the bacon then the cheese, put this for 1 minute under the broiler until just beginning to melt, then top with the second slice of bread. Put under the broiler again.

TOASTED CHEESE AND HAM SANDWICH
Either follow the directions above, using sliced hot boiled ham instead of bacon, or arrange the ham on a heated dish, and make thin sandwiches of bread, butter, and sliced cheese. Toast one side, turn and cover with another layer of thinly sliced cheese, brown under the broiler and put onto the hot ham. Broiled brisket of beef is also excellent with toasted cheese.

Fried sandwiches

Cooking time   *few minutes*

4–8 leftover meat sandwiches · 1 egg
3 tablespoons milk · seasoning
¼ cup butter or fat.

This method of reheating turns leftover sandwiches into a delicious hot snack. Naturally care must be taken that the meat is quite fresh – ham, tongue, and corned beef are particularly suitable. If desired open the sandwich and add a little prepared mustard and chutney for extra flavor. Beat the egg, milk, and seasoning, then brush each side of the sandwich. If the bread is stale, use a little more milk and allow these to soak for a few minutes. Heat the butter or fat and fry until crisp and brown. *Serves 4*

SOUPS

This section gives a variety of soups, from the classic clear consommé to easily made thick, sustaining vegetable soups which are almost 'a meal in themselves'.

Wise choice of soup

Select a clear soup to precede a substantial meal. Vegetable soups are filling so are excellent before a light main course. If this is fish or eggs, choose a meat soup. Fish soup is an unusual starter for a special dinner, and a good invalid dish. To save preparing an elaborate meal, make a really satisfying and sustaining soup that can be a meal in itself. Broths, chowders, and bisques are soups almost too filling for the first course of a meal. Served with cheese and fruit they are the answer to a one-course meal. Do not serve highly seasoned or spiced soups if the main course is rather delicately flavored, e.g. sole, chicken, or veal in a cream sauce, since this will affect the palate and prevent the enjoyment of the following course as much as one would wish.

Ways to serve soups

When serving a soup like the onion soup gratinée, which is put under the broiler to brown, use a flameproof container. If serving soup as a snack or part of a buffet meal, ordinary cups are possibly more comfortable to hold and manage than soup plates or proper soup cups. Cold soups look most attractive served in clear glass dishes instead of chilled soup cups.

To use leftover soups

These can be kept in the refrigerator and reheated or served cold. In order to avoid monotony, try adding a different flavoring, e.g. extra herbs or finely chopped mint give an interesting taste to a vegetable or potato soup; or mix with another flavoring, e.g. a little tomato purée is delicious added to an onion soup; curry powder carefully blended with a little milk or cream and stirred into a chicken soup provides an entirely different flavor.

Easy remedies when things are wrong

PROBLEM – if the soup is too salty, remember next time to add a little seasoning then taste before adding any more – vegetables contain mineral salts, so can give quite an amount of flavor.
TO REMEDY – stir in cream or milk or add a diced potato and simmer in the soup for awhile. The potato may be removed from the soup before serving.
PROBLEM – if the soup is lumpy, it is due to careless thickening with flour or cornstarch.
TO REMEDY – whisk hard with a metal whisk and the lumps will probably come out. Alternatively, press through a sieve and reheat.
PROBLEM – if the soup is lacking in flavor, it means it was not tasted during cooking.
TO REMEDY – (at the last minute), add garlic salt . . . paprika . . . a few drops of soy sauce or chili sauce . . . or blend in cream and chopped chives. Often the soup needs extra richness and a good knob of butter stirred in before serving gives this.

Making stock

BROWN STOCKS are those made from beef bones, mutton and game, and they should only be used for meat soups unless the recipe specifically states to the contrary, e.g. brown vegetable soup (see recipe page 35).

WHITE STOCKS are made from poultry bones (do not include any giblets or the body of the bird), and from veal. Use for vegetable soups, etc.

VEGETABLE STOCKS. If any vegetable stock from cooking vegetables is left, then this may be added to the other ingredients in a vegetable or meat and vegetable soup – unless it is very strongly flavored, e.g. cabbage, onion, turnip, or carrot.

Brown stock

Cooking time   *2½–3 hours*

About 2 lb. beef bones
water to cover (approximately 7½ cups)
seasoning · vegetables, if desired
bayleaf, if desired.

Wash the bones, put into the pan with the water, add seasoning, vegetables (onion, carrot, celery), and a bay leaf. Bring to a boil, remove any scum, then cover the pan and simmer gently for about 3 hours. Strain the stock well and store in the refrigerator or freezer.

White stock

Use the carcase of chicken or veal bones. If using chicken carcase, do not add giblets or any dark meat.

STOCK IN A PRESSURE COOKER

Ingredients as above, but reduce water to half and cook for about 45 minutes at 15 pounds pressure.

Aids to soup making

COOKING SOUPS IN A PRESSURE COOKER

Many soups may be prepared in a pressure cooker. The time varies, of course, according to the type of ingredients, but you need approximately one fourth of the cooking time for most vegetables, i.e. a soup that takes 1 hour in a saucepan cooks in 15 minutes in a pressure cooker. Here are the points to remember about soup making in a pressure cooker: you will need to use approximately half the usual amount of water or stock for long-cooking soups. (This is because you have little, if any, evaporation in a pressure cooker, which has been allowed for in the saucepan recipes.) Where the ordinary saucepan method for soup takes only a few minutes, decrease the amount of liquid by just under one third; when making soup, remember not to fill the cooker too full; you do not need the rack in the bottom of the pressure cooker.

Generally speaking, soups should be cooked at a 15 lb. pressure and the pressure then allowed to return to normal at room temperature.

Where soups are strained and thickened afterward, you will then treat the pressure cooker like an ordinary saucepan for thickening.

USING AN ELECTRIC BLENDER

Soups may be prepared in a blender where straining is indicated in the recipe. Vegetables, particularly tomatoes, retain the maximum amount of flavor if *lightly* cooked, so you produce a much better tomato soup if the tomatoes are puréed in the blender before cooking. This does NOT remove the seeds, however, and there will be tiny particles of skin. Preparation of mixed vegetables for soups by puréeing before cooking will reduce the cooking time to well under one half; but it has been found that onions, which are then cooked for a short time, tend to have a rather strong and, to some people, unpalatable flavor, so in any special recipe with a high percentage of onion it is better if the ingredients are fully cooked before being put into the blender to produce a smooth purée.

The blender container is usually made of heat-resisting material, but even so it is wise to warm it slightly for a minute under hot running water before putting in a very hot soup.

TERMS USED IN SOUP MAKING

A BROTH contains pieces of food in a clear, unthickened liquid, often has rice or barley.

A CONSOMMÉ means a clear soup, although this will often have a garnish of some kind.

A CHOWDER or bisque means a very filling soup, almost like a stew.

A CREAM SOUP should have a really creamy texture.

CLEAR SOUPS

These include consommé, which needs long slow cooking, then careful straining. To save time, there are cans of good quality consommé available and the classic garnishes may be added to these.

Beef tea

Cooking time   *2 hours*

1 lb. lean beef · 2½ cups water · ¼ teaspoon salt.

After removing all the fat, cut the meat into small pieces. Put these into a stone jar or double boiler, with the water and salt. Bring the water in the bottom portion just to a boil; then simmer very gently for at least 2 hours. Strain through cheesecloth, then let it cool sufficiently to skim off fat. Reheat, without boiling. Serve with crisp toast.

Serves 4

Note: Do not make large quantities of beef tea for it should not be kept for longer than a day.

Beef consommé

Cooking time   *1 hour*

¾ lb. beef foreshank · 5 cups good meat stock
seasoning · 1 onion · 1 carrot
small piece celery · sprig parsley · bay leaf
1 tablespoon sherry (optional).
TO CLEAR SOUP: 1 egg white and shell.

Cut the meat into small pieces, and put into a
saucepan with the remaining ingredients. Simmer
very gently for 1 hour, then strain through several
thicknesses of cheesecloth. Add sherry if desired.
To clear the consommé, put in a stiffly beaten egg
white and clean egg shell, gently simmer for a
further 20 minutes, then restrain.   *Serves 4*

Garnishes for consommé

There are a variety of soups which are made by
adding a garnish to a basic consommé.

CONSOMMÉ CELESTINE
Make thin pancakes and cut into wafer-thin strips.
Heat in the consommé.

VEAL CONSOMMÉ
Use the same ingredients as beef consommé plus
¾ lb. stewing veal. Omit the bay leaf, but add a very
little sherry to keep the pale color.

Consommé julienne

Add to beef consommé above:
1 large carrot · ½ medium turnip
1 leek *or* onion · small piece cabbage
2 tablespoons margarine.

Cut the vegetables into thin pieces about the size
and thickness of a matchstick. Melt margarine in a
saucepan, and sauté the vegetables in this until
just turning brown. Add about ¼ cup of the consommé, and cook gently until the vegetables are
quite tender. Remove any fat, then add the remaining consommé, and reheat gently.

Chicken consommé

Cooking time   *2 hours*

1 chicken carcass · 2–3 peppercorns · salt
pepper · 2 cloves · 1 carrot · 1 onion
chopped parsley.

Remove any remaining small pieces of meat from
the bones, chop finely and set aside, then break or
crack the bones and put in a saucepan with seasoning and diced vegetables. Cover with water, and
simmer gently for about 2 hours. Strain, add the
meat and chopped parsley; reheat.   *Serves 4*

GAME CONSOMMÉ
Make stock by boiling the carcass of any game along
with vegetables. Let stand until cool, remove any
fat, reheat, strain, and flavor with sherry.

VEGETABLE SOUPS

These have an endless variety – the simplest form of
vegetable soup is to simmer diced or grated vegetables in water and seasoning or in a meat or chicken
stock (see pages 32–33).
There are the purée soups where the vegetables are
cooked, puréed, then reheated, generally with a
sauce or cream to taste.
Finally, there are the cream soups, where a high
percentage of cream or creamy sauce is used.

Simple vegetable soup

Cooking time   *10–20 minutes*

2 carrots · 1 potato · 1 small turnip
few peas (fresh *or* frozen) · small onion
1 *or* 2 stalks celery · 3¾ cups water *or* white stock
seasoning. TO GARNISH: chopped parsley.

Peel and dice or grate the vegetables – the latter
saves about half the cooking time. Bring the water
or stock to a boil, add seasoning, then the vegetables.
Cook until tender. Taste and reseason, if desired.
Garnish with parsley.   *Serves 4*

Cream of vegetable soup

Cooking time   *45 minutes*

1¼ cups mixed prepared vegetables*
2½ cups water *or* white stock · ¼ teaspoon vinegar
seasoning · ¼ cup butter
3 tablespoons all-purpose flour · ⅔–1¼ cups milk.
TO GARNISH: paprika and/or parsley.

* Choose ½ cup sliced carrots · ¼ cup chopped onions
½ cup diced potatoes, *or* other vegetables in season.

Keep the prepared vegetables in cold water as you
prepare them until they are ready to cook – if you
have included any Jerusalem artichokes, add 1
tablespoon lemon juice to prevent discoloration.
Put into a saucepan with the water or stock, vinegar,
and seasoning. Simmer gently for 30–45 minutes.
Press through a sieve, then return the purée to
saucepan, and add the butter. Blend the flour with
the cold milk, stir into the boiling purée, and continue cooking, stirring constantly, until it forms a
smooth thick soup. Garnish with paprika and/or
parsley.   *Serves 4*

Brown vegetable soup

Use any of the vegetable soup recipes, but substitute a good brown stock for water or white stock and milk.

This makes a strongly-flavored and interesting soup which is ideal to serve before a light main course. The picture on page 19 shows a brown vegetable soup and salmon dumplings.

Cream of artichoke soup

Cooking time	45 minutes

1½ lb. Jerusalem artichokes · 2½ cups water or white stock · ¼ teaspoon vinegar · seasoning ¼ cup butter · 3 tablespoons all-purpose flour ¾–1¼ cups milk.
TO GARNISH: paprika.

Wash and peel the artichokes and, if large, cut into small pieces. Remember to keep the artichokes in cold water, with a tablespoon of lemon juice to prevent discoloration, until ready to cook them. Put into a saucepan with the water or stock, vinegar, and seasoning. Simmer gently for 30–45 minutes. Press through a sieve, then return the purée to the saucepan with the butter. Blend the flour with the cold milk, stir into boiling purée, and continue cooking, stirring constantly, until it forms a thick smooth soup. Garnish with paprika, and serve with toast. A few of the artichokes may be saved and cut into tiny pieces to float on the soup as a garnish.
Serves 4

CREAM OF BEET SOUP
Use raw beets. Dice and simmer for approximately 1 hour. Continue as above.

Asparagus soup

Cooking time	Just under 10 minutes

1 medium can asparagus · 2½ cups milk
2 tablespoons butter or margarine
3 tablespoons cornstarch or all-purpose flour
seasoning.

Open the can of asparagus, and reserve the liquid. Chop the asparagus into tiny pieces. Heat the butter or margarine, then stir in the cornstarch or flour. Add the milk and asparagus stock. Bring to a boil, taste, and season. Put in the asparagus. Heat for a few minutes, and serve.
Serves 4

Carrot soup

Cooking time	10 minutes

8 small carrots · 1 onion · 1¼ cup milk
2½ cups water · 1–2 chicken bouillon cubes
seasoning. TO GARNISH: chopped parsley or chives.

Grate the carrots and onion, and simmer for about 8 minutes, until tender, with the milk and water in which the bouillon cubes have been dissolved. Season well, and include a dash of sugar if desired. Pour into heated soup cups and garnish with the parsley or chives.
Serves 4

Cauliflower soup

Cooking time	30–35 minutes

1 medium cauliflower · 1 onion
2½ cups water or white stock · seasoning
2 tablespoons butter · ¼ cup all-purpose flour
1¼ cups milk.
TO GARNISH: cayenne pepper.

Cut the cauliflower stalk and some of the flowerets, reserving the rest. Put into a pan with the chopped onion, water, and seasoning and simmer gently until tender. Press through a sieve. Make a white sauce from the butter, flour, and milk; put in the cauliflower purée and reheat, adding a little extra milk if the sauce is too thick. Meanwhile, divide the remaining flowerets into very small pieces. Boil in salted water until just tender. Put into the soup, and serve at once garnished with cayenne pepper.
Serves 4–5

Variations

CREAM OF CAULIFLOWER SOUP
Use a little less water and add coffee cream after blending cauliflower purée with the sauce.

CHEESE AND CAULIFLOWER SOUP
Add ¼–¾ cup grated cheese to the soup, and heat until melted.

GOLDEN BALL CAULIFLOWER SOUP
Blend 1 egg yolk with a little whipping cream. Stir into the soup just before serving and thicken without boiling. Garnish with hard-cooked egg yolk, pressed through a sieve to look like mimosa.

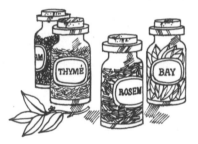

Celery chowder

Cooking time	30–35 minutes

1 cup celery · 1 onion · 2 medium potatoes
1¼ cups white stock or water · seasoning
2 tablespoons butter · 3 tablespoons all-purpose flour · 1¼ cups milk.
TO GARNISH: celery heart leaves or croutons (see page 46).

Finely chop the celery, chop or grate the onion, and finely dice the potatoes. Simmer the vegetables together in the stock or water until tender, seasoning well. Meanwhile, make a thin sauce of the butter, flour, and milk, add vegetable mixture to this. Heat thoroughly, season, and serve garnished with small celery heart leaves or croutons.
Serves 4

Cream of celery soup

Cooking time   *30 minutes*

1 large bunch celery · 3¾ cups white stock *or* water · ¼ cup all-purpose flour · ¼ cup butter ⅔ cup milk · ⅔ cup coffee cream *or* evaporated milk seasoning, including celery salt.
TO GARNISH: cayenne pepper.

If you do not wish to strain this soup, cut the celery into very tiny pieces. Simmer celery with the water or stock until tender, then strain, if desired. Meanwhile, make a white sauce from the flour, butter, and milk; this will be very thick, so the celery mixture or purée needs to be blended very slowly into this. Reheat, then add the cream and seasoning. Garnish with cayenne pepper.   *Serves 6*

Chestnut soup

Cooking time   *1 hour 10 minutes*

1 lb. chestnuts · 2½ cups water *or* white stock ¼ cup margarine *or* butter · 1¼ cups milk dash salt, cayenne pepper, and sugar, if desired.
TO GARNISH: Toast *or* croutons (see page 46).

With a sharp knife, make a slit in each chestnut shell, cover with water, and simmer for 15 minutes. Peel both the outer and inner shells from the nuts while still hot, then return to the saucepan with the fresh water or stock. Simmer gently for 45 minutes. Press the chestnuts through a sieve, and put the purée into the pan, with the margarine or butter, milk, and seasoning. Heat slowly, then serve with crisp pieces of toast or croutons. *Serves 4*

Corn soup

Cooking time   *Just under 10 minutes*

2 tablespoons butter *or* margarine
3 tablespoons cornstarch *or* ¼ cup all-purpose flour 1¼ cups water · 1 bouillon cube (preferably chicken) · 2½ cups milk · 1 (12 oz.) can sweet corn *or* mixed sweet corn and peppers *or* 1 (10 oz.) package frozen corn · seasoning.
TO GARNISH: little chopped chives *or* parsley.

Heat the butter or margarine, then stir in the cornstarch or flour. Cook gently for several minutes. Add the water, bouillon cube, and milk, and bring to a boil. Cook until thickened. Add the sweet corn, and heat for a few minutes. Season well, and garnish with chopped chives or parsley.   *Serves 4*

Cucumber purée soup

Cooking time   *20 minutes*

1 large *or* 2 medium cucumbers* · 1 onion little celery · 1¼ cups white stock 2 tablespoons butter · ¼ cup all-purpose flour 1¼ cups milk · seasoning.
TO GARNISH: parsley.

* If all the skin is left on a cucumber it gives a very bitter flavor but a little should be included to give a slight green color. Alternatively, the cucumber may be simmered in water for a few minutes before using this recipe.

Chop the cucumber and onion, and mix with the chopped celery. If celery is not obtainable, Belgian endive or celeriac (celery root) may be used instead. Put into a pan with the stock, and simmer until tender. Press through a sieve. Meanwhile, make a white sauce with the butter, flour, and milk, add the cucumber purée, and reheat. Season well. A little lemon juice or vinegar may be added when heated, but do not boil again. Garnish with chopped parsley.
Serves 4

Cream of mushroom soup

Cooking time   *15–20 minutes*

2 cups mushrooms* · ¼ cup butter *or* margarine ½ cup all-purpose flour · 2½ cups water *or* white stock · 1¾ cups milk · seasoning

* Mushroom stems may be used.

Chop mushrooms finely unless you wish to strain the soup. Melt the butter or margarine in a saucepan, sauté mushrooms for 5 minutes, stirring to prevent their discoloring. Stir in the flour, and cook for 3 minutes. Remove the pan from the heat, and gradually add water and milk. Bring to a boil, and cook until soup thickens. Season.   *Serves 4*

Lentil soup

Cooking time   *1½ hours*

1 cup washed lentils · 5 slices bacon, chopped 1 onion, chopped · 1 carrot 2½ cups water *or* any prepared stock · seasoning little chopped thyme *or* parsley 2 tablespoons butter · 3 tablespoons all-purpose flour · 1¼ cups milk.
TO GARNISH: chopped parsley.

Put the lentils (these may be soaked overnight, if desired), bacon, onion, carrot, and stock into a saucepan. Add seasoning and herbs – the seasoning MUST be added at the very start of cooking. Cover and simmer gently for about 1½ hours. Meanwhile, make a very thin sauce with the butter, flour, and milk, add the lentil purée and reheat. Check seasoning, and serve garnished with chopped parsley.
Serves 4

Variation

LENTIL AND TOMATO SOUP
Use ½ cup lentils and 1 cup chopped tomatoes.

Fish whirls, page 56

Chunky herring salad, page 24; Baked stuffed fish, page 55

Fish and cheese puff, page 56

Pea soup

Cooking time   *35–40 minutes*

1½ lb. peas (including pods) *or* pods from 2 lb. fresh
peas when young · 3¾ cups water *or* ham stock
small onion (optional) · seasoning
small sprig mint · dash sugar
good knob butter.
TO GARNISH: chopped mint *or* croutons (see page 46)
or peas, if desired.

Wash pods and shell the peas. Put pods and peas into
a saucepan with stock (reserving few peas, if desired,
for garnish), onion, seasoning, and mint, and simmer
until tender. Press through a sieve; this must be
done very vigorously, so that the flesh of the pods
is pushed through and only the skins are left.
Return to the pan, reheat, add a little sugar to taste
and a good knob of butter. If the pods are very
fleshy the soup may be a little thick when strained,
so add a small quantity of extra stock or milk.
Serve garnished with chopped mint or croutons or
a few freshly cooked peas.   *Serves 4*

Water cress soup

Cooking time   *11 minutes*

2 bunches water cress (about 4 cups)
1 tablespoon corn oil
2 teaspoons gravy flavoring
2½ cups water · 3 tablespoons cornstarch
6 tablespoons milk.

Wash the water cress thoroughly, reserve few sprigs
for garnish, and remove leaves from stems of
remainder. Sauté gently for 2–3 minutes in heated
oil. Add gravy flavoring and the water. Bring to a
boil, stirring constantly, then simmer for about 5
minutes. Strain if required. Mix cornstarch and
milk smoothly, add to the purée, and cook for 3
minutes, stirring constantly. Garnish with sprigs
of water cress.   *Serves 4*

Instead of corn oil, which makes this a good vegetarian soup, you may use 2 tablespoons butter, and
chicken stock in place of water.

Cream of spinach soup

Cooking time   *15 minutes*

1–1½ lb. fresh spinach *or* 1 (10 oz.) package frozen
spinach · 1 onion, (optional) · seasoning
2 tablespoons butter · ¼ cup all-purpose flour
2½ cups milk · 3–4 tablespoons whipping cream.
TO GARNISH: croutons (see page 46).

Cook the spinach in a minimum amount of water,
add the onion, if desired, and seasoning to taste.
Drain, then strain or chop (unless using frozen
spinach purée). While the spinach is cooking, prepare a thin white sauce with the butter, flour, and
milk, add the spinach and the cream, and reheat
gently, seasoning well. Serve with croutons.
Sprinkle with little grated nutmeg, if desired.
                                   Serves 4

Tomato soup

Cooking time   *45 minutes*

6 medium tomatoes (ripe) · 1 onion · 1 carrot
1 stalk celery · 2 slices bacon
2 tablespoons butter (optional) · 3¾ cups white
stock *or* water · seasoning · *bouquet garni*.

Peel and chop the tomatoes and onion, grate or dice
the peeled carrot, and chop the celery and bacon.
Heat the bacon in a pan, add the butter, then sauté
the vegetables in this; do not allow the bacon or
onion to brown. Add the stock, seasoning, and
bouquet garni (3 bay leaves, 3 sprigs parsley, and 1
sprig thyme, tied together), cover the soup, and
simmer gently for approximately 35 minutes.
Adjust seasoning. Strain, reheat, and serve at once.
                                   Serves 4

CREAM OF TOMATO SOUP
This often poses problems because the soup has a
tendency to curdle – the secret is in careful blending.
Prepare the purée as above, but use only 2½ cups
stock. Make a thin white sauce of 2 tablespoons
butter, ¼ cup all-purpose flour, and 1¼ cups milk,
season well. Reheat the strained tomato purée in
one pan. Whisk the HOT BUT NOT BOILING sauce
into the HOT BUT NOT BOILING purée, and serve
at once.

Dieter's chowder

Cooking time   *35 minutes*

2 tablespoons margarine · 1 large onion
1–2 slices bacon · 2 large tomatoes
2 stalks celery · ½ large *or* 1 small green sweet
pepper · very few mushrooms, (optional)
2 medium carrots · seasoning
5 cups water with little gravy flavoring
¼ small cabbage. TO GARNISH: chopped parsley.

Melt the margarine, and sauté diced onion until just
changing color, then put in the chopped bacon and
continue to cook for a few minutes. Peel and chop
tomatoes, and add all the other diced vegetables
(except the cabbage), seasoning, and the water mixed
with the gravy flavoring – the tomatoes will become
part of the liquid in cooking. Simmer for approximately 20 minutes. Add the finely chopped cabbage,
and cook for a further 10 minutes. Garnish with
chopped parsley.   *Serves 4*

Note: To make a more satisfying dish for non-dieting
members of the family, add a thick layer of grated
cheese on top before serving.

MEAT AND POULTRY SOUPS

The recipes in this section may be used as a basis for other soups, for example, the recipe for hare soup is very successful when made with rabbit or other game such as grouse or pheasant – but since the carcases of these game birds are smaller than that of a hare, use less wine, and allow 4 servings only.

The chicken soup recipe produces a richer soup if made with duck or goose, or a similar flavored soup with a turkey carcass. Naturally, since a turkey is much larger than a chicken, the amount of water etc. needs to be doubled and the soup will serve about 8 people.

Chicken broth

Cooking time   *30 minutes*

5 tablespoons Patna rice *or* barley
5 cups stock from cooking chicken
vegetables already cooked with chicken, with 1 cup fresh finely diced vegetables *or* strain away the vegetables and use 2–3 cups freshly diced vegetables
little cooked chicken · seasoning.
TO GARNISH: parsley · croutons.

If using pearl barley, blanch this first by putting into cold water, then bring the water to a boil, and strain. Add blanched barley or rice to the stock and the vegetables, and cook steadily for 15 minutes. Add tiny pieces of chicken, and continue heating for about 10 minutes. Add seasoning to taste, then pour into a heated bowl or tureen. Serve garnished with parsley and croutons.   *Serves 4*

Chicken soup

Cooking time   *1 hour 25 minutes*

1 chicken carcase · 6 cups water
½ cup diced cooked chicken · 1¼ cups milk
1 tablespoon cornstarch · 2 tablespoons butter
seasoning.

Simmer the carcase in the water for 1 hour, then strain. Add the cooked chicken meat and milk to the stock, and cook for a further 15 minutes. Press through a sieve, and blend with cornstarch. Add butter and seasoning, and cook for 10 minutes.
                    Serves 4

Giblet soup

Cooking time   *1¼ hours*

¼ cup butter *or* poultry fat · 1 small onion
1 tablespoon all-purpose flour
6¼ cups poultry stock *or* water
giblets from poultry · bayleaf · parsley
little sherry *or* port wine (optional).
TO GARNISH: parsley · croutons.

Heat the butter, and sauté the sliced onion in this. Stir in the flour, and cook gently for several minutes. Add the stock and giblets, and simmer until the giblets are very tender, add the bay leaf and sprig of parsley, remove the giblets from the stock, rub through a sieve or chop very finely. Return to the soup and reheat, add a little sherry or port wine, which is excellent in this soup, if desired. Remove bay leaf and parsley before serving, and garnish with finely chopped parsley and croutons.   *Serves 4*

Game soup

Cooking time   *1½ hours*

Carcase of 1 large *or* 2 small grouse *or* pheasants
⅓ cup butter · 2 carrots · 2 onions
1 piece celery *or* celeriac (celery root)
½ cup all-purpose flour · 3¾ cups brown stock
seasoning · 3 tablespoons red currant jelly
3–4 tablespoons sherry *or* port wine.

Break the carcase of the game into neat pieces. Sauté in the butter for several minutes, then add the carrots, onion, and celery or celeriac. Sauté the vegetables in the butter until golden. Add the flour and stir well, then gradually blend in the stock. Bring to a boil, stir well, and season. Cover and simmer for 1 hour. Drain the liquid into a second pan, rub the vegetables and any tiny pieces of game through a sieve into the liquid, and reheat with red currant jelly and sherry or port wine.   *Serves 4–6*

Kidney soup

Cooking time   *1½ hours*

½ lb. beef kidney* · 1 small onion
¼ cup butter · ¼ cup all-purpose flour
5 cups brown stock *or* water · seasoning
parsley · little port wine *or* Burgundy.

* To use lamb kidney the cooking time will be 30 minutes only, so reduce the amount of stock to 3¾ cups.

Chop the kidney and onion very finely, and sauté in hot butter for 1–2 minutes, making sure not to harden the outside of the meat. Blend in the flour and gradually add the stock. Bring to a boil, stir until smooth, add the seasoning and a sprig of parsley, then simmer gently for about 1½ hours. Remove the parsley, add the wine, and serve immediately.
                    Serves 4

Mulligatawny soup

Cooking time   *1 hour*

1 apple · 1 large carrot · 2 onions
¼ cup fat *or* drippings · ¼ cup all-purpose flour
1 tablespoon curry powder · 5 cups stock*
1 tablespoon chutney · 3 tablespoons seedless
white raisins · dash sugar · seasoning
little lemon juice *or* vinegar.

* Made by simmering lamb or mutton bones *or* a
small lamb's head.

Chop the apple and vegetables into tiny pieces,
sauté in the hot fat, then work in the flour and
curry powder. Add the stock, bring to a boil, and
simmer until thickened. Add remaining ingredients,
and simmer for about 45 minutes–1 hour. Press
through a sieve, and return to the pan to reheat.
Taste, adjusting seasoning if necessary, and add a
little extra sugar or lemon juice, if desired. *Serves 4*

Oxtail soup

Cooking time   *3¼ hours*

1–1½ lb. ox joints · ¼ cup shortening *or* margarine
1 small turnip · 3 medium carrots
1 large onion · 7½ cups brown stock *or* water
¼ teaspoon mixed herbs (sage, parsley, thyme,
rosemary, and bay leaves) · seasoning
½ cup all-purpose flour.

Soak the ox joints for approximately 1 hour, then
discard the water. Heat the shortening, slice the
vegetables, and sauté for about 5 minutes. Add the
stock, (reserving 1 cup), the ox joints, herbs, and
plenty of seasoning, and simmer gently for about
3 hours. Blend the flour with the 1 cup cold stock,
and stir this into the soup. Bring to a boil, and cook
for about 10 minutes. Remove the ox joints, cut the
meat from the bones, return to the soup, and reheat.
Since this soup will have a fair amount of fat it is
best made the day before required, so that you can
allow it to cool and then remove the fat from the
top.   *Serves 6–8*

Scotch broth

Cooking time   *2¾ hours*

3 tablespoons barley · ½ lb. stewing beef *or* mutton
5 cups water · 1 leek *or* onion, sliced
1 cup diced carrot · 1½ cups diced rutabaga · salt
pepper · ½ cup sliced cabbage.
TO GARNISH: 1 tablespoon chopped parsley.

Blanch the barley by putting into cold water, then
bring the water to a boil, and strain. Put the barley,
diced beef, and water into a pan, bring to a boil,
skim, and simmer gently for 1 hour. Add all the
prepared vegetables, except the cabbage and plenty
of seasoning, and simmer for a further 1½ hours. Add
the cabbage, and simmer an additional 15 minutes.
Skim off any excess fat from the broth, pour into a
heated tureen or soup cups and garnish with parsley.
                                                  Serves 4

FISH SOUPS

Fish makes an excellent soup which is ideal as a
light meal in itself – do not overcook the fish,
otherwise the flavor is lost and in the case of shellfish, the flesh becomes tough.

Fish soup

Cooking time   *55 minutes*

1 lb. fish* · ½ lb. fish trimmings (skin, head, and
bones) · 5 cups water
1 large onion *or* 2 leeks · 2 tablespoons margarine
¼ cup all-purpose flour · ⅔ cup milk
salt · pepper · 1 teaspoon chopped parsley.

* Whiting gives a very delicately flavored soup;
fresh haddock gives a moderately strong flavor;
cod has a very definite flavor.

Wash and clean fish and trimmings. Simmer trimmings in water for 10 minutes. Strain. Place fish
in a pan with the stock and sliced onion or leeks.
Bring to a boil and skim well. Poach gently for 10
minutes. Remove the fish and flake. Cook the stock
for 30 minutes longer. Strain, and rinse the pan.
Melt the margarine, add the flour, and cook, without coloring, for a few minutes. Add the stock and
milk, and return to a boil, stirring constantly. Add
the flaked fish, season, and poach gently for 5
minutes. Add the chopped parsley and serve. *Serves 4*

Mussel soup

Cooking time   *30 minutes*

2½ pints mussels · 3¾ cups water
1 finely chopped onion
3 tablespoons finely chopped celery
small bunch parsley · seasoning · ¼ cup rice
1 large peeled chopped tomato
squeeze lemon juice *or* little vinegar.
TO GARNISH: chopped parsley.

Scrub mussels, discarding any that are open and will
not close when sharply tapped. Always remove the
'beard' (the rather stringy part). Put into a large
saucepan with onion, celery, parsley, and seasoning
and heat slowly until mussels open. Remove mussels
from liquid, and take out of shells. Meanwhile,
reheat liquid, add rice, and simmer until tender with
the tomato. Remove sprig of parsley, add mussels
and lemon juice or vinegar. Reheat gently. Garnish
with chopped parsley.   *Serves 4*

Lobster chowder

Cooking time   *25–30 minutes*

1 small cooked lobster · 2½ cups water
1–2 slices bacon
1 teaspoon finely chopped onion · ½ cup all-purpose
flour · 1 medium potato, diced
1 cup milk *or* whipping cream · dash sugar
salt · pepper · crisp toast strips.

Remove flesh from lobster, cut in small pieces, and
set aside. Put shell only into pan with the water
and simmer gently for about 15 minutes. Strain,
and add enough water to make up to 2½ cups again.
Cut bacon into narrow strips. Put into a pan and
sauté lightly; add the onion and flour, and cook
gently without coloring. Gradually add the lobster
stock, stirring constantly. When the sauce has come
to a boil and thickened, add lobster and the remaining ingredients. Either reduce heat under pan to
cook very gently or put into a double boiler and
cook until it forms a thick creamy mixture. Serve
crisp strips of toast separately.   *Serves 4*

Scallop bisque

Cooking time   *20–40 minutes*

3 tablespoons oil for frying · 1 carrot
1 leek · 1 clove garlic
dash fennel (optional) · 4 peppercorns
½ lb. cod, flounder, *or* lemon sole
3 tablespoons cornstarch
1 (6 oz.) can tomato paste
⅔ cup dry white wine · ⅔ cup water
3¾ cups milk · 4 scallops
¼ cup whipping cream · salt.

Heat the oil in a deep pan. Chop the carrot, leek,
and garlic finely, and add to the oil with fennel and
peppercorns. Sauté lightly. Cut the fish into small
pieces. Add to the vegetables. Continue cooking
gently for 2–3 minutes. Add the cornstarch and
tomato paste. Mix well, then add the wine and
water. Bring to a boil, then add the milk. Cover,
and cook gently for about 20 minutes, or until the
vegetables are tender. Press through a sieve. Cut
the scallops into small pieces, add to the soup, and
return to low heat for about 10 minutes, or until the
scallops are tender. Stir in the cream, and season to
taste.   *Serves 4*

SOUPS FROM ABROAD AND LESS USUAL SOUPS

These provide a wide variety of flavors, from the
refreshing and unusual fruit soups to the richness
of the red wine soup.

Apple soup

Cooking time   *20 minutes*

3 medium fairly sharp baking apples
2½ cups water · 1¼ cups white wine
sugar to taste.
TO GARNISH: lemon slices.

Chop the apples but do not peel or core. Simmer in
the water until tender, then press through a sieve.
Add the white wine. Taste and stir in required sugar
while the apple mixture is still sufficiently warm
to make is dissolve completely. Serve very cold,
garnished with lemon slices.   *Serves 4*

SPICED APPLE SOUP
Add ½ teaspoon cinnamon, ¼ teaspoon nutmeg and ¼
teaspoon allspice to the apples while cooking.

Borsch

Cooking time   *40 minutes–1½ hours*

1 large raw beet *or* slightly more cooked beet
1 carrot · 1 onion · 2–3 tomatoes
clove garlic · little chopped celery
5 cups chicken *or* beef stock *or* water* · seasoning
vinegar.
TO GARNISH: little sour cream *or* cream cheese.

* Use only 3¾ cups with cooked beet.

Grate the beet and put into a pan with the grated
or chopped carrot and onion, tomatoes, crushed
garlic, and celery. Add the stock or water. Simmer
the raw beet for 1½ hours or cooked beet for about
40 minutes. Season, and add a little vinegar. Garnish
with sour cream or cream cheese before serving.
                                   Serves 4

Cheese soup

Cooking time   *25 minutes*

½ onion, finely chopped · ¼ cup butter
⅓ cup all-purpose flour · 2½ cups milk
2 teaspoons salt · dash pepper · 2½ cups white
stock · 3 carrots, finely chopped *or* grated
2 stalks celery *or* piece of celeriac (celery root),
finely chopped *or* grated · 2 cups grated Cheddar
cheese.
TO GARNISH: chopped parsley.

Sauté the onion in the butter until tender. Add the
flour, and cook slowly for 1 minute, stirring constantly. Add the milk, seasoning, and stock gradually, stirring constantly, and bring to a boil. Add
the carrots and celery, and cook until they are
tender. Stir in the cheese, and heat gently until
melted – do not overcook. Garnish with chopped
parsley before serving.   *Serves 4–6*

Greek lemon soup

Cooking time   *25 minutes*

5 cups chicken stock · 6 tablespoons rice flour
2 eggs · 1–2 tablespoons lemon juice · salt
pepper.

Heat the stock and sprinkle in the rice flour, stirring constantly until thickened and then stir
occasionally. Simmer for 20 minutes. Beat the eggs
with the lemon juice. Add about ⅓ cup of the very
hot stock to the eggs and lemon juice, stirring
constantly. Remove the soup from the heat, pour
in the egg mixture, and season with salt and pepper.
Serve at once. Do not boil the soup again after the
eggs have been added or it will curdle.   *Serves 6–8*

Hollandaise cream soup

Cooking time   *12–15 minutes*

2 tablespoons butter · 3 tablespoons cornstarch
3¾ cups chicken *or* veal stock *or* water with 1 chicken
bouillon cube
3 egg yolks · ⅔ cup whipping cream · seasoning
½ teaspoon chopped tarragon
½ teaspoon chopped parsley.
TO GARNISH: few peas.

Melt the butter in a pan, add the cornstarch and
cook for several minutes. Gradually add the stock,
bring to a boil, and simmer for 3 minutes, stirring
constantly. Beat together the egg yolks and cream,
and stir carefully into the soup. Cook WITHOUT
BOILING for a few minutes, stirring constantly.
Lastly add the seasoning, tarragon, and parsley.
Garnish, if desired, with cooked peas.   *Serves 4*

Minestrone soup

Cooking time   *2 hours 10 minutes*

⅓ cup kidney beans · 1 large onion
3 tablespoons olive oil · 1 clove garlic
2–3 slices bacon, diced · seasoning
3¾ cups water *or* white stock · 1 large diced carrot
3 tablespoons chopped celery
3 medium tomatoes *or* 1 (8 oz.) can tomatoes
2 cups finely shredded cabbage · ½ cup macaroni.
TO GARNISH: 1 tablespoon chopped parsley
grated Parmesan cheese.

Soak the kidney beans in water overnight. Chop
onion finely and sauté in the hot oil, with the
crushed garlic and bacon. Add drained beans, seasoning, and water, and simmer gently for about 1½
hours. Put in remaining vegetables, with the exception of the cabbage, and cook for a further 20
minutes, adding a little more water, if necessary.
Add cabbage and macaroni, and cook until both are
barely tender. Taste and add seasoning, if necessary.
Garnish with chopped parsley and the cheese.
   Serves 4

Note: A little red wine may be used in this recipe;
add it with the vegetables.

French onion soup

Cooking time   *30 minutes*

4 medium onions · ½ cup butter
5 cups brown stock · seasoning
4 slices French bread
¼–¾ cup grated Gruyère cheese.

Cut the onions into thin slices, and sauté in the hot
butter until pale gold. Do not allow to become too
dark. Add the stock and seasoning, and simmer for
approximately 20 minutes. Put the bread, which
may be toasted, if desired, into 4 heated soup cups,
add the soup, sprinkle the grated cheese on top of
the bread.   *Serves 4*

FRENCH ONION SOUP GRATINÉE
Make the soup as above, but brown the cheese under
a hot broiler – do not overcook. Illustrated on page
18.

SOUPS TO SERVE COLD

A cold soup is a most refreshing start to a meal.
Make sure it is very cold and serve in chilled dishes.

Jellied consommé

Cooking time   *1 hour*

¾ lb. beef foreshank · 5 cups strong beef stock
seasoning · 1 onion · 1 carrot
small piece celery · sprig parsley · bay leaf.
TO GARNISH: cucumber *or* lemon *or* smoked salmon.

Make consommé using method for Beef consommé
(see page 34). Let stand until cool to form a light
jelly. If the weather is hot, 2 teaspoons powdered
gelatin will help it set. Beat lightly before putting
in chilled soup cups. Garnish with slices of cucumber
or lemon or smoked salmon.   *Serves 4*

Iced cherry soup

Cooking time   *25 minutes*

1½ lb. *or* 1 (1 lb.) can red tart cherries
water · juice 1 lemon · sugar to taste.
TO GARNISH: few sprigs fresh mint.

Cover the fruit with water. Simmer gently, then
add lemon juice and sugar to taste. Reserving few
cherries for garnish, press through sieve and pour
into freezing trays to lightly freeze. Serve in chilled
soup cups decorated with remaining whole cherries
and mint leaves.   *Serves 4*

Gazpacho

Cooking time   *None*

Water · 6 medium tomatoes
1 medium cucumber · 1 onion *or* several scallions
1 or 2 cloves garlic · 1 small green sweet pepper
seasoning · little olive oil
lemon juice *or* white wine vinegar.

Put the water in the refrigerator to become very cold. Peel the tomatoes as this helps when the mixture is strained or placed in a blender, to give a smooth mixture. Peel the cucumber, and finely dice, reserving a little for garnish. Chop the tomatoes, onion, and garlic; add to the cucumber and either pound until smooth or press through a sieve; the sweet pepper may also be strained or chopped very finely, after removing all the seeds and core. (If using a blender, add a little water so none of the thick mixture is wasted.) Put the purée into a bowl, then gradually beat in seasoning, olive oil, and enough cold water to give a flowing consistency. Taste to check seasoning, and add lemon juice or vinegar. Serve garnished with remaining cucumber. This soup must be very cold, so put in the refrigerator until ready to serve and serve in ice cold soup cups.   *Serves 4*

Vichyssoise

Cooking time   *40 minutes*

¼ cup butter · 2 large onions, chopped
8 medium leeks, chopped · 3¾ cups chicken stock
or water with 2 chicken bouillon cubes
2 medium potatoes, chopped
1 tablespoon parsley, chopped
2 eggs *or* egg yolks · ⅔ cup whipping cream *or* milk
seasoning.
TO GARNISH: chopped chives *or* parsley.

Heat butter and sauté chopped onions and leeks until golden but not brown. Add stock, or water with chicken bouillon cubes, chopped potatoes and parsley. Simmer for 30 minutes, press through a sieve and return to pan. Blend eggs with cream, add to soup and cook WITHOUT BOILING for a few minutes. Season. Serve well chilled in ice cold soup cups, garnished with chives or parsley. Or place chilled soup cups in slightly larger bowls and surround with crushed ice.   *Serves 4–6*

Other soups to serve cold

Many soups, other than those given, may be served cold. Remember a thick purée soup or a soup thickened with flour becomes much thicker as it cools, so dilute the mixture with more liquid so the *cold* soup is the consistency of coffee cream. Here are some of the most successful cold soups:

APPLE SOUP (see page 44) – try this with crab apples.

ASPARAGUS SOUP (see page 35) – dilute with extra coffee cream, and serve with lemon wedges.

BORSCH (see page 44) – use more stock and garnish with cream cheese.

CORN SOUP (see page 36) – top with garlic flavored cream cheese.

CUCUMBER PURÉE SOUP (see page 36) – dilute with coffee cream and chicken stock, and serve with lemon.

MULLIGATAWNY (see page 43) – dilute with milk or coffee cream, garnish with raw cauliflowerets and/or diced green sweet pepper.

TOMATO SOUP (see page 41) – use extra stock and flavor with lemon juice. Freeze lightly before serving.

WAYS TO GARNISH SOUP

An attractive garnish makes a soup look more inviting and often creates an interesting taste.

CROUTONS are the most usual garnish and are particularly good in soft creamy soups, e.g. potato, pea and lentil soups.
For 4–6 people remove crusts from 2 slices of bread, and dice into ¼-inch cubes. Sauté in ¼ cup hot fat or butter. Drain well. Do not add to the soup until just before serving – or put croutons into a small dish and serve separately.

ALMONDS – blanched and browned under the broiler – are excellent with chicken, fruit, or lemon soups.

CHOPPED PARSLEY, CHIVES, OR MINT add color and flavor to vegetable and other soups.

CHOPPED HARD-COOKED EGG gives a contrast in color to tomato soup.

SLICED LEMON should garnish cold soups.

PAPRIKA gives color to white creamy soups.

Interesting breads to serve with soup

Most people like bread or rolls with soup and the following suggestions give a 'new look' to bread.

CHEESE AND CARAWAY SLICES
Cut slices of French bread. Spread with butter, sprinkle with finely grated Cheddar cheese and add a few caraway seeds. Heat for 1 minute under a hot broiler.

HAM FINGERS

Excellent with pea soup. Cut sandwiches of bread and butter and lean ham. Remove crusts, cut into narrow strips and fry in hot fat or butter for 1–2 minutes.

Garlic bread

Cooking time   *5–8 minutes*
Oven temperature   *450°F.*

½ cup butter
1 *or* 2 crushed cloves garlic *or* garlic salt to taste
1 long French loaf.

Cream the butter and garlic or garlic salt together. Make slices at regular intervals in the loaf. Press sides of loaf – this opens the cuts – and spread the garlic butter in slices. Put into a preheated 450°F. oven for 5–8 minutes until thoroughly heated. Excellent with soup or to serve with salads.
Serves 4–8

EMERGENCY SOUPS

With the large selection of canned and dehydrated soups on the market one can have a great variety of soups in the cupboard ready for an emergency. Remember canned soups are already cooked, so just need reheating, garnishing, and serving. Check the directions on the can for the correct amount of liquid to add. Dehydrated soups, on the other hand, consist of ingredients from which the liquid content has been removed; there are various types so follow directions for cooking given on the packet. Prepared soups may be used as a basis for interesting dishes. Try adding grated carrot or finely chopped water cress to chicken soup; a can of corn and chopped chives to celery soup; or poached eggs to a can of beef consommé.

SOUPS TO IMPRESS

There are some luxurious soups in this book – those using shellfish in particular – but the following are little known and so would be ideal when you want a soup that is quite out of the ordinary.

Sweet pepper soup

Cooking time   *12–15 minutes*

3¾ cups chicken stock *or* water and 2 bouillon cubes
1 medium grated *or* finely chopped onion
½ diced green sweet pepper
½ diced red sweet pepper (optional)
1–2 grated carrots · ¼ cup very small cauliflowerets
¼ cup peeled diced cucumber
4–5 medium sliced radishes · seasoning.

Put the stock into a saucepan, and bring to a boil, add all the vegetables and seasoning, cover, and simmer for 10 minutes only. Do not overcook, since the vegetables should retain their texture. Serve hot with crispbread and butter.
This may also be made into a delicious creamed soup which could be served hot or cold according to the weather . . . strain the soup after cooking for 15 minutes and reheat. Blend 1 egg yolk with ½ cup whipping cream, and stir into the hot, but not boiling soup. Reheat for a few minutes only, then stir in 3 tablespoons sherry.
Serves 4–6

Cream Julie

Cooking time   *30 minutes*

3 large ripe tomatoes · 1 cup mushrooms
¼ cup butter · 1 small onion
¼ cup all-purpose flour · 2½ cups white stock
seasoning · ⅓ cup very lean tender ham, diced.
TO SERVE: ⅔ cup whipping cream.

Wash the tomatoes and chop coarsely. Wash and peel the mushrooms if necessary (see page 162), then cut into neat thin slices. Sauté the mushrooms in the hot butter. Remove and reserve about half of these but keep those remaining in the pan. Add the chopped onion and the flour, and stir for several minutes, then gradually blend in the stock. Bring to a boil, and cook until slightly thickened. Add the tomatoes and seasoning, and simmer for about 20 minutes. Press through a sieve, reheat, add the reserved mushrooms and diced ham, then cook for several minutes. Pour into soup cups or plates, and serve with the lightly whipped cream. Do not add the cream to the soup while it is boiling – in fact it is better to allow everyone to help themselves.
Serves 4–5

Red wine soup

Cooking time   *10 minutes*

2½ cups inexpensive red wine
dash cinnamon · 1 teaspoon granulated sugar
4 whole cloves · 1¼ cups water · 3 egg yolks
little pepper.

Bring the wine, cinnamon, sugar, cloves, and water to a boil and simmer, without boiling, for about 8 minutes. Pour the hot liquid over the beaten egg yolks, stirring briskly, and add a little pepper to taste. Serve at once, hot.
Serves 4–6

Note: This may be chilled, if desired, and served with 1 tablespoon yogurt or sour cream in each plate or soup cup.

FISH

Fish is a nutritious and interesting food and the great variety of fish available and various methods of cooking mean that it should never be monotonous.

Whichever fish you buy, take care it is fresh – fresh fish is easily recognizable by bright eyes and scales, a pleasant fresh smell (it should never smell of ammonia), and the stiffness of the fish – it should never be 'flabby' and limp-looking. More detailed information is given under the various kinds of fish.

Wise choice of fish

For quick cooking have fish broiled or fried. For sustaining dishes serve fish with a good sauce.

Serve steamed or poached cod or sole to young children or elderly people, for this is the most easily digested fish and form of cooking.

Do not serve a white flesh fish in a white or creamy sauce before a fricassée of chicken or veal – choose shellfish or oily fish. Serve then cold or cook by frying, broiling, or serve with a piquant sauce to make a change in color and taste. If having a main course that is fried, avoid a very rich fish dish. Generally a similar species of fish, fat versus lean and caught in the same type of water (salt or fresh), may be substituted when necessary.

Ways to serve fish

The simplest fish dish looks more attractive if served in the attractive fluted scallop shells rather than on a plate. Put lobster and crab back in the shells to serve, even when hot, for the shell adds color. This may be polished with a very little oil if desired.

Fish cocktails may be served in cocktail glasses, or on shallow dishes, preferably well-chilled.

To serve leftover fish

TAKE CARE THAT LEFTOVER FISH IS NOT KEPT FOR TOO LONG A PERIOD SINCE IT DETERIORATES QUICKLY –

LEAN FISH – use in fish cakes, fish pie, or a fish salad.

OILY FISH (kippers in particular) – pound for a pâté to use as a sandwich filling.

SHELLFISH – use as potted fish, in fish salads, add to sauces.

SMOKED FISH – haddock – put into a Kedgeree, add to potato for fish cakes.

Easy remedies when things are wrong

PROBLEM – if fish breaks when cooking, it could be due to overcooking.

TO REMEDY – if overcooked, then serve with plenty of melted butter or with a sauce to give extra flavor and moisture.

PROBLEM – if fish is not overcooked but still breaks, this is doubtless due to too thin a coating of flour, etc. Do coat fish thoroughly, particularly cod.

TO REMEDY – arrange neatly on the serving dish, and top with a colorful garnish.

PROBLEM – if the fish is lacking in flavor, this is generally due to insufficient seasoning when poached or to overcooking.

TO REMEDY – add a good sauce or seasoned butter.

PROBLEM – if shellfish is tough, this is due to overcooking or defrosting frozen shellfish too quickly.

TO REMEDY – this fish could be chopped in smaller pieces so the toughness is less apparent.

Ways to garnish fish

WITH FRUIT

LEMON is the traditional garnish and certainly lemon juice gives extra 'bite' and flavor to fish. Serve lemon as slices – or wedges – or as butterflies. Cut the slices into quarters and arrange like wings. As twists – cut into fairly thin slices. Make a cut to the center. Twist so the slice stands upright. As halves – cut the lemon in a Vandyke or zigzag pattern, pull the halves apart.

With a knotted garnish on the halved lemon: insert the tip of a knife at the pointed end of the lemon, cut away the peel in a thin regular strip – do this carefully so the peel does not break. Continue until the peel is removed from half the lemon. Cut away the pulp. Twist the peel into a knot on top of the halved lemon.

ORANGE though rarely used – is excellent with cod and herrings.

WITH VEGETABLES

PARSLEY either chop the parsley – the easiest way to do this is to use kitchen scissors or chop the washed and well-dried parsley on a board with a knife, see page 11; or divide the parsley into small sprigs; or fry the sprigs of parsley: wash and dry them thoroughly, put into a frying basket, and lower into very hot deep fat for 1 minute only – remove quickly then fry again for 1 minute. Drain on paper towels.

CUCUMBER cut the cucumber into slices or form into twists as lemon.

Sauces to serve with fish

Most sauces based on a white sauce or béchamel sauce blend excellently with fish. Hollandaise and tartar sauce are classic accompaniments, but sauces with stronger flavoring such as tomato sauce and curry sauce are very good.

Kinds of fish

Fish is generally described under three groups – freshwater fish, which may be either oily or lean; saltwater fish, which may be either oily or lean; and shellfish. In addition there are fish roes, canned, and frozen fish.

SALTWATER FISH

Generally the flesh should be really white and 'milky' looking. The market forms for the fish are varied, usually depending upon the size of the species. They may be purchased either in fillets, or with larger fish in portions of fillets, and in slices which are generally called steaks or cutlets. The best known saltwater fish are:

BARRACUDA (oily) This game fish is not well known although those who have sampled it fresh or smoked find it delicious.

BASS (lean) The well flavored black sea bass found off the Atlantic and Pacific coasts are available whole or in fillets all year. The striped bass is often known as a rockfish. The saltwater species should not be confused with those found in freshwater. Cook like fresh salmon – best broiled or fried.

BLACK DRUM (lean) Found in the Atlantic as far north as New York down to the Rio Grande in the Gulf of Mexico, it is relished particularly in Texas and Louisiana.

BLOWFISH (lean) Also known as a puffer or sea squab, this fish has the capacity to gorge itself with air until nearly cylindrical. Only the flesh surrounding the backbone is eaten.

BLUEFISH (lean) Found from Florida to as far north as Massachussets, this delicately flavored fish averages 6–8 pounds and is generally available whole.

BUTTERFISH (oily) Averaging ½ pound this small fish is a delight to eat for much of the Eastern markets.

COD (lean) Called scrod or codling when young and small, this species of fish is one of the most important of the edible fish ranging from 10–100 pounds when fully grown. Its popularity is perhaps indicated by the numerous available forms – fillets, flaked, salted, shredded, smoked, steaks, and whole. Excellent all-purpose fish because of its definite flavor: particularly good in 'made-up' dishes. Poach, fry, bake or broil. It has large flakes, so when frying it is inclined to break unless floured well before being coated with egg and crumbs or batter.

CUSK (lean) Found from Cape Cod north as far as Greenland, the cusk is rarely marketed whole, although found filleted, smoked, and salted. When fresh, it may be used as a substitute for cod or haddock.

EEL (oily) Eels are oftentimes erroneously classified as freshwater fish. Actually they are both, since the eggs are hatched in the Atlantic. Later the mature eels migrate into European and American rivers for a portion of their life span before returning to the same Atlantic spawning grounds to repeat the cycle. Fish merchants will sell live eels in a tank of water or as the smoked delicacy.

FLOUNDER (lean) This family of fishes includes the sole members – lemon sole, dab, gray sole, and winter flounder, although the flavor and texture varies greatly from the imported Channel soles. It is popularly listed on menus as simply 'sole' and is customarily filleted or whole. May be cooked in most ways.

FLUKE (lean) Another of the flounder family the fluke is also known as a summer flounder. The unusually fine texture of the flesh makes it a popular fish to use in any flounder recipe.

GROUPER (lean) These friendly large clowns of the Atlantic have been tamed by researches while in their underwater homes. The smaller red grouper ranges from 5–15 pounds while the jewfish, found primarily off Florida's coastline, reaches up to 125 pounds. Recipes for red snapper or bass are suitable.

GRUNT (lean) All year the South Atlantic and warm tropical water abounds with this small species of fish. It is marketed whole.

HADDOCK (lean) A close relative of the cod, this smaller fish is becoming one of the most popular. It is found in many forms – whole, fillets, flaked, salted, and when smoked is called Finnan Haddie. A fish, not unlike cod but finer textured. Can be cooked by all methods.

HALIBUT (lean) The small chicken halibut may be purchased whole although steaks are the usual form for the mature halibut which averages 50–100 pounds. Because the taste is so good it may be cooked in quite simple ways.

KINGFISH (oily) Found in the Gulf and the South Atlantic, steaks and whole kingfish are marketed from November to March.

LINGCOD (lean) This fish which ranges from 4–30 pounds may be found as far north in the Pacific as Sitka, Alaska to Santa Barbara, California. It is not related to the cod family despite its name.

MACKEREL (oily) A small rich-flavored fish, it is found from April to November in many forms – fresh, frozen, whole, smoked, canned, and salted. Looks like a larger, more silvery herring. Cook as herrings; particularly good served with a thick gooseberry purée as sauce. The large market in frozen mackerel within the past few years has reduced the quantity of fish which are salted.

MULLET (oily) Striped mullet in the Pacific extend from Central California to Japan while those in the Atlantic may be found as far south as Brazil and northward to Cape Cod. They are available all year whole or filleted.

PILCHARD (oily) Tiny fish ranging from 1½–2 ounces each, much of the catch is canned and the remaining sold fresh whole.

POLLOCK (lean) This relative of the cod and haddock is frequently sold as frozen fillets under the name of deep-sea fillets or ocean-fresh fillets. Its texture remains firm when thawed and it may be prepared following either cod or haddock recipes.

POMPANO (oily) It is considered to be one of the finest of the eating fishes although the small number which are not consumed locally around the Gulf and South Atlantic command an exorbitant price.

PORGY (lean) Found dressed along the Atlantic seaboard this fish averages 1½–2 pounds. A somewhat larger variety may be called Scup which is from 2–4 pounds. It is also filleted.

RED DRUM (lean) Varying greatly from 2–25 pounds, this South Atlantic and Gulf Coast fish is also called redfish or spot bass. Depending upon its size, it may be whole, or cut into fillets or steaks.

RED SNAPPER (lean) This, the mutton fish, schoolmaster, yellowtail and the gray snapper are available all year whole, in steaks, or in fillets. Recipes for bass may be used successfully.

ROSEFISH (oily) Frequently frozen in fillets and designated 'ocean perch', this species and the redfish are a popular choice fish which has rather firm flesh with coarse flakes.

SALMON (oily) Ranging from 3–60 pounds many species such as the popular chinook, sockeye, and red salmon abound in the Pacific waters, migrating inland to freshwater rivers to spawn. A small catch of Kennebec are caught in the North Atlantic also. Besides the fresh and frozen steaks, much of the salmon available is canned or smoked.

SEA HERRING (oily) It is rare to see fresh herring; however, it is popular salted, smoked, and canned. When canned the term 'sardine' covers a number of small fish species. Make sure herrings are very firm and bright-eyed. May be broiled, fried, baked (with stuffing, if desired) or pickled and soused to have with salads.

SHAD (oily) When in season between February and April this fish is available whole or filleted. At other times, it may be purchased canned.

SHARK (oily) Fillets and chunks of this fish are sold all year.

SHEEPSHEAD (lean) It averages about 1½ pounds along the Atlantic and Gulf coasts, and it may be sold either whole or filleted.

SKATE (lean) This unusual shaped fish is a member of the ray family which has a broad diamond shape although it is very flat. The wings are the edible portion. An unusual fish which has a very firm flesh. Fry, bake or poach – it is recommended that the fish be steamed for a few minutes before frying.

SQUID (oily) The squid, cuttlefish, or inkfish as it is also frequently called is usually purchased dressed – the bone has been removed and the abdomen slit. Wash it very thoroughly.

SWORDFISH (oily) Steaks are customarily sold from this very popular fish. It is caught in the Atlantic and Pacific, and imported from the Mediterranean.

TUNA (oily) Although this may be purchased fresh in steaks most fish lovers are familiar with the crisp white flesh of the albacore and the slightly pink color of the blue fin.

WHITING (lean) Also called silver hake, this frequently frozen fish has become a popular newcomer to the 'fish and chips' shops. It averages 1–4 pounds. A fish that is light and easily digested. It may be used in place of lemon sole and is excellent cooked whole.

FRESHWATER FISH

Some of the fish given as freshwater are fish that migrate into rivers and lakes from the ocean. These fish may have a slightly 'muddy' flavor so wash in plenty of cold water before cooking.

BASS (lean) The number of species of freshwater bass abound – rock, calico, spotted, striped, large-mouthed, and small-mouthed to mention only a few. Many are reserved as game fishes. It belongs to the same family as the crappie, therefore the similarity of names.

BLUEGILL SUNFISH (lean) Another member of the crappie family, this fish is reserved as a game fish. The fish has firm and flabby flesh and averages 1 pound in the Great Lakes and Mississippi Valley.

BUFFALO FISH (lean) Ranging from 2–20 pounds, this Mississippi Valley fish and its varieties is similar to a carp in flavor if not preferred by many people. It is available whole, dressed, drawn, in steaks, or fillets.

BURBOT (lean) A freshwater member of the cod family and frequently called freshwater cod, recipes for cod or haddock may be used successfully.

CARP (lean) This is one of the few freshwater fish available in so many forms including: alive, whole, fillets, steaks and smoked. Large tanks permit its shipment alive. Unless a very small carp, this fish is too tough for broiling or frying.

CATFISH (lean) The Great Lakes and Mississippi Valley provides much of the bulk of this fish for market or sport. It is available skinned and dressed for those who dislike the job which is necessary before cooking.

CRAPPIE (lean) This fish is reserved as a game fish and is rarely available on the market. Depending upon the species, the average weight is 1–4 pounds.

LAKE HERRING (oily) This tiny 5–6 ounce species found in the Great Lakes is closely related to the whitefish rather than the sea herring. It is also called cisco.

LAKE TROUT (lean) Also called togue, this fish is marketed whole or drawn from northern lakes. It averages 6–8 pounds.

LAKE SALMON (lean) This fish is not to be confused with the fat salmon caught in saltwater. It is a game fish located in Maine and as far north as Labrador.

MULLET (oily) Larger than the saltwater mullet, this fish averages 2–5 pounds and is found throughout the United States in lakes, streams, and the Mississippi River.

MUSKELLUNGE (lean) Also called the musky, this is reserved as a game fish.

PICKEREL (lean) This 1½ pound fish is marketed whole, and is a very well known favorite.

PIKE (lean) Called many names such as jack pike, northern pike, or the lake pike, this species is a member of the same family as the muskellunge and the pickerel. It is found in rivers bordering the Great Lakes north to Alaska and the Arctic Circle.

SHEEPSHEAD (lean) Available whole or in fillets, this fish averages 2–8 pounds and is available all year. The flesh is known to be exceptionally tender.

SMELT (lean) Classified sometimes as a saltwater fish, the smelt migrates from the ocean to spawn in the Great Lakes and surrounding rivers. They are available from September to May although the season and run varies depending upon the location. May be poached, broiled, fried, baked, or cooked in white wine or apple cider. To prepare, remove the fins but leave head on to cook.

TROUT (lean) Numerous species are considered favorite game fish – brook (also called speckled, mountain or brown), golden, rainbow (salmon), and the steel head which is the rainbow trout when caught in saltwater. Keep well basted when cooking since the fish is rather dry. Ideal to cook almost immediately after being caught.

WHITEFISH (oily) The 1–2 pound species of this fish which, like the lake herring, may be called cisco are frequently found in the Great Lakes and other smaller northern lakes and streams. Within recent years government control of the lamprey eel has reduced the harm of the parasite upon the fish.

YELLOW PERCH (lean) Also called the yellow pike perch, this small 1–2 pound fish is plentiful in northern lakes and is marketed whole, filleted, or frozen.

SHELLFISH

The way to test if shellfish is fresh is to make sure there is no stale smell of ammonia – the color of the shell should be bright and the tails of the lobsters should spring back when tested (see page 52).

ABALONE Found particularly along California's coast this univalve mollusk is available fresh only in California. Some are canned for shipping however. Fresh abalone requires pounding before preparation and slight undercooking to prevent toughness.

CLAMS Both the East Coast and West Coast vie for the title claiming the excellence in clams. Those in the East are the soft-shell (long-necked) and the hard-shell (little-necked). The latter also enjoys the Indian name guahog. Those on the Pacific coast are razor clams, geoducks, and mud clams. Smaller than oysters, but may be served in the same way.

CRABS The Pacific crab, which is also called Dungeness, is the species available all year. Those from the Atlantic coast such as the hard-shell (blue), oyster, rock, and sweetwater have shorter seasons. It should be noted that the hard-shell (blue) is the same species as the soft-shell although caught at one of the times when the crab has just shed its shell during growth. Dress and serve hot or cold. Be sure to remove the stomach bag and grey-brown fingers. To cook put in boiling salted water, simmer for 20–25 minutes, rinse in cold water. Best selection is male crab, distinguished by larger claws.

CRAWFISH OR CRAYFISH Spelled either way, this is the same as the French écrevisse. It may be called a rock lobster in which case only the tail is eaten. Although no large claws, use as lobster.

LOBSTER Termed homard in French this crustacean is caught off the Florida coast and north in the Atlantic. It has 2 large heavy claws and should be cooked when alive. Some cooked meat is sold, and some is available canned. Serve hot or cold. To cook, wash well, tie claws and put into boiling water. Simmer for 20–25 minutes according to size, BUT NO MORE, then put into cold water. Hen lobster has a wide tail and red coral, which is delicious. The lobster should feel heavy for its size, and the tail should spring back when tested. Be sure to remove intestinal vein and the lady fingers.

MUSSELS The majority of mussel fame lies with the saltwater mollusk although a freshwater species is found in central U.S. and in Middle Europe. They are available live in the shell and canned. Serve raw as oysters in a sauce.

OYSTERS Those species of oysters both from the Atlantic coast and Pacific coast beds are available from September to May shucked, live in the shell, or canned. Generally served raw as hors d'oeuvre, may be used in sauces or as main dish, delicious as filling in omelets.

SCALLOPS This mollusk is well known for its beautiful shell. The smaller species, bay scallops are more tender and a pale pink or tan color, while the larger sea scallop which is more plentiful is both firmer and whiter in color. Use in sauces and main dishes. The roe (coral) should be firm and bright in color. Remove the black part and gristly fiber. Save shells to use in scalloped dishes.

SHRIMP Customarily the small and the jumbo shrimp are purchased headless. Today they are found in a variety of states – fresh, frozen, raw, cooked, shelled, unshelled, and de-veined. They come from the Gulf coast primarily.

TERRAPIN From October to March the diamond-back terrapin which is a freshwater and saltwater swamp turtle is available cooked, live in the shell, or canned. It is both very rare and expensive.

TURTLE Of the several species available, perhaps green turtle ranks as the most famous since it provides the famous turtle soup. It is available live in the shell and canned, as are the snapping turtle from New Orleans and the soft-shell turtle.

SMOKED FISH

COD This is filleted then cured. Cook as smoked haddock. Allow 6–8 oz. per person.

EEL An unusual but excellent hors d'oeuvre (see page 24). Allow approximately 1–1½ oz. eel fillets or 2–2½ oz. of the whole eel.

HADDOCK Either filleted and smoked or cured whole. Poach in water or milk, and serve with butter or a sauce. Top with poached egg, if desired. Take care not to overcook. Excellent as kedgeree. Allow 8–10 oz. per person.

SALMON Serve as hors d'oeuvre. Allow 1½–2 oz. per person.

SEA HERRINGS Herrings are smoked in various ways: Kippers may be fried, broiled, baked, or boiled. Bloaters are best broiled or fried. Buckling are served as smoked trout.

WHITING Cook as haddock, generally called 'golden fillets'. Allow 2 fillets per person.

CANNED FISH

Until the can is opened, this fish will keep indefinitely. When opened, refrigerate or use at once.

ANCHOVIES Sold either flat fillets or rolled. Add to sauces, use in salads, sandwiches etc.

CRAB Use in salads and sandwiches.

SEA HERRINGS Buy fresh herrings canned. Use in salads, sandwiches, or for reheating.

BUCKLING OR ROLLMOPS Buy in jars. Use in salads.

SALMON Use in salads, sandwich fillings, or in dishes such as fish pie, fish cakes.

SARDINES Use in salads, sandwich fillings, or serve on hot toast.

TUNA Found as solid pack, flakes, chunks, and pieces Use as salmon.

LOBSTER Use in salads and sandwiches.

PILCHARDS Use in salads, sandwiches, or for reheating.

SHRIMP Use as fresh.

FROZEN FISH

Many fish are obtainable frozen, sometimes they are coated ready to fry.
Follow the manufacturer's directions on the package for defrosting and cooking. Many fish may be cooked when frozen but frozen shellfish should be defrosted at room temperature.

FISH ROES

COD ROE This should first be steamed. Allow approximately 10–15 minutes per lb. and the roe is then ready to use. It may be skinned, then sliced, and fried in bacon drippings. The steamed, sliced roe may be brushed with melted fat and fried and used in place of, or mixed with, fish in fish pie. Fresh, it may also be used in a fish pâté (see page 25).

SMOKED COD ROE This is an excellent sandwich filling. Skin and mash with butter, seasoning, and a little lemon juice. Use in a pâté for hors d'oeuvre.

SOFT HERRING ROE Separate, wash and dry the soft roes, which are the sperm from the male, coat in a little flour, and sauté for a few minutes in butter or margarine. Serve on toast or put on top of cooked herrings.
Another excellent way of cooking the roe which

makes it easily digestible and, therefore, suitable for young children or invalids is to put on a plate with butter or margarine, a little seasoning and cream or milk. Cover with a second plate and steam over a pan of rapidly boiling water for approximately 10 minutes. Serve on hot toast garnished with paprika, butter, and/or chopped parsley. The cooked roe may be put into a white sauce or used instead of flaked fish in a fish pie.

HARD HERRING ROE Separate, wash, and dry the hard roes which are the eggs from the female.
To fry – coat in seasoned flour or egg and bread crumbs or batter, and fry in shallow or deep fat.
To broil – put into the broiler pan, not on the rack, brush with melted butter or margarine and broil – serve with broiled tomatoes.
As a pâté – steam the roe as instructed for soft roe but use little, if any, milk to give a drier mixture. Pound the roe until soft, add seasoning, a little extra butter if desired, and a squeeze of lemon juice. To give a more interesting color, a few drops of anchovy paste may be added; in which case use less salt.

STURGEON ROE (CAVIAR) One of the most expensive delicacies, although there is cheaper caviar than that which comes from Russia or Iran (which is considered the finest). Serve on brown toast or brown bread and butter topped with finely chopped hard-cooked egg and a squeeze of lemon. As an hors d'oeuvre, serve on a bed of lettuce with lemon and hot brown toast.

SALMON ROE Excellent when poached or sautéed.

SHAD ROE A choice favorite when sautéed in melted butter or broiled for several minutes, brushing frequently with melted butter.

To fillet or bone fish

Fish is easier to serve when it has been filleted, i.e. when the fish is taken off the bone. This is generally done by the fish dealer if requested, but it is worthwhile knowing how to do this. The method depends upon the type of fish – flat fish, for example, may be made into four small, or two large fillets as given below. Always choose a sharp knife, one with a point so this may be inserted under the flesh. If the tip of the knife is dipped in salt it has a better cutting edge; naturally this salt must be rinsed off the fish.

TO CUT FLAT FISH INTO FOUR FILLETS

Cut off the head with a sharp knife (for fish stock, the head provides a great deal of flavor). Make a deep incision down the back of the fish, i.e. on the side with the dark skin. Make a shallow cut around the edge of the flesh, avoiding the bones and fins. Insert the tip of the knife in the flesh and gradually loosen it away from the backbone, folding it over gently. Do not hurry or pull, otherwise some of the flesh may be left on the bone. Having removed one fillet from the back, turn the fish over and repeat this process, working this time from the tail rather than the head. Now remove the second fillet from the black side, then the white.

TO CUT FLAT FISH INTO TWO FILLETS

Remove the head, as given in the instructions above, then make a deep incision just above the tail, and a shallow cut around the edge of the fish. Put the tip of the knife under the tail, cut, and gently ease away the flesh, as given above. There is a tendency for there to be a thin 'break' in the center of these two fillets if the flesh is not thick, so handle carefully.

TO FILLET OTHER FISH

Cut off the head of the fish, then make a long slit under the stomach and remove intestines – retain roe where desired. With large fish, insert the knife under the backbone and gently ease this away from the flesh. This then leaves the whole fish without a backbone. Wash this in cold water to make sure all tiny particles of bone and intestines are removed, then cut the fish into two fillets – these may be skinned, if desired.
Fish containing a high percentage of bone to flesh, herrings for example, are generally boned before cooking. As the flesh of a herring is fine and delicate it is important to remove this carefully.

TO BONE HERRINGS

Scale, if necessary, by scraping with a knife from tail to head. Cut off head, slit along stomach. Remove the intestines and roe, which should be kept. The roe may be cooked with the fish or separately. Wash. Open the herring and put cut side downward onto a board. Run your thumb very firmly along the center, feeling the backbone; do this several times. Turn fish over; you will find the backbone completely loosened and easy to remove. Trim fins and tail, and cut fish into two fillets, if desired – herrings are not skinned.

To skin fish

Take the fillet in the left hand, holding it by the tip. Make a firm cut with a sharp knife just at the tip, then lift the flesh with the knife away from the skin; continue until all the flesh is free. Dip the edge of the knife in a little salt for a better cutting edge.
This is the correct way to skin fish, but if you are in a great hurry, put the fillets under a hot broiler for a moment, and the skin will come away easily.
The above method describes skinning fillets, but whole fish may be skinned in the same way, by first loosening the skin from the body in one place and then gently easing it away.

WAYS TO COOK FISH

While there are many interesting dishes made from fish, the basic methods of cooking are as follows:

Poaching fish

Suitable for smoked fish, fresh salmon, and fresh-water fish. While the term 'boiling' fish is often used, this is incorrect, since fish must not be boiled, it would break and the flavor be spoiled. It should be poached i.e. cooked gently; allow 1¼ cups water, ½ teaspoon salt to each portion of fish. Omit salt with smoked fish. If cooking several pieces of fish, do not increase the amount of water a great deal; allow a sufficient amount to cover the fish.
Put the fish into cold salted water, bring just to a boil, lower the heat, simmer for:
3 minutes – thin fillets of fish
5 minutes – thicker fillets
7 minutes – thick slices or steaks.
Carefully remove fish from water, drain, then serve with butter and lemon or a sauce.

Baking fish

Since fish has a dry flesh compared to meat, it should always be put into a greased dish, unless it is covered with liquid. In most cases the dish should be covered with a lid, greased foil or wax paper so that the flesh is kept moist.
An ideal way to bake is in wine. Use a preheated 350°F. oven and allow:
15 minutes for thin fillets of fish
20–25 minutes for thicker fillets or steaks
30–35 minutes for whole fish.
Baking is suitable for most fish – see individual recipes and page 55.

Broiling fish

This is suitable for all kinds of fish; however, it is rarely used for shellfish. Preheat the broiler before cooking the fish. Brush the rack of the broiler with melted butter or margarine to prevent the fish sticking or place the fish on a piece of greased foil. Put this on the rack. Brush the fish with melted butter or margarine, season lightly, and add a little lemon juice.

BROIL FISH FOR
2–3 minutes – thin fillets of fish
(These do not need turning)
5 minutes – thicker fillets
(These do not need turning but lower heat for last few minutes of cooking time)
9–10 minutes – thick slices or steaks
(Turn fish during cooking and brush second side with melted butter or margarine).

Frying fish

Suitable for all kinds of oily fish, freshwater fish, and some shellfish.
There are two methods of frying used for fish:
a) shallow frying, see below:
b) deep frying, see below.

SHALLOW-FRYING OR PAN-FRYING

Dry the fish very well after washing and coat in either seasoned flour or egg and bread crumbs. Heat approximately ¼ cup fat (enough to give a depth of a ¼ inch) for thin fish or about ⅓ cup fat for thicker pieces of fish. Test the temperature of the fat as when frying fish in deep fat. Put in the coated fish and cook for:
4 minutes – thin fillets of fish
(Turn after 2 minutes and cook for the same time on the second side)
5–6 minutes – thicker fillets
(Cook as above, then lower the heat for final 1–2 minutes)
7–9 minutes – thick pieces or whole fish
(Cook as thin fillets then lower heat for the final 3–5 minutes).

DEEP-FRYING

Minimum 2 cups fat *or* 2½ cups oil
4 portions fish
3 tablespoons all-purpose flour with seasoning either egg and bread crumb coating *or* batter coating (see following page).

Heat the deep fat with the frying basket in position to 375°F. Coat the dry fish with seasoned flour, then with egg and bread crumb or batter coating. Test to see if the fat or oil is sufficiently hot. A cube of bread should turn golden brown within 1 minute in fat (oil takes slightly under 1 minute to brown the bread). If the bread shows no signs of browning in this time, heat the fat or oil longer and test again. If the bread browns very much more quickly, the fat or oil is too hot. Remove pan from heat and cool, but remember that overheated fat or oil can give an unpleasant taste to food. Lower the fish carefully into the frying basket; never bend over the pan of hot fat in case it splutters. Reduce the heat slightly, so the fat does not continue to become hotter, cook for:

3 minutes – thin fillets of fish
4 minutes – thicker fillets of fish
5 minutes – thick pieces or steaks of fish.

Lift the fish in the frying basket out of the pan of hot fat, and hold the basket over the pan for a few seconds so that the surplus fat drains back into the pan. Tip the fish onto paper towels on a heated plate. This drains off excess fat and makes sure the fish is really crisp. Serve garnished with lemon and parsley and serve with fried potatoes.

COATING FISH FOR FRYING

There are three ways of coating fish:

1. FLOUR COATING – to 4 portions of fish allow:
¼–½ cup all-purpose flour · dash salt
dash pepper.

Wash and dry the fish thoroughly with paper towels. This makes certain the flour will adhere to it. Arrange the seasoned flour on either a piece of wax paper or on a flat surface. Press the fish onto the flour on one side, turn, and do the same with the second side. Make sure the fish is completely covered with flour; then lift onto a clean plate.

2. EGG AND BREAD CRUMBS – to 4 portions of fish or shrimp allow:
3–4 tablespoons all-purpose flour · dash salt
dash pepper · 1 egg · 1 tablespoon water
¼–⅓ cup toasted bread crumbs.

Wash and dry the fish well on paper towels. Coat

the fish with flour as above. Sometimes this step is omitted, but you will have a more even coating of egg and bread crumbs if flour is used first. Blend egg and water, then either put the fish into the egg and turn it with a spoon and knife or with 2 knives, or leave the fish on a plate and brush the egg over one side of the fish then turn and brush the second side. Whichever method is used, make certain that the fish is thoroughly coated. Put the bread crumbs either onto another plate or square of wax paper, or into a wax paper bag. Place the fish onto the bread crumbs, if on a plate or square of wax paper, and press firmly against them so they coat one side; then turn with 2 knives and coat the second side. Press the bread crumbs very firmly against the fish with a broad-bladed knife or spatula, to make certain they stick firmly and do not fall off and burn during cooking. A paper bag is the quickest and easiest way for coating but it sometimes spoils the shape of the fish unless used very carefully. Drop the fish into the bread crumbs in the bag, and shake up and down gently. This is particularly suitable for small portions of cod fillets, fish steaks, or shrimp. Remove the coated fish from the bag, and press the bread crumbs firmly against the fish with a knife or spatula. The fish is then ready to fry. Follow the directions for shallow or deep-frying (see previous page).

3. BATTER – to 4 portions of fish or shrimp allow:
1 cup all-purpose flour · dash salt · 1 egg
1 cup milk
3 tablespoons all-purpose flour with seasoning.

For a thinner coating batter, use an additional 3 tablespoons milk. Sift the flour with the salt, add the egg, and beat well, then gradually beat in the milk. Milk and water could be used for a more economical coating. Coat the fish with the seasoned flour. Dip the fish into the batter. Remove with a fork and spoon, and hold suspended over the batter so that any surplus may drop back into the bowl. This saves making any mess as you put the fish into the fat. It also avoids too thick a coating. Use the smaller percentage of milk for rather solid pieces of fish such as cod, and the thinner batter, i.e. using the additional milk, for thinner pieces of fish.

Fish cakes

Cooking time   *6 minutes*

½ lb. poached *or* steamed lean saltwater fish
2 cups mashed potatoes · 1 egg · seasoning.
TO COAT: 3–4 tablespoons seasoned flour · 1 egg
¼–⅓ cup toasted bread crumbs.
TO FRY: ¼–⅓ cup fat. TO GARNISH: parsley · lemon.

Remove all bones and skin from the fish; flake with a fork. Add the potatoes, egg, and seasoning, mix well, then divide into 8 round cakes. Coat the fish

cakes in seasoned flour, then in egg and bread crumbs (see previous page). Heat the fat in a skillet and fry the fish cakes for 2–3 minutes until golden brown on the underside. Turn, then cook for the same time on the second side. Remove from the skillet and drain on paper towels. Serve hot, garnished with parsley and lemon.   *Serves 4*

There is another way of binding fish cakes – instead of the egg use a thick panada (see page 182) made with 2 tablespoons margarine, ¼ cup all-purpose flour, and ⅔ cup milk and seasoning.

ANCHOVY FISHCAKES
Stir 2–3 drops of anchovy extract into the half-beaten egg or into the sauce.

PARSLEY FISHCAKES
Add 1–2 teaspoons chopped parsley to the mixture before cooking.

SALMON FISHCAKES
Use 8 oz. flaked canned salmon for the fish.

Baked stuffed fish

Many lean saltwater fish are excellent when stuffed and baked whole. The most suitable are small cod called codling or haddock.
Stuffings may vary a great deal . . . try Parsley stuffing (see page 189), Mushroom stuffing (see page 189), Sage and onion stuffing – particularly good with cod (see page 189).
Cut the head off the fish, clean it well and remove the backbone if possible. Season the flesh well, press in the stuffing and secure with either fine string or skewers. Lift into a well-greased roasting pan – if a fairly crisp skin is required, then brush this with melted butter, margarine or oil. If a softer skin is preferred, then grease the fish, place in an ovenproof casserole and cover tightly or cover with well-greased foil or wax paper. Bake in a preheated 350°F. oven if the fish is fairly large, allowing about 20 minutes per lb., or a preheated 375°F. oven if the fish is small, allowing a good 15 minutes per lb. Serve garnished with baked tomatoes, etc. Illustrated on page 39.

Fish pie

Cooking time   *25–30 minutes*
Oven temperature   *375°F.*

1 lb. lean saltwater fish poached *or* steamed
2¼ cups mashed potatoes · 2 tablespoons margarine
WHITE SAUCE: 2 tablespoons margarine *or* butter
¼ cup all-purpose flour · 1¼ cups milk
dash salt · dash pepper.
TO GARNISH: parsley.

Flake the cooked fish, put into a pie pan, then make the white sauce (see page 183). Cover the fish with the sauce, then spread the mashed potatoes on top, making sure this covers the sauce. Put tiny pieces of margarine on top. Bake for 25–30 minutes in a preheated 375°F. oven. Garnish with parsley and serve hot.   *Serves 4*

MIXED FISH PIE
Follow the directions above, but use a mixture of fish . . . flaked lean saltwater fish, canned or fresh salmon, and shellfish.

Fish whirls

Cooking time   *20 minutes*
Oven temperature   *375°F.*

8 fillets flounder *or* whiting · seasoning
squeeze lemon juice · ¼ cup butter
1½ cups milk · 1 cup cooked shelled shrimp
¼ cup all-purpose flour
3–4 tablespoons whipping cream.
TO GARNISH: chopped parsley.

Form the fillets into rolls, season, and add a squeeze
of lemon juice. Put onto a deep plate with half the
butter and a very little milk and steam for about
10 minutes, or bake in a preheated 375°F. oven for
approximately 20 minutes, or until just tender. Fill
the rolls with the shrimp halfway through the
cooking. Lift out of the butter and milk, and put
onto a very hot serving dish. Keep hot. Heat the
remaining butter, stir in the flour, and cook for
several minutes. Strain the liquid from cooking the
fish and add to the milk, blend this into the white
sauce. Bring to a boil, and cook until thickened,
season well, stir in the cream, then pour this sauce
around the fish, and garnish with chopped parsley.
Illustrated on page 38.   *Serves 4*

Fish puff

Cooking time   *30 minutes*
Oven temperature   *375°F.*

1 lb. cooked lean saltwater fish
1 cup mashed potatoes
2 tablespoons butter *or* margarine · 3 eggs
¼ cup milk · seasoning.

Flake the fish and blend it with the potatoes, melted
butter, 2 egg yolks, milk, and seasoning. Put into
a shallow ovenproof dish and bake in a preheated
375°F. oven for 20 minutes. Beat the egg whites until
very stiff, fold into the beaten yolk with plenty of
seasoning. Spread over the fish, and return to the
oven immediately. Leave for a further 10 minutes
until the top is brown.   *Serves 4*

FISH AND CHEESE PUFF
Follow the recipe above but add ½ cup very finely
grated Cheddar cheese and 2 teaspoons chopped
parsley to the stiffly beaten egg whites. Illustrated
on page 40.

Cod and bacon

Cooking time   *10 minutes*

4 cod steaks *or* pieces of cod fillet
dash pepper · squeeze of lemon juice
2 tablespoons butter *or* margarine
4 slices Canadian-style bacon · 4 tomatoes.
TO GARNISH: lemon · parsley.

Wash and dry the cod very well. Season with pepper
but do not use salt since the bacon is salty. Sprinkle
with lemon juice. Melt the butter or margarine,
brush the rack of the broiler pan with this, then put
on the fish, brush with a little more butter or
margarine and broil under a high heat for 5 minutes.
Turn over, brush with the remaining butter or
margarine, then place the bacon on top and the
halved tomatoes, which should be well seasoned.
Broil for a further 4–5 minutes. Garnish with lemon
and parsley before serving.   *Serves 4*

Cod in cider

Cooking time   *25–35 minutes*
Oven temperature   *375°F.*

4 cod steaks · seasoning · 2 onions
1 green sweet pepper · 1¼ cups apple cider
3 tablespoons all-purpose flour
1 tablespoon butter *or* margarine.

Tie the pieces of cod into neat circles or skewer in
position. Season, and put into the bottom of an
ovenproof baking dish. Add the thinly sliced onions,
the diced, deseeded pepper, and the cider. Cover with
foil or a lid and bake in a preheated 375°F. oven for
20–30 minutes, depending on the thickness of the
fish. Remove the cod from the liquid, and put onto
a heated serving dish. Blend the flour and butter or
margarine in a saucepan, and cook for 2 minutes,
then gradually add the liquid from cooking the fish,
onions, and pepper, and cook until moderately thick.
Pour over the cod.   *Serves 4*

Cod casserole

Cooking time   *25–30 minutes*
Oven temperature   *375°F.*

4 cod steaks · seasoning
1½ oz. butter *or* margarine · 4 large tomatoes
1 small onion
1 tablespoon chopped parsley *or* chives
3 tablespoons fish stock *or* water *or* white wine.

Form the cod into neat shapes and tie these if
possible. Season well. Use half the butter or margarine to grease an ovenproof baking dish, and put
the fish into this. Peel the tomatoes, and cut into
very thin slices. Peel the onion, and grate it finely.
Put half the tomatoes over the fish, then the onion
and parsley or chives, and the remaining tomatoes.
Season well. Add the liquid, and put the remaining
butter or margarine on top. Do not cover the dish.
Bake in a preheated 375°F. oven for approximately
30 minutes. This should be sufficiently moist to
make a sauce quite unnecessary.

         Serves 4

This way of cooking fish may be varied in a number
of ways and various kinds of lean saltwater fish may
be used.

58

Roast rib of beef, page 74

Rolled sirlion, page 74; and Yorkshire puddings, page 209

Chicken and ham galantine, page 337; and Chicken Chasseur, page 339

Cod Dugléré

Cooking time   *25–30 minutes*

1 tablespoon butter · 1 medium onion
3 tomatoes ·· 1 tablespoon chopped parsley
3 tablespoons white wine *or* apple cider
⅔ cup water
1 large package frozen cod steaks (approximately
1¼ lb.)
FOR THE SAUCE: 1 tablespoon butter
3 tablespoons all-purpose flour.
TO GARNISH: parsley.

Melt the butter, and sauté the chopped onion without browning until soft. Add the peel and de-seeded tomatoes, parsley, wine, and water, and place the cod steaks in this mixture. Poach very gently for 15 to 20 minutes. Meanwhile, make a white sauce with the butter and flour; add the tomato and wine mixture, bring to a boil, and stir until sauce has thickened. Pour over the fish and garnish with parsley.   *Serves 4*

Baked flounder and mushrooms

Cooking time   *Approximately 20 minutes*
Oven temperature   *375°F.*

4 large or 8 small flounder fillets
seasoning · ⅓ cup butter · squeeze lemon juice
½–1 cup mushrooms.

Skin the flounder if desired (see page 53), and season well. Spread with half the butter, and sprinkle with lemon juice. Slice the mushrooms very thinly. Arrange the fillets in a well-buttered, ovenproof baking dish. If the fillets are large they will need to be folded in half; if small put the four fillets only into the baking dish. Put the mushrooms on top of half the big fillets or over the four small fillets. Either fold the ungarnished half of the large fillets over the mushrooms or place the four other small fillets on top of the mushrooms. Season the fish very well, and top with the remaining butter. Cover with a lid or foil, and bake in a preheated 375°F. oven for approximately 20 minutes. If the fillets are very thick you may need to allow a little longer cooking time, but do not overcook.   *Serves 4*

Haddock and cucumber

Cooking time   *Approximately 15 minutes*

¼ cup butter *or* margarine · seasoning
4 haddock steaks · ½ small cucumber
either 1¼ cups cultured sour cream *or* coffee cream
and 1 tablespoon lemon juice.

Heat the butter, and fry the well seasoned haddock in this until nearly tender. Peel and slice the cucumber. Add to the haddock with the sour cream or cream and lemon juice. Season. Heat gently for about 5 minutes. The cucumber will not be particularly soft but this makes a very pleasant contrast in texture. If, however, it is required to be very soft, then it should be put in with the haddock, sautéed in the butter, and allowed to cook for the whole period.   *Serves 4*

Halibut bake

Cooking time   *25–30 minutes*
Oven temperature   *375°F.*

4 halibut steaks · ⅔ cup white wine
8 small onions or shallots
½ teaspoon finely chopped mixed fresh herbs (sage, parsley, thyme, rosemary, and bay leaves)
seasoning.

Put the halibut into an ovenproof casserole with the other ingredients. Cover tightly and bake in a preheated 375°F. oven for 25 minutes or until tender. Lift the halibut onto a heated serving dish, and top with the unthickened liquid and onions. If preferred, the halibut may be put onto a heated serving dish with the onions and the liquid strained and used as a white wine sauce. Halibut is such a rich fish that baking in a clear liquid like white wine is a very good way of cooking it.   *Serves 4*

Fried skate

Cooking time   *12–15 minutes*

4 portions skate · seasoning · ⅓ cup butter
1 tablespoon lemon juice *or* 1 tablespoon white, malt or wine vinegar.

Steam the skate for about 5 minutes. Dry well. Season, and fry in butter until tender, turning to cook both sides. Lift the fish onto a heated plate. Add the lemon juice or vinegar to the butter, heat this. Pour over the skate and serve immediately.
          Serves 4

Variations

1. Add a little chopped parsley to the butter.
2. Add tiny snippets of fresh lemon peel to the butter.
3. Add a few capers and diced gherkins to the butter.
4. Brown the butter, as given under halibut meunière (see page 62), and pour over the skate.

Grilled flounder with savory butter

Cooking time   *3–5 minutes*

FOR THE BUTTER: 1 crushed clove garlic (optional)
grated peel of 1 lemon · dash cayenne pepper
dash celery salt · seasoning · ⅓ cup butter
4 large *or* 8 small flounder fillets.
TO GARNISH: water cress.

Blend all the flavorings with the butter. Since none of this should be wasted, it is a good idea to spread about one-third over a piece of foil and fit this onto the rack of the broiler. If foil is not available, then put one-third of the savory butter into the broiler pan itself. Either lay the flounder over the foil or put into the broiler pan. Top with the remaining butter, spread this evenly over the fillets. Broil for 3 minutes for thin fillets, 5 minutes for thick fillets, or a little longer if necessary. Do not overcook. Put the fish on a heated serving dish, pour over the butter, and garnish with water cress.
          Serves 4

Flounder Bercy

Cooking time   30–40 minutes
Oven temperature   350°F.

4 large *or* 8 small flounder fillets
2 shallots *or* small onions · 2 teaspoons parsley
seasoning · 1¼ cups white wine
⅔ cup water *or* fish stock · 2 tablespoons butter
¼ cup all-purpose flour.

Fold fillets, put into a buttered ovenproof dish with the chopped shallots, parsley, seasoning, half the wine, and water or fish stock. Cover with buttered wax paper and bake in a preheated 350°F. oven for approximately 20 minutes. Heat butter, stir in flour, and cook gently for several minutes. Add remaining wine, and cook until smooth. Lift fillets onto a heated dish. To the sauce add unstrained liquid from the dish. Cook until smooth and thick. Pour over fish.   *Serves 4*

Flounder bonne femme

Cooking time   20 minutes
Oven temperature   350°F.

¼ cup butter · 4 large *or* 8 small flounder fillets
seasoning · little chopped parsley
1¼ cups white wine · ½–¾ cup mushrooms.
FOR THE SAUCE: 2 tablespoons butter
¼ cup all-purpose flour · ⅔ cup milk.

Grease an ovenproof dish with 1 tablespoon of the butter, and put fillets in. Add seasoning, parsley, and wine. Cook in a preheated 350°F. oven for approximately 20 minutes, or until just tender. Sauté sliced mushrooms in remaining butter. Meanwhile make a thick white sauce of the butter, flour, and milk. Lift fillets onto a heated dish and arrange mushrooms around them. Strain the wine liquid into the sauce. Stir briskly until very smooth, then pour over the fish. Serve in a border of mashed potato.   *Serves 4*

Flounder Véronique

Cooking time   45 minutes
Oven temperature   350°F.

2 medium whole flounder · 2–3 peppercorns
few stalks parsley · 1 small onion (optional)
1¼ cups water · seasoning · ¼ cup white wine
1 finely chopped shallot (optional)
⅔ cup coffee cream · ¼ lb. white grapes
2 tablespoons butter · ¼ cup all-purpose flour.

Skin and fillet each flounder. Put heads, skin, and bones into a saucepan with the peppercorns, parsley stalks, onion, and water. Simmer for 30 minutes. Strain off the liquid and use as stock. Season fillets, roll them skinned side in, and place upright on a buttered deep plate or ovenproof dish. Add the stock, wine, and shallot, cover, and poach in a preheated 350°F. oven or over a pan of boiling water until cooked. Keep fish hot, and drain off ⅔ cup liquid. Make up to 1¼ cups with cream. Peel the grapes and discard the seeds. Make a white sauce with the butter, flour, and cream liquid. Coat fish evenly with the sauce, and garnish with grapes, which should be heated for a few minutes in the sauce.   *Serves 4*

Eel with parsley sauce

Cooking time   45 minutes

2 lb. eels · sprig parsley · 2 slices lemon.
TO SERVE: parsley sauce (see page 183).
TO GARNISH: lemon · parsley.

Skin eels and cut into 2–3 inch lengths. Put into cold salted water, adding the parsley and lemon slices. Simmer gently for approximately 45 minutes. Drain, and serve with parsley sauce. Garnish with lemon and parsley.   *Serves 4*

Trout with almonds

Cooking time   13–15 minutes

4 trout (1 lb.) · seasoning
½–¾ cup butter · ⅓ cup blanched almonds
TO GARNISH: parsley · lemon.

Remove the backbones from the trout. Season fish lightly, and fry for about 10 minutes in the butter, until tender. Put onto a heated dish, and sauté the almonds for about 5 minutes, adding additional butter if needed. Pour over the fish. Garnish with parsley and lemon.   *Serves 4*

Halibut Meunière

Cooking time   10–12 minutes

¼ cup butter · 4 halibut steaks *or* flounder fillets
seasoning · little lemon juice
1 tablespoon chopped parsley
few capers (optional).
TO GARNISH: lemon slices.

Heat the butter, and fry the halibut or flounder for about 10 minutes. Lift onto a heated dish, and continue cooking butter until it is dark brown. Add seasoning, lemon juice, parsley, and capers and pour over the fish. Garnish with lemon slices.   *Serves 4*

Cooking fish with browned butter, as in the recipe above, is also successful using jumbo shrimp, skate, and indeed for most fish.

Carp with paprika sauce

Cooking time   30 minutes
Oven temperature   375°F.

1 carp *or* small cod (codling) *or* fresh haddock
1¼ cups cultured sour cream *or* coffee cream
blended with 1 tablespoon lemon juice
1–2 teaspoons paprika · seasoning
¼ cup butter · ⅔ cup fine fresh bread crumbs.

Wash the carp and cut into thin slices. Blend the sour cream with the paprika and seasoning. Spread half the butter on the bottom of an ovenproof dish with half the paprika cream. Put the fish on top, and cover with the remaining paprika cream, the bread crumbs and remaining butter. Bake in a preheated 375°F. oven for about 20 minutes, or until the fish is tender and the cream golden brown.   *Serves 4*

Coquilles St. Jacques bonne femme

Cooking time   *25 minutes*

4 scallops · 1¼ cups milk
¼ cup white wine · 2 tablespoons butter
¼ cup mushrooms · 3 tablespoons all-purpose flour
salt · pepper · 1 cup mashed potatoes.
TO GARNISH: sprigs parsley.

Slice scallops, and simmer in milk and wine until
tender – about 10 minutes. Remove, drain carefully,
and place in the deep shells, and keep hot. Melt
butter, and sauté sliced mushrooms until soft,
about 3–4 minutes. Add flour, and cook for a further
1–2 minutes. Stir in the fish liquid and bring to a
boil, stirring constantly. Boil gently for 5 minutes,
then season to taste. Pipe a firm border of mashed
potatoes around the edge of each scallop shell, and
pour the sauce over the fish. Reheat under the broiler
until lightly browned, and garnish with parsley.
Serves 4*

* If serving for a substantial main course this is
only enough for 2.

Coquilles St. Jacques

Cooking time   *Approximately 20 minutes*

4 medium scallops · 1¼ cups milk
little mashed potato · ¼ cup butter
¼ cup all-purpose flour · seasoning
1 tablespoon white wine *or* sherry
few toasted bread crumbs · ¼ cup grated Cheddar
cheese.

Simmer the scallops in milk for approximately 10
minutes, or until quite soft.* When cooked, put
scallops onto their shells. Pipe a border of mashed
potato around each. Melt butter, stir in flour, and
cook gently for 3 minutes. Gradually add the scallop
liquid, made up to 1¼ cups again. Cook sauce until
thick, adding seasoning and wine. Carefully mask
the tops of the scallops with this. Sprinkle with
bread crumbs and cheese, and put into a preheated
425°F. oven or under the broiler until heated through
and brown on top.   *Serves 4†*

* This must be done slowly, since too quick cooking
makes them tough.
† If serving for a substantial main course this is
only enough for 2.

Dressed crab

Cooking time   *None*

1 large cooked crab. TO GARNISH: parsley.

Pull off all claws and wipe the shell. Turn crab on
its back and take the body from the main shell.
Remove and discard the stomach bag and gray
fingers. These must not be eaten. Take out all meat,
putting dark and white into separate bowls, then
crack the top of the shell, and remove pieces so there
is a flat cavity to fill. Crack claws, and remove the
meat, adding it to the light meat. Arrange dark
and light meat alternately in the shell and garnish
with parsley. See picture on page 37.   *Serves 4*

Crab au gratin

Cooking time   *5 minutes*

1 dressed crab, see above · ⅓ cup fine fresh bread
crumbs · 1–2 tablespoons butter.

Prepare the dressed crab, as above, but omit any
garnish. Sprinkle the bread crumbs over the top
with the melted butter. Heat steadily under the
broiler until golden brown.   *Serves 4*

There are many ways of varying this particular dish.
1. The crab meat may be blended with a very little
curry powder and a few drops of Worcestershire
sauce.
2. Sauté a thinly sliced onion and a thinly sliced
peeled tomato until very tender. Add the prepared
crab meat, and season very well. Pile back into the
shell. Top with bread crumbs and butter, and brown
under the broiler.
3. Add a layer of finely grated cheese to the bread
crumbs before browning.

Scallops and bacon

Cooking time   *5 minutes*

4 scallops · seasoning · little lemon juice
4 slices bacon.

Remove the scallops from shells. Season, add a little
lemon juice. Wrap each in a bacon slice, secure with
a skewer. Fry or broil for 5 minutes.   *Serves 4**

* If serving for substantial main course this is only
enough for 2.

Lobster salad

Cooking time   *None*

2 medium lobsters · lettuce
approximately ⅔ cup mayonnaise · lemon
sliced tomatoes · cucumber.

Prepare the lobsters (see page 52). Crack the claws
with a light weight. If you have special lobster picks,
leave the meat in the cracked shells, otherwise
carefully remove the meat with a fine skewer. If
leaving the meat in the claws, arrange these beside
the body of the lobster. The meat in the body may
be removed, diced, and piled back again. If removing
the meat from the claws, blend with body meat.
Arrange on lettuce, top with mayonnaise, lemon,
tomatoes, and cucumber.   *Serves 4*

Note: To increase the number of servings, remove
all the flesh and arrange in the center of a ring of
hard-cooked eggs, tomatoes, cucumber etc., and
garnish with tiny claws.

Lobster Thermidor

Cooking time   *15 minutes*

2 tablespoons butter · ¼ cup all-purpose flour
1 cup milk · 3 tablespoons whipping cream
prepared mustard · seasoning
2 medium lobsters
1 small onion *or* shallot · ¼ cup butter
3 tablespoons white wine *or* sherry
2–4 tablespoons grated cheese, preferably Parmesan.

Make a sauce with the 2 tablespoons butter, flour, milk, cream, a little mustard, and seasoning. Add the diced lobster meat and heat gently. Sauté very finely chopped shallot or onion in the ¼ cup butter. Add to the lobster mixture with wine or sherry. Pile into lobster shells, cover tops with grated cheese, and brown under a hot broiler.   *Serves 4*

The essential ingredient in this dish is mustard.

Mussels marinière

Cooking time   *10 minutes*

2½ pints mussels · 1 small onion
2 or 3 stalks celery · seasoning   1 bunch parsley
1 tablespoon tarragon vinegar
little wine (optional).* TO GARNISH: chopped parsley.

* A good dry white wine, Graves, is excellent. If not using white wine add 1 tablespoon white wine vinegar as well as the tarragon vinegar.

Scrub mussels well, discarding any that are open and will not close when sharply tapped. Put into a large saucepan with 2½ cups water, the onion, celery, seasoning, parsley, vinegar, and wine. Heat slowly until mussels open. Sometimes you will find a small growth, looking like a weed, in the mussels – this must be removed with the beards and discarded. Remove half the shell, leaving each mussel on a half shell. Reboil the liquid, and strain over them. Garnish with chopped parsley.   *Serves 4*

Fried shrimp

Cooking time   *few minutes*

About 20–24 jumbo shrimp, cooked *or* raw
coating batter *or* egg and toasted bread crumbs
(see page 54) · fat *or* oil for deep frying.
TO GARNISH: lemon · parsley.

If using frozen shrimp, defrost at room temperature. Dry well before coating with batter or egg and bread crumbs. Heat the fat to approximately 365°F. – cube of bread will turn golden brown within about 1 minute. Put in the shrimp and fry steadily. Garnish with lemon and parsley.   *Serves 4*

Shrimp Provencale

Cooking time   *5–6 minutes*

1 small onion · 1 clove garlic
2 *or* 3 tomatoes · 3 tablespoons olive oil
about 20 jumbo shrimp, cooked *or* raw
little white wine · chopped parsley
seasoning.
TO GARNISH: extra chopped parsley.

Sauté the chopped onion, garlic and the tomatoes in oil. If using raw shrimp, add these with parsley and wine. Cook steadily for about 5–6 minutes. If using cooked shrimp, add wine, parsley, and seasoning to onion mixture and get this very hot before heating the shrimp for 2–3 minutes. Serve garnished with parsley.   *Serves 4*

Herring in sour cream sauce

Cooking time   *None*

4 large *or* 6 small rollmop herring (see page 65).
SOUR CREAM SAUCE: 1¼ cups cultured sour cream *or* use coffee cream and 2 extra teaspoons lemon juice *or* vinegar
2 teaspoons lemon juice *or* vinegar (use some from the jar of herrings if wished)
½–1 teaspoon dry mustard
1 small onion *or* several scallions *or* chives.
TO GARNISH: chopped parsley · 1 lemon.

Drain the liquid from the herring, and cut them into small pieces. Blend the sour cream with all the other ingredients, chopping the onion or scallions or chives very finely. Arrange the herring in a shallow dish, top with the cream, chopped parsley, and wedges of lemon. Serve with beets.   *Serves 4*

Fried herring in oatmeal

Cooking time   *10 minutes*

4 herring · 1 beaten egg
½–⅔ cup finely ground rolled oats
½ cup fat.
FOR THE SAUCE: ⅔ cup ketchup
4 pickled gherkins, chopped · 1 tablespoon capers.
TO GARNISH: lemon · parsley.

Clean and fillet the herring, wash, and dry thoroughly. Dip in beaten egg, then coat thoroughly with oatmeal. Heat fat in a skillet until hot. Fry the herring on each side over low heat for 4–5 minutes. Heat the ketchup in a small saucepan, and stir in gherkins and capers. Garnish fish with lemon and parsley, and serve with the sauce.   *Serves 4*

This is a traditional Scottish method of cooking fish, mustard sauce could be served instead.

Stockholm herring

Cooking time   *20–25 minutes*
Oven temperature   *375°F.*

4 large fresh herring · ¼ cup butter
1 tablespoon dry mustard · 3 large tomatoes
seasoning.
TOPPING: 2 onions · 2 tablespoons butter
2 lemons.
TO GARNISH: chopped parsley.

Remove the heads and roe from the herring, then clean and remove the back bones. Cream the butter with the mustard. Spread this over the herring, add the roe and season lightly, then fold over the herring again. Peel the tomatoes, slice thinly, and put at the bottom of an ovenproof dish, seasoning them lightly. Place the herring on top, then the onions, cut into wafer-thin slices, and the 2 tablespoons melted butter. Bake in a preheated 375°F. oven for approximately 15 minutes, remove and place thin rings of lemon over the onions. Return to the oven for 5–10 minutes until the fish and onions are quite tender. Garnish with chopped parsley.   *Serves 4*

Rollmop herring

Cooking time   *few minutes*

½ cup salt · 5 cups water · 8 herring
approximately 2½ cups malt vinegar
1–2 onions · 2–3 bay leaves · 2–3 gherkins
2–3 chili peppers
1–2 tablespoons mixed pickling spice (see page 312)
extra vinegar.

Make brine of the salt and water. Soak the herring in the brine for 2 hours if filleted, twice as long if whole. Remove from the brine, and put into a large shallow dish. Cover with vinegar, and let stand for several hours. Remove the fish from the vinegar, lay flat on a wooden board, then roll each fish or fillet around a small tablespoon of finely sliced onion and secure with a small wooden toothpick. Put into jars with bay leaves, gherkins, and chili peppers and cover with cold spiced vinegar (see below).   *Serves 4*

Note: Rollmops will keep refrigerated for 2–3 weeks.

SPICED VINEGAR

Measure the vinegar in which the herring have been soaking, and make up to 2½–3¼ cups (depending on the size of the jars) with additional vinegar. Allow 1 tablespoon mixed pickling spice (see page 312) to each 2½ cups vinegar, boil together for 15 minutes and let stand until cool.

Mackerel and gooseberry sauce

Cooking time   *20–30 minutes*
Oven temperature   *400°F.*

4 large mackerel · 2 tablespoons butter *or*
margarine · seasoning
3 cups green gooseberries
¼–⅓ cup granulated sugar · about ⅔ cup water.

Cut heads from mackerel, split them, and remove backbones. Brush with a little butter or margarine, and season well. Bake in a preheated 400°F. oven for approximately 20–30 minutes, depending on the size. Simmer gooseberries with sugar and water. Rub through a sieve or beat until smooth, then add remaining butter or margarine. Pour sauce over fish and serve.   *Serves 4*

Soused mackerel

Cooking time   *1 hour*
Oven temperature   *300°F.*

4 mackerel · 1 teaspoon mixed pickling spice (see page 312) · 1 teaspoon granulated sugar
⅔ cup water · 1 small onion
1 teaspoon cinnamon, nutmeg, or allspice
⅔ cup vinegar · 2 bay leaves.

Split the mackerel, and remove the backbones. Roll the fish. Put into a covered ovenproof casserole with all the other ingredients, and cook in a preheated 300°F. oven for 1 hour.   *Serves 4*

Herring may be cooked in the same way and, indeed, most lean saltwater fish and oily fish may be pickled like this. They are very good hot or cold. If serving cold, use some of the vinegar in the salad dressing.

Court-bouillon

This is the liquid often used for poaching fish, especially salmon. It may be varied according to personal taste, but generally consists of:

2½ cups water · 1 tablespoon lemon juice
few peppercorns · 1 sliced onion
1 teaspoon salt · bouquet garni (3 bay leaves, 3 sprigs parsley, 1 sprig thyme, tied together).

Instead of water, fish stock may be used or fish stock blended with a little white wine. Allow sufficient of the above ingredients to cover the fish and poach (see page 54).

Poached salmon

Cooking time. 20–25 minutes

Seasoning · 1¼–1½ lb. fresh salmon
lemon juice · 2 tablespoons butter · few drops
oil.

Season salmon, add a little lemon juice, and tie
carefully in a neat 'parcel' of buttered wax paper.
Put into cold salted water with a little lemon and
oil in the water. Bring slowly to a boil, and simmer
gently allowing 10 minutes per lb. Another way of
cooking relatively small pieces of salmon is to bring
the water to a boil as above, then remove the pan
from the heat. Cover the pan tightly, and leave the
fish in the water until it is cold. This method is
excellent if wishing to serve the fish cold, for there
is no possibility of it being overcooked and dry.

Serves 4

Salmon cream mold

Cooking time 10 minutes

⅔ cup aspic · 1 teaspoon unflavored gelatin
⅔ cup mayonnaise · 3 tablespoons whipping cream
½–¾ lb. cooked salmon · 2 hard-cooked eggs
2 sliced gherkins · seasoning.

When making the aspic jelly, dissolve the gelatin
in the liquid. Let stand until cool. Mix with the
mayonnaise, cream, flaked salmon, 1 of the chopped
hard-cooked eggs, and 1 of the gherkins. Season
well. Put into a rinsed mold, and chill until set.
Turn out, and decorate with the remaining egg and
gherkin. Serve with a lettuce salad.

Serves 4 as a main course or 6–8 as a first course

Salmon mousse

Cooking time 10 minutes

2 tablespoons butter
1 tablespoon finely chopped onion
¼ cup all-purpose flour · 1¼ cups milk
dash thyme · 1 bay leaf · little grated nutmeg
8 oz. salmon, *either* canned, *or* cooked fresh salmon

1 tablespoon unflavored gelatin
¼ cup pitted chopped ripe olives
2 stalks celery, diced · 1 red dessert apple*
3 tablespoons ketchup
¼ cup classic mayonnaise (see recipe page 186)
seasoning · juice 1 lemon.
TO GARNISH: ripe olives · cucumber and/or 1 apple
water cress.

* The apple in the mixture gives a crisp texture. One
tablespoon diced peeled cucumber may be used
instead.

Melt the butter in a saucepan, and gently sauté the
onion, until transparent but not brown. Stir in the
flour and cook gently for 3 minutes. Add milk
gradually, stirring constantly. Add the thyme, bay
leaf, and nutmeg, and simmer over low heat for 10
minutes. Remove bay leaf, and cool sauce. Flake
salmon finely, and gradually beat into the sauce.
Add gelatin, which has been dissolved in 3 tablespoons water, chopped olives, celery, and diced raw
apple. Stir in ketchup and mayonnaise, and season

to taste. Pile into a serving dish and chill. Just
before serving, garnish with another apple, cut into
slices and dipped in lemon juice to retain its color.
Fill the center of the mixture with more ripe olives,
rings of sliced cucumber and water cress. *Serves 4*

Salmon mornay

Cooking time 25–30 minutes
Oven temperature 375°F.

4 medium cooked potatoes
2 tablespoons margarine · 3 tablespoons milk
seasoning · medium can salmon *or* tuna fish
1¼ cups Béchamel sauce (see page 183)
½–¾ cup grated Cheddar cheese.
TO GARNISH: chopped parsley · 1 tomato.

Mash the potatoes and beat in the margarine, milk,
and seasoning. Line the sides and bottom of a
shallow ovenproof dish with the potatoes then put
the flaked fish on top. Make the sauce, stir in the
cheese, then spoon over fish. Bake in a preheated
375°F. oven until golden on top, garnish with parsley
and sliced tomato. *Serves 4*

Jugged kippers

Cooking time 5 minutes

kippers · boiling water.

Roll up the kippers. Put into a heatproof jug and
pour in enough rapidly boiling water to cover. Cover
jug and let it stand for 5 minutes in a warm place.
Remove the fish, and drain. Serve with a pat of
butter on top.

Fried bloaters

Cooking time 6 minutes

4 bloaters · little fat.

Break the heads off the bloaters. Heat the fat, and
put in the bloaters. Fry on each side until crisp and
golden brown. *Serves 4*

Broiled bloaters

Cooking time 7–8 minutes

4 bloaters · little margarine *or* drippings to fry
roe.

Break the head off each bloater, split open the back,
remove roe and backbone. Sauté the roe in a little
hot margarine or drippings until golden brown.
Preheat the broiler, grease the rack in the broiler,
place the fish on it, insides to heat. When brown,
turn and broil the skin side. Serve hot with the fried
roe. *Serves 4*

Pilchard squares

Cooking time   *35–40 minutes*
Oven temperature   *400°F.*

1 recipe short crust pastry (see page 215)
1 can pilchards · 1 small grated onion
2 teaspoons chopped parsley · seasoning
1 egg. TO GLAZE: little egg and milk.

Roll out the pastry, and cut into two equal-sized shapes. Mash the pilchards, add the onion, parsley, seasoning, and approximately half the beaten egg. Spread over one layer of pastry then top with the second layer. Seal the edges, and brush the top of the pastry with the remaining egg blended with a little milk. Bake in a preheated 400°F. oven for 35–40 minutes, lower the heat if necessary after about 20 minutes. Cut into squares, and serve hot with baked tomatoes or cold with salad.   *Serves 4*

EMERGENCY FISH DISHES

Making fish dishes in a hurry probably means using canned or frozen fish.

Cheese topped fish fingers

Cooking time   *10 minutes*

1 large package fish sticks *or* ready coated frozen fish · little butter *or* margarine
¼ cup grated Cheddar cheese · 4 tomatoes
seasoning.

Put the fish sticks or coated fish on the rack of the broiler pan, brush with a little melted butter or margarine, and cook according to the manufacturer's directions. When nearly cooked, top with the grated cheese, pressing this firmly into the fish. Broil for 2–3 minutes more only. While the fish is cooking put the halved and seasoned tomatoes on the rack of the broiler pan, or in the pan itself and cook. The cheese adds extra protein to the fish so enabling the dish to serve more people and be more sustaining.   *Serves 4–6*

Potato and fish salad

Cooking time   *None*

1 (15 oz.) can new potatoes
1 jar rollmop herrings · 1 (1 lb.) can beets
1 dessert apple · 1 teaspoon capers
2 teaspoons chopped gherkins
seasoning (optional).
TO GARNISH: lettuce · tomatoes
2 hard-cooked eggs.

Drain the potatoes, and dice neatly. Drain and dice the rollmop herring and the onions from the jar. Mix with the drained, diced beets, peeled and diced apple, capers, and gherkins. Toss and add seasoning if required, but the rollmop herrings are so well seasoned that it should not be necessary. Either pile neatly into the center of a dish or press into a bowl for a short time, then unmold. Arrange the lettuce, sliced tomatoes, and sliced hard-cooked eggs around the salad.   *Serves 4*

Hasty fish stew

Cooking time   *8 minutes*

1 can tomato soup · 1 medium can tuna fish *or* salmon · few cocktail onions.
TO GARNISH: few gherkins.

Heat the soup, put in canned fish (try to keep fairly large pieces) and onions. Heat for a few minutes. Serve topped with gherkin fans.   *Serves 4*

FISH DISHES TO IMPRESS

There are many fish dishes in the preceding pages and elsewhere in this book for special occasions, but the following should prove interesting.

Cream broiled salmon

Cooking time   *12–14 minutes*

4 fresh salmon steaks · seasoning · lemon juice
¼ cup butter · ⅔ cup whipping cream
grated peel of ½ lemon · squeeze lemon juice
½ teaspoon chopped chives.

Skewer, do not tie, the salmon into a neat shape. Season and flavor with a little lemon juice. Melt the butter, and brush the bottom of the broiler pan with half of this, arrange the salmon on this, and brush with the remaining butter. Broil quickly for about 3 minutes, turn carefully, and broil on the second side until golden. Then lower the heat, and cook until tender; the time will vary according to the thickness of the steaks but for approximately 1 inch thick steaks a total time of 12–14 minutes should be sufficient. Whip cream lightly, blend with lemon peel, juice, and chives. Two minutes before end of cooking time spoon over blended cream.   *Serves 4*

Fish cream

Cooking time   *15 minutes*

1½ lb. lean saltwater fish such as halibut
2 eggs · 1½ teaspoons unflavored gelatin
¼ cup fish stock *or* water
1¼ cups whipping cream · ¾–1 cup cooked shelled shrimp · 2 oz. smoked salmon · seasoning.
TO GARNISH: lettuce · cooked *or* canned asparagus tips · few shrimp · lemon.

Cook the fish by poaching or steaming, but make sure it is not overcooked or 'watery'. Drain well, and flake very finely. Beat the egg yolks. Soften the gelatin in the cold fish stock or water, then dissolve by standing the bowl in a pan of boiling water; add the egg yolks. Blend the fish into the gelatin mixture and, when cold, add the lightly whipped cream, chopped shrimp – save a few for garnish – and the smoked salmon cut into thin strips. Lastly fold in the seasoning and stiffly beaten egg whites. Put into a plain mold or ring mold, lightly greased with olive oil and chill until just firm. Turn out onto a bed of lettuce, and garnish with asparagus tips, the reserved shrimp and lemon twists.   *Serves 4*

MEAT

In this section you will find how to select the various cuts of meat for each method of cooking, along with traditional and new and exciting recipes.

Wise choice of meat

When wishing to make an economical dish, choose a casserole or stew using the cheaper cuts of beef, lamb, veal, etc. For a party, choose a casserole, but include wine, and interesting vegetables such as sweet peppers to make it exciting – this saves carving meats and if guests are late, the casserole will not spoil. When wishing to lose weight, choose roasted meats or broiled steak or chops. Select roasted lamb when fresh peas, new potatoes, and fresh mint are available, since these are perfect accompaniments.

Ways to serve meat

Garnish stewed meats with a border of diced mixed (macédoine) vegetables. Arrange chops around a pyramid of cooked rice or creamed potatoes with tomatoes and mushrooms in between – this looks much more inviting than when arranged flat on a serving dish. Try a crown roast for that special party – not at all difficult and most impressive.

To use leftover meat

Meat must be stored carefully to prevent harmful bacteria developing – this is particularly important with stews, casseroles, and ground meat preparations.
Stews and casseroles – Reheat and serve again. To be sure that the meat is thoroughly reheated, bring just to boiling point and maintain this temperature for at least 15 minutes. To avoid monotony, blend spices (curry powder, chili powder, etc.) with the gravy. Add chopped herbs, tomato purée, etc.
Roast meat – Serve cold with salads or reheat very carefully, taking care not to overcook; grind or chop and use in dishes like Shepherd's pie, etc. There are many recipes using cooked meat in this section.
Broiled or fried meat – There is less possibility of these being leftover, since it is easy to buy just the right quantity. Use as roast meat.

Easy remedies when things are wrong

PROBLEM – if roast meat is undercooked, this was because the meat was left in the oven for too short a period or the oven heat was too low.
TO REMEDY – if time permits, leave for a longer period, but this may mean that vegetables etc. are overcooked while being kept waiting, so slice the meat thinly and either put for a moment or so under the broiler or heat for a few minutes in the gravy.
PROBLEM – if the meat is rather dry, this is generally because it is overcooked.
TO REMEDY – since the meat is already cooked more than it should be, the best solution is to camouflage it by grinding and serving in a rather rich sauce.
PROBLEM – if the meat is tough, this could be because it was the wrong cut for that particular method of cooking; it could be that it was overcooked (liver in particular toughens with too much cooking).
TO REMEDY – as above, or grind the meat finely and use in patties, etc. The flavor will never be good but the toughness is less obvious.
YOU WILL FIND OTHER POINTS ABOUT SUCCESSFUL MEAT COOKING UNDER EACH SECTION – FRYING, BROILING, ETC.

Frozen meats

This means that the meat has been frozen quickly and at a low temperature so that it may be stored for a very long period. In most cases, frozen meat is better if completely defrosted before cooking, to retain maximum juiciness in thick cuts of meat and it should be allowed to defrost in the original wrapping in the refrigerator when time permits. The exceptions are prepared hamburgers and prepared meat products, and these may be cooked from the frozen state – be guided by directions on the package.

CHOOSING MEAT

In order to obtain the best result in cooking meat, it is important to select the right cuts. Your butcher will help you identify the meat and make recommendations as to what is a 'good buy' at various times of the year.

To choose pork

The fat of pork should be white and must be firm – do not buy pork if the fat looks 'flabby' and soft. The lean of pork should be pale pink and firm.

To choose lamb or mutton

Although lamb and mutton are given together in this section, it is important to allow longer cooking for mutton and to realize that unless it is of very good quality it is better to cook mutton by slower roasting and to avoid pan-frying or broiling.
Lamb will have a certain amount of fat (although generally less than mutton), which should be firm but rather transparent-looking; the lean should be paler pink than mutton. Mutton, when of good quality, should have firm white fat and the lean meat should be deep pink.

To choose beef

Beef should have some fat, this denotes a good quality and will give meat of a moist texture as well as being tender. The fat should be a very pale cream in color and look firm.

To choose veal

Veal spoils easily, so should be stored with great care. The fat of veal (of which there is very little) should be firm, white in color and dry looking. The lean should be very pale pink and firm in texture.

RETAIL CUTS OF BEEF

	Broil	Panbroil	Panfry	Roast	Braise	Cook in liquid
ROUND						
BOTTOM ROUND STEAK					X	
(POT-ROAST)						
(SWISS STEAK)						
CUBE STEAK	X					
EYE OF ROUND					X	
HEEL OF ROUND					X	X
ROLLED RUMP				X*	X	
ROUND STEAK					X	
SIRLOIN TIP ROAST				X*	X	
STANDING RUMP				X*	X	
TIP STEAK	X*	X*	X*		X	
TOP ROUND STEAK					X	
SIRLOIN						
BONELESS SIRLOIN STEAK	X	X	X			
CUBE STEAK	X					
FLAT BONE SIRLOIN STEAK	X	X	X			
PIN BONE SIRLOIN STEAK	X	X	X			
SIRLOIN TIP ROAST				X*	X	
TIP STEAK	X*	X*	X*		X	
WEDGE BONE SIRLOIN STEAK	X	X	X			
SHORT LOIN						
CLUB STEAK	X	X	X			
FILET MIGNON (TENDERLOIN)	X	X	X			
PORTERHOUSE STEAK	X	X	X			
T-BONE STEAK	X	X	X			
TOP LOIN STEAK	X	X	X			

Retail cuts of beef (continued)

	Broil	Panbroil	Panfry	Roast	Braise	Cook in liquid
RIB						
BONELESS RIB STEAK	X	X	X			
RIB EYE STEAK OR ROAST (DELMONICO)				X		
RIB STEAK	X	X	X			
STANDING RIB ROAST				X		
CHUCK						
ARM POT-ROAST (ARM STEAK)					X	
BLADE POT-ROAST (BLADE STEAK)					X	
BONELESS SHOULDER POT-ROAST (BONELESS SHOULDER STEAK)					X	
CHUCK SHORT RIBS					X	
CHUCK TENDER					X	
ENGLISH CUT (BOSTON CUT)					X	
INSIDE CHUCK ROLL					X	
PETITE STEAKS					X	
FORESHANK						
SHANK CROSS CUTS					X	X
BRISKET						
BEEF FOR STEW					X	X
CORNED BRISKET						X
FRESH BRISKET					X	X
SHORT PLATE						
PLATE BEEF					X	X
ROLLED PLATE					X	X
SKIRT STEAK FILLETS					X	X
SHORT RIBS					X	X
FLANK						
BEEF PATTIES	X	X	X			
FLANK STEAK	X*				X	
FLANK STEAK FILLETS					X	
ANY SECTION						
GROUND BEEF	X	X	X	X	X	

* denotes a high quality meat which may be cooked using this method

RETAIL CUTS OF LAMB

	Broil	Panbroil	Panfry	Roast	Braise	Cook in liquid
LEG						
AMERICAN LEG				X		
CENTER LEG				X		
COMBINATION LEG				X		
FRENCHED LEG				X		
HINDSHANK					X	X
LEG CHOP (LEG STEAK)	X	X	X			
LEG WITH SIRLOIN ON				X		
LEG WITH SIRLOIN OFF				X		
ROLLED DOUBLE SIRLOIN				X		
ROLLED LEG				X		
SHANK HALF OF LEG				X	X	
SIRLOIN CHOP	X	X	X			
SIRLOIN HALF OF LEG				X		
SIRLOIN ROAST				X		

Retail cuts of lamb (continued)

	Broil	Panbroil	Panfry	Roast	Braise	Cook in liquid
TRIMMED LOIN						
ENGLISH CHOP	X	X	X			
LOIN CHOPS	X	X	X			
LOIN ROAST				X		
ROLLED DOUBLE LOIN				X		
HOTEL RACK						
CROWN ROAST				X		
FRENCHED RIB CHOPS	X	X	X			
RIB CHOPS	X	X	X			
RIB ROAST				X		
SHOULDER						
ARM CHOP	X	X	X		X	
BLADE CHOP	X	X	X		X	
CUSHION SHOULDER				X		
NECK SLICES					X	X
ROLLED SHOULDER				X	X	
SARATOGA CHOPS	X	X	X		X	
SQUARE SHOULDER				X		
FORESHANK						
FORESHANK					X	X
BREAST						
BREAST	X	X	X	X	X	X
BRISKET PIECES	X	X	X	X	X	X
RIBLETS	X	X	X	X	X	X
RIBS	X	X	X	X	X	X
ROLLED BREAST	X	X	X	X	X	X
STUFFED BREAST	X	X	X	X	X	X
STUFFED CHOPS	X	X	X	X	X	X
ANY SECTION						
CUBES FOR KEBABS				X		
CUBE STEAK	X	X	X			
GROUND LAMB	X	X	X	X		
LAMB FOR STEW					X	X
LAMBURGERS	X	X	X			

RETAIL CUTS OF PORK

	Broil	Panbroil	Panfry	Roast	Braise	Cook in liquid
HAM (LEG)						
CANNED HAM				X		
FRESH HAM, BUTT HALF				X		
FRESH HAM, CENTER SLICE		X	X		X	
FRESH HAM, ROLLED				X		
FRESH HAM, SHANK PORTION				X		
SLICED COOKED HAM (BOILED HAM)	X		X			
SMOKED BOSTON SHOULDER ROLL				X		
SMOKED HAM, BUTT PORTION				X		X
SMOKED HAM, CENTER SLICE	X	X	X	X		
SMOKED HAM, SHANK PORTION				X		X
LOIN						
BACK RIBS				X	X	
BLADE CHOP	X		X		X	
BLADE LOIN ROAST				X		

Retail cuts of pork (continued)

	Broil	Panbroil	Panfry	Roast	Braise	Cook in liquid
BUTTERFLY CHOP			X		X	
CANADIAN-STYLE BACON	X	X	X	X		
CENTER LOIN ROAST				X		
COUNTRY STYLE BACKBONE				X	X	
LOIN CHOP	X		X		X	
RIB CHOP	X		X		X	
ROLLED LOIN ROAST				X		
SIRLOIN CHOP	X		X		X	
SIRLOIN ROAST				X		
SMOKED LOIN CHOP	X	X	X			
TENDERLOIN			X	X	X	
TOP LOIN CHOP	X		X		X	
BOSTON BUTT						
BLADE STEAK			X		X	
FRESH BOSTON BUTT	X		X	X		X
FRESH SAUSAGE	X	X	X			
PORKLET			X		X	
ROLLED BOSTON BUTT	X		X	X		X
SMOKED SAUSAGE	X	X	X			
SMOKED SHOULDER BUTT	X	X	X	X		X
TRIMMED JOWL						
JOWL BACON	X	X	X			X
FOREFOOT						
PIG'S FEET					X	X
PICNIC						
ARM ROAST				X		
ARM STEAK			X		X	
CANNED LUNCHEON MEAT	X	X	X			
CANNED PICNIC				X		
FRESH HOCK					X	X
FRESH PICNIC				X		
ROLLED FRESH PICNIC				X		
SMOKED HOCK						X
SMOKED PICNIC				X		X
BACON (BELLY)						
BARBECUE RIBS (SPARERIBS)	X			X	X	
SALT PORK		X	X			X
SLAB BACON	X	X	X		X	
SLICED BACON	X	X	X			

RETAIL CUTS OF VEAL

	Broil	Panbroil	Panfry	Roast	Braise	Cook in liquid
LEG						
BONELESS CUTLETS			X		X	
CENTER LEG				X	X	
CUBE STEAK	X	X	X			
HEEL OF ROUND					X	X
ROLLED CUTLETS (VEAL BIRDS)			X		X	
ROLLED DOUBLE SIRLOIN				X	X	
ROLLED LEG				X	X	
ROUND STEAK			X		X	
SHANK HALF OF LEG				X	X	
SIRLOIN ROAST				X	X	
SIRLOIN STEAK			X		X	
STANDING RUMP				X	X	

Retail cuts of veal (continued)

	Broil	Panbroil	Panfry	Roast	Braise	Cook in liquid
TRIMMED LOIN						
KIDNEY CHOP			X		X	
LOIN CHOP			X		X	
LOIN ROAST				X	X	
ROLLED LOIN				X	X	
HOTEL RACK						
CROWN ROAST				X		
FRENCH RIB CHOP			X		X	
RIB CHOP			X		X	
RIB ROAST				X		
SHOULDER						
ARM ROAST				X	X	
ARM STEAK			X		X	
BLADE ROAST				X	X	
BLADE STEAK			X		X	
NECK					X	X
ROLLED SHOULDER				X	X	
VEAL FOR STEW					X	X
FORESHANK						
FORESHANK					X	X
BREAST						
BREAST				X	X	X
BRISKET PIECES					X	X
BRISKET ROLLS					X	X
RIBLETS					X	X
ROLLED BREAST				X	X	X
STUFFED CHOPS			X		X	
ANY SECTION						
CITY CHICKEN			X		X	
CUBE STEAK	X					
GROUND VEAL	X	X	X	X	X	
MOCK CHICKEN LEGS			X		X	
ROLLED CUBE STEAKS (VEAL BIRDS)			X		X	
VEAL CHOPLETS			X		X	
VEAL FOR STEW					X	X
VEAL PATTIES			X		X	

To choose variety meats

Offal is the name given to special cuts of meat and the following information gives the most satisfactory methods of cooking them.

BRAINS – beef, veal, pork, and lamb may be served in a sauce or fried, etc.

CHITTERLINGS – the small intestines of calf, sold prepared by some butchers. Serve cold or fry in a little hot fat.

FEET – pig's, calf's, and lamb's. Generally used to make meat molds or brawn because they contain a great deal of gelatin (see pages 112 and 113).

EARS – rarely seen. Simmer gently until tender and serve cold.

FAGGOTS – generally sold cooked by some butchers. Made from liver, kidney, pork, with bread crumbs, onion, etc. (see page 110).

HEAD – pig's, calf's, and lamb's. Generally used in brawn (see page 112) or may be served hot.

HEART – beef, veal, pork, and lamb. When tender, may be stuffed and roasted or braised (see page 95).

KIDNEYS – veal, pork, and lamb – fry or grill. Beef kidney – generally used in stewing (see Steak and kidney pie, page 146, Steak and kidney pudding, page 158).

LIGHTS – lungs of the animal.

LIVER – veal, pork, and lamb – fry or grill. Beef – braise.

OXTAIL – Used as a stew (often called a ragout), or a soup (see page 43).

SUET – hard internal fat from mutton or beef used in suet pastry (see page 217).

SWEETBREADS – beef, veal, and lamb – come from the pancreas, throat, and heart of the animal. Very easily digested. Fresh sweetbreads are often difficult to obtain; many butchers now sell frozen sweetbreads. Use in a fricassée or braised or in various sauces (see page 182–187) or fried (see page 90).

TONGUE – beef, veal, pork, and lamb. May be purchased fresh, smoked, pickled, or corned. Pork and lamb are usually purchased cooked. May be boiled and pressed. Calf's, lamb's, pig's – use in the same way.

TRIPE – from the stomach of beef. Both plain and honeycomb are available fresh, canned, or pickled. Frequently it is purchased precooked with the final cooking still required. There are many ways of cooking this; several recipes are on pages 324–325.

To choose cooked meats

There is a wide range of ready cooked meats available either in cans or sold by weight. Since there is no shrinkage in cooking, allow about 3–5 oz. per person (generally one uses less in sandwiches than when served with a salad). Suggestions for visible signs of freshness are given.

BEEF AND OTHER COOKED FRESH MEATS – should look firm and the top of the meat cut should not look dry. The cut side exposed to the air does dry easily and the customer is justified in refusing to accept this first slice – good shops would not offer it.

BRAWN – similar to mold on page 60, fresh when the jelly is clear and firm – stale jelly contracts.

BRISKET, TONGUE (ready salted and cooked), – *corned beef* also sold in slices – fresh when the meat is clear reddish pink and not dry.

FRANKFURTERS – available singly as well as in cans and by the pound; the outside should look pleasantly moist.

FROZEN MEAT PIES – see comments page 145.

HAGGIS – traditional Scottish dish made of liver etc. Cook steadily in water for 1 hour, serve hot; prick the skin as it cooks to prevent the mixture breaking through. Should look firm and smell pleasant.

HAM – it is correct for prices to vary according to method of curing; ham on the bone is also generally more expensive than canned ham – see comments about freshness under beef and brisket.

LUNCHEON MEATS – blending of ham, pork, etc. relatively inexpensive – see comments on beef etc.

SALAMI – cooked sausages of various kinds (from garlic sausages to fairly inexpensive liver sausages, blood sausage, etc.) – see comments about beef – buy small quantities only to assess flavor.

The meat section in this book is divided up as follows:—
The first part deals with the more tender and therefore more expensive cuts of meat used for a) roasting, b) frying, c) broiling and d) dishes that need baking. The second part deals with the less tender and cheaper pieces of meat for cooking in liquid, stewing, cooking in a casserole, and braising.
The third part of the section is for meat dishes that are served cold (though many more are in the salad section), and ways to use leftover meat. The final page, as in each section, gives emergency meat dishes and meat dishes to impress.

ROASTING MEAT

Many people regard the method normally used for cooking meat i.e. in a pan in the oven, as baking rather than roasting, but the fact remains that when meat is called roasted, this is the method used. However, the old traditional method of roasting,

i.e. with the meat on a spit turned over or under the source of heat, can now be carried out with an electric spit specially fitted to either gas or electric broilers or ovens. The timing for spit roasted meat is exactly the same for quick roasting if high heat is used, or for slow roasting if low heat is used. Lean meats like beef should be brushed with fat once or twice (basted) to keep them moist, but fat meat – pork, lamb – needs no additional fat.

Quick roasting

Use a preheated 400°F. oven. This method is suitable only for the more expensive cuts of meat (see pages 69–73). Frozen meats and less expensive cuts are better roasted by the slower method. After the first 15 minutes the heat may be lowered to 375°F. Add potatoes to roast during cooking; transfer meat and potatoes to a heated dish while making gravy. Any surplus fat in the meat pan should be clarified (see page 86) and stored.

Slower roasting

Use a preheated 325°F. oven. This method is suitable for the less expensive cuts of meat, but not suitable for cooking meat bought for stewing or cooking in a casserole. Potatoes cannot be roasted, or a Yorkshire pudding cooked, at this lower heat.

To roast meats

Select one of the large tender cuts suggested for roasting. Place the meat on a wire rack, then in an open roasting pan. The fat side of the meat should be up to baste the meat naturally. A meat thermometer may be inserted into the thickest muscle portion not touching any bones, if desired. For rare roast to 140°F., medium 160°F., and well done meat 170°F. Do not cover the pan and do not add any water.

Roasting beef

CHOOSE: For quick or slow roasting those cuts suggested on the chart on pages 69–70.

ALLOW: $\frac{1}{2}$–$\frac{3}{4}$ lb. per person with bone; $\frac{1}{4}$–$\frac{1}{2}$ lb. per person without bone.

PREPARE: Spread 2 tablespoons fat or bacon drippings on lean part of the beef.

COOK: In an open roasting pan.
Quick roasting: 15 minutes per lb. plus an additional 15 minutes for rare beef; 20 minutes per lb. plus an additional 20 minutes medium.
Slow roasting: 25–35 minutes per lb. plus an additional 25–35 minutes.

SERVE: Hot with Yorkshire pudding (see page 209), horseradish relish, mustard. Thin gravy (see page 86). Cold with salad. Illustrated on pages 58–59.

Roasting lamb or mutton

CHOOSE: For quick or slow roasting those cuts suggested on the chart on pages 70–71.

ALLOW: $\frac{1}{2}$–$\frac{3}{4}$ lb. per person with bone; $\frac{1}{3}$–$\frac{1}{2}$ lb. person without bone.

PREPARE: Spread 1 tablespoon fat or bacon drippings on lean lamb, no fat on mutton. Stuff, if desired.

COOK: In an open roasting pan.
Quick roasting: 20–25 minutes per lb. plus an additional 20–25 minutes. Slow roasting: 35 minutes per lb. plus an additional 35 minutes.

SERVE: Hot lamb with Mint sauce (see page 186), Thin gravy (see page 86). Hot mutton with Onion sauce (see page 183), or Red currant jelly (see page 310), Thick gravy (see page 86). Cold with salad.

Roasting pork

CHOOSE: For quick or slow roasting those cuts suggested on the chart on pages 71–72.

ALLOW: ½–¾ lb. per person with bone; ⅓–½ lb. per person without bone.

PREPARE: Put in stuffing or cook this separately. For crisp 'crackling', score skin, brush with melted lard, clarified drippings or oil, sprinkle lightly with salt.

COOK: In open roasting tin.
Quick roasting: 25 minutes per lb. plus an additional 25 minutes. Slow roasting: 35 minutes per lb. plus an additional 35 minutes.

SERVE: Hot with Sage and onion stuffings (see page 189), Apple sauce (see page 184), Thick gravy (see page 86). Cold with salad. Illustrated on page 77.

Roasting veal

CHOOSE: For quick or slow roasting those cuts suggested on the chart on pages 72–73.

ALLOW: ½–¾ lb. per person with bone; ⅓–½ lb. per person without bone.

PREPARE: Use plenty of fat to keep veal moist. Stuff, if desired (see pages 188–190).

COOK: In an open roasting pan.
Quick roasting: 25 minutes per lb. plus an additional 25 minutes. Slow roasting: 35–40 minutes per lb. plus an additional 35–40 minutes.

SERVE: Hot with Veal stuffing (see page 189), Bacon rolls (see page 330), (sausages may also be put around meat during cooking), Thick gravy (see page 86). Cold with salad.

New ways of flavoring roast meats

BEEF

Sprinkle the top of the beef with salt and a little black pepper then spread with prepared mustard. Roast the beef as usual, but about 30 minutes before serving, brush the top of the beef with melted butter or oil, and press very finely chopped onion blended with chopped parsley and a little Worcestershire sauce over the one side.
Larded beef: This is ideal for lean beef.
Season the beef well and coat with a little flour, and brown both sides in hot fat. Cool sufficiently to handle, then thread long thin strips of bacon or salt pork through the beef – a larding needle is generally used for this, but a carpet needle, thin knife, or ice pick may be used.
Try stuffed beef for a change (see recipe this page).

LAMB

Split the skin of lamb and insert a cut clove of garlic in this. One clove gives a very delicate flavor – two a more definite one.
Spread a sprig of fresh rosemary over the lamb or chop the leaves from a sprig very finely, and sprinkle over the lamb during roasting.
Roast lamb in the usual way and about 25–30 minutes before serving, brush with melted red currant or cranberry jelly.
Stuff the lamb (see recipe on next page).

MUTTON

Lay the mutton on a bed of thickly sliced raw potatoes and thinly sliced raw onions, season well. This is generally called Mutton lyonnaise. The vegetables taste delicious – do not use this method if the mutton is very fat. Lamb could be cooked in the same way.
30 minutes before the end of cooking time sprinkle a little orange juice over the mutton – this is particularly good if the meat is rather fat. Try stuffed mutton (see recipe on next page).

PORK

Score the skin and brush with a little oil or melted fat to encourage crisp crackling. Press very finely grated orange peel over the oil or fat. 30 minutes before serving the pork sprinkle with orange juice and continue cooking.
Half-cook the pork, drain the surplus fat then stand the pork on a bed of thickly sliced dessert apples and very thinly sliced onions, season well, and continue cooking. (The surplus fat must be poured away otherwise the apples and onions are too greasy.)

VEAL

Veal that is larded before roasting has a particularly good taste. Insert long thin strips of bacon or salt pork through the veal at regular intervals – this gives additional flavor and helps to keep the lean veal meat pleasantly moist.
Make small pockets in the outside of the veal and insert a canned anchovy in each. Roast as usual or try anchovy and garlic leg of veal. Brush the veal with melted red currant jelly 30 minutes before the end of the cooking time.

Roast stuffed beef

Cooking time   *As page 74*

Rolled rump, Rolled sirloin tip roast, Rolled rib roast, or rib eye roast
Stuffing – Ham and horseradish stuffing (see page 189) or Savory rice stuffing (see page 189).

Make a slit halfway through the meat to give a 'pocket'. Insert the stuffing and tie or skewer to

secure. Roast as page 74, using the slower method of roasting.
Include the weight of the stuffing when calculating the roasting time.

Roast stuffed lamb

Cooking time   *As page 74*

Cuts as mutton, also rolled breast.
Stuffing – Sage and onion stuffing (see page 189), *or* Savory rice stuffing (see page 189), *or* Cucumber stuffing (see page 190).

Fill a 'pocket', made in the meat as suggested under mutton, with the stuffing. If the cut is large enough spread with the stuffing and roll. Roast using the slower or quicker method as page 74. Include the weight of the stuffing when calculating the roasting time.

Roast stuffed mutton

Cooking time   *As page 74*

Rolled leg, rolled double sirloin, rolled double loin, *or* rolled shoulder.
Stuffing – Prune and almond stuffing (see page 190) *or* Nut and celery stuffing (see page 190).

Make a slit halfway through the meat to give a 'pocket'. Insert the stuffing and tie or skewer. Alternatively, spread the stuffing over the meat, then roll and tie. Roast as page 74, using the slower or quicker method. Include the weight of the stuffing when calculating the roasting time.

Roast stuffed veal

Cooking time   *As page 75*

Rolled double sirloin, rolled leg, rolled loin, rolled shoulder, *or* rolled breast.
Stuffing – Veal stuffing (see page 189), *or* Sausage meat and ham stuffing (see page 188), *or* Savory rice stuffing (see page 189).

Fill a 'pocket' made in the meat as suggested under mutton, cover the meat with plenty of fat or lard it with bacon or salt pork as page 75. Roast as page 74, using the quicker method of roasting. Include the weight of the stuffing when calculating the roasting time.

Roast stuffed pork

Cooking time   *As page 75*

Rolled fresh ham, rolled loin roast, tenderloin, rolled boston butt, *or* rolled fresh picnic.
Stuffing – Sage and onion (see page 189) *or* Onion and apple stuffing (see page 189).

Fill a 'pocket' made in the meat as suggested under mutton. Score the fat, and brush with melted fat or oil. Roast as page 74, using the quicker method of roasting. Include the weight of the stuffing when calculating the roasting time.

Breast of lamb stuffed with eggs

Cooking time   *See page 74*

2 small *or* 1 large rolled breast of lamb. Veal stuffing, (see page 189), *or* Savory rice stuffing (see page 189) 3–4 hard-cooked eggs.

Spread the stuffing over the meat, then lay the shelled eggs on top of this. Roll very firmly and tie or skewer. Roast as the times given on page 75. Include the weight of the stuffing when calculating the roasting time. The weight of the eggs need not be counted, so when weighing, deduct 2 oz. for each egg used. Illustrated on page 103.   *Serves 4*

Roast stuffed chops

Cooking time   *See method*
Oven temperature   *400°F.*

4–8 lamb, mutton, pork, or veal rib *or* loin chops (depending upon size) · stuffing – see selection in section beginning page 188 · little fat (optional).

When chops are roasted instead of being fried or broiled they need less attention since they do not need turning. The meat may be removed from the bone so that it may be rolled neatly to form a round slice (often called a noisette). If using this method press the stuffing against the meat before rolling. If the bone is retained, press the stuffing against the side of the meat. Grease the roasting pan in the case of lean meat, and grease the top of the meat. Roast in a preheated 400°F. oven for 20 minutes for small cutlets, or up to 30 minutes for large cutlets. Pork and veal need a little longer.
Serves 4

Stuffed lamb hearts

Cooking time   *1½ hours*
Oven temperature   *375°F.*

8 lamb hearts · seasoning
stuffing – Sage and onion stuffing (see page 189), *or* Rice and raisin stuffing (see page 190), *or* Veal stuffing (see page 189).
¼ cup fat *or* butter.

Slit the hearts, remove the large veins and arteries then soak the hearts for 1 hour in a little cold salted water. Wash the hearts, dry them thoroughly, and season. Fill with stuffing, then tie or skewer each heart. Brown the hearts for a few minutes in the hot fat, in the meat pan. Roast in a preheated 375°F. oven for approximately 1½ hours. Serve the hearts with brown gravy.   *Serves 4*

Roast pork, page 69; Coconut stuffed peaches, page 339; and Stuffed tomatoes

Hungarian goulash, page 99

Blanquette of veal, page 109; Beef stew, page 97

Steak and kidney pie, page 146

82   Tomato beef olives, page 99; Deviled beef, page 98; Springtime hot pot, page 108; Fish and corn casserole, page 329; and Lamb and mushroom râgout, page 100

Steak and kidney pudding, page 158

Lamb or mutton chops jardinière, page 88; Creamed vegetables, page 322

Veal with paprika

Cooking time — *About 1 hour*
Oven temperature — *350°F.*

1¼ lb. rolled loin roast *or* tenderloin
¼ cup all-purpose flour · ¼ cup butter
2 onions · ¼ cup paprika · 3 medium tomatoes
seasoning · 1 tablespoon tomato paste
1¼ cups boiling water · 1 bay leaf
3 tablespoons whipping cream.

Cut veal into four portions and coat the pieces with flour. Heat half the butter in a pan. Add the floured veal, and cook for a few moments until golden all over. Transfer meat and fat to a preheated 350°F. oven, and roast until tender, about 25 minutes, basting occasionally. Meanwhile, sauté the chopped onion in the remaining butter. When tender, sprinkle in the paprika. Add the chopped tomatoes, seasoning the tomato paste. Stir well, and cook gently for 5 minutes. Gradually add the boiling water and the bay leaf. Cook fairly quickly for 20 minutes. Remove and discard the bay leaf. Stir the cream into the sauce, and reheat gently before coating the veal with it. Do not allow sauce to boil. *Serves 4*

GLAZED HAM

There are many glazes used to give extra flavor to the fat, and since sweet flavors blend excellently with ham, a fairly high percentage of sugar, honey, molasses or corn syrup may be used. It is important, however, that when once the ham is glazed it is not overcooked, for these sweet finishes burn very easily.

Quick glazes for ham

Many of the glazes for ham are very quick; unless stated to the contrary allow 30 minutes to complete the cooking in a preheated 375°F. oven. To prepare the ham for glazing, see recipe below.

BROWN SUGAR GLAZE
Press brown sugar over the scored fat; do this with a flat-bladed knife and a very firm movement. The brown sugar may be mixed with any chosen spice – cinnamon, nutmeg – or stick cloves into the fat.

FLOUR GLAZE
Although the word 'glaze' is used for this coating, it does not have the 'shine' one normally associates with a proper glaze. Blend ½ cup all-purpose flour, 1 teaspoon dry mustard, dash pepper, ⅓ cup brown sugar, ½ teaspoon cinnamon, ¼ teaspoon nutmeg, and ¼ teaspoon allspice. Press carefully over the scored fat of the ham. This is enough for a 4–5 lb. ham.

FRUIT GLAZE
Select a canned fruit in heavy syrup – pineapple, peaches, apricots, or cherries are the most suitable. Drain off about ⅔ cup of the syrup and blend with ⅓ cup brown sugar or ¼ cup honey, 1–2 teaspoons dry mustard (optional), ½ teaspoon spice (select either cinnamon, ginger, or cloves). Brush this glaze over the fat. This amount is enough for a 4–5 lb. ham. The canned fruit may be served cold around the meat or heated in the roasting pan with the ham.

HONEY GLAZE
Glaze the prepared ham with honey, then press cloves into this.

HONEY AND SPICE GLAZE
Sprinkle a mixture of ½ teaspoon cinnamon, ¼ teaspoon nutmeg, and ¼ teaspoon allspice over the scored fat, then brush with honey; in this way you brush the spice well into the fat.

MOLASSES GLAZE
Brush molasses over the scored fat. If this has a rather too definite flavor, then blend equal quantities of molasses and corn syrup.

Prune and orange glazed ham

Cooking time — *30 minutes*

Partially cooked ham, 4–5 lb. in weight.
GLAZE: ⅔ cup boiling water · 1 cup prunes
juice of 2–3 oranges (depending on size)
grated peel of 2–3 oranges
2 teaspoons prepared English mustard
⅓ cup brown sugar.

Bake the ham until 30 minutes cooking time remains. Score the fat with a sharp knife; this helps the fat to crisp and the meat looks more attractive if this is done neatly in a definite design. Coat with the glaze and return to a 375°F. oven to finish cooking, and until brown and crisp on top.
The 30 minutes cooking time above assumes the ham is hot when glazed. If it is partially cooked and has been allowed to cool, then the cooking time should be increased by about 20 minutes. To prepare the glaze: Pour the boiling water over the prunes; let stand either overnight or for several hours, depending upon the softness of the prunes, then add the orange juice. Remove the prunes from the liquid; there should be about ⅓ cup left. If the prunes are very dry they may absorb more liquid, in which case increase the amount of water slightly. If more liquid is left, then boil rapidly for a short time until reduced to ⅓ cup. Blend the juice with the orange peel, mustard, and brown sugar. Brush over the scored fat (see above) – use all the glaze. Heat prunes in the pan with the ham. *Serves 8*

Apricot and orange glazed ham

Cooking time — *See below*
Oven temperature — *375°F.*

1 smoked ham, approximately 4–5 lb. in weight.
TO GLAZE AND GARNISH: 3 medium oranges · 1 cup dried apricots · ⅓ cup brown sugar.

Soak the ham overnight in cold water if it is a dry-cured ham. If brine-cured, no soaking is required. Put into a pan of fresh cold water, bring the water to a boil, lower the heat, and simmer steadily, making sure the ham is completely covered during cooking. Allow 35 minutes per lb. plus an additional 10 minutes. When the ham is two-thirds cooked, (i.e. 1 hour 40 minutes to 2 hours) remove the water, cool sufficiently to handle then remove any skin. Score the fat with a sharp knife. While the ham is cooking prepare the glaze. Grate the peel from the oranges and squeeze the juice. Pour the juice over the apricots and simmer in a covered pan for about 30 minutes over low heat; drain this liquid, blend with the orange peel and sugar, brush over the ham and then bake in a preheated 375°F. oven for remaining cooking time. 15 minutes before serving, press apricots against glaze. *Serves 8*

To make gravy

There are various methods that may be used. Today many people prefer to use packaged gravy or gravy flavoring.

BROWN GRAVY

Pour off all the fat from the roasting pan except 1 tablespoon. For a thin gravy, blend in 1 tablespoon flour. For a thick gravy, blend in ¼ cup all-purpose flour. Cook in the fat stirring constantly, over a moderate heat until the mixture turns golden brown, taking care it does not burn. Add 1 cup liquid (water, bouillon, vegetable stock, or meat stock). Cook until the gravy thickens, stirring constantly, taste and correct the seasoning. Add a few drops gravy flavoring, if desired.

Note: The amount of flour will vary since some people prefer a very thin gravy. Others consider the only true gravy is the juice that runs from the roast meat. Naturally when meat is well cooked there is little juice, but rare beef provides a good quantity of natural gravy which should be served with the meat.

GRAVY TO SERVE WITH FRIED AND BROILED MEAT, SAUSAGES, ETC.

Although this is not considered correct, many people like it.
Measure out 1 cup liquid – water, stock, vegetable stock, or water and a bouillon cube. For a thin gravy, blend 2 tablespoons flour with a little of the liquid.
For a thick gravy, use 3 tablespoons flour. Put the remaining liquid in a saucepan, and bring to a boil. Gradually stir blended mixture into the liquid, bring to a boil and cook until thickened. To improve the flavor stir in 1–2 tablespoons fat or drippings plus a few drops of gravy flavoring, if desired. Cook for 2–3 minutes. Taste and season, if necessary.

Drippings from meat

When meat has been roasted the fat and juices, known as drippings should be put into a bowl to set. It may then be used in cooking, but to keep the drippings fresh it should be cleaned or 'clarified'. Sometimes there are pieces of fat that are cut away from meat before it is cooked. If these are put into a pan in the oven, and heated until crisp, you will obtain additional drippings.

TO CLARIFY DRIPPINGS

Drippings contain tiny particles of food and these, like all food, will become rancid in time and spoil the drippings. If you clear the dripping you remove the particles, and it will keep until you need it again.
Put the drippings into a large saucepan, and cover with cold water. Bring slowly to a boil, and boil steadily for 20 minutes. Do not have the heat very high, otherwise the drippings and water will boil over. After this time let the drippings cool slightly. Put a thick piece of cheesecloth or a fine sieve over a bowl, hold the saucepan firmly and pour drippings and water slowly through into the bowl. Let stand until the drippings are solid again. Lift the solidified fat away from the water and turn it upside down.

You will find a brown layer at the bottom. Scrape this away, it may be used in gravy. Put the clarified drippings in a bowl, in the refrigerator. The tiny particles of food will have been dissolved in the water, which is then discarded.

TO CLEAN THE MEAT PAN

After using a roasting pan for cooking the meat and often for making the gravy as well, it is both sticky and greasy. This will be much easier to wash if first wiped out thoroughly with paper towels.
If the pan has been used just for roasting, any drippings left should be used. There are directions for cleaning (clarifying) this above, so it may be used in cooking.

WHAT WENT WRONG WHEN ROAST MEAT WAS NOT SUCCESSFUL?

If roast meat was very hard and dry on the outside, the oven was too hot or insufficient fat was used.

If the roast meat was hard and too crisp on the outside, the oven was too hot and too *much* fat was put on the meat.

If the meat was tough, this was caused either by insufficient cooking time or by trying to roast less tender cut of meat (see page 74 for roasting meat, also slower method of roasting).
If the meat fell into small pieces when it was cut or carved, it was overcooked.

TO FRY MEAT

This is a quick and most convenient method of cooking very tender cuts of meat. In most cases, meat to be fried is either tender and young or it is meat which has been ground or cubed. Here are the points to remember:

1. For shallow frying, make certain that the oil or fat is hot before the meat goes in, with the exception of bacon, which goes into a cold skillet.
2. Seal the meat on either side, then turn down the heat immediately to make absolutely certain that you do not overcook the outside before the center of the meat is cooked.
3. Drain fried meats well.

TO DRAIN FRIED MEAT

1. Lift the meat onto paper towels.
2. Allow to drain for 30 seconds and then serve.

Methods of frying meat

SHALLOW-FRYING or PAN-FRYING

You need just enough oil or fat to cover the bottom of the skillet when melted, and give a depth of about ¼–½ inch, at the most.
The fat or oil should be heated only until a FAINT haze is seen. Fry the meat quickly on either side, then reduce the heat to make sure the meat is cooked through to the middle.

DEEP-FRYING

Put the oil or fat into a deep saucepan or deep fat fryer, and heat to 375°F., or until a faint haze is seen, or a cube of bread turns golden brown within a minute. Do not get the fat any hotter than this, otherwise the meat will burn. In order to remove the meat easily it may be put into a frying basket, and lowered into the hot fat or oil. After the outside of the meat is crisped or browned, lower the heat to make sure it cooks through to the center. Because the meat will be browned on both sides simultaneously, the cooking time can, therefore, be slightly reduced when frying meat in deep fat.
While any meat may be fried in deep fat, this method is generally used for meats that have been coated with egg and bread crumbs, for prepared meat dishes like croquettes, etc., and for frying coated pieces of young chicken.

PAN-BROILING

Although the pan may be rubbed with a very little fat this is not necessary except where the food is less fat than usual. Pan broiling is suitable for bacon, but not for Canadian-style bacon, and many types of pork sausages. Beef sausages, which often contain a smaller amount of fat, need shallow-frying.

Frying beef

CHOOSE: Steaks as given on pages 69–70.

ALLOW: ¼–½ lb. per person.

COOK: *Rare:* 1-inch thick steaks 2–3 minutes on a high heat on each side.
Medium: 2–3 minutes on a high heat on each side. Reduce the heat and fry 4–6 minutes, less if the meat is thinly cut.
Well done: 2–3 minutes on a high heat on each side. Reduce the heat and fry 6–10 minutes, less if the meat is thinly cut.
Minute steak: 1–2 minutes over high heat on each side.

SERVE: With fried tomatoes, mushrooms, or fried onion rings. Garnish with water cress.

Butter or oil or a mixture of butter and oil is an excellent fat in which to fry steak.

TOURNEDOS OF STEAK

A fillet steak cut from the tenderloin made into a round steak usually 2½ inches in diameter and 1-inch thick is called a tournedo. Generally a strip of pork fat or suet is wrapped around the outside then secured with a piece of string to help maintain its shape. If this has not been done for you, press the meat with your hands into a circle and then tie it. Each type of garnish gives its name to a tournedo steak. Unless specifically stated, the steaks may be fried or broiled.
One generally serves a tournedo on a circle or large crouton of fried bread. You may dispense with this if you wish, but it raises the meat and makes it look more impressive.

AFRICAINE – serve with fried bananas and horseradish relish.

ARLÉSIENNE – serve with fried eggplant slices and tomatoes, and top with Crisp fried onion rings (see page 165).

BARONNE – top with mushrooms, and serve with tomato paste and Béarnaise sauce (see page 185).

BELLE HÉLÈNE – serve with asparagus tips and truffle (mushrooms could be substituted).

CALCUTTA – serve with curry flavored rice (cook rice then fry a little curry powder in butter and sauté rice in this) and Brown sauce (see page 183), flavored with chutney.

CARLTON – top with chopped egg, and serve with Béarnaise sauce (see page 185) and strips of cooked tongue, mushrooms, and truffle.

CÉLERI – serve with braised celery.

CHASSEUR – serve with Chasseur sauce (see page 339).

CHÉRON – serve with artichoke hearts filled with diced cooked vegetables and topped with Béarnaise sauce (see page 185).

DREXEL – coat with Béarnaise sauce, and serve with tomato paste topped with truffle and shoestring potatoes.

DUMAS – coat with Onion sauce (see page 183), sprinkle with cheese and brown under the broiler. Top with slices of ham and serve with Potato croquettes (see page 167).

MAJESTIC – serve on a purée of cooked mushrooms and in a creamed potato border with Béarnaise sauce (see page 185).

MÉNAGÈRE – serve in a border of Duchesse potatoes (see page 167), top with tiny pieces of carrot, turnip and onions, and Brown sauce (see page 183) or Espagnole sauce (see page 184).

NESSELRODE – serve with a well seasoned purée of chestnuts and fried potatoes.

NIÇOISE – serve with cooked green beans and cherry tomatoes.

OTHELLO – top with a fried or poached egg.

D'ORSAY – top with stuffed olives and mushrooms.

PARISIENNE – top with asparagus tips and Béarnaise sauce (see page 185).

POMPADOUR – top with tomato paste and a slice of broiled or fried ham and truffle (or mushrooms).

SCRIBE – serve on cooked rice, top with a little pâté and Madeira sauce (see page 183).

Créole steak

Cooking time   *15 minutes*

1¼ lb. tenderloin *or* other tender steak
¼ cup butter · 2 onions · several stalks celery
1 (8 oz.) can tomatoes and ¼ cup beef bouillon *or* use
2–3 large peeled fresh tomatoes and ⅔ cup beef
bouillon · seasoning.
TO SERVE: boiled rice *or* noodles.
TO GARNISH: chopped parsley.

Cut the steak into neat strips, then sauté in the
hot butter with the peeled sliced onions and diced
celery. Add the tomatoes and bouillon, season, and
simmer for about 10 minutes. Serve in a border of
rice or noodles and garnish with chopped parsley.

Serves 4

Steak Diane

Cooking time   *few minutes*

1 very finely chopped onion *or* shallot
¼–⅓ cup butter · 4 very thin slices boneless sirloin
steak *or* 8 slices tenderloin steak
little Worcestershire sauce · little brandy
(optional).
TO GARNISH: chopped parsley.

Sauté the onion or shallot in the butter for 1–2
minutes. Add the steak and fry on each side. Place
on a heated plate. Add Worcestershire sauce and the
brandy to the butter, ignite, if desired, and pour
over the steaks. Garnish with chopped parsley.

Serves 4

Steak au poivre

Cooking time   *4–8 minutes*

4 tender steaks · ¼–⅓ cup butter
½–1 tablespoon crushed peppercorns · little brandy

Brush the steaks with plenty of butter, and press
finely crushed peppercorns into each side. Broil or
fry over high heat to personal taste. Place on a
heated dish, add a little brandy to the butter remaining in the pan. Heat and pour over the steaks.

Serves 4

Note: Crushed peppercorns are very hot. Unless a
very definite flavor is liked, broil or fry the steak
and serve with Poivrade sauce (see page 184).

Scrambled beef

Cooking time   *12–15 minutes*

¾ lb. tender steak · 1–2 onions
1–2 tomatoes · 1 green sweet pepper (optional)
¼ cup butter *or* margarine
2 teaspoons chopped mustard pickles · seasoning
3–4 eggs.
TO GARNISH: 4 slices bread.

Grind or chop the meat very finely. Peel and slice
the onions and tomatoes, and chop the pulp of the
sweet pepper into neat pieces. Heat the butter or
margarine in a pan, and cook the meat and vegetables
until just tender, adding the pickle and seasoning
when almost cooked. Blend a little more seasoning
with the eggs, pour into the meat mixture, and
scramble lightly – do not allow the mixture to
become too firm. Meanwhile toast the bread, and
arrange the meat mixture on a heated dish, garnished with triangles of toast. Serve with plenty
of butter and a crisp green salad. *Serves 4*

Frying lamb or mutton

CHOOSE: Cuts given on pages 70–71. Mutton is less
suitable.

ALLOW: 1–2 chops per person.

COOK: 3–4 minutes on each side on high heat, reduce
the heat and fry 6–8 minutes. Steam mutton chops
for 10 minutes first.

SERVE: With fried tomatoes or mushrooms. Garnish
with parsley or water cress.

GARNISHES FOR LAMB AND MUTTON CHOPS

AUX CONCOMBRES – serve with rings of peeled fried
cucumber.
DUCHESSE – coat and serve in a border of green peas,
cooked to a smooth purée. Serve with Espagnole
sauce (see page 184).
FINANCIÈRE – fry or broil and serve with cooked
onions and carrots.
ITALIENNE – marinate in equal parts of oil and vinegar
with mixed herbs. Drain, coat and fry. Serve with
mushrooms and chopped shallots.
JARDINIÈRE – coat and serve with a colorful garnish
of mixed spring vegetables.
MARÉCHALE – coat with beaten egg and grated cheese,
not bread crumbs. Serve with Bigarade sauce (see
page 184). Steam cutlets first for 10 minutes, then
coat and fry, to make sure the cheese is not overcooked.
NELSON (particularly suitable for mutton cutlets) –
after steaming spread with a Veal stuffing (see page
189), top with grated cheese and roast until tender.
Serve with a purée of onions.
RÉFORME – coat, but mix the bread crumbs with
very finely diced bacon or chopped ham. Garnish
with cooked strips of ham, mushrooms, and hard-
cooked eggs and serve with Poivrade sauce (see page
184). You may use strips of beets as a substitute for
ham.

Parmesan chops

Cooking time   25 minutes

8 small lamb *or* mutton chops · 1 egg
¼ cup grated Parmesan cheese
approximately ¼ cup toasted bread crumbs
fat for frying.

Simmer the chops very gently for about 15 minutes
in salted water or white stock. Drain and pat dry.
Coat with beaten egg and the cheese mixed with
the bread crumbs. Fry steadily until crisp and
golden brown. Drain, and serve with tomato sauce,
new or creamed potatoes and peas. Garnish with
paper frills.   *Serves 4*

Lamb chops Strasburg

Cooking time   10 minutes

8 lamb chops   seasoning
small quantity homemade liver pâté (see page 25)
or canned pâté · 8 thin slices lean ham.
TO COAT: 1 egg · ½ cup fried bread crumbs.
TO FRY: fat. TO GARNISH: asparagus tips.

Trim the chops, season, and spread the pâté over
one side. Cover with the ham. Coat in beaten egg and
the bread crumbs. Fry steadily in shallow or deep
fat until crisp and golden brown. Drain on paper
towels. Garnish with asparagus tips. Serve with
Brown sauce, Espagnole sauce, or Tomato sauce,
(see page 184).   *Serves 4*

Frying pork

CHOOSE: Chops as given on pages 71–72.

ALLOW: 1–2 chops per person.

COOK: Snip fat to crisp; 4–5 minutes on each side on
high heat, reduce the heat and fry for 35–40 minutes.

SERVE: With fried tomatoes or with heated rings of
canned pineapple. Garnish with water cress.

GARNISHES FOR PORK CHOPS

Due to the more pronounced flavor of pork in com-
parison to beef, lamb, and veal there are less classic
garnishes. Most fruit blends well with the richness
of pork – in particular prunes, peaches, pineapple,
apricots, oranges, and apples. The fruit may be
heated in the skillet or under the broiler for a few
minutes before serving with the meat.

OTHER GARNISHES FOR FRIED OR BROILED
PORK

A L'INDIENNE – the pork should be coated with well
seasoned flour blended with a little curry powder.
Fry or boil in the usual way, and serve with rice.

AUX FINES HERBES – broil the pork chops and serve
with Brown sauce (see page 183) to which should be
added finely chopped fresh sage, parsley, and chives.

SOUBISE – serve the chops on a bed of well seasoned
Crisp fried onion rings (see page 165).

Frying veal

CHOOSE: Chops or rolled cutlets as given on page 73.

ALLOW: ¼–½ lb. per person.

PREPARE: Coat with seasoned flour or flour, then egg
and bread crumbs.

COOK: Use ¼ cup butter; 5 minutes on each side on
high heat, reduce the heat and fry 10–15 minutes.

SERVE: With lemon slices.

Since veal is a very lean meat use plenty of butter
or butter and oil to fry.

Escalope of veal or Wiener Schnitzel

Cooking time   About 8–12 minutes

4 thin rolled cutlets · flour · seasoning
1 egg · fine fresh bread crumbs for coating
¼ cup butter.

Coat the veal with the seasoned flour, and then with
the egg and bread crumbs. To fry the veal you may
use approximately ¼ cup butter or, since butter is
inclined to discolor slightly with heating, although
it gives a lovely flavor, many people like to use ¼
cup butter and 3 tablespoons oil. You could use a
little fat, if desired. Heat the butter or butter and
oil, put in the veal, cook fairly quickly on each side
until crisp and brown. Reduce the heat, and cook
for a few minutes to make certain the veal, which
does need thorough cooking, is tender through to the
middle.   *Serves 4*

The following are suggestions for garnishes to veal.
Cutlets may be broiled or fried.

CORDON BLEU – there are two ways of making this
dish. Either have very large veal cutlets and cover
with a slice of Gruyère cheese and ham. Fold over
to make a sandwich, then coat and fry for longer
than usual since the veal will be double thickness.
Or, do not coat the veal, but fry in butter, top with
ham and cheese when nearly cooked, and put under
the broiler until melted.

CRACOVIENNE – garnish cutlets with strips of anchovy
fillets and serve with Madiera sauce (see page 183).

FLORENTINE – cutlets served on a bed of creamed
spinach.

HOLSTEIN – garnish with slices of hard-cooked egg, anchovy fillets, gherkins, and capers.

MAÎTRE D'HÔTEL – broil or fry cutlets, and top with Maître d'hôtel butter (see page 124).

A LA MARÉCHALE – coated cutlets fried and served with Bigarade sauce (see page 184).

A LA MILANAISE – cutlets coated with egg and, instead of plain bread crumbs, an equal quantity of bread crumbs and Parmesan cheese. Serve with cooked macaroni topped with Parmesan cheese.

SOUBISE – cutlets fried and served with onion purée.

VIENNOISE – serve with Brown sauce (see page 183), gherkins, olives, capers, anchovy fillets, and hard-cooked egg.

ZINGARA – fried veal cutlets – serve on top of cutlet-shaped pieces of broiled or boiled ham and Madeira sauce (see page 183).

Royal veal

Cooking time   *10–15 minutes*

4 boneless *or* rolled cutlets   ·   ¼ cup butter
1 cup button mushrooms   ·   ½ cup dry sherry
approximately ⅔ cup whipping thick cream
seasoning.
TO GARNISH: chopped parsley.

Gently fry veal in the butter until golden then set aside and keep hot. Sauté the mushrooms in the butter, and arrange over veal. Pour sherry into the pan, cook quickly for 5 minutes, remove from heat, and add cream and seasoning. Pour over veal and sprinkle with parsley.   *Serves 4*

Veal escalopes with pâté

Cooking time   *10–15 minutes*

4 large thin boneless cutlets   ·   ¼ cup liver pâté (see page 25)   ·   seasoning   ·   flour   ·   egg
bread crumbs   ·   ½ cup butter.

Spread the slices of veal with purchased or home-made pâté. Fold into a sandwich, coat in seasoned flour, egg, and bread crumbs, and fry in hot butter until crisp, brown and tender – see Escalope of veal.
                 Serves 4

Frying bacon

Place slices of bacon in a cold skillet over low heat. Fry until done to taste, turning frequently. The drippings may be poured off occasionally, if desired. Drain on paper towels.
For Canadian-style bacon, snip the fat edges to prevent curling. Place in a lightly greased cold skillet and fry until brown, turn and fry the second side. Drain on paper towels.

Fried liver and bacon

Cooking time   *8–10 minutes*

1–1¼ lb. sliced lamb *or* calf liver
3 tablespoons all-purpose flour   ·   seasoning
¼ cup butter *or* drippings   ·   4–8 slices bacon
2–4 tomatoes.

Dry the liver well. Coat the liver in the flour and seasoning; the amount of flour given is sufficient for a thin coating, and this prevents a rather hard outside to the liver. Heat the butter, add the liver, and fry steadily on the first side, then turn and fry on the second side. If the liver is fairly thick reduce the heat after about 5 minutes cooking, but do not overcook otherwise it will be tough.
Toward the end of the cooking time add the bacon and the halved or whole seasoned tomatoes, and cook with the liver. If the skillet is not sufficiently large it is advisable to fry the bacon and tomatoes before the liver and keep these hot while the liver is cooked. If desired, make gravy in the skillet, (see page 86).   *Serves 4*

Fried liver and orange

Cooking time   *12–15 minutes*

¼ cup butter   ·   1–1¼ lb. sliced lamb *or* calf liver
3 tablespoons all-purpose flour   ·   seasoning
finely grated peel of 2 oranges   ·   juice 2 oranges
1¼ cups meat stock
2 teaspoons arrowroot *or* cornstarch.
TO GARNISH: lettuce   ·   sliced orange.

Heat the butter. Coat the liver in seasoned flour mixed with the orange peel. Fry in the hot butter on each side for a few minutes, add the orange juice, and cook for 3 minutes. Remove the liver from the pan. Stir in the stock blended with the arrowroot or cornstarch, bring to a boil, and cook until smooth and clear. Serve separately. Garnish the liver with lettuce and sliced orange.   *Serves 4*

Fried sweetbreads

Cooking time   *55 minutes*

1–1¼ lb. sweetbreads   ·   water   ·   seasoning
1¼ cups white stock *or* water.
TO COAT: 1 egg   ·   ½ cup toasted bread crumbs.
TO FRY: fat. TO GARNISH: parsley   ·   lemon.

Wash the sweetbreads in cold water. If frozen allow to defrost before cooking. Blanch the sweetbreads – this is done by putting them into a saucepan with cold water to cover, then bring the water to a boil and discard it. The purpose is to whiten the sweetbreads. Season the stock or water, put in the sweet-breads and simmer for 45 minutes. Drain well, and allow the sweetbreads to cool enough to handle. Remove the skin then coat with the beaten egg and bread crumbs, and fry in hot fat until crisp and brown. Drain on paper towels. Garnish with parsley sprigs and lemon wedges. *Serves 4*

Frying sausages

It is important to prick fat sausages lightly before frying to prevent the meat breaking through the skins and spoiling the appearance of the sausages. This is unnecessary when cooking skinless sausages. As stated on page 87, pork sausages may be pan-broiled, i.e. cooking without additional fat. Place the sausages into a cold pan over low heat until the fat begins to flow from the sausages, then the heat may be slightly raised. Cook on one side until brown then turn. They will take approximately 10 minutes cooking but this will vary slightly according to the size or according to manufacturer's directions. Never undercook pork sausages. When cooking beef sausages put about 1–2 tablespoons fat into the pan, heat this, add the sausages and continue as above.

Frying kidneys

Wash and dry the kidneys and remove the very thin skin. Small lamb kidneys and slightly larger pork kidneys may be cooked whole but the larger calf kidneys should be halved or sliced. To give a slightly crisp outside, coat the meat with seasoned flour but for a softer outside do not coat. Fry steadily in hot butter or fat allowing approximately 8 minutes for kidneys that are sliced or for small lamb kidneys and a little longer for pork kidneys.

Deviled kidneys

Cooking time   *10 minutes*

8 lamb kidneys · ¼ cup butter
1 tablespoon vinegar · 2 tablespoons prepared mustard · seasoning.
TO SERVE: toast · bacon.

Gently fry the halved kidneys in butter for 8 minutes, turning occasionally. Stir in the vinegar, mustard, and a sprinkling of salt and pepper. Cook for 2 minutes more and serve on toast with bacon.
Serves 4

Meatballs

This form of serving meat is equally good for family meals or for a party. Meatballs are served in most European countries. When making these the mixture should be sufficiently moist for the small balls to remain tender during cooking.
Scandinavian meatballs are poached in liquid, but to give a crisp coating they may be fried in a little fat or butter then poached.

Cooking time   *20 minutes*

1 lb. ground meat (this can be ground beef *or* half beef and half pork *or* a mixture of beef, pork, and veal) · seasoning · 1 medium onion
⅛ cup butter *or* margarine · ⅔ cup fine fresh bread crumbs · ⅛ cup milk · ¼ cup all-purpose flour
1¾ cup beef bouillon.
TO GARNISH: chopped parsley.

Mix the meat, season this well. Chop the onion very finely or put through a grinder or grate. Fry in one-third of the butter for a few minutes, then blend with the meat. Put the bread crumbs into the milk for a few minutes to soften, then stir into the meat mixture. Beat well, form into about 18 tiny balls. Heat the remaining butter in a large shallow skillet. Coat the meatballs in the seasoned flour, and fry for several minutes until pale golden. Add the bouillon and simmer gently for 10–15 minutes. Garnish with chopped parsley. *Serves 4–5*

These meatballs may be varied by adding a little curry powder to the onion; by blending a dash mixed herbs (sage, parsley, thyme, rosemary, and bay leaves) with the meat, etc.; by adding ½–1 crushed clove garlic to the onion.

Veal balls

Cooking time   *15 minutes*

1 lb. veal for stew · 1 cup mashed potatoes
1 medium onion · seasoning · 1 egg
¼ cup butter *or* bacon drippings
1¼ cups cultured sour cream *or* 1¼ cups coffee cream and 1 tablespoon lemon juice.

Grind the veal, and blend with the mashed potatoes, very finely chopped or grated onion, seasoning, and egg. Form into small round balls, then flatten very slightly. Fry in the butter or bacon drippings until golden. Add sour cream or coffee cream and lemon juice and simmer for about 10 minutes. *Serves 4*

Scandinavian meatballs

Cooking time *20 minutes*

1 lb. veal *or* ½ lb. pork and ½ lb. veal
¼ cup melted butter *or* ¼ cup finely chopped beef suet
seasoning · ¼ teaspoon mace
¼ cup all-purpose flour · 1 egg
⅓ cup coffee *or* whipping cream.
FOR THE SAUCE: 2½ cups brown stock
¼ cup all-purpose flour *or* potato flour
2 tablespoons butter · ⅓ cup coffee *or* whipping cream.

Grind the meat twice until very fine, add the melted butter or the suet, seasoning, mace, and flour. Blend thoroughly, gradually beat in the egg and cream. Form into tiny balls with a teaspoon dipped in hot water then simmer gently in 1¾ cups of the stock. Drain and keep hot. Blend the flour with the remaining stock, stir into the pan and boil until thickened. Add the butter and the cream. Cook steadily until a creamy sauce; season well, then pour over the meatballs. *Serves 4–5*

Hamburgers

Cooking time *20 minutes*

2–3 onions · 1 lb. ground chuck steak *or* ground round steak · seasoning · ¼ cup fat
4 soft hamburger buns

Chop one onion very finely, and slice the others. Season the meat very well. Sauté the chopped onion in the fat for a few minutes, remove and blend with the meat. Form into 4 large patties, the size of the buns. Fry the meat and the sliced onions in the fat remaining in the skillet – do not overcook, the hamburgers should be slightly rare. To serve, slit buns – toast each half then top with the hamburgers and fried onions, and cover with the other bun half. *Serves 4*

This is a basic recipe which may be varied a great deal, e.g.
Blend ⅔ cup fine fresh bread crumbs with the meat and onions, with ¼ teaspoon mixed herbs (sage, parsley, thyme, rosemary, and bay leaves) and a small egg: add a grated raw medium potato to the meat, etc.: blend 2–4 tablespoons rolled oats with the meat and onions.

Soufflé fritters

Cooking time *20 minutes*

Ingredients as the meatballs (see page 91).
FRITTER BATTER: ⅓ cup all-purpose flour
½ teaspoon baking powder · seasoning · 2 eggs
⅓ cup milk.
TO FRY: fat or oil.

Make the meatballs as in the recipe, fry these in the fat but simmer for 5–10 minutes only. Remove from the stock and drain thoroughly in a sieve or on paper towels. Blend the flour with the baking powder, seasoning, egg yolks, and the milk then fold in the stiffly beaten egg whites. Dip each ball in the soufflé fritter mixture. Deep-fry until crisp and brown. *Serves 4–6*

Spanish potatoes

Cooking time *1½ hours*
Oven temperature *375°F.*

4 large potatoes · 1 large onion · 2 tomatoes
1 green sweet pepper · ¼ cup butter *or* margarine
dash garlic salt *or* 1 crushed clove garlic
4 cooked pork sausages *or* 6–8 slices cooked Canadian-style bacon *or* ham · seasoning.

Scrub the potatoes, and bake in their jackets in a preheated 375°F. oven for 1–1¼ hours, or until just soft. Meanwhile peel and slice the onion and tomatoes. Remove the center and seeds from the sweet pepper, and dice neatly. Heat the butter or margarine, and sauté the vegetables until just soft. Add the garlic salt or crushed clove garlic, the diced sausages, bacon, or ham, and heat thoroughly. Season well. When the potatoes are soft, cut a slice from the top and remove the pulp. Mash and season this, mix with sautéed vegetables, do not add butter since the filling is fairly rich. Pile the filling into the center of the shells then return to the oven to heat through. *Serves 4*

WHAT WENT WRONG WHEN FRIED MEAT WAS NOT SUCCESSFUL?

If the meat was greasy, it was fried in fat that was not sufficiently hot; or the meat was not drained on paper towels. Steaks, chops are not drained but coated meats, such as fried sweetbreads, should be drained. If the outside of the meat was very hard, the fat was too hot when the meat was put into the pan. If the meat was rather tough, it may be that it was not sufficiently tender for frying or that it was fried for too short a period. In certain cases (liver for example), overfrying makes the meat tough and hard.

TO BROIL MEAT

Broiling, like frying, is an excellent way of cooking tender cuts of meat. It must not be used for less tender meat since the process is so quick that the meat would be tough and inedible. Broiling is considered better than frying from the health point of view, since less fat is used and, therefore, the meat is more easily digested, and lower in calories. Broiled vegetables – mushrooms, tomatoes – may either be put in the pan under the rack or put on rack itself and broiled with the meat.

THE POINTS TO REMEMBER ARE:

1. Make sure the broiler is preheated before the meat is put underneath it, for it is essential to seal the outside of the meat quickly, to retain the maximum flavor and meat juice. The one time when the broiler is not preheated is when broiling ham. The ham should be put on the rack, then the broiler turned on – the reason for this is that the high heat causes the fat to curl (even when snipped) and burn before the rest of the meat is cooked.
2. Keep lean meat well brushed with melted butter or oil, so it does not become dry – steak and veal are the two leanest meats and also lean ham. Lamb, mutton, and pork need little, if any fat.
3. When turning meat under the broiler, do not pierce with a fork, but use two knives or tongs.
4. Broiled meats do not need draining before serving.

Choice of meat for broiling

The choice of meats for broiling is similar to that for frying – beef, lamb or mutton, pork, bacon, sausages are equally suitable for broiling as for frying. Liver, sweetbreads, and veal are more suitable for frying than broiling.

The timing for broiling is virtually the same as the time for frying. The meat is cooked quickly on each side, as the time given for frying, then the heat of the broiler is lowered for the remainder of the cooking or the broiler pan moved farther away from the source of the heat. It may be necessary to both lower the broiler pan position as well as lowering the heat, to make sure that the outside of the meat is not browned too quickly. Classic garnishes for broiled meats are found with the garnishes for fried meats in the previous section.

Stuffed steak

Cooking time   *10–12 minutes*

4 very thin large boneless sirloin steaks *or* boneless rib steaks · stuffing (select one from the section beginning on page 188 – Sage and onion is especially good) · ¼ cup butter.

Lay the steaks flat on a dish and spread half of each slice of meat with the stuffing, fold over like a sandwich, secure with a wooden toothpick, and brush with melted butter. Broil as for steak (see opposite page); and since the meat has now become much thicker it will need longer cooking than usual.

Serves 4

Steak and bacon patties

Cooking time   *5–10 minutes*

1 lb. ground sirloin steak *or* ground chuck steak
1 medium onion · seasoning
⅔ cup fine fresh bread crumbs · 1 egg
dash mixed herbs (sage, parsley, thyme, rosemary, and bay leaves)
4 slices bacon · 2–4 tablespoons butter.
TO GARNISH: cooked frozen *or* canned corn
halved tomatoes.

Put the steak and onion through a meat grinder, blend with the seasoning, bread crumbs, egg, and herbs. Form into 4 round patties. Wrap each slice of bacon around one of the patties. Secure with a wooden toothpick. Broil the patties, brushing the centers with some of the butter. Turn carefully with a spatula to prevent their breaking. Time as for steak. Garnish with cooked corn and broiled tomatoes, which should be well seasoned and brushed with the remaining butter.

Serves 4

STEAK AND BACON PATTIES HAWAIIAN STYLE
Cook the patties as above, and when turned onto the second side, top each patty with a ring of pineapple, brush this with butter and heat well.

Pork and apple patties

Cooking time   *11–16 minutes*

1 lb. fresh ham, center slice
¼ lb. pork sausage meat · seasoning
dash chopped fresh sage *or* dried sage
2 medium dessert apples · 1–2 tablespoons butter.

Grind the pork and blend with the sausage meat, seasoning, and sage. Form into 8 fairly flat patties. Core, but do not peel, the apples and cut into 8 rings. Sandwich the patties with 4 of the apple rings. Put under a hot broiler, cook for 10–15 minutes, turn, and cook for the same time on the second side. Top with the remaining apple rings and brush with a very little melted butter, lower the heat and cook for a further 5–10 minutes. Do not undercook pork.

Serves 4

TO BOIL MEAT

The term 'boiled meat', such as 'boiled ham' or 'boiled beef' is frequently used; but it must not be boiled fiercely. If meat is boiled rather than simmered, the flavor is spoiled and often the meat cut breaks into pieces. It appears cooked, but may still be very tough, and will not carve well. The liquid in which the meat is 'boiled' must therefore simmer only.

Ham, brisket of beef or beef tongue are frequently sold salted, which gives a better flavor, and in the case of brisket and beef tongue it also makes the meat a better color. Unless you are told that the meat is very lightly salted, it is advisable to soak overnight in cold water to cover. If time does not permit overnight soaking, then soak for several hours, changing the water once or twice.

Today much ham is sold very lightly cured and therefore soaking is unnecessary. Fresh brisket, etc. may also be used as the salted meats. Wash or wipe the meat well.

TO 'BOIL' MEAT

1. Put the meat into a large pan, cover with fresh cold water, adding vegetables (if stated in the recipe) and required seasoning. This means just pepper or peppercorns in the case of salted meats.
2. Bring the water to a boil. You may notice a thin layer of gray bubbles and sediment on top; to keep the liquid clear, remove this with a spoon onto a plate.
3. Cover the pan, then lower the heat. Simmer for time indicated for different meats.
4. When the meat is cooked, lift it onto a heated dish.
Use the stock for gravy.

'Boiling' beef

CHOOSE: Fresh or salt (corned) brisket.

ALLOW: 4–6 oz. fresh meat per person; ½ lb. salt meat per person (this shrinks more than fresh).

PREPARE: Wash or wipe fresh meat; soak salt meat (see notes above).

ADD: Water to cover, mixed vegetables, i.e. whole or sliced carrots, leeks, or onions, little turnip or rutabaga, bay leaf, pepper, and salt (with fresh meat).

COOK: 30 minutes per lb., plus an additional 30 minutes.

SERVE: Hot – with mixed vegetables and dumplings and unthickened stock in gravy boat, and prepared mustard.
Cold – cool in stock, serve with salad.

Boiled brisket of beef

Cooking time   *2 hours, salted;*
1½ hours, unsalted

2 lb. brisket of beef, salted (corned) *or* unsalted*
water to cover · 1 large onion · 4–5 cloves
2 carrots · 1 bay leaf · sprig parsley
1 tablespoon butter · 1 medium onion
¼ cup all-purpose flour · 1¼ cups brisket stock.
TO GARNISH: 1 large apple · butter for frying.

* When ordering salted brisket, remember it has to be in brine for several days to be at its best and you should therefore give the butcher ample notice.

If the beef is salted, soak for several hours in cold water, place in fresh cold water, bring to a boil gently, and simmer for 1 hour. Change the water. If beef is unsalted simply cover the meat with cold water. Add the peeled large onion studded with the cloves, the peeled quartered carrots, bay leaf, and parsley to the meat. Bring to a boil and simmer gently allowing 20 minutes per lb. plus an additional 20 minutes. Meanwhile, heat the butter in a small pan, add the chopped medium onion, and sauté until golden brown. Sprinkle in the flour, stir well, and cook for a few minutes. Gradually add the boiling stock from the beef, stirring constantly. Simmer gently for 20 minutes, stirring occasionally. When cooked, slice the meat, cover with the onion sauce, and garnish with slices of apple fried in butter.   *Serves 6*

PRESSED BRISKET OF BEEF
Cook salted brisket of beef as above. Remove from the liquid, and put the beef into a saucepan or a pan, dissolve 1 teaspoon unflavored gelatin in ⅔ cup of the hot stock. Pour over the beef, cover, and put a weight on top for several hours, or until cold and the jelly is set.

'Boiling' pork

CHOOSE: Head, fresh Boston butt, rolled Boston butt, and fresh hock rib.

ALLOW: ¼–⅓ lb. rolled pork per person; ⅓–¾ lb. other cuts per person, due to amount of bone.

PREPARE: Wash.

ADD: Water to cover. Pork is rarely cooked with vegetables. Cook head as in recipe for brawn (see page 112).

COOK: 30 minutes per lb., plus an additional 30 minutes.

SERVE: Not usually served hot.
Cold with salad. Remove meat from stock immediately after it is cooked. Let stock cool, remove layer of fat and clarify (see page 86).

'Boiling' lamb or mutton

CHOOSE: Rolled breast (could be stuffed).

ALLOW: ¼–½ lb. rolled lamb per person; due to amount of bone.

PREPARE: Wash.

ADD: Water to cover, mixed vegetables (see beef), salt and pepper.

COOK: Lamb – 1½ hours; Mutton – 2 hours.

SERVE: Hot with mixed vegetables, garrish with chopped parsley, Caper sauce (see page 183). Unthickened stock may be served separately. Not served cold.

Boiled lamb and caper sauce

Cooking time   *About 1½ hours*
also see method

1½ lb. lamb neck slices*
4–8 carrots · 4–8 onions
dash fresh *or* dried herbs · water
seasoning · bay leaf (optional).
CAPER SAUCE: 2 tablespoons butter *or* margarine
¼ cup all-purpose flour · ⅔ cup milk
⅔ cup lamb stock · 2–3 teaspoons capers
little caper vinegar.
TO GARNISH: cooked vegetables.

* This is not a generous amount of meat but the caper sauce adds to the food value of this dish, so a smaller amount of meat is needed. If using mutton, where the bones are larger, more meat is needed.

Cut the meat into neat pieces and put into a saucepan with the whole peeled carrots and onions. Add the herbs – in summer use a rather generous amount of mint – chopped or in leaves – then cover with water. Add the seasoning and bay leaf, if desired, and simmer for about 1½ hours in the case of lamb or a good 2 hours for mutton. Toward the end of the cooking time remove ⅔ cup of the lamb stock from the pan. Make the sauce with the butter or margarine, flour, milk, and lamb stock (see method page 183). Stir until thickened then add a little more milk or stock if a slightly thinner sauce is desired.

Add seasoning, the capers, and some of the vinegar from the jar of capers. Take care that the remaining capers in the jar are not left uncovered with vinegar; it is better to add a little ordinary vinegar if a sharper taste is desired. To serve the boiled lamb, remove from the stock and arrange on a heated dish garnished with freshly cooked vegetables; choose peas, beans, carrots etc. Serve the sauce over the top of the meat or in a gravy boat. Some of the clear unthickened stock may also be served.   *Serves 4*

'Boiling' veal

CHOOSE: Rolled breast (could be stuffed), head.

ALLOW: ¼–½ lb. per person.

PREPARE: Wash.

ADD: Water to cover, vegetables (see beef), bay leaf, little lemon juice, salt, pepper, or cook head as in recipe for brawn (see page 112).

COOK: 30 minutes per lb. plus an additional 30 minutes.

SERVE: Hot with the mixed vegetables and parsley sauce.
Cold; as a brawn (in the case of the head) or sliced with salad for other meat.

'Boiling' ham

CHOOSE: A whole or part of a smoked ham.

ALLOW: ¼–⅓ lb. per person without bone, ½–¾ lb. per person with bone.

PREPARE: Soak in cold water overnight or for some hours.

ADD: Water to cover. Vegetables may be added at the beginning or during cooking. Avoid adding salt, but season well with pepper.

COOK: 20 minutes per lb. plus an additional 20 minutes, although a very thick cut may need just a little longer.

SERVE: Hot; the traditional accompaniment is Pease pudding (see page 167), or with dumplings. Cold with salad. Let meat cool in the stock for this keeps it moist. Remove the rind (this may be added to soups and stews to give flavor then removed before serving), and coat the cold fat with toasted bread crumbs. Hot or cold ham is delicious with Cumberland sauce (see page 184).

WHAT WENT WRONG WHEN 'BOILED' MEAT WAS NOT SUCCESSFUL?

If it was dry and hard, this generally due to cooking too quickly or for too short a period. Always make certain that you have allowed the right time for this method of cooking and never cook too quickly.

If the meat broke badly when being lifted from the pan, it was cooked for too long and possibly too quickly, so that the outside was overcooked before the heat had penetrated through to the center.

TO BRAISE OR POT-ROAST MEAT

Braising is a form of cooking by moist heat that is often misnamed on a menu or in recipes. The dish that appears under 'braised beef' is frequently a pleasant stew. To braise meat or poultry correctly, the meat is browned in a small amount of hot fat then covered and cooked ABOVE a bed of vegetables etc. The correct name for the mixture used to give flavor to the meat is a mirepoix.
The fact that dishes are given the name 'braised' when this is not strictly true does not mean they are other than excellent.
Pot-roasting is very similar to braising. The meat is browned in a small amount of fat, then cooked in a small amount of liquid, tightly covered.

Braised hearts

Cooking time   *See below*

4 medium lamb hearts *or* 1¼ lb. calf heart *or* beef heart · ½ oz. flour · seasoning
dash dry mustard · ¼ cup butter *or* drippings
¼ cup diced Canadian-style bacon *or* ham
MIREPOIX: 3 onions
3 stalks celery (or use celeriac (celery root) instead) · 2 large potatoes · 1–2 bay leaves
few sprigs parsley · 3 peeled tomatoes
1¼ cups beef stock. TO GARNISH: forcemeat balls (see Forcemeat stuffing page 188).

Wash the hearts and dry thoroughly, remove the veins and arteries (the white tube-like parts). Lamb hearts may be left whole, or halved, calf heart or beef heart may be left in one piece or cut into neat strips. Coat in the flour, mixed with seasoning and the mustard and fry in half the butter or drippings then remove from the pan. Fry the bacon or ham for a few minutes, then remove from the pan. Heat the remaining butter or drippings, then sauté the sliced onions, diced celery or peeled diced celeriac, and diced potatoes. Add the bay leaves, parsley, tomatoes, and seasoning. Pour the stock on top. Place the hearts and bacon on top, cover the pan tightly and simmer slowly for 1½ hours for lamb hearts, 2 hours for calf heart and 2½ hours for beef heart. Lift the hearts and bacon onto a heated dish, press the vegetables through a sieve or put into an electric blender. Add to the stock, reheat and pour around the hearts. Garnish with the forcemeat balls.
Serves 4

BRAISED LIVER
Beef liver may be cooked in a similar way, but in order to keep this moist increase the amount of stock to 1½ cups and the potatoes to 3, or use ⅔ cup medium red wine and 1¼ cups beef stock. Simmer slowly for 2½ hours.

Tongue en papillotes*

Cooking time   *10–15 minutes*
Oven temperature   *425°F.*

4 large thin slices cooked tongue
2 teaspoons chopped parsley
2 teaspoons chopped shallot
2 teaspoons capers · 1 teaspoon chopped tarragon
(optional) · small can anchovies · dash pepper
4 slices bacon
4 small greaseproof paper bags *or* sheets of parchment paper.

* This method of cooking in heavy paper is traditionally French and it conserves much of the flavor.

Lay the slices of tongue on a board or large flat dish. Blend the parsley, shallot, capers, and tarragon with the chopped anchovies and oil from the can. Season with pepper; since the anchovies provide a strong salt flavor do not use salt. Put this mixture on each slice of tongue and roll firmly. Roll the bacon around the tongue rolls, and slip inside a greaseproof paper bag or wrap firmly in parchment paper, sealing like a parcel. Place on a baking sheet. Cook in a preheated 425°F. oven for 10–15 minutes, remove from the paper, and serve at once. This makes an excellent light lunch with a green salad.   *Serves 4*

Braised beef

Cooking time   *1¼ hours*

2 lb. beef – fresh brisket, rolled rump roast, sirloin tip roast, *or* eye of round
2 slices bacon.
MIREPOIX: 2 tablespoons butter · 1 slice bacon
2 large carrots · 1 large onion
1 stalk celery · 1 small turnip
bouquet garni · ⅔ cup beef bouillon and ⅔ cup medium red wine *or* 1¼ cups beef bouillon
seasoning.

Wipe the meat. Put the meat with the bacon into the pan and brown the meat gently on each side, then lift onto a dish. Prepare the mirepoix; heat the butter, sauté the chopped bacon, the thickly sliced vegetables then add the *bouquet garni* (3 bay leaves, 3 sprigs parsley, 1 sprig thyme, tied together), bouillon, wine and seasoning. Put the meat on top of this, cover with the bacon and a buttered piece of wax paper or foil, then cover tightly. Simmer very gently for 1¼ hours. Lift the meat onto a heated serving dish, top with the bacon, then strain the liquid from the vegetables, etc., and serve this as a thin sauce. If preferred, the vegetables may be pressed through a sieve and added to the liquid to give a thick sauce. or strain the liquid and use this as part of the stock in a Brown sauce (see page 183) or Espagnole sauce (see page 184).   *Serves 6*

Swiss steak special

Cooking time   *1¼ hours*
Oven temperature   *425°F.*

¼ cup butter · 1 clove garlic (optional)
1 package dehydrated onion soup
1½–2 lbs. beef arm pot-roast, blade pot-roast, inside chuck roll, *or* round steak, 1 inch thick
little black pepper · ¼ cup medium red wine
1 cup mushrooms.

Spread half the butter over the center of a piece of foil 15 by 15-inches double thickness, halve the garlic, and rub it over foil. Sprinkle half the package soup, after shaking well, over the butter. Place beef on this. Sprinkle a little black pepper on the beef, then the remainder of the soup and dot with the remaining butter. Pour the wine over this. Slice mushrooms and arrange around the beef. Fold the foil and make into a parcel to prevent juices running out. Bake in a preheated 425°F. oven for approximately 1¼ hours. Serve with boiled rice and a green vegetable.   *Serves 4*

Chops Americaine

Cooking time   *40 minutes*
Oven temperature   *400°F.*

4 thick lamb loin chops · 4 slices Canadian-style bacon · 3 large tomatoes
2 teaspoons Worcestershire sauce · seasoning
1 tablespoon oil.

Arrange the chops in a shallow ovenproof baking dish. Top with the bacon, then the peeled sliced tomatoes, the sauce, seasoning, and oil. Cook in a preheated 400°F. oven for 40 minutes then serve with a green salad.   *Serves 4*

Pot-roast

Cooking   *See below*

Meat · vegetables · water *or* stock
seasoning.

This method of cooking meat is ideal when you do not wish to use the oven. It is a good way of cooking the less tender cuts of beef – lamb – mutton – veal, but is not suitable for stewing meat. Pork and duck are, on the whole, too fat to cook by this method unless the fat is removed once or twice during cooking.
First brown the meat in a heavy saucepan. If the meat is very lean, add 2–4 tablespoons fat. Remove the meat from the pan onto a plate. If more than 2 tablespoons of fat remains, remove this too. Put a thick layer of vegetables – whole potatoes, carrots, turnips, onions – into the pan. Add enough water or stock to come a good halfway up the vegetables, then season. Put the meat on top of the vegetables. Now cover tightly; if the cover does not fit well, put a piece of foil under this, for it is essential that the pan does not boil dry.

BEEF; allow about 25–30 minutes per lb. plus an additional 25–30 minutes, depending upon how well-done you like it.

LAMB, MUTTON, PORK, VEAL; allow 35–40 minutes per lb. plus an additional 35–40 minutes.

The size of the vegetables must be fairly large so they are well-done but not overcooked. If you have a rack that fits into the pan, the meat may be put on this, with liquid underneath but no vegetables. The liquid in the pan makes a delicious gravy; thicken, if desired.

Mediterranean pot-roast

Cooking time   *2½–3 hours*

Approximately 2½–3 lb. beef (see pages 69–70 for suggested cuts).
3 tablespoons oil · 4 large fresh tomatoes
seasoning · dash marjoram · bay leaf
1–2 cloves garlic crushed · ⅔ cup beef bouillon *or* water.

Brown the meat on both sides in the hot oil in a heavy pan, add the peeled tomatoes and the remaining ingredients. Cover the pan tightly, and simmer very slowly. Turn the meat once or twice during cooking.   *Serves 6–7*

Pork with savory rice

Cooking time   *35–40 minutes*
Oven temperature   *400°F.*

¼ cup long-grain rice · 4 large pork chops
1 large onion · 3 large tomatoes · seasoning
1¼ cups canned tomato juice.

Cook the rice according to one of the methods on page 192 until nearly tender. Do not overcook, otherwise it will become sticky in this dish. Put the pork chops in an ovenproof dish, and roast uncovered in a preheated 400°F. oven for 15 minutes. Peel and slice the onion very thinly and the tomatoes rather thickly. Remove the pork from the oven, and top with the onion slices, then the rice, then the tomatoes. Season each layer well. Pour the tomato juice into the side of the dish, but not on top of the rice, etc. Return to the oven for a further 20–25 minutes, lowering the heat slightly if the mixture on top of the chops is becoming too brown.
Serves 4

TO STEW OR COOK MEAT IN A CASSEROLE

In the first case, the meat and vegetables are *cooked slowly* in stock or water in a covered saucepan on top of the range. In the second case, they are cooked in a covered container in the oven.

ADAPTING RECIPES FOR STEWS AND CASSEROLE DISHES:

The same recipe may be used for either stewing or cooking in a casserole...BUT ALWAYS ALLOW A LITTLE EXTRA LIQUID IF ADAPTING A CASSEROLE RECIPE FOR STEWING ON TOP OF THE RANGE, SINCE THERE IS MORE LOSS OF LIQUID DUE TO EVAPORATION. On the other hand, ALLOW A LITTLE LESS LIQUID OR THICKEN A LITTLE MORE if cooking a stew in the oven, since there is less evaporation. Cook for a slightly longer period in a preheated 300°F. oven – e.g. if stewing for 2 hours, allow 2¼–2½ hours in the oven.

TO PREPARE INGREDIENTS:

While more expensive cuts of meat may be used, stews and casseroles were designed for less expensive meats, since slow cooking makes them tender.
1. Wipe the meat; cut into convenient-sized pieces (if stated in the recipe), remove excess fat (remember *some* fat gives a good flavor) and gristle.
2. Prepare any vegetables, herbs, etc.
3. Coat meat in seasoned flour and fry if stated in the particular recipe.
4. Add the liquid, etc., and bring to a boil. Lower heat, and simmer for time given in recipe.
5. If the meat was not coated before stewing, you may have to thicken toward end of cooking time.
6. If dumplings are included, check there is sufficient liquid in the pan to cook these.
Allow 15–20 minutes cooking time, serve around the meat, etc.

If preparing a casserole

Follow steps 1, 2, 3 and 4 above.
Transfer the meat, vegetables and the liquid to an ovenproof casserole. Cover this tightly with a well fitting lid or with foil. Cook for the time given in the recipe. If dumplings are to be added they may either be cooked in boiling salted water in a saucepan on top of the range then added to the casserole just before serving, or the uncooked dumplings may be put on top of the liquid in the casserole 20 minutes before the end of the cooking time. When the dumplings are added the cover should not be replaced unless there is plenty of space between the dumplings and the cover to allow them to rise.

Beef stew

Cooking time   *2–2½ hours*

1–1½ lb. stewing beef · 2 tablespoons fat
2 onions · 4 carrots · 1 turnip and/or stalk celery
3¾ cups beef stock *or* water and 3 bouillon cubes
seasoning · dash mixed herbs (optional)
¼ cup all-purpose flour *or* 2 tablespoons cornstarch.
TO GARNISH: chopped parsley.

Remove excess fat and gristle from meat and cut into neat cubes. Heat the fat in a saucepan and sauté the meat in this for 2 minutes. Cut the peeled vegetables into neat pieces and add to the meat. Pour in all the stock except ¼ cup. Bring to a boil, add seasoning and herbs, and simmer slowly for 2–2½ hours, or until the meat is tender. Blend the flour or cornstarch with the remaining stock, add to the liquid in the pan and stir with a wooden spoon until the gravy has thickened. Serve garnished with chopped parsley. Illustrated on pages 57, 104.
Serves 4–5

BEEF STEW AND DUMPLINGS
Follow the recipe for beef stew above until the gravy has been thickened, but make sure there is plenty of stock in the saucepan before putting in the dumplings, since they absorb liquid very readily. Make the dumplings (see page 110), and add to the stew a good 15 minutes before the end of the cooking time. Allow the liquid to boil steadily so that the dumplings cook quickly and are light.

BEEF AND KIDNEY STEW
Use 1 lb. stewing beef and ¼–½ lb. beef kidney in the beef stew above.

Flemish stew

Cooking time   *2¼–2½ hours*

1–1½ lb. stewing beef · 8–12 small onions
2 tomatoes · clove garlic (optional)
3 tablespoons fat · *either* 3¾ cups Brown stock (see page 32) *or* use 1¾ cups Brown stock and 1¾ cups tomato juice · seasoning
2 teaspoons prepared mustard · 1 thick slice bread
¼ teaspoon mixed herbs (sage, parsley, thyme, rosemary, and bay leaves).

Cut the beef into neat strips, peel the onions and tomatoes, and crush the garlic. Sauté the vegetables then the meat in the hot fat, then add the liquid and seasoning to taste. Simmer slowly for approximately 2–2¼ hours. Spread the mustard on the slice of bread, from which the crusts have been removed and sprinkle with the herbs (fresh or dried). Put bread on top of the stew and leave for about 15 minutes. Beat hard with a wooden spoon until the bread breaks completely and thickens the liquid.

Serves 4–5

Speedy beef chop suey

Cooking time   *20 minutes*

4–6 oz. egg noodles · water · salt
1 (8 oz.) can tomatoes · ½ cup grated cheese
½–¾ lb. tender beef steak (see pages 69–70)
2 medium onions · 2–3 stalks celery
3 tablespoons oil · 1 cup bean sprouts (optional)
small piece cucumber
½–1 tablespoon soy sauce.

Boil the noodles for about 10 minutes only in salted water, or until nearly tender. Drain, and return to the pan with the tomatoes and cheese, and heat gently without cooking. Meanwhile, dice the steak and chop the onions and celery finely. Sauté gently in the oil until the meat is tender, adding the bean sprouts and tiny strips of cucumber and soy sauce toward the end of the cooking time. Arrange the tomato flavored noodles on a heated dish and top with the meat mixture.

Serves 4

Savory ground beef

Cooking time   *1¼ hours*

2 onions · 3–4 tomatoes · ¼ cup fat
¼ cup all-purpose flour · 2½ cups Brown stock (see page 32) · 1 lb. ground beef · seasoning.
TO GARNISH: chopped parsley · sliced tomato.

Peel onions and tomatoes, and cut into small pieces. Sauté the onion for 3 minutes in the hot fat, taking care it does not become too brown. Add the tomatoes and cook for a further 2 minutes. Remove the pan from the heat and gradually stir in the flour. Cook over low heat for 2–3 minutes, stirring constantly. Add the liquid slowly, following the same procedure as when adding milk in a white sauce. Bring to a boil and cook until a slightly thickened sauce. Add the meat; stir this well to break it into small pieces. Add the seasoning. Cook tightly covered for about 1 hour, stirring occasionally. Taste and reseason, if necessary. Garnish with chopped parsley and sliced tomato.

Serves 4

Deviled beef

Cooking time   *2 hours 40 minutes*

1–1½ lb. stewing beef · ¼ cup all-purpose flour
seasoning · 1 teaspoon curry powder
1 teaspoon dry mustard · dash cayenne pepper
¼ cup fat · 2½ cups beef bouillon
2 teaspoons Worcestershire sauce.
few drops chili sauce · 2 teaspoons vinegar
1 tablespoon chutney · 4–6 medium carrots
4 medium tomatoes · 1 cup peas.
TO SERVE: ½ cup long-grain rice.

Cut the beef into neat strips or cubes. Mix the flour, seasoning, curry powder, dry mustard, and cayenne pepper together. Coat the meat in this, and sauté in the hot fat for several minutes. Gradually blend in the stock, Worcestershire sauce, chili sauce, vinegar, and chutney. Bring to a boil, and cook until a thin sauce. Cover the pan and simmer for 1½ hours, then add the sliced carrots. Simmer for a further 30 minutes then add the tomatoes and peas. Taste and correct the seasoning, then continue cooking for another 30 minutes. Meanwhile, boil the rice (see page 192). Serve the beef and vegetables on a heated dish with the rice. Illustrated on page 82.

Serves 4–5

Chili con carne

Cooking time   *55 minutes–1½ hours*

¼ cup butter *or* margarine · 1 large onion
1 green sweet pepper · 2 stalks celery
¾–1 lb. ground beef *or* diced stewing beef
1 tablespoon chili powder* · ½ teaspoon salt
cayenne pepper · 2 teaspoons paprika
3 medium tomatoes *or* 1 (8 oz.) can tomatoes
1 (15½ oz.) can kidney beans *or* soaked and cooked kidney beans · ⅔ cup water.

* This is very hot. I suggest only one quarter of the quantity is used for the first time – increase as palate becomes used to the taste.

Heat the butter or margarine in a saucepan. Chop the onion, green pepper, and celery, and cook with the ground beef in the butter until just tender, then add the remaining ingredients. Bring just to a boil, lower the heat, and cook gently for approximately 55 minutes or 1¼ hours if diced meat is used. Stir halfway through cooking, and add a little more water, if necessary. Some people like to add ⅓ cup cooked rice to the recipe at the end of the cooking time.

Serves 4

Beef olives

Cooking time *2–2½ hours*
Oven temperature (if used) *300°F.*

1–1¼ lb. beef rump steak, top round steak, *or* inside chuck roll
1 onion · 1 carrot · ¼ cup fat · seasoning
1 bay leaf · 1¾ cups Brown stock (see page 32)
or water with 1–2 beef bouillon cubes
¼ cup all-purpose flour.
STUFFING: ⅔ cup fine fresh bread crumbs
¼–⅓ cup chopped beef suet · 1 tablespoon chopped parsley · 1 teaspoon dried thyme *or* savory
1 teaspoon grated lemon peel · seasoning · 1 egg
milk to mix.

Ask your butcher to thinly slice the beef into pieces about 4 × 3 inches. Prepare the stuffing by combining all ingredients. Spread some on each piece of flattened, beaten meat, roll up or form into a ball like an olive and secure with heavy white thread or very fine string. Peel and slice the onion and carrot. Heat the fat and sauté the onion and beef olives in it; add the carrot and seasoning, bay leaf, and stock blended with the flour, then cook until thickened. Cover and simmer slowly until tender, or transfer to a covered ovenproof casserole for 2½ hours in a preheated 300°F. oven. Remove string before serving. Arrange the beef olives and sauce in the center of a heated dish, with cooked mixed vegetables and a border of piped mashed potatoes.
Serves 4

Tomato beef olives

Cooking time *2–2¼ hours*
Oven temperature *300°F.*

1¼ lb. beef rump · ¼ cup all-purpose flour
1¼ cups Brown stock (see page 32)
4 large tomatoes *or* ⅓ cup tomato ketchup.
STUFFING: 2 onions
½ cup butter *or* fat *or* margarine
1 cup fine fresh bread crumbs · 2 tomatoes
1 tablespoon chopped parsley · seasoning.
SAVORY NOODLES: 4–6 oz. egg noodles
3 large tomatoes · 1 green sweet pepper.

Ask the butcher to cut the beef into thin slices, giving 4–5 pieces. To prepare the stuffing, chop the onions very finely, sauté in one-quarter of hot butter or fat, then blend with the bread crumbs, peeled chopped tomatoes, parsley, and seasoning. Spread over the slices of meat and roll firmly, then tie with heavy thread or very fine string. Heat ¼ cup of the remaining butter, and fry the beef olives in this, lift out of the butter into an ovenproof casserole. Stir the flour into the butter, and cook for 2–3 minutes, then gradually blend in the stock and 2 peeled chopped tomatoes or half the ketchup. Season well. Pour this sauce over the olives, then cook tightly covered in a preheated 300°F. oven for 2–2¼ hours. Meanwhile, boil the noodles in salted water until just tender; drain, sauté the sliced tomatoes and diced seeded pepper in the remaining butter, then mix with the noodles. Put the sauce on the serving dish, top with the olives and noodles and pour either the remaining tomato ketchup or well-seasoned strained tomato pulp (made from the remaining tomatoes) over the meat. Illustrated on page 82.
Serves 4–5

Paprika beef stew and dumplings

Cooking time *2 hours 25 minutes*

1¼ lb. stewing beef · ¼ cup all-purpose flour
2 teaspoons paprika · seasoning
¼ cup fat · 3 large onions
3¾ cups Brown stock (see page 32) · 4–6 carrots
2 tomatoes · dumplings (see page 110).

Cut the beef into neat pieces. Mix the flour with the paprika and seasoning. Coat the beef with this, and sauté in the hot fat, then add the sliced onions, and cook for about 5 minutes. Gradually blend in the stock, bring to a boil, and cook until thickened slightly. Add the carrots and the peeled sliced tomatoes, cover tightly, and simmer for 2 hours. Check there is sufficient liquid, add the dumplings, and boil quickly for a further 20 minutes. *Serves 4*

Hungarian goulash

Cooking time *2¼ hours*

½–¾ lb. stewing beef · ½–¾ lb. stewing veal
3 medium onions · 4 medium tomatoes
¼ cup all-purpose flour · 1–2 tablespoons paprika*
seasoning · ¼ cup fat · 1¾ cups beef bouillon†
⅓ cup unflavored yogurt.
TO GARNISH: dill pickle *or* gherkins.
TO SERVE: lettuce · green sweet pepper.

* this is NOT a hot flavor but a sweet one.
† this is a thick stew, but more liquid may be used if desired.

Dice the meats. Slice the onions, peel the tomatoes, and cut into thick slices. Blend the flour, paprika, and seasoning. Coat the meats in the flour mixture, sauté in the hot fat, then gradually blend in the bouillon. Bring to a boil and cook until thickened. Add the onions, and tomatoes. Cover the pan tightly, and simmer gently for 2 hours. Make sure that the liquid does not evaporate, since this is a very thick mixture. Just before serving, blend the yogurt into the mixture, or if preferred, the stew may be topped with the yogurt before serving. Garnish with a dill pickle or pickled gherkins. This is excellent served with additional pickled gherkins or pickles and with a crisp salad made just of lettuce and rings of green sweet pepper, and boiled rice or boiled noodles. Illustrated on page 78. *Serves 4–5*

Cassoulet

Cooking time   *5 hours*
Oven temperature   *300°F.*

1 lb. navy beans · 1 ham bone
3 tablespoons brown sugar · 1 tablespoon molasses
5 cups beef bouillon · ¼ cup drippings
1 lb. pork arm steak · 1 lb. stewing mutton *or*
lamb · 1 crushed clove garlic · 6 small onions
3 tablespoons tomato paste · *bouquet garni*
seasoning · 3 frankfurters
fine fresh bread crumbs.

Soak the beans in cold water overnight. Drain, and put them in a saucepan with the ham bone, sugar, and molasses. Cover with the bouillon, and simmer for 2 hours. Melt the drippings, and lightly brown the diced meat, then add the garlic, onions, tomato paste, *bouquet garni* (3 bay leaves, 3 sprigs parsley, and 1 sprig thyme, tied together), and seasoning. Simmer gently for a few minutes. Drain the beans, and reserve the stock. Put a layer of beans in a deep ovenproof casserole, then add the meat mixture, then beans and meat alternately, ending with the beans. Barely cover with some of the bouillon and cook in a preheated 300°F. oven for 3 hours. Add more liquid if needed. One hour before serving add the sausages cut up, cover with bread crumbs and continue cooking uncovered.   *Serves 7–8*

Irish stew

Cooking time   *Approximately 2¼ hours*

1–1½ lb. lamb *or* mutton arm chops *or* neck slices
2 large onions · about 4–6 medium peeled potatoes
1¾ cups white stock *or* water · seasoning.
TO GARNISH: chopped parsley.

Cut the meat into cubes, put into a saucepan with the sliced onions and half the sliced potatoes. Add the water or stock and seasoning, bring to a boil, and remove any scum from the surface. Cover tightly, lower the heat, and simmer gently for about 1½ hours. Slice the remaining potatoes, put into the stew, and continue cooking for a further 40 minutes. Taste and reseason, if necessary. Lift carefully onto a heated dish, and garnish with chopped parsley.   *Serves 4*

Lancashire hot pot

Cooking time   *2 hours*
Oven temperature   *375°F.*

6 medium potatoes · 1–1½ lb. mutton arm chops *or* neck slices · 2 lamb kidneys · 1 large onion
seasoning · ⅔ cup meat stock *or* water.

Arrange a layer of potatoes at the bottom of an ovenproof casserole. Cut the meat into cubes and remove the fat from the kidneys, then skin, core, and slice them. Place over the potatoes. Add the sliced onion, seasoning, and stock. Top with the remaining sliced potatoes then cover tightly. Bake in a preheated 375°F. oven for 2 hours, but remove the cover for the last 15 minutes. Serve with pickled red cabbage. Illustrated on page 102.   *Serves 4*

Lamb and mushroom ragoût

Cooking time   *1 hour 45 minutes*

1½–2 lb. lamb arm chops *or* neck slices (mutton could be used) · 3 cups beef *or* chicken stock *or* water
4 medium carrots
2 large *or* about 8–10 small onions
1 cup mushrooms · 1½ cups fresh beans
1⅓ cups fresh peas (*or* 1 (10 oz.) package frozen beans and 1 (10 oz.) package frozen peas) · seasoning
¼ cup all-purpose flour (optional).

Cut the meat into cubes. Put into a pan with the stock or water and the sliced or whole carrots and sliced or whole onions. Bring to a boil, and simmer steadily for 1 hour, then add the mushrooms, beans, peas, and seasoning. Simmer for a further 45 minutes. If using frozen beans and peas, the liquid may become rather thin, so simmer for the last 20 minutes uncovered. To thicken the liquid for gravy, blend the flour with a little cold water, stir into the ragoût, bring to a boil, and simmer for 5 minutes. Illustrated on page 82. If mutton is used in this recipe, it will take a little longer to cook. *Serves 4-5*

Lamb cutlets Lyonnaise

Cooking time   *55 minutes*
Oven temperature   *400°F.*

4 large potatoes · 2 medium onions
¼ cup fat
4 large *or* 8 small lamb loin chops *or* rib chops
4 bay leaves · 4 *or* 8 slices Canadian-style bacon
seasoning · ⅔ cup beef *or* chicken stock.

Peel and slice the potatoes and onions, sauté in the hot fat in a skillet for approximately 15 minutes, until half-cooked. Put the lamb into a shallow ovenproof casserole, top with whole or halved bay leaves, the bacon, and well seasoned potatoes and onions. Do not cover the dish. Pour the stock on top, and bake in a preheated 400°F. oven for approximately 40 minutes. Serve with pickled red cabbage.   *Serves 4*

This recipe may be made with mutton chops, but these will require approximately 1¼ hours cooking time.

Springtime hot pot

Cooking time   *2 hours*
Oven temperature   *300°F.*

1½–2 lb. lamb arm chops *or* neck slices
4 medium onions · 4–6 medium carrots
2½ cups brown stock · seasoning · 3–4 tomatoes
1⅓ cups fresh peas *or* 1 (10 oz.) package frozen peas
Herb dumplings (see recipe on page 110).

Cut the meat into neat pieces, arrange in an ovenproof casserole with the whole or sliced onions, whole or sliced carrots, stock, and seasoning. Cover tightly, and cook in a preheated 300°F. oven for about 1½ hours. Add the quartered tomatoes, peas, and the herb dumplings (check to see there is plenty of stock in the casserole). Do not cover again, but cook for a further 30 minutes.
If preferred, this may be cooked in a saucepan, but in this case use 3–3¾ cups stock. This is excellent with new season's lamb. Illustrated on page 82.   *Serves 4-5*

Frying pan barbeque, page 330

Lancashire hot pot, page 108

Breast of lamb, stuffed with eggs, page 76

Beef stew and dumplings, page 97

Roast capon in cider, page 121; Mashed or creamed potatoes nests, page 167

Chicken curry, page 135

Duck and orange, page 121

Roast turkey, page 120; Bacon rolls on skewers, page 330; Forcemeat stuffing, page 188;
Sausages, page 91; Christmas pudding, page 231

Chinese pork casserole

Cooking time *1½–2 hours*
Oven temperature *325°F.*

1½ lb. pork (for a luxurious dish, center slice fresh ham – for an economical dish, pork arm steak)
¼ cup all-purpose flour · seasoning
1 teaspoon dry mustard · 2 teaspoons granulated sugar · ¼ cup fat if using fresh ham *or* 2 tablespoons fat it using arm steak
½ lb. very tiny onions *or* shallots
⅔ cup chicken stock
1 (1 lb. 4 oz.) can pineapple rings
1 cup diced bamboo shoots *or* 2 cups bean sprouts *or* use ¾ cup diced peeled cucumber.

Cut the meat into neat pieces. Blend the flour with the seasoning, mustard, and sugar. Roll the meat in this. Melt the fat, and cook the coated meat in this for about 10 minutes, turning over once or twice. Watch carefully since the sugar helps this to brown quickly. Add the onions or shallots, and cook for 2–3 minutes. If there is rather a lot of fat from the pork, spoon out. Gradually blend in the stock and ¾ cup syrup from the can of pineapple. Bring to a boil, and allow to thicken. Transfer to an ovenproof casserole, cover tightly, and cook in a preheated 325°F. oven for 1½–2 hours, allowing the longer period for arm steak. If preferred, this may be simmered in a covered saucepan, but allow a total of 1¾ cups liquid instead of 1¼ cups, since some of this will evaporate. 15 minutes before serving, add the diced pineapple and bamboo shoots. Serve with boiled rice or noodles. *Serves 4–5*

Pork and bean casserole

Cooking time *40–45 minutes*
Oven temperature *375°F.*

¾ lb. pork arm steak · 1 bunch celery
1 large onion
1 (16 oz.) can baked beans in tomato sauce
1 cup fine fresh bread crumbs
2 tablespoons butter *or* margarine.

Dice the pork, and fry in a pan until golden colored and nearly tender. Put into a shallow ovenproof dish with the diced celery. Chop the onion finely, and sauté in the pork fat remaining in the pan, until nearly tender. Spread over the pork and celery. Top with the beans, then the bread crumbs and melted butter or margarine. Bake in a preheated 375°F. oven for approximately 30 minutes, or until the topping is crisp and brown. The contrast between the crisp celery (which does not have time to become very soft) and the tender beans and fairly fat meat is very pleasant and this makes a most economical dish. *Serves 4–6*

Blanquette of veal (1)

Cooking time *2¼ hours*

1¼ lb. stewing veal · 3 slices bacon
3 carrots · ½ lb. small onions *or* shallots
⅔ cup white wine · 1¼ cups water *or* chicken stock
seasoning · little milk · ¼ cup butter
½ cup all-purpose flour · 1 canned *or* ½ fresh red sweet pepper*

* If using fresh red sweet pepper cook for a short time in boiling salted water – until nearly soft.

Cut the veal and bacon into neat pieces, and slice the carrots. Blanch the veal and bacon by putting into cold water, bringing to a boil and discarding water. This gives a particularly white color to the meat. Put meat into a pan, add the carrots and whole peeled onions or shallots, pour the wine and water or stock on top. Cover and simmer gently for 2¼ hours, seasoning well. Drain off the liquid, measure, and add enough milk to give 2½ cups. Make a white sauce with the butter, flour, and liquid. Blend with the meat and vegetables then add the strips of red sweet pepper. *Serves 4–5*

Blanquette of veal (2)

Cooking time *1 hour 35 minutes*

1 lb. stewing veal · 2 onions
bouquet garni (3 bay leaves, 3 sprigs parsley and 1 sprig thyme, tied together)
2½ cups white stock *or* water and chicken bouillon cube · ¼ cup butter · ½ cup all-purpose flour
⅔ cup coffee cream *or* evaporated milk
1 *or* 2 egg yolks · 1 tablespoon lemon juice.
TO GARNISH: Bacon rolls (see page 330) · parsley lemon.

Put the diced veal, onions, and herbs into pan with the stock. Simmer gently for approximately 1½ hours, or until tender. Drain, and keep the meat hot. Make a sauce with the butter, flour, and 2½ cups of stock, simmer for 2 minutes. Add the cream or evaporated milk, and reheat. Stir in the egg yolk and lemon juice, reheat, but do not boil. Pour the sauce over the veal, and garnish with bacon rolls and chopped parsley and lemon. Illustrated on page 79. *Serves 4*

Liver and apple casserole

Cooking time *1 hour 40 minutes*
Oven temperature *350°F.*

1 lb. calf liver · ¼ cup all-purpose flour
seasoning · 1 teaspoon dry mustard · ¼ cup fat
2 medium baking apples · 2 medium onions
6 slices bacon · 1¼ cups water.

Cut liver into thin slices. Sift together the flour, seasoning, and the mustard, then coat the slices of liver. Brown liver lightly in heated fat. Fill a greased ovenproof casserole with alternate layers of liver, sliced and cored apples and onions, then top with pieces of bacon. Add water, cover casserole, and cook in a preheated 350°F. oven for 1½ hours, removing the cover for the last 20 minutes. Serve with mashed potatoes, mustard greens, and spinach. *Serves 4*

Oxtail ragoût

Cooking time   2½* hours

½ cup navy beans (optional) · water
2–2½ lb. ox joints · 3–4 onions *or* leeks
3–4 large carrots · ½ cup all-purpose flour
seasoning · ¼ cup fat · prepared mustard
1–2 beef bouillon cubes (optional).
TO GARNISH: parsley · freshly cooked vegetables.

If using dry navy beans these should be soaked overnight in cold water to cover. If the butcher has not cut the ox joints into neat pieces this should be done. Slice the onions or leeks and the carrots. Blend the flour with the seasoning, and coat the ox joints well, then fry in the hot fat until golden brown. Add the vegetables, cook for several minutes, then cover with water. Bring the water to a boil, stir until the mixture has thickened, stir in a little mustard to flavor and the stock cubes dissolved in some of the hot liquid . . . ox joints have such a rich flavor that meat stock is not necessary. If using dried beans put these in with the meat. Cover the pan, and simmer for nearly 2½ hours. This time should be adequate but sometimes the meat is rather tough, that is why cooking one day then reheating makes sure it is well cooked in addition to removing surplus fat. To cook and serve the same day, look at the stew at the end of the cooking time and if it seems rather greasy on top then spoon off any surplus fat or 'blot' this by laying a clean piece of white blotting paper on top. Top with chopped parsley and freshly cooked carrots, onions, peas, etc.

Oxtail stew may be flavored with wine, a *bouquet garni* (3 bay leaves, 3 sprigs parsley, and 1 sprig thyme, tied together), tomatoes.

If cooking one day and serving the next, allow the stew to become quite cold and 'set' then remove any surplus fat with a knife. Reheat thoroughly, top with the garnish.   *Serves 4–6*

* The cooking time above is the minimum to allow; it is better to plan to cook the stew one day and allow it to cool then reheat it . . . see recipe.

Faggots

Cooking time   1 hour 40 minutes
Oven temperature   425°F.

½ lb. pork arm steak · 1 lb. pork liver
1 pork kidney (heart could be used)
1 large onion · seasoning
⅔ cup fine fresh bread crumbs · 1 egg
¼ teaspoon dried sage and thyme *or* ½–1 teaspoon each freshly chopped herbs.

Put pork, liver, kidney, and onion into a pan with seasoning and water to half-cover. Simmer gently for 40 minutes, then drain. Grind or chop finely and blend with the remaining ingredients. Form into 9 balls about 2½–3 inches in diameter and, if you can get a pig's caul (this is a membrane), wrap each ball in a piece of this. If not, spread the mixture in a greased 8-inch layer cake pan, mark into squares and cover with greased foil. Bake in a preheated 425°F. oven. Baste with hot fat. Remove foil or caul before serving.   *Serves 4*

Ham Charlotte

Cooking time   30 minutes
Oven temperature   400°F.

4 large slices bread · ¼ cup butter *or* margarine *or* clarified drippings · thick white sauce made with 2 tablespoons butter, ¼ cup all-purpose flour and ⅔ cup milk · seasoning · 1 cup diced cooked ham.
TO GARNISH: 1–2 tomatoes · parsley.

Remove the crusts from the slices of bread, cut into strips. Heat the butter, margarine, or drippings and fry the bread until crisp and golden colored. Put half in the bottom of an ovenproof dish. Make the white sauce, season lightly (remember ham is sometimes very salt), add the diced ham. Spread the white sauce mixture over the layer of fried bread, then top with the remaining bread. Bake in a preheated 400°F. oven. Garnish with slices of tomato and parsley.   *Serves 4*

Variations
This may be varied by making a thick cheese sauce (see page 183) instead of white sauce.
Ground beef may be used instead of ham, and this may be blended with a thick Brown sauce or Mushroom sauce (see page 183), or a Tomato sauce (see page 184).
Ground lean lamb is also very good in this recipe and may be added to a thick Caper sauce (see page 183).

Dumplings for stews and casseroles

Dumplings make a stew or casserole more interesting and sustaining. To make sure they will be light:

1. Check that the mixture is firm enough to roll in balls but is not too stiff.
2. Check that the liquid is boiling before the dumplings are added.
3. Keep the liquid boiling steadily until the dumplings are cooked.

Cooking time   15–20 minutes

1 cup all-purpose flour · 1½ teaspoons baking powder · ½ teaspoon salt
⅓ cup chopped beef suet · water to mix.

Sift together the flour, baking powder, and the salt into a bowl. Add the suet and blend with a knife. Stir in enough water to bind the mixture, which should be soft enough to form into balls. Divide into 8–10 portions and roll into balls with lightly floured hands. Check that the liquid in the pan is boiling, add the dumplings, and cook for 15–20 minutes.   *Serves 4–5*

Herb dumplings

Cooking time   *15–20 minutes*

Ingredients as dumplings · 2–4 teaspoons chopped fresh herbs *or* ¼–1 teaspoon dried herbs (use all one herb – parsley, chives, *or* use mixed herbs such as sage, parsley, thyme, rosemary, and bay leaves).

Blend the herbs with the dry ingredients, and continue as dumplings. These are excellent with some stews, with boiled beef, chicken, etc. *Serves 4*

Potato dumplings

Cooking time   *40–45 minutes*

3 medium old potatoes (choose a 'floury' type) ¼ cup all-purpose flour · ¼ cup fine fresh bread crumbs · 2 tablespoons butter · 2 eggs seasoning · dash nutmeg · 5 cups water.

Boil or steam the potatoes in their jackets for approximately 30 minutes until barely soft but unbroken. If the potatoes are cooked this way they are less likely to become oversoft and 'watery' than when they are peeled. Mash the potatoes thoroughly, mix with the other ingredients; if the mixture seems too soft to handle add a little additional flour. Form into about 8 balls and cook steadily in boiling seasoned water for 10–15 minutes. Drain well. These are excellent served with stews.   *Serves 4–6*

WHAT WENT WRONG WHEN A STEW OR CASSEROLE WAS NOT SUCCESSFUL?

If the meat was tough, it was cooked for too short a period or too quickly; or it could have been very poor quality meat. In the first case, a second cooking could improve the tenderness. In the second case it might be better to strain off the liquid, put the meat through a grinder and return to the liquid.

If the stew or casserole was tasteless, this is due to insufficient flavoring – see page 172, dealing with herbs, spices, etc., for these add much flavor to stews. Always taste just before serving, for you may still want to adjust the flavor.

If the stew or casserole was too greasy, this could be due to using too much fat or leaving too much fat on the meat or using too little thickening. Most rich stews or stews containing a lot of fat, such as ox joints are better if the stew or casserole is allowed to cool then excess fat removed. If time does not permit this, then scoop off any fat with a spoon or remove by pressing white blotting paper against the top of the stew – this absorbs surplus fat. If you feel the greasiness is due to insufficient thickening, blend a little flour or cornstarch with a little cold stock or water, stir into the stew or casserole, allow to cook and thicken before serving ... allow ¼ cup all-purpose flour to each 2½ cups liquid, or 2 tablespoons cornstarch.

If the liquid in the stew or casserole was very 'watery', this again is due to insufficient thickening and perhaps not realising that vegetables contain a high percentage of water and, as they cook, they are likely to give additional water content to the gravy in the stew. Simply blend flour or cornstarch with a little cold water and add to the stew or casserole as suggested above. A quicker and easier way to thicken is to lay a slice of bread (with crusts removed) over the top of the stew or casserole, leave this until the bread becomes soft, then beat it into the stew with a wooden spoon. The bread completely disintegrates and thickens the gravy. See recipe for Flemish stew, on page 98, where this method is used.

OTHER METHODS OF COOKING MEAT

USING A COVERED ROASTING PAN

Choose one sufficiently deep so that large cuts of meat or poultry do not touch the top lid. In this way there is room for the fat to splash to the top and brown the outside of the meat or poultry. It does crisp the outside a little. If the meat or poultry fits tightly in to the pan, the outside will not brown or crisp; remove the cover for the last 30 minutes of cooking time for extra crispness. The advantage of a covered pan is that the oven keeps cleaner. Vegetables will not crisp if cooked round the meat or poultry in a covered pan, so the lid should be removed in plenty of time, or a separate pan used for these. When using a covered pan, allow about 15 minutes extra cooking time for the heat to penetrate or use a hotter oven, as suggested under foil

USING ALUMINIUM FOIL WHEN ROASTING

There are two ways of using foil:

1. Wrap the meat in a complete parcel. The meat is kept very moist, but it tends to have a slight flavor of steamed meat. You can avoid this by opening the foil and letting the meat brown towards the end of the cooking time. If using this method of cooking meat, you need to allow up to 15–20 minutes extra cooking time in order for the heat to penetrate through the piece of foil
2. Put the meat into a meat pan and then place a piece of foil over the top to take the place of the lid of a covered roaster. The foil should not actually touch the meat. This gives the effect of a covered pan and the meat browns. Allow about 15 minutes more cooking time.
If you do not wish to extend the cooking time, use a slightly hotter oven when cooking in foil, i.e. 25° higher. This does not produce a scorching result, as the meat is well protected.
With lean meat it is advisable to grease foil slightly before putting around meat; this prevents the possibility of the meat sticking to the foil.

Use as aluminium foil, but do not increase the
roasting time or oven temperature. Meat browns
in the wrapping but does not crisp – so open wrapping
as suggested for foil.

MEATS TO SERVE COLD

Most roasted and 'boiled' meats are excellent when
cold but the following recipes use economical meats
to make molds etc. More recipes for cold meat dishes
are included elsewhere in this book.

Savory ham horns

Cooking time   *None*

2 oz. cream cheese
3 tablespoons tomato sauce
little horseradish relish (optional)
few olives *or* gherkins *or* beets · seasoning
8 small slices cooked ham · lettuce.
TO GARNISH: olives · tomatoes.

Beat the cream cheese until light. Add the tomato
sauce, horseradish relish, and slices of olives or
gherkins or beets. Season well. Spread each slice
of meat with this mixture, and roll into a horn
shape. Serve on a bed of lettuce, and garnish with
olives and tomato roses.   *Serves 4*

Potted meat

Cooking time   *2 hours*

6 pig's feet · ¼ teaspoon mixed herbs* (sage,
parsley, thyme, rosemary, and bay leaves)
small bunch parsley · 2 bay leaves
1½ lb. beef flank steak *or* stewing beef · seasoning

* Fresh *or* dried.

Wash pig's feet. Put into a saucepan with the mixed
herbs, parsley, and bay leaves. Add strips of meat
and seasoning, then simmer gently in water to cover
for approximately 2 hours, or until the meat is quite
tender. Put the meat through a coarse grinder. You
may like to do it twice or grind it more finely.
Remove the meat from the feet and put this through
a grinder at the same time. Put the meat into a
bowl, and then boil the stock rapidly in a saucepan
until this is reduced to approximately 1¼ cups.
Strain over the meat, and allow to set.

Store tightly covered in the refrigerator. Use slices
for sandwich fillings, serve it in strips with salad,
or it is very good spread over slices of hot buttered
toast, covered with grated cheese and then browned
under the broiler.   *Serves 6–8*

Beef galantine

Cooking time   1½ *hours*

1 lb. ground beef · ½ lb. pork sausage meat
¼ cup butter *or* fat · 2 medium onions · 1 egg
¼ teaspoon dried herbs *or* ½ teaspoon chopped herbs
seasoning · ⅓ cup fine fresh bread crumbs
⅓ cup beef bouillon *or* milk · 2 hard-cooked eggs
TO COAT PAN: 2 tablespoons butter *or* fat
½ cup toasted bread crumbs.

Blend all the ingredients except the hard-cooked
eggs until a smooth mixture. Bouillon gives a more
savory taste – milk a milder flavor. Shell the hard-
cooked eggs. Grease the bottom and sides of a 9-inch
by 5-inch loaf pan, and coat with the bread crumbs.
Put half the meat mixture into the pan, add the eggs
then cover with the remaining meat mixture. Put
a piece of greased foil on top and steam for 1½ hours.
If more convenient, bake in a preheated 300°F. oven
for the same time. Turn out, and serve hot or cold.
                                            Serves 4–5

Variations on beef galantine

GALANTINE COATED WITH ASPIC
Do not coat the pan with butter and bread crumbs.
Bake or steam and allow to cool. Make 2½ cups aspic
(see page 332). Arrange small pieces of tomato,
gherkin, and hard-cooked egg on the top of the
galantine. Brush with a little cool aspic and allow to
set. When the garnish is firmly in position brush or
pour the remainder of the aspic over the top and
sides of the loaf.

GALANTINE COATED WITH CHAUDFROID
SAUCE
Coat the galantine with Chaudfroid sauce and
garnish with small pieces of gherkin, tomato, etc.
Page 337 gives information on coating food with this
cold sauce.

VEAL GALANTINE
Use ground veal and ham instead of beef and sausage
meat. Bind with coffee cream instead of bouillon or
milk.

Brawn

Cooking time   3 *hours**

1 calf's head · 1 teaspoon salt · dash pepper
small bunch parsley · dash mixed herbs (sage,
parsley, thyme, rosemary, and bay leaves)
½ lb. stewing beef · juice of ½ lemon.

The butcher will probably split the head, but if this
has not been done, it should be split down the center.
Wash carefully in plenty of cold water, lift out the
white part, i.e. the brain, wash this separately and

keep in a bowl. Put the calf's head into a large saucepan, cover with cold water, add the salt, pepper, parsley, and herbs. Cover tightly, and simmer gently for 1½ hours. When the head is cool enough to handle, remove all the meat, skinning the tongue. Cut the meat from the head into neat pieces and return to the stock. Dice the stewing beef into ½-inch cubes, and add to the saucepan with the lemon juice. Simmer steadily in the uncovered saucepan for a further 1½ hours. Remove the meat from the stock with a perforated spoon or put through a strainer, then pack into a large bowl. Strain enough of the liquid to cover. Let stand until set, turn out, and serve with salad.

The brains may be added to the meat when diced, or cooked in a little hot butter for 5–10 minutes and served separately on toast. They should be used the same day since they do not keep well.

* In a pressure cooker allow 25 minutes before skinning tongue etc., then a further 20 minutes at 15 lb. pressure.

Serves 6–8

BRAWN WITH LAMB'S, SHEEP'S OR PIG'S HEAD
These do not contain as much natural setting substance as a calf's head, but are less expensive. After removing the meat from the stock, continue as follows:
Measure 1¼ cups stock, strain into a saucepan and heat. Soften 1 teaspoon unflavored gelatin with 3 tablespoons cold water, pour the very hot stock over the gelatin, and stir until dissolved. Pour over the meat in the bowl.

Meat croquettes

Cooking time   *15–20 minutes*

1½ cups cooked meat · 2 tablespoons butter *or* margarine · ¼ cup all-purpose flour
⅔ cup milk · 2 teaspoons chopped parsley
2 teaspoons chopped gherkins
1 cup fine fresh bread crumbs · seasoning.
TO COAT: 1 egg · ½ cup toasted bread crumbs.
TO FRY: fat for deep-frying.

Grind the meat or chop very finely. Make a thick white sauce of the butter or margarine, flour, and milk, add the parsley, gherkins, and the meat. Blend well, then stir in the bread crumbs and seasoning. Let the mixture cool, form into about 8 finger shapes then brush with beaten egg and coat in the toasted bread crumbs. Deep-fry in hot fat until crisp and brown, then drain well on paper towels. Serve hot or cold.

Serves 4

Variations on meat croquettes

IF USING BEEF
Add a little grated horseradish or horseradish relish to the mixture or season well with prepared mustard.

IF USING LAMB OR MUTTON
Use chopped mint in addition to parsley or use instead of parsley. Add 2 teaspoons capers.

IF USING PORK
Add sage (chopped fresh or dried) to flavor with finely chopped shallots or chives.

IF USING VEAL
Blend 1–2 teaspoons paprika with the sauce.

IF USING CHICKEN
Blend ¼–⅓ cup finely chopped fried mushrooms with the sauce.

Beef and ham fritters

Cooking time   *8 minutes*

1½ cups cooked beef · ½ cup cooked ham
3 tablespoons finely chopped celery
1½ cups all-purpose flour · 2¼ teaspoons baking powder · ¼ teaspoon salt · 2 eggs · 1 cup milk
TO FRY: fat *or* oil for deep-frying.

Dice or grind the beef and ham, then stir in the celery. Make a thick batter with the flour, baking powder, salt, eggs, and milk. Coat the meat with the batter. Drop spoonfuls into hot shallow or deep fat or oil, and cook until crisp and golden brown. Drain on paper towels, and serve with a green salad.

Serves 4–6

Rissoles

Cooking time   *15–20 minutes*

1–1½ cups cooked meat
⅔ cup fine fresh bread crumbs
FOR THE SAUCE: 2 tablespoons fat
¼ cup all-purpose flour · ⅔ cup beef bouillon
dash mixed herbs (sage, parsley, thyme, rosemary, and bay leaves) · seasoning.
TO COAT: 1 tablespoon all-purpose flour · 1 egg
½ cup toasted bread crumbs.
TO FRY: ¼ cup fat.
TO GARNISH: sliced tomato · parsley.

Cut the cooked meat into very small pieces or put through a grinder. Mix with the bread crumbs and the thick sauce made with the fat, flour, and bouillon. If the saucepan is sufficiently large, add the meat and bread crumbs to the sauce, or mix in a bowl, adding the herbs and seasoning. Let stand until cool and firm. Divide into 4 large or 8 smaller portions. Put these onto a board, dusted with seasoned flour, and form into neat flat patties. Coat in beaten egg and bread crumbs. Heat the fat in a skillet and fry the rissoles for 2–3 minutes until golden brown. Turn and cook for the same time on the second side. Drain on paper towels. Garnish with tomato slices and parsley. Serve hot with Brown or a Tomato sauce (see pages 183, 184) or cold with salad.

Serves 4

Shepherd's pie

Cooking time 35–40 minutes
Oven temperature 375°F.

1–1½ cups cooked meat · 2 tablespoons drippings *or*
fat · 1 onion · 2 tomatoes
¼ teaspoon mixed herbs (sage, parsley, thyme, rosemary, and bay leaves) · seasoning
¾–1¼ cups beef bouillon *or* Brown sauce
2⅓ cups mashed potato
2 tablespoons butter *or* margarine.

Cut the cooked meat into neat pieces or put through
a grinder. Heat the drippings or fat, and sauté the
finely chopped onion for 3 minutes. Add the peeled,
chopped tomatoes and the meat, and heat together
for 2–3 minutes. Stir in the herbs, seasoning, and
finally the bouillon or brown sauce – the amount
varies according to whether you like a firm or soft
mixture. Put into a 9-inch pie pan, and cover with
the mashed potatoes, marking it with a fork, or
piping it. Put tiny pieces of butter on the potato to
help it to brown. Bake in a preheated 375°F. oven
for 35–40 minutes, or until the top is crisp and brown.
Serves 4

Corned beef Scotch eggs

Cooking time 8–10 minutes

1⅓ cups fine fresh bread crumbs
1½ cups flaked corned beef · seasoning
6 hard-cooked eggs.
FOR THE SAUCE: 2 tablespoons margarine
¼ cup all-purpose flour
⅔ cup milk *or* beef bouillon.
TO COAT: 1 egg · toasted bread crumbs.
TO FRY: fat for deep-frying.

To make the sauce, heat the margarine in a saucepan, stir in the flour, and cook for 2 minutes, then
add the liquid. Bring to a boil, and cook until thick,
stirring constantly. Add the bread crumbs and the
corned beef, season well. Press the mixture around
the outside of the shelled hard-cooked eggs. When
you have a neat shape, brush with beaten egg, toss
carefully in bread crumbs, and fry until crisp and
golden brown in hot fat. *Serves 4–6*

Corned beef hash

Cooking time 15 minutes

1½ cups corned beef · ⅓ cup fat
2 medium boiled potatoes · 2 medium onions
seasoning.
TO SERVE: 4 fried eggs (optional)
sliced tomato.

Dice but do not flake the corned beef. Heat two-
thirds of the fat in a skillet, add the sliced potatoes,
and brown gently for about 5 minutes, do not mash.
Add to the beef. Heat the remaining fat, and sauté
the finely chopped onions for 5 minutes, add to the
corned beef mixture, and season lightly. Return
this mixture to the skillet and heat thoroughly,
then pile into a pyramid shape on a heated dish.
This is excellent topped with fried eggs and garnished with a ring of raw sliced tomato. *Serves 4*

BEEF HASH
Cooked beef may be used. Dice the beef. Rare beef
is excellent served in this way.

EMERGENCY MEAT DISHES

The following recipes give interesting meat dishes
which may be prepared in a matter of minutes.

Cranberry ham

Cooking time 5 minutes

4 thick slices of cooked *or* canned ham
2 tablespoons fat
3 tablespoons cranberry sauce *or* jelly (red currant
jelly could be substituted).
TO GARNISH: cooked *or* canned peas
cooked *or* canned asparagus.

Fry the ham for 2–3 minutes in the hot fat, or brush
with the melted fat and heat under the broiler.
Spread with the cranberry sauce or jelly, and place
under a hot broiler until this bubbles, then serve
immediately. Arrange on a heated dish with a border
of the prepared vegetables. *Serves 4*

Kidneys in port wine

Cooking time 15 minutes

12–16 lamb kidneys · ¼ cup butter
1 small onion · ¼ cup all-purpose flour
seasoning · 1¼ cups beef stock · bay leaf
⅔ cup port wine.
TO SERVE: ½ cup long-grain rice.

Skin the kidneys, fry in the hot butter for several
minutes with the finely chopped onion. Do not allow
the meat or onion to brown. Stir in the flour and
seasoning. Cook for several minutes, then blend in
the stock, and bring to a boil. Add the bay leaf and
port wine, and simmer gently for about 8 minutes.
Remove the bay leaf and serve the kidneys in a
border of cooked rice (see page 192). *Serves 4–6*

Tongue in Madeira wine sauce

Cooking time 15 minutes

8 slices cooked tongue
1 teaspoon prepared mustard.
FOR THE SAUCE: 3 tablespoons butter *or* margarine
¼ cup all-purpose flour · ⅔ cup beef stock
¾ cup Madeira wine · 1 bay leaf
1 tablespoon red currant jelly · seasoning.
TO GARNISH: cooked *or* canned peas.

Spread the tongue very thinly with mustard. Heat
the butter or margarine in a large skillet. Stir in
the flour and cook for several minutes, then gradually blend in the stock and wine. Bring to a boil,
add the bay leaf, and simmer for 5 minutes, adding
the red currant jelly and seasoning well. Add the
tongue, and heat for a few minutes. Serve on large
heated dish surrounded with peas. *Serves 4*

MEAT DISHES TO IMPRESS

In this chapter on meat, the dishes vary from the very simple to the more unusual and elaborate. Other meat dishes may be found in the section on entertaining, page 331. Remember to select a meat dish that will not spoil unduly if kept waiting for a time. In the case of the Crown roast it would be wiser to choose lamb or pork, rather than veal which dries easily, if there is any possibility of the meal being slightly delayed.

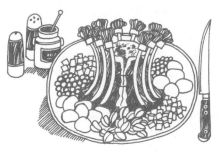

Crown roast

Cooking time   *See page 74*

This is a most impressive way to cook and serve lamb, pork, or veal.
You need at least 12 chops in the loin or loins (less will not give a good circle). The center may be filled with stuffing or with cooked mixed vegetables. Any of the stuffings in that section may be used but you may need a larger quantity than the recipe, since a Crown roast of 12 chops serves 6 people. Calculate the weight of the meat and stuffing and follow the directions for timing on pages 74–75.

At least 12 loin chops of meat (see above) stuffing (see above).
TO GARNISH: canned pitted red tart *or* candied cherries green olives (optional) · cooked vegetables.

Ask the butcher to prepare the meat for a Crown roast; since this takes time he will need reasonable warning. If he cannot do this then ask for the meat to be 'chined', i.e. cut between each chop so the meat may be rolled. You may have two small loins, so first skewer these into a circle then tie firmly with string or better still sew with thin string and a very firm needle. Prepare the stuffing and calculate the combined weight of the stuffing and the meat. Put the meat into a roasting pan; it is a good idea to put foil under the center of the meat so that the stuffing will not 'fall out' during cooking or when lifting the cooked roast out of the pan. Protect the ends of the bones with foil; since the meat is cut away from these. Roast as timing for the particular meat – page references above. The stuffing should be pressed firmly into the center of the meat and the top of this may be protected with foil, remove foil if you desire stuffing to brown and crisp. To serve: lift onto a large heated dish and top the end of each bone with a cherry and olive or put on paper frills. Surround with cooked vegetables.

Allow 2 chops per person

Roast spareribs and rice with sweet sour sauce

Cooking time   *50 minutes*
Oven temperature   *425°F.*

3–4 lb. back spareribs or pork blade loin chops*
FOR THE SAUCE: 3 tablespoons cornstarch
1 cup water
3 tablespoons mixed vinegar pickles
3 tablespoons vinegar · seasoning
1 tablespoon soy sauce *or* Worcestershire sauce
3 teaspoons brown sugar *or* corn syrup
TO GARNISH: cooked rice · lemon wedges.

* 1–1½ lb. tenderloin pork, diced and fried, may be used.

Put the meat into a roasting pan and roast in a preheated 425°F. oven for approximately 30 minutes. Pour off surplus fat and return to the oven for a further 15–20 minutes until crisp and brown. Blend the cornstarch with water, chop pickles fairly finely, then put all ingredients for the sauce into a pan and cook until thickened. Make a wide border of rice on a heated dish, arrange the meat on this. Pour the sauce into the center. Put lemon wedges around the edge.   *Serves 4*

Liver soufflé

Cooking time   *25–30 minutes*
Oven temperature   *375°F.*

1 small onion · ¼ cup butter *or* margarine
¼ cup all-purpose flour · ⅔ cup milk
¾ cup (calf *or* lamb) liver · seasoning
3 egg yolks · 4 egg whites.

Dice the onion, and sauté in the butter or margarine. Stir in the flour and cook for 2–3 minutes, add the milk, bring to a boil, and cook until thickened. Stir in the finely chopped raw liver, seasoning, and egg yolks and finally fold in the stiffly beaten egg whites. Put into a greased 1–1½ pint soufflé dish or ovenproof dish, and bake in a preheated 375°F. oven until well risen and golden colored. Do not overcook otherwise the moist texture of the liver is spoiled. Serve immediately. This is an excellent way of serving liver, which is a good source of iron, to people who normally are not fond of its rather definite flavor.   *Serves 4*

Liver and potato soufflé

Cooking time   *25–30 minutes*
Oven temperature   *375°F.*

¾ cup (calf *or* lamb) liver · ⅓ cup milk
2 tablespoons butter · 1¼ cups mashed potatoes
2 teaspoons chopped parsley · 4 eggs
seasoning.

Chop or grind the liver. Add the hot milk and melted butter to the potatoes, then blend with the liver. Add the parsley, egg yolks, and seasoning. Fold in the stiffly beaten egg whites. Put into a greased 1–1½ pint soufflé dish or ovenproof dish and bake in a preheated 375°F. oven for approximately 25–30 minutes, or until well risen and golden brown. Serve immediately.   *Serves 4*

POULTRY

Poultry today is of very high quality and compared with many other foods, it is relatively inexpensive, particularly in the case of chicken.

Wise choice of poultry

Choose steamed or 'boiled' chicken for an invalid, since it is so easily digested. If buying young chicken, fry or broil and serve with an interesting sauce or garnish – this retains the maximum flavor. Very young chicken has little flavor if roasted. When entertaining, a large turkey to give plenty of servings is often a relatively economical buy.
Choose duckling when new potatoes and garden peas are in season.

Ways to serve poultry

Serve pale-looking boiled chicken with a hard-cooked egg sauce which gives an interesting color. Add the chopped whites to the sauce, garnish with the chopped yolks, parsley, and paprika.
Serve duck with a colorful garnish of oranges, apricots, or cherries – (see page 121 and 137).
Have individual portions of cranberry sauce in halved orange skins to garnish turkey or chicken.
Serve hot fried chicken drumsticks with tartar sauce.

To use leftover poultry

Any leftover cooked poultry may be turned into an excellent stew, casserole, or curry – (see pages 133 and 134). Cook the sauce and vegetables well before putting in the pieces of poultry, to prevent these being overcooked.

Easy remedies when things are wrong

PROBLEM – if duck is tough, this is often because the bird was fairly old and needed longer cooking than usual – times for roasting are given on pages 119 and 120, but duck may be cooked for a little longer than the recommended time without drying.
TO REMEDY – reheat any parts remaining in a good brown sauce (see page 183).
PROBLEM – if goose or duck is greasy without a crisp skin, this could be due to roasting in a covered container or not pricking the skin as suggested.
TO REMEDY – replace the bird in a preheated 450°F. oven for 15–20 minutes – prick lightly when very hot.
PROBLEM – if the flesh off the body of poultry has a distinctly bitter taste, when the bird was drawn the gall bladder could have been broken in the body.
TO REMEDY – unfortunately, there is little one can do. The meat is quite harmless – serve with a rather well-seasoned sauce. It is quite likely that outer parts of the bird will be satisfactory, although it is surprising how this bitter taste can permeate the whole carcase.
PROBLEM – if the flesh of chicken or turkey is dry and tasteless, this is due to overcooking or insufficient fat; stuffing a bird also helps to give a moist texture.
TO REMEDY – serve with a rather rich 'buttery' sauce. When the bird is not being stuffed, put a good knob of butter inside, with a sprig of fresh herbs (rosemary is excellent).
PROBLEM – if stewing chicken is tough, this was either inadequate cooking or a very old fowl – look carefully when buying.
TO REMEDY – cook for a longer period or reheat slowly. Next time, put 2 peeled potatoes in the body – these help soften the flesh.

Types of poultry

CHICKEN . . . one has the older bird, generally known as a fowl; a roasting chicken and those specially bred to produce particularly plump birds called capons; smaller birds are often called broilers, and these birds may be fried, broiled or roasted. Tiny chickens are also called spring chickens.

TURKEYS . . . one rarely finds an old turkey – these are all generally plump roasting birds.

GOOSE . . . as turkey.

DUCK . . . a larger bird is called a duck, very young birds duckling.

CHOICE AND PREPARATION OF POULTRY

CHOOSE AND BUY POULTRY

While there is a very high standard of poultry available in this country, like any other food, you get the best produce if care is taken in selecting it.

TO CHOOSE FRESH ROASTING CHICKENS OR CAPONS

The flesh should look white and firm and the breastbone should feel soft and pliable. The legs should be bright yellow and fresh looking with firm, not limp claws. In the case of a cock, the comb should be firm and bright in color. A good chicken has a. broad breast, which means that you can carve slices from this. DO NOT BUY chickens that have little breast and very long legs, for you are paying for the weight of bone and not flesh.

TO CHOOSE STEWING FOWLS

It is quite correct for a stewing fowl to have a slightly yellow tinge to the skin, which indicates there is a certain amount of fat. Before buying, however, look at it very critically and see if the layer of fat is very thick. If it is, the fowl will be wasteful since the fat will run out during cooking and leave you with relatively little meat. Signs of freshness are the same for roasting chicken, above.

TO CHOOSE SPRING CHICKENS OR CHICKENS SOLD FOR ROASTING OR FRYING

These are always young chickens and have been bred specially for this particular purpose, but make sure they have a reasonable amount of flesh on the breast, otherwise you are really buying just skin and bone. Signs of freshness are the same as for roasting chicken, above.

TO CHOOSE CHICKEN PIECES

Chicken pieces are sold very frequently and they do enable the smaller family to buy the exact amount required. The same rules of firmness and fattiness apply with the pieces. In some recipes the breast gives a better result, which means you may select all breast meat. In the same way, legs are ideal to fry for a picnic dish. Look to see that the legs are well covered with flesh and that this is not too dark, which indicates staleness.

Note: A FRESH CHICKEN OF ANY KIND SHOULD HAVE NO UNPLEASANT SMELL.

TO CHOOSE DUCK OR GOOSE

The flesh should be a good cream color and fresh smelling. Avoid poultry with too much fat since this means the duck or goose will be very wasteful. While duck and goose never have the same amount of breast as chicken and turkey, feel to see there is a reasonable thickness. The legs should be firm-looking.

TO CHOOSE TURKEY

Apply the same test as chicken.

TO CHOOSE GUINEA FOWL

This should look firm in texture with a plump breast. Other points as chicken. Guinea fowl is cooked when fresh and not allowed to become 'high' as game.

Quantities of poultry to allow

CHICKEN 1. Large chickens should give you up to 8 portions and should be carved in slices (see page 144).
2. Smaller chickens yield 4 portions. You may either carve in slices or divide the bird into two wing and breast portions and two leg portions (see page 144).
3. For a small chicken, split in half or carve; yields 2 portions.

DUCK 1. A large duck yields 4 portions.
2. A small duck yields 2 portions, split in half or carve.

GUINEA FOWL As chicken.

GOOSE See amount under roast goose page 120.

TURKEY See amounts under roast turkey page 120.

TO PREPARE POULTRY

It must be remembered that poultry is handled, particularly if it has been trussed and cut into pieces, in the shop and it should, therefore, be washed well, both outside and inside the body. If roasting or frying, dry thoroughly with paper towels, so that there is no undue spitting when the bird goes into the fat.

TO PREPARE CHICKEN FOR COOKING

Most of the chickens that you buy today are already drawn and trussed, but it may well be that you are sent a chicken that needs drawing and trussing. Most shops will joint a chicken if you ask them to. Instructions are given on this and the next page, so that you can deal with the matter yourself if you wish. Boning may sound an extremely difficult operation. It is not particularly easy, but it can be done by an amateur with patience and it does produce a chicken that can be utilized for a party in the most economical way, since it gives a generous number of portions. It also saves any difficulties in carving since you slice across the bird. Once again, given reasonable notice, a butcher would probably do this for you. Other poultry may be jointed as chicken, but there is less need for this since they are generally cooked whole. Boning duck, turkey or goose is an excellent idea, especially for a buffet party.

To pluck poultry

Generally this is done for you and even if you are given an unplucked bird, a butcher probably will pluck this for you, for a small charge. The bird should be plucked as soon as possible after killing. Hold it firmly and pull out the feathers with a firm movement. Singe all over with a lighted candle after plucking, to remove the 'stubbles' from the base of the feathers.

To draw poultry

1. Cut off the feet and, if necessary, draw the sinews from the legs.
2. Hold the bird by the legs and singe, if desired.
3. Cut off the head and leave about 3 inches of neck.
4. Insert a small pointed knife at the end of the spine and split up the skin of the neck.
5. Pull away loose skin and cut off the neck close to the shoulder.
6. Remove crop and windpipe.
7. Cut round vent. Put in fingers and loosen the inside – be careful not to break the gall bladder (attached to the liver).
8. Firmly draw out all the inside, and cut the gall bladder from the liver without piercing it.
9. Put the neck, liver, gizzard, heart, and kidneys into a bowl of cold water and wash thoroughly. Use these to make stock or gravy by simmering gently.
10. Wipe inside of bird with a clean damp cloth.

In the case of a large turkey, the sinews must be drawn from the legs, so it is advisable to have this done by a butcher, if possible.

To truss poultry

A chicken is trussed to keep it in good shape while cooking. Stuff the chicken before trussing.
1. Put in the stuffing at the breast opening. If two kinds of stuffing are being used, one kind may be put in at the tail opening.
2. Fold the skin firmly over the back at the neck and secure, if desired.
3. Press the legs down firmly at the sides of the bird.
4. Put a skewer right through the bird just under the thighs.
5. Turn the bird over and tie the wings with a skewer.
6. Pass string under the ends of the skewer and cross over at the back.
7. Turn the bird over and tie the string around the tail, securing the ends of the legs.

To bone a chicken

1. Use a really sharp small knife and commence at the breast with the neck towards you.
2. First loosen the skin at the neck of the bird. This is easier to do with the tips of your fingers than with the knife. Continue loosening the skin on the breast away from the flesh; do not tear the skin.
3. Take the knife and cut the wishbone away from the flesh. Do this carefully so no meat is left on the bone. Remove the wishbone.
4. Turn the bird so that the breast is on the table and use the point of the knife to first cut the shoulder joints, then to cut away the shoulder bones and remove.
5. Put the tip of the knife into the skin by the wings and neatly cut away the bones from the wings – the tips are better removed completely.
6. Lift skin away from the thighs. Cut the thigh joints away from the body, then gradually cut the flesh away from both thighbones and drumsticks.
7. You may leave the small pieces of bone at the bottom of the drumsticks, i.e. jointing drumstick to foot of bird – this helps to remould the bird into its familiar shape.
8. Having removed wishbone, shoulder bones, wings, and legs, you have now to work carefully to remove complete breast bones and backbone and finally cut off the tail.
9. The bird is now flattened flesh.
10. Put the stuffing – you need at least twice the usual amount – first onto the breast of the boned bird, then put a little down the center of the leg flesh and wings.

11. Fold the skin at the neck end very firmly over stuffing to keep this from falling out during cooking.

12. Press flesh over stuffing in legs and wings.

13. Form the flesh and stuffing back into the shape of the unboned bird – this is not difficult to do, since the flesh is soft and pliable.

14. Tie legs and wings firmly into position – arrange the bones at the end of legs against the body of the bird.

15. Roast in the usual way – allowing just over normal time for weight of bird and stuffing, since this is now solid flesh.

16. To carve, all you need to do is to cut slices right across the bird, so everyone will have both light meat, stuffing, and dark meat.

17. The bones may be used to make excellent stock.

Other poultry may be boned in the same way. Naturally large turkeys take longer to do and it may be possible to have this done professionally providing notice is given, for it does take time.

To cut up a chicken

1. Cut the chicken in half. Cut through the skin between the leg and the body and pull back the leg. Continue cutting through the joint.

2. To divide the dark meat, cut through the joint between the drumstick and the thighbone.

3. To divide the white meat, first lift the wing and cut through the skin to uncover the joint. Cut through the joint and along the ribs, leaving some breast meat on the wing portion.

A duck may be prepared in the same way, but naturally this is rarely necessary since roasting whole or cooking in a casserole are the usual ways of cooking duck. It is not suitable for frying or broiling, since it is more fat than a chicken.
Goose and turkey are too large to cook in pieces.

To cut up a chicken French style

This method of cutting a chicken produces a large number of pieces and is, therefore, economical. Choose a bird 2½–3 lb. in weight. Remove the giblets, and thoroughly clean the inside of the bird; trim the wings and legs.

1. Cut off the legs – pull gently from the bird and cut through joint. Cut each leg into 2 pieces.

2. Cut off the wings – pinch a piece of flesh between the thumb and first finger before cutting.

3. Cut the body in half, cutting through the rib cage.

4. Cut the breast diagonally across into 2 pieces. Tap the knife gently with a heavy weight to cut through the bone.

5. Cut the back into 3 pieces. The back pieces are cooked and used to build up the center of the dish when serving. They would not normally be served as portions.

6. Flesh from these pieces may be used in dishes where small chicken pieces are required.

7. Use the chicken pieces for a variety of fried and casserole dishes.

Frozen and canned poultry

Never cook poultry when it is frozen and do not defrost by immersing it in hot water, allow to thaw out gradually. Times to allow are given in the roasting details which follow. Defrosting is best carried out overnight by leaving the bird, still in its package, to thaw naturally at room temperature or on a shelf in the refrigerator. In an emergency, poultry may be thawed more rapidly by submerging in *cold* water for 2–3 hours. Leave the bird in its package and change the water frequently. Do not thaw by plunging into hot water. This robs the flesh of flavor. All the recipes given in this section are equally suitable for frozen as well as fresh poultry. While the quality of frozen poultry is very high, in that only the youngest and most tender birds are considered worth freezing, one must remember that a little flavor is lost. Therefore, if you are buying frozen poultry it is as well to choose a dish in which plenty of flavor is provided.

Since canned chicken, or chicken in glass jars, is already cooked, it may be used in recipes where the chicken is reheated, or chicken breasts or whole chickens may be coated with egg and bread crumbs and fried or broiled; do not overcook – simply heat. Other poultry is not preserved in the same way.

TO ROAST POULTRY

The information on roasting, given on page 74, may be followed when roasting poultry, and it is possible to use either the quicker method of roasting or the slower one.

If roasting poultry in a 425°F. oven, the temperature may be reduced to 375°F. after the first 15 minutes. Take care not to overcook the bird. Times for roasting are given on the next page, but while this is a very good guide it does sometimes happen that a bird takes a little longer because it is particularly thick on the breast or legs, for its weight. On the other hand, a bird that has fairly big bones and a small amount of flesh could take 5–10 minutes shorter cooking time. You will be able to judge this by the appearance, but be on the safe side and have a look during cooking because if you overcook poultry you lose some of the moist texture and flavor. Remember the weight of stuffing must be included in the total cooking time.

RECIPES FOR ROASTING

Given below are the traditional ways of roasting poultry – these are followed by more unusual recipes.

Roasting chicken

CHOOSE: quick roasting . . . good quality roasting fowl or capon, or frozen bird (which should be defrosted at room temperature).
Slow roasting . . . as above, or young stewing fowl – this could be steamed for 1–1½ hours then roasted for 20 minutes per lb. plus an additional 20 minutes.

ALLOW: 2½–3 lb. bird for 4 people (weight when trussed).

PREPARE: wash and dry trussed bird. Put in the stuffing. Cover breast with bacon ends and pieces (obtainable from many grocers), inexpensive bacon, butter, clarified drippings or fat.

COOK: covered roasting pan or aluminium foil*
excellent. Remove cover or open foil for last 30
minutes.
Quick roasting – 15 minutes per lb. plus an additional
15 minutes (weight stuffed after trussing).
Slow roasting – 25–30 minutes per lb. plus an
additional 30 minutes.

SERVE: hot with veal or sausage meat stuffing, bacon
rolls (see page 330), sausages, bread sauce (see page
185), or thickened gravy.
Cold with salad.

* see comments about timing on page 74.

Roasting turkey

CHOOSE: quick roasting . . . good quality bird or
frozen bird (large frozen birds need up to 48 hours to
defrost completely) or follow package instructions.
Slow roasting . . . very practical at Christmas time
for fresh or frozen turkeys.

ALLOW: up to ¾ lb. per person, due to weight of bone.

PREPARE: as chicken.

COOK: covered roasting pan or aluminium foil*
excellent. Remove cover or open foil for last 30
minutes.
Below are the accepted times for roasting turkey,
but with the modern broad-breasted turkeys, it is
advisable to be somewhat generous.
Quick roasting – 15 minutes per lb. plus an additional
15 minutes, up to a total of 12 lb. including stuffing;
for extra lb. over this weight, allow 12 minutes only.
Slow roasting – 25–30 minutes per lb. plus an additional 30 minutes, up to a total of 12 lb. including
weight of stuffing; for every extra lb. over this
weight, allow 20–25 minutes per lb.

SERVE: as chicken, although the variety of stuffings
that may be used is very great (see chapter on
stuffings). Many people prefer cranberry sauce to
bread sauce. Illustrated on p. 108.

* see comments about timing on page 74.

Roasting Guinea fowl

Although this is cooked for the same time as
chicken, one has the choice of treating it as chicken,
i.e. stuffing it, etc., or leaving it unstuffed and
serving with the same accompaniments as game.
Guinea fowl can be very dry, so be generous in the
amount of fat used.

Roasting duck or goose

CHOOSE: young birds or frozen birds. The latter
should be defrosted at room temperature – in the
case of a large goose, this could take up to 24 hours.

ALLOW: duck – this has large bones and relatively
little meat on the breast. One small duck therefore,
serves 2 people, a larger duck serves 4 people.
Goose – the bones are very large in proportion to the
flesh; allow ¾–1 lb. per person.

PREPARE: wash and dry trussed bird. Put in the stuffing, but this may be cooked separately to avoid it
becoming too greasy. No fat is necessary. Cook in
an open roasting pan.

COOK: quick roasting – 15 minutes per lb. plus an
additional 15 minutes (weight including stuffing).
Slow roasting – 25–30 minutes per lb. plus an additional 30 minutes. Duck and goose can be rather fat;
this may be counteracted if the skin is pricked very
lightly with a fine skewer. Do this after 30 minutes
with duck, 1 hour for goose, and again towards the
end of the cooking time; the excess fat spurts out.
Do not prick too deeply, otherwise fat soaks into
flesh.

SERVE: hot with sage and onion or other stuffings
(see page 188 onward), apple sauce, thickened gravy,
orange salad, or bigarade sauce. Cold with salad.

Apricot stuffed chicken

Cooking time   *1 hour 20 minutes*
Oven temperature   *425°F.*

1 (1 lb. 14 oz.) can apricots
savory rice stuffing (see page 189)
3 lb. chicken · 3–4 tablespoons butter.

Drain the juice from the apricots. Put half the juice
into a pan, and heat until only 3 tablespoons of
juice are left. Chop all apricots, reserving 8 for
garnish, add to the savory rice stuffing; add the
concentrated hot juice, and mix. Stuff the bird,
spread butter over the breast, and wrap in aluminium
foil. Roast for 1 hour in a preheated 425°F. oven,
then open foil so bird browns. Add the remaining
apricots and juice to the roasting pan and cook for
a further 15 minutes.   *Serves 4*

Ashanti fowl

Cooking time   *See method*
Oven temperature   *425°F. then 400°F.*

FOR THE STUFFING: ⅔ cup fine fresh bread crumbs
1 large onion · 3 large tomatoes
1 cup smooth peanut butter · salt to taste
¼ teaspoon cayenne pepper (optional)
4½–5½ lb. roasting chicken · ¼ cup butter
3 tablespoons all-purpose flour.

Prepare bread crumbs, chop onion, and peel and chop
tomatoes. Sauté onion, tomatoes, then add peanut
butter, bread crumbs, salt, and pepper. If possible,
bone chicken (see page 118) and lay flat. Stuff with
prepared stuffing. Tie into a neat shape then dot
with butter and sprinkle with flour, or stuff whole
in the usual way. Roast for 15 minutes per lb. plus
an additional 15 minutes in a hot oven, reducing to
moderately hot after 15–20 minutes until crisp and
brown.   *Serves 6–8*

Roast chicken with butter and parsley

Cooking time   *See method*
Oven temperature   *425°F. then 375°F.*

4½–5½ lb. chicken · 4 sprigs parsley
⅔ cup butter · seasoning · ⅔ cup cold water

Stuff the chicken with chopped parsley, half the
butter, and seasoning. Spread the remaining butter
all over the chicken. Calculate the cooking time and

allow 20 minutes per lb. plus an additional 20 minutes, for the bird is roasted in a preheated 425°F. oven for 7 minutes only, after which the heat should be reduced to 375°F. Pour water into the pan after 7 minutes roasting and continue cooking. The bird has a delicious flavor and moist texture. *Serves 6–8*

Roast goose with chestnuts and onions

Cooking time   *As page 120*
Oven temperature   *As page 120*

Roast the goose as the table on page 120. Meanwhile shell the chestnuts (see page 190), and peel the onions. Approximately 30 minutes before the end of the cooking time, pour the fat out of the pan except for about 2 tablespoons. Return the goose to the pan with the nuts and onions. Finish roasting, and serve with the vegetables around the goose.
Servings depend on the weight of the bird.

Roast capon in cider

Cooking time   *As page 119*
Oven temperature   *As page 119*

1 capon · butter *or* shortening
stuffing, if desired (see below)
2½ cups apple cider *or* dry white wine
approximately 8 small onions · 1–2 green sweet peppers · 4–8 tomatoes · 10 slices bacon.

Coat the capon with butter or shortening and stuff, if desired, although this is not essential in this recipe as the cider helps to keep the flesh very moist. Check the cooking time against the table on page 119 and roast in the usual way. 45 minutes before the end of the cooking time, pour the cider over the capon. Spoon this over again once or twice to make sure the capon is absorbing the cider. If there is an excessive amount of fat in the pan, some of this may be drained before adding the cider. Put in the onions and the halved green peppers or wide strips of green pepper (make sure the seeds and core are carefully removed). Continue cooking for a further 30 minutes, then add the tomatoes and the finely diced bacon. Continue cooking until the end of the roasting time, spoon the cider over the capon again. Place onto a heated serving plate with the vegetables. The cider may be served as an unthickened sauce, if desired, but it may be thickened – allow 3 tablespoons cornstarch or ¼ cup all-purpose flour to the total amount of cider. This rather thin sauce is excellent with capon. Illustrated on p. 105.
Serves 6–8 depending on the weight of the bird.

Duck and orange

Cooking time   *As page 120*
Oven temperature   *As page 120*

1 duck or 2 small duckling
bigarade sauce (see page 184)
TO GARNISH: 2–3 oranges · lettuce.

Roast the duck on ducklings as page 120. Stuffing is generally omitted to avoid conflicting flavors. Meanwhile, make the sauce (see page 184). Peel oranges and remove outside pith. Use a very sharp knife to cut orange into sections. Carve the duck or cut into pieces and coat with the sauce. Garnish with the orange segments and lettuce. Illustrated on p. 107. *Serves 4*

Duck Maréchale

Cooking time   *As page 120*
Oven temperature   *As page 120*

1 duck *or* 2 small duckling.
TO GARNISH: 1 (1 lb.) can pitted red tart cherries
2 large oranges.
TO SERVE: bigarade sauce (see page 184).

Roast the duck or ducklings as page 120. As the cherries and oranges provide such a selection of flavor, it is advisable that the duck is not stuffed. Prepare the bigarade sauce, but use 3 or 4 tablespoons of syrup from the can of cherries as part of the liquid. Heat the cherries and the orange segments in the remaining cherry syrup. Carve the duck or ducklings or cut into pieces, then arrange on a heated dish. Garnish with the hot drained cherries and orange segments. Serve the bigarade sauce separately. *Serves 4*

Sweet sour duckling

Cooking time   *See below*

1 large duck *or* 2 small ducklings
3 tablespoons clear honey *or* corn syrup
3 tablespoons lemon juice *or* white vinegar
3 tablespoons orange juice · 1 tablespoon brandy.

Cook the duck or ducklings as the time given on page 120. 20 minutes before the end of the cooking time, remove the duck from the roasting pan, drain the fat, then return the duck to the pan and brush the outside with the glaze made by blending the honey or syrup, lemon juice or vinegar, orange juice, and brandy. Return to the oven for 10 minutes, remove and brush again with the glaze, some of which will have dripped into the pan. Continue cooking. In this method, stuffing may be omitted, if desired, or serve with orange rice stuffing (see page 190). *Serves 4*

TO FRY POULTRY

Since chicken is the poultry usually fried, directions are given for this. Diced turkey could be fried, duck and goose are generally considered too fat.

TO PREPARE CHICKEN FOR FRYING

1. The chicken pieces should be well dried with paper towels or a cloth.
2. They can then be coated with seasoned flour; allow approximately ¼ cup all-purpose flour, ¼ teaspoon salt, and dash pepper for 4 small pieces, or double this for a thick coat.
3. They may be coated with egg and bread crumbs.
4. They may be coated with batter. This is better for deep frying, but not as good for shallow frying. Coat chicken in the same way as fish (see page 54).

To fry chicken in shallow fat

Cooking time   *15–20 minutes*

4 chicken pieces
TO COAT: seasoned flour *or* egg and toasted bread crumbs.
TO FRY: ¼ cup butter, oil *or* shortening.

Coat the chicken pieces with seasoned flour or egg and bread crumbs. Heat the butter, oil, or shortening in a skillet. It should be at least ½ inch deep. Fry chicken fairly quickly until brown on the under side, turn and brown on the second side, then lower heat and cook fairly slowly to cook completely through. Drain on paper towels. Serve with fried tomatoes, mushrooms, etc., and a green salad, or vegetables, or with a garnish.   *Serves 4*

To fry chicken in deep fat

Cooking time   *12–15 minutes*

4 chicken pieces · coating
TO FRY: 1 pan deep fat *or* oil, *or* deep fat fryer.

The chicken pieces may be coated with seasoned flour, egg and crisp bread crumbs or batter for deep frying; however flour gives the least attractive appearance. Heat the fat. To test if the right heat, lower a small cube of bread into the fat, and it should turn golden brown in 1 minute. Do not have the fat or oil any hotter, otherwise the chicken becomes too brown on the outside before being cooked through. Put in the chicken pieces, (they are easier to remove if a frying basket is used), and cook until golden brown. Either lower the heat or remove the pan carefully from the heat and allow the chicken to continue cooking for the time given, to make sure it is tender. Drain on paper towels. Serve with the same accompaniments as chicken fried in shallow fat, or with a garnish.   *Serves 4*

Chicken Cordon Bleu

Cooking time   *15–20 minutes*

4 chicken breasts *or* 2 small frying chickens*
4 slices ham · 4 slices Gruyère *or* Cheddar cheese
little seasoned flour · egg · bread crumbs
fat *or* oil for frying.

* make sure they have nice meaty breasts.

If using frozen chicken breasts allow these to defrost at room temperature. If using whole chickens, cut away the breast with a sharp knife. Slit the breasts lengthwise so you have 8 slices in all, then sandwich these with ham and cheese. Dip in seasoned flour, then in egg and bread crumbs. Fry until crisp and golden brown in hot fat, then lower the heat, and cook steadily for about 15–20 minutes. Drain on paper towels.   *Serves 4*

The rest of the chicken may be fried as a separate dish, or used in many of the dishes in this section.

Chicken à la Kiev

Cooking time   *12–15 minutes*

4 very tiny spring chickens or 2 larger birds (they must be very young to ensure flesh being cooked)
½ cup butter.
TO COAT: 1–2 eggs · ¾ cup toasted bread crumbs.
TO FRY: olive oil.

Choose either very tiny chickens and bone these completely (see page 118), or use the breast and wings of 2 larger chickens (making 4 portions), removing the tiny bones from the wings. Flatten the meat. Put a pat of the butter onto each portion of chicken or whole spring chicken, roll firmly, coat in beaten egg and bread crumbs, and fry in hot oil until golden brown. Drain well on paper towels, and serve with water cress, vegetables, or salad.   *Serves 4*

Deviled chicken

Cooking time   *15–20 minutes*

1 young frying chicken · 2–3 onions
4 slices bacon · ¼ cup butter
FOR THE SAUCE: ¼ cup butter · ½ teaspoon curry powder · ¼ cup all-purpose flour · seasoning
1¼ cups milk · 2–3 teaspoons prepared mustard
few drops Worcestershire sauce
¼ cup coffee or whipping cream.
TO GARNISH: 4 bacon rolls. (See page 330).

If using a frozen chicken allow this to defrost at room temperature. Cut the chicken into 4 pieces. Slice the onions thinly and dice the bacon, then heat the butter in a large skillet and fry the chicken until golden brown on the outside. Lower the heat, and continue cooking until tender. Meanwhile, heat the butter for the sauce, stir in the curry powder and flour, cook for several minutes, add a lavish amount of seasoning, then blend in the milk, bring to a boil, and cook until the sauce has thickened, stirring well. Remove from the heat, add the mustard, Worcestershire sauce, and cream. Arrange the fried chicken on a heated dish, coat with sauce and garnish with bacon rolls.   *Serves 4*

Chicken Maryland

Cooking time   *15 minutes*

2½ lb. frying chicken · 1 egg
toasted bread crumbs · 2 sautéed bananas (see below).
TO FRY: fat or oil.
TO GARNISH: bacon rolls (see page 330)
water cress · corn fritters (see below).

Cut the chicken into 4–6 pieces and coat each piece with egg and bread crumbs. Fry the chicken quickly until golden brown in a depth of ½-inch hot fat, turning once. Reduce the heat, and cook gently until tender, on both sides. Drain, and serve on a heated dish with baked bananas and garnished with bacon rolls, water cress, and corn fritters. *Serves 4*

Sautéed bananas

Cooking time   *5 minutes*

2 firm bananas or plantain bananas
flour or egg and bread crumbs.
TO FRY: fat or oil.

Cut the bananas into halves, or quarters lengthwise, if large. Coat with a little flour or egg and crumbs. Sauté for a few minutes in hot fat. *Serves 4*

Corn fritters

Cooking time   *4–5 minutes*

1 egg · 3 tablespoons all-purpose flour
¼ teaspoon baking powder · salt
cayenne pepper · 1 teaspoon Worcestershire sauce
1 (12 oz.) can corn kernels *or* 1 (10 oz.) package frozen cooked corn.
TO FRY: fat *or* oil.

Make a batter with the beaten egg, flour, baking powder, and seasonings. Beat well and mix in the Worcestershire sauce and the drained corn. Gently fry a tablespoon of the batter in a little hot fat, turning once, for 4–5 minutes until golden brown. Continue until the batter is used. *Serves 4*

Fried chicken with orange and almond sauce

Cooking time   *25–30 minutes*

2½ lb. frying chicken · seasoning · paprika
¼ cup butter *or* oil · 3 oranges
1 tablespoon granulated sugar
⅓ cup toasted flaked almonds.

Cut the chicken into 4 pieces, and season well. Heat the butter or oil in a large skillet and fry the chicken until golden brown all over. Cover the pan, reduce the heat, and cook gently for 20 minutes, or until the chicken is tender. Meanwhile, squeeze the juice from 2 of the oranges, remove the skin and pith from the third and cut into segments. Remove the chicken from the skillet, and arrange on a heated serving dish. Drain the excess butter or oil from the skillet,

and add the orange juice, orange segments, and sugar to the skillet. Bring slowly to a boil, stirring constantly, and boil rapidly for 2–3 minutes. Adjust seasoning, pour over the chicken, sprinkle with the almonds, and serve. *Serves 4*

Sweet and sour chicken

Cooking time   *30 minutes*

⅓ cup oil · 1 clove garlic · 4 chicken pieces
¼ cup all-purpose flour · seasoning
1 (16 oz.) can pineapple pieces or chunks
few purple and green grapes · few slices preserved ginger · 2 cups bean sprouts.
FOR THE SAUCE: 2 teaspoons cornstarch
1 tablespoon soy sauce · 3 tablespoons vinegar
¼ cup granulated sugar *or* honey
⅔ cup chicken stock · ⅔ cup pineapple syrup.
TO GARNISH: little finely chopped canned pineapple and stem ginger.

Heat the oil, and sauté the crushed garlic. Coat the chicken with the flour and seasoning, and fry until browned on all sides. If preferred, the chicken may be cut into neat cubes before cooking. Lower the heat, add pineapple pieces, grapes, and ginger. Continue cooking over low heat for 15–20 minutes, or until tender, adding the bean sprouts toward the end. For the sauce, blend all the ingredients together, put into a pan, and boil for 2–3 minutes, stirring constantly. Garnish the chicken with pineapple and ginger, and serve with the sauce. *Serves 4*

Chicken with paprika sauce

Cooking time   *20–25 minutes*

8 slices bacon · ¼ cup butter
4 pieces young frying chicken · salt
1 tablespoon paprika · 1¼ cups cultured sour cream *or* coffee cream and 1 tablespoon lemon juice
boiled rice (see page 194).

Fry the bacon in a large skillet over low heat for 8–10 minutes, or until evenly browned, turning occasionally. Remove from the pan and keep warm. Fry the chicken pieces in the bacon fat and the butter until they are golden, then add a little hot water, and simmer until they are quite tender, seasoning with salt and paprika. Add the cream gradually, stirring constantly, until the sauce thickens. Put boiled rice in the center of a dish, layer the bacon over it, then cover with the chicken. *Serves 4*

TO BROIL POULTRY

Since chicken is the type of poultry usually broiled, directions are given for this only. Turkey flesh is too thick for this purpose and duck and goose are considered better roasted. Chickens for broiling, like frying, must be young, since the whole object when you broil is to cook quickly.

Broiled chicken

Cooking time   *15 minutes*

4 pieces young chicken or 2 halved chickens
seasoning · ¼–½ cup melted butter *or* oil.
TO GARNISH: Maître d'hôtel *or* parsley butter (see below).

Season the chicken well. Place the pieces, skin side down, in the bottom of the broiler pan or on the rack, and brush with the butter or oil. Preheat the broiler. Cook the chicken for 5 minutes. Turn the pieces over, brush well with additional melted butter or oil and cook for a further 5 minutes. Reduce heat, or move broiler further from the source of heat, and continue until cooked. Brush with butter or oil occasionally during cooking. Serve immediately, garnished with parsley butter. Tomatoes may be broiled at the same time and also bacon slices.

Serves 4

Maître d'hôtel butter or parsley butter

Cooking time   *None*

Squeeze lemon juice
1 tablespoon chopped parsley · seasoning
¼ cup butter.

Work the lemon juice, parsley, and seasoning into the butter. Put into a cool place, cut in neat pieces.

Spatchcock of chicken

Cooking time   *15 minutes*

4 very small young spring chickens
¼–½ cup butter *or* shortening · seasoning
4 tomatoes
TO GARNISH: parsley · lettuce *or* water cress.

Cut the chickens along the backbone, so they may be pressed out flat (this is what is meant by spatchcock of chicken). Brush the chickens with the melted butter or shortening, and season well. Place in the bottom of the broiler or on the rack. Heat the broiler, cook the chickens for 5 minutes. Reduce heat, and continue broiling until cooked through. The tomatoes may be broiled at the same time as chickens, either put in the bottom of the broiler or on the rack. Serve the chickens with the broiled tomatoes, and garnished with chopped parsley and lettuce or water cress.

Serves 4

Ways to flavor broiled chicken

There are a number of ways in which broiled chicken may be flavored. These make no difference to the cooking time, as given above.

LEMON CHICKEN – blend the grated peel and juice of 1 lemon with the butter used to brush the chicken.

MUSTARD TOPPING – blend 2 teaspoons prepared mustard with the butter used to brush the chicken.

MUSTARD CRUMB TOPPING – blend 3–4 teaspoons prepared mustard with the butter used to brush the chicken. Brown the chicken on one side, turn, and press about ½ cup fine fresh bread crumbs over the chicken pieces. Continue cooking until crisp and brown.

DEVILED CHICKEN – blend 1 tablespoon prepared mustard with 1 teaspoon Worcestershire sauce and ¼ teaspoon cayenne pepper, then mix with the butter used to brush the chicken. This is particularly good served with a well flavored mustard sauce.

TO POT-ROAST POULTRY

Since turkey and goose are too large to put into most saucepans and the latter, like duck, too fat for this method of cooking, it is only chicken and guinea fowl that are usually pot-roasted.

Pot-roast chicken

Cooking time   *Depending on weight of chicken*

¼ cup fat *or* oil · 1 roasting chicken
1¼ cups white stock *or* water *or* ⅔ cup white stock and ⅓ cup red *or* white wine *or* apple cider
4 medium carrots · ½ lb. small onions
seasoning.

Heat the fat or oil in a large pan. Sauté the chicken in this until golden brown. Put in the stock or other liquid with the vegetables, which should be left whole. Put the chicken on top, add seasoning, and cover tightly. If you are not satisfied that the cover is tight, put a piece of aluminium foil underneath. Cook over low heat for approximately 15 minutes per lb. plus an additional 15 minutes; always include weight of stuffing, for pot-roasting chickens may be stuffed. The chicken will not be very crisp, but since it is not immersed in the liquid, it does taste like roast chicken.

Serves 4–8 depending on the weight of the bird.

Duck and apricot sauce, page 137; Smoked salmon, page 24; Potato croquettes, page 167; Peas, page 163; Broccoli, page 161; Meringues, page 298

126   Chicken and bacon pie, page 148; Simple vegetable soup, page 34

Roast pheasant, page 139; Game chips, page 140; and Fried crumbs, page 140

Raised pie, page 157

Pressed tongue, page 337; and salad, page 168

Boiled brisket of beef, page 93; and salad, page 168

Sausage, bacon, kidney and egg breakfast grill, page 321

Pot-roast poultry in a pressure cooker

Cooking time   *See below*

1 chicken or Guinea fowl · stuffing, if desired
seasoning · 3 tablespoons all-purpose flour
2 tablespoons fat *or* oil · ⅔ cup water.

Calculate the weight of the bird plus the stuffing. Coat thinly in well seasoned flour, and brown uncovered in the hot fat in the pressure cooker. Remove the bird from the fat. For guinea fowl, put very fat bacon slices over the breast. Put approximately ⅔ cup water in the pressure cooker, place the bird on the trivet (rack) of the cooker and bring up to pressure, according to the manufacturer's instructions. Allow 5 minutes per lb. at 15 lb. pressure. Allow to drop back to normal at room temperature. If desired, the bird may be put on a bed of whole vegetables instead of the trivet and the liquid added – the vegetables will be very soft for soup or to add to gravy.

Serves 4–8 depending on the weight of the bird

TO POT-ROAST A STEWING FOWL

Cooking time   *Depending on weight of fowl*

Ingredients as pot-roast chicken. Pour away any surplus fat after browning the fowl. Pack freshly prepared vegetables around the fowl during the period of cooking. Cook very slowly and allow 30 minutes per lb. plus an additional 1 hour. The vegetables will be very soft at the end of the cooking time – use to flavor gravy or use for soup.

TO STEW POULTRY OR SERVE IN A CASSEROLE

To stew poultry

Chicken is the most usual poultry to stew, although small turkeys may be cooked using the slow method for chickens, then roasted for a short period in a very hot oven. The advantage of this method is that shrinkage is reduced to a minimum, and it is therefore an economical method of cooking turkey. Critics of this method however find that the flesh tastes more like stewed poultry than roast.
A very fat goose or duck may be simmered very slowly in water, as in the slow method, for about 1 hour for goose or ½ hour for duck, removed from the liquid, cooled, dried well, then roasted as usual – deducting the simmering time from the usual time allowed for roasting. This removes excess fat – but the method described under roasting goose and duck on page 120 should solve this problem.

To stew chicken

The water should never be allowed to boil hard since you will not get a good taste or texture – let the water move only slightly when once it has come to a boil. If you are sure the stewing fowl is reasonably young, then you can allow 30 minutes per lb. plus an additional 30 minutes – if moderately young allow an additional 1 hour, but if you have grave doubts as to whether it is tough then it is better to use the very slow method below.

If you wish to have good stock as well as a tender chicken, this is a good way to cook the bird. Vegetables may be added (see stewed chicken and vegetables, this page). If you do not need a great deal of stock, then only half cover the bird with water, season lightly, and cover the breast with a little butter – this gives a stronger flavor to the flesh of the bird.

VERY SLOW METHOD

Put the bird into a large container, completely cover with water, and add seasoning to taste. Cover tightly, and simmer slowly, allowing 30 minutes per lb. plus an additional 2 hours. Make sure the water has only an occasional bubble on the surface.

QUICKER METHOD

Put 1 or 2 potatoes inside the bird as the steam from these helps to make it tender and keep it moist. Put into a steamer over a pan of rapidly boiling water. Add a little seasoning, and allow 40 minutes per lb.

QUANTITY TO ALLOW

There is considerable shrinkage in a stewing fowl due to the amount of fat (which when clarified after cooking is excellent to use). Allow a generous amount when buying a stewing fowl – ¾–1 lb. per person is usual; although modern stewing fowls tend to be very plump with small bones (this weight is when trussed).

Stewed chicken and vegetables

Cooking time   *See method*

1 stewing fowl · 5 slices bacon · 1 large onion
seasoning · 2½ cups water · 1¾ cups diced mixed
root vegetables (onion, carrot, turnip, potatoes)
¼ cup all-purpose flour · ⅔ cup milk.
TO GARNISH: chopped parsley.

Wash chicken and cut into neat pieces. Dice bacon and put into a pan with chopped onion, chicken pieces, seasoning, and water. Cover and simmer gently until tender. This will depend upon the weight of the bird and method used – for a 4 lb. bird (weight when trussed) stewed by the quicker method this means cooking for 4 × 40 minutes i.e. 2 hours 40 minutes. If cooked by the slower method it means 4 hours. Add the vegetables about 45 minutes before the chicken will be cooked. Blend flour with the milk, and stir into the liquid. Bring to a boil, stirring well, and cook until smooth and thickened. Taste and reseason, if necessary. Garnish with chopped parsley.

Serves 4–8 depending on the weight of the bird

Chicken supreme

Cooking time *20 minutes*

1 stewed *or* steamed chicken
FOR THE SAUCE: ¼ cup butter *or* margarine
½ cup all-purpose flour · 1¼ cups chicken stock (see method) · 1¼ cups milk · seasoning
2 egg yolks · ⅓ cup coffee *or* whipping cream.
TO GARNISH: parsley.

Slice the boiled chicken or cut into pieces, and keep hot in a little of the chicken stock. Strain 1¼ cups stock from the liquid. Heat the butter or margarine, then blend in the flour, and cook for several minutes. Gradually stir in the chicken stock and milk. Add seasoning, bring to a boil, and cook until a smooth thick sauce. Remove from the heat. Blend the egg yolks and cream and strain into the hot sauce, stirring constantly. Cook for several minutes without boiling. Either coat the chicken with the sauce or serve separately. If coating the chicken, lift the meat from the stock and drain well. If serving separately, the chicken may be served in a very little stock, if desired. Garnish with sprigs of parsley or chopped parsley.
The amount of sauce is enough for 6–8 people, and the number or portions will depend upon the weight of the bird.

To cook poultry in a casserole

The most popular poultry to use in a casserole is chicken, since it blends with a variety of flavorings. Duck may also be casseroled very successfully; since this contains a high percentage of fat it is a good idea to cook the casserole one day before required, allow it to cool, remove the fat and reheat (see page 86 for ways to remove surplus fat).
Leftover turkey and goose make excellent casserole dishes.

Coq au vin

Cooking time *50 minutes*

1 cup mushrooms · 4–8 small shallots *or* onions
¼–⅓ butter *or* oil · 5 slices bacon *or* fat pork
1 young chicken *or* chicken pieces · 1 clove garlic
¼ cup all-purpose flour
2½ cups red wine *or* 1¾ cups chicken stock and ⅔ cup red wine · seasoning.

Slice the mushrooms, and sauté with the onions in butter until tender and the onions golden brown. Fry the diced bacon, remove, and add the chicken pieces. Cook steadily for about 10 minutes, until golden on the outside. Remove from the butter, and stir in the crushed garlic and the flour. Cook for about 3–4 minutes, then gradually add the wine or stock and wine. Add seasoning, and bring just to a boil. Simmer until a smooth sauce. Return the chicken, mushrooms, and onions to the sauce, season well, and simmer for approximately 30 minutes, or until the chicken is tender. *Serves 4*

Chicken in cider

Cooking time *35–40 minutes*

3½ lb. chicken *or* chicken pieces · 1 onion
1 large carrot · ¼ cup butter · seasoning
1 tablespoon all-purpose flour · 1¼ cups apple cider
finely chopped parsley.

Cut the chicken into 8 pieces, and slice the onion and carrot. Melt the butter in a large skillet, and brown the chicken joints quickly all over. Remove from the skillet and keep warm. Add the sliced onion and carrot to the fat, and sauté gently for 5 minutes. Sprinkle in seasoning and flour, and cook for several minutes, then add the cider. Bring to a boil, stirring constantly. Return the chicken to the skillet, and cover tightly. Simmer gently for 25–30 minutes. Garnish with finely chopped parsley.
Serves 4

Blanquette of chicken (1)

Cooking time *2¼ hours*

1 stewing fowl · water · 4 onions · 8 cloves, optional · 4 carrots · bouquet garni
seasoning.
1 recipe white sauce, coating consistency (see page 183) · ⅓ cup milk *or* coffee *or* whipping cream
2 egg yolks.
TO GARNISH: parsley.

Put the stewing fowl into a saucepan and barely cover with water. Giblets may be cooked at the same time, but do not use the liver since it takes away the delicate flavor. Add onions stuck with cloves, carrots, *bouquet garni* (3 bay leaves, 3 sprigs parsley, and 1 sprig thyme, tied together), and seasoning. Bring to a boil and skim, then lower the heat, and simmer for about 2¼ hours. Make the white sauce. Lift chicken onto a heated dish and strain 1¼ cups of the liquid into the white sauce. Blend milk or cream with egg yolks, stir into the hot sauce, and cook until thickened well, but DO NOT BOIL. Cut the chicken into pieces and serve with sauce. Garnish with parsley. *Serves 4*

Blanquette of chicken (2)

Cooking time *1 hour for young chicken*
2–2½ hours for stewing fowl

3 slices bacon · 3 carrots
4 pieces chicken *or* stewing fowl
½ lb. small onions *or* shallots · ⅔ cup white wine
1¼ cups water *or* white stock · seasoning
little milk · ¼ cup butter · ½ cup all-purpose flour · 1 canned *or* ½ fresh red sweet pepper*

* If using fresh pepper, cook for a short time in salted water.

Dice the bacon, and slice the carrots. Blanch the bacon and chicken with boiling water, discard water and place meat in pan. Add the onions and carrots, and pour on the white wine and stock. Cover and bring to a boil. Simmer gently for 2 hours, seasoning to taste. Drain off the liquid and measure, add enough milk to give 2½ cups. Make a white sauce with this, using the butter and flour. Stir back into the stew and add the strips of sweet pepper. Pour into a heated serving dish. The carrots could be omitted and 1 cup mushrooms sautéed in butter added to the sauce instead.   *Serves 4*

Jardinière chicken

Cooking time   *20–25 minutes*

1 small young chicken · seasoning
¼–⅓ cup melted butter · 1 lb. mixed spring vegetables (1 cup sliced carrots (*or* diced)
½ cup shelled peas, 1 cup chopped beans)
1 recipe brown sauce (see page 183).

Prepare the chicken by cutting in half and skewering flat, if necessary. Heat the broiler. Season chicken well, place skin side down in bottom of broiler, brush with melted butter, and cook for 5 minutes. Turn the chicken over, brush well with melted butter, and cook for a further 5 minutes. Reduce heat or move broiler further from the source of heat, and continue cooking until tender. Cook the young mixed carrots, peas, and beans. Make brown sauce. Serve chicken coated with the sauce.
Serves 4

Chicken curry

Cooking time   *2¼–2½ hours*

1 chicken *or* chicken pieces · ¼ cup butter
1 small onion · 1 small apple
1 tablespoon curry powder · 3 tablespoons all-purpose flour · 2½ cups chicken stock
1 or 2 chili peppers (optional) · dash ginger
dash turmeric · 1 tablespoon chutney
squeeze lemon juice · seasoning
¾ cup flaked coconut
3 tablespoons seedless white raisins
TO GARNISH: green sweet pepper.
TO SERVE: ¼–⅓ cup long-grain rice.

Cut the chicken into pieces and fry in the hot butter for 5 minutes, then remove. Sauté the chopped onion and apple for a few minutes, then add the curry powder and flour. Cook for 2–3 minutes, then care-

fully blend in most of the stock. Bring to a boil and cook until a thin sauce. Add the spices, chutney, lemon juice, and seasoning then return the chicken to the sauce. Pour the heated remaining stock over the coconut and let stand for a few minutes, then add the strained liquid to the curry. If preferred, fresh coconut or coconut milk may be used. Add the raisins, and simmer very gently for approximately 2 hours. Garnish with sweet pepper, and serve with boiled rice (see page 194). For a picture of this recipe see page 106.   *Serves 4*

Lemon chicken

Cooking time   *3–4 hours*
Oven temperature   *275°F.*

1 lemon · 1 large stewing fowl
½ lb. small onions · celery · 4 medium carrots
3 bay leaves · 3 white peppercorns · water
seasoning · 1 cup mushrooms · ¼ cup butter
1 egg · ⅓ cup whipping cream · ⅔ cup sherry
1 cup blanched almonds.

Squeeze lemon juice all over the outside of the bird. Put the lemon skin inside after removing all the seeds. Put the chicken into a flameproof casserole, with the whole onions, diced celery and carrots, bay leaves, and peppercorns. Cover with water to come within 1 inch from the top, and season lightly. Cover tightly and cook in a preheated 275°F. oven for 3–4 hours. When tender, remove chicken from liquid and keep warm. Boil remaining stock rapidly to reduce to one half original volume. Sauté mushrooms in the butter. Beat egg and cream, gradually adding 1¼ cups of the boiling stock and stirring constantly until thick and smooth. Add mushrooms, sherry, and blanched almonds. Replace the chicken, and surround with sauce.   *Serves 4*

TO STEAM CHICKEN

Put the well-washed chicken into a steamer over a pan of boiling water. If the stewing fowl is very fat, it needs seasoning only. If, on the other hand, it is quite a lean bird it is a good idea to either brush with a little melted butter or wrap in buttered paper. Do not steam too quickly. A young bird needs just about 20 minutes for each lb. plus an additional 20 minutes.
This is a very good way of cooking baby spring chickens as well as roasting fowls, particularly if you intend to allow them to get cold and serve with salad. An older stewing fowl needs a minimum of 30 minutes per lb. plus an additional 30 minutes.
The water underneath, unless you cook the giblets in this, has very little flavor from the chicken.

Duck and leek casserole

Cooking time   *2½ hours*
Oven temperature   *300°F.*

6 medium leeks · seasoning
1 teaspoon finely chopped sage · 1 duck
1¼ cups duck stock (made by simmering the giblets)
3 tablespoons port wine.

Wash and slice the leeks thickly. Put half into the bottom of an ovenproof casserole; top with seasoning, half the sage, the duck cut into pieces, and stock mixed with the port wine. Cover with remaining leeks, season well, and add remaining sage. Cover tightly, and cook in a preheated 300°F. oven for 2½ hours. Serve with creamed or baked potatoes. This is a surprisingly rich dish, so, if preferred, the duck and leeks may be lifted onto a serving dish and the liquid diluted with an equal amount of stock, then thickened – allow ¼ cup all-purpose flour to each 1¼ cups liquid. This counteracts the fat content.
Serves 4

Chicken galantine

Cooking time   *2 hours and time to make stock*
1 large roasting chicken
1 lb. pork sausage meat · 5–8 slices bacon
⅔ cup fine fresh bread crumbs · 2 eggs
1 tablespoon chopped parsley
grated peel and juice of 1 lemon · seasoning
TO SIMMER: 3¾ cups white stock
package unflavored gelatin.

Bone the chicken (see page 118) and, if time permits, simmer the bones to make the stock. Mix all the ingredients for the stuffing together, and spread over the boned chicken, as method on page 118. Tie or skewer the chicken firmly, and put into a large saucepan with the stock. Simmer VERY SLOWLY for 2 hours. When cooked, strain off 2½ cups stock and dissolve the gelatin in this. Allow to cool and just begin to stiffen. Lift the chicken onto a wire rack and turn on its breast, then brush the back with some of the half-set gelatin, and allow this to set firmly. Meanwhile keep the remaining gelatin from becoming too stiff. Turn the chicken over so the breast is up, and cover the body with the gelatin mixture. Serve with salad.   *Serves 8*

DUCK GALANTINE
Use a large roasting duck. Reduce sausage meat to ½ lb. and increase amount of bread crumbs to 2 cups. Use 2 teaspoons chopped parsley and ½ teaspoon finely chopped fresh sage. Bone duck and skin, then continue as chicken.

DISHES TO USE COOKED POULTRY

Store cooked poultry carefully since it deteriorates easily.

Turkey croquettes

Cooking time   *15 minutes*

FOR THE SAUCE: 2 tablespoons butter *or* margarine ¼ cup all-purpose flour · ⅔ cup milk *or* chicken stock · seasoning · 1½ cups chopped cooked turkey.
TO COAT: 1 egg · toasted bread crumbs.
TO FRY: fat.
TO GARNISH: canned *or* cooked asparagus tips.

Make a thick white sauce with the butter, flour, and milk and season well. Add the chopped turkey and allow mixture to cool slightly. Form into croquette shapes. Coat in egg and crumbs. Fry in shallow fat until crisp and golden brown on each side. Garnish with asparagus tips.   *Serves 4*

Pilaf of duck or goose

Cooking time   *30 minutes*

1 cup medium *or* long-grain rice · ¼ cup butter
1 onion · ⅔ cup currants
¼ cup blanched almonds
2 large tomatoes · seasoning
1 teaspoon granulated sugar
2½ cups chicken stock *or* water with 1 chicken bouillon cube · 1½ cups diced cooked duck *or* goose
TO GARNISH: ¼–½ cup toasted blanched almonds.

Sauté rice in butter for 2–3 minutes. Add the finely chopped onion, currants, and chopped almonds, and sauté for a few minutes. Peel and slice the tomatoes, and mix with seasoning and sugar. Add to the rice mixture, then add hot stock quickly. Cover tightly and cook at very low heat for about 20 minutes, or until the stock is completely absorbed. Add the diced, skinned duck or goose, and cook for 5 minutes. Garnish with the almonds.   *Serves 4*

Turkey à la king

Cooking time   *20 minutes*

¼ cup butter *or* margarine · ½ cup mushrooms
½–1 red *or* green sweet pepper
2 tablespoons extra butter *or* chicken fat
¼ cup all-purpose flour · ⅔ cup milk and ⅔ cup chicken stock *or* 1¼ cups milk · seasoning
1 egg · 1–1½ cups diced cooked turkey
3–4 tablespoons coffee cream.
TO GARNISH: chopped parsley.
TO SERVE: hot buttered toast.

Heat the butter in a pan, add the sliced mushrooms and sliced pepper (removing core and seeds), and sauté gently until tender. Make a white sauce with the 2 tablespoons butter, flour, and milk, season well. When the sauce is thick, add the egg and cream blended well together. Cook gently without boiling for 2–3 minutes. Add turkey, cooked mushrooms, and pepper, and heat together for a few minutes. Garnish with chopped parsley, and serve on hot buttered toast.

Serves 4

EMERGENCY POULTRY DISHES

When time is short, one of the easiest foods to buy is a cooked chicken. A cooked duck may be used in the second recipe.

Chicken and asparagus cream

Cooking time	10–15 minutes

1 cooked chicken *or* chicken pieces · ¼ cup butter
1 small can asparagus *or* 1 (10 oz.) package frozen asparagus, cooked · ⅔ cup coffee cream
¼ cup mayonnaise · seasoning

Cut the chicken into pieces, and heat thoroughly in the butter in a skillet. Open the can of asparagus, and strain the liquid into the top of a double boiler. Add the cream, mayonnaise, and seasoning and heat over boiling water until blended. Arrange the chicken on a serving dish, pour over the sauce and garnish with the asparagus. This dish is not suitable for duck, since it is very rich.

Serves 4

Speedy coq au vin

Cooking time	20 minutes

1 cooked chicken *or* chicken pieces
1¼ cups cheap red wine
approximately ¼ cup cocktail onions
1 (2½ oz.) can mushrooms *or* 1 cup small fresh mushrooms · seasoning · ¼ cup all-purpose flour
2 tablespoons butter.

Cut the chicken into pieces; put into a saucepan with 1 cup of the wine and the remaining ingredients, except the flour and butter. Heat for approximately 10 minutes. Blend the flour with the remainder of the wine, and stir into the liquid with the butter. Continue cooking for a further 10 minutes. Taste and season well. Many people find all wine too strong, so if preferred, use half wine and half chicken stock.
Cooked duck may be used instead of chicken, as Canard au vin.

Serves 4

POULTRY DISHES TO IMPRESS

Most poultry, when well cooked and served, is suitable for a special occasion, but the following recipes are particularly impressive.

Chicken with walnuts

Cooking time	About 10 minutes

¼ cup walnuts · 1 small onion
1 small red sweet pepper · ¼ cup oil
1½ cups cooked chicken, cut in strips
1¼ cups white stock · 3 tablespoons cornstarch
1 teaspoon granulated sugar
1 tablespoon soy sauce · 3 tablespoons sherry
1 (8 oz.) can water chestnuts, drained and sliced
cooked rice.

Sauté the coarsely broken walnuts, sliced onion, and sliced sweet pepper in the oil until the onion and pepper are tender, but not brown. Stir in the chicken, and add the stock. Mix the cornstarch and sugar together smoothly with the soy sauce, add to ingredients in pan, and simmer gently for 3 minutes, stirring constantly. Add the sherry and water chestnuts and warm through. Serve hot with cooked rice.

Serves 4

Duck and apricot sauce

Cooking time	See below
Oven temperature	400°F.

2 small ducklings *or* 1 large duck
very little honey.
SAUCE: 1 (1 lb. 14 oz.) can apricot halves
juice 1 lemon · water
1 tablespoon arrowroot *or* cornstarch
3–4 tablespoons apricot brandy.
TO GARNISH: water cress.

Roast the ducklings in a preheated 400°F. oven for 1¼–1½ hours, depending on the size, prick as directed on page 120. After 45 minutes roasting, or 1 hour in the case of a large duck, brush the skin with a little honey (dilute this with water or syrup from the canned apricots if very thick). This gives a very crisp skin. Return to the oven and continue roasting. A little time before the ducks are ready to serve, make the sauce. Strain the liquid from the can of apricots. Add the lemon juice and enough water to give 1¼ cups liquid. For a more savory sauce use ⅔ cup apricot syrup and ⅔ cup well strained stock (made from simmering the giblets). Blend with the arrowroot. Put into the saucepan and cook until smooth, thickened, and clear. Taste and, if necessary, add a small amount of sugar or honey, since the sauce should be slightly sweet but not sticky. To give a shine to the sauce, you may either add 1 teaspoon strained fat from the ducks, or a small knob of butter. Place the ducklings on a heated dish. Put the apricot halves into the sauce and heat for just a few moments. Stir in the apricot brandy, and heat but do not boil. Pour over the ducklings and garnish with water cress. The sauce may be ignited, if desired. Illustrated on p. 125.

*Serves 4 with generous portions,
6 with smaller portions*

DUCK AND CHERRY SAUCE
Follow directions for duck and apricot sauce, but use canned Bing cherries and cherry brandy. If fresh cherries are available these may be simmered with a little sugar and water and used instead of canned fruit.

GAME, CARVING AND MEAT PIES

GAME

Wise choice of game

Choose rabbit, hare, or pigeons for economy; other game is less easily available. It may have a closed season, in which case one often has little choice. Naturally, older game must be used for casserole dishes, younger game roasted.

Ways to serve game

Serve roast game with the recommended accompaniments, and it is delicious with a venison or game sauce.

To use leftover game

Heat in a casserole in a well seasoned sauce.

Easy remedies when things are wrong

PROBLEM – if the game has a very strong taste, it was hung for too long a period. This is very much a matter of personal taste.
TO REMEDY – choose a very highly flavored sauce to serve with the game.
PROBLEM – if the game is tough, this is due either to insufficient cooking or choosing the wrong method of cooking (the game may have been old and therefore needed longer, slower cooking) or the game was inadequately hung. It is a great mistake to eat game when it is freshly killed. It needs a few days to hang; this, however, does not give the strong 'gamey' flavor which many people like very much and other people dislike. It takes longer to give this strong flavor, except in very warm weather.
TO REMEDY – tough game may be very tough and it is better, if it has been roasted, to put it into a casserole at once and continue cooking until tender in a well flavored sauce.
PROBLEM – if the game is dry, this is due to insufficient fat being used on or in the bird; as recommended on page 139, lard is spread over the bird and a little put inside. Another interesting filling for the bird is to use cream cheese or cream cheese blended with a little lard. Naturally, this gives a delightfully unusual flavor.

To buy game

Choose birds which have good plump breasts and tender legs, if desiring to roast. Where the legs appear sinewy it is probably better to choose a method of casseroling.
Make certain the game is hung for your particular taste before buying. You can tell if this will be 'high' (word used to describe strong smelling game) by its smell.

TO ROAST GAME

Game has a tendency to dry during cooking, so it is advisable to place a small piece of fat, 3–4 tablespoons, inside the bird. As game has a definite flavor, pure lard is excellent for this.

To save last minute frying, cook the game chips and crumbs earlier in the day. Drain the game chips and put these and the crumbs on separate ovenproof plates or tins. Reheat for a few minutes in the oven just before serving.

Roast grouse

Cooking time — *35–50 minutes*
Oven temperature — *425°F.*

1 large young grouse *or* 2 smaller ones
seasoning · lard.

Wash and dry the grouse well, season lightly, put
2–3 tablespoons lard inside and cover the outside
with a thin layer of lard. Roast in a preheated
425°F. oven for the first 15 minutes. If a very young
bird, you may continue roasting for a further 15–20
minutes, but if any doubt as to whether the bird is
young and tender, lower the heat to 350°F. and roast
a further 45 minutes. Serve with accompaniments
(see below). *Serves 2–4*

GAME: How to cook

NAME	IMPORTANT POINTS	ACCOMPANIMENTS	COOKING TIMES AND TEMPERATURES
CAPERCAILZIE OR WOOD GROUSE	This has a whitish breast, a little like turkey, but game-like legs; almost size of turkey, rare but delicious	As grouse or turkey	15 minutes per lb. plus an additional 15 minutes in 425°F. oven for first hour, then lower to 350°F. oven
CYGNET	Young swan, rare, with fish-like flavor	Sage and onion (see page 189 or Chestnut stuffing (see page 190)	Braise with Brown sauce (see page 183) for about 3 hours in 300°F. oven
GOLDEN PLOVER	As grouse but do not draw	As grouse	As grouse
GROUSE	Roast if young. Older birds best casseroled. Must be well hung before cooking	Redcurrant jelly (see page 310) or Bread sauce, (see page 185) game chips, Fried crumbs, (see page 140) and Water cress	35–55 minutes (see above) or approximately 2 hours in casserole (see page 140)
HARE	Excellent roasted when young. If older, try Jugged Hare	See Jugged Hare, page 142	See Jugged Hare, page 142
LEVERET	Young hare. As hare	As hare	As hare
MALLARD	Wild duck. See duck, page 120	As duck	As duck
ORTOLAN OR GARDEN BUNTING	Do not draw. Cook (as quail) in vine leaves, for same time	As duck	25 minutes
PARTRIDGE, RUFFLED GROUSE, OR BOBWHITE	Do not hang more than 3 days. At its best when legs yellow. Can be roasted when young, halved, then fried or broiled when very young	As grouse	30 minutes
PHEASANT	Roast as grouse	As grouse Chestnut stuffing (see page 190) ideal, or use sliced fried mushrooms, alone or mixed with chestnut stuffing. Illustrated on page 127	15 minutes per lb. plus an additional 15 minutes
PIGEON	Very cheap and excellent value. Roast if young	See recipes	See recipes
PLOVER	As golden plover		
PTARMIGAN	Type of grouse. Should be cooked as grouse	As grouse	As grouse
QUAIL	As pigeon	As pigeon	As pigeon
RABBIT	Can be roasted, casseroled, put in pies	See recipes	See recipes

NAME	IMPORTANT POINTS	ACCOMPANIMENTS	COOKING TIMES AND TEMPERATURES
SNIPE	Small birds can be roasted when young. Handle carefully as skins may break. May also be put into casseroles or puddings	As grouse	As grouse
SQUAB	Young pigeon, or rook. Very young chickens sometimes called squab	As pigeon	As very small and young could be fried or broiled for about 15 minutes
TEAL	Type of small wild duck. May be cooked as duck	As duck. Excellent with orange salad and bigarade sauce, or in casserole	25 minutes for very tiny bird – up to 35 minutes
VENISON	Flesh of deer. Moderate hanging for several days improves flavor. Young venison may be identified by blue vein. Roast only the most tender cuts. Baste well. Other cuts can be casseroled	Cumberland sauce or Espagnole sauce, redcurrant jelly, watercress, or as mutton	20 minutes per lb. plus an additional 20 minutes for roasting; 2–3 hours casserole
WIDGEON	Type of wild duck. Cook as teal or duck	As duck	25 minutes
WOODCOCK	Do not draw intestines. Delicious. When roasting, put toast underneath. May also be halved and fried	As grouse	25–30 minutes

Game chips

Cooking time   *few minutes*

4 large potatoes   ·   lard for frying.

Cut the peeled potatoes into wafer-thin slices, deep-fry in lard until crisp and golden. Illustrated on page 127.   *Serves 4–6*

Fried crumbs

Cooking time   *few minutes*

2 cups fairly coarse soft bread crumbs
¼ cup lard.

Sauté the bread crumbs in the hot lard until crisp and brown. If the crumbs can be put into a fine-meshed strainer they may be fried for about 30 seconds to 1 minute in deep hot lard *after* frying the game chips. Illustrated on page 127.   *Serves 4*

Grouse casserole

Cooking time   2½–3 hours
Oven temperature   300°F.

¼ cup all-purpose flour   ·   2 medium grouse
5 slices bacon   ·   ¼ cup fat
1 onion   ·   4 carrots   ·   ½ rutabaga
1¼ cups chicken *or* game stock   ·   seasoning
4 tomatoes   ·   bay leaf.

Flour the grouse, and dice the bacon. Fry the grouse in the hot fat for 10 minutes, adding the bacon halfway through. Remove and put into a casserole. Sauté the chopped onion, carrots, and diced rutabaga in the fat for a few minutes. Gradually add the stock,

bring to a boil, and cook until thickened and smooth. Season well. Pour over the grouse, adding the tomatoes and bay leaf, and cover tightly. Cook gently for about 2½ hours in a preheated 300°F. oven. Remove bay leaf before serving.   *Serves 4*

CASSEROLES OF GAME

Other game may be cooked in exactly the same way as the grouse casserole on this page. This is, however, a fairly economical casserole and it may be made more interesting and exciting.
Add peeled chestnuts to the casserole, with a little red wine.

RICE STUFFING – most game is not stuffed, but a rice stuffing could be used, if desired; this is particularly good for a game casserole.

ORANGE FLAVOR – use the recipe for grouse casserole, but add the finely grated peel and juice of 2 oranges.

The amount of liquid in the grouse casserole is fairly small; if you wish additional gravy, increase this to 1¾ cups.

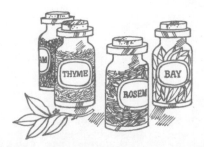

Stuffed pigeons

Cooking time   *See method*
Oven temperature   *425°F. or 375°F.*

FOR THE STUFFING: 2 hard-cooked eggs
1 cup fine fresh bread crumbs · ¼ cup chopped beef
suet · seasoning
a little grated nutmeg
1 tablespoon chopped parsley · 1 egg
4 small pigeons · 3–4 tablespoons lard.

To make the stuffing, chop the hard-cooked eggs
and blend with the bread crumbs, suet, seasoning,
nutmeg, and parsley, then bind with the egg. Put
the stuffing into each of the pigeons, then cover the
birds with the lard. If very young, cook in a preheated
425°F. oven for approximately 35 minutes. However,
pigeons tend to have a fairly firm flesh and so it is
better to cook slightly older birds in a preheated
375°F. oven for approximately 1¼ hours. Baste the
pigeons well during cooking, or if preferred, wrap
each pigeon in foil, after covering with lard as
above, and cook for approximately 1 hour 25 minutes
in a 375°F. oven, opening the foil for the last 10–15
minutes. In this way you are sure they are really
moist. *Serves 4*

Stuffed jugged pigeons

Cooking time   *1 hour*
Oven temperature   *450°F.*

FOR THE SAUCE: 1 shallot · 2 mushrooms
1 tablespoon butter · ⅔ cup Brown sauce (see
page 183) · 1 tablespoon jellied consommé, when
available · ¼ cup sherry.
FOR THE STUFFING: ⅓ cup milk
1 thick slice bread, without crusts · 2 shallots
2 mushrooms · ¼ cup chopped ham *or* bacon
1 small sprig parsley
hearts and livers of pigeons · seasoning
2 large *or* 4 small pigeons
2 *or* 4 slices of bread *or* toast · little fat
few mushrooms. TO GARNISH: mushrooms
few cooked carrots · water cress.

Make the sauce by sautéeing the sliced shallot and
mushrooms in the hot butter, then add the brown
sauce and jellied consommé. Simmer very gently
for 20 minutes, then add the sherry, and strain the
sauce, if desired. Make the stuffing by pouring the
hot milk over the bread, beat until smooth. Chop
the shallots, mushrooms, ham or bacon, parsley and
the hearts and livers, then add to the bread mixture;
season. Stuff the pigeons with this, arrange them
on slices of bread or toast and cover with fat. Bake
in a preheated 450°F. oven for 30–35 minutes, adding
a few mushrooms after 15 minutes. Lift onto a heated

dish with bread underneath each pigeon, pour some
of the sauce over each one. Garnish with mushrooms,
a few cooked carrots, and water cress, and serve the
remaining sauce separately. *Serves 4*

Game pie

Cooking time   *1 hour 30 minutes*
Oven temperature   *450°F. then 375°F.*

1 grouse *or* pheasant *or* 2–3 smaller birds (such as
pigeon) · ¼ cup all-purpose flour · 1 *or* 2 hard-
cooked eggs · 2 slices Canadian-style bacon
1 small finely chopped onion · 1 cup chopped
mushrooms · seasoning
1¼ cups game *or* chicken stock
1 recipe flaky *or* rough puff pastry (see page 216)
little egg *or* milk.

Cut the uncooked bird or birds into neat pieces and
flour these. Slice the egg or eggs and cut the bacon
into neat strips. Arrange together with the onion
and mushrooms in a deep pie pan or ovenproof
casserole. Season well, and pour over the stock.
Cover with the pastry, and brush with a little egg or
milk. Put into a preheated 450°F. oven for 10 minutes.
Put a piece of paper over the pastry, lower the heat
to 375°F. and cook for a further 1¼ hours. *Serves 4*

Stuffed rabbit or hare

Cooking time   *1½ hours*
Oven temperature   *400°F.*

1 young rabbit *or* young hare (leveret)
either Sage and onion stuffing (see page 189) *or*
Veal stuffing (see page 189) *or*
½ lb. sausage meat · 2–4 tablespoons fat
4–5 slices bacon
Onion sauce (see page 183) (optional).

Wash the rabbit in cold water to which a little
vinegar is added to whiten the flesh. Dry well. Stuff
the body of the rabbit (the head may be left attached,
although most people today like to remove this
before cooking). Heat the fat in a roasting pan or
ovenproof casserole, put in the rabbit, and spoon
hot fat over this. Cover rabbit with bacon, cover
tightly. Cook in a preheated 400°F. oven for about
1½ hours reducing the heat for the last 15 minutes,
if necessary. Serve with roast potatoes and a green
vegetable. The liver, etc. of the rabbit may be
simmered to make stock for gravy. If you are not
using a stuffing, an onion sauce is excellent with
roast rabbit. *Serves 4–6*

Jugged hare

Cooking time   *3 hours 45 minutes*
Oven temperature   *325°F.*

1 hare, cut into pieces (save as much blood as possible)
1 onion · few carrots
¼ cup bacon drippings *or* lard · ½ cup all-purpose
flour · ⅔ cup port wine
1 tablespoon red currant jelly · seasoning
Veal stuffing (see page 189).
TO GARNISH: water cress · parsley.

Cook the liver of the hare for 30 minutes in 3¾ cups
salted water. Soak the hare in cold water and a
little vinegar. Sauté the chopped onion and carrots
in the drippings. Stir in the flour and add the liver
stock. Bring to a boil, and cook until thickened.
Stir in blood of hare, port wine, redcurrant jelly,
and plenty of seasoning. Mash the liver or press
through a sieve, stir into sauce or put with the sauce
into an electric blender, switch on for a few seconds
until smooth. Cover the hare with the sauce and
simmer very slowly for about 3 hours in a saucepan.
Make the stuffing, roll into balls and bake in a
preheated 325°F. oven for 20 minutes. Arrange hare
on a heated dish, unless serving in a casserole. Coat
with most of the sauce, serve the remaining
separately. Garnish with balls of stuffing, water
cress and parsley, if desired.   *Serves 4*

Deviled rabbit

Cooking time   *1½ hours*

1 rabbit · 5 slices bacon · 1 large onion
about 1½ cups diced mixed root vegetables
1 teaspoon curry powder
1 teaspoon Worcestershire sauce
2½ cups water · seasoning · ¼ cup all-purpose
flour · ⅔ cup milk.
TO GARNISH: chopped parsley.

Wash the rabbit in cold water, to which a little
vinegar has been added to whiten the flesh. Cut the
meat into pieces. Dice the bacon, and put into a pan
with the rabbit, chopped onion, vegetables, curry
powder, and Worcestershire sauce. Fry for a few
minutes, then add the water, and bring to a boil;
season well. Cover tightly, and simmer gently for
about 1½ hours, or until the rabbit is tender. Blend
the flour with the milk, and stir into the liquid.
Bring to a boil, stirring constantly, and cook until
smooth and thickened. Taste and reseason if necessary. Garnish with chopped parsley.   *Serves 4*

Rabbit loaf

Cooking time   *1–2 hours*
Oven temperature   *375°F.*

1 rabbit · 1 large onion · 2 tablespoons fat
5 slices streaky bacon · ½ lb. pork sausage meat
seasoning · ¼ cup milk *or* rabbit stock
little margarine · toasted bread crumbs if baking
or fine fresh bread crumbs if steaming.

Cut all the meat from the rabbit bones with a sharp
knife and use the bones and liver to make stock to
serve with the loaf, if serving hot. Sauté the onion
in the fat. Grind the rabbit flesh and bacon. Add to
the sausage meat and fried onion. Other flavorings
may be added, if desired – chopped parsley, a little
sage, garlic or garlic salt, chopped celery or celery
salt. Blend and season well. Gradually moisten
with the milk or the rabbit stock. Grease a mold or
ovenproof casserole with the margarine and coat
with the bread crumbs. Put in the rabbit mixture,
and cover with foil or greased wax paper. Either
steam for about 2 hours or bake in a preheated
375°F. oven for 1–1¼ hours. Turn out and serve hot
with gravy and mixed vegetables or cold with salad.
Illustrated on page 154.   *Serves 4*

EMERGENCY GAME DISHES

Since game is both an expensive and fairly rare
food, there are really no emergency dishes one
could make with it.

GAME DISHES TO IMPRESS

Most game makes an impressive dish because of its
comparative scarcity and fairly high price if it has
to be purchased; naturally in the locality, where it
can be shot, it can be a very cheap food.
The following recipe with quail is a most interesting
one, but if quail is not available, it can be made with
other game, since the vine leaves give a most
delicious taste.

Quail with vine leaves

Cooking time   *35–45 minutes*
Oven temperature   *425°F.*

4 small quail · seasoning
about 20 young vine leaves
8 slices bacon
4 slices toast · a little liver pâté, if desired
1¼ cups Brown sauce (see page 183) *or* Espagnole
sauce (see page 184) · 3 tablespoons sherry
small bunch white grapes (optional).

Clean and season the birds, wrap them in a layer of
vine leaves, then in the bacon and roast in a preheated 425°F. oven. Unwrap the birds – the vine leaves
may be discarded or served as an accompaniment.
Put the quails on toast, and spread with liver pâté,

if desired. Strain any juice from the pan into the sauce then add the sherry. Either coat the birds with this sauce and top with the grapes or garnish the quail with grapes and serve the sauce separately.

Serves 4

Pheasant terrine

Cooking time	*1¼–1¾ hours*
Oven temperature	*350°F.*

1 large pheasant
6 slices bacon
seasoning · 1 tablespoon sherry
¼ cup game stock (made from carcass bones)

Cut the breast away from the bones of the bird, slicing this carefully. Remove the remaining meat from the bones. Put this, with the giblets and bacon, through a grinder, using all the skin; or chop the pheasant meat, giblets and bacon very finely. Grease a 2½ pint ovenproof bowl or mold. Put one-third of the minced pheasant at the bottom of the bowl. Cover this with half the sliced breast, seasoning each layer well. Continue with another one-third of the minced pheasant, then the remaining breast, and finally the remaining ground pheasant. Mix the sherry with the stock and seasoning and pour over the meat. Cover with buttered wax paper or foil and cook in a preheated 350°F. oven for approximately 1¼ hours. If the pheasant is not very young, allow up to 1¾ hours.

Serves 4

CARVING

Good carving is a skill which may be acquired with continual practice. In order to be able to carve well, it is essential that the meat or poultry is correctly cooked – if it is underdone then it can be more difficult to carve because it is tough (the exception, of course, being underdone beef); if overcooked then the meat crumbles and it is impossible to obtain good slices.

To carve well

A very sharp knife is necessary for good carving, this may be an electric carving knife which is suitable for carving and cutting all meats, bread, etc., and which does not need the usual sharpening, or a special carving knife which should not be used for general purposes. Keep the knife very sharp, so invest in a steel (see below).
The heat of the meat blunts the cutting edge after a fairly short time, so if ever you need to carve for a very large party try to borrow or invest in a second knife, because you would not wish to stop and sharpen the knife since the meat would get cold.

HOW TO CARVE

Always use a carving fork which not only holds the meat or poultry in position, but has a guard which protects the carver if the knife should slip. An ordinary fork will not give this protection. Get into the habit of carving the meat where possible away from yourself – this minimizes the risk of cuts should the knife slip.
Remove the string or skewers from the part of the meat where you will be carving, but in the case of large cuts do not remove all the skewers, or all the string at once since this holds the meat in a good shape.
The skewers or string are generally removed from poultry all at one time.
With meat one carves across the grain of the meat – see next column.

TO SHARPEN A CARVING KNIFE

The correct action when sharpening a carving knife is to hold the cutting edge against the steel at an angle of not more than 15° – too sharp an angle does not give a good result.
1. Draw the cutting edge of the knife across the steel – away from you – use a brisk but steady movement.

2. Turn the blade and draw the cutting edge towards you using the same movement.
3. Continue like this, but at the same time move the knife so you sharpen from the tip to the base.

Store your carving knife carefully, since knives may be harmed when a weight is placed upon the cutting edge.
If using an electric knife sharpener, follow the directions given by the manufacturer.

TO CARVE BEEF

BONED AND ROLLED – these roasts are the easiest to carve, so it is worth asking the butcher to bone and roll a difficult cut until you are used to carving – then you simply cut thin slices across the meat. Lay these neatly on the plates or dish.

MEAT ON THE BONE – you can carve these cuts with the meat flat on the dish.
For a standing rib roast, remove the backbone from the ribs. Cut from the meat across to the rib as it lies flat on the plate. To loosen the slice from the rib, cut vertically along the rib.

TO CARVE VEAL

The method of carving depends on the specific cut. Leg or shoulder is carved downward or around the bone as lamb, loin cut downward into chops, tenderloin carved across as beef.

TO CARVE LAMB OR MUTTON

This is generally carved in thicker slices than beef, although naturally this is a matter of personal preference. The grain of the meat means that slices are cut downwards in most cases.

LOIN CHOPS, RIB CHOPS, CROWN ROAST – these are cut into chops and it is important to ask the butcher to 'chine' the meat, or chop it through the bone for easier carving.

LEG – make the first slice in the center of the leg and cut a 'V' shaped slice for the first portion, allowing the knife to go down to the bone. After this, carve slices from either side of this cut portion.

SQUARE CUT SHOULDER – here one follows the contour of the bones, cutting slices round it. If the bone at the end of the shoulder is held in a napkin it gives one a firmer hold. This means dispensing with a carving fork for a time, so take particular care in cutting. A rolled shoulder will lessen carving problems for this rather difficult cut.

SADDLE – since this is a double loin make very long slices first across the center of the cut – cutting these downward. Next cut rather slanting slices from the remainder of the meat.

TO CARVE PORK AND HAM

Cut leg or shoulder of pork in the same way as lamb. Loin of pork should be easy to cut, since the skin is scored before cooking to give good crackling, and the butcher generally saws through the bones. Cut slices downward.

Ham on the bone is cut from the shank end toward the thicker part of the ham. Press the carving fork firmly into the flesh to hold this steady. Ideally one needs a thinner more flexible knife for carving ham than one generally uses for carving other meats. Rolled ham is cut thinly across the meat.

TO CARVE POULTRY

This depends upon the size of the birds – since it is recommended in the case of turkeys and large chickens that the leg is removed for carving – this may be done in the kitchen. Poultry scissors are invaluable for cutting legs from chickens, or cutting ducks into serving pieces into serving pieces – or when using a knife, find the junction of the thigh bone with the tip of the knife, insert this into the flesh and gradually pull the leg away from the body. The same action is used when removing wings – with practice this becomes quite easy. If poultry is completely boned, then carve like a rolled meat.

When carving a large chicken, duck, turkey, or goose, try to complete carving the flesh from one side of the bird before beginning on the second side, for cut surfaces dry quickly, whereas the skin of the poultry prevents this happening.

TO CARVE A CHICKEN

The method by which this is carved depends on the size of the bird. Small spring chickens – serve one per person. If slightly larger, cut into halves – you cut firmly downward, slightly to one side of the center of the breast bone; this is quite easy to do with a sharp knife.

Medium chickens can be cut into pieces rather than carved. To do this, cut away the two legs (these may be cut again into four pieces, i.e. two drum sticks and two thigh joints). The breast meat may be cut away on either side of the breast bone with the wings, or the wings may be cut away from the body first, then the breast made into two pieces. This will give 6 or 8 portions altogether – four leg portions, two breast and wing portions, or two wings and two breast portions. Sometimes the ladies are given the breast and wings, and the men the legs, but in most families one leg and half the breast is served – so the medium chicken serves 4 people. The wings are included as part of a breast portion, but naturally this depends upon personal preference.

The large chicken is carved by first either cutting or pulling off the leg on one side. This enables you to cut large slices from the breast. When sufficient meat from the breast has been cut, carve the meat from the leg – see turkey.

TO CARVE A DUCK

Small ducklings may be cut in half, as tiny chickens, since there is not a lot of meat on the breast. Larger birds will be cut into four pieces – two from the breast, and two from the legs. For a very large duck, rather thick slices may be carved from the breast instead of serving the breast uncut. The flesh from the legs may be carved in the same way as turkey.

TO CARVE A TURKEY

Either cut off the leg on one side, or pull it well away from the body. This enables you to cut large slices from the breast. Cut long thin slices of meat across the breast meat – the fact that the leg is removed makes this very easy. Carve slices of stuffing as well. Next cut slices from the leg – where the leg is very large and 'meaty' this can be done by carving across the leg until one comes to the bone. The final pieces are cut into narrow thick slices. Where the legs are smaller it is easier to cut slices around the bone. Give each person a little light meat, dark meat, and stuffing.

TO CARVE A GOOSE

Carve in the same way as a turkey, there will be considerably less breast on most geese, however.

TO CARVE GAME

Small birds are served whole or halved, larger birds carved or cut like chicken. Venison is carved like lamb.

Roasted hare and large rabbits are carved by cutting long slices on either side of the back bone, then carving round the bones in the legs.

MEAT PIES AND PUDDINGS

The recipes in this section cover a wide range of meat pies and some steamed puddings. Many of these are traditional.

Wise choice of pies and puddings

For a cold meal, choose one of the raised pies, i.e. veal and ham, chicken and ham or pork. Most of the other pies could be served cold, but on the whole, are nicer hot. For a very cold day, choose a steamed pudding – and it is interesting to note that the Sea pie, which is the traditional name, is really a steamed pudding.

Ways to serve pies and puddings

The way the pies are served will depend very much on the particular recipe. Many of the pies are given in portions for four people, but they could be baked in individual pie dishes, or in a small casserole topped with pastry.

To use leftover pies and puddings

IF ANY RAISED PIES – WHETHER HOME MADE OR PURCHASED FROM A SHOP – ARE LEFTOVER, THE GREATEST CARE MUST BE TAKEN TO STORE THEM IN THE REFRIGERATOR, AND TO USE THEM UP QUICKLY. IF THEY CANNOT BE EATEN WITHIN 24 HOURS, IT IS ADVISABLE TO DISCARD THEM, FOR MANY CASES OF MILD FOOD POISONING CAN BE TRACED TO EATING STALE PIES. Other pies which may be reheated cause less problems, but read the remarks under reheating stews and casseroles, page 68. Steamed pudding may be resteamed but naturally should be stored in the refrigerator, because the meat is highly perishable.

Easy remedies when things are wrong

PROBLEM – if a steamed pudding is not as light as it should be, this is either due to the fact that the suet crust pastry was made too dry or the water did not boil sufficiently quickly for the first 1½ hours.
TO REMEDY – there is little one can do to remedy the pudding crust once it has been cooked.
PROBLEM – if the meat in a pie or pudding is tough, this is due to inadequate cooking of the meat – remember it is often a cheaper cut of meat which does need a long cooking period.
TO REMEDY – cover the pastry to prevent overbrowning and continue cooking. The suet crust pastry in a steamed pudding is not harmed in the slightest by extra cooking.

To make a perfect pie

1. Follow the instructions for making the particular pastry.
2. Make sure the meat is adequately cooked before putting it into the pie pan, or allow sufficient time for this to be cooked in the pie.
3. To prevent the pastry sinking in on top of the meat, fill the pie pan very full.
4. To make sure the pastry is crisp, make a slit on top to allow the steam to escape.
5. Make pies look interesting by glazing the pastry and decorating this with pastry leaves, etc.

WAYS OF DECORATING MEAT PIES

LEAVES: Cut along strips of pastry, then cut the strips across to form a leaf or diamond shape. Make marks on these with a knife to look like the veins of a leaf.
TASSELS: Cut strips of pastry, and divide these into 3- or 4-inch lengths. With the tip of a knife, cut at intervals, then roll the pastry to form a tassel.

ROSES: Cut strips of pastry. Roll one end very firmly for about ¼ inch to make the center of the rose. Roll the rest around loosely. Press down at intervals with your fingers to form rose petals.

TO GLAZE PASTRY

Meat pies should be glazed. This gives an attractive color and shine to the pastry. The pastry may be brushed with milk, but it is a much better color if brushed with beaten egg yolk. The egg may be blended with 1 tablespoon water so that the coating is not too thick.

Steak and kidney pie

Cooking time   *1 hour 55 minutes**
Oven temperature   *425°F. then 325°F.*

1¼–1½ lb. stewing beef
2 lamb kidneys *or* ¼ lb. beef kidney
1 tablespoon all-purpose flour · seasoning
1 recipe rough puff *or* flaky *or* puff pastry
water *or* beef bouillon.
TO GLAZE: 1 tablespoon milk *or* 1 beaten egg.

Method 1. Cut the beef and kidney into 1-inch cubes, and mix well. Roll in the seasoned flour; or cut thin narrow strips of the beef, and cut the kidney into tiny pieces. Put a piece of kidney on each strip of stewing steak and roll firmly, then toss in seasoned flour. Stand an egg cup in the center of a 9-inch pie pan or an ovenproof casserole to support the pastry. Put the meat into the pie pan, and pour in enough water or bouillon to come halfway up the meat. Do not put more in, as it may boil out in cooking. Roll out the pastry, and cover the pie. Use any scraps of pastry left to form leaves or a tassel or roses to decorate the pie. Brush the top of the pie with the milk or egg, pressing the decoration in position. Make a tiny slit in the pastry over the egg cup to allow the steam to escape. Bake in a preheated 425°F. oven for about 25 minutes, to enable the pastry to rise. Put a piece of wax paper over the top of the pie, then lower the heat to 325°F. and cook for a further 1½ hours.* When serving, have a gravy boat of hot bouillon available to pour into the pie to make extra gravy, if desired. (See picture page 80).

* longer if the meat is tough.

Method 2. Prepare the meat as above and cook as stewed beef and kidney (see page 97) until nearly tender. Put the meat into a pie pan and let stand until cool. Roll out the pastry, and cover the pie. Bake in a preheated 425°F. oven for 25 minutes, then lower the heat to 300°F. for a further 10 minutes.
Serves 4

Always stand the pie pan on a baking sheet in case any bouillon boils out; this also enables you to remove the pie more easily from the oven.

STEAK AND ONION PIE
Use 1 large sliced onion instead of the kidney.

STEAK AND OYSTER PIE
Ingredients as steak and kidney pie with about 6 oysters, which should be halved and added to the meat. Scallops could be used instead, if desired. The combination of shellfish and meat is an excellent one.

Cornish pasty

Cooking time   *50 minutes*
Oven temperature   *425°F. then 350°F.*

Double recipe short crust pastry (see page 215)
¾–1 lb. uncooked rump roast *or* good quality stewing steak · 2 medium potatoes
2 medium onions · seasoning
3 tablespoons beef bouillon *or* water.
TO GLAZE: little milk *or* beaten egg.

Make the short crust pastry. Roll into 4 circles, each approximately 8 inches in diameter. Cut the meat, the peeled potatoes and onions into ¼-inch cubes and put onto a plate. Mix with the seasoning, and put into the center of each pastry circle. Add the bouillon or water to the meat mixture. Brush the edges of the pastry with a little water and press together lightly, over the filling, so that they will not open during cooking. Flute the edges. Lift the pasties, keeping fluted edge uppermost, on to a lightly greased baking sheet, using a spatula. Brush the pastry with a little milk or beaten egg. Bake in a preheated 425°F. oven for 25 minutes, then lower the heat to 350°F. for a further 25 minutes to make sure the meat and vegetables are cooked. Serve hot or cold.
Serves 4

Mushroom beef pie

Cooking time   *35–40 minutes*
Oven temperature   *400°F.*

1 onion · ⅓ cup shortening *or* butter
¾ lb. cooked meat · ¼ cup all-purpose flour
⅔ cup brown stock *or* water and beef bouillon cube
1¼ cups milk · 1 cup mushrooms
1 (8 oz.) can cooked peas · seasoning
1 recipe short crust pastry (see page 215).
TO GLAZE: milk *or* egg.

Chop the onion finely, and sauté in two-thirds of the shortening or butter, add the diced meat, and cook for several minutes. Stir in the flour, cook for several minutes, then gradually blend in the stock or water and bouillon cube and the milk. Bring to a boil, and cook until a smooth sauce. Meanwhile sauté the sliced mushrooms in the remaining shortening or butter (this prevents the mushrooms darkening the sauce). Stir the mushrooms and peas into the sauce, season, and put into a 2½ pint pie pan or ovenproof casserole. Cover with pastry, brush with a little milk or beaten egg, and bake in a preheated 400°F. oven for 35 minutes, or until crisp and golden brown.
Serves 4

Croustade of beef

Cooking time   *See method*
Oven temperature   *See method*

1 recipe short crust pastry (see page 215)
$\frac{1}{2}-\frac{3}{4}$ cup mushrooms · 2 tablespoons butter
seasoning · approximately 1 lb. beef tenderloin or
boneless sirloin *cut in one piece*, 3–4 inches thick.

Roll out the pastry very thinly to a neat rectangle.
Chop the mushrooms finely, and blend with the butter and seasoning to form an almost paste-like
consistency. Spread this over the center of the
pastry, leaving the ends uncovered. Put the piece
of steak on top, season lightly and wrap it up in the
pastry dough. Tuck in the ends and seal the edges
with water. Put onto a lightly greased baking sheet.
If you like steak rare, allow 20–25 minutes in a
preheated 400°F. oven, then lower the heat to 350°F.
and cook for a further 20 minutes. If you like it
medium, when the heat is lowered to 350°F. allow
30–40 minutes. If you like it well done, allow a good
40 minutes at 350°F. Serve with Mushroom sauce or
Brown sauce (see page 183). This is often known as
Boeuf en croute.   *Serves 4*

Lamb pies

Cooking time   *$1\frac{1}{2}$ hours*
Oven temperature   *375°F.*
                      then 300°F.

$\frac{1}{2}$ lb. lamb · 1 small onion, finely chopped
1 tablespoon bacon drippings
1 tablespoon parsley · 1 tablespoon thick gravy
1 tablespoon tomato ketchup · seasoning
1 recipe short crust pastry (see page 215)
little beaten egg.

Grind the lamb, and sauté the onion in the melted
drippings. Add to the lamb, parsley, gravy, and
ketchup and season well. Line muffin pans with
circles of pastry and moisten the edges. Fill with
the lamb mixture, and cover with a second circle of
pastry. Seal, crimp the edges, and make a small slit
in the top to allow steam to escape. Decorate with
pastry leaves, if desired, and brush with beaten egg.
Bake in a preheated 375°F. oven for 25 minutes,
reduce heat to 300°F. and bake for a further 1 hour.
If desired, this recipe may be made using cooked
lamb, in which case the cooking time is 25 minutes
in a 375°F. oven.   *Serves 4*

Lamb and celery pasty

Cooking time   *45 minutes*
Oven temperature   *400°F.*

1 recipe short crust pastry (see page 215)
$\frac{3}{4}$ lb. cooked lamb · 1 ($10\frac{1}{2}$ oz.) can cream of celery
soup. TO GLAZE: little milk.

Make the pastry, halve, and roll each half into an
8-inch circle. Put one piece of pastry into a pie pan
or ovenproof dish, cover with the diced or ground
lamb and half the soup. Place the second pastry
circle on top, seal and neaten the edges; decorate
with a rose and leaves of pastry and brush with
milk. Bake in a preheated 400°F. oven for 45 minutes
and serve with the remaining heated soup as a sauce.
     Serves 4

Mutton pie

Cooking time   *2 hours*
Oven temperature   *475°F.*
                      then 350°F.

8 small mutton *or* lamb rib chops · 8 small onions
$\frac{1}{4}$ cup fat · $\frac{1}{4}$ cup all-purpose flour · $1\frac{3}{4}$ cups water
seasoning · 8 small tomatoes · few capers
1 recipe flaky *or* short crust pastry (see page 215 or
page 216) · little milk.

Brown the mutton and then the onions in the fat.
Stir in the flour, and cook for a few minutes. Add
the water, bring to a boil, and stir until smooth.
Season well, cover the pan, and simmer 1 hour.
Remove onions and mutton from the stock. Arrange
in a 9-inch pie pan, so that all the bones are standing
upright in the center of the dish. Put in the tomatoes,
capers, and some of the gravy. Cover with pastry,
allowing bones to pierce this in the center, and
brush with a little milk. Bake in a preheated 475°F.
oven for approximately 45 minutes, then reduce the
heat to 250°F. for 20–25 minutes.   *Serves 4*

Kidney, bacon, and mushroom pie

Cooking time   *55 minutes*
Oven temperature   *450°F. then 375°F.*

$\frac{3}{4}$ lb. lamb kidneys · $\frac{1}{2}$ lb. Canadian-style bacon
2–4 tablespoons fat · 2 cups mushrooms · 1 onion
2 teaspoons all-purpose flour · $\frac{2}{3}$ cup meat stock
seasoning · 1 recipe flaky pastry (see page 216)
little milk.

Peel and halve the kidneys, and cut the bacon into
strips. Sauté in the fat, then put layers of bacon,
kidneys, and sliced mushrooms into a 9-inch pie pan.
Add sliced onion to the fat in the pan, and sauté
until soft. Stir in the flour, and cook for 2–3 minutes.
Add the stock and seasoning, and bring to a boil,
cook until thickened. Pour into the pie pan, top
with pastry, and glaze with the milk. Bake in a
preheated 450°F. oven for 15–20 minutes, then reduce
the heat to 375°F. for the remaining time. Serve with
Mashed or Duchesse potatoes (see page 167), baked
tomatoes, green vegetables or salad. This may also
be served cold with salad.   *Serves 4*

Chicken giblet pie

| Cooking time | 2 hours 10 minutes |
| Oven temperature | 425°F. then 350°F. |

½–¾ lb. chicken giblets (i.e. 2 sets) · water
seasoning · little flour
Double recipe short crust pastry (see page 215)
3–4 hard-cooked eggs · ½ lb. Canadian-style bacon
little milk or beaten egg.

Simmer giblets in water to cover until tender.
Strain off nearly all the stock, reserving about 3
tablespoons. Cut all meat from the neck of the
chicken – chop liver, heart, and kidney finely, and
sprinkle lightly with well-seasoned flour. Roll out
half the pastry and line an 8-inch pie pan with this.
Cover pastry with half the giblet meat, the sliced
hard-cooked eggs, and bacon. Pour stock over this,
and cover with the remaining giblet meat. Roll out
the remaining pastry and place over the top, then
decorate with pastry leaves. Brush with milk or
little beaten egg, and bake in a preheated 425°F.
oven for about 20 minutes, lower heat to 350°F. for a
further 20 minutes. The hard-cooked eggs may be
omitted and replaced by 1–1½ cups sliced mushrooms
or 4 boiled, chopped onions, if desired.   *Serves 4*

GIBLETS FROM DUCK, GOOSE OR TURKEY
Substitute duck giblets for the chicken giblets. The
other ingredients can be the same.

Chicken and bacon pie

| Cooking time | 45 minutes |
| Oven temperature | 400°F. |

2 cups diced cooked chicken · 4 slices Canadian-
style bacon · ¼ cup butter
½–1 cup small mushrooms · ¼ cup all-purpose flour
1¼ cups milk or ⅔ cup milk and ⅔ cup chicken stock
seasoning · 1 recipe short crust pastry (see page
215). TO GLAZE: 1 egg or a little milk.

Dice the chicken into neat pieces, and dice the
bacon. Heat half the butter, and fry the bacon and
mushrooms in this for a few minutes. Heat the
remaining butter, stir in the flour, and cook for
2–3 minutes. Add the milk or milk and stock, then
season. Bring to a boil and cook until thickened.
Add the chicken, bacon, and mushrooms. Put into
an 8-inch pie pan – cover with the short crust pastry,
brush with egg or milk, and bake in a preheated
400°F. oven for approximately 30 minutes. Illustrated
on page 126.   *Serves 4*

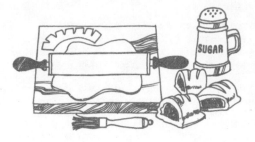

Sausage rolls

| Cooking time | 15–20 minutes |
| Oven temperature | 450°F. |

1 recipe rough puff or flaky or puff pastry (see page
216) · ½ lb. sausage meat.
TO GLAZE: 1 egg · 1 teaspoon water.

Roll the pastry into a long strip, then roll the
sausage meat into a long thin strip on a floured
board. Place the sausage meat onto the pastry,
brush the edges with water, fold over, seal, and flute
these together. Cut the roll into 12 medium or 16–18
small pieces. Put these onto an ungreased baking
sheet and make 2 or 3 slits on top of each roll with a
sharp knife or kitchen scissors to allow the steam
to escape when baking. Beat the egg and water
together, and brush over the rolls. Bake in a preheated 450°F. oven for 15–20 minutes. Look at the
sausage rolls after 10 minutes and if they appear to
be browning rather quickly, lower the heat to 375°F.
to finish cooking. It is important that the sausage
meat is well cooked without overbrowning the
pastry. Lift the sausage rolls onto a wire cooling
rack with a spatula.
     Makes 12 medium or 16–18 small sausage rolls.

Sweetbread vol-au-vents

| Cooking time | 20 minutes |
| Oven temperature | 450°F. |

¾ lb. veal sweetbreads
1 recipe puff pastry (see page 217) · 1 egg
¼ cup fine fresh breadcrumbs · 1½ cups raw mushrooms, finely chopped · 1 tablespoon capers
⅔ cup thick white sauce (see page 183). TO FRY: fat.
TO GARNISH: slices of mushroom.

First blanch the sweetbreads (see page 90). Roll out
the pastry to ¼-inch thick. Cut out four 4-inch patty
shells (bouchées or vol-au-vent cases). Brush the
tops with a little egg, and bake in a preheated
450°F. oven for 20 minutes, or until golden and crisp.
Coat the sweetbreads in egg and bread crumbs, and
fry until crisp and tender. Meanwhile add the
mushrooms and capers to the sauce and simmer for
7 minutes. Arrange the pastry cases on individual
plates, pile in the sweetbreads and top with the
sauce. Garnish with slices of mushroom. Serve with
creamed spinach and potatoes.   *Serves 4*

Cheese pudding, page 211; Cheese soufflé, page 207; Cheese and shrimp flan, page 330; Welsh rabbit, page 30

Fresh vegetables, pages 160–167

151

Scotch orange salad, page 170; Sausage salad, page 331

Savory ham rolls, page 171; and mixed salad, page 168

Hors d'oeuvres with eggs, page 23; Rabbit loaf, page 142; Pineapple fruit salad, page 330

Stuffed baked potatoes, pages 167 and 330

Potato cakes with scrambled eggs, page 321

Turkey vol-au-vent

Cooking time   *35 minutes*
Oven temperature   *475°F. then 400°F.*

1 cup mushrooms · 2 tablespoons butter
¼ cup all-purpose flour · 1¼ cups poultry stock *or*
milk · seasoning · 1 recipe puff pastry (see page
217) · 1 cup diced turkey pieces from carcase and
wings. TO GLAZE: little beaten egg.

Wash and slice the mushrooms. Melt the butter in a
saucepan, and add the flour. Pour in the stock or
milk, bring to a boil, and stir until the sauce is
thick, then season. Add the pieces of turkey and the
mushrooms, and heat gently for 5 minutes. Meanwhile, roll out the pastry and cut into a large circle.
With a small cutter or saucer, press a circle into the
middle of the pastry. Glaze the top and sides with a
little beaten egg. Bake in a preheated 475°F. oven
for 10 minutes, then lower the heat to 400°F. for
10–12 minutes. Carefully cut off the lid of the vol-au-
vent and remove the dough. Return the pastry shell
and the lid to the oven to dry out for 5–8 minutes.
Fill the shell with the hot turkey mixture, and
replace the lid. Serve immediately.   *Serves 4*

TO MAKE RAISED PIES

The reason these are called raised pies is because the
pastry can be moulded with the hands, rather than
putting it into a bowl or mold, (see Raised pork pie
below). This pastry is very easy to handle, provided
it is kept warm. The usual fillings for this kind of
pie are pork, or veal and ham; the chicken and ham
pie on the next page may also be made with hot
water crust pastry. Although some people enjoy this
pastry when it is hot, raised pies are generally
served cold. See picture page 128.

Raised pork pie

Cooking time   *2½ hours*
Oven temperature   *350°F.*

1 recipe raised pastry (see page 331)
5 bacon slices · 1½ lb. pork tenderloin
salt · pepper · ginger · 1 egg
1 pig's foot · ½ onion
4 black peppercorns · 1 bay leaf · 5 cups water.

Make the pastry and shape it into a pie with your
hands. Be sure to leave about one-third of the pastry
for the lid. You can mold the pie around a suitable
can or saucepan which must be greased slightly.

Alternatively if using an ovenproof casserole, cut
2 circles of pastry for the top and bottom, the same
diameter as the casserole, and a strip the circumference of the dish. Line the pastry with the bacon.
Dice the pork and sprinkle with salt, pepper, and
ginger, and fill the pie. Add 3 tablespoons of water.
Turn the sides of the pie inward, and place on the
lid. Decorate as wished, but there must be a central
vent left for the pie jelly to be poured in after the
pie has cooked. This is traditionally camouflaged
with a 'rose' made of pastry. Brush over with beaten
egg and bake in a preheated 350°F. oven for about
2½ hours. Let stand until cool, meanwhile place pig's
foot, onion, peppercorns, and bay leaf in the water
and simmer uncovered for 1½ hours. Reduce the water
to ¾ cup in this way. Strain and let stand until cool.
This is the pie jelly. Just before it sets, pour it into
the cold pie a little at a time. When the pie is full
put in the refrigerator until required. Illustrated on
page 128.   *Serves 4–5*

Veal and ham pie

Cooking time   *2¼ hours*
Oven temperature   *375°F.*

1 recipe raised pastry (see page 331)
1 lb. veal tenderloin · ½ lb. ham · seasoning
¼ teaspoon grated lemon peel · 1–2 hard-cooked
eggs · ⅔ cup water *or* bone stock · 1 egg
1 teaspoon unflavored gelatin
½ teaspoon gravy flavoring.

Make the pastry and keep warm in a bowl until
ready to use. Remove pastry from bowl and with
two-thirds of the dough line a 9-inch by 5-inch loaf
pan. Wash and dry the veal and ham, removing any
skin and cut into 1 inch cubes. Roll the meat in
seasoning and lemon peel. Place half the meat in
the bottom of the pastry lined pan. Cut each egg in
half. Place on top of the meat and cover with the
remaining meat. Pour into the pie ¼ cup of the water
or stock. Turn the top edges of the pastry lining in,
over the meat, and moisten it all around. Roll out
the remaining one-third of pastry to make a lid.
Press down well all around the edges and cut at
¼-inch intervals with a sharp knife to seal. Make a
hole in the center, brush with beaten egg, decorate
with pastry leaves, and brush with beaten egg once
again. Bake in a preheated 375°F. oven for 2–2¼
hours. Let stand until cool. Melt the gelatin in
remaining water or stock, and stir in the meat
extract. When the pie is cool and the gelatin mixture
just setting, pour into the pie through the hole in
the center. Let set completely before serving.

Serves 4–5

Chicken and ham pie

Cooking time   *Approximately 1½ hours*
Oven temperature   *400°F.*

1 small cooked stewing fowl *or* ½ larger fowl
1 bay leaf · seasoning · dash mixed herbs (sage,
parsley, thyme, rosemary, and bay leaves)
¼ lb. Canadian-style bacon *or* cooked ham
1 recipe short crust pastry (see page 215)
⅓ cup chicken stock *or* 2 tablespoons milk *or* beaten
egg and milk.
FOR THE PIE JELLY: 1 teaspoon unflavored gelatin
¼ cup chicken stock.

Cut all the bones away from the chicken, and simmer
them with the bay leaf, seasoning, and herbs. Meanwhile, dice the chicken and bacon and mix together.
Roll out the pastry and line the bottom and sides of
a 3-pint ovenproof casserole, fill with the chicken
mixture and the stock. Make a circle of pastry to
cover the filling. Lay this on top, and seal the edges
firmly. Do not press the top pastry down too hard,
since there must be room to pour in the jellied stock
after cooking. Make a slit in the center of the top
pastry and use any remaining pastry left to form
leaves, a rose, or a tassel. Brush with the milk or
beaten egg and milk to glaze. Bake in a preheated
400°F. oven for about 1¼–1½ hours. If the pie is becoming too brown reduce the heat slightly. Let stand
until cool before removing from the casserole. When
the pie is cool, fill with jellied stock. To make this,
dissolve the gelatin in the chicken stock and pour
through slit in top of pie. Make a wax paper funnel
for easy pouring.   *Serves 4*

MEAT PUDDINGS

A meat pudding is an ideal dish in cold weather. It
has the great advantage that it may be left untended,
except for filling up the water in the pan or steamer.
If a steamer, i.e. a container with holes at the
bottom over a pan of water is not available, stand
the ovenproof bowl on a small pan or pastry cutter
in a saucepan half filled with water. A string handle
enables the basin to be lifted out easily and safely.
Tie string round top of bowl; form a double loop of
string, and twist string over this for added support.
A strong band of foil under the bowl also helps to lift
it out.

FOR A PERFECT PUDDING:
1. Line the bowl with the suet crust pastry – there
are two ways in which this can be done:
a) form all the pastry into a large circle, rolling
this out thinly. Cut out one-quarter of the dough
in a wedge shape – put to one side for the lid. Lower
the remaining dough into the bowl, seal the edges
together.
b) insert the complete circle of pastry into the
bowl, and pull gently until it forms an even layer.
Trim away the surplus pastry to use as the lid.
2. Do not overfill the bowl with meat, otherwise
some of the juice will boil out in cooking.
3. Cover the pudding – lay the circle of pastry on
top of the meat, moisten, and seal edges and press
together.
4. Grease a piece of wax paper and lay over the
pudding, making a pleat across the center so that

the pastry may rise. Cover with more wax paper or
foil or a cloth.
5. Put over boiling water and cook as given in the
recipe for Steak and kidney pudding.

Rabbit and mushroom Pudding

Cooking time   *3 hours*

1 recipe suet crust pastry (see page 217) · 1 rabbit
seasoning · ¼ cup all-purpose flour
4 slices Canadian-style bacon · 1 cup mushrooms
2 small onions · 1 teaspoon sage · water.

Make the suet crust pastry. Cut the rabbit into
neat pieces, and coat with well-seasoned flour. Chop
the bacon, mushrooms, and onions. Line a greased
ovenproof bowl with some of the pastry, and roll
out the remaining pastry to form a lid. Fill the pastry
with the rabbit, bacon, mushrooms, onions, sage,
and enough water to cover the meat. Moisten the
edges and press the lid onto the pudding. Cover with
greased wax paper and foil. Steam for 3 hours.
      Serves 4

Steak and kidney pudding

Cooking time   *4 hours*

1½ lb. stewing beef
2 lamb kidneys *or* ½ lb. beef kidney
1 tablespoon all-purpose flour · seasoning
approximately ⅔ cup water *or* meat stock
1 recipe suet crust pastry (see page 217).

Trim the beef, and cut into thin strips. Cut the
kidney into small pieces. Either place a piece of
kidney on each strip of steak and roll firmly, or mix
the kidney and steak together. Put the flour and
seasoning onto a plate, and toss the meat in this
until well coated. Use one of the two methods of
lining a bowl with pastry (see previous column).
When the bowl is lined, put in the meat and enough
water or stock to come two-thirds of the way up the
bowl. Do not fill to the top or the liquid will boil
out. Roll out the pastry for the lid, and put this over
the filled pudding. Cover with either greased wax
paper or foil or a cloth dipped in boiling water and
floured. Fix firmly round the top of the bowl. Put
the pudding into a steamer; stand this over a saucepan of boiling water, making sure that it is balanced
steadily. Steam for 4 hours. Allow the water to boil
rapidly for the first 2 hours; add more boiling water
when necessary. Serve with thickened gravy or pour
vegetable stock into the pudding, after cutting, to
give it extra gravy. Illustrated on page 83.
      Serves 4–6

SMALL STEAK AND KIDNEY PUDDINGS

As a large pudding takes a long time to cook, you may prefer to make small ones. Use old coffee cups, mugs, or custard cups. A pudding sufficient for 1 person needs approximately 2 hours steaming.

Sea pie

Cooking time   *about 2 hours 30 minutes*

2 tablespoons fat · 2 onions · ½–1 lb. stewing beef · 3 tablespoons all-purpose flour
seasoning · 2½ cups stock or water and a beef bouillon cube · 4–6 carrots · 1 turnip
1 recipe suet crust pastry (see page 217).

Heat fat in a saucepan and sauté chopped onions for a few minutes. Cut beef into neat pieces and coat in seasoned flour, then cook in the fat for a few minutes. Gradually add stock. Bring to a boil, add diced carrots and turnip with extra seasoning if required. Simmer gently for approximately 2 hours. Make the pastry. Roll into a circle the size of the meat mixture, and place on top of the meat mixture, first making sure there is plenty of liquid in pan. If the cover is deep enough to let pastry rise without sticking to it, put on, otherwise leave uncovered. Cook steadily for approximately 30 minutes.   *Serves 4*

EMERGENCY PIES

A pie takes a long time to make and it cannot, therefore, be called an 'emergency' dish. However, purchased pies may be made more interesting by a selection of colorful vegetables arranged around them. The following gives two ways in which a topping may be put on meat as a quick 'pie'.

Meat cobbler

Cooking time   *20–25 minutes*
Oven temperature   *425°F.*

Large can beef stew. FOR THE COBBLER: 1½ cups all-purpose flour · 2¼ teaspoons baking powder
¼ teaspoon salt · dash pepper · 2 tablespoons butter or margarine · milk to mix.

Put the beef stew into an ovenproof dish, and heat for about 4 minutes. Sift the flour together with the baking powder, salt, and pepper, rub in the butter or margarine, then bind to a soft rolling consistency with the milk. Roll out, and cut into a neat circle. Arrange on top of the meat and bake in a preheated 425°F. oven for 15–20 minutes.   *Serves 4*

Beef and vegetable crumble

Cooking time   *30 minutes*
Oven temperature   *375°F.*

Large can of beef stew with vegetables
1 cup all-purpose flour · dash salt
3 tablespoons butter or margarine
¼ cup finely grated cheese.

Put the meat into an ovenproof dish. Sift flour and salt, rub in butter or margarine, and add cheese. Press over top of meat and bake in a preheated 375°F. oven for approximately 30 minutes.   *Serves 4*

PIES AND PUDDINGS TO IMPRESS

Most of the pies and puddings in this section may be served for a rather special occasion, with perhaps rather luxurious additions. For example the steak and kidney pudding could have oysters added, or the chicken pies, asparagus and mushrooms. The following, however, are excellent for party occasions.

Ham and mushroom pudding

Cooking time   *2½–3 hours*

1¼ lb. smoked ham center slice · 2 medium onions
2 cups small mushrooms · 4 tomatoes
seasoning · dash mixed herbs (sage, parsley, thyme, rosemary, and bay leaves) · 1 recipe suet crust pastry (see page 217).

If the ham is fairly salty, soak overnight in water to cover. This is most important since the flavor will be very concentrated in the pudding. Dice the ham neatly, and blend with the sliced onions and mushrooms, the peeled and sliced tomatoes, seasoning, and mixed herbs. Line an ovenproof bowl with part of the suet crust pastry, put in the ham mixture, half fill with water, cover with the suet crust lid and greased wax paper or foil (see page 158) and steam for 2½–3 hours.

     Serves 4–5

Chicken and asparagus pie

Cooking time   *1 hour 20 minutes*
Oven temperature   *450°F. then 350°F.*

1 young chicken, approximately 3 lb.
2 small onions · ¼ cup butter · ½ cup all-purpose flour · 1⅓ cups milk · ⅔ cup coffee or whipping cream · seasoning · 1 (14 oz.) can asparagus or small quantity cooked asparagus
1 recipe flaky or rough puff pastry (see page 216)
TO GLAZE: milk or egg.

Cut the uncooked meat away from the bones of the chicken – these bones may be the basis for an excellent stock. Sauté the sliced onions in the butter, stir in the flour, cook for 2–3 minutes, add the milk and cream and make into a smooth sauce. Season well and blend with diced chicken, and asparagus; if using canned asparagus a little of the liquid in the can may be added to the sauce. Put into a 9-inch pie pan, top with pastry, decorate with pastry leaves, and glaze (see page 145). Bake in a preheated 450°F. oven for 20 minutes, then lower the heat to 375°F. and bake for a further 45 minutes to 1 hour. Cover the pastry with foil if it appears to be browning too much.   *Serves 4–6*

VEGETABLES

Wise choice of vegetables

There is a selection of vegetables in season throughout the year, so try to make the best use of these. Choose frozen or canned vegetables when the fresh produce is not available or when you wish to save time . . . it is very pleasant to be able to enjoy frozen or canned garden peas in the middle of winter

Ways to serve vegetables

Serve vegetables as soon as possible after they are cooked. Serve young vegetables or vegetable dishes as a separate course, so their flavor may be fully appreciated.

To use leftover vegetables

Leftover vegetable water should not be discarded, since it contains vitamins and mineral salts. Use it to make gravy or to add to soups or sauces, or add a bouillon cube to the hot liquid and drink this. Leftover vegetables may be added to salads or fried (see page 165).

Easy remedies when things are wrong

PROBLEM – if vegetables lack flavor it is often because they are overcooked. It may be because too large pieces of the vegetable were cooked . . . shred green vegetables finely; cauliflower may be cooked whole, but it cooks in a shorter time (and therefore retains more flavor) if it is cut into pieces. There is no remedy if the vegetables are tasteless, except to try and give them extra flavor with melted butter, chopped chives, or coat them with a sauce.

Buying vegetables

Green vegetables are fresh when they are firm and crisp. A cabbage should feel firm and have a good heart, except in the case of beet greens or turnip greens when there is little heart. Spinach should be bright green and dry. Yellow-looking leaves or a slightly damp texture in the case of spinach indicates a stale vegetable.
Root vegetables should be firm and with as few marks as possible.
If buying ready-washed vegetables, care must be taken to use them quickly, for they deteriorate more quickly than vegetables which still have soil on them.

Canned vegetables

These are cooked in the process of canning, so need heating only. When the can has been opened, however, the vegetables must be used quickly, since they are then as perishable as ordinary cooked vegetables.

Dried vegetables

Dried vegetables may be one of two types – the ordinary dried vegetables which need soaking in cold water for some hours, or better still overnight, before cooking; or the more modern A.F.D. (accelerated freeze dried) type, which should be cooked as the directions on the packet, i.e. in quite a short time, without soaking.

Frozen vegetables

There is an excellent selection of these available. Buy carefully. Store and cook as recommended by the manufacturer. Do not refreeze after thawing. Do not allow frozen vegetables to remain for too long a period at room temperature before cooking. When once the vegetables have been cooked they are then as perishable as ordinary cooked vegetables.

To store vegetables

Fresh vegetables need to be stored in a cool place, but where they cannot be affected by frost if the weather is exceptionally cold. Spread out the vegetables to allow good air circulation – a vegetable rack is ideal.
Frozen vegetables should be stored in the freezing compartment of the refrigerator – follow the frozen food and refrigerator manufacturers' recommendations about length of storage; or they may be stored in a home freezer.

VEGETABLES

Where vegetables are imported, it is difficult to give the time of year available since they come from so many different parts of the world.

VEGETABLE, SEASON, AND SERVING	TO PREPARE	TO COOK
ARTICHOKES, GLOBE September to May Allow 1 per person	Wash, cut away stem to the level of the leaves, discard outer or discolored leaves	Cook in boiling salted water for 30 minutes. Serve with melted butter, white or cheese sauce
ARTICHOKES, JERUSALEM November to January Allow 1½ lb. to serve 4	Scrub, peel or scrape. Soak in cold water, add a few drops lemon juice to prevent discoloration	Cook for about 30 minutes in boiling salted water, serve with melted butter, white or cheese sauce
ASPARAGUS February to June Allow 1½ lb. to serve 4	Wash carefully, then break off tough thick stalk	Either steam or boil the tied bunch upright in salted water in a tall pan for 20–25 minutes, serve with melted butter
BEANS, Green and Wax Available all year Allow 1 lb. to serve 4	Wash and remove ends. Beans may be left whole, thinly sliced lengthwise, or cut into 1-inch crosswise pieces	Cook steadily in boiling salted water for about 15 minutes
BEANS, LIMA July to November Allow 3 lb. unshelled to serve 4	Wash and shell just before cooking. Cut pod open with a sharp knife or scissors	Cook steadily in boiling salted water for about 20 minutes
BEETS Available all year	Cut off tops, leaving 2 inches remaining, wash well, and leave whole	Cook in boiling salted water about 35 minutes, or until soft, test by pressing gently. Cool and serve sliced or diced; or serve with parsley sauce
BROCCOLI Available all year Allow 1½ lb. to serve 4	Wash well, remove any withered leaves	Cook large broccoli heads and sprouting broccoli like CAULIFLOWER, serve with melted butter or white sauce. Cook broccoli spears as ASPARAGUS to retain the firmness of the stems, serve with melted butter (see page 23)
BRUSSELS SPROUTS November to January Allow 1½ lb. to serve 4	Remove outer withered leaves, wash in cold water with dash salt to remove any small insects, mark a cross with a sharp knife at bottom of each sprout	Boil rapidly in salted water for about 10 minutes
CABBAGE – RED, GREEN or SAVOY Available all year Allow 1½ lb. (1 head) to serve 4	Remove any withered leaves, wash, shred finely with sharp knife	Boil rapidly in only a little salted water for about 10 minutes, or cook in the water which clings to the washed leaves, or serve raw in salads. A little lemon juice or few drops of vinegar added helps to retain color in red cabbage
CARROTS Available all year Allow 1¼ lb. to serve 4	Wash well, peel or scrape; leave whole if small, slice if large	Cook in boiling salted water for 25–30 minutes
CAULIFLOWER Available all year Allow 2 lb. (1 head) to serve 4	Cut off thick stalk and outer leaves. Cook whole, or divide into flowerets	Cook whole cauliflower in boiling salted water for 15–20 minutes, flowerets for about 10 minutes
CELERIAC (Celery root) October to April Allow 1½ lb. to serve 4	Cut off leaves and tough fibers. Wash and peel	Cook as CELERY or boil whole for 40–50 minutes. Serve in salads

VEGETABLE, SEASON, AND SERVING	TO PREPARE	TO COOK
CELERY Available all year Allow 1 bunch to serve 4	Generally eaten raw and in salads. Wash thoroughly, remove any coarse strings, serve in sticks or chopped	Wash, divide into 1-inch pieces, cook in boiling salted water for about 20 minutes, serve with white, parsley, or cheese sauce. May also be braised
CHARD OR SWISS CHARD or SEAKALE Available all year Allow 2 lb. to serve 4	Wash, trim as necessary	Cook as CELERY
CHICORY Available all year Allow 2 lb. to serve 4	Wash several times, remove damaged leaves, drain, serve in salads	Cook as LETTUCE
CORN ON THE COB May to October	Refrigerate unhusked. Husk and remove silks when ready to use	Boil in salted water for about 3–4 minutes – to prevent toughness, do not boil too quickly or for too long Serve with melted butter
EGGPLANTS Available all year allow 1½ lb. to serve 4	Wash and remove any hard stalk. Score and salt skin, let stand for 20 minutes – to give milder flavor	Bake in casserole with knob of margarine and little milk for 30 minutes. May be stuffed or fried like potatoes. Cook for about 6–8 minutes in boiling salted water
GARLIC Available throughout the year	Use very sparingly for flavor. A 'clove' is one small portion	
GREENS Available all year Allow 2 lb. to serve 4 Collards, Beet Tops, Escardle, Kale, Mustard Greens, Turnip Greens	Wash several times, remove damaged leaves, and drain	Cook only in the water clinging to the leaves for about 3–10 minutes, or until soft
KOHLRABI June to October Allow 1 medium per person	Remove leaves, pare and cube or slice	Boil in salted water for about 25 minutes, or until tender
LEEKS Available all year Allow 2 lb. to serve 4	Cut off roots and outer leaves. Split down the middle and wash very thoroughly	Boil for 30 minutes in salted water, serve with white or cheese sauce. Use instead of onions in soups or stews
LETTUCE Available all year Allow 2 lb. to serve 4 Iceberg, Boston, Bibb, Leaf, Romaine	Normally served in salads. Pull apart, wash several times, drain, shred with fingers	May be cooked like cabbage or in a little butter in covered pan for 15–20 minutes, or until soft; or may be braised
MUSHROOMS Available all year Allow 1 lb. to serve 4	Wash or wipe, trim stem end. If large, peel, remove stems and cook separately. Cook small button mushrooms whole	Fry or broil in butter, bake in a covered casserole for about 30 minutes, or stew in milk and thicken liquid with a little flour
OKRA June to November Allow 1 lb. to serve 4	Wash, remove stems and leave small pods whole, cut large ones into ½-inch slices	Boil in salted water for about 10 minutes, or until tender
ONIONS Available all year Allow 1½ lb. to serve 4	Peel under cold running water and slice; or leave whole if cooking as a separate vegetable	Put in soups or stews; fry with meat or savory dishes. Boil whole onions for 1 hour in salted water or sliced onions 10–15 minutes, and serve with white sauce

VEGETABLE, SEASON, AND SERVING	TO PREPARE	TO COOK
PARSNIPS Available all year Allow 1½ lb. (6 medium) to serve 4	Wash, scrape or pare, leave whole, slice, quarter, or cut into strips	Boil in salted water for about 30 minutes. Put in soups or stews, but do not have too many, as flavor is strong. Very good baked around meat
PEAS September to June Allow 3 lb. to serve 4	Shell and wash just before ready to cook	Cook steadily in boiling water for 10–15 minutes. Serve with melted butter. Add sprig of mint and teaspoon of sugar when cooking to improve flavor
SWEET RED OR GREEN PEPPERS April to December Allow 1 per person	Remove stems, membranes, and seeds, wash. Keep whole if stuffing, or shred, or cut into slices	Eat raw with salad; fry about 3–5 minutes; add to sauces, egg dishes, casseroles. Stuff as a main dish and bake, may be parboiled previously
POTATOES, NEW May to August Allow 1½ lb. (10–12 small) to serve 4	Wash and leave whole	Boil in salted water for about 20 minutes, or until tender
POTATOES Available all year Allow 2 lb. (6 medium) to serve 4	To boil: peel thinly or scrape. Wash, cut into large pieces, if necessary. To bake: wash thoroughly, grease skin, if desired, prick skin	Put in boiling salted water and cook for 20–25 minutes. Bake in a preheated 375°F. oven for approximately 1 hour. May also be fried, roasted, or steamed
RUTABAGAS October to April Allow 2 medium to serve 4	Wash and pare thinly. Cut into pieces or small cubes	Boil in salted water for about 30 minutes for pieces or 20 minutes for cube, or until tender
SAUERKRAUT Imported	Made by fermenting cabbage. Can be obtained ready-prepared	Heat with butter and flavorings (see page 322)
SCALLIONS Available all year Allow 2 bunches to serve 4	Wash and remove any loose skin	Boil in salted water for about 8–10 minutes, or until barely tender
SPINACH Available all year Allow 2 lb. to serve 4	As GREENS, wash several times, remove damaged leaves, drain	As GREENS, or put into a heavy pan with a little salt and boil rapidly for about 15 minutes. Turn onto a board and chop finely, then return to the pan with a little milk and butter and reheat
SQUASH, SUMMER Available all year Allow 2 lb. to serve 4 Zucchini – dark green Chayote – light green Straightneck – yellow Crookneck – yellow Pattypan – white Scalloped – white	Wash, remove blossom and stem ends, cut into neat pieces but do not pare	Boil in salted water for about 10–15 minutes, or until tender
SQUASH, WINTER October to February Allow 3 lb. to serve 4 Acorn – small Banana – large Buttercup – large Butternut – small Hubbard – large	Small: cut in half, remove fibers and seeds Large: cut into pieces, remove fibers and seeds	Boil in salted water for about 15–20 minutes, or until tender, drain Bake in a preheated 400°F. oven for about 25–30 minutes, or until tender

VEGETABLE, SEASON, AND SERVING	TO PREPARE	TO COOK
SWEET POTATOES OR YAMS Available all year Allow 6 medium to serve 4	Wash but do not pare	Cook in boiling salted water for about 30–35 minutes, or until tender. Chestnut flavor excellent roasted
TOMATOES Available all year, best from summer to fall Allow 6 medium to serve 4	Wash; slice or use whole. Delicious raw. Put into boiling water for 1 minute to remove skin	Cook covered for about 8–10 minutes, or until tender without adding water. May also be baked, broiled, roasted
TURNIPS Available all year Allow 6 medium to serve 4	Scrape or pare, wash, leave whole, dice or slice if desired	Put into soups and stews. When young they are very good cooked in boiling salted water for 25–30 minutes, until tender, then mashed

LEGUME, SEASON, AND SERVING	TO PREPARE	TO COOK
BEANS, NAVY or KIDNEY Available all year	Generally purchased dried. Soak overnight in cold water	Drain, cover with cold salted water, simmer gently for 2–3 hours. Drain, toss in butter and chopped parsley or serve with white sauce
LENTILS Available all year	Soak overnight in water	Put into pan with water, add salt, simmer gently until tender
PEAS, DRIED	Prepare and cook as NAVY BEANS	

BASIC WAYS OF COOKING VEGETABLES

A simple method of cooking vegetables often retains the maximum of flavor.

To cook in water

Cooking time   *See tables*

Use the minimum quantity of water. In the case of green vegetables this means about ½–1 inch only in the pan. In the case of root vegetables you will need enough to cover. Bring the water to a boil, add salt to taste – remember with a small quantity of water you do not need as much salt. Prepare the vegetables as given in the table, then add them gradually to the boiling water; in this way one is certain the water always keeps boiling. When all the vegetables have been put into the pan, cover tightly, and cook for as short a time as possible. Naturally, it depends upon personal taste as to how well-cooked one likes vegetables, but the more lightly cooked they are the more they retain flavor and vitamins.

Potatoes are excellent if cooked in their skins and peeled afterward.

Drain the vegetables when tender, and toss in a knob of butter or margarine. Serve at once.

To steam vegetables

Put vegetables into a steamer over a pan of boiling water, season lightly, cover the steamer, and cook for the shortest time possible. This method is not suitable for green vegetables, but very good for root vegetables.

To cook in butter

Young peas, beans, diced carrots, etc., may be cooked in butter or margarine. Prepare as in the table. Put into a pan with a generous amount of butter or margarine (¼ cup for each 1 lb. of prepared vegetables). Season lightly, cover tightly and cook steadily, shaking the pan occasionally to prevent the vegetables burning. If desired, 3–4 tablespoons liquid (white stock or water) may be added to prevent any possibility of this happening.

To braise

This method means the vegetables are served in a rich brown sauce (see page 166 under Braised celery). Other vegetables may be cooked in this way.

To fry vegetables

The method depends on the type of vegetable.

TO FRY POTATOES

Prepare these by peeling (new potatoes may be peeled and fried whole or fried in their skins). Cut into the required shape; some popular ones are . . .

CHIPPED POTATOES: Cut into wafer-thin slices such as for Game chips. (See page 140).

SLICED POTATOES: (often called French fried when cooked): Cut into strips about ¼ inch thick.

MATCHSTICKS: Cut into matchstick thin pieces.

RIBBON: Peel the potato pulp in such a way as to give long thin ribbons such as obtained from peeling an apple into a long spiral strip.

SOUFFLÉ POTATOES: See below. Dry the potatoes and keep covered until ready to fry.

TO SHALLOW FRY

Heat enough fat or oil in a pan to give a depth of about ¼–½ inch, put in the potatoes, and fry until golden, turn as you cook. Chipped potatoes and sliced potatoes are better if fried twice, so remove from the pan, reheat fat, and fry for a second time, drain on paper towels. This method takes 4–6 minutes.

TO DEEP FRY

Heat the fat or oil in a pan or deep fat fryer to 375°F. – do not have it too hot, since the potatoes should cook steadily for the first time. A cube of day-old bread should take at least 1 minute to turn pale golden if using fat, a slightly shorter time with oil. Put in the potatoes and fry steadily until tender. Remove and reheat until very hot (bread should brown in ¼ minute with fat, about 20 seconds with oil). Put in the potatoes, and fry for about 1 minute, or until crisp and golden brown. Drain on paper towels. The thinner potatoes and game chips need one frying only. This method takes 3–4 minutes. For soufflé potatoes, one needs deep fat and a slightly 'waxy', not a 'floury' type of potato. Give a first frying as above but let potatoes become quite cold after this. Reheat the fat, put in the potato slices, and fry until golden – they will puff up like a soufflé.

TO FRY ONIONS

Peel and slice the onions into rings. Dry well on paper towels.

FOR SOFT ONION RINGS

Choose shallow fat (see potatoes) and fry gently until tender. This method takes about 8 minutes.

FOR CRISP ONION RINGS

Separate the rings and dip in milk, then toss in well-seasoned flour. Choose deep fat – (see potatoes). This method take about 5 minutes.

OTHER VEGETABLES THAT ARE EXCELLENT FRIED:

CARROTS: Only when young – slice, fry in shallow fat . . . 6–8 minutes.
CUCUMBER: Slice; if using shallow fat, do not coat, if using deep fat, coat . . . 4–6 minutes.
EGG PLANTS: Slice, coat in seasoned flour, use deep or shallow fat . . . 4–6 minutes.
LEEKS: As onions – wash well and cut into rings . . . 5–8 minutes.

SWEET PEPPERS: Cut into rings, discarding seeds and core. Do not coat, fry steadily in shallow fat . . . 5–8 minutes.
SWEET POTATOES: As ordinary potatoes.

To roast vegetables

Cooking time   *Approximately 1 hour*
Oven temperature   *425°F.*

Heat about ¼ cup fat in a pan, unless roasting around the meat. Prepare the vegetables (see the table), roll around in the fat until evenly coated, and roast in a preheated 425°F. oven for approximately 1 hour. Potatoes and parsnips are more 'floury', if parboiled for approximately 10–20 minutes before roasting.

Eggplant and tomato bake

Cooking time   *1 hour*
Oven temperature   *375°F.*
2 medium eggplants · 4 medium ripe tomatoes seasoning · 3 tablespoons oil
3 tablespoons parsley.

Cut the eggplant into thin slices. Peel and slice the tomatoes. Season the eggplants well, and let stand for a short time before cooking, this tends to remove the slightly bitter flavor from the skin. Sauté the eggplants in the hot oil for 3–4 minutes until evenly coated. Put a layer of seasoned tomatoes and chopped parsley in a small ovenproof casserole, top with a layer of eggplants and a final layer of tomatoes. Cover tightly. Bake in a preheated 375°F. oven for approximately 55 minutes.   *Serves 4*

Bean loaf

Cooking time   *1 hour*
Oven temperature   *350°F.*

1 (16 oz.) can baked beans
1 cup fine fresh bread crumbs · ½ cup chopped walnuts · 1 medium onion · seasoning · 1 egg
1 tablespoon chopped parsley · 3 tablespoons milk
¼ cup butter *or* margarine.
TO GARNISH: tomatoes.

Blend the beans with the bread crumbs, nuts, the very finely chopped onion, seasoning, egg, parsley, milk and half the butter or margarine. Grease a 9-inch by 5-inch loaf pan with the remaining butter or margarine, and put in the mixture. Cover with greased foil, and bake in a preheated 350°F. over for 1 hour. Turn out and garnish with baked tomatoes.   *Serves 4*

Savory beets

Cooking time   *20 minutes*

¼ cup butter *or* margarine · 1 large onion
¼ cup all-purpose flour · ⅔ cup water
3 tablespoons vinegar · 2 teaspoons granulated sugar · 2 large *or* 4 small beets
4 slices bacon · seasoning

Heat the butter or margarine, and sauté the thinly sliced onion for a few minutes. Stir in the flour, and cook for several minutes, then gradually blend in the water, vinegar, and sugar. Bring to a boil and cook until thickened. Remove from the heat, and add the sliced beets. Broil the bacon, chop half the slices and stir into the beet mixture, then add seasoning to taste. Put into a heated dish, and top with the remaining chopped bacon. This is very good with sausages. *Serves 4*

Scalloped cabbage and celery

Cooking time 20–25 minutes

1 small red *or* green cabbage
1 small bunch celery
FOR THE SAUCE: 2 tablespoons butter *or* margarine
¼ cup all-purpose flour · ⅔ cup milk
⅔ cup vegetable stock · ⅔ cup fine fresh bread crumbs · 2 tablespoons butter *or* bacon drippings
seasoning.

Shred the cabbage, and dice the celery. Make a thin white sauce with the butter or margarine, flour, milk, and vegetable stock (from cooking the vegetables). Naturally the stock cannot be added until after the vegetables are cooked but it is a good idea to start the sauce, so the vegetables are not allowed to stand for any length of time.
Sauté the bread crumbs in the hot butter or bacon drippings. Cook the cabbage and celery in boiling salted water in the same pan for about 5 minutes only. Drain, retaining the stock required for the sauce. Blend with the sauce, add the vegetables, season well, put into a shallow flameproof dish, top with the crumbs, and brown under a hot broiler. The crisp texture of the celery blends well with the sauce. *Serves 4–6*

Cauliflower cheese

Cooking time 25–30 minutes

1 cauliflower.
FOR THE SAUCE: 2 tablespoons butter *or* margarine
¼ cup all-purpose flour · seasoning
½ teaspoon prepared mustard · 1¼ cups milk
1–1½ cups* grated Cheddar cheese (optional).
TO GARNISH: chopped parsley · toast.

* use more if desired.

Prepare and cook the whole cauliflower (or separate into cauliflowerets) until just soft – do not overcook. Make a sauce of the butter or margarine, flour, seasoning, and milk or use half milk and half cauliflower stock. Put the cauliflower into a heated serving dish. Stir the cheese into the hot sauce. Coat the cauliflower, and serve at once garnished with the parsley and triangles of hot toast. *Serves 4–5*

Celeriac (celery root) hotpot

Cooking time 1¼ hours
Oven temperature 350°F.
1 large *or* 2 small celeriac (celery root)
¼ cup butter · ⅔ cup coffee cream · seasoning.

Peel and cut the celeriac into ¼-inch slices. Heat the butter with the cream, and season this generously. Put the celeriac into a small ovenproof casserole and top with the butter and cream. Bake in a preheated 350°F. oven for approximately 1¼ hours. This is excellent to accompany meat or fish dishes.
It may be varied by topping the vegetable with grated cheese about 25 minutes before serving.
Serves 4

Braised celery

Cooking time 45 minutes

1 large *or* 2 small bunches celery · 1 large onion
2 large tomatoes · ¼ cup butter *or* margarine
bouquet garni · water · seasoning.

Wash the celery well, remove the outer stalks and chop these finely, but divide the remaining celery into thick neat pieces. Quarter the onion and halve the tomatoes. Sauté the well dried thick pieces of celery in the hot butter or margarine for several minutes. Remove from the pan, and add the onion, tomatoes, chopped celery, and *bouquet garni* (3 bay leaves, 3 sprigs parsley, 1 sprig thyme, tied together), with just enough water to cover. Season this well, and replace the celery in the pan, seasoning lightly. Cover tightly and cook very slowly. Remove the celery from the pan and place on a heated dish, press the vegetable mixture through a sieve to form a purée then pour over the celery. *Serves 4–6*

Stuffed sweet peppers and tomatoes

Cooking time 35 minutes
Oven temperature 400°F.

2 large green sweet peppers · 8 medium tomatoes
4 slices finely chopped bacon · 1 cup finely chopped mushrooms · 1 cup fine fresh bread crumbs
½ teaspoon mixed herbs (sage, parsley, thyme, rosemary, and bay leaves) · seasoning · 1 egg
2 tablespoons butter.
FOR THE TOPPING: ⅔ cup fine fresh bread crumbs
½ cup finely grated Cheddar cheese.
TO GARNISH: little chopped parsley.

Halve peppers lengthwise, remove cores and seeds, boil for 5 minutes only in salted water, then drain. Cut a slice from the top of each tomato, chop these slices finely, and mix with scooped-out pulp. Fry bacon and mushrooms for a few minutes only, mix with tomato pulp, bread crumbs, herbs, and seasoning, then bind with the egg. Press filling into peppers and tomatoes. Grease a large, shallow ovenproof dish with half the butter, put in the vegetables and top with the remaining butter. Cover tightly and bake in a preheated 400°F. oven for approximately 20 minutes. Remove the cover and top the vegetables with the crumbs and cheese, then brown for a few minutes only under a hot broiler. Garnish with parsley. Illustrated on p. 176. *Serves 4*

Zucchini provençal

Cooking time 20 minutes

¾–1 lb. small zucchini · ¼ cup butter *or* margarine
or a little oil · 1–2 cloves crushed garlic
1 large sliced onion · 1 (1 lb. 12 oz.) can tomatoes
or 4 peeled chopped tomatoes plus ⅔ cup water
seasoning.

Wash the zucchini and cut into 1-inch slices – do not peel. Heat the butter in a large skillet or large saucepan, sauté the garlic and onion in this, add the tomatoes, and simmer for a few minutes. Put in the zucchini and seasoning, cover the pan, lower the heat, and cook for approximately 10 to 15 minutes, until the zucchini are tender. *Serves 4–6*

Barbecued corn

Cooking time   *15 minutes*

4 ears sweet corn · seasoning · 2 tablespoons
butter · ½–1 teaspoon curry powder
few drops Tabasco *or* Worcestershire sauce
4 slices bacon.

Husk the corn, place in boiling water, return to the
boil and cook for 3–4 minutes, salting this toward
the end of the cooking time. Drain the corn. Blend
a generous amount of seasoning into the butter with
the curry powder and Tabasco sauce and spread
thinly over the corn, then wrap a slice of bacon
around each ear. Secure with a toothpick, and broil
for about 5 minutes.   *Serves 4*

Paprika mushrooms

Cooking time   *10 minutes*

2 tablespoons butter
1¼ cups coffee cream *or* ⅔ cup whipping cream and
⅔ cup milk · 1–2 teaspoons paprika
1–1½ cups mushrooms · seasoning.

Heat the butter in a saucepan, then add the cream
blended with the paprika, the mushrooms, and
seasoning. Cover the pan and cook steadily for 4–5
minutes.   *Serves 4*

Pease pudding

Cooking time   *3½ hours*

1 lb. split peas · water · seasoning
bouquet garni · 1 medium onion
2–4 tablespoons butter *or* margarine
2 small eggs *or* egg yolks.

Soak the peas overnight in cold water to cover.
Then discard the water, and put into a pan, cover
with fresh water, add seasoning, *bouquet garni* (3 bay
leaves, 3 sprigs parsley, 1 sprig thyme, tied together),
and onion. Cover the pan, and simmer very gently
for 2½ hours, or until the peas are tender. Either
beat hard with a wooden spoon or press the peas
through a sieve; the herbs and onion may be discarded, if desired or strained also. Beat in the butter
and the eggs, taste, and season very well. Put into a
greased ovenproof bowl or casserole and cover with
foil. Steam for 1 hour (see page 158 – puddings).
           Serves 4

Mashed or creamed potatoes

Cooking time   *25 minutes*

6 medium peeled potatoes · water · seasoning
4 tablespoons butter *or* margarine · ⅓ cup milk.
TO GARNISH: chopped parsley.

Cook the potatoes steadily in boiling salted water
until soft; do not overcook. Drain, then mash with
a fork or potato masher. Beat the butter and milk
into the potatoes; these will be a better color if the
milk is heated. Season well. Mashed potatoes may
be used in many ways; the picture on page 105 shows
these formed into a nest and filled with cooked
ground beef. They may be made into Duchesse
potatoes – see next column – do not add milk to the
potatoes when wishing to brown and pipe into a
definite shape.   *Serves 4*

Potato cakes are made by adding enough flour to
mashed potatoes to form into neat shapes, then
fried (see picture page 156).

Duchesse potatoes

Cooking time   *20 minutes*
Oven temperature   *375°F.*

1–2 egg yolks · ¼ cup butter
4 medium mashed potatoes · seasoning.

Beat egg yolks and butter into potatoes. Season
well. Pipe into large rosettes on a greased baking
sheet and bake in a preheated 375°F. oven for 20
minutes.   *Serves 4*

Baked potatoes or jacket potatoes

Cooking time   *See method*

4 large old potatoes · butter *or* margarine.

Wash and prick the potatoes several times with a
sharp knife. It is important to prick the potatoes to
prevent the skins breaking. To give these a crisp
skin they may be greased very lightly. The time and
temperature for baking may vary a great deal
according to the other dishes in the oven. In a preheated 375°F. oven a large potato will take about
1¼ hours. If baking more slowly increase the cooking
time. When cooked they feel soft to the touch. Make
a cross in the center of each potato or split this to
allow the steam to escape. Top with butter or
margarine, or flavor with seasoning and chives and
top with cream or cottage cheese, or top with
grated cheese. Other toppings are ground ham or
other meat. Illustrated on p. 155.   *Serves 4*

Potato croquettes

Cooking time   *few minutes*

4 medium potatoes mashed · flour · seasoning
1 egg · fine toasted bread crumbs
little fat for frying.

The mashed potatoes should be firm enough to form
into a finger or croquette shapes; if necessary work
in a little flour. Coat the shapes with seasoned
flour, brush with beaten egg, and roll in bread
crumbs. Fry in a little fat until crisp and brown.
Drain very thoroughly on page towels. Illustrated
on p. 125.   *Serves 4*

POTATO CHEESE CROQUETTES:
Add approximately ½ cup grated cheese to the
mashed potatoes. A very little finely grated cheese
may be added to the bread crumbs for coating.

Scalloped potatoes

Cooking time   *1¼–2 hours, see below*
Oven temperature   *375°F. or 300°F.*

4–6 medium potatoes · seasoning · ¼ cup butter
approximately 1¼ cups milk.

Slice the peeled potatoes very thinly, and arrange
in an ovenproof dish. Season each layer, and add a
little of the butter and milk. Either bake in a preheated 375°F. oven for 1¼ hours or in a 300°F. oven
for 2 hours.   *Serves 4–5*

SALADS, HERBS, AND SPICES

SALADS

A good salad can turn a plain main dish into an exciting one, or a salad can become a meal in itself.

Wise choice of salads

These vary so much that the choice is limitless. Select refreshing flavors to blend with rich foods, e.g. orange salad with duck. Experiment with new mixtures. Serve a green or other salad with hot meat, fish, etc.

Ways to serve salads

Serve the salads in individual dishes, in orange skins, on flat plates, or in salad bowls.

To use leftover salads

On the whole, leftover salads are not successful – use as quickly as possible.

Easy remedies when things are wrong

PROBLEM – if a green salad is lacking in flavor this could be because the ingredients were inadequately dried after washing – always shake dry.
TO REMEDY – add a little more dressing.

TO PREPARE SALADS

Wash and shake green salad ingredients well or put these onto a cloth, pick up the ends and whirl the cloth around so all moisture is absorbed. Do not pat lettuce or greens hard since they easily can be bruised.

Prepare other ingredients as the vegetable table, serving them chopped, sliced, or diced, as desired. A good salad should be tossed in a dressing, either add oil, vinegar and seasoning to taste or toss in a prepared dressing such as mayonnaise or French dressing.

Green salad

Cooking time   None

1 head lettuce · little water cress
small piece cucumber
small piece green sweet pepper · oil · vinegar
seasoning.

The ingredients for a green salad should, as the name suggests, be green ingredients only, so do not add tomatoes, hard-cooked eggs, beets, etc. Shred the lettuce, sprig the water cress, then slice the cucumber and the green pepper. Toss together in a bowl with dressing to taste. Belgian endive, chicory, mustard greens, and garden cress could be added, if desired. *Serves 4–6*

SIMPLE SALADS

CUCUMBER SALAD: Peel the cucumber, if desired, slice very thinly, put on a plate, cover, and let stand for 1–2 hours. Pour off surplus moisture, season well, and serve with oil, vinegar, seasoning, and chopped parsley. The dressing may be added immediately if desired, but then the natural moisture from the cucumber cannot be removed.

SWEET PEPPER SALAD: Cut red and green sweet peppers into very thin slices, toss in oil, vinegar, and seasoning.

TOMATO SALAD: Peel the tomatoes if desired, slice thinly, put onto a plate, add finely chopped chives oil, vinegar, seasoning, and a pinch sugar.

Mixed salad

Cooking time   None

Ingredients as green salad · 2 tomatoes
few radishes · few scallions
2 hard-cooked eggs.

Any salad which contains a variety of ingredients could be called a 'mixed salad', but the accepted form is to blend sliced tomatoes, radishes, onions, and eggs with the ingredients in a green salad. Either toss in a French dressing or mayonnaise or serve the latter separately. *Serves 4–8*

Potato salad

Cooking time   *20–25 minutes*

4 medium potatoes · ⅓–½ cup mayonnaise
2 teaspoons finely chopped *or* grated onion *or* chopped
chives · seasoning
3–4 teaspoons finely chopped parsley.
TO GARNISH: chopped parsley.

There is a saying that a potato salad should be
'mixed when hot and eaten when cold'. This is
correct, because if the mayonnaise is added to the
hot potatoes it blends much better. However,
potato salad is often a good way of using leftover
cooked potatoes.
Cook potatoes by boiling – do not scrape new potatoes; remove the skin if necessary. When potatoes
are cool enough to handle, dice, put into a bowl and
mix with the remaining ingredients. Pile into a
serving dish and top with a little extra parsley.
Serves 4–6

Potato mixed salad

Cooking time   *None*

2–3 medium cooked potatoes · 2 tomatoes
cooked green beans.
TO GARNISH: ripe olives · dressing.

Slice or dice the potatoes and tomatoes, blend with
the beans, and garnish with the olives. Top with
dressing, which may be oil, vinegar, and seasoning
or mayonnaise (shown picture page 276). If preferred
mix the ingredients together and toss in dressing.
Serves 4–5

Orange salad

Cooking time   *None*

1 head lettuce · 2 large oranges
¾ teaspoon dry mustard · ¼ teaspoon salt
dash pepper · ½ teaspoon granulated sugar
2 tablespoons oil
2 tablespoons vinegar *or* lemon juice.

Wash and dry lettuce and arrange on small plates.
Peel oranges and remove white pith. Then, using
a very sharp knife, cut sections from the oranges.
Arrange on the lettuce. Put the mustard onto a
flat plate and add the seasonings. Gradually blend
in the oil and vinegar. Pour over the salad. *Serves 4*

Cole slaw

Cooking time   *None*

1 small Savoy *or* firm white cabbage
3 tablespoons olive oil
1 tablespoon vinegar · salt · pepper
2–3 tablespoons mayonnaise.

Shred the cabbage finely. Mix all the other ingredients in a bowl. Pour them over the cabbage and
toss. Let stand a little before serving. *Serves 4–6*

Cole slaw may be varied by adding grated carrot, or
finely diced celery or dessert apple to the cabbage.

Russian salad

Cooking time   *None*

1⅓ cups cooked peas* · 2 medium potatoes*
1½ cups green beans*
1 medium cooked turnip* · 1¼ cups cooked carrots*
3 tablespoons oil · 1 tablespoon vinegar
seasoning · lettuce, (optional)
mayonnaise (see either recipe page 186).

* Or use cooked frozen mixed vegetables.

Neatly dice all the vegetables. Put into a large
bowl, and pour the oil and vinegar over the surface,
then season well. Let stand for several hours,
turning gently in the dressing from time to time so
that the vegetables are not broken. When ready to
serve, pile onto a dish – a bed of lettuce, if desired –
and form into a pyramid. Pour over just enough
mayonnaise to coat. *Serves 4–6*

SALADS WITH RICE

Cooked rice makes an excellent basis for a salad
since it blends with most flavorings. If possible, mix
the rice with the dressing while it is hot to enable
it to absorb the various flavorings. Use a long-grain
or medium-grain rice and cook as one of the methods
given on page 192. When a recipe says 1 cup cooked
rice, this means ⅓ cup uncooked rice.

Shrimp and rice salad

Cooking time   *None*

1 cup cooked rice · 1 fresh *or* canned red sweet
pepper · ⅔ cup cooked peas
¼ cup French dressing *or* use mayonnaise to taste
approximately 1 cup shelled cooked shrimp
2 cans anchovy fillets

Blend rice with sliced or diced sweet pepper, and
the remaining ingredients. (See picture page 273).
Serves 4–6

Rice and mushroom salad

Cooking time   *None*

⅔ cup cooked rice · 1 cup small raw mushrooms
1 green sweet pepper · French dressing.

Blend the rice with the well washed, sliced mushrooms, thinly sliced or diced sweet pepper and toss
in dressing. (See picture page 276). *Serves 3–4*

SALADS WITH FISH

Most fish is excellent in or with a salad. Fish salads range from the classic Salad Niçoise to those with new blendings of flavors.

Fish medley salad

Cooking time   *None*

Approximately 1½ pints cooked mussels (see page 64) *or* canned mussels · 2–3 oz. smoked eel
lettuce. TO GARNISH: olives
cooked *or* canned asparagus
purple and white grapes.

Arrange the mussels and diced eel on the lettuce. Garnish with the remaining ingredients, or if preferred, all the ingredients may be tossed together.
Serves 4–5

Scotch orange

Cooking time   *None*

2 large oranges · 1 medium can fruit cocktail
2–4 oz. smoked salmon · ⅓ cup white vermouth *or* ¼ cup apple cider and 1 tablespoon lemon juice.
TO GARNISH: cucumber · chicory.

Halve the oranges, remove the pulp carefully, then discard pith and seeds and reserve the shell. Mix the orange pulp, well-drained fruit cocktail, and shredded smoked salmon with the vermouth or apple cider and lemon juice. Cut the edges of the orange shells into a zigzag pattern, and put in the fish and fruit mixture. Garnish with cucumber twists and chicory. Illustrated on page 152. *Serves 4*

Rollmops and orange salad

Cooking time   *None*

4 rollmops (prepared herring fillets)
1–2 oranges.

Serve the rollmops either whole or cut into pieces with slices or segments of orange. (See picture page 276).
Serves 4

Salad Niçoise

Cooking time   *None*

1 (7 oz.) can tuna · 1 head lettuce
1 small can anchovy fillets · 3–4 tomatoes
2 hard-cooked eggs · 1 small green sweet pepper
ripe olives · few lima beans
vinaigrette dressing (see page 186).

Drain the oil from the tuna (this may be blended with the dressing, if desired). Mix the ingredients together, slicing the tomatoes and eggs or cutting into quarters. Cut the sweet pepper into strips. Mix together and toss in the vinaigrette dressing. Illustrated on page 177.
Serves 4

SALADS WITH EGGS AND CHEESE

Both hard-cooked and scrambled eggs are excellent in salads. The hard-cooked eggs may be sliced, served whole, or stuffed (see picture page 154) and suggestions below.

Most cheese is excellent with salads.
Serve grated Cheddar, Gruyère, etc. with either sharp flavored salads or with fruit.
Danish Blue or Stilton is also excellent in a salad with vegetables and/or fruit; both cream cheese and cottage cheese (low on calories) blend well with fruit (see recipe below and picture page 275).

Egg and sea food salad

Cooking time   *10 minutes*

4 eggs · 1 can anchovy fillets · lemon juice
pepper · about 1 cup shelled cooked shrimp.
TO GARNISH: mustard greens and garden cress.

Hard cook the eggs for 10 minutes only, then crack the shells and plunge into cold water to prevent a dark line forming round the yolk. Shell and quarter. Drain the oil from the anchovies, and blend with lemon juice and pepper, to taste, to form a good dressing. Arrange the eggs, anchovies, and shrimp on the mustard greens and garden cress and top with, or serve with, the dressing. (See picture page 276).
Serves 4

Stuffed hard-cooked egg salad

Cooking time   *10 minutes*

4–6 hard-cooked eggs (cooked for 10 minutes then cooled quickly) · stuffing – see suggestions below. Ingredients as green salad.

Halve the hard-cooked eggs, remove the yolks and blend with the stuffing selected. Pile back into the whites (or pipe if sufficiently smooth), and serve on green salad. Illustrated on page 154.

TO STUFF: blend 1–2 teaspoons anchovy paste. Add chopped shrimp or crab meat. Flavor with curry powder and chutney. Blend with finely diced ham or chicken. Mash sardines and blend with the yolks.

Cottage cheese salad

Cooking time   *None*

1 large head lettuce · 1 medium can fruit cocktail
approximately 2 cups cottage cheese
½–1 cup halved walnuts · either yogurt, cultured sour cream *or* a little Low calorie salad dressing (See page 186). Illustrated on page 275.

Wash the lettuce and shake it dry. Arrange in a large shallow salad bowl to give the impression of a whole lettuce once again. Drain the fruit cocktail. Beat the cottage cheese along with some of the walnuts which may be left in halves or chopped coarsely, but save the remaining for garnish. Pile the cottage cheese mixture onto the lettuce. Surround with a ring of fruit cocktail. Top with yogurt, cultured sour cream or salad dressing, and more walnut halves. A few pieces of dates may also be put on this, but should be avoided by dieters.

Serves 4

SALADS WITH MEAT

Many meats may form the basis of an interesting salad. On page 153 the color picture shows rolls of ham in a salad. These may be filled with mixed vegetables in a thick mayonnaise; cream cheese or cottage cheese blended with herbs; chopped hard-cooked eggs or cucumber in mayonnaise.

The color picture on page 276 shows a salami salad. Salami may be blended with vegetables of every kind and also with fairly sharp fruit, if desired. Since the types of salami vary considerably, it is always possible to choose one flavor to blend with your choice of ingredients. See also illustration on page 177.

EMERGENCY VEGETABLES AND SALAD DISHES

The very excellent range of canned and frozen vegetables enables interesting dishes to be prepared very quickly. Canned vegetables may be tossed in a dressing or mayonnaise for salads. The vegetables may be heated and tossed in butter and herbs to serve as an accompaniment to a meal. The following recipe uses carrots but is equally good with asparagus or mixed vegetables.

Carrot and cheese bake

Cooking time   *20 minutes*
Oven temperature   *275°F.*

1 (1 lb.) can carrots · 3 eggs · seasoning
¾ cup grated cheese.

Open the can of carrots, and slice if whole. Place in a very shallow ovenproof dish. Beat the eggs, season, and mix with ⅓ cup liquid from the can. Pour over the carrots. Sprinkle with grated cheese, and bake

in a preheated 275°F. oven for 20 minutes; by this time the eggs will not be completely set but almost like a sauce. If you require a firmer consistency, bake for an additional 15 minutes.   *Serves 4–6*

VEGETABLES AND SALADS TO IMPRESS

The most important thing about a salad or a vegetable dish is that it must complement the other foods being served. The following recipes use less well known vegetables or fruit and may highlight your menu.

Ratatouille

Cooking time   *45 minutes–1¼ hours*

2 large onions *or* about 8 very tiny onions
6 medium tomatoes
1 large zucchini *or* 4–6 small zucchini
4 small egg plant · 1 red and 1 green sweet pepper
3–4 tablespoons oil *or* ¼ cup butter
1–2 cloves garlic · sprig thyme · 2 bay leaves
seasoning · little chopped parsley.

Chop the onions or halve the tiny onions. Peel the tomatoes, cut in half, sprinkle with salt, and turn upside down to drain. Peel the large zucchini and cut in large chunks or wash and thickly slice the small zucchini; remove stems from the egg plant, cut in half, scoop out slightly and cut into chunks. Seed, core and slice the sweet peppers. Heat the oil or butter in a heavy pan and gently sauté the onions and crushed garlic. Add the tomatoes, large or small zucchini, egg plant, sweet peppers, thyme, and bay leaves. Season well, cover tightly, and simmer slowly until the vegetables are tender; the difference in cooking time depends on the size of the pieces of vegetable. Remove bay leaves and serve, piping hot, sprinkled with parsley.   *Serves 4*

Avocado salad

Cooking time   *None*

3 avocados · 2 tomatoes
1 onion, finely chopped · 3 tablespoons oil
1 teaspoon coriander (optional)
2 teaspoons Tabasco sauce · lettuce.
TO GARNISH: 2 sliced tomatoes.

Peel the avocados, then remove and discard the pits. Peel tomatoes; chop pears and tomatoes coarsely, and stir in onion. Fold into blended oil, coriander, and Tabasco sauce, pile on a bed of lettuce in a salad bowl, and garnish with sliced tomatoes. Chill if possible before serving.   *Serves 4*

Avocado and grapefruit salad

Cooking time   *None*

1–2 avocados · grapefruit · green sweet pepper
tomato · water cress · chicory
lettuce *or* garden cress, as liked
French dressing (see page 186).

Cut the avocados into slices, divide the grapefruit into sections, and finely slice the sweet pepper. Place on the prepared ingredients remaining, and serve with French dressing.   *Serves 4*

HERBS AND SPICES

Keep a good selection of spices and herbs in your kitchen, for a well-flavored dish is more interesting and it can tempt even a jaded palate, since it acts upon the taste buds and stimulates the gastric juices.

Spices are obtainable in various forms (see page 181), the most convenient being ground – sold in small jars or cans – which keep almost indefinitely in a cool, dry place.

Many herbs may be grown in a garden or in a window box. When fresh herbs are unobtainable, use dried herbs – either those you have prepared yourself or purchased.

Herbs

Many of these may be grown in the garden – some of those spices given in the list of herbs may also be grown. The initial A means an annual; B is biennial; P a perennial. Unless stated to the contrary, all are easy to dry or may be obtained in dried form.

TO DRY HERBS

Wash them after picking in hot weather, dry well in a cloth, then lay them on baking sheets, padded with plenty of paper and a piece of cheesecloth over the top. Dry very slowly at room temperature or in a 200°F. oven (with the door ajar) until brittle. Crumble, then store in tightly covered containers or jars. In very hot weather they may be dried in the sun. Tie in bundles and protect from flies and dust by putting cheesecloth over them. Parsley is a better color if dried for a few minutes in a hot oven

ANGELICA (B) – bought crystallized – home treatment to crystallize is difficult. Use: stems and leaf stalks in desserts, or for decoration.

BALM (P) – Use: in stuffings and drinks – slight lemon flavor.

BASIL (A) – a) Lemon, b) Sweet – rather like bay leaf. Use: as bay leaves. A mild clove flavor, use as cloves and for tomatoes, seafoods.

BAY (LAUREL) (P) The leaf from the laurel tree – Use: 1–2 leaves in stews, soups, meat, fish, and poultry dishes, or even custard.

BORAGE (A) – slight cucumber taste. Leaves excellent in salads, pickles, or if put into custards, then removed. Use flowers and leaves in drinks.

BOUQUET GARNI – A bouquet of herbs, usually parsley, thyme, and bay leaf, tied together, although other herbs or flavorings may be added. Dried herbs should be tied in a piece of cheesecloth for easy removal.

BURNET OR SALAD BURNET (P) – slight taste of cucumber. Use leaves only when young to add to salad.

CARAWAY (B) – Use: gather seeds, dry – see spices.

CELERY SEED OR FLAKES (A) – generally available: whole or ground, into salt. Use: in soups, sauces, and vegetable dishes.

CHERVIL (A) – Use: fine parsley-like leaves for soups, salads, egg and fish dishes – it withers quickly, so not for garnishing.

CHIVES (P) – has a more delicate flavor than onion, chop and use in omelets, main dishes, soups, sauces, and salads.

CLARY (P) – Use: when dried in salads or with vegetables. Fresh leaves may be put into salads.

CORIANDER (A) – Use: see spices.

CUMIN (A) – Use: see spices.

DILL (seeds of plant) – dried when ripe. Use: for pickles.

DILL WEED (A) – Use: chopped leaves can be used in sauces, salads, with eggs, Scandinavian dishes and salmon.

FENNEL (P) – not available commercially. Use: add chopped fine leaves to sauce to serve with fish or for flavoring pickles and soups.

FENNEL (FLORENCE) (A) – this is very large, with aniseed-like taste. Use thick stalks as raw vegetable in salads or cooked like celery. Leaves as above.

GARLIC (A) – Use: very sparingly to give strong onion flavor in salads, stews, etc.

HORSERADISH (A) – Use: the grated root has a 'hot' flavor and is used for sauces for meat and fish.

MARJORAM (SWEET) (A) – member of mint family. Sweeter and more delicate than oregano. Use: excellent with lamb and vegetables.

MINT (P) – Use: for mint sauce. Can be put into fruit drinks, chop and use in salads. There are several varieties of mint, each of which has a slightly different flavor, including, of course, peppermint.

OREGANO (P) – also called wild marjoram. Member of mint family. Use: in Italian or Spanish dishes, excellent combined with tomato dishes.

PARSLEY (B) or sow annually – Use: the most useful herb to give flavor and provide a garnish.

PENNYROYAL (P) – a member of the mint family. Use: sparingly in main dishes, sausages and forcemeat stuffings – very strong.

PURSLANE (A) – Use: in salads or may be cooked as a green vegetable.

ROSEMARY (P) – Use: put a sprig inside a roasting fowl instead of stuffing, or with rabbit, lamb, veal, pork, chicken, dumplings, and chopped in salads.

RUE (P) – Use: an old fashioned herb tea. The leaves are very bitter.

SAGE (P) – Use: chopped fresh sage leaves for sage and onion stuffing, pork and poultry.

SAVORY (P) – Use: when cooking lima and other beans, peas, lentils, in stuffings, and in soups and stews.

SORREL (P) – Use: the acid tasting leaves are cut up for use in omelets, soups and salads; or cook like spinach.

TARRAGON (P) – Use: the chief use of this herb is for making tarragon vinegar. To do this, put a few sprigs in vinegar, and leave in the bottle. Add a

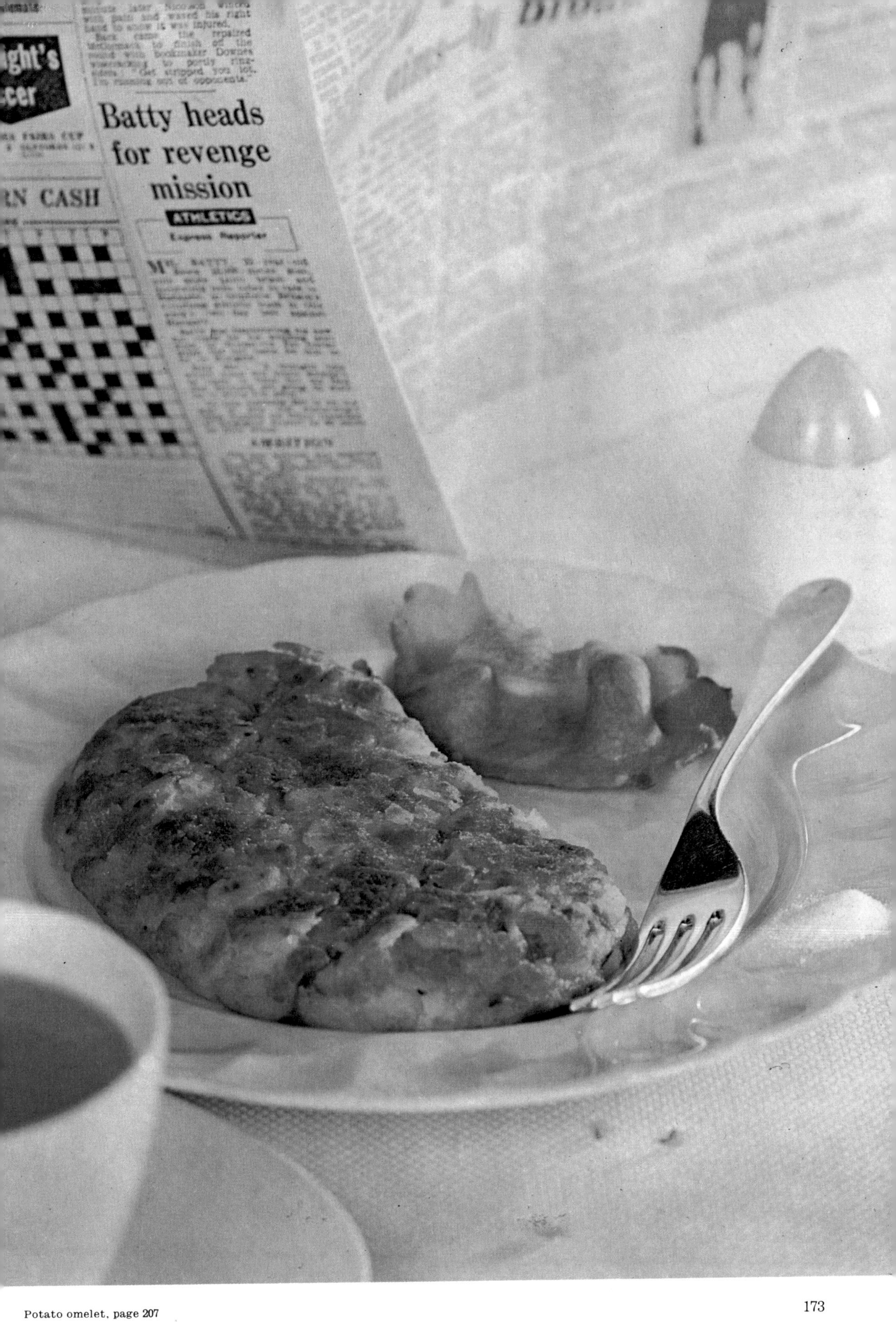

Potato omelet, page 207

Potato nursery shapes, page 323

Stuffed sweet peppers and tomatoes, page 166

Salad Niçoise, page 170; Mixed meat salad, page 171; Kebabs and saffron rice, page 330

Blackberry and apple dumplings, page 218

Apricot tart with flaky pastry, page 216

Pasta, page 193

little chopped tarragon to mayonnaise to serve with fish or chicken. A few leaves may be added to a salad, egg dish, poultry or seafood.

THYME (P) – Use: in stuffings, add to soups, mayonnaise, salads, meat and fish dishes, onion. Found in bouquet garni. There are several varieties of thyme including the very delicious lemon thyme.

Spices

ALLSPICE (from dried berry of an evergreen tree) – not a mixture of spices as often supposed, but its flavor is very like a combination of cinnamon, cloves and nutmeg. Generally available, whole and ground. Use in: cakes, puddings, some drinks. Top a milk pudding with this. Stir a pinch into a stew.

ANISE (from very tiny seeds of plant) resembles flavor of licorice candy – Generally available; whole and ground. Use in: candy, cakes, puddings, pickling and with fresh fruits.

CARAWAY (seeds of plant) – Generally available: seeds or ground. Use in: cakes, biscuits; but in Scandinavia in particular the seeds are added to meat dishes, and to cooked cabbage. Cook red or green cabbage in the usual way, toss in butter and caraway seeds.
There is a Danish cheese with caraway seeds called Danbo.

CARDAMON – (seeds of plant) – a member of ginger family. Generally available: whole or ground. Use in: Danish pastries, one of the principal ingredients in curry powder. Add a little to vinegar when pickling.

CINNAMON (from the bark stripped from the young branches of the tree) – Generally available: rather large pieces (usually called stick) or ground. Use in: cakes, puddings, and drinks. Add to apples, pears, or rhubarb when cooking.

CLOVES (unopened flower buds of the tree) – Generally available: whole or ground. Use in: the most usual spice to put with apples in a pie, also in cakes, puddings and punches. Onion is studded with cloves when making bread sauce. Excellent in stews, and soups.

CORIANDER (seeds of plant) – Generally available: whole or ground. Use: one of main ingredients in curry, good in breads, fruit pies, and soups.

CUMIN (seeds of plant) – Generally available: whole or ground. Use: mainly as a curry ingredient. Add to soups – particularly lentil soup for a new taste.

CURRY POWDER – (blend of spices). May include up to twelve spices: allspice, cassia, cardamon, cloves, coriander, fennel, mace, mustard, several peppers and turmeric.

GINGER (from the root of the plant) – Generally available as: fresh (rather rare – known as green ginger), crystallized (in sugar), preserved (in syrup), ground. Use in: cakes, parkin, gingerbread, biscuits, puddings, cookies, frostings. Add a little to hambergers. Also to curries. Making gingerade.

MACE (red membrane covering nutmeg) – more pungent flavor. Generally available: blades or ground. Use: as nutmeg – see below.

MIXED PICKLING SPICE – Generally available in a blend of 10–16 spices: peppercorns, mustard seed, chili, etc. Use in: pickling or preparing vinegar.

MUSTARD (seeds of plant) – Generally available: whole, ground, or prepared (English, French mustard, etc.). Use: as a condiment. With meat dishes, as a flavoring in many savory dishes.

NUTMEG (seeds of tree) – Generally available: whole (grate to use) or ground. Use: as flavoring for puddings, (particularly baked custards), cakes, cookies, drinks, and soups. Add to mashed young turnips or rutabagas.

PAPRIKA (not true pepper plant – dried fruit from sweet pepper-capsicum) – Generally available: ground. Interesting color (red) – for garnish in sauces, pastas, eggs, potatoes, salads, and goulash.

PEPPER – Black (dried immature fruit – stronger) – Generally available: peppercorns, ground, coarse ground or cracked. Use: most usual condiment of all – as seasoning in all main dishes (generally with salt). White (dried mature fruit with hull removed) – slightly more subtle flavor, available and used as black pepper.

PEPPER, CAYENNE (not true pepper plant – dried hot pepper – capsicum) – Generally available: ground. Interesting color (red – very hot, but can be used VERY sparingly as garnish) – to flavor dishes, especially cheese pastry.

PEPPER, CHILI (from the very hot chilis – type of capsicum) – Generally available in: whole dried pods or a ground blend of chili peppers, red peppers, oregano, garlic powder, and cumin. Use: as cayenne – most famous use in Chili con carne.

POPPY (seeds of plant) – contains a tiny drop of an oil (fragrant). Generally available: whole. Use: in rolls, cakes, rice, or fish.

SAFFRON (dried orange stigma of a crocus-like plant) – most expensive spice of all. Each blossom with its three stigmas is picked by hand. To give one pound, 75,000 flowers are needed. Generally available in: strands (soak these in water and strain) or powder. Use: to flavor cakes, biscuits and rice.

SESAME (seeds of plant) – Generally available: seeds. Use: as topping for breads, green salads, cookies, a butter spread, and candy.

TURMERIC (root of ginger family) – Generally available: ground. Use: in pickles, with pork, fish, and chicken – as an ingredient in curry.

VANILLA BEAN (pod of plant) – Generally available: dried bean, or prepared with sugar (vanilla sugar) or as an extract. Use: cut bean through center, put into jar of sugar, store, and then use this sugar as flavoring in cakes, cookies, and sauces. Or put pod into milk for puddings, heat gently, remove pod, rinse in cold water, allow to dry and store to reuse later. Beans keep for a long time. Add few drops vanilla extract to cakes, puddings, and candy.

SAUCES

A good sauce adds not only interest to a dish, but flavor and food value also.

Wise choice of sauces

While there are some sauces which are traditional accompaniments to certain dishes, try various other flavors – for example, an Espagnole sauce is very good with roast chicken.

Ways to serve sauces

The sauce may either be poured over the food and the garnish added, or it may be served separately.

To use leftover sauces

If any sauce is leftover, cover it carefully and reheat gently. Occasionally, a sauce becomes very stiff with standing, in which case add a little extra liquid; on the other hand, some sauces tend to become thinner as they stand – when reheating, you will need to cook for sufficiently long a period to evaporate the surplus moisture, or to add a little extra thickening.

Easy remedies when things are wrong

PROBLEM – if the sauce is lumpy, this is often due to insufficient cooking of the flour or to the fact that the liquid has not been properly incorporated.
TO REMEDY – whisk sharply.
PROBLEM – if a skin forms on the top of a sauce while it had to be kept waiting, this is due to the fact that the sauce was left uncovered.
TO REMEDY – cover with damp paper, see below.

Consistencies of sauces

These may vary considerably: a coating sauce is generally used to serve with dishes and it should just coat the back of a spoon; a thin sauce is used to blend with vegetable purées for soup, etc.; a thick sauce, called a panada, is used to bind ingredients together, as in fish cakes.

To make a perfect sauce

1. Follow the directions for the amount of fat, flour or thickener, and liquid.
2. Make sure that the flour is adequately blended with the fat.
3. Stir well as the sauce thickens or whisk very briskly. If stirring the sauce, do this thoroughly (see instructions under blending method of white sauce opposite).
4. If the sauce is to be left on the range, either turn the heat down very low or transfer the sauce to the top of a double boiler to prevent any possibility of it burning.
5. If the sauce has become slightly thick with standing, dilute it with extra liquid. The choice of liquid will, of course, depend on the recipe.
6. If leaving a sauce for any length of time a skin will form on top. This may be prevented by cutting a circle of wax paper exactly the size of the saucepan, dip the paper in cold water, shake reasonably dry and lay this gently over the top of the sauce. Do not press down otherwise some of the mixture will be wasted when removing the paper. When ready to reheat the sauce, remove the paper gently, and stir or whisk the sauce.
7. Always taste a sauce before serving and adjust the seasoning.

White sauce (1)

Cooking time   *5–8 minutes*

2 tablespoons butter *or* margarine
3 tablespoons all-purpose flour
1¼ cups milk for coating consistency; 2½ cups milk for thin sauce for soups; ⅔ cup milk for a thick sauce (panada) or binding consistency · seasoning.

Heat the butter gently, remove from the heat and stir in the flour. Return to the heat and cook gently for a few minutes so that the mixture does not brown. Again remove the pan from the heat and gradually blend in the cold milk. Bring to a boil and cook, stirring with a wooden spoon, until smooth. Season well. If any lumps have formed, whisk sharply.   *Serves 4*

White sauce (2)

This is known as a 'blending' method, for the flour is blended with the liquid, rather than being made into a mixture with the butter or margarine, as above.

Cooking time   *5–10 minutes*

3 tablespoons all-purpose flour · seasoning
1¼ cups milk · 1–2 tablespoons butter *or* margarine.

Mix the flour with the seasoning in a bowl and gradually add one fourth of the milk, stirring with a wooden spoon until you have a smooth paste. Put the remaining milk into a saucepan, bring to a boil taking care it does not boil over. Pour the boiling milk slowly over the flour mixture, stirring constantly. Tip the sauce back into the saucepan and put over a low heat. Stir until the mixture boils, then continue cooking for 3 minutes, stirring constantly. Add the butter. When stirring a sauce, make sure that the wooden spoon scrapes across the bottom and into the corners of the pan. If the sauce becomes a little lumpy, remove pan from the heat, beat the sauce with a wooden spoon, or better still with a hand whisk, until it becomes smooth. Taste and re-season if necessary.
       Serves 4 small or 2 large portions

Variations to white sauces (1) or (2)

ANCHOVY SAUCE
Stir in chopped anchovies or 1 teaspoon anchovy paste.

BÉCHAMEL SAUCE
Simmer pieces of very finely chopped onion, carrot, and celery in milk. Strain and make as white sauce.

CAPER SAUCE
Use ⅔ cup milk and ⅔ cup stock. Add 2 teaspoons capers or a little caper vinegar.

CHEESE SAUCE
Stir in ¾–1½ cups grated Cheddar cheese when sauce has thickened, and add a little dry mustard. (Mornay sauce, see page 66.)

CREAMED TOMATO SAUCE
Whisk a tomato paste (which should be hot but not boiling) into hot white sauce. Do not boil.

ECONOMICAL HOLLANDAISE SAUCE
Make white sauce, remove from heat, and beat in 1 egg, and tablespoon lemon juice or vinegar. Cook gently without boiling for a few minutes.

HORSERADISH SAUCE (HOT)
Beat about 1 tablespoon vinegar and 3 tablespoons grated horseradish into white sauce. Add a small amount of cream and dash sugar.

MAÎTRE D'HÔTEL SAUCE
As white sauce, but use half fish stock. Add 2 teaspoons chopped parsley and ¼ cup whipping cream just before serving.

MUSHROOM SAUCE
Cook ¼ cup chopped mushrooms in the milk, then use milk to make white sauce. Add cooked mushrooms and reheat.

MUSTARD CREAM SAUCE
Blend ½–1 tablespoon dry mustard with the flour. Proceed as white sauce, stirring in a little extra milk or cream.

ONION SAUCE
Boil 3 onions, chop or slice, and add to sauce – use a little onion stock.

PARSLEY SAUCE
Add 1–2 teaspoons chopped parsley and a squeeze lemon juice.

TARTAR SAUCE (HOT)
Make white sauce, then beat in 2 egg yolks, 1 tablespoon cream, 1 tablespoon chopped gherkins, 1 teaspoon chopped parsley and a squeeze lemon juice. Cook gently for a few minutes without boiling.

Brown sauce

Cooking time   *5–8 minutes*

2 tablespoons lard *or* bacon drippings
3 tablespoons all-purpose flour
1¼ cups meat stock *or* water and beef bouillon cube
seasoning.

The method of making is the same as for white sauce (1), see this page. A sauce with more flavor is made by frying a finely chopped onion and carrot in the lard, then adding flour, etc. If frying vegetables for a brown sauce, use ¼ cup lard and allow 15 minutes cooking time. The sauce should be strained before using. Brown sauce may also be made by the blending method. The quantities are the same as above. Blend the flour with the stock, put into a saucepan with the seasoning, add the lard or drippings and cook until thickened. Should you wish to add vegetables in this method, then the chopped onion and carrot must be added to the stock. This should be simmered for about 15 minutes, strained, made up to 1¼ cups again and the sauce made as above.
          Serves 4

MADEIRA SAUCE
Use half stock and half Madeira wine.

Espagnole sauce

Cooking time   50 minutes

2 tablespoons butter · small piece of onion
2 large mushrooms · 2 large tomatoes
1 slice bacon · 3 tablespoons all-purpose flour
1¼ cups beef bouillon · *bouquet garni*
seasoning · 3 tablespoons sherry.

Melt the butter in a pan, chop the onion, and mushrooms, and slice the tomatoes. Sauté in the butter for 5 minutes with chopped bacon, stirring well. Next stir in the flour and cook again for 5 minutes. Gradually blend in the cold bouillon, add the *bouquet garni*, bring to a boil and simmer for 40 minutes. Season well, strain and reheat with sherry. *Serves 4*

SAUCE POIVRADE
Add 12 peppercorns with the *bouquet garni* in the Espagnole sauce above. Strain and add 2–3 tablespoons brandy.

Apple sauce

Cooking time   20 minutes

3 medium apples · ⅔ cup water
1 tablespoon granulated sugar
1 tablespoon butter *or* margarine.

Peel, core, and thinly slice the apples. Put into a pan with the water, sugar and butter or margarine. Cook gently until soft, then press through a sieve or beat with a wooden spoon until smooth.   *Serves 4*

Bigarade sauce

Cooking time   1 hour 10 minutes

1 bitter orange, preferably Seville · ⅔ cup water
Espagnole sauce, above
1 tablespoon lemon juice
3 tablespoons port wine *or* claret.

Pare the rind from the orange, discarding any white pith. Cut into wafer-thin strips and simmer these in the water for about 10 minutes. Strain the Espagnole sauce carefully, reheat with the orange rind, orange juice, lemon juice, and wine. A little sugar may be added, if desired.   *Serves 4–6*

Cumberland sauce

Cooking time   15 minutes

⅔ cup water* · grated peel and juice 1 lemon
grated peel and juice 2 oranges
1 teaspoon cornstarch *or* arrowroot
3 tablespoons water *or* port wine
¼ cup redcurrant *or* apple jelly.

* or use half wine and half water.

Put water and fruit peels into a saucepan and simmer for about 5 minutes. Strain if desired, then return liquid to pan, but finely grated peels are very soft and look attractive in the sauce. Add the fruit juice and cornstarch or arrowroot blended with the 3 tablespoons water or wine. Bring to a boil and add jelly. Cook until clear.   *Serves 4*

Cranberry sauce

Cooking time   15 minutes

2–3 cups cranberries · ⅔ cup water
½–1 cup granulated sugar*
1–2 tablespoons butter
3 tablespoons port wine (optional).

* up to ¾ cup for a very sweet sauce.

Simmer the cranberries in the water. Press through a sieve, add sugar to taste and butter. For an unstrained sauce, make a syrup of the water and sugar, drop in the cranberries and cook until a thick mixture, then add the butter. If desired, a little port wine may be added to this sauce, in which case use slightly less water.   *Serves 4*

Tomato sauce (1)

Cooking time   About 20 minutes

1 small chopped onion · 1 carrot
1 clove garlic · 2 tablespoons butter *or* margarine
1 small grated apple
1 can tomato paste
2 teaspoons cornstarch · ⅔ cup water
dash granulated sugar · salt · pepper.

Dice onion and carrot, and crush the garlic. Sauté for a few minutes in butter or margarine, then add grated apple. Add the tomato paste, the cornstarch blended with the water, and seasoning. Bring to a boil and stir until smooth. Simmer gently for about 10 minutes, taste and re-season.   *Serves 4*

Tomato sauce (2)

Cooking time   About 30 minutes

1 small onion · 1 carrot · 1–2 cloves garlic
2 tablespoons butter
5 large fresh tomatoes *or* 1 lb. can tomatoes
3 tablespoons all purpose flour
⅔ cup beef bouillon *or* liquid from can
salt · pepper · dash granulated sugar
1 bay leaf.

Dice onion, and carrot, and crush the garlic. Heat butter and sauté them in this. Do not brown. Add tomatoes and simmer for a few minutes with canned tomatoes, rather longer with fresh ones. Take time doing this since it improves the flavor of the sauce. Blend flour with bouillon, add to other ingredients; simmer gently for about 30 minutes. Stir from time to time. Press through a sieve or beat with a wooden spoon; add seasonings and sugar. The bay leaf may be added at the same time as the tomatoes, but for a milder flavor add it with the bouillon.   *Serves 4*

Curry sauce and simple curries

Simple curries may be made by adding meat, fish, or vegetables to the sauce below. If using cooked meat, uncooked vegetables or raw fish, simmer sauce for 30 minutes–1 hour, then add meat, fish, or diced vegetables and simmer for 25–30 minutes. If using shellfish or cooked fish, heat for 5 minutes only in the thickened sauce. Raw meat must be simmered in the sauce for several hours, adding extra liquid if needed.

Cooking time   *See notes below*

¼ cup margarine *or* butter · 1 onion · 1 apple
¼ cup flour · 1 tablespoon curry powder
1 teaspoon curry paste (optional)
1¾–2½ cups stock* · salt · pepper
dash sugar
1 tablespoon flaked coconut**
1 tablespoon seedless white raisins
1 tablespoon chutney
squeeze lemon juice *or* a few drops vinegar.

* Use meat stock for meat curries; fish stock or a little water for fish curries; water with a little gravy flavoring for vegetable or egg curries.

** Or chopped fresh coconut – a little coconut milk may also be added.

Heat butter or margarine and sauté finely chopped onion and apple until soft. Stir in the flour and curry powder (more or less of this may be used as desired) and paste. Cook gently for several minutes. Gradually stir in stock, bring to a boil and cook until thickened, then add remaining ingredients, tasting at the end to make sure there is sufficient seasoning and sweetening. Add the food to be curried and continue as above. Serve with boiled Patna rice, chutney, and side dishes.

Tangy barbecue sauce

Cooking time   *None*

½ small onion · 1 clove garlic
1 sprig parsley · ⅔ cup tomato ketchup
3 tablespoons wine vinegar
3 tablespoons oil *or* melted butter
1 teaspoon Worcestershire sauce
ground pepper to taste.

Mince onion, garlic, and parsley and put into a large screw top jar with all the other ingredients. Cover and shake vigorously until all ingredients are well blended. Let stand for 24 hours, shaking occasionally. Use as a basting sauce for the last 30–35 minutes of cooking, or increase the amount of liquid by adding ⅔ cup beef bouillon or water and use as a sauce to serve with pork chops.   *Serves 4–6*

Sweet sour sauce

Cooking time   *5–10 minutes*

3 tablespoons vinegar
2 tablespoons granulated sugar
1½ teaspoons tomato ketchup *or* tomato paste
1 tablespoon cornstarch
1½ teaspoons soy sauce · ⅔ cup water · salt
2 teaspoons oil
¼ cup crushed pineapple *or*, for a more spicy flavor, about ¼ cup finely chopped Mustard pickles.
⅓ cup very finely chopped onions, scallions, *or* pickled onions.

Blend vinegar, sugar, tomato ketchup or tomato paste, cornstarch, and soy sauce with the water. Put into a saucepan and cook until thick. Add the salt and oil and continue cooking for a few minutes. Lastly, stir in the pineapple or mustard pickle and onion.   *Serves 4*

Bread sauce

Cooking time   *few minutes*

1 onion · 4–5 cloves, if desired · 2½ cups milk
1 cup fine dry bread crumbs · ¼ cup margarine
seasoning.

Peel the onion and if using cloves, stick these firmly into onion. Put into milk, along with other ingredients. Slowly bring milk to a boil. Remove from heat and let stand in a warm place for as long as possible. Just before the meal is ready, heat the sauce gently, beating it with a wooden spoon. Remove onion before putting into sauce boat.
     Serves 8

Venison sauce (game sauce)

Cooking time   *30 minutes*

1 onion · 6–8 cloves · ⅔ cup fine ale *or* beer
1 tablespoon vinegar · 3 tablespoons cold water
2 anchovies · seasoning.

Peel onion and stick it with cloves. Put the ale, vinegar, and water into a pan. Add the onion, cloves, and the anchovies. Season with salt and pepper, and simmer for ½ hour. Strain before serving.   *Serves 4*

Béarnaise sauce

Cooking time   *15 minutes*

1 shallot · ½–1 tablespoon tarragon
sprig thyme · 1 bay leaf
3 tablespoons vinegar
ingredients as for Hollandaise sauce (see page 186).

Place the chopped shallot, chopped tarragon, thyme, and bay leaf in 3 tablespoons vinegar (this may be white wine vinegar; if fresh tarragon is not available use all or part tarragon vinegar) in a pan. Heat the mixture, and simmer for 2–3 minutes. Strain, then proceed as for Hollandaise sauce (see next page). Béarnaise sauce may be varied by adding a very little tomato paste to the sauce when thickened; this is often given the name of Choron sauce.   *Serves 4*

Hollandaise sauce

Cooking time   *10–15 minutes*

2 egg yolks · pinch cayenne pepper
salt and pepper
2–3 tablespoons lemon juice *or* white wine vinegar
¼–½ cup butter.

Use a double boiler, if possible, if not a flameproof bowl over a saucepan may be used. Put the egg yolks, seasonings, and lemon juice or vinegar into the top of the pan or bowl. Whisk over hot water until the sauce begins to thicken. Add the butter, in very small pieces, whisking in each piece until completely melted before adding the next – *do not allow to boil* or it will curdle. If the sauce is too thick, add a little cream.   *Serves 4*

Classic mayonnaise

Cooking time   *None*

1 egg yolk · dash salt, white pepper, and dry mustard · dash sugar (optional)
⅓–½ cup olive oil · 1 tablespoon vinegar
1 tablespoon warm water.

Put the egg yolk and seasonings into a mixing bowl. Gradually beat in the oil, drop by drop, beating constantly until the mixture is thick. When it becomes creamy, stop adding oil, for too much will make the mixture curdle.* Beat in the vinegar gradually, then the warm water. Use when fresh.   *Serves 4*

* If this does happen, break another egg into a bowl and add the curdled mixture drop by drop, beating hard.

While the amount of olive oil given is usual, some people like to use more oil and it is possible to incorporate as much as ¾ cup oil into the one egg yolk, but naturally it does make a very 'oily' rich mayonnaise.

LEMON MAYONNAISE
Follow the directions for mayonnaise, but gradually add an extra tablespoon lemon juice and ¼ teaspoon very finely grated lemon peel.

TARTAR SAUCE
Make mayonnaise as above then add ½–1 tablespoon chopped parsley, 2–3 tablespoons chopped gherkins (or fresh cucumber) and 1–2 teaspoons chopped capers.

Mayonnaise without eggs

Cooking time   *None*

1 teaspoon dry mustard · 1 teaspoon granulated sugar · ¼ teaspoon salt · dash pepper
1 small can evaporated milk · 1¼ cups olive oil
3–4 tablespoons wine vinegar.

Put the mustard into a bowl with sugar, salt, and pepper. Add the evaporated milk. Mix and beat in the olive oil, drop by drop. Add the vinegar, when the mixture thickens. Season to taste.   *Serves 4*

Uncooked cucumber sauce

Cooking time   *None*

1 small cucumber · 1 tablespoon lemon juice
seasoning
¼ cup cultured sour cream *or* mayonnaise*
few drops chili sauce *or* Worcestershire sauce.

* Purchased or homemade.

Grate the cucumber; if the skin is tender, all or some of this, may be included. Blend with the remaining ingredients. This sauce is excellent with fish.   *Serves 6–8*

Chaudfroid sauce

Cooking time   *None*

1 teaspoon unflavored gelatin · ¼ cup cold water
1¼ cups thick mayonnaise *or* salad dressing.

Sprinkle the gelatin on the water, and let soften. Cool and mix with the mayonnaise or salad dressing.   *Serves 4*

Vinaigrette dressing or sauce

Cooking time   *None*

½ cup oil
¼ cup vinegar (use wine vinegar, cider vinegar, *or* a mixture of wine and tarragon vinegars)
chopped fresh herbs to taste (chives, parsley, tarragon, etc.) · few capers · salt · pepper
dash dry mustard
dash granulated sugar (optional).

Often it is assumed that vinaigrette dressing and French dressing are identical – the above gives an interesting dressing, similar, but not exactly the same as French dressing. See method below.   *Serves 4*

FRENCH DRESSING
Proportions of oil and vinegar (or use lemon juice instead of vinegar) as dressing above. Mix dry ingredients together in a bowl or saucer, then add oil and vinegar and mix thoroughly – or shake together in a covered container. Herbs may be added but are not essential – this is the difference between the dressings.

Horseradish cream

Cooking time   *None*

little dry mustard · salt · pepper
dash granulated sugar · ⅔ cup whipping cream
3 tablespoons grated horseradish
1 tablespoon white vinegar.

Mix all the seasonings with the cream, and whip lightly. Add the horseradish and vinegar.   *Serves 4*

Mint sauce

Cooking time   *None*

¼ cup fresh mint leaves · 2 teaspoons granulated sugar
1½ teaspoons hot water · 3 tablespoons vinegar.

Wash and dry the mint leaves, put onto a chopping board with 1 teaspoon sugar (this helps to chop the mint finely). Chop until fine, then put into a sauce-boat. Add the remaining sugar, stir in the hot water, and let stand for a few minutes to dissolve sugar. Add the vinegar. *Serves 4*

Sweet white sauce

Cooking time   *5–8 minutes*

1 tablespoon cornstarch · 1¼ cups milk
3 tablespoons granulated sugar · 1 tablespoon butter · little vanilla extract.

Blend the cornstarch with a little cold milk. Bring the remaining milk to a boil. Pour over the corn-starch and return to the pan with the sugar. Bring the sauce to a boil, stirring constantly. Add the butter, and vanilla extract. Continue cooking steadily, stirring well. *Serves 4*

FLAVORINGS FOR SWEET WHITE SAUCE

COFFEE – blend 1 teaspoon instant coffee with the butter.

CHOCOLATE – blend 1–2 teaspoons of cocoa or ½–1 tablespoon chocolate drink powder with the corn-starch. As cocoa or chocolate thickens very slightly, use 1¼ cups milk plus an extra tablespoon milk.

Egg custard sauce

Cooking time   *10–15 minutes*

1 large egg *or* 2 egg yolks*
2–3 tablespoons granulated sugar
1¼ cups milk.

* If using 2 egg yolks, you get a somewhat thicker cus-tard. If wanting a very thick egg custard for a trifle, 2 egg yolks and 1 white may be used to this amount of sugar and milk.

Beat the egg or egg yolks and the sugar together. Add the warmed milk, beating well. Strain the mixture into the top of a double boiler with hot *but not boiling* water underneath. Cook slowly, stirring occasionally with a wooden spoon, until the mixture is sufficiently thick to coat the spoon. If no double boiler is available, cook the custard in a flame-proof bowl, that balances safely, over hot water, or if the heat on the top of the range can be turned down very low, cook in an ordinary saucepan but the custard must not be allowed to boil otherwise it will curdle. *Serves 3–4*

Brandy butter

Cooking time   *None*

½ cup butter · 1¼ cups confectioners' sugar
½ teaspoon vanilla extract
about 2–3 tablespoons brandy.

Cream the butter until it is light and fluffy, gradu-ally beat in the sifted confectioners' sugar.
Add the vanilla and sufficient brandy to give a good flavor. Continue beating until it is the consistency of whipped cream. Pile or pipe into a pyramid shape on a small dish. *Serves 4*

Chocolate sauce

Cooking time   *few minutes*

3 tablespoons water · 1 teaspoon granulated sugar
1 tablespoon corn syrup
1 tablespoon cocoa *or* 3 tablespoons chocolate drink powder.

Put all ingredients into a pan or the top of a double boiler and heat gently, stirring constantly.

Jam sauce

Cooking time   *few minutes*

½–1 cup jam
3 tablespoons granulated sugar
juice of 1 lemon · 1¼ cups water
2 teaspoons arrowroot *or* cornstarch.

Put the jam, sugar, and lemon juice into a saucepan with most of the water, and bring to a boil. Blend the arrowroot or cornstarch with the remaining water, stir into the jam mixture, and continue cooking until clear. *Serves 4*

Melba sauce

Cooking time   *few minutes*

1¼ cups fresh raspberries* · 1¼ cups water
¼ cup sugar · 3–4 tablespoons redcurrant jelly
2 teaspoons arrowroot *or* cornstarch.

Put the raspberries, most of the water, the sugar, and jelly into a saucepan. Blend the arrowroot or cornstarch with the remaining water, and add to the raspberry mixture. Bring to a boil, and cook until smooth and thickened. Strain, if desired, and allow to cool. *Serves 4–6*

* If using canned fruit, measure the liquid from the can and add sufficient water to give 1¼ cups. In the case of frozen raspberries assess the amount of liquid as the raspberries defrost, and add water to give desired consistency.

Lemon hard sauce

Cooking time   *None*

⅓ cup butter
2 cups confectioners' sugar · 3 tablespoons lemon juice · finely grated peel of 1 lemon.

Cream softened butter with the sifted confectioners' sugar. Gradually beat in the lemon juice and peel.
Serves 4

Brandy lemon sauce

Cooking time   *15–20 minutes*

2–3 lemons · 1¼ cups water · ½ cup granulated sugar · 2 teaspoons cornstarch · ¼ cup brandy.

Cut the lemon peel into matchstick-thin pieces. Soak for 1 hour, then simmer in the water for 10–15 minutes until tender. Add the sugar, the cornstarch blended with the lemon juice, and boil until thick. Add the brandy, serve hot. *Serves 4–5*

STUFFINGS

A stuffing adds flavor and interest to meat, fish, poultry, and vegetable dishes. By making A STUFFING TO GO WITH THE DISH you are probably having a more economical meal, for this helps to make the more costly meat or poultry serve more people.

Wise choice of stuffing

Choose a flavor that either is sufficiently mild that it does not 'overshadow' the main food, e.g. veal stuffing with chicken or veal, or choose one that counteracts richness, e.g. sage and onion stuffing with duck or pork.
On the other hand there are times when you can give an unexpected touch to a meal, by including a really unusual stuffing.

To serve stuffing

The stuffing may be cooked with the meat or poultry, and carved as you carve this, or it can be served separately, or made a little more firm in texture, rolled in balls and baked.

To use leftover stuffing

Add to a casserole, or slice and fry.

Easy remedies when things are wrong

PROBLEM – if the stuffing lacks flavor this is probably because it was too dry or overcooked.
TO REMEDY – beat a little melted butter and chopped fresh herbs into the hot stuffing.

Cooking times for stuffings

No set time is given for cooking stuffings, for this will depend upon the time taken to cook the meat, poultry, etc. If the stuffing is made into balls, it will take approximately 20–30 minutes to cook and heat in a preheated 300°–350°F. oven. When a cooking time is given at the top of the stuffing recipe it refers to the cooking of an ingredient in the stuffing.

Forcemeat

This is the name often given to all stuffings but in this book it refers to a particular flavor for stuffing, recipe below. Good for all meats, chicken, or turkey.

QUANTITIES OF STUFFING

These are enough for an average-sized bird or roast – use 2–3 times as much for a turkey or goose.

Forcemeat stuffing

Cooking time   *None*

¼ lb. pork *or* beef sausage meat
1 tablespoon chopped parsley
dash mixed herbs (dried *or* fresh sage, parsley, thyme, rosemary, and bay leaves) · seasoning
1 egg · ¼ cup fine fresh bread crumbs (optional).

Mix all the ingredients together. It is advisable to add the bread crumbs if stuffing balls are desired.

When using this stuffing for poultry, the cooked finely chopped giblets or just the liver may be added.
Serves 4–6

MEAT STUFFINGS

Sausage meat is an excellent stuffing because of its moist texture. To give a more interesting flavor it may be blended with parsley and herbs to taste as in the forcemeat recipe. It may be mixed with lightly fried chopped onions; or with raisins and chopped walnuts, etc. Another meat that gives a good flavor in stuffings is ham, and this is combined with sausage meat in the recipe below.

Sausage meat and ham stuffing

Cooking time   *None*

1 small apple · 1 small onion
½ cup cooked ham
grated peel and juice of 1 lemon
¼ lb. pork or beef sausage meat · pepper.

Peel and grate the apple and onion, chop the ham, then blend all the ingredients together. Use for most meats or poultry.
Serves 4

Kidney and rice stuffing

Cooking time   *15 minutes*

¼ cup butter *or* fat · 2 medium onions
½ cup long-grain rice
½–¾ cup pork *or* lamb kidney · ⅔ cup beef bouillon
seasoning · ½–1 teaspoon mixed herbs (sage,
parsley, thyme, rosemary, and bay leaves).

Heat the butter or fat and sauté the chopped onions,
rice, and chopped kidney in this. Add the bouillon,
seasoning, and herbs, and simmer for 10 minutes
until the liquid is absorbed and the rice nearly
tender. Use for pork, chicken, and duck.   *Serves 4*

Ham and horseradish stuffing

Cooking time   *None*

⅔ cup uncooked ham *or* bacon · 1 green sweet pepper
¼ cup shredded beef suet · 1 cup fine fresh bread
crumbs · 2 teaspoons freshly grated horseradish
1 egg · seasoning.

Chop or grind the ham or bacon finely. Dice the
flesh of the pepper. Mix all the ingredients together.
Use with beef or other meat.   *Serves 4*

HERB STUFFINGS

Where possible use fresh herbs in stuffing, but if
dried herbs have to be used instead allow approximately half the given quantity.

Rosemary butter stuffing

Cooking time   *3–4 minutes*

¼ cup butter · 2 cups dry bread crumbs
1 tablespoon fresh rosemary · 1 medium onion
1 egg · seasoning.

Heat the butter and sauté the bread crumbs in this
until golden brown and crisp. Add the chopped
rosemary, onion, egg, and seasoning. Excellent for
chicken, turkey, or veal.   *Serves 4–5*

Sage and onion stuffing

Cooking time   *10–20 minutes*

2–3 large onions · 1¼ cups water · seasoning
¾–1 cup fine dry bread crumbs
1–2 teaspoons dried *or* chopped fresh sage
1 egg (optional).

Peel the onions, chop if desiring a short cooking
time. Put into the water, add seasoning, and cook
until slightly soft. Remove from the stock, chop,
then add to the remaining ingredients. Bind with
the egg or onion stock. Use for pork or duck.
   Serves 4

Veal or parsley stuffing

Cooking time   *None*

¼ cup shredded beef suet *or* melted butter *or*
margarine
½ teaspoon mixed dried herbs (sage, parsley, thyme,
rosemary, and bay leaves) *or* 1 teaspoon fresh
chopped herbs · grated peel and juice of ½ lemon
1 cup fine dry bread crumbs · 1 egg · seasoning
2–4 teaspoons chopped parsley (more, if desired).

Mix all the ingredients together. If desired, a little
stock or milk may be added to give a soft stuffing.
This is the most usual stuffing of all and may be
used with meat, fish, poultry, or vegetables. The
cooked giblets or cooked liver from poultry may be
finely chopped and added, if desired.   *Serves 4–6*

VEGETABLE STUFFINGS

Many vegetables can be used in stuffings and the
following recipes include some with the most
interesting flavors.

Rice stuffing

Cooking time   *15 minutes*

3 tablespoons oil *or* ¼ cup lard · 2 medium onions
1 green sweet pepper · 1 red sweet pepper
½ cup long-grain rice · 1 cup celery
seasoning · 1¼ cups beef bouillon
¼ cup seedless raisins.

Heat the oil or fat and sauté the chopped onions,
diced green and red pepper. Add the rice, chopped
celery, seasoning, and bouillon. Simmer for 10
minutes until the rice has absorbed the bouillon
but not quite cooked. Add raisins. Use with poultry
or meats.   *Serves 6–8*

Mushroom stuffing

Cooking time   *5–6 minutes*

¼ cup butter *or* margarine · 1 small onion
seasoning · 1⅓ cups fine fresh bread crumbs
2 teaspoons chopped parsley · ½ cup mushrooms.

Heat the butter or margarine, sauté the chopped and
well seasoned onion in this, then add to the crumbs,
parsley, and chopped mushrooms. Use for fish, meat,
or poultry. Excellent in beef olives (see page 99).
   Serves 4–5

Onion and apple stuffing

Cooking time   *10 minutes*

3 medium onions · water · seasoning
3 medium dessert *or* cooking apples
2 teaspoons granulated sugar
½–1 teaspoon chopped fresh sage.

Peel the onions and cook for 10 minutes only in
water with seasoning to taste. Drain (use the stock
in gravy) and chop, then blend with the peeled
chopped apples, and the remaining ingredients. This
is a more 'crumbly' stuffing than usual so should not
be rolled into balls. Use with pork and other meat,
duck or goose.   *Serves 4–6*

Cucumber stuffing

Cooking time   *None*

½ medium cucumber
grated peel and juice of 1 lemon
⅔ cup fine fresh bread crumbs · 2 large tomatoes
seasoning.

Peel and grate cucumber, blend with lemon peel,
juice, bread crumbs, peeled chopped tomatoes, and
seasoning. Use with meat or fish. *Serves 4–6*

Nut and celery stuffing

Cooking time   *10 minutes*

¼ cup butter *or* margarine
1 small bunch celery · 2 large carrots
2–3 tablespoons chopped parsley · ¾–1 cup chopped
nuts (either cashews, walnuts, *or* peanuts)
seasoning.

Heat the butter or margarine, sauté the very finely
chopped celery and grated carrots in this, then add
the remaining ingredients. Excellent with meat and
vegetable dishes. *Serves 6–8*

FRUIT STUFFINGS

Fruit blends well with most meats and with the
richer poultry, in particular duck and goose, and
even with some fish (herrings, mackerel), fruit
stuffings are an excellent choice. Included in the
fruit stuffings is chestnut stuffing, and, since there
are many ways of preparing this stuffing, two recipes
are given. In recipe (2) canned chestnut purée may
be used; this is not recommended for recipe (1).

Chestnut stuffing (1)

Cooking time   *25 minutes*

1 lb. chestnuts · water
1¾ cups ham *or* poultry stock · 2 bay leaves
¾ cup cooked ham · ⅓ cup butter *or* margarine
seasoning.

Slit the skins of the chestnuts, and boil steadily for
5–10 minutes in water. Remove one chestnut at a
time and discard the shell and inner skin while still
warm. Keep the remaining chestnuts in the hot
water while waiting to skin them. Put the shelled
chestnuts into the stock, add the bay leaves, and
simmer for 15–20 minutes. Remove the chestnuts
from the stock and either chop them or press
through a sieve. Discard bay leaves. Mix with the
chopped ham, butter or margarine, and season well.
Excellent for turkey or chicken but may be used
for meats. To make a more substantial stuffing,
blend with ⅔ cup fine fresh bread crumbs and 1 teaspoon chopped mixed herbs (sage, parsley, thyme,
rosemary, and bay leaves). *Serves 6*

Chestnut stuffing (2)

Cooking time   *15–20 minutes*

1 lb. chestnuts* · water
3 tablespoons milk · ¼ cup butter
seasoning · ½ cup chopped celery'(optional)
½ cup fine dry bread crumbs.

* Or canned unsweetened chestnut purée.

Slit and boil the chestnuts for 10 minutes, then
shell as recipe above. Return to fresh water, season,
and boil for another 5–10 minutes, drain, strain, and
mix with the remaining ingredients. *Serves 6*

Rice and raisin stuffing

Cooking time   *15 minutes*

½ cup long-grain rice
¼ cup butter *or* 3 tablespoons oil
grated peel of 1 lemon · 1¼ cups water
seasoning · juice of 1 lemon · 2 large carrots
⅔ cup seedless raisins · ¾ cup blanched almonds.

Sauté the rice in the butter or oil, add the lemon
peel and water, then bring to a boil. Season well,
and simmer until rice is nearly tender, adding the
lemon juice toward the end of the time. Cool slightly,
add the grated carrots, raisins, and slivered almonds.
Use with pork chops or other meats. *Serves 4–6*

Prune and almond stuffing

Cooking time   *None*

1 cup pitted prunes *or* 1¼ cups prunes with pits
1¼ cups fine fresh bread crumbs
⅔ cup beef bouillon *or* ⅔ cup milk for a milder stuffing
⅔ cup blanched almonds
¼ cup butter *or* margarine
2 medium apples · seasoning.

Soak the prunes overnight in cold water, then discard the water and chop fairly finely. Soak the
bread in the bouillon or milk, and when quite soft,
beat with a wooden spoon. Add the prunes, chopped
almonds, melted butter or margarine, and grated
apple. Season well – this is an excellent stuffing for
goose or pork. If using with a goose, double the
quantities. *Serves 4–6*

Orange rice stuffing

Cooking time   *15 minutes*

2 tablespoons finely chopped onion
2 tablespoons butter *or* margarine · 2–3 large
oranges · ½ cup medium *or* long-grain rice
beef bouillon · seasoning · ½ teaspoon chopped
sage.

Sauté the onion in the hot butter or margarine.
Grate the peel from the oranges and squeeze the
juice. Add the peel to the onion, then the rice, and
mix well. Measure the juice and add enough bouillon
to make 2½ cups. Pour over the rice, and sprinkle
with seasoning and sage. Bring to a boil and simmer
in an uncovered pan for about 10 minutes, until the
rice is nearly tender and has absorbed all the liquid.
This stuffing is excellent with ducklings or with
ham, bacon, or pork. *Serves 4–6*

PASTA AND RICE

These two foods may be used in many dishes, since they have the great advantage that they are both economical to buy and they combine with so many basic ingredients.

Wise choice of pasta and rice

In the case of pasta, this is quite a problem, since there are so many varieties . . . for example, the picture on page 180 shows: ravioli and cannelloni (both forms of pasta which are stuffed), wheels and shells (often cooked to serve instead of potatoes), vermicelli and seed pasta (frequently just used to garnish soups), and ribbon, twisted and green noodles (used in many dishes). The picture also shows Italian rice, which is ideal for risotto. Many pasta shapes are interchangeable, since they have the same flavor and result in cooking.
Rice, while having the same flavor, varies a great deal in the way it cooks, so choose long-grain rice (Patna is one type) for main dishes where it is particularly important that the rice grains are not sticky; use a medium-grain for both main and desserts where a certain amount of stickiness is quite pleasant – croquettes, for example; use a short-grain rice for puddings to give a creamy texture.

Ways to serve pasta and rice

Pasta is generally served as a main dish, whereas rice is popular as both a dessert and main dish. In this section, main dishes only are given.

To use leftover pasta and rice

Pasta and rice may both be reheated (see recipe page 323). Rice is excellent in salads.

Easy remedies when things are wrong

PROBLEM – if pasta or rice is sticky, this is due to incorrect cooking, overcooking, or to using insufficient water – see below.
TO REMEDY – rinse as suggested in the recipes for cooking.

To cook pasta

PASTA – the name given to the macaroni family – needs cooking in plenty of boiling salted water. Use 5 cups water and approximately 1 teaspoon salt to each 4 oz. pasta. Cook as described in spaghetti below, and use a large pan, for the pasta will become sticky if it has no freedom of movement. Pasta is cooked when it is *just* soft to the touch – do not overcook.
Frying noodles, another method of cooking, is on page 193.
Remember pasta absorbs a lot of water. For example, 1 cup uncooked macaroni means at least 2 cups when cooked.

To cook spaghetti

Cooking time   *10–12 minutes*

5–7 cups water · 1 teaspoon salt
4–6 oz. spaghetti.

Put the water and salt into the largest saucepan available and bring to a boil. Put the ends of the spaghetti into the boiling water, and hold until they soften. Turn the spaghetti slightly so that the softened ends form a circle in the water. Hold the spaghetti until a little more is tender. Turn again, and finally put in the complete length. Allow the spaghetti to boil steadily for approximately 10–12 minutes. Halfway through the cooking time, lift it in the water with two metal spoons to separate the pieces so there is no possibility of their sticking. Test to see if *just* soft and when cooked, drain. Do not overcook.   *Serves 4*

To cook rice

The method of cooking depends upon the type of rice. On page 194 are three ways of boiling rice, all of which are successful, so it is a matter of personal taste which one is chosen. When boiling rice, do not overcook; the grains should feel firm to the touch but when tasted should not have a hard center. Remember rice absorbs a lot of water. 1 cup uncooked rice means 3 cups when cooked.

TO RINSE PASTA OR RICE

This removes the starch from the outside of the cooked pasta or rice. Put the cooked pasta or rice into a fine sieve, pour over *cold* water if reheating, or use boiling water if serving immediately; continue until no longer sticky. Shake the sieve to remove surplus moisture, then dry rice on baking sheets in a 250°F. oven. Pasta may then be served with the appropriate sauce.

EASY WAYS OF SERVING PASTA

Cook the pasta – macaroni or spaghetti are the most suitable for these recipes – and serve:

a) Return the pasta to the saucepan, add a little butter or margarine and chopped parsley. Serve with grated cheese.

b) Spaghetti Milanaise – cook the spaghetti and serve with tomato sauce; either of the recipes on page 184 are suitable.

c) Cook the pasta and serve with cheese sauce; or as suggested on page 323 for macaroni cheese.

Spaghetti with tomato and red pepper sauce

Cooking time   *1 hour*

2 tablespoons oil · 1 clove garlic
1 onion, sliced
1 lb. cooked pork *or* beef, chopped
4 large tomatoes
1 red sweet pepper
3 tablespoons parsley · hot water *or* beef bouillon
salt · pepper. TO SERVE: 1 lb. spaghetti
Parmesan *or* Gruyère cheese · green salad.

Start cooking the sauce first since it takes longer than the spaghetti. Heat the oil in a pan, and sauté the garlic, onion, and pork or beef. Remove the garlic; add chopped, peeled tomatoes, sliced red pepper, and parsley. Cook for 5 minutes before adding sufficient hot water or bouillon to make a sauce. Add salt and pepper last. Simmer until tomatoes are reduced to a pulp, stirring occasionally. The longer you cook the better, but make sure the sauce does not become too dry – if making early in the day to reheat, leave it a little thin. Cook the spaghetti in the usual way, drain, and mix well with plenty of grated cheese, then pile on a large dish. Pour the sauce on top and serve with extra cheese and green salad.
Serves 8–12 as an hors d'oeuvre or 4–6 as a main course.

Cream cheese noodles

Cooking time   *50 minutes*
Oven temperature   *375°F*

8 oz. thin egg noodles · seasoning
1–1½ cups cottage *or* cream cheese
2 tablespoons grated Parmesan cheese
3 tablespoons parsley · 1 small onion, chopped
3 eggs · ¼ cup butter

Cook the noodles until tender in boiling salted water; strain. Add all the other ingredients. Bake in a greased ovenproof casserole for approximately 30 minutes in a preheated 375°F. oven.   *Serves 4*

Spaghetti Bolognese

Cooking time   *1 hour*

2–3 tablespoons butter · 1 tablespoon olive oil
½–1 clove garlic (optional) · 1 onion, finely chopped
1 cup mushrooms · 1 carrot, shredded
approximately ½ lb. ground beef
1 (8 oz.) can tomatoes *or* 1 (6 oz.) can tomato paste
or 4 fresh tomatoes · seasoning
1¼ cups beef bouillon if using canned tomatoes, *or*
1½ cups if using fresh tomatoes *or* paste
1 cup red wine · 6–8 oz. spaghetti · grated cheese.

Heat the butter and oil in a pan, then gently sauté the crushed garlic, onion, mushrooms and carrot for several minutes. Add the meat and the remaining ingredients, and simmer until the sauce has thickened. Cook the spaghetti as given on page 191; and drain. Pour the sauce on top, and serve with grated cheese. Illustrated on page 149.
Serves 6–8 as an hors d'oeuvre or 4 as a main course.

To make ravioli

Cooking time   *8 minutes*

4 cups all-purpose flour · ½ teaspoon salt
2 eggs · Filling (see p. 193).

Sift the flour and salt. Add the eggs and enough water to make a pliable dough. Knead well, then let stand for 30 minutes. Roll out to PAPER THINNESS, and cut in half. Let dry for a short time. Space spoonfuls of the filling on one half, lay other half on top, and press very firmly around the filling. Cut into 1½-inch squares, and make sure each square is firmly sealed. Drop into a pan of rapidly boiling salted water, and cook for 8 minutes. Remove carefully, and serve at once with grated cheese, and tomato sauce. If desired, the ravioli may be fried in deep fat instead. Serve with cheese.   *Serves 4*

TO FILL RAVIOLI

These fillings should be blended together so that they form an almost paste-like consistency.

1. Drained canned stewing steak blended with a chopped sautéed onion or tomato.
2. A very thick cheese sauce made with 2 tablespoons butter, ¼ cup all-purpose flour, ⅔ cup milk, 1 cup cheese and seasoning mixed with ¼ cup fine fresh bread crumbs.
3. Creamed spinach, grated cheese, and egg.
4. Cream cheese, and grated Parmesan cheese, bound together with an egg yolk.
5. Fried, finely chopped cube steak, onions, and diced cooked potato, bound together with the liquid from the rare steak.

Gnocchi

Cooking time   *10–15 minutes*

2½ cups milk · seasoning · 1 cup semolina flour
¼ cup grated cheese · ¼ cup butter
1 beaten egg. TO GARNISH: tomatoes · parsley.

Warm the milk, adding a sprinkling of seasoning. Sift in the semolina, and bring to a boil, stirring. Cook gently for 2–3 minutes until thickened. Remove from the heat and add ¼ cup of the grated cheese and half of the butter. Beat in the egg. Stir over low heat, without boiling, for a minute or two. Turn out onto an oiled or moistened plate, and spread ¼ inch thick. Cool, cut into circles about the size of a half dollar. Arrange in overlapping rows on a buttered dish. Sprinkle with the remaining cheese, and dot with remaining butter. Heat under the broiler, slowly at first, then more quickly to brown; or bake in a preheated over (425°F.) until hot and golden. Garnish with sliced tomatoes and parsley.

Serves 4

Potato gnocchi

Cooking time   *30–35 minutes*

5 medium potatoes, peeled
seasoning · 2 cups all-purpose flour · 1 egg
1 tablespoon butter.

Boil the potatoes steadily in salted water until just tender. Either press the potatoes through a sieve or put through a potato ricer. Mix with the other ingredients. Form into balls or flat cakes, and cook in boiling salted water for 10 minutes. Drain and serve with plenty of grated Parmesan cheese and tomato sauce (see page 184). *Serves 4*

KNOW PASTA

While very few shops stock all the many varieties of pasta shapes, you will find quite a few of them are available. For your guidance, here are the most popular ones:

BUCATINI – very thin macaroni.
CANNELLONI – small sheets of pasta stuffed and rolled.
CAPELLINI – almost as fine as fidelini.
CAPPELLETI – cone-shaped pasta, usually stuffed.
CAVATELLI – cave-shaped pieces.
DITALI – largest size tubes of cut macaroni.
DITALINI – smallest size tubes of cut macaroni.
FARFALLE – bows in all sizes.

FETTUCCINE – long, wide egg noodles.
FIDELINE – finest spaghetti. Comes 'nested'.
FUSILLI – twisted macaroni with hole through it. Considered supreme achievement of spaghetti worker's art.
GNOCCHI – small semolina dumplings, eaten with cheese.
LASAGNE – ribbons of pasta, used in baked dishes.
LINGUINE – flat, ribbon-like spaghetti, often served with fish.
MACCHERONI – generic term for larger pasta varieties. Outside Italy, the name is commonly used to describe the thick, pipe-stem tubes of pasta.
MARUZZE – large shell macaroni.
MEZZANI – grooved quills.
PASTINE – very small round forms, used for soup and for feeding to babies.
RAVIOLI – stuffed pasta squares.
RIGATONI – ribbed macaroni, sometimes stuffed.
SEMINI – 'little seeds' used in soups.
SPAGHETTI – long, thin round pasta used with sauces.
SPIEDINI – chewy, horn-shaped, and grooved. Designed to hold sauce.
STELLETTE – little stars, used in soups.
TORTELLINI – doughnut-shaped rings with filling in center.
VERDI – 'green' pastas which have been mixed with spinach.
VERMICELLI – long, thin, round pasta used in soups.
YOLANDA – twists of noodles.
ZITA – cut macaroni tubes, slightly curved, usually served with meat sauce. (Some shapes are illustrated on page 180.)

To fry noodles

Cooking time   *10 minutes*

4 oz. noodles
3–4 tablespoons oil *or* use pan of deep oil.

Boil noodles until they are soft, but not sticky. Drain in a sieve, or colander, and rinse with cold water. Heat the oil until a very faint haze is seen, then put in the noodles, and fry until crisp and golden; drain well. Serve as an accompaniment to sweet and sour dishes; or they make an interesting hors d'oeuvre served with lots of grated cheese and a tomato salad. *Serves 4*

BOILING RICE

For boiled rice to serve with main dishes: choose long-grain.
For boiled rice to serve in rice croquettes, etc.: choose medium or short-grain.
For boiled rice to serve as a dessert: choose short-grain.

The three basic methods of cooking rice

METHOD 1

For ½ cup rice allow 5 cups boiling salted water. Put in the rice, and cook rapidly for approximately 14–15 minutes. Drain, and rinse in boiling water, put onto flat sheets in a 250°F. oven to dry for a short time.

METHOD 2

For each 1 cup rice, allow 2 cups water. Put the rice, cold water, and salt to taste, into a saucepan with a tightly fitting cover. Bring to a boil, stir briskly with a fork, lower the heat, cover, and simmer gently for 15 minutes. By this time the water will have been absorbed and every grain of rice cooked, but not sticky.

METHOD 3

Use the same proportions as method 2, but put into the top of a double boiler over boiling water. Cook for approximately 30 minutes covered tightly.

In methods 2 and 3 it is not necessary to rinse the rice.

Mutton risotto

Cooking time   *25–30 minutes*

2 onions · 2 large tomatoes
¼ cup long-grain *or* medium-grain *or* Italian rice (see page 193 for notes on various types of rice)
¼ cup margarine *or* butter *or* use 3 tablespoons oil
2½ cups beef bouillon · seasoning
1½ cups diced cooked mutton (or lamb)
¼ cup seedless white raisins.
TO GARNISH: chopped parsley. TO SERVE: grated cheese.

Peel and slice both the onions and tomatoes. Wash and dry the rice. Heat the margarine, butter, or oil and sauté the vegetables and rice in this, do not allow the onions to brown. Add the bouillon, bring to a boil, season, then cook for 10 minutes. Add the mutton, and stir the rice mixture thoroughly, lower the heat and continue cooking in an uncovered pan until the rice is tender and the liquid absorbed. Stir in the raisins just before serving (if these are put in too soon they tend to give a rather odd color to the rice). Pile onto a heated serving dish, and garnish with chopped parsley. Serve with grated cheese.   *Serves 4*

Kedgeree

Cooking time   *30 minutes*

½ lb. smoked haddock · ¾ cup long-grain rice
1 onion · ¼ cup butter · 2 hard-cooked eggs
pepper · salt · cayenne pepper
chopped parsley · onions (optional).

Pour boiling water over the haddock, and let stand for 5 minutes. Remove any bones and skin, and flake coarsely. Bring 2½ cups salted water to a boil, in a large saucepan, add the rice, cover tightly and cook over very low heat until all the water is absorbed, about 25 minutes. Meanwhile sauté chopped onion in a little of the butter until soft and transparent. Chop egg whites and sieve the yolks. Stir flaked fish, onion, egg whites, and remaining butter into the cooked rice, and season rather highly. Heat through gently and pile on a flat heated dish. Make a big yellow cross over the top with the sieved egg yolks and scatter whole dish with parsley. Top with fried sliced onions, if desired.   *Serves 4*

Jambalaya

Cooking time   *25 minutes*

3 tablespoons olive oil · 1 medium onion
2 stalks celery *or* canned celery *or* Belgian endive
1¼ cups cooked long-grain rice
1 (8 oz.) can peeled tomatoes
½ lb. frankfurters *or* cooked meat
seasoning · 1 tablespoon chopped parsley
grated Parmesan cheese.

Heat the oil in a skillet, and sauté the onion and celery over low heat until soft and golden. Add the rice, and stir until thoroughly mixed. Add the tomatoes, frankfurters, seasoning, and parsley. Cook and heat gently. Serve very hot with grated Parmesan cheese.   *Serves 4*

Oriental chicken and rice salad

Cooking time   *20 minutes*

½–¾ cup rice (medium *or* long-grain)
cut clove garlic (optional)
¼ cup salad oil
1 tablespoon vinegar (preferably wine *or* tarragon)
seasoning · 1 tablespoon currants
1 large tomato, peeled, de-seeded, and chopped
1 green sweet pepper, finely sliced
3 tablespoons chopped walnuts (optional)
1 cup cooked chicken, cut into bite-size pieces.

Cook the rice as described or use leftover rice; in which case you will need about 1½–2¼ cups when cooked (this is a very filling salad suitable for a main meal). If using leftover cooked rice, warm through so it absorbs the flavors well. Rub a large bowl with garlic, and in it mix together the oil, vinegar, and seasoning. Add the hot rice, and mix thoroughly. Stir in the remaining ingredients and lastly the chicken. Cover and set aside in a cool place for the flavors to blend. When cold transfer to a serving dish.   *Serves 4*

Salmon and rice croquettes

Cooking time   *35–40 minutes*
Oven temperature   *375°F.*

¼ cup rice (preferably medium-grain)
1 (1 lb.) can salmon · seasoning
2 teaspoons lemon juice · 1 egg
3–4 tablespoons fine dry bread crumbs.
TO GARNISH: water cress · lemon.

Cook rice (see opposite). Flake the salmon with a fork. Add seasoning and lemon juice. Blend well together, form into croquettes, and let stand for 15 minutes (to settle firmly into shape). Brush with egg, and roll in crumbs. Place in a buttered oven-proof dish and bake in a preheated 375°F. oven for 15–20 minutes. Garnish with water cress and lemon slices.   *Serves 4*

EMERGENCY DISHES WITH PASTA OR RICE

The very popular canned macaroni and spaghetti mean that cooked dishes using pasta may be made very quickly; below are suggestions to give a more original touch to these.

Spaghetti and bacon bake

Cooking time   *10 minutes*

1 medium can spaghetti in tomato sauce
4 slices bacon · ½ cup fine dry bread crumbs
½ cup grated Cheddar cheese.

Warm the spaghetti. Cut the bacon into narrow, long strips and fry these in a skillet. Tip the hot spaghetti into a dish, top with the crumbs, and cheese, and brown under the broiler. Arrange the lattice of bacon on top.   *Serves 4*

Speedy risotto

Cooking time   *20 minutes*

½–¾ cup Italian or long-grain rice · water
seasoning · 2 tablespoons butter *or* margarine
small can luncheon meat, diced
1 onion · 2 tomatoes
TO SERVE: grated cheese.

Cook rice (see opposite). Meanwhile, heat the butter or margarine, sauté the luncheon meat, the grated or thinly sliced onion and the peeled, sliced tomatoes in this, season well. When the rice is cooked, blend with the meat mixture, pile into a heated dish, and serve with cheese.   *Serves 4*

PASTA AND RICE DISHES TO IMPRESS

Both pasta and rice dishes can look so colorful that they are most impressive. They are excellent for family or party meals. The following paella is rather costly for a family occasion, but the lobster could be omitted. The lasagne is an excellent recipe for any occasion; if the wide ribbon noodles are not obtainable then use ordinary noodles. Try to use the three kinds of cheese to give a variety of flavors.

Paella

Cooking time   *40 minutes*

1 small chicken, or use part of a cooked chicken
1 onion · 1 clove garlic
3 tablespoons olive oil
5 cups chicken stock (made from simmering the bones and giblets of the chicken)
2 medium tomatoes · ½ cup rice
little saffron, if possible
1 small cooked lobster or 1 (1 lb.) can lobster
8–10 large shelled cooked shrimp
6–8 mussels · 1 (10 oz.) package frozen peas
1 red sweet pepper or ½ can pimientos.

Cut the chicken, onion, and garlic and sauté in the oil until golden. Add half the chicken stock, and simmer for 15 minutes. Add the tomatoes, peeled, and chopped, the rice, and the remaining stock. Simmer for 5 minutes, stir in the saffron (if using the strands you will need about 12 – soak in 3–4 tablespoons cold water for about 30 minutes, strain and use liquid; if using powder you need about ¼ teaspoon blended with 1 tablespoon water). Arrange the lobster pieces, shrimp, mussels, and peas attractively with the red pepper. Continue cooking until the rice is cooked and has absorbed most of the liquid, 15–20 minutes.   *Serves 4*

Lasagne

Cooking time   *1½ hours*
Oven temperature   *400°F.*

7 oz. lasagna (this is a wide ribbon noodle; use either the plain type *or* the green, spinach flavored shown in the picture on page 180).
Bolognese sauce (see page 192) · 1 (3 oz.) package cream cheese
4–6 oz. Gruyère cheese, sliced thinly
¼ cup grated Parmesan cheese.

Cook the lasagna in boiling salted water for about 15 minutes, or until tender. Drain, and if using long pieces, put these over the top of a saucepan to dry out. Cut into convenient lengths. Make the sauce. Put a layer of the lasagna into a buttered dish, then a layer of sauce, a little cream cheese, Gruyère cheese, and Parmesan cheese. Fill the dish like this, ending with the Parmesan cheese. Bake in a preheated 400°F. oven for approximately 30 minutes.   *Serves 4*

EGGS

Since eggs provide an inexpensive protein food, they are essential in family menus.

Wise choice of egg dishes

This depends upon the occasion – and the time available. Omelets are suitable for most meals or for a first course; a soufflé is one of the most impressive of all dishes.

Ways to serve eggs

There is a variety of ways of serving eggs – try adding a lightly boiled or poached egg to a clear soup; a fried egg on top of broiled white fish (this saves making a sauce); while frying eggs, add a little chili powder or sauce or Worcestershire sauce.

To use leftover eggs

Hard-cooked eggs may be used for main dishes or sandwiches. Cut omelets into strips as a garnish; pancakes (if not filled) can be reheated in hot fat.

Easy remedies when things are wrong

PROBLEM – if eggs are tough and leathery, this is due to overcooking.
TO REMEDY – there is nothing one can do.
PROBLEM – if scrambled egg is watery, this is due to too quick cooking.
TO REMEDY – strain off liquid and beat a good knob of butter into the egg.

Hard-cooked eggs

Cooking time   *3½–10 minutes*

eggs · water

There are basically two methods of hard-cooking an egg. In the first, which gives a lighter egg white, the egg is put into cold water and the water brought to a boil. If using this method allow 3½ minutes for a lightly set egg (or even 3 minutes if very lightly set); up to 8–10 minutes for a hard-cooked egg. The other method is to put the egg into boiling water, in which case allow 4 minutes for a lightly set egg (3½ minutes for very lightly set); up to 10 minutes for a hard-cooked egg.

Eggs au gratin

Cooking time   *45 minutes*
Oven temperature   *300°–325° F.*

4 eggs · 1¼ cups milk · seasoning
1 cup grated Cheddar cheese.
TO GARNISH: 2 tomatoes.

Beat the eggs, add the warm milk, seasoning, and grated cheese. Put into a greased, ovenproof baking dish and stand in a pan of water, then bake for about 40 minutes in a preheated 300°–325°F. oven. Peel and slice the tomatoes thinly, place on top of the egg mixture and return to the oven for 5 minutes. The mixture should be lightly set. Serve with hot toast.
Serves 4

EGGS AND MUSHROOMS AU GRATIN
Sauté about 1 cup sliced mushrooms in butter. Put at the bottom of the dish, then cover with the mixture as Eggs au gratin.

Egg and vegetable cutlets

Cooking time   *8–10 minutes*

4–5 hard-cooked eggs
2–3 cups diced and cooked mixed vegetables
⅓ cup fine fresh bread crumbs
½ recipe (⅔ cup) thick white sauce (1) (see page 183)
seasoning. TO COAT: 1 egg · crisp bread crumbs
fat *or* oil for frying.

Chop eggs. Mix with other ingredients and form into 4 large or 8 small cutlet shapes. Brush with beaten egg and roll in bread crumbs. Fry in hot fat or oil until crisp and golden brown. Serve hot or cold.
Serves 4

Fluffy baked eggs, page 209; Bacon pancakes, page 321; Hot grapefruit, page 321

Baked apples Californian, page 236

Mixed fruit salad, page 253

200

Game pie, page 141; Shrimp vol-au-vents, page 332; Picture frame flan, page 337;
Cheese tomato cases, page 322; Cherry slices, page 280

Blackcurrant tart, page 338; Marmalade tart, page 338; Honey tart, page 219; Jam tart, page 219; and Coconut cheesecake, pages 331 and 338

201

Potato pan scones, page 291

Sultana almond twist, page 289; Chelsea buns, page 277; Tea cakes, page 290;
Scotch pancakes, page 289; Fruit and nut loaf, page 290

Flowerpot loaf, page 289; Swedish tea ring, page 278; Chelsea buns, page 277; Breads made with yeast, page 288

Deviled eggs – hot

Cooking time   *30 minutes*
Oven temperature   *350°F.*

1 medium onion · ¼ cup butter *or* margarine
¼ teaspoon prepared mustard
¼ teaspoon curry powder · seasoning
8 hard-cooked eggs.
SAUCE: 2 tablespoons butter *or* margarine
¼ cup all-purpose flour
½–1 teaspoon curry powder · 1¼ cups milk
few drops Worcestershire sauce · seasoning.
TOPPING: ⅔ cup fine fresh bread crumbs
2 tablespoons butter *or* margarine.

Chop the onion very finely, then sauté in the hot
butter or margarine, stir in the mustard, curry
powder, and seasoning. Cut the eggs in half lengthwise, remove the yolks, chop, and blend with the
onion mixture, pack into whites, put cut side downward in a long shallow ovenproof dish. Make a sauce
of the butter, flour blended with the curry powder,
milk, and Worcestershire sauce, taste and season
well. Pour over the eggs – do this carefully so they
are not disturbed in the dish. Top with the crumbs
and butter or margarine – in tiny pieces – and bake
for approximately 15–20 minutes in a preheated
350°F. oven until the top is crisp and brown, or if
preferred put under a hot broiler.   *Serves 4*

Scotch eggs

Cooking time   *5–8 minutes*

4 hard-cooked eggs · ¾–1 lb. sausage meat
1 tablespoon seasoned all-purpose flour · 1 egg
½ cup toasted bread crumbs.
TO FRY: oil *or* fat. TO GARNISH: parsley · tomatoes.

Shell the hard-cooked eggs. Press the sausage meat
into neat squares on a floured board. Wrap the eggs
in the sausage meat, making sure this is completely
sealed without any air space or cracks. Brush with
the beaten egg. Roll in the bread crumbs (see page
54 for coating in egg and bread crumbs). Heat the fat
or oil, and test that the temperature is not too hot.
When a piece of stale bread becomes golden brown
in 1 minute with oil, 1½ minutes if using fat, put in
the Scotch eggs. Fry steadily for approximately 5–8
minutes until crisp and golden brown. Remove,
drain on paper towels and serve hot or cold, garnished
with parsley and tomatoes.   *Serves 4*

TO BAKE: it is possible to cook these in the oven.
Allow approximately 20–25 minutes in a preheated
375°F. oven. Illustrated on page 131.

Pâté eggs

Cooking time   *None*

4 hard-cooked eggs
2 tablespoons pâté
either 1 tablespoon butter *or* 1½ teaspoons whipping
cream
green salad. TO GARNISH: 1 *or* 2 gherkins
small piece of red sweet pepper *or* tomato.

Cut the eggs in half lengthwise, remove the yolks,
and mash or sieve these, then blend with the pâté,
and butter or cream. Pile or pipe back into the egg
whites. Put on a bed of green salad and garnish with
tiny pieces of gherkin and/or red pepper or tomato.
    Serves 4 as an hors d'oeuvre or 2 as a main course.

Fried eggs

Cooking time   *few minutes*

bacon drippings, *or* other fat, *or* butter · eggs.

Heat enough bacon drippings or other choice of fat
in a skillet; lightly cover it (little if any fat is needed
in a plastic resin treated skillet). Break the eggs
into a cup or saucer and lower into the fat. Cook the
egg slowly. If desired, spoon a little hot fat over the
yolk to form a film on the surface. The egg may be
turned over when the white is set.

Poached eggs

Cooking times   *few minutes*

4 eggs · margarine *or* butter · salt.
TO SERVE: 4 slices bread · extra butter.

Like all egg dishes, poached eggs must be served the
moment they are cooked, so toast and butter the
bread while they cook. Crack the shells and pour
the eggs into a cup or saucer. To use an egg poacher,
put a piece of margarine or butter, about the size
of a hazelnut, into each cup; when this is melted,
carefully slide an egg into the cup, adding a dash of
salt, if desired. Cover and allow the water in the
pan underneath to boil steadily for about 3½–4
minutes. Slide the egg on to the buttered toast and
serve.

Alternative method:

Put a small piece of margarine or butter into an old
cup and stand it in a pan of boiling water until the
fat melts. Pour in egg, cover the saucepan, and cook
as before.

Or the following method is preferred by many people
since it gives a lighter result:
Bring 1½–2 inches water to a boil in either a saucepan
or a skillet. Add 1 tablespoon vinegar if desired,
since it prevents the whites from spreading. Put in
a dash of salt. Break eggs gently into a saucer, and
slide into the boiling water, cook for about 3 minutes,
or until whites are set. Drain the eggs carefully with
a slotted spatula, and serve on prepared toast.
        Serves 4

TO SERVE POACHED EGGS FOR A LIGHT MEAL

EGGS FLORENTINE: put the eggs on a bed of cooked spinach and top with a cheese sauce.

EGGS AND HADDOCK: top poached haddock with poached eggs.

Scrambled eggs

Cooking time   *few minutes*

Seasoning · 4 eggs
¼–½ cup milk *or* cream
1–2 tablespoons margarine *or* butter.

Beat the seasoned eggs lightly. Add 2 tablespoons milk for each egg if you like a soft mixture. Heat the margarine or butter in a skillet, pour in the eggs, and cook gently, stirring well from the bottom until the mixture starts to thicken. Turn the heat down very low, and continue stirring until egg mixture is lightly cooked through.   *Serves 2*

Note: if you are making scrambled eggs for a large number of people, use a large skillet pan otherwise the mixture tends to get very hard on the outside before the center is set. A double boiler or flame-proof bowl over hot water is an easy and very efficient way of cooking scrambled eggs.

TO FLAVOR SCRAMBLED EGGS

Many foods may be added to scrambled eggs:
FISH: Toss flaked cooked fish or shellfish in the butter before adding the eggs.
MEAT: Blend cooked ham with the eggs (other meats may be tossed in the butter before adding eggs).

MAKING OMELETS

An omelet is one of the many ways of turning eggs into main meals, and the omelets may be varied in several ways.

1. For a substantial serving allow 2 eggs per person and, if making omelets for a number of people, do not try to cook too many eggs at a time. It is better to use 4–6 eggs at the maximum, i.e. an omelet for 2–3 people, in a 7–8-inch pan. If you try to cook a larger number, the process is too slow and the eggs tend to toughen.
2. For a plain (or French) type omelet, whisk the eggs lightly with seasoning, adding a little water, if desired. Allow about 1 tablespoon water for each egg.
3. Heat 1 tablespoon butter or oil in the omelet pan, add the whisked eggs and allow the mixture to set lightly on the bottom. Then work the mixture by loosening the omelet from the sides of the pan, at the same time tilting it so that the liquid mixture flows underneath. Continue until all liquid has set. Fold or roll away from the handle and tip onto a heated dish. Serve immediately.
4. For a soufflé omelet, the whites and yolks are separated and the stiffly beaten whites folded into the beaten yolks, then seasoned. This tends to be a drier, but of course a thicker and lighter omelet – and may be set without turning if, given a minute or so cooking in the usual way, it is then put under

a moderately hot broiler, or even finished cooking in the oven if the handle of the pan permits. While a soufflé omelet may be flavored with the ingredients suggested below it may also be served as a dessert (see page 236).

Plain omelet

Cooking time   *few minutes*

6 eggs · ¼ cup water · salt
pepper · ¼ cup butter.

Whisk the eggs, water, and seasoning. Heat butter in a large skillet or omelet pan and pour in the omelet mixture. Allow to set lightly on the bottom. Loosen the omelet from the sides of the skillet, tilting the skillet from side to side, so the liquid mixture flows underneath. Continue until all the liquid is lightly set. Fold or roll away from the handle. Tip onto a heated dish and serve at once.   *Serves 3*

FLAVORING AN OMELET

There are many ways in which an omelet may be given additional flavor. Some of the most popular are given below . . . quantities of flavoring are per person.

CHEESE: add 3–4 tablespoons grated cheese to the egg mixture just before folding.

MUSHROOM: sauté ¼–½ cup sliced mushrooms in a little butter, add to the eggs before cooking or to the omelet before folding.

PARSLEY OR OTHER HERBS: add ½–1 teaspoon dried or fresh herbs to the eggs.

Kidney omelet

Cooking time   *10–13 minutes*

2–3 lamb kidneys · ⅓ cup butter · tiny onion (optional)
3 tablespoons all-purpose flour
seasoning
3–4 tablespoons red wine *or* port wine and 3–4 table-spoons beef bouillon (*or* ½ cup beef bouillon only)
4–5 eggs · seasoning · 3 tablespoons water.

Skin and dice the kidneys, then sauté in ¼ cup butter, with the finely chopped onion, until nearly tender. Stir in the flour and seasoning, then blend in the liquid. Bring to a boil and simmer for 1–2 minutes. Meanwhile, prepare the eggs and make the omelet in the usual way. Put the kidney filling inside the omelet, fold or roll away from the handle and tip onto a heated dish.   *Serves 2–3*

Potato omelet

Cooking time   *10–12 minutes*

¼ cup butter · 2 small boiled diced potatoes
4 eggs · ½ teaspoon salt · dash pepper.

Heat the butter in a skillet. Add potatoes, and sauté
until golden. Beat the eggs lightly and season. Add
to the potatoes, and cook quickly as for an ordinary
omelet (see opposite page). Take care potatoes are
evenly distributed. Cook for a further 5 minutes.
Fold over and serve at once. Illustrated on page 173.
Serves 2

SEASONING A PAN

If a new pan is seasoned before being used, food is
less likely to stick. This is not necessary in the
case of a plastic resin treated surface. To season
a pan, sprinkle a little salt into the hot pan, rub
this into the metal with soft paper. Heat a small
amount of fat and rub this well into the pan. Ideally,
one should keep a special pan or skillet for omelets,
which may also be used for pancakes.

LOOKING AFTER AN OMELET PAN OR SKILLET

Wherever possible the pan should be wiped out with
soft paper rather than washing it on the inside.
Never allow butter or fat to become too hot so food
burns in the pan.

SOUFFLÉS

A soufflé depends on the way in which eggs are
incorporated for its light texture, so remember:

IN A HOT SOUFFLÉ

1. Do not have the soufflé mixture too stiff.

2. Do not use too great a weight of flavoring, otherwise the eggs cannot make the mixture rise as much
as one would wish. This is particularly important in
ham soufflé, vegetable soufflé, and fruit soufflé. In
the case of a cheese and vegetable soufflé, the
vegetables are put at the bottom of the dish.
3. Choose a dish sufficiently small so that the soufflé
may rise above it when cooked. '
4. While an equal number of egg yolks and whites
may be used, and obviously the soufflé has greater
nutritional value if this is done, one has a lighter
result if more whites than yolks are used. Fold the
whites into the mixture lightly and carefully.
5. Do not bake the soufflé too slowly, otherwise it
could be rather dry and leathery – tastes vary as to
how firm it should be – many people like the center
to be slightly soft. The cooking times given allow
the soufflé to be just lightly set; for a softer inside
shorten the recommended cooking time by 5
minutes. The mixture should be ready to serve when
golden colored and firm on top.
6. Serve the soufflé the moment it comes out of the
oven, to prevent it from dropping.

IN A COLD SOUFFLÉ

1. Prepare the soufflé or serving dish as given in the
recipe so the mixture may stand well above the top
of the dish.

2. Always allow the egg yolk mixture to be slightly
set BEFORE incorporating the egg whites so they
may be evenly distributed and held throughout the
mixture. If the egg yolk mixture is too thin, then
the egg whites rise to the top while the egg yolk
mixture sinks. (See page 240.)

Main dish soufflés

A soufflé is ideal for a light supper or lunch dish.
The cheese soufflé gives the basic proportions; however, flaked cooked fish, chopped ham, or chopped
chicken may be used instead.
When making a ham (or other meat or fish) soufflé
use approximately ½ cup chopped meat or fish and
half milk and half meat or fish stock.

Cheese soufflé

Cooking time   *50–60 minutes*
Oven temperature   *350°F.*

2 tablespoons melted butter *or* margarine
¼ cup all-purpose flour
¾–1 cup milk · 3 egg yolks
¾–1 cup grated cheese*   4 egg whites
seasoning.

* All Cheddar or half Cheddar and half Parmesan –
all Parmesan gives a very dry texture.

Blend the butter and flour together, add the milk
and stir (if you like a soft fairly 'runny' middle to
a soufflé then use the greater quantity of milk).
Beat in the egg yolks and the cheese, fold in the
stiffly beaten egg whites, taste, and season. If preferred, the seasoning may be added with the flour,
but by adding it at this point, it may be adjusted
better. Put into a 1 pint soufflé dish or ovenproof
casserole, smooth on top with a spatula, and bake
in a preheated 350°F. oven for 50–60 minutes until
well risen and golden brown, or until a knife when
inserted halfway between the edge and the center
comes out clean. Plan the baking time carefully
so that it may be served immediately. Illustrated
on page 150.   *Serves 4*

Sweet soufflés

A sweet soufflé may be hot or cold; a basic recipe for
a hot sweet soufflé is given on page 208 along with
suggested flavorings.

Vanilla soufflé

Cooking time   About 25 minutes
Oven temperature   375°F.

1 tablespoon cornstarch
⅔–1 cup milk (see comments in cheese soufflé)
2 tablespoons butter · ¼ cup granulated sugar
½–1 teaspoon vanilla extract · 3 egg yolks
4 egg whites.
TO DECORATE: little sifted confectioners' sugar.

Blend the cornstarch with the milk, put into a pan, and cook until thickened. Blend in the butter, sugar, and vanilla extract. Beat in the egg yolks, let cook slightly then fold in the stiffly beaten egg whites. Put into a 1 pint buttered soufflé dish or ovenproof casserole (sweet soufflés stick more than ones containing cheese) and bake in a preheated 375°F. oven for about 25 minutes, or until golden colored. Sift the confectioners' sugar on top before serving. Jam sauce is an excellent accompaniment.   *Serves 4*

FLAVORINGS FOR SWEET SOUFFLÉS:

ALMOND or other flavoring may be used instead of vanilla.
FRUIT: use fruit juice or syrup instead of milk and add ¼–⅓ cup finely chopped fruit.
Rum or other liqueur may be added as part of the liquid . . . crème de menthe is particularly good.

BATTERS

A batter made with egg, flour, etc. is used in many ways, among the most famous being pancakes and Yorkshire pudding. The basic batter is given below:

Basic batter

1 cup all-purpose flour · dash of salt
1 egg · 1¼ cups milk.*

* Or use part milk and part water.

Sift the flour and salt into a bowl large enough to allow for beating in the liquid. Break the egg into a small bowl, then add it to the flour. Add about one fourth of the milk or milk and water, and stir carefully with a wooden spoon until the flour is blended. Beat really hard until it is smooth. Either beat in the remaining liquid or let the batter stand for 10–15 minutes, then gradually add the remaining liquid. When the batter becomes thinner, use a whisk to help incorporate air. The batter is then ready to use. Many people consider it better to let this stand in a cold place for a short time, particularly when baking the batter, as in a Yorkshire pudding.

Use the same recipe as for basic batter, but use 2 eggs instead of 1, and add 1 tablespoon oil to the smooth batter. By adding oil, the pancakes become crisper in cooking.

Thin pancakes

Cooking time   4 minutes

1 tablespoon lard *or* shortening *or* oil
Basic batter (see recipe opposite)
flavoring (sugar and lemon) *or* filling (see page opposite).

Put lard, shortening, or oil into a small skillet and heat until a faint haze rises. It is important to have a thin covering of batter only, so pour the batter from a pitcher or spoon; add only enough to make a paper-thin covering in the skillet. Cook steadily on the first side for about 2 minutes, then turn or toss the pancake (see below). Cook for a further 2 minutes on the second side. The pancake is then ready. Either put in the filling at once, or remove from the pan and place on a heated dish. After making each pancake, heat a little extra lard or oil before cooking the next.   *Makes 8–12*

TO KEEP PANCAKES HOT

When cooked, put each pancake onto a heated dish, or onto a sheet of wax paper sprinkled with granulated sugar on a heated dish. Either keep hot in the oven, with the heat turned very low, or keep hot by placing the dish over a saucepan of hot water. Serve as quickly as possible. For a large family, make the pancakes, wrap them in aluminum foil, and fry again for ½–1 minute on each side before serving.

TO TURN A PANCAKE

Shake the pan (see 'to toss a pancake'). Insert a broad-bladed spatula under each pancake, then gently turn the pancake over.

TO TOSS A PANCAKE

This needs practice but is not as difficult as it sounds.
1. Shake the pan before you attempt to toss the pancake. If it moves easily in the pan, it is sufficiently cooked on the underside; if it seems to be sticking, allow another ½ minute over a steady heat.
2. Take the pan in your right hand, if you are right-handed, or your left if you normally use your left hand. Hold it very securely but have your wrist quite relaxed, not stiff and taut. Practise this with an empty pan.
3. Point the pan downwards slightly, then give one sharp, upward flick. The pancake will rise out of the pan, turn in the air and should drop back into the pan with the cooked side up, if you do not draw the pan backwards. Illustrated on page 221.

LOOKING AFTER A SKILLET USED FOR PANCAKES

So that pancakes do not stick in cooking, follow directions for the care of an omelet pan (page 207).

Lemon pancakes

Cooking time   *4 minutes*

Pancakes (see recipe opposite) · lemon
granulated sugar.

Make the pancakes as method opposite, place a pancake onto a piece of sugared wax paper, roll and serve
on a heated dish with lemon slices or wedges and
sugar.

Fruit pancakes

Cooking time   *4 minutes*

Pancakes (see recipe opposite)
canned, cooked, or sweetened ripe fruit.

Cook the pancakes, keep hot (see opposite) and then
fill with well-drained canned, cooked, or sweetened
ripe fruit.

Cheese pancakes

Cooking time   *10–15 minutes*

Pancakes (see recipe opposite) · Cheese sauce (see
page 183).
TOPPING: 2 oz. grated cheese.

Make the pancakes and also the cheese sauce. Keep
the pancakes hot, and fill each one with hot sauce
just before serving. Roll, top with grated cheese, and
serve as soon as possible.   *Serves 4*

Yorkshire pudding

Cooking time   *30–40 minutes large*
                      15–20 minutes small
Oven temperature   *450°F. then 375°F.*

Batter as pancakes (see recipe opposite)
2 tablespoons lard *or* well clarified drippings.

Make the batter, and let stand, if desired. Put the
lard into a 13 inch by 9 inch or 9 inch square pan; the
cooking time will depend upon the depth of the mixture. If preferred divide the lard between muffin
pans. Heat the lard in the pan for 4–5 minutes. Pour
or spoon in the batter, and place on the top rack of
a preheated 450°F. oven. Bake 10–15 minutes for a
large pudding; 5–8 minutes for smaller ones, then
lower the heat to 375°F. if the batter shows signs of
browning too quickly. Serve the beef and vegetables
before the Yorkshire pudding, so that it remains
crisp. Cut a large pudding into neat pieces. Illustrated on page 59.   *Serves 4–5*

Toad-in-the-hole

Cooking time   *35–40 minutes*
Oven temperature   *450°F. then 375°F.*

Batter as pancakes (see recipe opposite)
2 tablespoons lard *or* well clarified drippings
1 lb. sausages.

Make the batter, and let stand, if desired. Put the
fat into a 13 inch by 9 inch or 9 inch square pan, and
heat for about 4 minutes. Add the sausages, and heat
for 8–10 minutes, depending upon the size. Pour the
batter over the sausages and bake in a preheated
450°F. oven for about 10 minutes, or until beginning
to rise. Lower the heat to 375°F., and bake until
golden brown. Halved tomatoes and mushrooms
may be added to the sausages; halved kidneys or
pork chops may be cooked in the same way. Always
heat the meat first before adding the batter, since
this prevents it from sticking to the tin. Illustrated
on page 131.   *Serves 4*

EMERGENCY EGG DISHES

It might be true to say that eggs are an emergency
food, since whatever method of cooking is chosen
they may be cooked and served within minutes.

EGG DISHES TO IMPRESS

An egg is the basis for so many dishes – it is the
reason for sponge cakes rising, etc. but the following
two recipes, although very simple, are very effective.

Spanish omelet

Cooking time   *10 minutes*

1 large onion · 1 green sweet pepper
2 tomatoes · 1 cooked potato (optional)
few shelled cooked shrimp · ⅓ cup butter *or* oil
6 eggs · seasoning.

Dice or slice the onion and the flesh of the pepper.
Peel and chop the tomatoes and the potato. The
shrimp may be cut into pieces if very large. Heat
half the butter, and sauté the onion in this until
tender, add the other ingredients, and heat thoroughly. Beat the eggs, add the seasoning; a little
water could be added but this is not essential since
the water in the vegetables makes a soft omelet. If
the vegetables have been heated in the omelet pan,
tip onto a plate and heat the remaining butter.
Blend the vegetables with the egg, and pour into the
pan, cook as directed in omelets (see page 206), but
do not fold, serve flat.   *Serves 3–4*

Fluffy baked eggs

Cooking time   *5–8 minutes*
Oven temperature   *400°F.*

4 slices bread · butter · 4 eggs · seasoning.

Toast the bread, and spread with butter. Separate
the egg yolks and whites. Whisk the whites until
very stiff, seasoning well. Make a ring on each slice
of toast with the whites, drop a yolk in the center,
and bake until set. Serve with ham or bacon. Illustrated on page 197.   *Serves 4*

CHEESE

Every country produces some kind of cheese and today these types of cheese are either exported or produced in most countries, so that the choice is almost bewildering.

Wise choice of cheese

The opposite page gives a good selection of cheese, but it is important to select the right cheese when cooking. Cheddar is an excellent cooking cheese, so are Gruyère, Swiss and Parmesan. The liking for cottage cheese is growing, and this has the great advantage of being low in calories, so may be included in a dieter's menu.

Ways to serve cheese

When serving cheese at the end of a meal, take time to make the cheese board look interesting. Make sure that the cheese is not too cold; if it is the type that may be stored in a refrigerator, bring it out a little before the meal, so it is at room temperature, which brings out the flavor.

To use leftover cheese

Grate if it is the cooking type and use in cooked dishes, or use in salads.

Easy remedies when things are wrong

PROBLEM – if the cheese in a sauce or dish is tough, this is due to overcooking, or cooking at too high a temperature, or even using too much cheese (a soup topped with cheese then broiled must have a thin layer of cheese only). It could, of course, be due to using a cheese that was unsuitable for cooking, see above and opposite.
TO REMEDY – unfortunately, there is little one can do on such occasions.
PROBLEM – if the cheese curdles in a sauce, this is due to cooking too quickly so the protein in the cheese coagulates.
TO REMEDY – either put into an electric blender for a minute or whisk hard, or strain – the sauce is never as satisfactory.

CHEESE

This is one of the most important of all protein foods and it may be served uncooked as well as cooked. It is important to include it in the diet as often as possible.
For young children and elderly people, cheese is more easily digested if finely grated and sprinkled over vegetables, salads, or soups. Cooked cheese is less easy to digest. Opposite is a list of some of the cheeses available, stating whether they are suitable for cooking.

Variety and origin

AMERICAN – U.S.A., includes cheddar, Colby, washed-curd, and stirred curd. Range from deep yellow to creamy white and mild to sharp flavor. Hard cheese.

BRICK – U.S.A., semi-soft cheese, creamy yellow interior with light gray or brown surface which is occasionally covered with a yellow wax coating.

BEL PAESE – Italy. Soft, mild, rather sweet cheese. Creamy yellow interior, gray surface.

BLEU – (BLUE) France. Soft, faint blue veining. Medium strong. Creamy white interior.

BRIE – France, like Camembert, best when really ripe. If firm and unyielding, is NOT ripe. Soft, mold-ripened cheese, creamy yellow interior, light brown surface. Mild to pungent flavor.

CACIOCAVALLO – Italy, very hard cheese, white interior with tan surface. Use grated for cooking.

CAMEMBERT – France. Test like Brie. Soft, mold-ripened with creamy yellow interior, gray-white surface.

CHEDDAR – England, hard cheese, color ranges from yellow to nearly white. Close and creamy texture;

'nutty' flavor strengthens as cheese matures. Good for cooking.

CHESHIRE – The oldest known English cheese, first made more than 700 years ago. A mellow, hard open-textured cheese, good for cooking. Red and white Cheshires have similar flavor.

COTTAGE CHEESE – Origin unknown. A low-calorie, white, soft, mild crumbly cheese made from skim milk, excellent in salads. Curd size may vary.

CREAM CHEESE – U.S.A. Soft, white, mild, unripened and easy to spread. Good for cooking.

EDAM – Holland, semi-soft to hard with red-coated surface and mild nutlike flavor. Creamy yellow interior. Cooks well.

EMMENTHAL – Switzerland. Firm cheese with large holes, nutlike flavor, light yellow color, milder than Gruyère, but not as good for cooking.

GJETOST – Norway. Dark brown goat's milk cheese, mild and rather sweet, caramel color.

GORGONZOLA – Italy, semi-soft with turquoise veins. Beige surface with light yellow interior, strongly flavored.

GOUDA – Holland, semi-soft to hard with red-coated surface and creamy yellow interior. Nutlike flavor slightly stronger than Edam. Cooks well.

GRUYÈRE – Switzerland, hard, light yellow color, similar to Swiss but stronger flavor and smaller holes. Cooks very well.

LIMBURGER – Belgium, semi-soft with creamy white interior and light brown surface. Mild taste, very pungent odor.

MOZZARELLA – Italy. A soft, mild cheese. Also called Scamorza.

MUENSTER – Germany, semi-soft cheese with many small openings throughout, creamy yellow interior with a gold surface.

MYSOST – Norway, dark brown cow's milk cheese, caramel colored but light than Gjetost.

NEUFCHATEL – France, soft, unripened, white color. Similar to cream cheese but lower in butterfat.

PARMESAN – Italy. Very hard creamy white color cheese for cooking, grates easily. Not suitable for dessert.

PASTEURIZED PROCESS CHEESE – A blend of both aged and fresh cheeses which are shredded, mixed, then pasteurized (heated). It melts easily when reheated. Flavoring materials may be added.

PASTEURIZED PROCESS CHEESE FOOD – prepared similarly to process cheese except uses less cheese and adds either nonfat dry milk or whey solids and water. In addition, it has a milder flavor and softer texture.

PORT DU SALUT – France, similar to Gouda, semi-soft, mellow with fairly strong flavor.

PROVOLONE – Italy, firm cheese with flavor ranging from mellow to sharp. Light creamy white interior with light brown surface.

RICOTTA – Italy, soft, unripened, nutlike flavor.

ROMANO – Italy, very hard cheese similar to Parmesan. Creamy yellow interior with a dark green surface.

ROQUEFORT – France, semi-soft cheese with blue-green veins. White interior is somewhat crumbly, sharp and peppery flavor.

SAMSOE – Denmark, semi-soft with holes similar to Swiss. Mild, cooks well.

STILTON – Close texture with blue veins. Strong, good flavor. Milder than Gorgonzola or Roquefort. Wrinkled surface with creamy white interior.

To store cheese

Cheddar cheese and similar types may be stored in the refrigerator, but should be kept in plastic boxes or covered with foil and put in a shelf near the bottom. The softer cheeses, such as Brie and Cam-embert, are completely spoiled if refrigerated.

Cheese pudding

Cooking time	25–35 minutes
Oven temperature	425°F.

1¼ cups milk · 2 tablespoons butter or margarine
1⅓ cups fine fresh bread crumbs · 1 cup grated cheese · seasoning · 1 or 2 eggs.

Bring the milk to a boil. Add the butter or margarine and bread crumbs, and let stand for 5 minutes. Add the cheese, and season well. Stir in the eggs. Pour into a well greased ovenproof dish, and bake in preheated 425°F. oven until brown on top. Serve at once. Cooking time depends upon depth of dish. Illustrated on page 150. *Serves 3–4*

Cheese and ham pudding

Cooking time	25–35 minutes
Oven temperature	425°F.

Ingredients as cheese pudding
½ cup finely chopped cooked ham.

Prepare the pudding as above, then add the ham with the cheese. This is particularly good served with creamed spinach. *Serves 4*

Cheese bread and butter pudding

Cooking time	45–50 minutes
Oven temperature	325°F.

4 large slices buttered bread
1–1½ cups grated Cheddar cheese · salt · pepper dry mustard · 1 teaspoon Worcestershire sauce
2 eggs · 1¾ cups milk.

Discard the bread crusts, and then cut each slice into six squares. Fill a greased 9-inch pie pan with alternate layers of bread, cheese, seasoning to taste, and Worcestershire sauce. Beat eggs and milk, and strain over cheese. Sprinkle top with cheese, and bake in a preheated 325°F. oven for 45–50 minutes. *Serves 4–5*

Cheese Charlotte

Cooking time   *few minutes*

¼ cup grated Cheddar cheese · few slices thinly
cut brown and white bread and butter · 3 eggs
2 teaspoons unflavored gelatin · ¼ cup water
⅔ cup whipping cream *or* evaporated milk
⅔ (3 oz.) package cream cheese
½ teaspoon prepared French mustard · dash salt
cayenne pepper.
TO GARNISH: blanched almonds · water cress.

Line a buttered Charlotte mold or salad mold with
strips of the bread, alternating white and brown.
Beat the egg yolks until thick, and add the gelatin,
first soaked then dissolved in the very hot water.
Stir in the cream or evaporated milk, cheeses, and
seasonings, then fold in the stiffly beaten whites.
Spoon the mixture into the mold and chill. Turn
out, and serve garnished with almonds and water
cress.   *Serves 4*

Cheese frankfurters

Cooking time   *10–15 minutes*
Oven temperature   *400°F.*

8 frankfurters · 4 oz. Cheddar *or* process cheese
8 slices bacon.

Slit each sausage, and cut the cheese into 8 strips.
Insert a strip in the center of each sausage. Wrap
a slice of bacon around each sausage, and secure
with toothpick. Put into an ovenproof dish and
bake in a preheated 400°F. oven until the bacon is
crisp.   *Serves 4*

Cheese meringues

Cooking time   *few minutes*

2 egg whites · ¼ cup finely grated Parmesan cheese
seasoning. TO FRY: oil *or* fat.
TO COAT: grated cheese.

Beat the egg whites until very stiff, then fold in the
cheese and seasoning. Drop spoonfuls in hot oil or
fat, and fry until brown. Drain on paper towels and
top with more cheese.   *Makes 18*

Cheese rafts

Cooking time   *15 minutes*
Oven temperature   *400°F.*

¼ cup butter · 4 slices bread
4 slices Cheddar *or* process cheese the same size as
the bread · 4 rings pineapple · 2 tomatoes.

Butter the bread on both sides. Put onto a baking
sheet, then top with the cheese and pineapple rings
– which should be well drained if using canned fruit.
Bake for 10 minutes, then put a halved tomato in the
center of each pineapple ring, and return to the oven
for a further 5 minutes.   *Serves 4*

English monkey

Cooking time   *About 10 minutes*

2 tablespoons butter · ⅔ cup milk
⅔ cup fine fresh bread crumbs · 1 cup grated cheese
1 beaten egg · salt · pepper
prepared mustard · Worcestershire sauce
4 slices toast. TO GARNISH: 1 tomato.

Melt butter, add milk and bread crumbs. When very
hot, add the cheese and egg. Add all seasonings. Stir
together until thick and creamy. Pour onto toast,
garnish with sliced tomato.   *Serves 4*

Cheese and bacon flan

Cooking time   *35–40 minutes*
Oven temperature   *425°F. 375°F.*

1 recipe short crust pastry · 3 slices bacon
2 eggs
seasoning including 1 teaspoon dry mustard
1¼ cups milk
1 cup grated Cheddar *or* Gruyère cheese
2 teaspoons chopped onion *or* shallot.

Roll out the pastry and line an 8-inch flan ring or
layer cake pan. Prick the shell with a fork and
bake in a preheated 425°F. oven for 8 minutes. Chop
the bacon and fry until crisp. Beat the eggs with the
seasoning, add the hot milk, bacon, cheese, and
onion. Pour or spoon into the pastry shell. Return to
the oven but lower the heat to 375°F. and cook until
the filling is set. Serve hot or cold with salad.
         Serves 4–5

Corn cheese tarts

Cooking time   *8–10 minutes*
Oven temperature   *425°F.*

1 recipe economical cheese pastry
1 (12 oz.) can corn (not creamed variety)
1 (3 oz.) package cream cheese
¼–½ cup grated Parmesan *or* Cheddar cheese
2 teaspoons chopped parsley · seasoning.

Roll out the pastry and cut into circles to line 12
muffin pans. Prick the shells with a fork and bake
in a preheated 425°F. oven for 8–10 minutes. Drain
the corn and blend with the cream cheese and
Cheddar cheese, then add the parsley and seasoning.
Pile into the pastry shells. Either serve cold, or
reheat gently.   *Makes 12*

Quick macaroni and cheese

Cooking time   *15 minutes*

1¾ cups quick cooking elbow length macaroni
7½ cups water · seasoning.
CHEESE SAUCE: 3 tablespoons butter
¼ cup all-purpose flour · 1¾–2 cups milk
seasoning including dash cayenne pepper
1 cup grated Cheddar cheese.
FOR THE TOPPING: ¼–½ cup grated Cheddar cheese
¼ cup toasted bread crumbs.
TO GARNISH: 1 tomato · few sprigs parsley.

Boil the macaroni in the water with salt to taste
for about 7 minutes (see remarks about quantity of
water for pasta on page 191), add pepper as well, if
desired. Melt the butter, stir in the flour, and cook
for 2 minutes, gradually blend in the milk, bring to
a boil, and cook until thickened and smooth, season
well, and add cheese. Drain the macaroni and blend
with the sauce, put into a 1 quart ovenproof casserole, top with the cheese and crumbs, and brown
under a hot broiler. Garnish with tomato and
parsley.   *Serves 4–6*

EMERGENCY DISHES WITH CHEESE

Cheese and fresh bread, crispbread, or crackers with
a tomato and followed by fresh fruit is surely the
easiest and one of the best emergency meals of all.
The following suggestions for cooked cheese dishes
can all be prepared within a very short time.

Cheese boxes

Cooking time   *None*

Fresh French bread *or* unsliced loaf · butter
cheese.
TO GARNISH: nuts *or* dates.

Cut the bread into slices about ¾ inch thick, then
cut into squares or strips. Spread with butter on
each side. Grate the cheese finely – the type of
cheese does not matter – then roll the bread in this.
Press a nut or date on top.
To give variety, use cream cheese instead of butter;
if this is rather hard it may be softened with a little
cream or milk.   *Allow 1–2 per person*

Swiss omelet

Cooking time   *10–15 minutes*
Oven temperature   *375°F.*

6 eggs · seasoning
3 tablespoons coffee cream *or* milk
1 cup grated Cheddar *or* Gruyère *or* Swiss cheese
little butter.
TO GARNISH: 1 tomato · few sprigs parsley.

Beat the eggs with the seasoning and milk, then
add the cheese. Butter a shallow ovenproof dish very
well. Pour in the cheese mixture and bake in a
preheated 375°F. oven for 10–15 minutes. This may
either be barely firm or lightly set, according to
personal taste. Garnish with sliced tomato and
parsley. For a softer center, half the eggs could be
put into the dish, then the cheese added, then the
rest of the eggs put on top.   *Serves 3–4*

Toasted cheese sandwich

Cooking time   *5 minutes*

4 slices bread · butter
4 slices Cheddar *or* Gruyère *or* Swiss *or* processed
cheese.

Toast the bread, spread with butter, then top with
the cheese and return to the broiler for several
minutes. This recipe may be varied as follows:

YORK CHEESE – lay a slice of cooked ham on the toast,
cover with cheese and broil.

VEGETABLE CHEESE – put hot cooked asparagus, celery,
or other vegetables on the toast, top with cheese and
brown.

CHEESE DISHES TO IMPRESS

A cheese soufflé is one of the most impressive of all
dishes – the recipe for this is on page 207, but fondue
is becoming very popular, it certainly is not difficult
and makes a most 'important-looking' centerpiece
to the table.

Fondue

The most sophisticated form of dip is a fondue. This
depends upon the right proportions of cheese and
wine, but chiefly on being able to keep the mixture
hot and *not* allowing it to boil. If the cheese does
become too hot it curdles.
Cubes of toast or fresh bread should be put on plates
around the hot cheese mixture. Each person takes a
cube of toast or bread on a long fork; dips into
fondue.

Cheese fondue

Cooking time   *10–15 minutes*

2 tablespoons butter
4 cups (1 lb.) grated Gruyère *or* half Gruyère and half
Swiss *or* use Cheddar cheese · seasoning
1¼ cups Graves *or* other dry white wine
1–2 tablespoons brandy *or* Curaçao (apple cider
could be used).

Butter the bottom and sides of an earthenware
casserole, copper or fireproof dish (unsalted butter
is ideal for this). Add the grated cheese, seasoning,
and wine. Keep warm over low heat, and stir occasionally. If desired, add a little brandy or Curaçao.
Cornstarch may be used to prevent the mixture
curdling; blend 2 teaspoons cornstarch with a little
of the wine, add to the cheeses, etc.   *Serves 4*

For a more exotic fondue add a little kirsch. For a
milder-flavored fondue, use Cheddar cheese. For a
more piquant fondue rub a cut clove of garlic on the
bottom and sides of the casserole before buttering
it. Add also a little dry mustard or nutmeg.

PIES AND PASTRIES

Wise choice of pastry

Choose one of the richer, light pastries – flaky, puff, rough puff – if you want the crust to rise. Use a flan (fleur) or cracker crumb pastry for sweet flans.

Ways to serve pastry

Most pastry may be served hot or cold – the light pastries (puff, etc.) are better when reheated a little to freshen them. Pastry may be made into small or large shells; it may be cut into strips or other shapes; it is, in fact, most versatile.

To use leftover pastry

If possible, reheat the pastry gently to recrisp.

Easy remedies when things are wrong

PROBLEM – if the pastry crumbles before baking, this is due to too much fat or too little liquid.
TO REMEDY – press pastry into a neat ball, sprinkle with a little water or egg yolk, gather up the dough lightly, knead carefully and roll out. This is not ideal treatment, but can 'save the day'.
PROBLEM – if the pastry crumbles when baked, this is due to the reasons above or, in the case of tartlet shell, handling too roughly.
TO REMEDY – there is little one can do when once the pastry has broken, but lift with a spatula or broad-bladed knife.
PROBLEM – if the pastry is tough, this is due to too much water, overhandling or too low an oven temperature.
TO REMEDY – there is little one can do, except where suitable to mask with a savory or sweet sauce.
PROBLEM – if the pastry loses it shape in cooking, this is often due to the same reasons as tough pastry.
TO REMEDY – there is little one can do – where suitable serve cut in portions, garnish or decorate to camouflage.
PROBLEM – if the pastry in a vol-au-vent is soft, this is due to the filling being put in too early.
TO REMEDY – there is nothing one can do – allow to dry out and cool before filling.

PASTRY MAKING

Good pastry is delicious, but many people feel pastry making is an art – this may be true to a degree, for some people do make perfect pastry without any apparent effort; on the whole though most people can make good pastry if they learn the technique and follow the directions carefully.

Types of pastry

There are many types of pastry, which are covered in this book.

PASTRIES MADE BY 'RUBBING IN'
Short crust ... sweet short crust ... and cheese pastry. Proportions of fat in the recipes vary.

PASTRIES MADE BY CREAMING
Flan (fleur) pastry, cracker crust (made with crumbs). See recipes for amounts of fat.

PASTRIES MADE BY HEATING FAT WITH LIQUID
Choux pastry and hot water crust pastry, (see page 331). Proportions of fat as particular recipe.

PASTRIES MADE BY FOLDING AND ROLLING
Flaky ... rough puff ... puff. Proportions of fat vary.

PASTRY MADE BY ADDING FAT TO FLOUR
Suet crust.

Amounts of pastry

To save space, recipes often say '1 recipe pastry' or ½ recipe pastry'. This means to make the recipe as it is given or reduce each ingredient accordingly.

To make good pastry

1. Measure the ingredients carefully.
2. Keep both ingredients and utensils as cold as possible. It helps to have cool hands, so in hot weather, when most people's hands become slightly sticky, it is a good idea to run cold water over your wrists as well as your hands to keep them cool.
3. Use a large bowl to give room to work.
4. Keep the pastry light as follows:
a) Sift the flour with the salt.
b) When rubbing fat into the flour lift the mixture well into the air.
c) Rub the fat lightly into the flour.
d) When folding and rolling, handle the rolling pin firmly but lightly.
5. Measure the liquid carefully; the amount in recipes is an approximate guide only, since different brands of flour absorb different amounts of water. The humidity of the atmosphere also affects the water absorption capacity.
6. Roll out the pastry carefully, as bad rolling will spoil the shape.
7. Bake at the correct temperature.

To bake a pie shell

Place the pastry into the pie pan and prick both the bottom and the sides thoroughly with a fork. The usual baking temperature is 425°F. for 8–10 minutes unless otherwise stated.

Short crust pastry

Cooking time   *As individual recipe*

2 cups all-purpose flour · ¾ teaspoon salt
⅔ cup lard *or* ⅔ cup plus 1–2 tablespoons shortening
approximately 4–5 tablespoons cold *or* ice water.

The flour may be all-purpose or self-rising (the former was considered correct, but today many people prefer to use self-rising flour). When using self-rising flour, the flavor and texture of the pastry will differ slightly. The salt should be omitted. The fat may be all lard, all shortening, all margarine or a combination of two of them. All butter is not recommended.
Sift the flour and salt into a mixing bowl. Rub in the lard until the mixture is like fine crumbs. Sprinkle the water gradually over the surface. The mixture is the right consistency when it can be gathered into a ball, leaving the bowl quite clean. Do not use hard pressure. Put the pastry onto a lightly floured pastry board, and roll to the required shape with a lightly floured rolling pin or one covered with a fine knitted stocking.

SOME USES OF SHORT CRUST PASTRY

Jam tarts; fruit tarts or fruit pies; jam turnovers; apple dumplings, etc. Meat pies – although rough puff, flaky or puff pastry is often preferred. Sausage rolls – although rough puff, puff or flaky pastry is often preferred. Cornish pasties and other patties, etc.

Sweet short crust pastry

Cooking time   *As individual recipe*

2 cups all-purpose flour · ¾ teaspoon salt
1 tablespoon granulated sugar
⅔ cup lard *or* ⅔ cup plus 1–2 tablespoons shortening
approximately 4–5 tablespoons cold water.

Read the comments on this page regarding flour for short crust pastry. Margarine or butter is generally used for sweet short crust pastry, but you may use a mixture of these as explained above.

Sift the flour and salt into a mixing bowl, add the sugar. Rub in the fat and continue as short crust pastry.
Sweet short crust pastry is used for sweet flans or tarts.

Cheese pastry (1)

Cooking time   *As individual recipe*

1 cup all-purpose flour · seasoning
dash dry mustard
¼ cup butter *or* margarine
¼ cup very finely grated Cheddar cheese
approximately 3 tablespoons water.

Sift the flour and seasoning into the mixing bowl. Add the butter or margarine, and continue as short crust pastry (see this page). When the fat has been thoroughly blended with the flour, stir in the cheese, and continue as short crust pastry.

Note: This pastry is a little difficult to handle because the cheese makes it richer than short crust, so keep your hands very cool.

Rich cheese pastry (2)

Cooking time   *As individual recipe*

1 cup all-purpose flour · seasoning
dash cayenne pepper (optional)
dash celery salt (optional)
¼ cup butter *or* margarine
½ cup grated Cheddar cheese
1 egg yolk · approximately 1–2 teaspoons water.

Sift flour and seasoning, rub in butter, add cheese and bind with egg yolk. If necessary, add just a very little water. Roll out to required shape and use as individual recipe.

USES OF CHEESE PASTRY

Cheese pastry is used in savories such as Cheese straws, (see page 299) and sometimes in savoury flan shells (such as Cheese and shrimp flan, page 330, Tomato cheese cases, page 322, or Corn cheese tarts, page 212) – due to the fact that the richer cheese pastry is fragile to handle, recipe 1 (more economical) is the more suitable for these.

Flan pastry (fleur pastry)

Cooking time   *As individual recipe*

1½ cups all-purpose flour · ¼ teaspoon salt
⅓ cup margarine *or* butter · ¼ cup sugar
1 egg yolk · approximately 3 tablespoons water.

Sift flour with salt. Cream butter and sugar until soft and light. Add flour, egg yolk, and enough water to make a rolling consistency. Roll out carefully and line a flan ring (see page 220) or a round layer cake pan.
This will be enough for a 7–8-inch flan.

USES OF FLAN PASTRY

Since this is a sweet crust it is used only for sweet flans or tarts.

Flaky pastry

Cooking time   *As individual recipe*

2 cups all-purpose flour · ¼ teaspoon salt
¾ cup fat* · 8–10 tablespoons cold water to mix
¼ teaspoon lemon juice.

* The fat in this recipe may be ½ cup butter *or* margarine and ¼ cup shortening, *or* all butter. A very light crust is made by adding ¼ cup chopped beef suet to the flour, then using ½ cup butter for putting on the pastry – the apricot tart illustrated on page 179 is made with this flaky pastry.

Cream the fat or fats until even in texture, and shape into a block on a plate, spreading it evenly. Mark into 4 equal portions. Chill in the refrigerator until firm.
Sift the flour and salt together in a bowl. Rub one portion of the fat into the flour. Add the water and lemon juice and mix with a round-ended knife into a dough. Knead the dough on a floured board until smooth and even in texture. Leave to rest for 10

minutes in the refrigerator before rolling out.
Roll into a rectangle about 18 × 6 inches, or 3 times as long as it is wide. Mark into thirds. Cut another quarter of the fat into small knobs and put evenly over top two-thirds of the dough. Fold the lower, uncovered section of the dough over the center, and the top third down, envelope style. Press the edges with the rolling pin to seal. Give pastry one quarter turn clockwise. Press with rolling pin in 2 or 3 places to distribute the air. Re-roll and add another quarter of the fat. Fold and seal edges as before. Repeat the process to incorporate the final quarter of the fat. Fold, seal and roll twice more. Allow the pastry to relax in the refrigerator for at least 20 minutes before using. Ideally, the pastry should be allowed to relax in the refrigerator for 10 minutes between each rolling. When shaped, and before putting in the oven, the pastry should be chilled once again.

NOTES ON FLAKY PASTRY

Even rolling, straight sides and square corners, as well as careful folding, are essential when making flaky pastry, so that the layers are regular, giving even rising and flaking. To help the rising in the oven, the folded edges of the pastry should be trimmed off with a sharp knife. During the baking the starch must absorb the fat, and the air that has been incorporated during rolling will expand and cause the pastry to rise. The flakes of the pastry should be even. It is essential to allow sufficient time for the pastry to cook through and for the outside to become crisp and evenly brown. Once the pastry has set the oven temperature should be lowered to prevent over-browning.
If the pastry is not required immediately it may be prepared ready for the final rolling and shaping, then wrapped in wax paper and stored in the refrigerator for 24–48 hours. It must be well protected so that moisture cannot escape, causing the outside to harden.

USES OF FLAKY PASTRY

This is similar to rough puff, or puff, or may take the place of short crust pastry in pies, such as Pear rafts (page 219) or Open fruit pie (page 218).

Rough puff pastry

Cooking time   *As individual recipe*

2 cups all-purpose flour · ½ teaspoon salt
½ cup fat, preferably lard
1 tablespoon lemon juice, if desired
approximately ⅓ cup water.

Sift the flour and salt into a mixing bowl. Cut the fat into neat pieces, and put into the flour. When the fat has been added, mix with the lemon juice and sufficient water to form a stiff dough. Do not rub the fat into the flour before adding the lemon juice and water – it should remain in pieces. Shake a little flour onto a pastry board and put the dough on this. Shape it into a rectangle and roll lightly with a floured rolling pin into a long strip. Fold neatly in three. Seal the ends, rib, etc. (see flaky pastry, above). Give the pastry a half turn and repeat the rolling twice more.

Puff pastry

Cooking time   *As individual recipe*

2 cups all-purpose flour · ¼ teaspoon salt
approximately 1 cup very cold water
few drops lemon juice · 1 cup chilled shortening
(preferably butter).

Sift flour and salt, mix to a rolling consistency with
water and lemon juice. Roll carefully into an 18 × 6-
inch rectangle. Knead the chilled butter under cold
running water until pliable, then form into a 6-inch
square and place in center of pastry. Fold over the
bottom section of pastry, and then the top so that
the butter is covered. Turn dough a quarter turn, seal
edges, and 'rib' (as flaky pastry, see previous page).
Roll out and fold dough in the same manner again.
Turn, seal edges, and 'rib' again. Repeat 5 times, so
making 7 rollings and 7 foldings in all. Put pastry
in the refrigerator for 15 minutes between each rolling to prevent it becoming sticky and soft. Always
place in the refrigerator once again just before
rolling for the last time and preferably for ½–1 hour
before baking. Puff pastry should rise to 4–5 times
the original height of the dough.

USES OF ROUGH PUFF AND PUFF PASTRY

These are used in any recipe where you need a really
well risen crust, e.g. vol-au-vent cases, jam turnovers etc. The two recipes are interchangeable.

Suet crust pastry

Cooking time   *As individual recipe*

2 cups all-purpose flour · ¼ teaspoon salt
1 cup finely chopped suet
approximately 4–5 tablespoons cold water.

You may use all-purpose flour in suet crust pastry
without any raising agent, but most people prefer
a suet crust to rise slightly and add 1 teaspoon of
baking powder to each 1 cup flour. If you buy butcher's suet, remove the skin and chop or grate it
finely. It is easier to chop if a small amount of flour
is put onto the chopping board.

Sift the flour and the salt into a mixing bowl. Add
the suet, and mix into the flour with a knife. Gradually stir the water into the flour and suet mixture
until it is soft enough to form into a ball but firm
enough to roll out. Use as individual recipes.

USES OF SUET CRUST PASTRY

This is used for both savory and sweet crusts which
may be steamed – as in steak and kidney pudding or
fruit pudding – or baked.

Biscuit crumb pastry or crust

Cooking time   *10 minutes*
Oven temperature   *325°F.*

1½ cups (approximately 20) graham crackers
¼ cup granulated sugar
¼–½ cup soft butter *or* margarine
1 tablespoon water (optional).

Crush the biscuits finely, add sugar, and rub in the
margarine. Press into an 8–9-inch pie pan, bringing
mixture up the sides of the pan. Bake in a preheated
325°F. oven for 10 minutes for extra crispness, or
chill in the refrigerator.

USES OF BISCUIT CRUMB PASTRY

This is used for fruit and other flans.

Choux pastry

This is a rather different type of pastry which is
used only for special purposes – Eclairs and Cream
buns, see page 220.

CHOUX PASTRY

Cooking time   *As individual recipe*

1 cup water · ½ cup butter *or* margarine
1 cup all-purpose flour · 3 eggs plus 1 yolk.

Heat water, margarine or butter, and sugar and
bring to a boil. Stir in the flour all at once. Return
pan to a low heat and cook very gently but thoroughly, stirring all the time, until the mixture is dry
enough to form a ball and leave the pan clean.
Remove pan from heat and add well-beaten eggs
slowly, beating until the mixture is smooth. Use as
individual recipes.

USES OF CHOUX PASTRY

This is used for making Eclairs and Cream buns (see
recipe page 220).

Fruit pie

Cooking time   *40–50 minutes**
Oven temperature   *425°F. then 350°F.*

2 recipes short crust *or* sweet short crust pastry
fruit (see below) · ½–1 cup granulated sugar
⅓–¾ cup water.

* Dependent upon fruit used.

Roll out the pastry; this must be larger than the
top of the pie pan to allow for the depth. Prepare
the fruit. Line a 9-inch pie pan with the pastry and
put into the pie pan with the sugar and water. Hard
fruit (apples, firm plums, etc.) need the larger
amount of water; soft fruits (blackcurrants, etc.)
the smaller amount. Add any extra flavoring, e.g.
2–3 cloves or a little lemon peel and lemon juice to
apples. Cover with the top crust. Cut away surplus,
press the edges of the pastry together firmly and

decorate. Place the pie on a baking sheet and bake in a preheated 425°F. oven for 15–20 minutes. Reduce the heat to 350°F. for a further 20 minutes for soft fruit, and 30 minutes for hard fruit. Sprinkle with granulated sugar before serving. *Serves 4–5*

FILLINGS FOR FRUIT PIES

Use any fruit that is in season; the following are particularly interesting ways to vary fruit pies. There are many canned fruit pie fillings which may be used in place of fresh fruit.

APPLE AND RAISIN PIE: Add 1⅓ cups seedless raisins to 6 medium apples, sliced. If the raisins are fairly dry, heat for a few minutes in water, then use this liquid in the pie. Add normal larger amount of sugar.

APPLE AND PRUNE PIE: Allow 1 cup dried prunes to each 6 medium apples, sliced. Soak the prunes overnight in water or water and orange juice to cover, unless sufficiently tender to omit this step. Put with the apples in the pie pan, or if rather hard simmer gently for a time, then add to apples and sugar. Juice in which the dried prunes were soaked may be used in the pie.

CHERRY AND ALMOND PIE: Add about 1–1½ cups slivered or flaked blanched almonds to each 2 (1 lb. cans) pitted red tart cherries.

Bakewell tart

Cooking time	*40–45 minutes*
Oven temperature	*375°F.*

1 recipe short crust pastry
⅓ cup butter *or* margarine · ⅓ cup granulated sugar
1 egg · ¼ cup all-purpose flour
¾ cup finely ground almonds
½ cup fine fresh cake crumbs · 3 tablespoons milk
¼ cup raspberry jam.
TO TOP: little sugar.

Make the pastry and roll thinly into a circle large enough to line a 7-inch flan ring (on a baking sheet) or an 8-inch layer cake pan. Cream the margarine and sugar together until very light. Beat in the egg, fold in the sifted flour, the ground almonds, cake crumbs, and the milk. Spread the bottom of the pastry with raspberry jam. Place the filling on top, and spread evenly with a knife. Bake in a preheated 375°F. oven for 40–45 minutes. Cool slightly, remove flan ring or turn out of cake pan, and dust lightly with confectioners' sugar. *Serves 6*

Open fruit pie

Cooking time	*40–50 minutes*
Oven temperature	*425°F. then 350°F.*

1 recipe short or sweet short crust pastry *or* flaky pastry.
FILLING: 1 lb. fruit · ⅓ cup granulated sugar
1–2 tablespoons water, if required
little flour *or* cornstarch, *or* semolina flour
1 tablespoon granulated sugar.

Roll out half the pastry to fit an 8-inch pie pan. Put the pastry into the pan and neaten the edges. To prevent the fruit from making the bottom crust soggy, shake a little flour or ½ teaspoon cornstarch or 1 teaspoon semolina flour over the bottom, then add a sprinkling of sugar. This absorbs the juice. Prepare the fruit and put into the pastry with the ⅓ cup sugar. Soft fruit requires no water; apples need 1 tablespoon; underripe plums or apricots need 3 tablespoons. Brush the rim of the pastry with water. Cut remaining pastry in strips, arrange around edge and make criss cross strips over fruit (see picture page 201). Decorate edge and proceed as for fruit pie (see page 217). *Serves 4–5*

Fruit pies may be made with flaky pastry instead of short or sweet short crust – roll pastry out fairly thin, since it will rise slightly (see pages 215, 216).

HONEY AND RAISIN PIE
Spread the bottom crust with honey and cover with a layer of seedless raisins.

MINCEMEAT PIE
Spread the bottom crust with approximately 6 oz. prepared purchased mincemeat or about 1 cup mincement (see page 338).

Apple dumplings

Cooking time	*50–60 minutes*
Oven temperature	*425°F. then 350°F.*

2 recipes short crust pastry *or* sweet short crust pastry · 6 large baking apples
3 tablespoons brown sugar · 6 cloves (optional)
3 teaspoons lemon juice to flavor (optional).

Make the pastry and roll into 6 neat squares. Peel and core the apples. Put 1 teaspoon of the sugar, a clove, and a ½ teaspoon lemon juice into the center of each apple. Place each apple on a square of pastry. Brush the edges of the pastry with a little water, then gather them around the apple. Leave the edges in a square shape, like an envelope, or mould them gently with your hands around the apple. Lift the dumplings carefully onto a baking sheet, brush pastry with a little milk, or beaten egg, and bake in a preheated 425°F. oven for 15–20 minutes, until the pastry is set and beginning to turn golden brown. Lower the heat to 350°F., and bake for a further 35–40 minutes to make sure the apples are cooked through to the center. Serve hot accompanied with sauce or cream. *Serves 4*

BLACKBERRY AND APPLE DUMPLINGS
Ingredients as above, but fill the centre of each apple with raw blackberries and sugar, or well-drained canned blackberries. Bake as above, and decorate with extra blackberries (see picture page 178).

Jam roly poly

Cooking time   2 hours or 35–40 minutes
Oven temperature   375°F.

¾ recipe suet crust (page 217)   ·   5–6 tablespoons jam.

Roll the pastry into a neat oblong about ¼-inch thick. Spread with jam, being careful not to take this right to the edges. Turn in side edges. Roll lightly like a Swiss roll.
To steam: wrap the pudding in greased wax paper, then in a floured cloth, or use greased foil without a cloth. In either case wrap the roly poly lightly to allow space for it to rise in cooking. Put into the steamer and cook for 2 hours over rapidly boiling water.
To bake: put the pudding on to a greased baking sheet and bake in the center of a preheated 375°F. oven for 45 minutes.   *Serves 4*

Instead of jam, the suet crust may be filled with mincemeat.

Jam turnovers

Cooking time   15 minutes
Oven temperature   475°F.

1 recipe flaky or puff pastry   ·   ⅓ cup jam.

Roll out the pastry and cut into 4 neat squares. Put some of the jam in the center of each square and brush the edges of the pastry with a little water. Fold over to make a triangle, then firmly press the edges together with a fork to prevent the jam running out when baking. Put a spatula under each turnover and lift onto a baking sheet. Bake in a preheated 475°F. oven for approximately 15 minutes or until the pastry is golden brown and crisp.
    Serves 4

Jam tart

Cooking time   Approximately 20 minutes
Oven temperature   400°F.

1 recipe short crust pastry
approximately ½ cup jam.

Make the pastry, put onto a lightly floured board, and shape it with your hands into a neat circle. Roll out the pastry, measure by placing an 8-inch pie pan on top to see if you have the correct size and shape. You need a good rim of pastry around the pan when measuring to allow for the depth in the pan when lining it. When you have a sufficiently large piece of pastry, fold this over the rolling pin to support it as it is lowered into the pan. Press the pastry down. Trim around the edge of the pastry with a knife. Be careful that you do not stretch the pastry or cut in toward the center of the pan, or you will not have a neat edge. There are various ways to decorate the edge of a tart (see page 338 and picture page 201). Spread the jam in the center of the pastry. Bake in a preheated 400°F. oven for approximately 20 minutes. When the pastry looks golden brown it is cooked.   *Serves 4*

Honey tart

Cooking time   20–25 minutes
Oven temperature   425°F.

1 recipe short crust pastry
2–3 tablespoons honey
2 tablespoons fine soft bread crumbs.

Bake on 8-inch pie shell (see page 215). While the honey can be put into the uncooked pastry, baking the pie shell first is a better method as it gives crisper pastry. Put the warmed honey over the half-cooked pastry, cover with the bread crumbs and return to the center of the oven for a further 10–15 minutes (see picture page 201).   *Serves 4*

Lemon meringue pie

Cooking time   55 minutes
Oven temperature   425°F. then 275°F.

½ recipe short crust pastry.
FOR THE FILLING: ¼ cup cornstarch
1¼ cups water   ·   ¼ cup margarine
½ cup granulated sugar   ·   2 egg yolks   ·   2 lemons.
MERINGUE: 2 egg whites   ·   ¼ cup granulated sugar.

Line a pie pan with the pastry and bake the shell in a preheated 425°F. oven for 8–10 minutes. Blend the cornstarch with the cold water. Put into a saucepan, and cook gently until thickened. Add the margarine, sugar, egg yolks, and the very finely grated lemon peels and finally the lemon juice. Pour into the pastry shell. Beat the egg whites until stiff and fold in nearly all the sugar. Pile on top of the lemon filling and sprinkle with the remaining sugar. Bake in a preheated 275°F. oven for 45 minutes, when the meringue should feel firm to the touch. Do not bake the meringue more quickly, otherwise it will not stay crisp when cold.   *Serves 4*

Pear 'rafts'

Cooking time   15–20 minutes
Oven temperature   450°F.

½ recipe flaky *or* rough puff pastry
3 tablespoons granulated sugar
2 large ripe pears   ·   juice of 1 lemon
¼ cup strained apricot jam
3 tablespoons water.
TO DECORATE: ¼ cup chopped walnuts.

Roll out the pastry, and cut into 4 equal-sized pieces, mold these lightly to be rather the shape of a halved pear and dust well with the sugar. Bake in a preheated 450°F. oven for about 15 minutes, or until crisp and golden. Meanwhile, peel and core the pears and halve. Poach in a syrup made of the lemon juice, jam, and water for a few minutes, turning the pears in the hot syrup until coated. Remove from the syrup and put onto the pastry. Top with chopped nuts. If any syrup is not used, pour it over the pastry and brush over the pears. If serving cold, put the cold pears into the cold pastry, to keep this crisp. Illustrated on page 272.   *Serves 4*

Éclairs

Cooking time   *35–40 minutes*
Oven temperature   *400°F. then 375°F.*

Choux pastry (see page 217).
TO FILL: ¾ cup whipping cream.
TO DECORATE: chocolate or coffee flavored confectioner's sugar frosting (see page 283).

Pipe mixture into thin rectangular shapes on well greased and floured baking sheets – either lift the nozzle when the desired length is reached or cut with kitchen scissors. Bake in a preheated 400°F. oven for 25 minutes then reduce the temperature to 375°F. and bake for the remaining 10–15 minutes. When cooked, cool, split, fill with whipped cream, and spread with frosting.   *Makes 15–18*

Cream buns

Cooking time   *35–40 minutes*
Oven temperature   *400°F. then 375°F.*

Choux pastry (see page 217)
TO FILL: ¾ cup whipping cream.
TO DECORATE: chocolate flavored confectioners' sugar frosting (see page 283) or sifted confectioners' sugar.

There are several ways to shape cream buns. The most simple is to grease and flour muffin pans and put in a spoonful of the mixture, or pile some of the mixture onto well greased and floured baking sheets. The correct method, however, is to put the mixture into a piping bag and force through large plain nozzles onto the floured and greased baking sheets. Bake in a preheated 400°F. oven for 15 minutes. Reduce the heat to 375°F. and bake for a further 20 minutes. (If you have a large roasting tin which can be put right over the cakes while in the oven, use this, for it helps to give a far better shape to them. The tin should be light in weight and allow several inches in height, for the buns will rise considerably as they cook. It is, however, quite possible to bake the buns without the tin.) At the end of this time the buns should be pale golden and feel very firm and crisp. Cool them gradually away from drafts. You may sometimes find when you split the buns that there is a little uncooked pastry left in the center. This should be taken out carefully, and if you feel it necessary, the buns returned for a few minutes to a slightly warm oven to dry. When buns are cold, split them and fill with whipped cream. Top with chocolate frosting or sifted confectioners' sugar.   *12 large buns*

To make a flan

A fruit flan is one of the most attractive desserts – in order to be really good: make the flan as described, bake the pastry shell and allow to cool, then fill with cold well-drained fruit, and cover with *cool* glaze.

To line a flan case

Choose short crust, sweet short crust (see page 215) or flan pastry (see page 216).
Roll out pastry to an approximate size. To measure, place flan ring or layer cake pan lightly on the pastry and allow the diameter of the pan plus 2 inches all round. If using a layer cake pan, grease very lightly. With a flan ring, unless new, greasing is not necessary. It is easy to get the pastry flan out of the ring if you stand the ring on a layer cake pan turned upside down. Then remove the ring and slide flan shell onto the wire rack or serving plate. To take the pastry from the pastry board or table to the layer cake pan or flan ring, lay pastry over the rolling pin, to act as a support. Arrange pastry in position over the pan or flan ring. Slide away rolling pin. Press pastry firmly into bottom of pan with the side of the forefinger. Press pastry firmly against sides of pan.
Use a knife to trim the edge of the pastry, with your left hand forefinger along the top of the pastry, cutting steadily behind it in a clockwise direction. This prevents the knife cutting into the edges and any stretching of the pastry.
Or, if the edge of the pan is sharp, roll the rolling pin firmly over the pastry.
It is now ready to make an edge on the flan, to fill it, or to bake the shell in a preheated 425°F. oven for 8–10 minutes.

TO MAKE AN ATTRACTIVE EDGE

Fluted flan rings are available, and, traditionally, one uses a plain flan ring for a flan which is not a dessert and a fluted one for a sweet flan. If you bake a flan shell in a layer cake pan or flan ring and want a slightly decorated edge, do this as follows:

A FLUTED EDGE

Pinch pastry between forefinger and thumb at about ¼-inch intervals and pull pastry down about ⅛–¼ inch from the top.

A PINCHED EDGE

Take pastry between forefinger and thumb at regular intervals and pull toward the center of the flan shell, which gives an even line on the top and a slightly pulled-in effect.

To make and fill a flan case

Cooking time   *8–10 minutes*
Oven temperature   *425°F.*

½ recipe short crust *or* sweet short crust pastry *or* 1 recipe flan pastry · *either* 1 large can fruit *or* ¾–1 lb. fruit with a little water and sugar *or* frozen fruit
arrowroot *or* cornstarch glaze.

Make the pastry and line a flan ring. Bake the pastry shell in a preheated 425°F. oven for 8–10 minutes. Prepare the fruit – when using canned fruit, drain the fruit over a fine sieve so that it is quite dry, and you have not wasted any of the syrup. To make sure it is very dry place the fruit on paper towels to drain before actually putting into the flan. When using cooked fruit – make a syrup of approximately 1 cup water and ¼–½ cup granulated sugar. Bring to a boil, then add the prepared fruit. Simmer very gently until just soft, but not broken. Remove, drain as for canned fruit, and cool. When using frozen fruit – allow to defrost but not to become over-defrosted. Drain as canned fruit, but when making the glaze allow a little less liquid since there will be further defrosting while the fruit actually stands in the pastry shell. Arrange the well drained cold fruit in the cold pastry shell. Make glaze, blending

How to make pancakes, page 208

Prune and pear compôte page 235; Apple fritters, page 236

Cream chocolate cloud, page 241

Christmas pudding, page 231

Jam suet pudding, pages 232 and 329

Steamed sponge pudding page 233

3 teaspoons arrowroot or cornstarch with 1½ cups fruit syrup and boiling for a few minutes until clear, cool, then spoon or brush over the fruit.   *Serves 4*

Apple and almond flan

Cooking time   *8–10 minutes*
Oven temperature   *425°F.*

½ recipe short crust *or* sweet short crust
PASTRY CREAM: 2 tablespoons cornstarch
1¼ cups milk · ¼ cup granulated sugar
¼ teaspoon vanilla extract · 1 egg
1 egg yolk. FILLING: ¾ cup granulated sugar
juice ½ lemon · ¾ cup water
6 large baking apples.
GLAZE: ¼ cup strained apricot jam
3 tablespoons syrup from cooking the apples.
TO DECORATE: 4–5 maraschino cherries
leaves of angelica · 16 whole blanched almonds.

Roll out pastry and make flan shell as on page 220, then bake the shell in a preheated 425°F. oven for about 8–10 minutes. Let stand until cool. While the pastry is cooking make the pastry cream, and prepare the filling. Blend the cornstarch with most of the milk, bring the remaining milk to a boil, then pour over the cornstarch, stirring constantly, return to the pan, and cook until thickened, adding the sugar and vanilla extract. Cool slightly, then stir in the whisked egg and yolk, return to the pan, and cook without boiling for about 3 minutes (a double boiler could be used for a longer period, if desired). For the filling, dissolve the sugar in the lemon juice and water over low heat. Cook quickly for a few minutes until syrupy. Cook apple slices in this syrup until barely tender. Put the cool pastry cream into the cool shell and arrange cold, well drained apple slices on top of the cream. Boil together the jam and 3 tablespoons syrup from cooking the apples for 4 minutes. Cool slightly, then brush on apple slices. Fill the center of the flan with maraschino cherries and angelica leaves, and make a border of almonds.   *Serves 6–8*

EMERGENCY PASTRY DISHES

Pastry dishes today may be made in a very short space of time, for it is possible to buy excellent frozen and package pastry mixes. Store and use these as directed on the package.

PASTRY DISHES TO IMPRESS

Many pastry dishes are impressive, as you will see from the pictures. The following are very suitable for special occasions.

Hazel nut flan

Cooking time   *8–10 minutes*
Oven temperature   *425°F.*

1 recipe short *or* sweet short crust pastry.
FOR THE FILLING: 16 marshmallows

⅓ cup milk · ½–1 cup hazelnuts or filberts
1 (8½ oz.) can crushed pineapple
1–2 dessert apples · 3 tablespoons granulated sugar
(optional) · few candied *or* maraschino cherries
¼ cup whipping cream *or* evaporated milk.

Line a 9-inch pie pan with the pastry and bake the shell in a preheated 425°F. oven for 8–10 minutes. Let stand until cool. Put the marshmallows (reserving four) and the milk into a saucepan large enough to hold the remaining ingredients, and put over a VERY LOW HEAT until the marshmallows are half melted; cool, then add the nuts, drained pineapple, most of the diced apple (leaving the peel on if a pretty color), the sugar, if desired, and most of the cherries. Lastly, fold in the whipped cream or evaporated milk (see page 238). Put into the pastry shell and top with the four marshmallows, cherries, and segments of apple – add these just before serving or sprinkle with lemon juice so that they do not discolor. Serve cold.   *Serves 6*

Jellied apricot pie

Cooking time   *25 minutes*
Oven temperature   *400°F.*

1 recipe sweet short crust pastry
1 (1 lb. 14 oz.) can apricots · water
1 package lemon gelatin · 1 egg yolk
3 tablespoons granulated sugar. TOPPING: cup whipping cream · 1 egg white · 3 tablespoons granulated sugar · 2 apricots from can · ¼ cup toasted blanched almonds*

* to blanch: put into boiling water for about 1 minute, skin, then toast under the broiler or in the oven.

Roll out the pastry and line an 8-inch flan ring or pie pan and bake the shell in a preheated 425°F. oven for 8–10 minutes. Meanwhile, drain the apricots from the can. Measure the syrup and add enough water to make 1¾ cups. Heat and dissolve the gelatin in this. Beat the egg yolk and sugar in a bowl, pour over the hot but not boiling purée, and then let stand until beginning to set. Chop or sift the apricots if preferred, reserving 2 for decoration. Blend with the gelatin. Let the pastry cool, then put in the cold gelatin mixture. Beat the cream until it just holds its shape. Beat the egg white until very stiff, then fold in the sugar and the cream. Pile on top of the filling and decorate with the sliced apricots and almonds, if desired.   *Serves 4–6*

Other canned or cooked fruits could be used in the same way: try raspberries, strawberries, or blackcurrants.

HOT PUDDINGS

Hot puddings may range from the rich, traditional Christmas pudding to a light sponge pudding, baked fruit crumble, or egg custard.

Wise choice of hot puddings

It is good menu planning to make a steamed sponge pudding or a pudding filled with fruit to follow a light or cold main course, or to serve an egg custard, or pudding based on an egg custard, after a fairly substantial main course.

Many of the puddings in this section are ideal for invalids, since they are easily digested.

Ways to serve hot puddings

The method of serving depends on the particular pudding. Most recipes in this section are for large puddings, serving 4–6 people, but, as you will see in the suggestions below, an appreciable amount of time is saved if they are cooked in individual containers or molds.

To use leftover hot puddings

Portions of steamed plain sponge or Christmas pudding may be resteamed or cut into slices and fried (see below).

Part of an egg custard may be served again or put into the electric blender and made into a pouring sauce.

A milk pudding (particularly a rice pudding) may be made into a most delicious cold dessert a condé (see page 239).

Easy remedies when things are wrong

PROBLEM – if a steamed sponge or suet pudding is heavy, this could be due to an error in the method of mixing (see page 267), or because the water did not boil sufficiently quickly.

TO REMEDY – there is little one can do except to camouflage the pudding with a particularly good sauce.

PROBLEM – if an egg custard, or pudding based on an egg custard, curdles (i.e. has holes in it and a layer of water), this is due to too high heat in steaming or baking (see page 233).

TO REMEDY – the custard can never be as good, but remove from the dish carefully so as to leave the 'watery' part behind, or in the case of a plain egg custard, put into an electric blender; switch on and turn the custard into a pouring sauce to serve with fruit, etc.

Adjusting the cooking times

Cooking times are given for large puddings. To save time, use individual molds, little castle pudding pans (small, cylindrical dariole molds) tightly covered metal containers such as baking powder cans, or even old coffee cups. The cooking time can then be reduced to just over a quarter, i.e. instead of 2 hours the little puddings need 35–40 minutes.

Poor knight's fritters

Cooking time   *5 minutes*

8 slices of bread *or* plain pudding *or* cake
butter · jam. TO COAT: 1 egg
3 tablespoons milk. TO FRY: butter *or* oil.
TO DECORATE: sugar.

If using bread, spread with butter and jam, then sandwich together. Pudding or cake needs no butter. Beat the egg and milk, dip the sandwiches in this, then fry in enough butter or oil to cover bottom of a pan. Drain on paper towels, and coat with sugar.
Serves 4

STEAMED PUDDINGS

The following recipes are for steamed puddings. Information on lining bowls with suet crust pastry is given on page 158 and directions on covering puddings, making string handles, etc., so they are easily removed from the saucepan or steamer, on the same page.

Apple Brown Betty pudding

2 cups fine fresh brown bread crumbs · 3 medium baking apples · ¼ cup currants, seedless white raisins, chopped mixed candied peel, or combination
¼ teaspoon cinnamon · dash nutmeg
dash allspice · 3 tablespoons granulated sugar
¼ cup butter or margarine · 1 tablespoon corn syrup · 2 teaspoons warm water.

Grease a 3 pint ovenproof bowl, and sprinkle some of the bread crumbs around the inside. Fill the bowl with alternate layers of thinly sliced apples, currants, bread crumbs, spices and sugar, ending with bread crumbs. Put the butter or margarine in tiny pieces on top. Mix the corn syrup with the water and pour over the top. Cover well, and steam for 1½–2 hours. *Serves 4–6*

Brigade pudding

Cooking time   *2½ hours*

1 recipe suet crust pastry (see page 217)
2 apples · 1⅓ cups fine fresh bread crumbs
⅓ cup currants · 1 tablespoon orange marmalade
¼ cup corn syrup.

Roll out the suet crust pastry, and line the sides of a greased 2 pint ovenproof bowl, keeping some of the pastry for the top. Slice the apples finely or grate them. Mix with the remaining ingredients. Put into the pastry shell, and cover with the remaining pastry. Put greased wax paper and a pudding cloth or foil on top, and steam for 2½ hours. *Serves 4–6*

Christmas pudding

Cooking time   *4–8 hours*

3 cups (1 lb.) seedless raisins · 2 cups seedless white raisins · 2 cups currants · 1 cup chopped mixed candied peel · ½ cup blanched almonds
½ cup all-purpose flour · 2 teaspoons cinnamon
1 teaspoon nutmeg · ½ teaspoon allspice
1¼ cups sugar* · 2⅔ cups fine fresh white bread crumbs · grated peel 1 lemon · ¾ cup chopped beef suet · 4 eggs
⅔ cup whisky, ale or beer, or milk, or orange juice.

* granulated or brown.

Mix together the raisins, white raisins, currants, candied peel, and chopped almonds. Sift the flour and spices together, and add to fruit mixture with sugar, bread crumbs, lemon peel, and suet. Beat eggs into mixture with the whisky, or stale ale or beer, or milk, or orange juice. Stir well – let stand over-

night, if desired, then stir again, and make a wish. Divide mixture between the greased ovenproof bowls. Use one 5 pint, two 2½ pint or 1¼ pint bowls. Cover first with greased wax paper and then with foil, or with a paste made by blending flour and water. Steam or boil for 4–8 hours depending on size. Uncover and let stand until cool. Re-cover with fresh wax paper and foil, and store in a cool, dry place. On Christmas Day steam or boil for a further 3 hours. Serve with brandy butter, or hard sauce, or lightly whipped and sweetened cream, or one of the sauces on page 187 or page 232. *Serves 14–16*

This pudding may be varied in many ways: A large grated baking apple gives a softer texture and 1 large grated carrot and/or ¾ cup flaked coconut a 'nutty' taste. Add chopped prunes too, if desired.

Apricot Christmas pudding

Cooking time   *4–8 hours*

3 cups (1 lb.) dried apricots · 2 cups seedless white raisins · 1½ cups chopped mixed candied peel
1 cup halved candied cherries
1 cup blanched chopped almonds · 1 cup chopped walnuts · grated peel of 2 oranges
grated peel of 1 lemon · 1¼ cups granulated sugar
2⅔ cups fine fresh bread crumbs · ½ cup all-purpose flour · ½ cup butter · 4 eggs · ⅔ cup liquid (this may be orange and lemon juice or fruit juice mixed with a light sherry or milk).

Chop the apricots – do not soak them, mix with all the remaining ingredients, melting the butter. Continue as the Christmas pudding (previous column). This pudding keeps quite well; should not be made more than 2 weeks before Christmas. Illustrated on page 108. *Serves 12–14*

Chocolate pudding

Cooking time   *1¾ hours*

½ cup all-purpose flour · ¾ teaspoon baking powder
dash salt · 3 tablespoons cocoa
¾ cup fine fresh bread crumbs · ⅓ cup chopped beef suet · ¼ cup granulated sugar
egg and milk or milk to mix
few drops vanilla extract.

Sift together the flour, baking powder, salt and cocoa, add all the other ingredients except the liquid, and mix thoroughly. Beat the egg and milk, adding vanilla essence. Stir sufficient liquid into the mixture to give a slightly sticky consistency.

Grease and flour a 1 pint ovenproof bowl and put in the mixture. Cover with greased wax paper, and steam or boil for approximately 1¾ hours. Serve with Chocolate sauce or Egg custard sauce (see page 187).

Serves 4

Collegiate puddings

Cooking time	*See method*
Oven temperature	*400°F.*

1¼ cups fine fresh bread crumbs · ⅓ cup seedless white raisins · ¼ cup granulated sugar
½ teaspoon baking powder
¾ cup finely chopped beef suet
¼ cup currants · dash each of nutmeg, cloves, cinnamon, and salt.

Mix together all the dry ingredients, add beaten eggs, and stir well. Put the mixture into well-greased individual molds and either bake in a preheated 400°F. oven for 25 minutes, or steam for 35 minutes. Serve with Brandy butter or white sauce flavored with brandy or Brandy lemon sauce (see page 187). If you wish to use one bowl, steam for 1½ hours or bake in a preheated 350°F. oven for 1¼ hours.

Serves 4–6

Halfpay pudding

Cooking time	*1½–2 hours*

⅓ cup chopped beef suet *or* margarine · 1⅓ cups bread crumbs · ½ cup all-purpose flour · ¾ teaspoon baking powder · dash salt
3 tablespoons corn syrup · ½ cup seedless white raisins · ½ cup currants · milk *or* egg and milk to mix.

Mix together the suet, bread crumbs and sifted dry ingredients. If using margarine, melt this and add in place of the suet. Add the corn syrup, white raisins, and currants, and stir thoroughly. Add the milk or egg and milk to give a sticky consistency. Half-fill a greased 3 pint ovenproof bowl, cover with greased wax paper and steam for 1½–2 hours.

Serves 4–5

Note: If desired, 3–4 tablespoons corn syrup may be put at the bottom of the bowl to give a sauce.

Fruit suet pudding

Cooking time	*2 hours*

1 recipe suet crust pastry · 5 medium baking apples (1 lb.), pared and diced *or* rhubarb *or* plums
¼–⅓ cup granulated sugar · little water.

Make the pastry and line the bowl as described on page 158. Fill with the prepared fruit, sugar, and about 3 tablespoons water, the amount depending on the juiciness of the fruit. Roll out the remaining pastry and press over the top of the pudding. Cover with greased wax paper or foil and steam over boiling water for approximately 2 hours, making sure the water boils vigorously. Turn out onto a heated dish and serve with whipped cream or Egg custard sauce (see page 187).

Serves 4–6

Fruit dumplings

1½ cups all-purpose flour · 2¼ teaspoons baking powder · ½ teaspoon salt · 3 tablespoons margarine *or* butter · ½ cup granulated sugar · water to bind · 1 lb. prepared fruit (apples, plums, berry fruits or frozen fruits) · 2 tablespoons granulated sugar, for sprinkling.

Sift together the flour, baking powder, and the salt, rub in the margarine or butter, add one fourth of the sugar, and water to bind. Form into 8 small balls. Put the fruit with the remaining sugar and approximately 1¼ cups water into a large saucepan. Heat until the liquid is boiling or until the fruit is beginning to soften, in the case of very hard plums etc. Drop in the dumplings and cook steadily for 20 minutes. Sprinkle with sugar before serving.

Serves 4–6

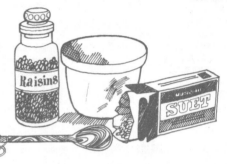

Pressure cooker puddings

A pressure cooker is suitable for cooking many puddings and it does save a considerable amount of time. Note the instructions about steaming for part of the time before pressure cooking. This allows the leavening agent to work and gives a light pudding. The following puddings are given as examples of timing. Follow the manufacturer's instructions as to the method of putting on pressure weight. If in a hurry the pressure may be reduced immediately, but remember this can cause cracking if you are using a glass or china bowl. It is safer to allow the temperature to drop back at room temperature.

Brigade pudding

Cooking time	*50 minutes*

Make Brigade pudding (see page 231). Put the bowl on the rack in the cooker with 5 cups boiling water. Fix the lid, but do not put on pressure weight. Steam for 20 minutes. Bring to 5 lb. pressure, lower the heat, cook for 30 minutes. Let pressure drop at room temperature.

Serves 4–6

Suet pudding

Cooking time	*50 minutes*

Make the Jam suet pudding (see page 329). Stand on the rack in the pressure cooker with 5 cups boiling water. Fix lid, but do not put on pressure weight. Cook as for Brigade pudding (see above). This method could be used for a Steak and kidney pudding (see page 158), but allow 20 minutes steaming and 1 hour at 15 lb. pressure. Let pressure drop at room temperature.

Serves 4

Sponge puddings

The same technique should be used when making a sponge pudding as when making a sponge cake, so read the directions from page 267 onward.

Steamed sponge pudding

Cooking time *1½ hours*

½ cup butter *or* margarine · ½ cup granulated sugar
2 eggs · 1 cup all-purpose flour · 1½ teaspoons baking powder · ¼ teaspoon salt · 1 tablespoon milk.

Cream margarine and sugar together until soft and light. Add eggs gradually, then stir in the flour sifted together with the baking powder and the salt, then the milk. Grease a 2 pint ovenproof bowl and pour the mixture into this. Cover with wax paper or foil and put in a steamer over a saucepan of rapidly boiling water. Steam for at least 1½ hours. Turn out onto a heated dish and serve immediately with any sweet sauce. *Serves 4*

This recipe may be varied in several ways
JAM – place 3–4 tablespoons jam at the bottom of the bowl. Illustrated on page 228.

FRUIT – add ⅓ cup currants, ⅓ cup seedless white raisins, and ⅓ cup chopped mixed candied peel but omit the milk. Serve with custard.

GINGER – sift 1 level teaspoon ginger with the flour and add ¼–⅓ cup diced candied ginger with the flour.

SYRUP (often called golden cap pudding) – put corn syrup at the bottom of the bowl and serve with Sweet syrup sauce (see page 330).

LEMON – add the finely grated peel of 1 lemon to the butter and sugar, and mix with 1 tablespoon lemon juice instead of milk. Put Lemon curd (see page 311) or lemon marmalade at the bottom of the bowl and serve with Lemon sauce (see page 329).

CHOCOLATE – substitute 1 tablespoon cocoa for 1 tablespoon flour. Chopped walnuts and ⅓ cup currants, ⅓ cup seedless white raisins, and ⅓ cup chopped mixed candied peel may be added.

EGG CUSTARDS

The following recipes are all based upon an egg custard and in order that this shall be successful remember:
1. Use the right proportion of eggs and liquid – too few eggs will give a custard that does not set.
2. Cook slowly – if steaming the custard or pudding then the water must be hot, but NOT BOILING.
If baking, stand the custard or pudding in a pan of water, so this 'slows up' the cooking process. The pan of cold water, known as a 'bain marie', is most effective if it is not used for the first 10–15 minutes cooking time; in this way the water in it will always be cooler than the custard temperature.

Steamed egg custard

Cooking time *1¼ hours*

2 eggs · 1 tablespoon sugar
1¾ cups milk · little freshly grated nutmeg.

Beat the eggs with a fork, add the sugar and the warmed milk; the milk must not boil or it will curdle the eggs. Pour into a greased pie pan or ovenproof bowl and top with grated nutmeg. Put the bowl into a steamer over very hot water and cook steadily for about 1¼ hours, being careful that the water does not boil since this will curdle the custard. Cool slightly and turn out, if desired. *Serves 4*

Baked egg custard

Cooking time *1¼–1½ hours*
Oven temperature *275°F.*

4 eggs *or* egg yolks · 3–4 tablespoons granulated sugar · 2½ cups milk · little freshly grated nutmeg.

Beat the eggs and sugar together. Pour over the hot but not boiling milk. Pour into a pie pan and top with grated nutmeg. Stand in another container of cold water. Bake for approximately 1¼–1½ hours in a preheated 275°F. oven until quite firm. For a less firm custard, use only 2–3 eggs. *Serves 4*

Steamed mocha pudding

Cooking time *2½ hours*
Oven temperature *275°F.*

4 egg yolks · 2 egg whites · ¼ cup granulated sugar · ½ cup chocolate drink powder · 1¾ cups milk · ⅔ cup very strong coffee · ½ cup seedless white raisins · ¼ cup chopped candied cherries
½ cup chopped nuts (optional)
¼ cup finely chopped candied peel
3 tablespoons sherry (optional).

Beat the eggs, sugar, and chocolate drink powder together. Pour over the milk and coffee. Add the remaining ingredients. Pour into a greased ovenproof bowl and steam gently WITHOUT BOILING for approximately 2½ hours, or bake in a preheated 275°F. oven for about the same time, standing the dish in another of warm water. Cover the pudding with well-buttered wax paper or foil. If serving cold, decorate with a little whipped cream and chocolate curls. *Serves 4–5*

Pressure cooking: Stand pudding on rack in the cooker with 5 cups boiling water. In this pudding, since there is no flour, bring to 15 lb. pressure and cook for 8 minutes.

Bread and butter pudding

Cooking time   *1 hour*
Oven temperature   *325°F.*

1 recipe Baked egg custard (see page 233)
2 large *or* 4 small slices bread · little butter
⅓ cup currants, *or* ⅓ cup seedless white raisins, *or* ⅓ cup chopped mixed candied peel, *or* a combination
little extra sugar.

Prepare the egg custard as previous page. Remove the crusts from the bread, butter thinly. Cut into neat squares or triangles, and arrange in a pie pan. Add the currants, and pour the custard over the top. Let stand for 30 minutes. Sprinkle the top with a little sugar, and bake in a preheated 325°F. oven for approximately 1 hour. If the pudding appears to be cooking too quickly after 45 minutes, lower the heat.
Serves 4

Queen of puddings

Cooking time   *55 minutes – 1 hour*
Oven temperature   *325°F.*

2 eggs · ½ cup granulated sugar · 1¼ cups milk
⅔ cup fine fresh cake *or* bread crumbs · 1 lemon
little jam.

Beat the egg yolks with half the sugar. Pour over the hot but not boiling milk. Put the bread crumbs and finely grated lemon peel into a bowl, and strain the egg mixture over them. Put a little jam in the bottom of a pie pan, and pour in the mixture. Bake in a preheated 325°F. oven for 35–40 minutes, or until firm. Spread jam over the top. Beat the egg whites until stiff, and fold in the remaining sugar, spread over the jam. Return to the oven for approximately 20 minutes. Serve hot. *Serves 4*

Finger pudding

Cooking time   *1 hour*

¼ cup granulated sugar · 2 eggs, separated
¾ cup finely ground almonds
½ teaspoon grated lemon peel
¼ teaspoon cloves
¾ teaspoon cinnamon · 3 tablespoons butter
½ cup crushed lady fingers *or* vanilla wafers.

Beat sugar and egg yolks until creamy. Add almonds, lemon peel, cloves, cinnamon, melted butter, and crushed cookies. Fold in stiffly beaten egg whites. Turn into a greased mold, or ovenproof bowl, and steam gently for 1 hour. Do not allow water to boil rapidly, otherwise pudding will curdle. *Serves 4*

Viennese pudding

Cooking time   *2½ hours*

¼ cup granulated sugar
¼ cup water · 2¼ cups milk
1 cup diced bread, without crusts
3 tablespoons granulated sugar · 4 egg yolks
2 egg whites · ⅓ cup seedless white raisins
¼ cup chopped candied cherries
½ cup chopped nuts (optional)
¼ cup finely chopped candied peel
3 tablespoons sherry (optional)

Put the granulated sugar and water into a heavy pan, stir until the sugar has dissolved, then boil steadily until 380°–390°F. on a candy thermometer. Cool slightly, then add the milk, heat without boiling, until the milk has absorbed the caramel, then pour over the diced bread. Let stand for at least 30 minutes. Add all the remaining ingredients to the caramel mixture, beating the eggs very well before they are put in. Pour into a greased ovenproof bowl and steam gently, without boiling, for approximately 2½ hours. Cool for 3 minutes in the bowl, so the pudding has a chance to set, then turn out carefully onto a heated dish. Serve accompanied with whipped or coffee cream poured over the pudding, or with sherry-flavored custard. *Serves 4–5*

Rice pudding

Cooking time   *2–3 hours*
Oven temperature   *300°F.*

¼–½ cup round short grain (often called Carolina) rice · 2¼ cups milk
little butter *or* chopped beef suet
granulated sugar to taste.

Soak the rice in the milk for 1 hour before cooking, or cover with a little water and put into a preheated 400°F. oven for about 10–15 minutes, or until the rice has absorbed the water; pour over the milk. Add a knob of butter or suet, to give extra creaminess, and sugar to taste. Cook in a preheated 300°F. oven for about 2–3 hours. *Serves 4*

FRUIT RICE PUDDING
Use the recipe above, but cook the rice in a very thin fruit purée or syrup instead of milk.

CARAMEL RICE PUDDING
Use recipe above, plus an additional ¼ cup granulated sugar and 3 tablespoons water. Put the sugar and water into a pan, stir until the sugar has dissolved, allow to brown, then add the milk and heat with the caramel, taking care not to boil rapidly. Pour over the rice, add sugar, etc. and continue as recipe.

Semolina pudding

Cooking time   *See method*
Oven temperature   *250°F.*

2¼ cups milk · 3–4 tablespoons granulated sugar
good ⅓ cup semolina.

Bring the milk to a boil, add the sugar, and gradually whisk in the semolina. Stir very briskly until thickened and smooth. Cook for about 10 minutes on top of the range or transfer to a pie pan and cook in a preheated 250°F. oven for approximately 45 minutes.

Serves 4

Fruit Charlotte

Cooking time — *50 minutes*
Oven temperature — *375°F.*

1 lb. prepared fruit – apples, plums, etc.
granulated sugar for cooking fruit · water
4 slices bread · ¼–⅓ cup butter
¼ cup brown sugar.

Cook the fruit with sugar and water for a few minutes. Remove a few pieces of fruit while still firm, to use for decoration. Cook the rest until a soft, thick purée. Cut the bread into neat strips and sauté on each side in the hot butter until crisp and golden brown. Drain, and pack one-third of the strips into a Charlotte mold or a 9-inch pie pan, and sprinkle with sugar. Cover with well-drained fruit purée, more slices of crisp bread, more sugar, then purée and a final layer of the crisp bread and sugar. Bake in a preheated 375°F. oven for about 35 minutes. Turn out and decorate with fruit. Serve accompanied with whipped or coffee cream.

Serves 4

Fruit crumble

Cooking time — *35 minutes*
Oven temperature — *375°F.*

1 lb. fruit · granulated sugar to taste · water
FOR THE TOPPING: 1 cup all-purpose flour
¼ cup butter *or* margarine · ⅓ cup granulated sugar.

Put the fruit, sugar, and a very little water, into a 9-inch pie pan. Soft berry fruits, such as raspberries and blackcurrants, will need no water at all. Heat for about 10–15 minutes. To make the topping, sift the flour, and rub the butter into it. Add the sugar, and sprinkle the crumbs evenly over the fruit, pressing down fairly firmly. This makes certain the crust may be cut into neat slices. Bake in a preheated 375°F. oven for about 25 minutes, or until crisp and golden brown. Serve hot or cold.

Serves 4

Eve's pudding

Cooking time — *45–50 minutes*
Oven temperature — *375°F.*

4 medium baking apples · ¼ cup granulated sugar
⅓ cup water · ⅓ cup butter *or* margarine
⅓ cup granulated sugar · 2 eggs
1 cup all-purpose flour
1½ teaspoons baking powder · ¼ teaspoon salt.

Peel, core, and slice the apples. Put into a 9-inch pie pan with the sugar and water, and bake in a preheated 375°F. oven for approximately 10 minutes. Cream together the butter and sugar, gradually beat in the eggs, and stir in the flour sifted together with the baking powder and the salt. Spread this mixture over the hot apples, and return to oven for a further 35–40 minutes. Sprinkle with sugar before serving.

Serves 4

Apple amber

Cooking time — *See method*
Oven temperature — *350°F.*

3–4 medium apples · very little water
½–⅔ cup granulated sugar · 2 eggs.

Simmer the apples with very little water and half the sugar. When a thick, smooth pulp add the beaten egg yolks. Pour into an ovenproof dish and bake in a preheated 350°F. oven for approximately 30 minutes. Whisk the egg whites until very stiff, fold in the remaining sugar and pile on top of apple mixture. Return to oven and brown meringue for 20 minutes if serving hot. If serving cold, place in 300°F. oven for about 1 hour.

Serves 4

Prune and pear compôte

Cooking time — *1 hour*

1 cup prunes · ⅔ cup water
⅔ cup white wine · 3–4 medium firm pears
¼ cup granulated sugar · ¼ cup strained apricot jam
TO DECORATE: 1 orange.

Put the prunes into a bowl, add water and wine to cover. Let stand overnight to soak, then simmer until nearly tender. Peel the pears, put into the pan with the prunes, sugar, and jam and simmer until tender. Decorate with sliced orange. Illustrated on page 222.

Serves 4–6

Apricot almond sponge

Cooking time — *50 minutes*
Oven temperature — *350°F.*

8–12 fresh apricots
grated peel and juice of 1 lemon
3 tablespoons water · ¼–⅓ cup granulated sugar
¼ cup blanched almonds.
FOR THE SPONGE CAKE: ½ cup margarine
½ cup granulated sugar · grated peel of 1 lemon
2 eggs · 1¼ cups all-purpose flour
¾ teaspoon baking powder · ¼ teaspoon salt
3 tablespoons lemon juice.
FOR THE TOPPING: ½ cup blanched almonds
tablespoon granulated sugar
grated peel of 1 lemon.

Wipe apricots and put at the bottom of an ovenproof dish with the lemon peel and juice, water, sugar, and almonds. Cream together margarine, sugar, and grated lemon peel until soft and light, then gradually beat in the eggs and fold in the flour and lemon juice to give a soft, spreading consistency. Cover the apricots with the batter, top with halved blanched almonds and sugar mixed with grated lemon peel, and bake in a preheated 350°F. oven for approximately 50 minutes, or until firm to the touch. Serve with Harlequin sauce – see below. Illustrated on page 271.

Serves 4–6

HARLEQUIN SAUCE

Gradually blend 1 tablespoon cornstarch with 1¼ cups water in a pan. Add juice of 1 lemon, 3 tablespoons apricot jam, and 3–4 tablespoons granulated sugar, and stir over moderate heat until thickened and clear; add ¼ cup chopped candied cherries and ¼–½ cup flaked, blanched almonds.

Soufflé sweet omelet

Cooking time   *few minutes*

6 eggs · ¼ cup water *or* milk (coffee cream could be used) · ¼ cup granulated sugar · ¼ cup butter
FLAVORING: see below.

Separate the eggs and beat the yolks with the liquid and sugar. Fold in the stiffly beaten egg whites. Heat the butter and pour in the egg mixture, allow this to set lightly at the bottom. The omelet may then be put under a broiler to complete cooking, or the pan put into the oven (if it has no handle). The reason for this method of cooking is that the omelet is particularly thick and the bottom would be over-cooked by the time the top was set if it were cooked in the normal way.   *Serves 3–4*

FLAVORINGS FOR SWEET OMELETS

JAM: Fill the omelet with hot jam, and pour hot jam on top before serving.

FRUIT: Fill and top with fruit purée as for jam.

NUT: Fill with ¼–½ cup chopped blanched almonds. Top with confectioners' sugar and ¼ cup blanched almonds. Brown under the broiler.

Baked apples Californian

Cooking time   *40–50 minutes*
Oven temperature   *400°F.*

4 medium baking apples · 2 tablespoons butter
¼ cup brown sugar · 1 (8 oz.) can fruit cocktail
sprinkle cinnamon.

Prepare apples by coring and slitting skins. Put into a buttered ovenproof dish, top with the remaining butter and the sugar. Pour the syrup from the canned fruit into the dish. Cook as baked apples opposite. For the last 10 minutes of the cooking time, add the fruit cocktail and a little cinnamon. Illustrated on page 198.   *Serves 4*

FRUIT FRITTERS

These are easily and quickly prepared, since the fruit is coated with batter – either a sweet one or a very light type – then fried in hot oil or fat until crisp. The oil or fat must be hot to crisp the outside quickly, approximately 375°F. To test: put a cube of day old bread into the oil – it should turn golden (NOT brown) in 30 seconds; in fat within 1 minute. Put in the fritters. Fry quickly for 1 minute, then reduce heat to finish cooking.

Plain batter

1 cup all-purpose flour
1½ teaspoons baking powder · ¼ teaspoon salt
3–4 tablespoons granulated sugar (optional)
1 egg · ⅔ cup milk · 2 teaspoons melted butter.

Sift together the flour, baking powder, salt, and sugar. Beat egg with milk and butter. Add to the dry ingredients, and beat until smooth.

Fluffy light fritter batter

1 cup all-purpose flour · dash salt
2 eggs · ⅔ cup milk and water.

Sift flour and salt, beat in egg yolks, milk, and water. Finally fold in stiffly beaten egg whites.

Apple fritters

Cooking time   *few minutes*

3 large baking apples · 1 tablespoon all-purpose flour · 1 tablespoon granulated sugar (optional)
1 recipe Fluffy fritter batter (see above)
TO FRY: oil or fat. TO COAT: granulated sugar.
TO DECORATE: 1 lemon

Peel and core the apples, and slice fairly thinly (this makes sure they may be adequately cooked without overbrowning the outside). Dust with flour – this helps the batter to adhere. The sugar may be added to the flour, if desired. Dip in the batter. Test oil as previous column – while shallow frying may be used it is better if deep frying is chosen – then put in the fritters, and fry steadily until crisp and golden brown. Drain on paper towels and sprinkle with sugar. Decorate with slices of lemon. Illustrated on page 222.   *Serves 4*

FOR OTHER FRUIT FRITTERS CHOOSE:

FRESH: firm bananas, firm ripe apricots or plums, greengage plums, halved cored small pears (ripe), pineapple rings.
CANNED: well-drained canned pineapple rings, halved peaches, pears.

WAYS TO COOK FRUIT

Cooked fruit is not only a popular dessert by itself, but it is the basis for other puddings and desserts.

1. If you want the fruit to maintain its shape it is better to cook it in the oven, or to poach it.
2. If you need a very thick purée, so little water may be used in the recipe, it is better to cook the fruit in the top of a double boiler over boiling water to prevent the possibility of the purée burning in the pan.
3. If you are trying to lose weight or are following a diabetic diet, use powdered or liquid sugar substitute instead of sugar (these are easier to dissolve than tablets).
Follow the manufacturer's instructions as to the quantity to allow.

Stewed fruit

TO EACH LB. FRUIT ALLOW:

¼ cup sugar, honey, or corn syrup
¼ cup water with very juicy soft fruits (raspberries, etc.)
⅓ cup water with ripe, quite juicy fruit (rhubarb, ripe apricots, etc.)
1¼ cups water with firm, hard fruit (firm plums, under-ripe gooseberries, etc.)
2½ cups water with dried fruit (soak the fruit overnight in this)
1 tablespoon lemon juice improves the flavor.

Cooking times

Soft fruit – up to 10 minutes
Hard fruit – up to 20 minutes
Dried fruit – up to 1 hour.

Prepare the fruit, peeling and removing the seeds where necessary. Put into a saucepan with the water and sugar, cover the pan, and cook gently until the fruit is soft.

To poach fruit

Cooking time – as stewed fruit
QUANTITIES – allow the same proportions of sugar, honey, or corn syrup and water as for stewed fruit.

This term is used for cooking fruit in the sugar syrup, the advantage being that the fruit keeps a better shape than when stewed. Put the sugar and water into the saucepan. Heat until the sugar has dissolved, then add the prepared fruit, cover the pan, and simmer gently until the fruit is tender but still unbroken.

Oven-cooked fruit

Oven temperature   *See method*

QUANTITIES – Allow the same proportions of sugar, honey, or corn syrup and water as for stewed fruit.

Cooking times
Soft fruit – up to 15 minutes
Hard fruit – up to 30 minutes
Dried fruit – 1¼ hours.

Put the prepared fruit, sugar, and water into a casserole. Cover and cook until tender in a preheated 350°F. oven; or if more convenient allow approximately double the cooking time above in a preheated 250°F. oven.

Fruit purée

Cooking time   *Depending on fruit*

1 lb. prepared fruit
¼ cup water with very soft fruits, *or* ⅔ cup water with ripe, quite juicy fruit, *or* 1¼ cups water with firm fruit
¼–⅓ cup granulated sugar.

Cook the prepared fruit with the water and sugar until you have a smooth thick mixture. Strain, if desired.   *Gives approximately 2½ cups purée*

To bake fruit

Cooking time   *See method*
Oven temperature   *See method*

Apples are the fruit usually baked, although bananas, oranges, and similar fruit may be baked.

APPLES: Allow 1 medium to large apple per person. Wash and dry the apples. Remove the core and stand in an ovenproof baking dish. Slit the skin around the apple with the tip of a sharp knife to prevent it bursting in cooking. The center may be filled before baking with: 2 teaspoons currants, seedless white raisins, or chopped mixed candied peel; 2 teaspoons granulated sugar; 1 tablespoon butter, 2 teaspoons brown sugar; 1 tablespoon blackberry jelly; 1 tablespoon corn syrup. Bake for 40–50 minutes in a preheated 375°F. oven. Illustrated on page 315.

ORANGES: Allow 1 large seedless orange or 2 smaller ones or 3 of the tangerine-type fruit (real tangerines have seeds, but there are many of this family which are seedless). To 4 oranges, or the equivalent, allow ¼ cup granulated sugar, ¼ cup water or orange juice, ¼ cup butter. Heat the sugar, water, and butter in an ovenproof dish until it forms a liquid syrup. Remove the peel and pith from the fruit. Put the whole or halved fruit into the syrup. Spoon this over the fruit. Bake in a preheated 300°F. oven for 20–30 minutes. Do not overbake.

BANANAS: Allow 2 small or medium bananas per person. To 8 bananas you need the same quantity of butter, sugar, and liquid (this may be orange juice or for special occasions brandy or rum) as for orange recipe. Bake for 20–25 minutes as oranges above.

To fry fruit

Many fruits may be fried, the most successful are

FRESH: apples (sweet type best), firm bananas, oranges, peaches, pears, pineapple.

CANNED: apricots, peaches, pears, pineapple.

Cooking time   *10 minutes*

¼–⅓ cup brown sugar · 2–4 tablespoons butter
4 large peaches *or* the equivalent in other fruit juice
1–2 oranges · 1–2 tablespoons brandy (optional).

Put the sugar and butter into a skillet, and stir until the sugar has dissolved and formed a golden mixture. Put in the prepared fruit and fry in this for a few minutes, turning round until coated. Fresh peaches, pears, and bananas should be skinned or peeled and halved; the other fruits peeled and cut into thick slices. Add the orange juice, and simmer for about 5 minutes, pour in the brandy and warm thoroughly. Serve at once.   *Serves 4*

COLD AND FROZEN DESSERTS

Cold desserts are not only delicious but practical, since they may be prepared well before the meal.

Wise choice of cold desserts

The choice varies a great deal, from cold cooked fruit or fresh fruit salads to soufflés or frozen desserts. Choose a refreshing fruit-flavored dessert if the main course is fairly rich; a creamy dessert after a more simple main course.

Ways to serve cold desserts

Choose attractive clear glass dishes, so the colors of fruits may be seen; interesting shaped molds for gelatin desserts. The classic soufflé dishes do not detract from a delicately decorated soufflé.

To use leftover cold desserts

Store in a cool place and serve again. Whisk gelatin mixture and fold into lightly whipped cream.

Easy remedies when things are wrong

PROBLEM – if a gelatin mixture does not set, this could be due to too much liquid or too little gelatin; using fresh pineapple; insufficient chilling time.
TO REMEDY – add a little more gelatin – but if fresh pineapple is put into a gelatin mixture it destroys the setting quality completely. Remove the pineapple, use with ice cream; thicken the gelatin mixture with cornstarch and use as a sauce.
PROBLEM – if the egg whites rise to the top in a cold soufflé, this is due to their being added before the jellied mixture was sufficiently thick.
TO REMEDY – stir very gently and serve in glasses or serve as a 2-layered sweet.

To whip cream

Put the cream into a fairly large deep bowl, so there is no splashing. Use a rotary or electric mixer, beat briskly until the cream begins to hold a shape, then slowly to make sure this is not over-whipped – if this happens the cream curdles and has a thick curd and watery 'whey'. If the cream is very rich, it is better to use a fork towards the end of whipping. Cream to use in soufflés and ice cream should not be too stiff – it should just hold its shape. Sugar may be added to the cream when nearly stiff; allow 1–4 teaspoons sugar to each ⅔ cup cream.

To lighten cream

Cream has a lighter texture if blended with an egg white. Allow 1 egg white to each ⅔ cup cream. Whip the cream and egg white in separate bowls and fold together just before using. The sugar may be whipped into either the cream or the egg white when stiff.

To whip evaporated milk

Follow the manufacturers' recommendations for any particular brand of evaporated milk; the best way to whip is either:
To boil the can of milk in a saucepan of water for 15 minutes (allow plenty of water) and then whip the milk. Store the milk in the refrigerator over-

night before beating, if possible (very chilled milk may whip without boiling).

OR to obtain a stiffer mixture, boil can in water, open the can while the milk is warm – do this carefully so it does not splash and scald the hand. Dissolve 1 teaspoon gelatin in 3 tablespoons water, add to the hot milk, refrigerate, and beat.

Yogurt

Yogurt is produced from milk which is treated with a bacteriological culture; it is nutritious yet low in calories. Today one may buy unflavored yogurt, and both flavored yogurt and the type where it is blended with fruits.

Yogurt may be served as a dessert, either by itself, sweetened, if desired, or as a topping for fruit. The following recipe makes a delicious dessert.

Yogurt whip

Cooking time   *None*

1 package fruit flavored gelatin · 1 cup hot water
1 cup cold water · approximately 1 cup fresh fruit
1¼ cups unflavored yogurt, or choose flavor to blend with gelatin and fruit. TO DECORATE: fresh fruit.

Dissolve the gelatin in the hot water, add the cold water, allow to set lightly, then beat sharply adding the fruit and yogurt. Pile into glasses and chill until quite firm. Top with more fruit.   *Serves 4–6*

Fruit condé

Cooking time   *few minutes*

1 recipe Rice pudding (see page 234)
⅓ cup whipping cream
medium can fruit
2 teaspoons cornstarch *or* arrowroot.

Put the rice pudding into a bowl, and beat in the cream. Taste, and add a little sugar, if desired. Spoon into a serving dish. Strain the fruit from the syrup and arrange the fruit in an attractive design on top of the creamy cold rice. Measure the syrup and if necessary, add a little water to make this up to 1¼ cups. Blend the cornstarch or arrowroot with ½ cup of the syrup, and put the remaining syrup into a saucepan and heat. Stir the cornstarch mixture into the hot syrup and continue cooking, stirring constantly, until the mixture thickens and becomes clear. Let stand until cool, then spread or brush over the fruit.

To give a little more color and flavor to the glaze, add 1 tablespoon redcurrant jelly to coat red fruits or strained apricot jam to coat yellow fruits or fruit cocktail.   *Serves 4*

Fruit snow

Cooking time   *None*

2 egg whites · 2½ cups fruit purée (see page 237)

Beat the egg whites until very stiff. Fold into the cold fruit purée, and pile into sundae glasses.
              Serves 4

Fruit fool

Cooking time   *15 minutes*

1 lb. fruit* · sugar to taste
minimum quantity of water (see method)
2 recipes egg custard sauce using 4 egg yolks plus 2 egg whites (see page 187).
TO DECORATE: little whipping cream
fruit or candied cherries · angelica.

* blackcurrants, gooseberries, (about 4 cups) and apples (about 3 medium) are some of the best fruits to choose.

Cook the fruit with sugar to taste and little, if any, water. In the case of blackcurrants, these may be cooked in a double boiler without any water, for it is essential that the purée is very thick. Use ¼ cup water only with apples and gooseberries. One way of obtaining a very thick purée with apples is to bake them in their skins rather than cook in water. When the fruit is soft, beat or strain if it contains seeds and skin. While the fruit is cooking, make the custard sauce. Beat the thick fruit purée into the custard. Tint if necessary to give a pleasant pale color. Put into glasses or a shallow bowl and chill thoroughly. Top with whipped cream and either whole fruit or cherries and angelica.   *Serves 4–6*

Summer pudding

Cooking time   *10–15 minutes*

1¼ lb. fruit (use redcurrants and raspberries; rhubarb; mixed red and blackcurrants, etc.)
very little water · sugar to taste
6 slices white bread.

Cook the fruit until just tender with the water and sugar. Line a bowl with thin pieces of bread – make sure there are no gaps in this. Fill the center with the sweetened fruit and juice. Put thin slices of bread over the top and a saucer and a small weight on top to encourage the juice to soak through the bread. Let stand for 24 hours in a cool place or refrigerator. Turn out and serve with whipped cream or pudding.   *Serves 4–6*

Although this is called a Summer pudding, it may be made throughout the year with the fruits in season – it looks more attractive if a red or dark colored fruit is used, since this soaks through the bread and colors it an attractive pink.

Fruit meringue

Cooking time   *15 minutes*

1 lb. fruit · sugar to taste · minimum of water.
FOR MERINGUE: 2 egg whites · ¼ cup granulated
sugar.

Cook the fruit by poaching or stewing (see page 237).
Put into an attractive flameproof dish. Beat the egg
whites until very stiff, gradually add the sugar – see
method described on page 298. Pile on top of the
fruit and put under a hot broiler for a few minutes
to brown, or brown in a preheated 275°F. oven for
45 minutes. If preferred to serve cold, then use ½ cup
granulated sugar and cook in a preheated 200°F.
oven for approximately 1 hour.   *Serves 4*

Pear dessert

Cooking time   *25 minutes*

1 cup prunes · ¼ cup granulated sugar
1 teaspoon vanilla extract · 1 lemon
6 small firm pears.

Soak the prunes overnight in water to cover. Drain,
then blend together prune syrup, sugar, and vanilla
and boil for 5 minutes. Add prunes, lemon slices,
and peeled, cored whole pears (core from base with
an apple corer, but try to keep fruit unbroken and
stems on). Cover and simmer for 20 minutes or until
pears are tender. Serve very cold with either coffee
cream or whipping cream spooned over or ice cream.
                                                         Serves 6

Caramel oranges

Cooking time   *5 minutes*

FOR CARAMEL: ⅓ cup granulated sugar · ½ cup water
4 firm oranges, seedless if possible.
TO SERVE: chopped nuts · cream.

Put the sugar with ¼ cup water, into a pan. Warm,
stirring until the sugar has dissolved. Add an
additional ¼ cup water to this. Boil steadily, without stirring, until between 350°F.–370°F. is reached
on a candy thermometer. Pour over the prepared
oranges, which should be peeled with a sharp knife
to remove all the outer pith. Serve with nuts and
coffee cream.   *Serves 4*

COLD SOUFFLÉS

A cold soufflé is a delicious cold sweet.

To prepare a soufflé dish

Choose a sufficiently small dish so the mixture will
come above this – almost as if it has risen. Make a
thick band of wax paper or aluminum foil – this
may be double or treble thickness. Butter the part
that will go above the soufflé dish. Tie or pin it very
firmly so that the paper is standing above the top of
the soufflé dish. This will support the mixture after
the egg whites are added. When the soufflé has set,
very carefully remove the paper. The easiest way
to do this is to dip a knife in hot water and very
gently ease this around the inside of the paper.

Fruit soufflé

Cooking time   *few minutes*

1¼ cups *thick* fruit purée (see page 237)
½ package gelatin (use lemon gelatin with apricots,
etc., strawberry gelatin with red fruits) *or* use ½
envelope unflavored gelatin
⅓ cup water · 3 eggs · 2–4 tablespoons granulated
sugar · ⅔ cup whipping cream.
TO DECORATE: little whipping cream
few blanched almonds (see page 255) *or* other nuts.

Strain the fruit purée; dissolve the gelatin in the
cold water, then stand in a bowl over hot water
until completely dissolved, add to the fruit purée.
Beat the egg yolks and sugar until thick and creamy,
pour onto the fruit mixture. Let stand until beginning to stiffen. Fold in the lightly whipped cream
and stiffly beaten egg whites. Put into a 1 pint
prepared soufflé dish and let stand until set. Remove
the paper and decorate with a delicate piping of
whipped cream and almonds.   *Serves 4*

Economical lemon soufflé

Cooking time   *few minutes*

⅔ cup evaporated milk
grated peel and juice of 1 lemon · water
1 package lemon gelatin · 1 egg.
TO DECORATE: ¼ cup chopped blanched almonds.

Whip the evaporated milk as page 238. Measure the
lemon juice and add enough hot water to give 1¼
cups liquid. Dissolve the gelatin in this, and beat
into the beaten egg yolk and lemon peel. Cool, and
when beginning to stiffen, fold in the whipped
evaporated milk and stiffly beaten egg white. Put
into the prepared pint soufflé dish and chill until
set. Make a very narrow border of almonds around
the top of the soufflé.   *Serves 4*

Chocolate mousse

Cooking time   *5 minutes*

4 oz. bar plain milk chocolate · 3 tablespoons milk
2 egg whites.

Melt the chocolate and milk in a saucepan over low
heat. Let stand until cool. Add stiffly beaten egg
whites. Put into a dish and chill.   *Serves 4*

Note: this is also delicious made with orange juice
instead of milk.

Caramel mousse

Cooking time   *few minutes*

FOR CARAMEL: ¾ cup granulated sugar · ⅓ cup water.
FOR SOUFFLÉ MIXTURE: 3 egg yolks · 3 whole eggs
¼ cup granulated sugar · grated peel 2 lemons
⅔ cup whipping cream · 2 envelopes unflavored
gelatin · juice 3 lemons · 2 egg whites
TO DECORATE: ⅔ cup whipping cream · pistachio
nuts.

Put the sugar and the water in a pan. Stir until the
sugar is dissolved, and simmer slowly until 350°F.–
370°F. is reached on a candy thermometer. Remove
from the heat, add ¼ cup cold water carefully, stir
and pour into a bowl to cool. Put the yolks and whole
eggs into a bowl with the ¼ cup sugar and lemon peel
and beat until thick over low heat. Remove from the
heat, cool a little, stir in the caramel, the half-
whipped cream and the gelatin dissolved in the
lemon juice. Allow to thicken, then fold in the
stiffly beaten egg whites. Pour into a lightly oiled
mold to set. Turn onto a serving dish and decorate
with whipped cream and nuts.   *Serves 4–6*

Cream chocolate cloud

Cooking time   *few minutes*

¼ cup semisweet chocolate pieces · 2 eggs
⅔ cup whipping cream · few toasted blanched
almonds.

Place the chocolate into a bowl (reserving a few
pieces for decoration) and melt gently over hot
water; do not allow the chocolate to become too
hot. Remove from hot water. Separate the egg
whites from the yolks, and stir the yolks into the
melted chocolate, then beat hard until a light mixture. Beat the whites until stiff, then fold into the
mixture and let stand to set slightly. Whip the
cream, and fold half of it into the chocolate mixture.
Spoon half the chocolate into individual glass dishes
or stemmed glasses. Add a layer of whipped cream
and another layer of the chocolate mixture. Just
before serving, decorate with whipped cream, the
reserved chocolate, and toasted almonds. Illustrated
on page 241.   *Serves 3*

Peach mousse

Cooking time   *few minutes*

6 fresh ripe peaches · ½ package lemon gelatin
⅔ cup boiling water · 1 (5½ oz.) can evaporated milk
or ⅔ cup whipping cream. TO DECORATE: little whipping
cream *or* evaporated milk · angelica.

Peel and strain four of the peaches, halve, stone, and
slice the remaining two. Dissolve the gelatin in the
boiling water, chill until thick, and then beat well.
Beat the evaporated milk or cream until firm enough
to hold its shape. Whip the two mixtures together,
and fold in the strained peaches. Let stand until
set in four glasses. Arrange the peach slices on top
of the mousse, and decorate with beaten evaporated
milk or cream and angelica.   *Serves 4*

Butterscotch pudding

Cooking time   *6 minutes*

¼ cup butter · ½ cup brown sugar
½ cup fine semolina flour · 2½ cups milk.
TO DECORATE: 1 (1 oz.) square unsweetened chocolate
¼–½ cup walnuts · ⅔ cup whipping cream.

Melt the butter in a saucepan over low heat. Add
sugar and semolina flour and stir. Cook gently for
3 minutes. Add milk gradually, stirring constantly.
Continue stirring until mixture boils and thickens.
Simmer for 2–3 minutes. Pour into 6 sundae glasses
or individual dishes rinsed in cold water. Chill.
Decorate with grated chocolate, chopped walnuts,
and whipped cream.   *Serves 6*

Coffee honeycomb mold

Cooking time   *15 minutes*

1 (13 oz.) can evaporated milk · water · 3 eggs,
separated · ¼ cup granulated sugar · vanilla
extract · 4 envelopes unflavored gelatin
1 tablespoon instant coffee · ½ cup boiling water
TO DECORATE: fruit.

To the evaporated milk add enough water to give
3¾ cups. Heat the milk and water and pour onto egg
yolks and sugar, strain and return to the pan. Heat,
stirring until mixture thickens, do not allow custard
to boil, add a few drops of vanilla extract. Dissolve
the gelatin and instant coffee in the boiling water,
and add to the custard, making sure that both
mixtures are of similar temperature. Quickly fold
in the stiffly beaten egg whites. Pour into a wet
1½ quart fancy mold and chill until firm. Turn out
and decorate with fruit.   *Serves 6–8*

Queen Mab's pudding

Cooking time   *5–10 minutes*

Double recipe Egg custard sauce (see page 187)
2 tablespoons unflavored gelatin
¼ cup hot water · ¼ cup chopped candied cherries
½ cup chopped mixed candied peel
⅔ cup whipping cream. TO DECORATE: ⅓ cup whipping
cream · candied cherries.

Make the custard as instructed thick enough to coat
a spoon. Dissolve the gelatin in the hot water, and
stir into hot custard. Add chopped candied cherries,
candied peel, and whipped cream. Put into a mold.
Chill or let stand. When set, turn out of mold and
decorate with whipped cream and cherries. *Serves 4*

Florence cream

Cooking time *2 hours*

¼ cup granulated sugar
3 tablespoons water · 2½ cups milk
4 egg yolks · 2 egg whites
2 tablespoons granulated sugar
½ cup blanched chopped almonds
1 tablespoon butter.
TO DECORATE: ⅔ cup whipping cream · 2 tablespoons granulated sugar · ¼–½ cup blanched slivered almonds.

Put the ¼ cup sugar and water into a heavy saucepan, stir until the sugar has dissolved, then boil steadily until it reaches 380°F.–390°F. on a candy thermometer. Remove from the heat, let stand until cool, and then add the milk. Return to low heat, and stir gently until the milk has absorbed the caramel – do not heat too quickly otherwise the liquid could curdle. Beat the egg yolks and whites with the sugar, add the caramel flavored milk, then the almonds (these may be toasted slightly under the broiler, if desired). Pour into a buttered mold or ovenproof bowl, and cover with buttered wax paper or foil. Steam over hot, but not boiling water, for about 2 hours. Either serve in the dish or turn out when cool. When quite cold decorate with whipped sweetened cream and toasted almonds. Serve with meringue strips. *Serves 4*

Tipsy cake

Cooking time *10–12 minutes*

two 9-inch round sponge cakes (see page 267)
2–3 kinds jam · 2 teaspoons granulated sugar
⅔–1¼ cups sherry *or* port wine
1¼ cups crumbled macaroons (see page 298)
1 recipe Baked egg custard (see page 187) *or* 1 package vanilla pudding.
TO DECORATE: candied cherries · nuts, etc.

Split each cake layer. Put 1 slice into a dish, spread with 1 kind of jam. Add sugar to sherry or port wine, and moisten with this. Sprinkle macaroon crumbs on top. Put on second slice of cake, spread with different flavored jam, sprinkling of sherry, etc. Continue like this, using all slices of cake. Pour very hot custard over and let stand until cold. To prevent skin forming as custard cools, cover with a deep bowl. Decorate with cherries, nuts, etc.
Serves 6–8

RICH TIPSY CAKE
Follow the directions for the Tipsy cake above, but use approximately 1¾ cups whipping cream, whipped instead of custard. To have a lighter cream, beat 1¼ cups whipping cream until nearly stiff enough to hold its shape, then gradually beat in ⅔ cup coffee cream. Sweeten to taste.

Traditional rich trifle

Cooking time *5 minutes*

one 9-inch round layer sponge cake (see page 267)
raspberry jam · 6 macaroons (see page 298)
12 ratafia biscuits *or* ladyfingers
¼ pint sherry and brandy *or* sherry
grated peel ½ lemon · ¼ cup blanched slivered almonds. FOR CUSTARD:* 1¼ cups milk · 1 egg
1 egg yolk · 2 tablespoons granulated sugar.
TO DECORATE: 1¼ cups whipping cream
2 tablespoons granulated sugar · 1 egg white
candied cherries · angelica · ratafia biscuits *or* ladyfingers · blanched slivered almonds (see page 255).

* A slightly thicker custard layer can be made, if desired, by using double quantities.

Split the sponge cakes in half and spread with jam. Place in the bottom of a glass dish with the macaroons and most of the ratafia biscuits. Soak with sherry and brandy, or just sherry, and sprinkle with the lemon peel and almonds. Let stand for about 30 minutes. Make the custard by warming the milk; do not let it boil. Beat the eggs and sugar together, then beat in warm milk. Return to the pan and cook over low heat, stirring until the custard thickens. Strain, let cool slightly, then pour over the soaked sponges. Let stand until cold. Beat the cream until thick, and add the sugar. Beat the egg white until stiff, then fold into the cream. Pile on top of the trifle and decorate with cherries, angelica, a few ratafia biscuits, and blanched slivered almonds.
Serves 8

Raspberry trifle

Cooking time *5 minutes*

1 can raspberries* · one 9-inch round layer cake (see page 267) · little jam
1 package raspberry gelatin · 1 recipe Egg custard sauce (see page 187) *or* use double recipe for a thicker custard layer · blanched almonds (optional)
12 ratafias *or* ladyfingers (optional)
1¼ cups whipping cream · little granulated sugar
TO DECORATE: ½ cup blanched flaked almonds
¼ cup pistachio nuts · candied cherries.
* Or use 1 (10 oz.) package frozen fruit *or* 2 cups fresh fruit mashed with sugar.

Open the can of raspberries, drain, and reserve the syrup. Split the sponge cakes and spread with jam. Arrange the sponge cakes and some of the raspberries in the bottom of a bowl. Moisten with raspberry syrup, and cover with slightly warm raspberry gelatin, made with slightly less water than usual, and allow to set. Make the custard and, when cool, pour over the set gelatin; blanched almonds and ratafias may be added to this, if desired. Allow the custard to set, putting a plate over the top of the bowl to prevent a skin forming. Beat the cream until just stiff. Add sugar to taste and spread over the custard, marking with a fork. Toast the almonds gently under the broiler or for about 5 minutes in a 350°F. oven. Cool and scatter round the edge of the trifle, adding a few pistachio nuts as well. Arrange the remaining raspberries, nuts, and candied cherries in a design in the center. *Serves 6–8*

Charlotte Russe

Cooking time   *None*

1 package lemon gelatin · candied cherries
angelica · 7–8 ladyfingers
1 egg white (optional) · 1 envelope unflavoured
gelatin · 3 tablespoons cold water
⅔ cup whipping cream* · 3 tablespoons milk
3 tablespoons granulated sugar
½–1 teaspoon vanilla extract.

* It is not satisfactory to substitute evaporated
milk for cream in this dish due to the very delicate
flavor.

Use a Charlotte mold or 2½ cup soufflé dish or similar
straight-sided mold. Prepare lemon gelatin, cool,
and pour a ¼-inch layer into the bottom of the mold.
Chill until set firm. Decorate with cherry slices and
small pieces of angelica. Pour in additional gelatin
to a depth of about ½-inch. Chill until gelatin is
thick, but not firm. Split ladyfingers and trim ends
to fit neatly around the edges of mold. The sides of
the ladyfingers may be brushed with egg white to
help stick them together. Put the cut ends into the
gelatin with the split side facing the center of the
mold. Fit the fingers closely together, leaving no
gaps. Return to the refrigerator to set firm.
Soak unflavored gelatin in cold water. Whip cream
well, add milk, sugar, and vanilla extract and
continue whipping. Dissolve gelatin over hot water
and add to cream mixture, folding in carefully.
Continue stirring gently until almost set. Pour
onto prepared mold and chill until set firm. Trim
ladyfingers level with top of the mixture. Unmold
onto a serving dish. Decorate with remaining
chopped lemon gelatin around the bottom of the
Charlotte.   *Serves 4*

Fruit gelatin

Cooking time   *few minutes*

8 oz. canned, frozen, *or* fresh fruit·
package flavored gelatin.

Defrost frozen fruit and measure the liquid from
this or canned fruit. Add sufficient water to give
1 cup liquid. Bring the liquid to a boil, pour over
the gelatin and stir until dissolved. Stir in 1 cup
cold water. Either mix the fruit with the slightly
thickened gelatin or set a layer of gelatin in a
mold, add some of the fruit, cover with additional
gelatin, set and continue filling the mold in this
way. To unmold, dip in hot water for a few seconds.
See pictures on pages 314 and 315.   *Serves 4*

ICE CREAM AND FROZEN DESSERTS

These are frozen in the freezing compartment of the
refrigerator or in a freezer – use ice cube trays, or
ordinary metal containers, or molds.

ICE CREAM

When using a refrigerator it is advisable to turn the
cold control to the lowest setting for 30 minutes
before the mixture is put in. The quicker ice cream
is frozen, the better it will be. Turn the control
back to normal setting when the ice cream is firm.

CREAM, ETC: Always choose a mixture sufficiently
rich in butterfat, i.e. that includes cream or evaporated milk. Do not overbeat the cream or it will
give a solid texture to the ice cream.

SUGAR: Although granulated sugar may be used in
an ice cream, it is better to choose confectioners'
sugar since it gives a smoother texture to the mixture – make the mixture sweet, but remember that
too much sugar hinders freezing.

BEATING: Most ice creams have a lighter texture if
the mixture is frozen until nearly firm, then removed
from the refrigerator, turned into a bowl and beaten
vigorously; this incorporates air. The ice cream
should then be refrozen until firm.

SHERBETS

Sherbets and similar mixtures do not need quick
freezing; keep the refrigerator indicator at the
normal setting. The addition of gelatin is not
essential but it helps to keep the mixture smooth
without 'splinters' of ice, if being stored for some
time before serving. The addition of egg whites also
gives a very light texture.

Economical ice cream

Cooking time   *10–15 minutes*

1 recipe Egg custard sauce (see page 187) and use egg
yolks only · ⅔ cup whipping cream *or* whipped
evaporated milk (see page 255) · 3–4 tablespoons
granulated *or* confectioners' sugar · flavoring, see
below.

Allow the custard to cool, then fold in the whipped
cream, sugar, and flavoring. Beat egg whites left
from the custard, and fold into the mixture last of
all. Pour into ice cube trays and freeze until firm,
remove, turn into a bowl and beat briskly, then
refreeze until firm.   *Serves 4–5*

TO FLAVOR:

FRUIT – use ⅔ cup mashed or strained fresh bananas,
strawberries, etc., or a smooth purée from canned
or fresh fruit see picture, page 223.

CHOCOLATE – add ¼ cup cocoa or chocolate drink
powder to the custard.

VANILLA – add 1 teaspoon vanilla extract to the
custard.

Rich ice cream

Cooking time   *None*

1¼ cups evaporated milk *or* 1¼ cups whipping cream
¼ cup granulated sugar *or* confectioners'
2 beaten egg whites · flavoring as preferred.
Method as previous recipe.   *Serves 4*

Lemon sherbet

Cooking time   *5 minutes*

2–3 large lemons · 1¼ cups water
1 teaspoon unflavored gelatin *or* about a one fourth
lemon package gelatin
⅓–½ cup granulated sugar · 1 egg white

Peel the rind thinly from the lemons and simmer
for 5 minutes only with the water. Strain, and dissolve the gelatin in the liquid, with the sugar.
Squeeze the juice from the lemons (you should have
about ⅔ cup, but if the lemons give little juice use
another). Freeze until the mixture is just beginning
to stiffen, turn out, and fold into the stiffly beaten
egg white, then refreeze. If desired, the egg white
may be put into the mixture before freezing, but a
lighter texture is given by the method given above.
        Serves 4

ORANGE SHERBET

As above – use ¾ cup orange juice for a definite flavor
– see picture page 223.

Apricot sherbet

Cooking time   *10–15 minutes*

1 lb. fresh apricots · 1 lemon · 1¼ cups water
1 teaspoon unflavored gelatin, (optional)
⅓ cup granulated sugar · 1 egg white

Cook the fruit with the lemon peel, juice, and water
until tender, then beat or strain. Dissolve the gelatin
in the hot purée with the sugar. Freeze until the
mixture is beginning to stiffen, then continue as
lemon sherbet.   *Serves 4*

OTHER FIRM FRUITS SHOULD BE TREATED IN
THE SAME WAY.

SHERBETS FROM FRESH FRUIT: Proportions as apricot
sherbet, but make the syrup of the water, sugar, and
lemon peel and juice, dissolve the gelatin in this,
then strain onto the mashed fruit purée. With acid
fruits the lemon could be omitted. Continue as
lemon sherbet.

SHERBETS FROM CANNED FRUIT: Strain the fruit, add to
the syrup with the lemon juice. If storing, use
gelatin; dissolve this in a little hot water, add to
the purée then continue as lemon sherbet.

DESSERTS WITH ICE CREAM

These may be made with homemade ice cream or
with purchased ice cream.

Fruit Melba

Cooking time   *few minutes*

Melba sauce (see page 187) · fresh fruit – peaches,
ripe apricots, pineapples, strawberries, etc. *or*
canned fruit · ice cream.
TO DECORATE: whipping cream (optional).

Make the Melba sauce and allow it to become quite
cold. Prepare the fresh fruit by skinning, peeling,
etc. Make sure that fresh or canned fruits are cut
into bite-sized pieces. Spoon the ice cream into
sundae glasses, arrange the fruit round this, top
with the Melba sauce, and decorate with whipping
cream, if desired. (If using the quantity of Melba
sauce given and 1 pint ice cream, allow 1 medium
peach or equivalent per person.)   *Serves 6*

Baked Alaska

Cooking time   *3 minutes*
Oven temperature   *475°F.*

1 8-inch layer Sponge cake (see page 267)
1 pint to 1 quart ice cream
approximately 4–6 oz. fresh, canned, *or* frozen fruit.
MERINGUE: 4–5 egg whites · sugar.*

* Allow either 2–3 tablespoons granulated sugar per
egg white or, if you have a very sweet tooth, ¼ cup
per egg white.

Choose an ovenproof casserole, so the dessert may
be served and baked in the same container, and
place the sponge cake in this, soaking with a little
fruit syrup if using canned or frozen fruit. Top with
the very firm block of ice cream and fruit. Make
the meringue by beating the egg whites until very
stiff, then folding the sugar in gradually. Pile or
pipe the merigue mixture over the entire sponge
cake and ice cream – taking care no ice cream is
left uncovered, otherwise it will melt. Put into a
preheated 475°F. oven for about 3 minutes only, until
golden brown. Remove from the oven and serve at
once.   *Serves 6*

Simnel cake, page 262; Hot cross buns, page 278; Pashka, page 339; Economical Easter biscuits, page 297; Ground rice tarts, page 331

Wholewheat griddle scones, page 291

Shortcake (with strawberries), page 263

Marshmallow devil's food cake, page 281; Raisin apple meringue, page 338

Rich Christmas cake, page 263

Gingerbread with apple sauce, page 266

Lemon fruit slices, page 280; Chocolate iced short bread, page 299; Melting moments, page 324; Parkin, page 266

COUPE JACQUES – top well-drained canned, frozen, or fresh fruit with ice cream and melba sauce, (if desired). Top with whipped cream.

ICE CREAM AND LIQUEUR – put the ice cream into a glass and serve with a generous measure of cherry brandy, crème de menthe (see picture page 223); curaçao. Decorate with a twist of lemon peel.

FRUIT AND ICE CREAM – arrange fruit around ice cream (cherries are shown in the picture on page 223), top with a twist of orange peel and cherries on sticks. Make layer sundaes with sliced or whole fresh sweetened ripe fruit, whipped cream, and ice cream, (strawberries are shown in the picture on page 223).

EMERGENCY PUDDINGS AND DESSERTS

One of the best and quickest desserts is fresh fruit. Serve an attractive selection on the table or make into a fruit salad – separate fruits are unusual.

Mixed fruit salad

There are several ways of making this.

1. Prepare all fresh fruit – oranges and tangerines, etc. as page 169; peel and de-seed grapes; peel apples, bananas, and pears; peel peaches by dipping in hot water for about 30 seconds, then pulling away the skin. Cut away the peel from pineapples; fresh ripe apricots, plums, etc., need no peeling; remove the pits from cherries, if desired. Cut the fruit into neat pieces, put into a bowl, add sugar and a little white wine or kirsch or orange juice.
2. Prepare fruit as above, but cover with a syrup made by boiling sugar and water ($\frac{1}{4}$–$\frac{1}{2}$ cup granulated sugar to each 1$\frac{1}{4}$ cups water) and flavoring this with orange and/or lemon juice.
3. Open a can of fruit and blend this with fresh fruit. Illustrated on p. 199.

Apple and ginger meringue

Cooking time   *20 minutes*

3 large baking apples · $\frac{1}{4}$ cup granulated sugar
3 *or* 4 pieces candied ginger
2 egg whites · 3 tablespoons granulated sugar.

Peel, core, and slice apples then cook with sugar and a minimum quantity of water until tender. Press through a sieve. Add sliced ginger, pour into a dish, and cool. Beat egg whites until stiff, gradually beat in sugar. When very stiff heap into center of apple purée. Place the meringue under the broiler for a few seconds, or until pale golden. Illustrated on page 272.   *Serves 4*

PUDDINGS AND DESSERTS TO IMPRESS

Although not difficult, an Alaska is always an impressive dessert and the following recipe would be an excellent choice at Christmas time. If desired, the mincemeat may be cooked for a time, cooled slightly, then put on the sponge cake – this brings out the flavor of the mincemeat; but it must not touch the ice cream, just be around it, otherwise this will melt. The combination of flavors in the soufflé makes it an outstanding dessert.

Christmas Alaska

Cooking time   *3–5 minutes*
Oven temperature   *475°F.*

1 8-inch layer Sponge cake · 3–4 tablespoons brandy, sherry, *or* rum · $\frac{1}{4}$ cup mincemeat
1 pint to 1 quart vanilla ice cream · 4 egg whites
$\frac{1}{2}$–1 cup granulated sugar. TO DECORATE: small sprig holly.

Put the sponge cake into an ovenproof dish, then sprinkle with the brandy, sherry, or rum. If the cake is fairly dry use more brandy or blend this with a little fruit juice – the cake should be fairly soft. Spread with the mincemeat, then top with the ice cream. Beat the egg whites until so stiff you could turn the bowl upside down. Gradually beat in half the sugar then fold in the remainder. Pile or pipe over the ice cream, making sure it is completely covered. The larger quantity of sugar produces a more crisp topped meringue but it is very sweet. Brown for a few minutes only in a preheated 475°F. oven. While it may be served at once, this will stand for approximately 20 minutes without the ice cream melting. Top with the holly.   *Serves 4–6*

Chocolate brandy soufflé

Cooking time   *10–15 minutes*

3 eggs · $\frac{1}{4}$–$\frac{1}{2}$ cup granulated sugar
1$\frac{1}{4}$ cups milk · 3 (1 oz.) squares unsweetened chocolate · 3 tablespoons brandy
1 tablespoon unflavored gelatin · few drops vanilla extract · 1$\frac{1}{4}$ cups whipping cream.
TO DECORATE: some of the cream
$\frac{1}{4}$–$\frac{1}{2}$ cup chopped blanched almonds.

Separate egg yolks from the whites. Put yolks with sugar and milk into top of a double boiler and cook over hot water until just beginning to thicken. Meanwhile melt the chocolate then add to the milk mixture and stir until just beginning to thicken and forms a thick coating on the back of a wooden spoon. Blend the brandy and gelatin in a small bowl, stand over hot water until dissolved, then stir into the hot chocolate custard with the vanilla extract. Let stand until cool and beginning to stiffen slightly, then fold in most of the whipped cream and the stiffly beaten egg whites. Put into a prepared 1 pint soufflé dish, and decorate with the remaining whipped cream and almonds.   *Serves 4–5*

CAKES

A homemade cake is always appreciated by the family and cake-making is a most satisfactory form of cooking, for a perfectly baked cake is a pleasure to look at as well as to eat.

Wise choice of cakes

The choice of flavoring is a matter of personal taste, but choose the rubbed-in mixture (or one-stage method of mixing, page 259) when in a hurry; if you want cakes to store for a future occasion, choose meringues, rich fruit cakes, or gingerbreads. The lightest cakes are produced by the whisking method and the most economical with a yeast mixture.

Ways to serve cakes

While cakes may be served with coffee, remember fruit cakes and cheese are excellent instead of a dessert. Some plainer cakes may be sliced and buttered.

To use leftover cakes

A cake may be freshened by a brief warming period in the oven; rich fruit cakes may be stored for weeks (improving in flavor as they mature); plainer cakes may be sliced and buttered or toasted and buttered. Pieces of cake may also be sliced and fried as a quick fritter (see below).

Easy remedies when things are wrong

PROBLEM – if a cake is heavy or sunken in the center, this is due to a) too much liquid in the mixture; b) removing the cake from the oven before it is completely cooked (test carefully); c) incorrect oven temperature—if the heat is *too low* the cake *will not rise*, but if the heat is *too high* the outside sets too quickly and the cake *cannot* rise.

TO REMEDY – cut the center out of the cake with a pastry cutter and serve as a ring cake.

PROBLEM – if a cake is very dark and hard on the outside or on the top or on the bottom – if completely over-cooked the oven temperature was too high or the cake was left in the oven for too long a period. If only the top or only the bottom is overcooked, the cake may have been placed in the wrong position in the oven.

TO REMEDY – rub a grater over the overcooked surface. If the cake itself is overcooked, soak with fruit juice or sherry.

PROBLEM – if the fruit sank in a cake, the fruit was damp – see opposite; the cake batter was too wet or too light to support the weight of the fruit.

TO REMEDY – nothing can really be done. If very bad, slice the cake through the center and make two shallow cakes – the top one plain, the bottom one fruit.

PROBLEM – if a cake rises to a peak and cracks, this is due to too much beating or leavening agent, too dry a mixture, or filling the pan too full.

TO REMEDY – cut a slice off the top; frost the bottom of the cake rather than the top.

PROBLEM – if a cake fails to rise, this can be due to the same reasons as a heavy cake – see first point; also insufficient leavening agent. Remember really *rich* cakes do not rise in the same way as a light cake.

TO REMEDY – if very heavy in texture, slice, fry in hot butter, and roll in sugar as a fritter. Often, however, the cake is perfect – it just does not look as deep as expected.

To make cakes

It is absolutely essential that instructions are followed, not only for ingredients but also for method of handling. There must always be a well-balanced relationship between the amount of fat and eggs used, and if the proportions are altered the result could be a failure.

FLOUR TO USE IN CAKE MAKING

Unless stated to the contrary, flour in yeast cakes and buns is always plain; no leavening agent is required since this is provided by the yeast.

CHOICE OF FAT

Butter or margarine is ideal for most cakes. Where margarine is given before butter, this would give a slightly lighter texture.

CHOICE OF SUGAR

Granulated sugar is generally specified although occasionally brown sugar is suggested to provide a slightly different flavor and color.

To bake cakes

In this, as in every cook book, great care is taken to give correct baking times and temperatures. Every oven varies to a degree and even two ovens of a similar make can produce slightly different results, so regard any instructions as approximate only. Look at your own range instruction book and if it varies from the recommendation in the recipe follow your own instructions if you have found them reliable in the past.

POSITIONS IN THE OVEN FOR BAKING CAKES AND BISCUITS

Large cakes should be baked in the center of the oven. Small cakes, unless specifically stated to the contrary, should be baked in or toward the hotter part of the oven, which is the top portion. Shallow layer cakes are baked toward the hotter part of the oven.

To weigh and measure

FLOUR, SUGAR, CORNSTARCH – should be sifted then put into a measuring cup gently without packing, except in the case of brown sugar.

SYRUP, MOLASSES, HONEY – to measure syrup etc., either flour the bowl of the spoon, or dip the spoon in boiling water, dry, then use while warm.

FATS, BUTTER, SHORTENING ETC. – with a cup measure of fat, pack soft fat firmly into the measure. For butter or margarine use the handy markings on the stick. For soft fats such as shortening or lard, pack firmly into a measuring cup. Alternatively use a liquid cup measure and displace the amount required with water. For example, to measure ¼ cup

shortening, fill a 1-cup measure to the ¾-cup mark. Add shortening until the water rises to 1 cup. Drain the water and use the shortening as required.

Preparing ingredients for cakes, etc.

DRIED FRUIT – wash in cold water (unless packed as pre-cleaned), drain in sieve, and dry on baking sheets at room temperature for 48 hours, then store in jars.

ALMONDS, ETC. – blanch by putting them in boiling water for ½–1 minute. (Other nuts should be heated in the oven until skins can be rubbed off). Remove and dry in a cloth, then remove the skins – this is known as blanching – for chestnuts see page 190. Chop neatly, halve, flake or cut into long strips – known as slivering almonds.

CONFECTIONERS' SUGAR, FLOUR – press through a sieve to remove lumps from the sugar. Store confectioners' sugar (and brown sugar) in tightly covered containers to prevent it becoming lumpy. Flour should be sifted to obtain an accurate measure, then sifted with other dry ingredients to distribute the particles throughout and prevent lumps of a leavening agent, salt, or spice from occuring.

COCONUT, NUTS – flaked coconut and chopped blanched almonds may be tinted by rubbing into a few drops of coloring on a plate. Dry before using. Coconut or blanched almonds may be toasted slowly under the broiler or in the oven, until golden brown.

CANDIED CHERRIES – these are very heavy due to the weight of syrup. They are better if halved before being added to cakes, and they should be lightly floured. In order to be quite certain they will not sink to the bottom of the cake it is important to follow the recipe carefully, and they can be washed in COLD water, (which lightens their weight) then dried carefully before being put into cakes.

Types of cakes

The method of mixing is used to describe the various cakes.

RUBBING-IN METHOD – see page 257. Used for – small and large plain cakes. Method of mixing – fat is rubbed into flour lightly using the fingertips, lifting and allowing the mixture to fall back into the bowl until it resembles fine bread crumbs before rest of ingredients are added.

CREAMING METHOD – see page 259. Used for – small and large light cakes; rich cakes such as Christmas cake, etc. Method of mixing – fat is creamed with the sugar before other ingredients are added.

MELTING METHOD – (see page 265). Used for – gingerbread, etc. Method of mixing – fat, etc., is melted before being added to other ingredients.

WHISKING METHOD – (see page 267). Used for – very light cakes such as a true sponge. Method of mixing – eggs and sugar are beaten until very light and a pale color before incorporating other ingredients.

CONSISTENCIES OF CAKE BATTER AND DOUGHS

The word 'consistency' is used to describe the appearance and texture of the unbaked combined ingredients.

POURING CONSISTENCY – softest of all. The mixture pours easily from the bowl into the pan.

SOFT DROPPING CONSISTENCY – drops from the spoon within about 3 seconds.

FIRM OR SLOW DROPPING CONSISTENCY – drops from the spoon when given a sharp flick.

STICKY CONSISTENCY – too soft to roll but firm enough to stand in points when handled with a spatula.

In addition a soft rolling consistency is used for some yeast doughs – firm rolling consistency for some biscuits and pastry.

THE TOOLS YOU USE

A wooden spoon or electric mixer is ideal for creaming, or if the mixture is very hard and time limited, use your hands.
A metal spoon is best for folding flour, etc., into a light mixture to maintain a large volume.
A whisk is necessary to beat eggs and sugar; egg whites, etc. Choose either: a flat whisk or rotary beater or an electric mixer.
Electric mixers are excellent in cake making – remember where the speed may be adjusted that you use a steady (medium) speed for creaming; a higher speed for hard beating. On the whole it is better to add the flour by hand, or if you wish to use the mixer use the lowest possible speed. Utilize the manufacturer's recommended speed for your particular model.

SIZES OF CAKE PANS

In most recipes, the size of the cake pan is given and this determines the cooking time, which must be adjusted if you wish to make the cake in a slightly smaller or larger pan. As an example, assume that the cake recipe has been given for two 9-inch layer cake pans and you wish to bake it in two 8-inch layer cake pans (providing there is not too great a quantity of mixture). This means a deeper cake and the mixture will take a little longer to bake, so allow approximately an extra 5 to 10 minutes. Similarly to use a 13-inch by 9-inch pan, the time is approximately the same as for two 8-inch layer cake pans. Cup cakes which are two-thirds full will take approximately 10 minutes less time.

TO PREPARE CAKE PANS

There are on the market today plastic resin treated cake pans which tend to prevent sticking and these should be satisfactory if they are neither greased nor floured. Because they have a very special and generally expensive finish, wipe most carefully after

use and never take the cake out of the pan with a knife that might scratch it. Light sponge cakes may generally be baked in a pan which is greased with melted shortening or olive oil, and dusted very lightly with flour. To do this, shake a little flour over the pan, then turn the pan on its side and tap very firmly to coat the pan and to shake out the surplus flour. Richer cakes, such as a fruit cake, are always better if baked in a lined pan (see below).

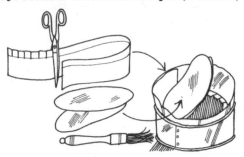

LINING A CAKE PAN

Place the pan on top of 2–4 thicknesses of wax paper and trace around it. Cut on the inside of the pencilled tracing. Grease each circle of paper and stick together.
Make a strip of wax paper, 2–4 thicknesses, long enough to go around the sides of the pan with an overlap of 1–2 inches, and 2 inches deeper than the pan. Fold up 1 inch along the bottom of the strip, and cut slanting slits up to the marking, about ½ inch apart. Place the strip of paper inside the pan, which should be lightly greased, allowing the slit ends to overlap on the bottom of the pan. Press the seam firmly together, then insert the circle of wax for the bottom.
For extra protection against excessive browning, place 2–3 layers of newspaper or heavy brown paper under the wax paper. For further protection, tie a double or treble band of brown paper around the outside of the pan, so it stands up well above the rim. If possible, these pans should not be washed. Turn cake out of pan, and while the pan is still hot, wipe with a soft paper or cloth. Cakes keep moist if an apple slice is stored with the cake in a tightly covered container – keep separate from bread or pastry.

HALVING OR DOUBLING QUANTITIES

One would imagine that if the quantities are halved and baked in a smaller pan, half the cooking time should be allowed. In fact, a little over half the cooking time is needed. If the quantities are doubled, it is rarely necessary to double the cooking time, as an additional ¼–⅓ of the original cooking time is enough. For the best results, this is generally not recommended.

SHAPES OF PANS

Some of the most usual and useful cake pans are:
1. BAKING SHEET – for cookies, etc.
2. FLAN RING – similar to a round layer cake pan without the bottom. It is placed on a baking sheet. A pie pan or layer cake pan may be substituted.
3. JELLY ROLL PAN – may also be known as a Swiss roll pan. The standard size is a 15½-inch by 15½-inch pan.
4. LOAF PANS – for loaf cakes and bread.
5. MUFFIN PANS – for cup cakes, also for small pastry tarts; fancy shaped ones may be obtained (hearts, diamonds, etc.)
6. ROUND LAYER CAKE PANS – shallow pans for cakes which have a filling – the 8-inch or the 9-inch layer cake pan are generally used. Some have a removable bottom. You need a pair at least.
7. RECTANGULAR CAKE PAN – for single layer cakes the 12-inch by 9-inch cake pan is generally recommended.
8. SQUARE CAKE PAN – for small single layer cakes either an 8-inch or a 9-inch square cake pan may be used.
9. TUBE PAN – useful, for cakes look attractive and are easy to cut – angel food cakes are generally baked in these. It is also known as a Bundt pan. For angel cakes, it should never be greased.
10. SPRING FORM PAN – for deeper single layer cakes, particularly for richer cakes – 3-inches deep. 8-inch, 9-inch or 10-inch sizes are usually used.

Rubbing-in method

While basic ingredients vary in cakes made by the rubbing-in method, the procedure of incorporating the fat into the flour is as follows:
1. Sift together the dry ingredients (except sugar) into a large mixing bowl.
2. Rub the fat into the dry ingredients, with the tips of the fingers. Do this well above the bowl so that as the ingredients drop back again you are incorporating air. Continue until the mixture resembles fine bread crumbs.
3. Add sugar, fruit, etc., according to the particular recipe.
4. Bind with egg or eggs and milk to the desired consistency. These cakes have a minimum amount of egg or milk for a fairly firm texture. If a softer and more moist texture is desired, add a little additional milk.
5. Put into the prepared pan or onto prepared baking sheet as the particular recipe.

WHEN USING THE RUBBING-IN METHOD REMEMBER:

1. Temperature – keep fat, etc., reasonably cool to prevent the unbaked cake from becoming over-sticky.
2. Mixing – rub fat into the dry ingredients, until a uniform texture – large uneven pieces of fat mean heavy patches in the baked cake.
3. Consistency – this type of cake must be fairly dry when mixed – see description of consistencies opposite and in the recipes – if too soft the cake or cakes will be heavy.
4. Baking – unless stated to the contrary, cakes or a large cake made by this method need fairly quick baking.
5. Turning out – many cakes made by this method are very 'short', i.e. light and crumbly, and should be allowed to cool for a short time before being removed from the pan or pans.
6. Storing – put the cakes in a tightly covered container away from pastry, bread, and cookies; but most cakes made by this method are best when eaten fresh – if stale they may be warmed for a few minutes in the oven.

TO TEST CAKES MADE BY THE RUBBING-IN METHOD

SMALL CAKES – press firmly on the sides and the cakes are cooked when firm and no impression is left by the fingertip.
LARGE CAKES – press firmly on top and if the cake feels firm remove it from the oven – the cake should have shrunk slightly away from the sides of the pan. As cakes made by the rubbing-in method are of a firm texture, fairly firm pressure is needed to test.

Cherry coconut buns

Cooking time *12–15 minutes*
Oven temperature *425°F.*

1½ cups all-purpose flour · 2½ teaspoons baking powder · ¼ teaspoon salt · ⅓ cup butter *or* margarine · ½ cup granulated sugar · ¾ cup flaked coconut · ½ cup candied cherries · 1 egg
1 egg yolk · approximately ½ cup milk.
TO DECORATE: 1 egg white · ⅓ cup flaked coconut
6–8 candied cherries.

Sift together the flour, baking powder, and the salt, rub in the butter or margarine until the mixture looks like fine bread crumbs, add the sugar, coconut, halved cherries, the egg, and egg yolk. Add enough milk to make a soft consistency. Put the dough in 12–16 small heaps on the baking sheets as described in rock buns, (see next page), but flatten slightly. Brush with egg white, sprinkle with coconut, and press half a candied cherry on top of each bun. Bake in a preheated 425°F. oven for 12–15 minutes. Test as instructions on this page. Allow the buns to cool for a few minutes on the baking sheets, then lift onto a wire rack. Eat when fresh. *Makes 12–16*

Lemon buns

Cooking time *12–15 minutes*
Oven temperature *425°F.*

Ingredients as Rock buns, but omit currants, seedless white raisins, and chopped mixed candied peel. Add ½–¾ cup chopped candied lemon peel and grated peel of 1 lemon; bind with lemon juice instead of milk. TO DECORATE: 1–2 tablespoons Lemon curd. (see page 311).

Prepare as rock buns (next page) and put onto the baking sheets. Make a small well in the center of each bun with a fingertip dipped in flour, or the handle of a teaspoon, and put in a small quantity of lemon curd. Bake as rock buns. *Makes 12–16*

Rock cakes or buns

Cooking time   *12–15 minutes*
Oven temperature   *425°F.*

2 cups all-purpose flour · 3 teaspoons baking powder · ½ teaspoon salt · ½ cup margarine ½ cup granulated sugar · ½ cup currants ½ cup seedless white raisins · ½ cup chopped mixed candied peel · 1 egg · approximately 3 table-spoons milk.
TO GLAZE: little sugar.

Sift the flour, baking powder, and salt into bowl, then rub in the margarine until the mixture looks like fine bread crumbs. Add the sugar, currants, raisins, candied peel, beaten egg and enough milk to give a sticky consistency, (see page 256). Put the mixture in 12 small 'heaps' onto well greased baking sheets or one large sheet, allowing room for the mixture to spread out. The easiest way to do this is with two spoons or forks – do not make the cakes too smooth on top. Sprinkle the tops of the cakes with sugar before baking. Bake in a preheated 425°F. oven for approximately 12–15 minutes. Test as instructions given on page 257. Allow the cakes to cool for a few minutes on the baking sheet, then lift on to a wire rack. Eat when fresh. *Makes 12*

Chocolate orange cupcakes

Cooking time   *12 minutes*
Oven temperature   *425°F.*

1½ cups all-purpose flour · 2¼ teaspoons baking powder · ¼ teaspoon salt · ½ cup margarine ½ cup chocolate drink powder · ½ cup granulated sugar · grated peel 2 oranges · 1 egg 3 tablespoons orange juice.
TO DECORATE: orange frosting made from 1 cup sifted confectioners' sugar · 1 tablespoon orange juice.

Sift the flour, baking powder, and salt into a bowl. Rub the margarine into the flour mixture, do this lightly since there is a fairly high percentage of margarine. Add chocolate drink powder, sugar, orange peel, egg, and orange juice. Mix well and put into greased and floured muffin pans, bake in a pre-heated 425°F. oven for 12 minutes. When cold, coat the top of each cupcake with frosting made by blending the sifted confectioners' sugar and juice.
Makes 12–16

Almond and chocolate chip cake

Cooking time   *1–1¼ hours*
Oven temperature   *350°F.*

2 cups all-purpose flour · 3 teaspoons baking powder · ½ teaspoon salt · ½ cup butter *or* mar-garine · ¾ cup granulated sugar · ½ cup slivered almonds · ½ cup semi-sweet chocolate pieces *or* 3 (1 oz.) squares semi-sweet chocolate · 1 egg 1 egg yolk · approximately 6 tablespoons milk.
TO DECORATE: 1 egg white · ¼–½ cup slivered almonds 1 tablespoon semi-sweet chocolate pieces *or* 1 (1 oz.) square semi-sweet chocolate.

Sift the flour, baking powder, and salt into a mixing bowl, rub in the butter or margarine until like fine bread crumbs. Add the sugar, almonds, the chopped chocolate, egg, egg yolk and enough milk to give a sticky consistency. Place in a greased 9-inch by 5-inch loaf pan. When the mixture is in the pan, brush with egg white and top with the ¼–½ cup almonds. Brush these with egg white when on the cake, so they shine. Bake in a preheated 350°F. oven for 1–1¼ hours. Remove from the oven and while the cake is still warm, sprinkle the chopped chocolate over the top. *12 portions*

Date and walnut bread

Cooking time   *1 hour*
Oven temperature   *350°F.*

2 cups all-purpose flour · 3 teaspoons baking powder · ½ teaspoon salt · ½ cup margarine *or* shortening · ½ cup granulated sugar · ½ cup chopped walnuts · ¾ cup chopped stoned dates 1 egg · approximately ½ cup milk.
TO DECORATE: walnut halves and dates.

Sift the flour with the baking powder and the salt, rub in the margarine or shortening as in 'Cut and come again' cake or bread; add the sugar, walnuts, dates, egg, and milk to bind. Place in a greased 9-inch by 5-inch loaf pan. Press the walnut halves and dates on top, then bake as 'Cut and come again' cake, or bread (see page 291). *12 portions*

Lemon crumble squares

Cooking time   *45 minutes*
Oven temperature   *350°F.*

2 cups all-purpose flour · 3 teaspoons baking powder · ½ teaspoon salt · ⅔ cup butter *or* mar-garine · ⅔ cup granulated sugar · ½–1 cup chop-ped candied citron peel · 2 eggs · ¼ cup lemon juice.
TOPPING: 2 tablespoons butter *or* margarine ½ cup all-purpose flour · ¼ cup granulated sugar grated peel of 2 lemons · 3 tablespoons strained lemon marmalade.

Sift the flour with the baking powder and the salt into a mixing bowl. Rub in the butter or margarine until like fine bread crumbs. Add the sugar, peel,

eggs, and lemon juice to make a sticky consistency. Put into a greased and floured 8-inch square pan. Smooth the surface with a knife. To make the crumble – rub the butter or margarine into the flour, add the sugar and lemon peel. Spread the unbaked cake with marmalade. Sprinkle the crumble on top, and bake in a preheated 350°F. oven for approximately 45 minutes. Remove from the pan carefully.
9 medium or 16 small portions

Orange marmalade cake

Cooking time 20–25 minutes
Oven temperature 375°F.

3 cups all-purpose flour · 4½ teaspoons baking powder · ¾ teaspoon salt · 1¼ cups granulated sugar · 3 tablespoons orange marmalade
grated peel of 2 oranges · 2 eggs
approximately ⅔ cup orange juice.
TO FILL: ⅔ cup whipping cream · ¼ cup orange marmalade.

Sift the flour together with the baking powder and salt into a mixing bowl, rub in the butter or margarine, add the sugar, marmalade, orange peel, eggs, and the juice. Grease and flour two 8-inch layer cake pans. Bake in a preheated 375°F. oven for approximately 20–25 minutes or, until firm. When cool, fill with whipped cream and the marmalade. Eat when fresh.
10 portions

Spiced crumble cake

Cooking time 45–55 minutes
Oven temperature 350°F.

2 cups all-purpose flour · 3 teaspoons baking powder · ½ teaspoon salt · ½ teaspoon cinnamon
¼ teaspoon nutmeg · ¼ teaspoon allspice
⅔ cup butter *or* margarine · ½ cup granulated sugar
1 tablespoon molasses *or* corn syrup · 2 eggs
1 cup chopped mixed candied peel · ½ cup currants
½ cup seedless white raisins · ½ cup chopped walnuts · approximately 3 tablespoons milk.
TOPPING: ½ cup all-purpose flour · ¼ teaspoon cinnamon · dash nutmeg · dash allspice
2 tablespoons butter *or* margarine · ¼ cup granulated sugar · ½ cup chopped walnuts.

Sift the flour, baking powder, salt, and spice into a mixing bowl. Rub in the butter or margarine until like fine bread crumbs. Add the sugar, molasses, or corn syrup. Beat in the eggs, add the fruit, and walnuts, blend well, then gradually add enough milk to give a sticky consistency. Put into a greased and floured 8-inch layer cake pan preferably with a removable bottom. Smooth flat on top. For the crumble – sift the flour and spices together, rub in the butter or margarine, then add the sugar and nuts. Press on top of the cake. Bake in a preheated 350°F. oven for approximately 45 minutes. To remove from the pan push up the bottom carefully. If the cake pan is inverted in the usual way, the topping is likely to fall off. This crumble topping may be put onto any fairly plain cake.
8–10 portions

Creaming method

While basic ingredients vary in cakes made by the creaming method, the procedure of incorporating eggs, flour, etc., into the fat is as follows:
1. Put the fat into the mixing bowl and beat with a wooden spoon, or an electric mixer, until soft and light adding the sugar gradually – if the bowl is put onto a folded cloth it stands more firmly on the table and makes less noise.
2. Beat the egg or eggs well in a second bowl.
3. Gradually add a little beaten egg to the creamed fat mixture, beating well as you do so. Continue adding more egg – if the mixture shows signs of 'curdling' then add a little sifted flour.
4. Sift the flour or sift together the dry ingredients.
5. Gradually fold the flour into the creamed fat mixture – do this gently using a metal spoon to maintain a large volume.
6. Add extra liquid, fruit, etc., as the recipe.
7. Put into prepared pan or pans and continue as individual recipe.

WHEN USING THE CREAMING METHOD REMEMBER:

1. Temperature – keep fat soft to facilitate creaming – do not melt this since it prevents the mixture becoming soft and light – the purpose of creaming is to blend the fat and sugar, and also to incorporate air. Eggs should be at room temperature – cold eggs directly from the refrigerator are likely to curdle.
2. Mixing – follow directions for creaming. Cream in a clockwise direction, if the spoon is turned in a counterclockwise direction from time to time it rests the arm. Add the beaten eggs vigorously to the mixture – add the flour GENTLY AND CAREFULLY – overhandling flour results in uneven air holes.
3. Consistency – although recipes vary, this cake mixture is generally fairly soft – see page 256. If too soft the cake may fall in the middle.
4. Baking – temperatures vary a great deal – generally the richer the cake the lower the baking temperature.
5. Turning out – small cakes and light large cakes may be turned out within a few minutes after removing from the oven; rich cakes are often better if cooled in the pan.
6. Storing – in a tightly covered container away from pastry, bread, and cookies. Most cakes made by this method keep reasonably well; very rich plain or fruit cakes keep for some considerable period.

TO TEST CAKES MADE BY THE CREAMING METHOD

SMALL CAKES – press gently but firmly on top of one or two small cakes, and the cakes are done when no impression is left by the fingertip.

LARGE CAKES – plain – press gently but firmly on top of the cake, and if no impression is made the cake may be tested with a very fine warm skewer or a wooden toothpick. If this comes away quite clean, then remove the cake from the oven. A further test is if the cake has shrunk slightly away from the sides of the pan.

LARGE CAKES – rich fruit – test by pressing, see above, then bring the cake from the oven and listen carefully. An uncooked fruit cake makes a distinct 'humming' sound – a cooked cake is quiet.

Angel whispers

Cooking time *12–15 minutes*
Oven temperature *425°F.*

⅓ cup margarine *or* butter · ½ cup granulated sugar
¼ teaspoon vanilla extract · 2 eggs
¾ cup all-purpose flour · 1 teaspoon baking powder
dash salt · ¼ cup cornstarch · ¼ cup milk.

Cream margarine or butter, sugar, and vanilla extract until soft and light colored. Beat in the egg yolks. Sift together the flour, baking powder, salt and cornstarch, fold into the egg yolk mixture, with the milk, and finally fold in the stiffly beaten egg whites. Half fill lined muffin pans. Bake in a preheated 425°F. oven for 12–15 minutes. These cakes are particularly light, due to the method of mixing. They may be used in place of an ordinary sponge cake for decorating. *Makes 8–10*

Butterfly cakes

Cooking time *As specific recipe*
Oven temperature *As specific recipe*

Mixture as Angel whispers *or* Butter Sandwich
⅔ cup whipping cream, whipped *or* Butter frosting made with ¼ cup butter, etc. (see page 283)
little jam · confectioners' sugar.

Make and bake the cakes and, when cool, cut a slice from the top of each cake. Cut this slice down the center to make the 'wings'. Whip the cream or make the butter frosting. Spread the top of the cakes with the jam, then put the whipped cream or butter frosting on top, or pipe this, if desired. Press the two wings in position, pipe or spoon a little extra cream or buttered frosting down the center and dust with sifted confectioners' sugar. *Makes 12–16*

Cupcakes

Cooking time *12 minutes*
Oven temperature *375°F.*

⅓ cup butter *or* margarine · ⅓ cup granulated sugar
2 eggs · 1 cup all-purpose flour · 1½ teaspoons baking powder · ¼ teaspoon salt
approximately ¼ cup milk · confectioners' sugar frosting using 1½ cups confectioners' sugar, etc. (see page 283).

Cream the butter or margarine and sugar until soft and light, gradually beat in the eggs. Add the sifted dry ingredients carefully, then stir in the milk. Half fill lined muffin pans and bake toward the top of a preheated 375°F. oven for approximately 12 minutes. The cupcakes will have risen toward the tops of the paper cases, but there should be plenty of space to coat with the frosting. *Makes 9*

Queen cakes

Cooking time *15 minutes*
Oven temperature *400°F.*

⅓ cup butter *or* margarine · ⅓ cup granulated sugar
½ teaspoon vanilla extract · 2 eggs · 1 cup all-purpose flour · 1½ teaspoons baking powder
¼ teaspoon salt · ⅓–⅔ cup seedless white raisins
1 tablespoon hot water · confectioners' sugar frosting (see page 283).

Cream together the butter or margarine and sugar until light and fluffy, and add the vanilla extract. Beat in the eggs one at a time. Fold in the flour sifted with the baking powder and the salt, then the raisins and hot water. Two-thirds fill lined muffin pans and bake in a preheated 400°F. oven for 15 minutes. Turn out and cool on a wire rack. Frost, if desired with confectioners' sugar frosting.
Makes 10–12

TO FLAVOR SMALL CAKES

Use either the Angel whispers, or the Queen cakes without the fruit, or Butter sandwich.

CHERRY CAKES
Add ½–¾ cup chopped candied cherries to any of the mixtures and top each cake with a halved cherry before baking. If using the Angel whispers, there is a possibility of the cherries falling to the bottom since the dough is very light, so Queen cakes is better to use.

CHOCOLATE CAKES
Omit ¼ cup of flour in either of the recipes and use ¼ cup chocolate drink powder; or omit 2 tablespoons flour and use 2 tablespoons cocoa.

HONEY CAKES
Substitute 2 tablespoons honey for 3 tablespoons sugar. Flavor the cakes with a little grated lemon peel.

Lamingtons

Cooking time *45–50 minutes*
Oven temperature *350°F.*

⅔ cup butter · 1 cup granulated sugar
¼ teaspoon vanilla extract · 3 eggs · 2½ cups all-purpose flour · 3¾ teaspoons baking powder
½ teaspoon salt · ⅓ cup milk.
TO FILL: raspberry jam.
TO COAT: 1¾ cups confectioners' sugar · ¼ cup cocoa
¼ cup boiling water.
TO DECORATE: 2¼ cups flaked coconut.

Cream the butter and sugar with the vanilla extract. Add the eggs gradually. Fold in the flour, sifted with the baking powder and the salt, alternately with the milk. Spread into a greased 8-inch square cake pan and bake in a preheated 350°F. oven for 45–50 minutes. Cool and store overnight in a tightly covered container. Next day slit the cake horizontally and spread the bottom piece with raspberry jam. Place the two pieces together again, and cut the cake into 2-inch squares. Place the confectioners' sugar and cocoa in a bowl, and make a well in the center. Slowly pour the boiling water into it. Stir with a wooden spoon, gradually working in the confectioners' sugar and cocoa. Add a little more water, if necessary. Keep the frosting thin by placing it over a pan of hot water. Put a square of the cake onto the prongs of a fork and dip into the chocolate frosting, allow any excess to drip back into the bowl. Roll in the coconut, and place on a wire rack until set.

16 portions

Madeleines

Cooking time   *12–15 minutes*
Oven temperature   *400° F.*

Ingredients as Queen cakes without the fruit (see page 260) *or* as Butter sandwich.
TO DECORATE: approximately ¼ cup apricot *or* raspberry jam · ¾–1 cup flaked coconut
5–6 candied cherries · very little angelica.

Make the cake as directed and half fill greased and floured dariole molds. (If you are unable to obtain dariole molds use deep muffin pans, cylindrical shaped tins or custard cups.) Bake in a preheated 400°F. oven for approximately 12 minutes. Turn out and if the tops are at all uneven, cut these flat with a sharp knife. Brush the tops of the cakes and the sides with warm jam, then roll in coconut. Top each with a halved candied cherry and tiny leaves of angelica. *Makes 12–18*

Butter or Victoria Sandwich

Cooking time   *20–25 minutes (layer cake)*
             10–15 minutes (cupcakes)
Oven temperature   *350° F.*

½ cup butter · ½ cup granulated sugar · 2 eggs
1 cup all-purpose flour · 1½ teaspoons baking powder · ¼ teaspoon salt.
Makes one 8-inch layer cake or 12–15 cupcakes

Cooking time   *20–25 minutes*
Oven temperature   *350° F.*

¾ cup butter · ¾ cup granulated sugar · 3 eggs
1½ cups all-purpose flour · 2¼ teaspoons baking powder · ¼ teaspoon salt.
Makes two 8-inch layer cakes or one 9-inch layer cake

Cooking time   *20–25 minutes*
Oven temperature   *350° F.*

1 cup butter · 1 cup granulated sugar · 4 eggs
2 cups all-purpose flour · 3 teaspoons baking powder · ½ teaspoon salt.
Makes two 9-inch layer cakes

Cooking time   *40–45 minutes*
Oven temperature   *350° F.*

1½ cups butter · 1½ cups granulated sugar
6 eggs · 3 cups all-purpose flour · 4½ teaspoons baking powder · ¾ teaspoon salt.
Makes one 13-inch by 9-inch cake
TO FILL: little jam.
TO DECORATE: confectioners' sugar *or* granulated sugar.

Cream butter and sugar until soft and light. Beat the eggs well then gradually beat into the butter mixture adding a little sifted flour if it shows signs

of curdling. Lastly fold in the sifted flour – (see page 259). The mixture should be a soft consistency, so if necessary add a very little water. Put into the greased and floured pan or pans and bake as above. Test as page 259. Turn out carefully onto a folded cloth on the palm of the hand, and reverse on to a wire rack to prevent wire marking top of cake. When cold, fill the layers or split and fill with jam, then top with sugar.

Variations in flavor to Victoria sandwich
A Victoria sandwich is an excellent basis for various flavorings:

CHOCOLATE
Omit ¼ cup flour and use ¾ cup flour and ¼ cup chocolate drink powder, or substitute 2 tablespoons cocoa for 2 tablespoons flour.

COFFEE
Blend 2–3 teaspoons instant coffee with 1 tablespoon warm water, for a recipe using 2 eggs, and add to the mixture after beating in the eggs.

LEMON OR ORANGE
Blend the grated peel of 1–2 lemons or oranges with the margarine or butter and sugar. Use 2 medium eggs plus 1 tablespoon fruit juice rather than 2 large eggs.

Rich Cherry cake

Cooking time   *40–45 minutes*
Oven temperature   *350° F.*

¾ cup butter · ¾ cup granulated sugar
3 large eggs · 1½ cups all-purpose flour
½ teaspoon baking powder · ½ cup finely ground almonds · ½ cup candied cherries.

Cream the butter and sugar in a bowl until soft and light. Beat the eggs, and add gradually to the creamed mixture. If the mixture shows signs of curdling, add a little flour. Sift the flour and baking powder together, and mix with the ground almonds. Halve the cherries and toss in the flour mixture, then fold the flour mixture into the bowl. Put into a greased and floured 9-inch square pan and bake in a preheated 350°F. oven for approximately 40–45 minutes, or until firm to the touch. Test as instructions on page 259 and turn out carefully.

12–14 portions

By using a very small amount of baking powder the cherries do not drop in this mixture, but do not add any liquid or increase the number of eggs.

Rich Dundee cake

Cooking time	2 hours
Oven temperature	325°F.

1 cup butter *or* margarine · 1 cup granulated *or* brown sugar · 4 eggs · 2½ cups all-purpose flour 1 teaspoon baking powder · 1 teaspoon cake spice ½ cup chopped blanched almonds · ¼ cup candied cherries · 1 cup seedless white raisins · 1 cup currants · 1½ cups chopped mixed candied peel approximately 3 tablespoons milk.
TO DECORATE: ½ cup blanched almonds.

Cream the butter and sugar together until soft and light. Gradually add the beaten eggs. Sift the dry ingredients together. Mix the chopped almonds, floured cherries, raisins, currants and mixed peel together. Stir in the flour and enough milk to make a slow dropping consistency, then lastly put in the fruit. Put into a greased and floured 9-inch spring form pan. Cover with halved blanched almonds and brush with a little egg white from egg shells, to glaze. Bake in a preheated 325°F. oven for 2 hours, reducing the heat after 1½ hours, if desired. Cool slightly in the pan before turning onto a wire rack.
14–16 portions

Madeira cake

Cooking time	¾–1 hour
Oven temperature	325°F.

¾ cup butter · ¾–1 cup granulated sugar 3 large eggs · 2 cups all-purpose flour 2 teaspoons baking powder · approximately 3 tablespoons milk.
TO DECORATE: 1 tablespoon granulated sugar, piece of candied lemon peel.

Cream the butter and sugar until soft and light, the larger amount of sugar helps to give a very fine texture. Beat the eggs and add gradually to the creamed butter mixture. Should this show signs of curdling, fold in a little sifted flour. Fold in sifted dry ingredients then the milk. Put into a greased and floured 8-inch spring form pan, sprinkle the sugar on top. Bake in a preheated 325°F. oven for approximately 45 minutes. Halfway through the baking time, place the peel on top of the cake, and if it seems to be getting a little too brown, lower the heat slightly. If preferred, the lemon peel may be put on the cake before baking, and covered halfway through baking with a piece of aluminum foil to prevent it becoming dry or burned. Test as instructions on page 259, then let stand in the pan for 2–3 minutes, turn out carefully onto a wire rack – make sure this is the right way up so the marks of the rack are on the bottom of the cake. *12–14 portions*

Variations on Madeira cake

A Madeira cake is an excellent basis for other light cakes. The recipe above is a fairly rich one and may be made more economical by decreasing the eggs and amounts of butter and sugar as follows:

ECONOMICAL MADEIRA CAKE
Use ½ cup margarine and ½–⅔ cup granulated sugar, then, when well beaten, add 2 large eggs, 2 cups all-purpose flour sifted with 3 teaspoons baking powder and approximately 4 tablespoons milk or enough to

give a soft dropping consistency. Bake as given in the recipe.

LIGHT FRUIT CAKE
Add approximately ⅓ cup currants, ⅓ cup seedless white raisins and 1 cup chopped mixed dried fruit to either the richer or plainer Madeira cake. Bake as given in the recipe.

COCONUT CAKE
Omit ½ cup flour in either the richer or plainer Madeira cake, add ¾ cup flaked coconut instead. Top with a little additional coconut and bake as given in the recipe.

CARAWAY CAKE
Add approximately 1 tablespoon caraway seeds to the flour (a little more or less according to personal taste) in either the richer or plainer Madeira cake. Bake as given in the recipe.

Simnel cake

Ingredients as Rich Dundee cake, see this page. The cake spice may be increased to 2 teaspoons, and a little cinnamon and nutmeg may also be added, if desired.

MARZIPAN
2 cups finely ground almonds · ½ cup granulated sugar · 1 cup confectioners' sugar · few drops lemon extract · 2 egg yolks.
TO DECORATE: egg white and apricot jam if desired, see below.

Prepare the cake. Put half into a well greased and floured 9-inch spring form pan. Make the marzipan, see directions on page 285. Use just under half the marzipan and roll this out to a circle approximately 9 inches in diameter. Put over the unbaked cake, then top with the remaining cake. Bake as Rich Dundee cake, this page. Turn cake out when cold, brush top with a little egg white or apricot jam, cover with a circle of marzipan. If any is left it may be formed into a decoration to go onto the cake. This is traditionally baked in a deep round pan, and decorated with an Easter design of eggs, baby chickens, etc., (see page 245). Brush the marzipan with egg white and brown this either in the oven for a few minutes, or under a broiler with the heat turned very low. *14–16 portions*

Golden Christmas cake

Cooking time   *See below*
Oven temperature   *325°F. then 300°F.*

1¼ cups butter · 1¼ cups granulated sugar
1 tablespoon corn syrup · grated peel 1 lemon
grated peel 1 orange · 5 large eggs
3 tablespoons brandy *or* sherry · 3 cups all-purpose
flour · 2 lb. seedless white raisins *or* seedless white
raisins and raisins · ½ cup chopped dried apricots
1 cup chopped walnuts · 1 cup chopped citron
chopped angelica (optional) · 1 cup chopped candied cherries* · 1 cup chopped candied pineapple.

* if possible half green cherries; half red.

Cream the butter and sugar with the corn syrup and
lemon and orange peels. Continue beating until the
mixture, is soft and light. Beat the eggs and liquid,
and gradually beat into the creamed butter mixture,
adding a little sifted flour if it begins to curdle. Mix
the prepared fruit with the walnuts, citron, angelica,
candied cherries, and pineapple. Stir into the cake
thoroughly with the flour, but do not overbeat. Put
into a well greased and floured 9-inch spring form
pan and bake in a preheated 325°F. oven for 1–1½
hours, then lower the heat to 300°F. for a further
1½–2 hours. Test as instructions on page 259 since
baking times vary a great deal in cooking rich cakes.
Let stand in the pan until completely cold, then
turn out carefully, and put on a wire cooling rack.
Keep wrapped in paper in a tightly covered container until ready to frost. Some people like to bake
rich cakes very slowly, but baking with two temperatures in this way gives a wonderfully moist
cake. Do look at the cake, however, the first time
you make it – after 1 hour's baking it should just be
changing to pale golden – if too dark, lower the heat.
Marzipan may be placed on the cake, if desired (see
page 285) and then frosted with Royal or any of the
frostings given on page 284 and following.

Serves 30–36 portions

Rich Christmas or Wedding cake

Cooking time   *See below*
Oven temperature   *325°F. then 300°F.*

1¼ cups butter · 1¼ cups brown sugar
1 tablespoon molasses · grated peel of 2 lemons
5 large eggs · 3 tablespoons brandy *or* rum *or* sherry
3 cups all-purpose flour · ¼ teaspoon allspice
¼ teaspoon nutmeg ·, 1½ teaspoons cinnamon
4 cups currants · 2 cups seedless white raisins
2 cups seedless raisins · 1 cup blanched chopped
almonds · 1 cup chopped mixed candied peel
½ cup chopped candied cherries.

Cream the butter and sugar with the molasses and
lemon peels, then continue as Golden Christmas
cake, baking for the same period of time. Pack the
mixture firmly into the pan so it slices well. When
cooked this makes a wonderful celebration cake.
Give this and the golden Christmas cake time to
mature – 6 weeks is ideal.
For a two tier traditional wedding cake – use this
for the bottom tier and half quantity for top tier,
baking this in a 6–7-inch round deep pan. In the case

of the larger but more shallow cake, bake for 2½
hours, and nearly 3 hours for the deeper cake. Reduce
the heat after the first hour. Illustrated on page 249.

30–36 portions

Devil's food cake

Cooking time   *20–25 minutes*
Oven temperature   *350°F.*

⅓ cup butter *or* shortening · 1¼ cups granulated
sugar · ¼ teaspoon vanilla extract · 2 eggs
2 (1 oz.) squares unsweetened chocolate · 1 cup
milk, preferably sour *or* buttermilk · 1¼ cups all-
purpose flour · 1¾ teaspoons baking powder
¼ teaspoon salt · ½ teaspoon baking soda.
TO DECORATE: boiled frosting, see page 286
1 (1 oz.) square unsweetened chocolate.

Cream the butter and sugar with the vanilla extract.
Gradually beat in the beaten eggs. Melt the chocolate, cool, then add to the creamed mixture. Alternately, add the milk with the sifted dry ingredients.
Put into two greased and floured 8 or 9-inch layer
cake pans, and bake in a preheated 350°F. oven for
approximately 20–25 minutes. Turn out and fill with
some of the frosting, then top with the remaining
frosting. Allow this to set and become firm, then
decorate with a trail of the melted chocolate.

12–14 portions

Shortcake

Cooking time   *15 minutes*
Oven temperature   *375°F.*

¾ cup butter · ⅓ cup granulated sugar · 1 egg
2¼ cups all-purpose flour · 1 teaspoon baking
powder.
FILLING AND TOPPING: whipped cream · fruit.

Cream butter and sugar until light and fluffy, add
the beaten egg. Stir in the flour sifted with the
baking powder, and knead lightly. Press out in two
8-inch greased and floured layer cake pans. Bake in
a preheated 375°F. oven for 15 minutes, or until pale
golden. Remove from the oven, turn out carefully
and cool. Sandwich together and top with cream and
fruit, see pictures on pages 247 and 314.
This is a combination of cake and biscuit in texture.
Recipes vary, but this is a rich mixture that keeps
several days. *6–8 portions*

Economical shortcake

Cooking time — *15 minutes*
Oven temperature — *425°F.*

3 cups all-purpose flour · 4½ teaspoons baking powder · ¾ teaspoon salt · ¼ cup margarine
½ cup granulated sugar · approximately ⅔–¾ cup milk.
FILLING AND TOPPING: whipped cream *or* whipped evaporated milk · fruit.

Sift the flour, baking powder, and salt into a mixing bowl, then rub in the margarine, add the sugar, and make a soft rolling consistency with the milk. Roll out into two 8-inch circles, put into greased and floured 8-inch layer cake pans, and bake in a preheated 425°F. oven for about 15 minutes. Cool and sandwich together with whipped cream and fruit. Top with additional whipped cream and fruit. Eat when fresh. *Serves 8–10*

Jiffy cake

Cooking time — *35 minutes*
Oven temperature — *350°F.*

¾ cup margarine · ¾ cup castor sugar · 2 eggs
2 cups all-purpose flour · 2 teaspoons baking powder · ⅓ cup milk *or* fruit juice *or* apple cider (this gives an excellent taste to plain cakes).

Put all the ingredients into a large mixing bowl, then beat for 2–3 minutes on medium speed. Spoon the batter into a greased and floured 9-inch round layer pan and bake in a preheated 350°F. oven for about 35 minutes. The cake may be iced if desired. *6–8 portions*

Toffee cake

Cooking time — *50 minutes*
Oven temperature — *325°F.*

¾ cup brown sugar · ⅔ cup butter · ⅓ cup milk
¼ cup granulated sugar · 2 eggs · 2 cups all-purpose flour · 3 teaspoons baking powder
½ teaspoon salt.

Put the brown sugar, 2 tablespoons of the butter and the milk into a heavy pan, and stir until the sugar has dissolved, then allow the mixture to reach 234°F., or the 'soft ball' stage (see page 305). Cream the remaining butter and sugar until soft and light, beat in the warm sweet syrup very gradually to prevent the mixture curdling; if this happens add some of the flour. Beat in the eggs, and fold in the remaining flour. Put into a 9-inch layer cake pan lined with greased wax paper, and bake in a preheated 325°F. oven for 50 minutes. This cake is delicious plain or may be covered with Boiled frosting (see page 286). *8 portions*

Upside down cake

Cooking time — *1 hour*
Oven temperature — *350°F.*

BOTTOM OF CAKE: approximately 8 oz. fresh fruit *or* well-drained canned fruit (apricots, peaches, pineapple) · ¼ cup butter · ¼ cup brown sugar
1 tablespoon corn syrup *or* honey.
FOR THE CAKE: ⅔ cup butter *or* margarine
⅔ cup granulated sugar · 3 eggs · 1½ cups all-purpose flour · 2¼ teaspoons baking powder
¼ teaspoon salt.

Prepare the fruit; melt the butter, and pour into the bottom of a 9-inch square pan. Top with the sugar and corn syrup, then arrange the fruit on this glaze. Cream the butter or margarine and sugar, gradually beat in the eggs, then fold in the flour sifted together with the baking powder and the salt. Spread over the fruit, then bake in a preheated 350°F. oven for approximately 1 hour. Turn out and serve hot or cold. *Serves 6 as dessert or 8 portions for tea*

Coffee almond cake

Cooking time — *45 minutes*
Oven temperature — *325°F.*

⅔ cup margarine · ⅔ cup granulated sugar
2 tablespoons instant coffee · 3 eggs
1½ cups all-purpose flour · 2¼ teaspoons baking powder · ¼ teaspoon salt · ⅓ cup ground almonds
⅓ cup blanched almonds.
TO FROST: 2 cups sifted confectioners' sugar
¼ cup butter · 1–2 teaspoons instant coffee
8 whole blanched almonds.

Cream the margarine and sugar until soft and light, adding the instant coffee toward the end of the creaming. Gradually beat in the eggs, then fold in the flour, sifted together with the baking powder and the salt, ground almonds, and finely chopped almonds. Put into an 8-inch round layer cake pan lined with greased wax paper and bake in a preheated 325°F. oven for approximately 45 minutes. Let stand until cool. Blend the confectioners' sugar with the butter and coffee, and beat until smooth. Spread over top of cake; decorate with blanched almonds. *8–10 portions*

Chocolate spice cake

Cooking time — *45–50 minutes*
Oven temperature — *350°F.*

⅔ cup butter *or* margarine · ⅔ cup granulated sugar
1 cup semi-sweet chocolate pieces · 3 eggs
1½ cups all-purpose flour · 2¼ teaspoons baking powder · ¼ teaspoon salt · ½ teaspoon cinnamon
¼ teaspoon nutmeg · ¼ teaspoon allspice
grated peel of 1 orange.
TO FROST: 2 cups sifted confectioners' sugar
juice of 1 orange · few drops orange food coloring, *or* 2 drops yellow and 3 drops red · candied cherries
angelica (optional) · few blanched almonds.

Cream the butter or margarine and sugar until soft and light. Melt ⅔ cup of the chocolate in a bowl over hot water, cool slightly, then beat into the creamed mixture. Gradually fold in the egg yolks, then beat hard, add the flour sifted together with the baking powder, salt, the spices, grated orange peel, the very finely chopped remaining chocolate, and lastly the stiffly beaten egg whites. Put into an 8-inch square cake pan lined with greased wax paper and bake in a preheated 350°F. oven for approximately 50 minutes, or until just firm to the touch – do not overbake. When cool, top with orange frosting made by blending sifted confectioners' sugar with the orange juice to give a spreading consistency. This may be tinted to a slightly deeper color, if desired. Let the frosting set, then cut the cake into squares with a knife dipped in hot water. Decorate with halved candied cherries, angelica leaves and blanched almonds.

8 large cakes, or 16 small ones

Melting method

While basic ingredients vary in cakes made by the melting method – the procedure of incorporating the fat, etc., into the flour is as follows:

1. Put the fat, sugar, and corn syrup or molasses into a saucepan, heat until the fat is melted – cool unless stated to the contrary.
2. Sift together the dry ingredients into a bowl.
3. Add the melted ingredients, and beat together briskly with a wooden spoon.
4. Add egg, liquid, etc., according to the recipe.
5. Put into prepared pan or pans and continue as individual recipe.

WHEN USING THE MELTING METHOD REMEMBER:

1. Temperature – although the fat, etc., is melted it is generally cooled before adding to the flour. Do not allow the fat, etc., to heat for too long a period in the saucepan otherwise it may burn, or will be wasted by overheating.
2. Mixing – follow directions in melting method – unless stated to the contrary, this method of cake making demands brisk beating to mix ingredients.
3. Consistency – although recipes vary, generally cakes made by this method should have a soft pouring consistency, see description of consistencies on page 256 and in the recipes.
4. Baking – temperatures in the oven will vary but most of these cakes should be cooked at fairly high heat.
5. Turning out – in many cases cakes made with a lot of molasses, etc., should be cooled in the pan, otherwise they break when turned out very hot. Handle with care since they are very delicate.
6. Storing – put the cakes in a tightly covered container, away from pastry, bread, and cookies. Most cakes made by this method keep well – in fact many are better if kept for some days or even weeks before being cut. Remove the paper used to line the pan from moist gingerbreads and similar cakes while warm.

TO TEST CAKES MADE BY THE MELTING METHOD

SMALL CAKES – press gently but firmly on top of one or two small cakes, and the cakes are cooked when no impression is left by the fingertip.

LARGE CAKES – first press gently but firmly on top of the cake. If no impression is made, the cake may be tested with a very fine warm skewer or a wooden toothpick. If this comes away quite clean then remove the cake from the oven. A further test is if the cake has shrunk slightly away from the sides of the pan.
It is important NOT to remove cakes made by this method from the oven until reasonably sure they are cooked, for if even slightly under-done a sudden draft could make them fall in the center.

Rich brownies

Cooking time — *30–35 minutes*
Oven temperature — *350°F.*

½ cup butter · 4 (1 oz.) squares unsweetened chocolate · 4 eggs · ¾ cup granulated sugar
1 cup all-purpose flour · 1½ teaspoons baking powder · ½ teaspoon salt · 1 cup finely ground almonds *or* very finely chopped walnuts.

Put the butter and chocolate into a bowl over hot water. Heat until the chocolate has melted. Beat the eggs and sugar until thick and light. Fold the chocolate mixture into the eggs, and then the sifted dry ingredients and nuts. Grease a 13-inch by 9-inch cake pan. Pour in the mixture, and bake in a preheated 350°F. oven for approximately 30 minutes. Test by pressing firmly on the top; the cake should be quite firm. Let cool slightly, then cut into squares or strips. Brownies should be rather soft and sticky in the middle so do not overbake. *Makes 12–16*

Coffee muffins

Cooking time — *20 minutes*
Oven temperature — *375°F.*

1½ cups all-purpose flour · 2¼ teaspoons baking powder · ¼ teaspoon salt · ¾ cup walnuts *or* pecans · 3 tablespoons butter · ⅔ cup strong coffee · ¼ cup brown sugar · 1 large egg.

Sift the flour together with the baking powder and salt, add the chopped nuts. Melt the butter with the coffee and brown sugar, cool slightly, then add to the flour mixture. Beat well, and lastly stir in the egg. Half fill well greased or paper lined muffin pans. Bake in a preheated 375°F. oven for approximately 20 minutes, or until firm. Serve hot or cold with butter. *Makes 9–12*

Honey cake

Cooking time — *1 hour*
Oven temperature — *350–375°F.*

2 cups all-purpose flour · 1 teaspoon baking powder · 1 teaspoon cinnamon · ½ teaspoon salt
½ cup sugar · ⅔ cup milk · 1 tablespoon butter
¼ cup honey.

Sift the dry ingredients. Warm the milk, butter and honey. Stir onto the flour, etc., and beat well. Put into a floured loaf pan and bake in a preheated 350–375°F. oven for 1 hour. *10–12 portions*

Moist grapefruit cake

Cooking time *1¼ hours*
Oven temperature *300°F.*

1 cup all-purpose flour · ⅓ cup granulated sugar
grated peel 1 grapefruit · 1 teaspoon baking soda
½ cup butter · ½ cup grapefruit marmalade*
½ cup grapefruit juice · 1 egg
TOPPING: ½ cup brown sugar · grapefruit juice.

* or use lemon *or* orange marmalade.

Sift the dry ingredients into a mixing bowl. Put the butter, marmalade, and half the juice into a saucepan and heat until the butter had melted. Cool slightly and add to the dry ingredients. Warm the remaining juice in the saucepan to make sure none of the marmalade, etc. is wasted. Pour over the ingredients in the mixing bowl, and beat thoroughly. Lastly beat in the egg. Put into a 9-inch square pan lined with greased wax paper and bake in a preheated 300°F. oven for approximately 1¼ hours. When cooked, cool for about 10 minutes in the pan, then turn out onto a wire rack with a plate underneath. Heat the brown sugar and grapefruit juice and spoon over the top of the warm cake. *10–12 portions*

Boiled fruit cake

Cooking time *1 hour*
Oven temperature *350°F.*

1¼ cups water *or* preferably strained moderately strong tea · ⅓ cup shortening
⅓ cup sugar, preferably brown · ⅓ cup currants
⅓ cup seedless white raisins · ⅓ cup chopped mixed candied fruit · 2½ cups all-purpose flour
3¾ teaspoons baking powder · ½ teaspoon salt
½ teaspoon cinnamon · ¼ teaspoon nutmeg
¼ teaspoon allspice · 1 teaspoon baking soda.

Boil the liquid, shortening, sugar, currants, raisins, and peel together in a pan for 2 or 3 minutes. Allow to cool slightly. Meanwhile, sift together the dry ingredients. Add liquid and beat thoroughly. Pour into a greased and floured 9-inch spring form pan. Bake in a preheated 350°F. oven for 45 minutes. This is an exceptionally economical cake that does not dry easily. *10–12 portions*

Gingerbread

Cooking time *1¼–1½ hours*
Oven temperature *300°F.*

2 cups all-purpose flour · ¼ cup granulated sugar
½ teaspoon nutmeg · ½ teaspoon cinnamon
½ teaspoon allspice · 1 teaspoon baking soda
1–2 teaspoons ginger · ½ cup butter *or* margarine
⅔ cup molasses · 3 tablespoons corn syrup
⅔ cup milk · 1 egg.
TO DECORATE: 2 tablespoons stem, preserved, *or* crystallized ginger.

Sift the dry ingredients into a mixing bowl. Put the butter or margarine, molasses and corn syrup into a saucepan and heat until the butter has melted. Then cool slightly and add to the dry ingredients. Warm the milk in the saucepan to make sure none of the molasses mixture is wasted. Pour over the ingredients in the mixing bowl and beat thoroughly. Lastly beat in the egg. Line an 8-inch square cake pan with greased wax paper. Pour in the batter and bake in the center of a preheated 300°F. oven for 1¼ to 1½ hours. Test carefully before removing from the oven, (see previous page for testing cakes made by melting method). Let the gingerbread cool in the pan for about 10 minutes, then turn on to a wire rack. Store in a tightly covered container for several days before cutting to allow the flavor to mature. This cake is delicious served with fresh apple sauce as a dessert – or give a piece of gingerbread and a crisp apple to children for a snack, (the molasses in gingerbread is an excellent source of iron).
10–12 portions

If desired decorate with sliced ginger, see picture on page 250.

Parkin

Cooking time *1–1¼ hours*
Oven temperature *300°F.*

½ cup butter *or* shortening and butter mixed
½ cup molasses *or* corn syrup *or* a mixture of both
⅔ cup brown sugar · 1–2 teaspoons ginger
¼ teaspoon allspice · ¼ teaspoon nutmeg
½ teaspoon cinnamon · 1½ cups all-purpose flour
1 teaspoon baking soda · 2 cups rolled oats, coarsely ground in a blender.
This may be adjusted to personal taste – more oats give a shorter, crumbly texture; more flour a finer, smoother texture.

Melt the butter, molasses, and brown sugar together in a pan, use while warm. Sift the dry ingredients together, then add the oats. Stir in the butter mixture, beat hard, then put into a prepared 9-inch square pan and bake in a preheated 300°F. oven for approximately 1–1¼ hours. Turn out carefully when warm, remove the paper, and store in a tightly covered container for several days before cutting. Recipes for Parkin vary a great deal – there is no liquid in the above recipe, but up to ½ cup milk may be added to give a softer, more moist Parkin. Illustrated on page 252. *10–12 portions*

INDIVIDUAL PARKINS
The previous recipe may also be adapted to make a cookie-like cake. Use only ¼ cup fat and ¼ cup granulated sugar – no liquid – and stir the mixture well. Allow to cool, then add 1 small egg to bind, and take small pieces of the mixture and roll into balls with lightly floured fingers. Put onto well-greased baking sheets and top with a blanched almond, or scatter flaked blanched almonds on top. Bake in a preheated 350°F. oven for approximately 10 minutes. Cool on the baking sheets before removing. Serve while fresh. *12–14 cakes*

Whisking method

While basic ingredients vary in cakes made by the whisking method – the procedure of incorporating the eggs and sugar with the flour, etc., is as follows:
1. Put the eggs and sugar into a mixing bowl. Whisk or beat briskly until the mixture is thick enough to see the mark of the whisk or electric mixer beater – this takes some time. The bowl may be placed on a folded cloth and steadied with the hand not whisking.
2. This can be done more quickly by standing the bowl over a saucepan of *hot*, not boiling, water – take care the eggs do not set around the sides of the bowl – once the egg and sugar mixture has become thick, remove from the heat, and continue whisking until cool.
3. Sift together the dry ingredients once or twice, since it is essential that it is free from any lumps – and it should be kept in a warm place.
4. Fold the sifted dry ingredients into the eggs and sugar with a metal spoon until thoroughly blended.
5. Add melted butter, hot water, or other ingredients given in individual recipes.
6. Put into prepared pan or pans and continue as individual recipe.

WHEN USING THE WHISKING METHOD REMEMBER:

1. Temperature – eggs and sugar whisk better if not too cold – also if the eggs are more than 24 hours old.
2. Mixing – follow directions for whisking, but remember that too energetic a movement when putting the flour into the eggs and sugar can spoil this cake completely, since it destroys the light texture achieved by whisking the eggs and sugar.
3. Consistency – although recipes vary a little in this type of cake, generally they should have a soft dropping consistency so that the unbaked cake mixture falls easily from the spoon. If too stiff then the cake is dry and unpalatable; if too soft the cake tends to be 'rubbery'.
4. Baking – temperatures will vary but most cakes made this way may be baked moderately quickly.
5. Turning out – these cakes are very fragile, so should cool for a few minutes in the pan – unless stated to the contrary. Cool away from a draft since if near cold air the surface tends to wrinkle.
6. Storing – put the cakes in a tightly covered container away from pastry, bread, and cookies. Most cakes made by this method do not keep for a very long period, and are better eaten fresh.

TO TEST CAKES MADE BY THE WHISKING METHOD

SMALL CAKES – press gently but firmly on top of one or two small cakes, and the cakes are cooked when no impression is left by the fingertip. These cakes are very fragile, so do not press too hard.
LARGE CAKES – press gently but firmly on top of the cake, and if no impression is made, the cake may be tested with a very fine warm skewer or a wooden toothpick. If this comes away quite clean, then remove the cake from the oven. These cakes are very fragile so do not press too hard. A further test is if the cake has shrunk slightly away from the sides of the pan.

Sponge cake

Cooking time	*14–16 minutes*
Oven temperature	*350°F.*

2 eggs · ⅓–½ cup granulated sugar* · ½ cup all-purpose flour · ¾ teaspoon baking powder
dash salt.

Makes one 8-inch layer cake

Cooking time	*15–20 minutes*
Oven temperature	*350°F.*

3 eggs · ⅓–½ cup granulated sugar* · ¾ cup all-purpose flour · 1 teaspoon baking powder
¼ teaspoon salt.
Makes two 8-inch layer cakes or one 9-inch layer cake

Cooking time	*15–20 minutes*
Oven temperature	*350°F.*

4 eggs · ½–⅔ cup granulated sugar* · 1 cup all-purpose flour · 1½ teaspoons baking powder
¼ teaspoon salt.
Makes two 9-inch layer cakes
TO FILL: little jam.
TO DECORATE: granulated *or* confectioners' sugar.

* the larger amount of sugar gives a lighter cake.

Beat the eggs and sugar until thick, see this page. Fold in the flour sifted with the baking powder and the salt as described. If the eggs are small, add 2–3 teaspoons hot water. Divide mixture between the greased and floured, or floured and sugared, pan or pans and bake as above. Test as above. Turn out carefully. When cold, fill the layers or split and fill with jam and top with sugar. An even lighter texture is given if the egg yolks and sugar are beaten first, then the beaten egg whites added to them.
Coating – this type of cake is improved by coating the pan with equal quantities of flour and sugar to give a crisp surface.

Swiss roll or jelly roll

Cooking time	*6–9 minutes*
Oven temperature	*425°F.*

2 eggs · ⅓–½ cup granulated sugar* · ½ cup all-purpose flour · ¾ teaspoon baking powder
dash salt · 1 tablespoon hot water.
TO FILL: ¼ cup jam.
TO DECORATE: granulated or confectioners' sugar.

* The larger amount of sugar gives a lighter sponge.

Line a 13-inch by 9-inch cake pan with greased wax paper. Cut the paper neatly at the corners so the cake will turn out a perfect shape. Put the eggs and sugar into a bowl and beat until light and thick. If desired, the eggs and sugar may be beaten in a bowl over hot, but not boiling, water. With a metal spoon, fold in the flour, sifted together with the baking powder and the salt, then fold in the hot water. Pour the mixture into the prepared pan and bake in a pre-heated 425°F. oven for 6–9 minutes. Test by pressing gently but firmly with the forefinger, and if no impression is left, turn the Swiss roll onto a sheet of sugared paper. Trim off the crisp edges and spread with warm jam. To roll a Swiss roll, make a shallow cut in the roll ½–1 inch from the end nearest to you. Fold this over firmly, lift the paper under the sponge, and use this to help form the cake into a neat roll. Cool away from drafts.   *4–6 portions*

Mocha cake

Cooking time   *10–12 minutes*
Oven temperature   *375°F.*

3 eggs · ½ cup granulated sugar · ¾ cup all-purpose flour · 1 teaspoon baking powder
dash salt · ¼ cup chocolate drink powder
1 tablespoon instant coffee · 1 tablespoon warm water.
TO FILL: ⅔ cup whipping cream.
TO DECORATE: little confectioners' sugar.

Beat the eggs and sugar until thick – see directions on page 267, sift together the flour, baking powder, salt and chocolate drink powder, then fold into the egg mixture, along with the instant coffee mixed with the tablespoon warm water. Put into two greased and floured 8-inch layer cake pans and bake in a preheated 375°F. oven for 10–12 minutes, or until firm. Turn out carefully onto a wire rack. When cold, fill with whipped cream, and top with sifted confectioners' sugar.   *6–8 portions*

NUT CAKE
Use the sponge cake or Swiss roll recipe, but instead of the flour use very finely chopped or ground nuts. Finely ground or blanched and chopped almonds may be used, but finely chopped unblanched almonds also give a good flavor. Filberts or walnuts may also be used.

Harlequin cake

Cooking time   *See below*
Oven temperature   *See below*

Two 8-inch layer Sponge cakes (see page 267) using ½ cup granulated sugar · few drops red food coloring · few drops green coloring.
TO FILL: little jam.
TO DECORATE: 1½ cups confectioners' sugar
¼ cup butter · little lemon juice · coloring if desired.

Make the cake as given. Grease and flour two 8-inch layer pans. Divide one third of the cake batter between the pans in small spoonfuls. Divide the remaining cake mixture in half and tint one half pale pink and one pale green. Put spoonfuls of the colored batter into the pans and bake as directed. Fill the two cakes with jam. Blend the confectioners' sugar and butter, beat until smooth, add the lemon juice, and spread over the top of the cake.   *6–8 portions*

Doughnuts with raisins

Cooking time   *8–10 minutes*

1 cup seedless raisins · ½ cup milk
1 cup all-purpose flour · 1½ teaspoons baking powder · ¼ teaspoon salt · 3 tablespoons granulated sugar · 1 egg.
TO FRY: fat.
TO COAT: ¼ cup granulated sugar.

Put the raisins into the mixing bowl with the milk and let stand for about 10 minutes so they may swell. Add the flour sifted with the baking powder and the salt, the sugar, and egg and beat well. Heat the fat in a pan or deep fat fryer to 375°F., add spoonfuls of the mixture and fry steadily for 2–3 minutes, then turn and brown on the second side. To test, press firmly with the back of the knife at the side of the doughnut and if no batter oozes out they are ready. Remove, drain on paper towels, then roll in sugar.
        8–10 portions

Yeast doughs

Both basic ingredients and the method of incorporating the yeast may vary, since modern teaching of baking with yeast is designed to make it as simple and quick as possible, but the following is one basic method of incorporating the ingredients:

1. Cream fresh yeast with a little sugar, add the lukewarm (110°F.) liquid and a sprinkling of flour.
2. Put into a warm place for the mixture to bubble – this will take approximately 15–20 minutes. To use dry yeast follow the special directions in each recipe, and page 288.
3. Meanwhile, put the flour into a warm bowl adding fat, etc., as given in the individual recipes.
4. Mix the yeast liquid with the flour, etc., and knead lightly until well blended.
5. Cover the bowl with a clean cloth, or put the whole of the mixture into a very large plastic bag. Put into a warm place and let rise until approximately doubled in bulk. This time will vary according to the richness of the dough, for an average size cake this will be from 1–2 hours.
6. Turn the dough onto a lightly floured board and knead lightly but firmly, pushing the dough with the heel of the hand. Continue like this until when pressed with a floured finger no impression of a finger mark is left and the dough is smooth and elastic.
7. Shape the dough as required, and put it into a pan or on baking sheets.
8. Let rise for approximately 20 minutes, always depending on the recipe, then bake as instructed.

Doughnuts, page 278

Apricot almond sponge, page 235

Pear 'rafts', page 219; Apple and ginger meringue, page 253

Shrimp and rice salad, page 169

Sandwich gâteau, page 30; Open sandwiches, page 31

Rollmops and orange salad, page 170; Potato mixed salad, page 169; Salad with meat, page 171;
Rice and mushroom salad, page 169; Egg and seafood, page 170

WHEN USING A YEAST DOUGH REMEMBER:

1. Temperature – since yeast is a living plant it needs warmth as well as food in the form of water, sugar, etc., to make it grow, and it is when the yeast grows that it makes dough very light. It is therefore essential that all ingredients and utensils in contact with yeast are kept pleasantly warm. If too hot on the other hand, the yeast may be killed before its work is done. That is why all liquid used should be lukewarm, i.e. approximately 110°F.
2. Mixing – this will vary according to the recipe. Some yeast cakes are too sticky to be kneaded well, but they must be mixed very thoroughly so that the yeast is evenly distributed. If not well kneaded or well mixed, the cake will have a very uneven texture.
3. Consistency – this type of cake should be fairly soft when mixed. The description of the consistency is given in the individual recipes.
4. Baking – unless stated to the contrary, cakes or a large cake made by this method need quick baking. This inactivates the yeast in the oven and prevents further rising.
5. Turning out – most cakes made by the yeast method are of a fairly firm texture and may be turned out of the pan, or lifted from the baking sheet, at once. In fact it is a good idea to do this since one method of testing yeast cooking is to knock the cake on the bottom with the knuckle to see if it sounds hollow, if it does the cake is adequately cooked.
6. Storing – put yeast cakes in a tightly covered container away from other cakes. If plain they may be stored with bread, but they should never be stored with pastry or cookies. If rich, keep in a separate container. There are a few yeast cakes that are rich and will keep, but generally they are better eaten fresh. They may be warmed for a few minutes in the oven to freshen.

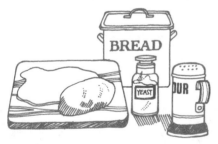

TO TEST CAKES MADE BY USING YEAST

SMALL CAKES AND BUNS – press firmly on the sides and the cakes are cooked when firm and no impression is left by the fingertips. Turn upside down and knock – see below.

LARGE CAKES – press firmly on top and if the cake feels firm, remove from the oven – the cake should have shrunk away from the sides of the pan – for less rich cakes turn out of the pan onto a clean cloth held on the palm of the hand, or on a wire rack – knock the cake and if it sounds hollow the cake is cooked – if it does not, then return to the oven for a short time.

Plain bun dough

Cooking time	*As individual recipe*
Oven temperature	*As individual recipe*

1 cake compressed yeast *or* 1 package active dry yeast · 3 tablespoons granulated sugar
1¼ cups milk *or* milk and water · 4 cups all-purpose flour · ¼ teaspoon salt.

Follow the directions given under bread making for mixing compressed or dry yeast with the warm milk or milk and water (see page 288). Meanwhile, blend the remaining sugar with the flour and salt. Continue as bread making and directions on this page and page 288, then shape the dough into the individual buns, etc.

Richer yeast dough

Cooking time	*As individual recipe*
Oven temperature	*As individual recipe*

1 cake compressed yeast *or* 1 package active dry yeast · ¼ cup granulated sugar · 1 cup milk
4 cups all-purpose flour · ¼ teaspoon salt
¼–½ cup butter *or* margarine · 1 egg.

When mixing this dough follow the directions at the beginning of this section. If using dry yeast, sprinkle this on top of the lukewarm (110°F.) milk, blended with 1 teaspoon of the sugar then continue as for compressed yeast. Continue as bread making and directions on this page and page 288, then shape the dough into individual buns, etc.

Chelsea buns

Cooking time	20 minutes
Oven temperature	400°F.

½ recipe Plain bread dough *or* ½ recipe Richer yeast dough (see above).
FILLING: 2 tablespoons melted butter · ½ cup seedless white raisins · ½ cup currants
¼ cup chopped mixed candied peel
¼ cup brown sugar.
TO GLAZE: honey.

Allow the dough to rise for the first time, see page 268. Knead thoroughly and roll to a rectangle 12 inches by 9 inches. Brush with the melted butter and cover with the currants, raisins, and candied peel. Sprinkle with the brown sugar. Roll up from the longest side like a jelly roll and seal the edge. Cut into 9 equal-sized pieces, and place these face downward in a lightly greased 8-inch square cake pan. Cover with a cloth or put inside a greased plastic bag, and let stand in a warm place until the dough is doubled in bulk – about 30 minutes. Uncover and bake in a preheated 400°F. oven for 20 minutes. Brush the buns while hot with a wet brush dipped in honey. Illustrated on page 204. *Makes 9*

Hot Cross buns

Cooking time   *See method*
Oven temperature   *See method*

1 recipe Plain dough *or* 1 recipe Richer yeast dough
with 1 teaspoon cinnamon, ½ teaspoon nutmeg, and
¼ teaspoon allspice · ¼ cup currants
¼ cup seedless white raisins · ½ cup chopped mixed
candied peel.
TO GLAZE: ¼ cup granulated sugar
3 tablespoons hot water.

Prepare the dough as the recipe selected, but sift the
spices with the flour and add the fruit. Let rise as
given in the recipe at the beginning of this section.
Form into balls and place onto slightly heated
greased baking sheets, mark the form of a cross on
the buns and let stand once more for 20 minutes in a
warm place. Mark the cross lightly if necessary. If
using the plain bun dough, bake in a preheated
425°F. oven for approximately 12 minutes. If using
the richer dough, then bake in a preheated 375°F.
oven for 15 minutes or 20 minutes. Remove the buns
from the oven, brush with the sugar blended with
hot water to give a good shine. Serve hot or reheated.
Traditionally they are made on Good Friday.
Illustrated on page 245.   *Makes 16–20*

More yeast buns and cakes

SWISS BUNS
Use either the plain bun dough or the richer yeast
dough. Form into finger shapes, let rise, and bake as
Hot Cross buns depending upon the type of dough
used. When cooked and cool top with confectioners'
sugar frosting.

CURRANT SQUARES
Use ½ recipe plain bun dough, add ¾–1 cup currants
to the flour. After rising for the first time, form into

a square to fit an 8-inch square pan. Mark into
squares and let rise until doubled in bulk – approximately 30 minutes. Bake in a preheated 400°F. oven
for 20 minutes then, when cold, coat with confectioners' sugar frosting made with 1½–2 cups confectioners' sugar, etc., (see page 283).

Swedish tea ring

Cooking time   *30–35 minutes*
Oven temperature   *350°F.*

1 recipe Plain bun dough or 1 recipe Richer yeast
dough (see page 277).
FILLING: 2 tablespoons melted butter · ¼ cup brown
sugar · 2 teaspoons cinnamon.
TO DECORATE: lemon flavored confectioners' sugar
frosting made with ¾ cup confectioners' sugar, 1
tablespoon lemon juice · candied cherries.

Allow the dough to rise for the first time, (see page
268). Knead thoroughly and roll into a rectangle
10 inches by 8 inches. Brush with the melted butter,
sprinkle the sugar and cinnamon over the dough,
and roll up from the longest side like a jelly roll.
Seal the edge and join ends together to form a ring
so that the sealed edge is underneath. Place on a
lightly greased baking sheet. With kitchen scissors,
cut slashes at an angle 1 inch apart to within ¼ inch
of the center. Turn sections on their sides so that the
filling shows. Cover with greased plastic or a cloth
and let rise for about 30 minutes, or until the dough
has doubled in bulk and feels springy. Bake in a preheated 350°F. oven for 30–35 minutes. Remove from
baking sheet, and cool on a wire rack. When cool,
decorate with the frosting made by blending the
sifted confectioners' sugar and lemon juice. Top
with cherries. Illustrated on page 204.

Doughnuts with yeast

Cooking time   *6–7 minutes*

Ingredients as basic bread (see page 288) *or* Plain bun
dough (see page 277) · lard for deep frying
¼–⅓ cup granulated sugar.

Allow the dough to rise, then form into small round
balls and let rise on a slightly heated baking sheet
for 15 minutes. Heat the lard to 375°F. To test, put in
a cube of day-old bread – it should turn golden brown
within 1 minute. Put in one batch of doughnuts, and
lower heat immediately so they do not brown too
quickly on the outside. Cook steadily for about 6–7
minutes, turning over once. Remove and drain on
paper towels, then roll in sugar. Heat fat again and
continue.
(If desired the dough may be cut into rings with a
well floured double cutter.)

JAM DOUGHNUTS
put a little jam in the center of the dough then form
into a round again before rising the second time.

CREAM DOUGHNUTS
split when cold and fill with whipped cream and jam.

SPICED DOUGHNUTS
sift a little cinnamon or cake spice with the flour.
Illustrated on page 270.

Easy ways to decorate a sponge cake

There are many simple ways in which a homemade or purchased cake may be transformed into a delicious dessert for family or guests by layering the cake and using one of the following fillings.

COCONUT: Fill a sponge cake with whipped cream, blended with chopped candied cherries and flaked coconut. Decorate with confectioners' sugar frosting (see page 283) on top of the cake, surrounded with a border of coconut and candied cherries.

COFFEE WALNUT: Fill a sponge cake with coffee flavoured butter frosting (see page 283). Coat the sides with the frosting and roll in chopped walnuts. Top the cake either with the frosting alone or with frosting and halved walnuts.

CHOCONUT: Fill a plain or chocolate sponge cake with vanilla flavored butter frosting, mixed with chopped nuts and chopped chocolate (see page 283). Coat the sides of the cake with chocolate flavored butter frosting and chopped nuts (see page 284). Cover the top of the cake with frosting and chopped nuts.

FROSTED WALNUT: Make the Madeira cake on page 262 but add 1 cup chopped walnuts to the flour. Make the Boiled frosting on page 286 using 3 egg whites etc. Split the cake into three layers and fill with some of the frosting. Coat the cake with frosting and decorate with walnut halves.

KIRSCH PINEAPPLE: Chop fresh or canned pineapple and soak this for a while in kirsch. Canned pineapple should be well drained. Blend with whipped cream and use to fill a sponge cake. Leave for a while so the sponge becomes fairly moist. Top with whipped cream and pineapple.

LEMON: Fill a sponge cake with lemon flavored butter frosting. Coat the sides of the cake with the frosting and brown flaked almonds. Top with lemon flavored confectioners sugar frosting and a piping of butter frosting.

ORANGE: Frost using orange flavored butter frosting instead of lemon . . . this may be varied by adding well drained canned mandarin oranges to the butter frosting.

STRAWBERRY: Blend fresh or well drained canned or frozen strawberries with whipped cream and chopped nuts. Use this to fill a sponge cake. Top with whipped cream and fruit.

Brandy snap cake

| Cooking time | 20–25 minutes, 8–12 minutes |
| Oven temperature | 350°F., 325°F. |

two 9-inch layers Victoria sandwich (see page 261) but sift 1–1½ teaspoons ginger with the flour
Brandy snaps (see page 297).
FILLING AND FROSTING: ginger butter frosting made with; ½ cup butter · 2 cups sifted confectioners' sugar · ¼–⅓ cup finely chopped candied or well-drained preserved ginger · ⅔ cup whipping cream.

Make and bake the ginger Victoria sandwich cake. Make and bake the brandy snaps, but twist into 12–13 horn shapes – to do this twist the cooked biscuits round well greased cream horn tins, if available, instead of the handle of a wooden spoon as on page 297. Leave the remaining ginger snap mixture unrolled and, when quite cold and crisp, break it into fairly small pieces. Cream the butter and sugar together until quite soft and light. Add the ginger, use about one-third of the mixture to fill the two layers and spread the remaining around sides and top of the cake. Coat the sides of the cake with the crushed brandy snaps. Pipe a rose of whipped cream into each of the horn shapes and place on top of the cake, (see picture page 251). The final decoration for this cake must be done just before serving, since brandy snaps become soft when exposed to the air for any period of time, but the cake itself may be baked and kept for 1 or even 2 days before decorating. *8–12 portions*

Chocolate layer cake

| Cooking time | 20–23 minutes |
| Oven temperature | 350°F. |

two 8-inch layers Victoria sandwich (see page 261)
FILLING AND FROSTING: 1 cup semi-sweet chocolate pieces · ½ cup butter
2 cups sifted confectioners' sugar.

Make and bake the Victoria sandwich. Melt the chocolate pieces in a bowl over hot water, cool, then add the butter and blend thoroughly, lastly adding the confectioners' sugar. Use some of this mixture to fill the cake, then cover the top and sides with the remaining frosting. Sweep the top and side frosting in peaks. *8–10 portions*

Chocolate cake

Cooking time   *25 minutes*
Oven temperature   *375°F.*

¾ cup butter *or* margarine · ¾ cup granulated sugar
3 eggs · 1¼ cups all-purpose flour
1¾ teaspoons baking powder · ¼ teaspoon salt
¼ cup cocoa · ⅓ cup milk. TO DECORATE: Chocolate
butter frosting made with ½ cup butter etc. (see
page 283) · ½ cup flaked almonds
Confectioners' sugar frosting made with 2 cups
confectioners' sugar etc. (see page 283)
few drops red coloring.

Cream the butter and sugar until soft and light.
Separate the eggs. Gradually beat the egg yolks
into the butter mixture. Fold in the sifted dry
ingredients, mixing to a soft dropping consistency
with the milk. Beat the egg whites until stiff, fold
into the mixture and put into two greased and
floured 8-inch layer cake pans. Bake in a preheated
375°F. oven for approximately 20 minutes. Cool on
a wire rack. Place some chocolate frosting in a
piping bag. Using the remainder, fill the cake and
frost the outside. Roll the cake in flaked almonds,
retaining a few for final decoration. Pipe whirls of
the frosting around the top edge and place a piece
of almond on each whirl. Color the confectioners'
sugar pale pink and fill the center with this, (see
picture page 269).   *8 portions*

Glazed cherry slices

Cooking time   *40–45 minutes*
Oven temperature   *325°F.*

Ingredients as Rich cherry cake on page 261.
TOPPING: 1 (16 oz.) can pitted red tart or Bing cherries
3 tablespoons redcurrant jelly (see page 310)
2 teaspoons arrowroot or cornstarch.

Make the cherry cake as the recipe page 261 but
spread the mixture into a 9-inch square pan, and
bake in a preheated 325°F. oven for approximately
40 minutes. Let stand until cool. Drain the cherries
carefully, and measure 1¼ cups syrup from the can
– if not enough syrup then add fresh fruit juice
(orange or lemon) to give the full amount. Put the
jelly and the fruit syrup blended with the arrowroot
or cornstarch into a saucepan and boil until thick
and clear. Cool slightly, and brush the top of the
cake with half the glaze. Arrange the cherries on
top, then glaze these with the cool syrup. Let stand
until completely cold, then cut into strips. Illustrated on page 200.   *12–16 portions*

Lemon fruit slices

Cooking time   *45 minutes*
Oven temperature   *325°F.*

Ingredients as Madeira cake (see page 262)
grated peel of 2 lemons · 1 tablespoon lemon juice
1 cup chopped mixed candied peel
½ cup seedless white raisins   ½ cup currants.
TO DECORATE: ¼ cup sieved apricot jam
Confectioners' sugar frosting made with 2 cups
confectioners' sugar
approximately 2 tablespoons lemon juice.

Prepare the Madeira cake, adding the grated lemon
peel to the butter mixture, and using lemon juice
as part of the liquid. Stir in the candied peel, raisins,
and currants, then place into a 9-inch square pan.
Bake in a preheated 325°F. oven for approximately
45 minutes. Let stand until cool, then brush the
top with the apricot jam and coat with the lemon
flavored frosting.   *12–16 portions*

ORANGE FRUIT SLICES
Use orange juice instead of lemon and decorate with
drained mandarin orange slices – serve at once.

CHERRY FRUIT SLICES
Tint the frosting pink and decorate with candied
cherries and angelica cut into small leaf shapes.
Illustrated on page 252.

Lady Baltimore cake

Cooking time   *30 minutes (including frosting)*
Oven temperature   *350°F.*

¾ cup margarine *or* butter · ¾ cup granulated sugar
3 eggs · 1½ cups all-purpose flour
2¼ teaspoons baking powder · ¼ teaspoon salt.
FOR THE FROSTING: ingredients as Boiled frosting
(see page 286), using 3 egg whites etc.
½ cup seedless raisins
¼ cup chopped walnuts · ⅓ cup finely chopped dried
figs · ¼ cup chopped blanched almonds (optional).

Cream the margarine or butter with the sugar until
soft and light. Gradually beat in the eggs, then fold
in the flour sifted together with the baking powder
and the salt. If the eggs are not very large, add a
few teaspoons water to give a soft dropping consistency. Bake in two greased and floured 8-inch
layer cake pans in a preheated 350°F. oven for
approximately 17–20 minutes. Let stand until cool.
Make the frosting given on page 286, then remove
half and put into a bowl, add the raisins, walnuts,
figs, and almonds, if desired. Fill the layers together
with this and use the plain frosting for the top. If
preferred, add double the quantities of raisins etc.
to *all* the frosting and use as a filling and coating.
                        8 portions

Austrian cherry cake

Cooking time   *15–20 minutes*
Oven temperature   *375°F.*

1½ cups butter *or* margarine · 1½ cups granulated sugar · 3 eggs · 3 cups all-purpose flour
4½ teaspoons baking powder · ¼ teaspoon salt
2 teaspoons cocoa · approximately 2 tablespoons boiling water.
FOR THE FILLING AND TO DECORATE: ½–¾ cup Filberts *or* hazelnuts · ¼ cup canned *or* fresh ripe cherries
vanilla butter frosting (double recipe) (see page 283) *or* 1¼ cups whipping cream
¼ cup toasted flaked almonds.

Grease and line three 8-inch layer cake pans. Cream the butter and sugar until light and fluffy. Beat in the eggs, and then fold in the flour sifted together with the baking powder and the salt, adding sufficient warm water to form a soft dropping consistency. Divide two-thirds of the mixture between two of the pans. Sift the cocoa into the remaining batter, stir, then add the water. Spread this evenly in the third pan. Bake in a preheated 375°F. oven for approximately 15–20 minutes. Chop the nuts, leaving about 12 for decoration; cut the cherries into small pieces, saving a few for decoration. Add nuts and cherries to the butter frosting or whipped cream. Sandwich the three layers together, placing the chocolate layer in the center. Spread the butter frosting evenly around the sides of the cake, then coat with toasted flaked almonds. Spread the remaining frosting on top, and decorate with nuts and cherries.   *8 portions*

Marshmallow Devil's food cake

Cooking time   *50 minutes*
Oven temperature   *325–350°F.*

Devil's food cake (see page 263)
marshmallow frosting (see page 286) try and select white marshmallows.

1 (1 oz.) square unsweetened chocolate.

Prepare the Devil's food cake as the recipe, but instead of baking in two 8–9-inch layer cake pans bake for approximately 50 minutes in a 3–3½ pint greased ovenproof bowl or pudding mold in a very moderate oven. Turn out and cool. Coat with the marshmallow frosting and top with grated chocolate, see picture page 248. If a thicker layer of frosting is required use 36 marshmallows, etc.
            10 portions

Nutty meringue cake

Cooking time   *25 minutes or 1½ hours*
Oven temperature   *350°F. or 200°F.*

5 egg whites · 1¼ cups granulated sugar
1¼ cups finely chopped nuts (walnuts *or* almonds)
1 teaspoon lemon juice *or* vinegar.
TO FILL: fresh fruit and whipping cream *or* lemon curd (see page 311) and whipping cream.

First cut three circles of wax paper 8 inches in diameter. Oil three 8-inch layer cake pans, place the wax paper in the bottom, then brush with oil or melted butter. Remember to oil the sides of the pans. Beat the egg whites until very stiff, gradually beat in half the sugar, then fold in the remaining sugar with the nuts and lemon juice or vinegar. Spoon the mixture into the pans. There are two ways of baking this. If you are going to serve it the day it is baked or the day after, then bake in a preheated 350°F. oven for about 25 minutes, when it will be crisp outside but soft inside. If you wish to store it for several days, then bake in a preheated 200°F. oven for approximately 1½ hours, or until crisp. Remove the paper carefully and, when cold, put into a tightly covered container with fresh wax paper between each layer. Fill with fresh fruit and whipped cream or with lemon gelatin and whipped cream.
            8–10 portions

Peach ring

Cooking time   *10–12 minutes*
Oven temperature   *400°F.*

2 eggs · ¼ cup granulated sugar
¼ teaspoon vanilla extract · ½ cup all-purpose flour
¾ teaspoon baking powder · dash salt
1 tablespoon cocoa.
TO DECORATE: 1 (1 lb. 14 oz.) can sliced peaches
¾ cup peach liquid · 1¼ cups whipping cream
candied cherry.

Beat the eggs, sugar, and vanilla extract until thick, light, and fluffy. Carefully fold in the flour sifted together with the baking powder, salt, and cocoa with a metal spoon. Pour into a greased and floured 7-inch tube pan or an 8-inch layer cake pan, and bake in a preheated 400°F. oven for about 10–12 minutes. Cool on a wire rack. Drain the syrup from the can of fruit, pour the syrup over the cake and allow to soak in. Whip the cream and spread over the top. Decorate by placing peach slices round the outside, and pile the remainder in the center. Top with a cherry.   *8–10 portions*

Strawberry roll

Cooking time   *9 minutes*
Oven temperature   *425°F.*

FOR THE SPONGE: 3 eggs · ½ cup granulated sugar
¾ cup all-purpose flour · 1 teaspoon baking powder
dash salt · 2 tablespoons melted but cooled butter
1 tablespoon hot water · sugar for rolling.
TO FILL: ¾ cup whipping cream · 2 cups sliced strawberries · sugar to taste.
TO TOP: whipped cream · 6–8 whole strawberries.

Make the Swiss roll and bake as page 267. Turn onto sugared wax paper, then place another piece of paper over the top and roll firmly. The butter will enable this cake to be kept for about 24 hours. Unroll, then fill with the whipped cream and sliced sweetened fruit. Re-roll, then top with whipped cream and whole fruit.   *4–6 portions*

Sunshine cake

Cooking time	*approximately 35–40 minutes*
Oven temperature	*375°F.*

¼ cup margarine *or* butter   ·   ¾ cup granulated sugar
5 egg yolks   ·   1¼ cups all-purpose flour
2¼ teaspoons baking powder   ·   ¼ teaspoon salt
¼ cup milk
TO MOISTEN: juice of 2 oranges   ·   a squeeze lemon juice   ·   water, if necessary   ·   ¼ cup granulated sugar.
TO FILL: fresh fruit.

Cream the margarine or butter and sugar until soft and light, then gradually beat in the egg yolks, adding a little flour if the mixture shows signs of curdling, then fold in the sifted dry ingredients and the milk. Well grease and flour a 9-inch by 3½-inch tube pan. Pour the batter into the pan. Bake in a preheated 375°F. oven for approximately 35–40 minutes. Test to see if cooked by pressing firmly on top. Turn out – store until ready to prepare. Place on the serving plate. Measure the orange juice and lemon juice and add enough water to yield ⅔ cup liquid. Heat this with the sugar, then spoon over the cake. If you have stored the cake for more than two days it may become a little dry, in which case use slightly more liquid. Fill the center with summer fruits, sweetened to taste.
8 portions

EMERGENCY CAKES

There are many ways in which cakes may be prepared when in a hurry.
If you have a freezer, an extra sponge cake may always be made when baking and kept in reserve. Otherwise purchased fresh or frozen, or box cakes may be filled with ice cream and fruit, whipped cream, etc., as suggested on page 279. Purchased cakes may be moistened if necessary with extra fruit juice, sherry or a suitable liqueur before adding fruit etc., (try kirsch with cherries, or apricot brandy with apricots). If you have time, make up quick cakes such as raisin doughnuts (see page 268).

CAKES TO IMPRESS

Most cakes in this section look impressive as well as having an extremely good flavor. The more artistically they are decorated or filled, the more they will be admired. Cakes which make use of meringue, such as Nutty meringue cake, opposite, are always a success. The following yeast cakes always look very special, but are much simpler to prepare than many people imagine.

Savarin

Cooking time	*30 minutes*
Oven temperature	*425°F.*

1 cup all-purpose flour   ·   ¼ cake compressed yeast *or* ½ teaspoon active dry yeast
1 teaspoon granulated sugar   ·   ⅓ cup warm milk (110°F.)   ·   ¼ cup margarine *or* butter   ·   2 eggs.
FOR THE SYRUP: ⅔ cup water   ·   ¼ cup granulated sugar   ·   2–3 tablespoons rum.
TO DECORATE: ⅔ cup whipping cream   ·   canned *or* fresh fruit.

Put the flour in a bowl. Cream the yeast with the sugar in a second bowl, add the warm milk; or whisk the dry yeast into the milk, adding the sugar. Sprinkle on a little flour and let stand in a warm place for approximately 10 minutes. Melt the margarine. Add the remaining flour and all the other ingredients to the yeast mixture and beat well. Pour into a well-greased and floured 8-inch layer cake pan and let stand at room temperature for 25 minutes, or until well risen. Bake in a preheated 425°F. oven for approximately 30 minutes. Meanwhile, heat the ingredients for the syrup. Turn the cake out of the pan, prick while hot with a fine knitting needle, and pour the syrup over the top. When cold, decorate with piped whipped cream and canned or fresh fruit.   *6–9 portions*

Rum Babas

Cooking time	*10 minutes*
Oven temperature	*425°F.*

Ingredients as for Savarin, plus 3 tablespoons currants, if desired   ·   syrup as for Savarin.
FOR THE TOPPING: ⅔ cup whipping cream
candied cherries   ·   angelica   ·   nuts.

Make the Savarin, adding the currants with the flour. Put into well-greased and floured muffin pans or proper rum baba tins (tiny flan rings). Let stand in a warm place for 15–20 minutes, then bake in a preheated 425°F. oven for approximately 10 minutes. Meanwhile, heat the ingredients for the syrup. Turn out the cakes, prick as Savarin, and soak with the syrup. When cold, top with whipped cream, candied cherries, angelica leaves, and nuts.
Makes 6–9

FROSTINGS

To frost cakes well takes time and practice, but it is worthwhile, for the results are so satisfying.

Wise choice of frostings

Use confectioners' sugar frosting or Butter frosting on cakes that will be eaten within a short time – these are not suitable for rich cakes.

To use leftover frosting

Cover with a damp cloth or put in a plastic bag.

Easy remedies when things are wrong

There is little that can go wrong with the icing itself – if too soft, add a little extra sugar; if too hard, a little extra moisture.

SUCCESSFUL FROSTINGS
Successful frostings depend upon careful blending of the ingredients. Where confectioners' sugar is used this should be sifted so it is quite smooth, the one exception is confectioners' sugar frosting where the liquid may be poured onto the sugar before sifting, the mixture then left for awhile and beaten hard. Take time to frost a cake so it is evenly coated, practise piping and work out a simple but effective design.

confectioners' sugar. Other size cakes in proportion – naturally the amount used when coating the sides depends on the depth of the cake.

FLAVORINGS TO ADD
Based on 2 cups confectioners' sugar, etc.

ALMOND AND OTHER FLAVORINGS – a few drops.

CHOCOLATE – 1 tablespoon sifted cocoa, 1 tablespoon melted butter – to keep gloss, or 2 (1 oz.) melted unsweetened chocolate squares.

MOCHA – add cocoa or chocolate, mix with coffee instead of water.

ORANGE OR LEMON – mix with either juice instead of

COFFEE – use strong coffee instead of water.

SPICED – Add a dash of spice.
Color with few drops of coloring.

Confectioners' sugar frosting

This frosting is the easiest to make and ideal for covering small cakes, cookies, and light cakes. It cannot be used for piping except for a flowing design, i.e. 'writing' or feathering. It tends to crack after a day or so.

TO MAKE
Blend 2 cups sifted confectioners' sugar with approximately 2 tablespoons warm water – for fragile cakes use a little more water in this frosting.

AMOUNTS TO USE
Top of an 8–9 inch cake – 2 cups confectioners' sugar etc. Top and sides of an 8–9 inch cake – 4 cups (1 lb.)

Butter frosting

This soft frosting is used for covering cakes, for piping and for a filling.

TO MAKE
Cream ¼ cup butter with ¾–1 cup sifted confectioners' sugar – the amount of sugar may vary according to flavoring or if a firm or soft mixture is required. The more sugar, the 'crisper' the mixture.

AMOUNTS TO USE
Top of an 8-inch cake – ¼ cup butter, etc. Other size cakes in proportion – naturally the amount used

when coating the sides and piping will vary according to depth of cake, and the generosity of the piping, etc.

FLAVORINGS TO ADD FOR BUTTER FROSTING
Based on ½ cup butter, etc.

CHOCOLATE – 2 teaspoons sifted cocoa, 2 tablespoons chocolate drink powder or 2 (1 oz.) squares unsweetened chocolate, melted, and a few drops vanilla.

LEMON – 2–4 teaspoons VERY finely grated lemon peel and 2 tablespoons lemon juice.

ORANGE – as lemon but add 2–3 tablespoons peel.

COCONUT – ½ cup flaked coconut.

COFFEE – 2 teaspoons instant coffee dissolved in 4 teaspoons water – add gradually to prevent curdling.

RUM – ¼ teaspoon flavoring or 2 tablespoons rum.

VANILLA AND OTHER FLAVORING – add few drops essence. Color butter frosting with a few drops of coloring.

Royal frosting

This frosting is an excellent coating for rich cakes, and perfect for piping, since it holds its shape. It should not be used on very light cakes, since it becomes too hard.

TO MAKE
Whisk 1 egg white lightly, add 2 cups sifted confectioners' sugar and 1 tablespoon lemon juice. Beat hard until the frosting is very white and shiny and holds its shape – the more this frosting is beaten the better it will be in color and consistency.

AMOUNTS TO USE
Top of a 9-inch cake, plus a little for piping – 1½ egg whites, etc. Top and sides of a 9-inch cake, plus a little for piping – 4 egg whites, etc.
Ideally, one should have two coats for a rich cake – which gives a better finish, so increase the amounts above by at least 50% for two coats and piping. If making up all the frosting at once, keep extra covered with damp paper or a damp cloth to keep it soft.

To pipe with Royal frosting

Before piping onto a cake for the very first time, it is a good idea to practise either on a board or a less important cake. For writing or straight lines you need a plain nozzle. For borders and simple designs you need a star nozzle. There are many more other shaped nozzles to form flower, leaf, or rose shapes.

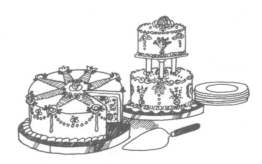

To make flowers in Royal frosting

Here are two ways to pipe flowers in Royal frosting: In order to build up the petals of a raised flower, it is useful to work with a frosting nail. Secure tiny pieces of greased wax paper on the frosting nail or plastic nail (these are available at most hardware stores), and make a small cone shape of frosting with a rose nozzle. Make a slight ribbon band round this with a writing nozzle. This gives the heart of the rose. Gradually build up the shape of the rose by attaching curved bands to form petals. If you cannot obtain a frosting nail, then you can work onto a slightly greased wooden toothpick. The idea of the nail or the stick is that you can turn it as you pipe, so getting the flow of frosting to give a real petal shape. Overlap petals slightly and tilt the nozzle to form the more open outside petals. When making the petals for the flatter types of flowers, i.e. daisies, pansies, blossoms, violets, etc., small squares of wax paper – placed on to a board or secured to frosting nails – are used. Hold the nozzle at a slightly more oblique angle to form the flat petals. Other flowers such as carnations may be piped, using your own imagination or copying a real flower.
When the flowers are hardened and set, lift the paper off the frosting nail and peel away from the frosting or gently pull the toothpick away from the frosting.

To coat a cake

MARZIPAN: Brush the top of the cake with sieved apricot jam. Roll out the marzipan on a sugared board or table, using just under half the quantity for the top of the cake. Lay the cake on top of this marzipan, or lift the cake the right way up again and press the top marzipan to this. Roll out the remainder of the marzipan to a strip exactly the depth of the cake, and about ⅛-inch longer than the circumference. Either brush the sides of the cake or the strip with apricot jam or egg white, then roll the cake along the strip rather like a hoop. Neaten the sides by rolling a jam jar or rolling pin, held upright, round the sides of the cake, and you can roll the top of the cake with a rolling pin. Allow the marzipan to dry for 48 hours to avoid any oil 'soaking through' the frosting, or if the marzipan is handled very gently this waiting can be eliminated.

ROYAL FROSTING: Make the frosting recipe (see page 284) and check it is a good coating consistency. Place almost half the frosting on top of the cake, smooth around with a spatula, working the frosting to remove bubbles. Either use the spatula in a slightly dragging movement or hold it at both ends at an angle to pull surplus frosting toward you. This is much easier if the blade of the spatula is sufficiently long to sweep across the whole width of the cake. If it is too short, you have to keep repeating the process and this means uneven spreading. If frosting top and sides, however, it is better to put all the frosting on top of the cake and move this from the top down the sides. Smooth the frosting with a clean spatula, holding it to the sides of the cake with one hand and turning the cake completely and smoothly with the other. If you are putting two coats of frosting onto the cake, always allow the first coat to dry before the second is applied. Keep the frosting for the second coat the right consistency by covering the bowl with paper or a damp cloth.

If you put the cake on its board or plate, onto a turntable or an upturned bowl, it may be rotated easily.

Marzipan or almond paste

This frosting is used for the 'undercoat' on rich cakes, such as Wedding, Christmas cakes, etc., but it is also a very effective coating and decoration (see Simnel Cake page 262).

Marzipan is very simple to make, but if over-handled it becomes very oily and this oil can soak through the frosting and spoil the color. There are several ways of overcoming this – experts can coat a cake with marzipan and handle it so little that the oil does not come through, so they can put the first coating of frosting on immediately. This has the advantage that the marzipan keeps very moist. If the marzipan is coated with egg white, the oil soaks through less – if left for a minimum of 48 hours before covering with frosting it dries out.

TO MAKE
Mix 1 cup finely ground almonds with ¼ cup granulated sugar and ¼ cup sifted confectioners' sugar, bind with a few drops almond extract and an egg yolk. (A whiter marzipan is made if the ingredients are blended with egg white, or use a whole egg, if desired.)

AMOUNTS TO USE
Top of a 9-inch cake – 1½ cups finely ground almonds, etc. Top and sides of a 9-inch cake – 3 cups finely ground almonds, etc. Other size cakes in proportion – naturally the amount used when coating depends on the depth of the cake and the thickness of the marzipan – the above gives a moderately thick layer. Marzipan may be colored with a few drops of coloring and may be flavored with a little sherry, if desired – in this case, increase the amount of confectioners' sugar slightly.

DECORATIONS IN MARZIPAN

The picture on page 245 shows marzipan used to decorate a Simnel cake. If marzipan is tinted it is excellent for making flowers. Take tiny pieces of marzipan, dip your fingers in a little sifted confectioners' sugar so the marzipan does not stick, then gradually form the desired shape. When the marzipan flower has been formed, it should be allowed to dry for 48 hours before it is put onto the cake. If it is not possible to leave the flowers for this length of time, place them on the cake just before serving, otherwise they may spoil the color of the cake.

As well as flowers, animals, etc., may be formed from marzipan.

Fondant plastic frosting

This frosting is one of the most successful for giving a perfect coating on a cake. It may be used on rich or plain cakes. It is firm enough to support the weight of tiers on a wedding fruit cake, yet never becomes as hard as Royal frosting.

TO MAKE
Dissolve 2 envelopes gelatin in ¼ cup hot water in a large pan. Add ½ cup liquid glucose and 4½ teaspoons glycerin and stir until blended, then mix with 8 cups (2 lb.) sifted confectioners' sugar. Knead very well, then roll out to desired size to cover the cake, sprinkling the rolling pin and board with equal quantities of sifted confectioners' sugar and cornflour.

AMOUNTS TO USE
For top of cake only, 8-inch cake, 5 cups (1¼ lb.) confectioners' sugar, etc., 10-inch cake, 7 cups (1¾ lb.) confectioners' sugar, etc., 12-inch cake, 11 cups (2¾ lb.) confectioners' sugar, etc. For top and sides,

8-inch cake 12 cups (3 lb.) confectioners' sugar, etc., 10-inch cake 18 cups (4½ lb.) confectioners' sugar, etc., 12-inch cake 26–28 cups (6½–7 lb.) confectioners' sugar, etc.

Plastic frosting is generally put over marzipan in place of Royal frosting. If you do not wish to use marzipan, brush the cake with sieved apricot jam to prevent the cake from crumbling, or you may coat the cake with a thin layer of confectioners' sugar frosting.

TO COAT A CAKE WITH FONDANT PLASTIC FROSTING

Make absolutely certain the frosting is rolled out to a sufficiently large shape. Remember it has to go over the top and drop down the sides of the cake. When you are satisfied that the frosting is the right size, move this gently and carefully on the board to make absolutely certain it does not stick and crack. Lift one end of the frosting and slip the sugared rolling pin underneath. Gradually ease the frosting over the rolling pin, so this supports the weight. Bring the rolling pin with the frosting over it to the cake and position the frosting so that it only needs lowering gently on to the cake. This is quite an easy movement. Slip the rolling pin away and allow the frosting to drop slowly onto the cake. Gently press the frosting against the cake and then trim away the bottom edges; do this slowly and carefully to make sure you have sufficient frosting. Once the cake is covered, press the frosting against it firmly and then 'polish' it with the palm of your hand; the more you 'polish' the more glossy and attractive it looks.

Fondant plastic frosting for flowers

Dissolve 1 teaspoon unflavored gelatin in 1 tablespoon hot water in a saucepan, then add just under 1 teaspoon glycerin and 2 tablespoons liquid glucose. Mix in 2 cups sifted confectioners' sugar. Work while warm, tinting if desired – the more you knead the better it is. Take off tiny pieces and mold as petals for flowers.

To form the flowers, take a small piece of frosting and make either the center of a flower or the first petal depending upon the shape chosen. In some cases, e.g. a rose, it is best to work the coloring into the frosting at the start. If you are making a great variety of flowers, you may prefer to mold them all in white frosting and tint by applying food colorings with a very fine paint brush. Remember that this will give a very much stronger color, so it is important to try out first. You may find it better to dilute the coloring with egg white or water.

Boiled frosting

Frosting using 1 egg, etc., will top an 8-inch cake. Frosting using 2 eggs, etc., will top and coat the sides of an 8-inch cake, or give thin coating on a 9-inch cake.
Frosting using 3 eggs, etc., will give 1–2 layers of filling, and top and coat the sides of an 8-inch cake, or a 9-inch cake.
When increasing the amount of sugar, the water need not be increased quite so much – otherwise it will lengthen the boiling time.

¾–1 cup granulated sugar (use the higher amount for a firmer frosting) · ⅔ cup water
1 large egg white · dash cream of tartar.

Put the sugar and water into a heavy saucepan and stir until the sugar has dissolved, then boil steadily without stirring, until the mixture reaches 238°F., i.e. a little forms into a soft ball when dropped into cold water. If the weather is very wet or humid, then boil to 240°F. to make sure of a good result. Remove the pan from the heat, then gradually pour onto the stiffly beaten egg whites, adding the cream of tartar. Beat until stiffened slightly and white, then use very quickly as the frosting hardens. This is NOT a frosting for a smooth coat, it looks more attractive if swirled into peaks.

Marshmallow topping and frosting

MARSHMALLOW TOPPING: This is very simple to make by heating 24 marshmallows in the top of a double boiler until the mixture is slightly fluffy, then spread over the top of the cake. It is ideal for sponge cakes. Care must be taken that the heat is very low, otherwise the marshmallows may burn. A double boiler may also be used.

MARSHMALLOW FROSTING: Melt 24 marshmallows slowly in 1 tablespoon milk in the top of a double boiler, then remove from the heat and let stand until cool. Beat 2 egg whites until stiff, then add 3 tablespoons granulated sugar and beat again until mixture is shiny and stands in firm peaks. Fold into the marshmallow mixture, then let stand for about 7–10 minutes before using. The frosting, may be tinted, if desired. Cover the top and sides of the cake with the frosting and leave in a cool place until ready to serve. If you find the frosting clings to the knife when you slice the cake, dip the knife into hot water. This amount will cover an 8-inch cake.

BREADS, BISCUITS, AND SCONES

Homemade bread provides one of the most delightful 'cooking smells' and its flavor should be as good as its appearance and smell.

Wise choice of breads and biscuits

Choose baking powder breads when in a hurry, or make a batch of biscuits. For breakfast time, prepare yeast rolls and leave them in the refrigerator to rise.

Ways to serve breads and biscuits

Bread is served at almost every meal; biscuits are generally associated with breakfast, but a hot biscuit is excellent for supper or even to accompany coffee.

To use leftover breads and biscuits

Leftover bread or scones are delicious toasted. Bread may be fried, used in Charlottes (see page 110), bread and butter pudding (see page 234), cinnamon doughnuts, rusks, etc.
Make your own crisp bread crumbs for coating fish etc. – crush the bread with a rolling pin or use an electric blender for fine crumbs, then bake in a very moderate oven until golden brown. Roll until fine, store in tightly covered container.

Easy remedies when things are wrong

PROBLEM – if bread and biscuits are dry, this is due to too dry a mixture; too slow baking; or over-handling.
TO REMEDY – dip quickly in milk, bake for a few minutes and serve hot.
PROBLEM – if the bread is very open and not of a smooth even texture, this is generally caused by either too much liquid or over-handling in kneading.
If you have a rather gray crumb, which looks unattractive and causes the bread to taste slightly heavy, it can be due to 'over-rising' or over-fermentation.
If there is a strong smell of yeast from the finished bread, it is either due to too high a proportion of yeast or again, 'over-rising'.
Tiny white spots on the crust of the loaf when baked means that the dough had a chance to form a skin while 'rising'. This is avoided by covering carefully and allowing the bread to 'rise' steadily rather than too rapidly. A bad color can be given to the crust of the bread by using too much flour in shaping.
TO REMEDY – the cooked bread cannot be changed, so use it in cooking.

FLOUR TO USE IN BREAD MAKING, ETC.

Unless stated to the contrary, flour in yeast bread is always all-purpose; no leavening agent is required since this is provided by the yeast.

POSITIONS IN THE OVEN FOR BAKING BREADS, ETC.

Large loaves should be baked in the center of the oven.
Small rolls and biscuits should be baked in the hottest part of the oven, the top.

TO USE DRIED YEAST

Allow 1 package active dry yeast in any yeast recipe instead of 1 cake compressed yeast. Warm the liquid in the recipe, add 1 teaspoon sugar, and sprinkle the yeast on top. Other types of yeast, such as instant blending ones should be used according to the manufacturers' directions.

RISING

Dough should be allowed to rise in a warm place for about 1 hour, or until doubled in bulk. Excessive heat will kill the yeast however. Modern experiments show that dough will 'rise' in colder places, e.g. a refrigerator – see below.

Bread making with yeast

Cooking time   See method
Oven temperature   425°F.

5¼ cups all-purpose flour ·· 1½ teaspoons salt
1 tablespoon lard · 1 cake compressed yeast *or* 1 package active dry yeast and 1 teaspoon sugar *or* 2 teaspoons dried yeast and 1 teaspoon sugar
1¾ cups warm water (110°F.).

Sift flour and salt, rub in the lard. Blend the compressed yeast and water, or follow directions for dry yeast, let stand until the mixture is frothy, approximately 10 minutes.

1. Mix the dry ingredients with the yeast liquid using a wooden spoon.
2. Work to a firm dough with the hand, adding extra flour if needed, until the sides of the bowl are clean.
3. Turn the dough onto a lightly floured board or table and knead thoroughly, to stretch and develop the gluten. To do this, fold the dough toward you then push down and away with the base of the palm of the hand (often called the heel). Continue until the dough feels firm and elastic and no longer sticky, approximately 10 minutes. Shape the dough into a ball.
4. Place in a lightly greased large plastic bag loosely tied, or a large saucepan with a cover, or back into the bowl covered with a table napkin and allow to rise until doubled in bulk, and the dough springs back when pressed with a floured finger. This is known as 'rising'.
5. Let rise for approximately 1 hour in a warm place. Overnight rise – up to 12 hours (or up to 24 hours) in a refrigerator – NOT the freezing compartment. Refrigerator risen dough must be returned to room temperature before shaping – let stand for about 20 minutes.
6. Turn risen dough onto a lightly floured board or table. Flatten firmly with knuckles to knock out air bubbles, then knead to make dough firm and ready for shaping. When kneading or shaping bread use only a little flour. Too much flour spoils the color of the crust.
7. For a large loaf, grease and warm a 9-inch by 5-inch loaf pan. Stretch the dough into an oblong the same width as the pan. Fold into 3 and turn over so the seam is underneath. Smooth over the top, tuck in ends and place in pan. For 2 small loaves divide dough into 2 and shape as above. Place in 2 warmed greased 7-inch by 3-inch loaf pans. For 18 rolls, lightly grease 1 or 2 baking sheets. Divide dough into 18 equal pieces. Roll each piece into a ball or chosen

shape, using the palm of the hand lightly. Place rolls on baking sheet, about 1 inch apart.
8. Either cover the pans with a cloth or slip into plastic bags to rise. Let stand until the dough comes to the top of the pans, or the rolls are doubled in bulk, approximately 15 minutes for rolls and 30–40 minutes for bread, in a warm place.
Refrigerator – rolls 6–8 hours or overnight; bread up to 16 hours.
9. To bake the dough, remove the plastic bags or cloth. Put into a preheated 425°F. oven. Bake large loaf for approximately 40 minutes; smaller loaves for approximately 30 minutes; rolls 12–15 minutes. The heat may be reduced slightly if the loaves seem to be browning too much.
10. To test if cooked, the loaves should have shrunk from the sides of the tin and sound hollow when tapped underneath with the knuckles.
This recipe yields 1 large loaf or 2 small loaves or 18 rolls. It may be used for 6 rolls and a Crown loaf and Poppy Seed braid. Illustrated on page 204.

Variations on basic white bread

BROWN BREAD – use whole wheat flour half and half all-purpose flour. Make as white bread, but use a little extra liquid.

FRUIT BREAD – add 1–1½ cups mixed dried fruit (currants, candied orange and lemon peel, and seedless white raisins) to the flour.

MALT BREAD – add 1 cup plus 2 tablespoons Ovaltine to the flour.

MILK BREAD – use milk instead of water. Skim milk makes a lighter bread; whole milk a richer one.

WHOLE WHEAT BREAD – yeast breads made from whole wheat flour do not require kneading. They may be allowed to rise once in the pan rather than rising twice.

Crown loaf

Cooking time   25–30 minutes
Oven temperature   425°F.

⅓ the white bread dough. TO GLAZE: ½ egg
1½ teaspoons water · dash granulated sugar.
TO DECORATE: poppy seeds.

Divide the risen kneaded dough into 6 and shape as for rolls. Place in a greased 8-inch round layer cake pan, 5 rolls to form a ring and the sixth in the center. Let rise in a lightly greased plastic bag until the dough springs back when pressed with a floured finger (about 30 minutes at room temperature). Brush with egg glaze made by blending egg, water, and sugar, before baking. Sprinkle a few poppy seeds on top if desired. Bake as for loaves in white bread recipe opposite.

Poppy seed braid

Cooking time *25–30 minutes*
Oven temperature *425°F.*

⅓ the white bread dough. TO GLAZE: ½ egg
1½ teaspoons water · dash granulated sugar.
TO DECORATE: poppy seeds (optional).

Divide the risen kneaded dough into 3 and shape each piece into a long thin roll about 10–12 inches long. Gather the 3 ends together and braid. Tuck both ends underneath. Place on a lightly greased baking sheet in a greased plastic bag, and let rise until the dough springs back when pressed with a floured finger (about 30 minutes at room temperature). Brush with egg glaze made by blending egg, water, and sugar, and sprinkle with poppy seeds. Bake as for loaves in white bread recipe on the opposite page.

Cheese bread

Cooking time *See method*
Oven temperature *425°F., 375°F.*

⅔ cup milk · ¼ cup lard *or* margarine
1 teaspoon salt · package active dry yeast
1 teaspoon granulated sugar · ¾ cup water
6 cups all-purpose flour · dash pepper
¾ cup finely grated Cheddar cheese and ¼ cup grated Parmesan *or* Cheshire cheese *or* 1 cup Cheddar cheese
1 egg · small knob butter.

Heat the milk with half the lard and salt, then let cool slightly. Add the milk to the water. Add the sugar. Sprinkle the yeast into the slightly warm milk mixture and let stand for approximately 10 minutes, or until frothy. Sift flour and pepper together. Rub in the remaining lard. Add the cheese, egg, and yeast liquid. Knead together until smooth. Let stand in a covered bowl in a warm place for approximately 1 hour. Turn out and knead again. Form into one large or two small loaves. Put into one 9-inch by 5-inch loaf pan or two 8-inch by 4-inch loaf pans which are warmed and greased. Let rise again for approximately 20 minutes. Brush with a little melted butter to give a shiny crust. Bake in a preheated 425°F. oven for approximately 15 minutes, then lower the heat to 375°F. for a further 15–20 minutes for the small loaves, or 30–40 minutes for the large loaf. *Makes 2 small or 1 large loaf*

Flowerpot loaves

Any bread may be baked in a flowerpot, and the earthenware surface of this gives excellent results. Buy new flowerpots and before using for the first time, season by greasing well and bake empty in a 425°F. oven for about ½ hour. Repeat, if possible, several times. This prevents loaves from sticking. Do not put into water once they have been seasoned.

The flowerpot loaves in the picture page 204 were made by mixing equal quantities of white and whole wheat flour, and following the recipe on opposite page. The risen dough was put into the well greased 4½–5-inch high flowerpots – the tops brushed with water blended with a dash of salt and whole wheat or crushed cornflakes – then baked as small loaves – opposite page.

Baking powder bread

Cooking time *Approximately 25 minutes*
Oven temperature *425°F.*

4 cups all-purpose flour · 1 teaspoon salt
5½ teaspoons baking powder
¼ cup margarine *or* shortening
approximately 1¼ cups milk.

Sift the flour, salt, and baking powder into a bowl. Rub in the margarine until quite fine. Mix very lightly to a light spongy dough with the milk. Shape into two small loaves and place in two 8-inch by 4-inch loaf pans, or in one 9-inch square pan. Bake in a preheated 425°F. oven for approximately 25 minutes *Makes 2 small loaves*

Scotch pancakes or scones

Cooking time *4–5 minutes*

1 cup all-purpose flour · 1½ teaspoons baking powder ¼ teaspoon salt
3 tablespoons granulated sugar · 1 egg
⅔ cup milk · 2 tablespoons melted butter *or* margarine (optional).

Sift together the dry ingredients. Beat in first the egg, then the milk. Lastly, stir in the melted margarine; this is not essential, but it does help to keep the pancakes moist. Grease and warm a griddle, or skillet. To test if correct temperature, drop a teaspoon of the batter on the griddle and if it becomes golden brown within 1 minute it is ready. Drop the batter onto the griddle with a tablespoon. Cook for about 2 minutes, then turn and cook for a further 2 minutes. To test whether cooked, press firmly with the back of a spatula, and if no batter comes from the sides and pancakes feel firm, serve at once with butter and jam, if desired, or fold in a table napkin to keep moist until required. Illustrated on page 203.
About 12 pancakes

Sultana almond twist

Cooking time *20–25 minutes*
Oven temperature *425°F.*

4 cups all-purpose flour · 1 teaspoon salt
1 tablespoon lard · ½ cup sultanas · ¾ cup flaked blanched almonds · ½ cake compressed yeast *or* ½ package active dry yeast and 1 teaspoon sugar
1¼ cups warm water (110°F.) · little milk to glaze.

Sift the flour and salt, then rub in the lard. Add the sultanas and half the chopped almonds. If using compressed yeast, blend this with the warm water or if using dry yeast follow the directions on page 288. Let stand for approximately 10 minutes until the mixture is frothy then continue as the recipe for bread with yeast on page 288. When the dough has risen, knead thoroughly and then form into two or three long strips. Place on a greased baking sheet. Join this at one end then twist or braid loosely (to allow room for the dough to rise again). Let rise for approximately 30 minutes at room temperature. Brush the twist very lightly with milk, and sprinkle with the remaining almonds. Bake in a preheated 425°F. oven for approximately 20 minutes, or until golden. Illustrated on page 203.

Tea cakes

Cooking time   *8–10 minutes*

Ingredients as bread (page 288) *or* plain bun dough (page 277), little fat.

Prepare the dough, and allow it to rise, then knead well, and divide into about 12–20 portions.* Form these into neat flat ¼-inch thick circles or roll out the dough and cut into circles. Put onto a warmed baking sheet and let rise for approximately 15 minutes in a warm place. Heat a griddle (often called a bakestone or girdle) or an electric frying pan or the bottom of a skillet – see comments under Scotch pancakes. Test if sufficiently hot by shaking on a little flour; this should turn golden circles in 1 minute. Put the tea cakes onto the lightly greased hot griddle and cook steadily for 2–3 minutes until golden brown, turn, and cook for the same time on the second side. Lower the heat and cook until firm to the touch. Illustrated on page 203.

* Makes 18–20 from the bread dough or 10–12 from the bun dough.

Coffee and prune bread

Cooking time   *1 hour*
Oven temperature   *350°F.*

3 tablespoons instant coffee
3 tablespoons water · ⅔ cup milk
1 cup pitted dried prunes · 3 cups all-purpose flour
4½ teaspoons baking powder · ½ cup granulated sugar · ¾ teaspoon salt · 1 cup chopped nuts (blanched almonds *or* walnuts)
¼ cup butter *or* margarine · 2 eggs.
TO DECORATE: walnuts.

Blend the coffee, water, and the milk together. Cut the prunes into small pieces with kitchen scissors. Pour the liquid over the prunes. If dry, they need soaking for about 1 hour, if soft and moist for 30 minutes only. Blend the flour, baking powder, sugar, salt, and nuts together. Melt the butter or margarine, then let stand until cool. Pour the butter over the flour, add the prunes and liquid, and beat thoroughly. Lastly stir in the eggs. Line a 9-inch by 5-inch loaf pan with greased wax paper, put in the bread dough, smooth the surface and lightly press walnuts on this. Bake in a preheated 350°F. oven for approximately 1 hour, or until firm to the touch. Turn out of the pan but do not remove the paper until ready to serve the loaf. *16–20 slices*

Fruit and nut loaf

Cooking time   *1¼–1½ hours*
Oven temperature   *350°F.*

½ cup butter *or* margarine
3 cups all-purpose flour · 4½ teaspoons baking powder · 1 teaspoon salt · ½ teaspoon allspice
½ teaspoon cinnamon · ¾ cup granulated sugar
¾ cup Ovaltine · ⅓ cup seedless white raisins
½ cup currants · 1 cup chopped mixed candied peel
¼ cup chopped candied cherries
¾ cup chopped nuts · 2 eggs
1 cup milk.

Melt butter or margarine and cool. Sift together dry ingredients and add the raisins, currants, peel, cherries, and nuts. Beat the eggs, then add the milk with the melted butter. Beat into the remaining ingredients and mix thoroughly. Line a 9-inch by 5-inch loaf pan with greased wax paper or well grease the pan. Bake in a preheated 350°F. oven for approximately 1¼ hours. This keeps well for several days. Good with butter and cheese. Illustrated on page 290. *Makes 1 loaf*

Walnut and date bread

Cooking time   *50–55 minutes*
Oven temperature   *375°F.*

3 cups all-purpose flour
3 teaspoons baking powder · ¾ teaspoon salt
¼ cup butter *or* margarine · 1½–2 cups dates
1 cup walnuts · ¼ cup sugar
⅔ cup water · ¼ cup milk · 2 eggs.

Sift the flour, baking powder and salt together, then rub in the butter or margarine. Chop the dates and the nuts. Add the nuts and sugar to the flour, but put the dates and water into a pan and heat for a few minutes – this softens the dates and gives a moist bread. Add the dates and liquid to the flour mixture, stir in the milk and the beaten eggs. Put into a 9-inch by 5-inch greased and floured loaf pan and bake for 45 minutes in a preheated 375°F. oven, then look at the loaf and if necessary lower the heat slightly for the remaining cooking time.
Makes 1 loaf

Oaties

Cooking time   *20–25 minutes*
Oven temperature   *350°F.*

1 cup all-purpose flour
2½ teaspoons baking powder
¾ teaspoon salt · 1¼ cups rolled oats
¼ cup granulated sugar · ¼ cup molasses
½ cup butter *or* margarine.
TO DECORATE: rolled oats.

Sift the flour, baking powder, and salt together, then add oats. Put the sugar, molasses, and butter into a saucepan, and heat until just melted. Cool slightly, then stir into the flour mixture until all the ingredients are thoroughly combined. Press into a greased 8-inch layer cake pan, sprinkle with rolled oats and bake in a preheated 350°F. oven for 20–25 minutes. Cut into wedges before completely cool. Serve with butter and jam or cheese. *8 portions*

Plain scones

Cooking time — *Approximately 10 minutes*
Oven temperature — *450°F.*

2 cups all-purpose flour
1 teaspoon cream of tartar plus ½ teaspoon baking soda *or* 5 teaspoons baking powder
¼ teaspoon salt · 2–4 tablespoons butter *or* margarine · 3 tablespoons granulated sugar
approximately ¾ cup milk.

Sift flour, cream of tartar, baking soda, and salt into a bowl. Rub in the butter, then add the sugar. Mix to a soft rolling consistency with the milk. Roll out to ½–¾ inch thick and cut into circles. Put onto an ungreased baking sheet, unless cheese, oatmeal, or molasses are in the ingredients. Bake in a preheated 450°F. oven for approximately 10 minutes. To test if cooked, press firmly at the sides. Scones are cooked when firm to the touch. Illustrated on page 314.

Makes 8–12

Variations – sweet

BROWN SCONES
Use half whole wheat flour and half all-purpose flour.

CHERRY SCONES
Add ½ cup finely chopped candied cherries to the flour. Grease the baking sheet well since the cherries may stick at the bottom.

DATE SCONES
Add ½ cup finely chopped MOIST dates to the flour.

LEMON OR ORANGE SCONES
Add the finely grated peel of 1–2 lemons or oranges, to the flour. Use some of the juice to replace some of the milk. Either add ½ cup chopped candied lemon or orange peel or marmalade to the dough. If using marmalade, the sugar may be omitted.

MOLASSES SCONES
Add 1–2 tablespoons molasses to the dough before adding the milk, and omit the sugar.

Variations – savory

CHEESE SCONES
Add dash salt, celery salt, pepper, and mustard to the flour. Add ½–1 cup finely grated cheese after rubbing in the butter or margarine. Omit the sugar.

HAM SCONES
Add ¼–½ cup finely chopped ham to the flour. Omit the sugar.

HERB SCONES
Add 1–2 teaspoons dried herbs to the flour or 2–3 teaspoons finely chopped fresh herbs. Omit the sugar.

Griddle scones

Cooking time — *10 minutes*

Ingredients as any scone mixture · little fat.

Make the scone mixture as the recipe, take care this is not too soft, since scones tend to spread out more when cooked on a griddle than when baked in the oven. Heat the griddle (sometimes called a bakestone or girdle) or when not available use a skillet (see Scotch pancakes page 289). Roll out the scone dough to be thinner than usual – ⅓-inch at the maximum. Test the hot griddle by shaking a little flour onto this; it is the correct heat when the flour turns golden brown within 1 minute. Grease lightly, cook the scones for 3 minutes, or until golden on the first side, turn, and cook for the same time on the second side. Lower the heat and cook for a further 3–4 minutes. Test as page 289. The scones in the picture page 246 are wholewheat griddle scones.

Makes 10–12

Potato pan scones

Cooking time — *8 minutes*

1 cup mashed boiled potatoes · 1 cup all-purpose flour · 1½ teaspoons baking powder
¼ teaspoon salt · 2 tablespoons butter *or* margarine
2–4 tablespoons granulated sugar · ⅔ cup seedless white raisins, raisins, *or* currants
approximately 1 tablespoon milk · little fat.

The mashed potatoes should be very dry and 'floury', and should not have been mashed with milk and butter, (see comments below). Sift the flour, baking powder, and salt into a second bowl, rub in the butter or margarine, then add the potatoes, sugar, and raisins. Blend thoroughly, then add just enough milk to make a firm rolling consistency. Form into one circle the size of the skillet. Heat the skillet, test the heat – see griddle scones recipe – and grease lightly. While the scones may be cooked on a griddle they are excellent in an ordinary skillet since the potatoes are already cooked and the cooking time is comparatively brief. Put in the scone circle. Cook steadily for approximately 3 minutes, turn, then mark into sections while still half cooked. Continue cooking until firm. Makes 4 large or 8 smaller wedge-shaped scones. If using potatoes mashed with milk omit the butter or margarine, and work in sufficient flour to give a firm rolling consistency. Add raisins and sugar to taste or make into a savory scone by adding seasoning and about ½ cup grated cheese. Illustrated on page 202.

'Cut and come again' cake, or bread

Cooking time — *1 hour*
Oven temperature — *350°F.*

2 cups all-purpose flour · 3 teaspoons baking powder · ½ teaspoon salt · ½ cup margarine
½ cup sugar – granulated *or* brown · ½ cup currants
½ cup seedless white raisins · ½ cup chopped mixed candied peel · 1 egg · approximately ½ cup milk.

Sift the flour with the baking powder and the salt into a mixing bowl, then rub in the margarine until the mixture looks like fine bread crumbs. Add the sugar, currants, raisins, candied peel, egg, and milk. Grease and flour a 9-inch by 5-inch loaf pan. Put in the mixture and smooth the surface. Bake in a preheated 350°F. oven for approximately 1 hour. Test as instructions given on page 257. Allow to cool for 2 minutes in the pan, then turn out. Eat when fresh, although this is delicious to butter the following day.

12 portions

COOKIES

Homemade cookies are not only delicious to eat but extremely practical, for they may be stored for some considerable time; so bake them when you have time to spare.

Wise choice of cookies

Bake brandy snaps (see page 291) for special occasions, fill with whipped cream or use as a decoration – for Brandy snap cake see page 279. Serve Meringues for dessert or for coffee. Pack Anzacs, Walnut crisps or Coconut pyramids for picnics, since they are not as fragile as some cookies.

Ways to serve cookies

Arrange them on flat plates or trays or in attractive dishes

To use leftover cookies

Leftover cookies may be reheated to crisp and freshen; or use as crumbs in place of cake or bread crumbs.

Easy remedies when things are wrong

PROBLEM – if biscuits spread badly in cooking, this is due to too much fat, too much liquid (in a recipe using this), or too cool an oven temperature.
TO REMEDY – trim biscuits with a sharp knife or a cookie cutter.
PROBLEM – if cookies or meringues 'stick' on the baking sheet, it was not greased enough.
TO REMEDY – warm the sheet of cookies, lift them off carefully with a damp, warm spatula.
PROBLEM – if cookies are not crisp, this is due to insufficient baking, being left in the air too long, or, kept in a container that was not airtight.
TO REMEDY – bake for a few minutes.
PROBLEM – if biscuits are very hard, this is due to too little fat or over-baking.
TO REMEDY – place a slice of bread or a piece of apple in the container to soften.

TO MAKE PERFECT COOKIES

Cookies on the whole need steady cooking, so they do not become too brown on the outside before they are cooked through to the middle. If the cookies are not quite crisp when they come out of the oven, they may easily be re-baked. Very rich cookies should be allowed to cool on the baking sheet for awhile since they are extremely fragile.

FLOUR TO USE IN COOKIES

Unless stated to the contrary, it is advisable to use all-purpose flour since the cookies will keep a better shape.

TO BAKE COOKIES

Unless stated to the contrary, most cookies should be baked in the center of the oven so they do not become too brown on the top.

TO DECORATE COOKIES

Cookies may be decorated by sandwiching two together with Butter frosting (see page 283) or jam, and topping with sifted confectioners' sugar.
It is important, however, to put this between the cookies just before serving them, otherwise they become too soft. Cookies may also be frosted, and one of the most attractive decorations is feathering (see below). Children enjoy cookies decorated with their own initials.

Toasted cheese and ham sandwich, page 31

296   Chocolate coconut pyramids, page 305; Coconut ice, page 305; Chocolate coated fudge, page 305; Fondant, page 306;
Marzipan candy, page 304; Economy fudge, page 306; Peppermint creams, page 307; Crème de menthe jellies, page 307

FEATHERING

To produce this attractive design, cover the cookies with a plain layer of confectioners' sugar frosting. Tint the remaining frosting and either pipe lines across the cookie, or dip a skewer in the colored frosting and make lines. Take a knife and pull the colored frosting toward you at regular intervals, or pull it first toward you and then away from you to make a design.

This decoration may also be used on cakes. Do not frost cookies until the day of serving because they will lose their crispness.

Anzacs

Cooking time	*15 minutes*
Oven temperature	*350°F.*

½ cup butter · 1 tablespoon corn syrup
1 cup all-purpose flour · ½ teaspoon baking powder
⅓ cup rolled oats · ½ cup flaked coconut
½ cup granulated sugar
little milk (if necessary).

Soften the butter slightly, then cream with the corn syrup. Add the remaining ingredients. Work in 1 teaspoon milk if necessary. Roll into small balls and put well spaced onto greased baking sheets. Bake in a preheated 350°F. oven for approximately 15 minutes. Cool for a few minutes on baking sheets, then lift onto a wire rack. *Makes 18–20*

VARIATIONS

Omit rolled oats and use 1½ cups all-purpose flour, ¾ cup coconut.
Omit coconut and use 1½ cups all-purpose flour and ½ cup rolled oats.

Brandy snaps

Cooking time	*8–12 minutes*
Oven temperature	*325°F.*

¼ cup margarine *or* butter · ¼ cup granulated sugar
3 tablespoons corn syrup · ½ cup all-purpose flour
¼ teaspoon baking powder · dash salt
½–1 teaspoon ginger.

Put margarine or butter, sugar, and corn syrup into a saucepan, and heat until the margarine has melted. Sift flour, baking powder, salt, and ginger together, then stir into the margarine mixture. Put a teaspoon of mixture on well greased baking sheets very well spaced – allowing room for the mixture to spread. Bake in a preheated 325°F. oven for 8–12 minutes, or until becoming firm around the edges – time the baking so that one sheet is ready to come from the oven at a time. Cool for 2 minutes, then roll around the greased handle of a wooden spoon. Hold in position for a few seconds, then remove spoon. *Makes 12–14*

TO ROLL BRANDY SNAPS

Grease the handle of a wooden spoon, lift one cookie from the baking sheet, and press around spoon, with the top of the biscuit on the outside. Hold in position for a few seconds to give the cookie a chance to set. Slip handle out, and put cookie on a wire rack.

Work quickly since when the cookies start to harden they cannot be removed from the baking sheet. If this happens, return to the oven for a minute. Store away from other biscuits in a tightly covered container.

Rich Easter cookies

Cooking time	*15–20 minutes*
Oven temperature	*375°F.*

¾ cup butter · ½ cup granulated sugar
2 egg yolks · ⅓ cup currants
2 cups all-purpose flour.

Cream butter and sugar until light, then beat in egg yolks and currants. Work in flour and, when mixed, gather together. Wrap in wax paper and place in the refrigerator overnight. Next day, roll out lightly with a floured rolling pin on floured wax paper to about ¼-inch thick. If the mixture seems too soft for cutting, return to the refrigerator until firm again, then cut into circles about 3½ inches in diameter, plain or fluted, remove the trimmings, and lift the cookies with a floured spatula onto baking sheets, placing well apart. Chill for about 20 minutes before cooking. Bake in a preheated 375°F. oven for 15–20 minutes. Since the cookies are very buttery they are likely to spread and lose their shape. Cool on the baking sheets. These are richer than a standard Easter cookie and the way they spread in the oven may explain why they are called Easter cakes in old cookbooks. *Makes 18*

Economical Easter cookies

Cooking time	*15–20 minutes*
Oven temperature	*325°F.*

½ cup butter · ½ cup granulated sugar
2 cups all-purpose flour · 1 teaspoon cinnamon
¼ teaspoon nutmeg · ¼ teaspoon allspice
¾–1 cup currants · 2–3 tablespoons milk *or*
1 egg yolk.

Cream the butter and sugar, add the flour sifted together with the spices. Add currants, milk or egg yolk to bind. Roll the dough out thinly, cut into rather large circles, put onto lightly greased baking sheets and bake in a preheated 325°F. oven for 15–20 minutes, or until golden brown, see picture page 245. *Makes 12–14*

Coconut pyramids

Cooking time	*20 minutes*
Oven temperature	*350°F.*

2 egg whites · 2⅔ cups flaked coconut
¼ cup granulated sugar · 1 tablespoon cornstarch.

Beat egg whites until stiff but not dry, then add the remaining ingredients. Form into pyramid shapes with slightly moistened fingers and put on a well greased and floured baking sheet. Bake in a preheated 350°F. oven for approximately 20 minutes. Cool slightly, and remove from the baking sheet with a spatula. *Makes 12–15*

Grantham gingerbread cookies

Cooking time   20 minutes
Oven temperature   350°F.

2 cups all-purpose flour   ·   ⅓ cup margarine
¾ cup granulated sugar   ·   ½ teaspoon nutmeg
1–2 teaspoons ginger   ·   1 small egg
1–2 tablespoons lemon juice.
FOR COATING: little rice flour, ground rice or semolina
flour.

Sift the flour into a mixing bowl. Rub in the margarine, then add the sugar and spices. Stir in the
egg and enough lemon juice to give a firm rolling
consistency. This dough is easier to handle if placed
in the refrigerator for several hours. Dust the pastry
board with the rice flour (or alternative), and roll
out the dough to about ½ inch thick, then cut into
circles of 2½–3 inches in diameter. Put onto lightly
greased baking sheets and bake in a preheated
350°F. oven for approximately 20 minutes, or until
firm to the touch. Cool for a few minutes on the
sheets, then lift onto a wire rack. Store in a tightly
closed container away from cakes – these are better
eaten fresh. They may be coated with a thin layer
of confectioners' sugar frosting, if desired.
                                              Makes 12

Oatmeal flapjacks

Cooking time   15–20 minutes
Oven temperature   375°F.

¼ cup butter or margarine   ·   ¼ cup sugar, granulated
or brown, or 3 tablespoons granulated sugar and 4
teaspoons corn syrup   ·   1¼ cups rolled oats
dash salt.

Heat the butter or margarine, and stir in the other
ingredients. Press into an 8-inch greased and floured
layer cake pan and bake in a preheated 375°F. oven
for approximately 15 minutes; check after about 10
minutes and, if the flapjacks are becoming too
brown, lower the heat for the remaining cooking
time. Mark into squares or triangles while hot, and
remove from the pan before completely cold. For a
richer cookie, increase butter to ⅓ cup and sugar to
⅓ cup.   Makes 6–8

Macaroons

Cooking time   15–20 minutes
Oven temperature   375°F.

2 egg whites   ·   ⅔ cup granulated sugar
few drops almond extract   ·   1½ cups finely ground
almonds.
TO DECORATE: 12 blanched almonds.

Beat egg whites lightly, add sugar, extract and
ground almonds; if the egg whites are small add
a little water to give a soft rolling consistency;
if large, add a little more ground almonds. Roll
in balls, put on a well greased and floured baking
sheet, allowing room to spread. Top with almonds.
Bake in a preheated 375°F. oven for approximately
20 minutes. Cool slightly and remove from the sheet
with a spatula.   Makes 12

Variations on macaroons

COCONUT MACAROONS
Use 2 cups flaked coconut in place of the ground
almonds.

CHOCOLATE MACAROONS
Add ½ cup chocolate drink powder or ¼ cup sifted
cocoa to the dough. This means either omitting
¼ cup of the ground almonds, or adding a few drops
of water to give the desired consistency.

Walnut crisps

Cooking time   15 minutes
Oven temperature   375°F.

1 cup all-purpose flour   ·   1½ teaspoons baking
powder   ·   ¼ teaspoon salt   ·   ½ cup brown sugar
¼ cup margarine or shortening   ·   ¼ cup walnuts
½ cup semisweet chocolate pieces   ·   1 egg.
TO DECORATE: 12 walnut halves or pieces.

Sift the flour together with the baking powder and
salt into a bowl. Add the sugar and margarine.
Chop the walnuts, and add with the chocolate to
the other ingredients. Mix with a fork for about
1 minute, at the same time pressing out the lumps
of margarine. Blend in the beaten egg. Spoon into
rough heaps on a greased baking sheet, allowing
room to spread, and place a piece of walnut in the
centre of each cookie. Bake in a preheated 375°F.
oven for approximately 15 minutes. Allow to cool
slightly on the pan before placing onto a wire rack.
(See picture, page 293).   Makes 12–14

Meringues

METHODS OF ADDING SUGAR IN MERINGUES: this recipe
gives three methods of adding sugar to the egg
whites. It is important that this is done carefully,
otherwise the texture of the meringues will be
spoiled.

Cooking time   1½–2 hours
Oven temperature   250°F.

2 egg whites   ·   ½ cup granulated sugar (or use ½
cup sifted confectioners' sugar and ¼ cup granulated
sugar).

Beat the egg whites until so stiff you can turn the
bowl upside down. Gradually and gently fold in the
sugar, or gradually beat in half the sugar then fold
in that remaining, or gradually beat in all the sugar
– particularly suitable with an electric mixer.
Lightly brush a baking sheet with oil or melted
butter. Either spoon the mixture onto this to give

neat mounds or pipe with a plain or fluted large nozzle in a cloth bag. Bake in a preheated 250°F. oven for 1½–2 hours depending on size. Remove from sheet and store in a tightly covered container until ready to fill. Sandwich together with whipped cream just before serving. Illustrated on page 125.

Makes 10–12 large or 24 small

FLAVORING FOR MERINGUES

The flavoring for meringues needs to be added very carefully, otherwise the texture of the egg whites could be spoiled.

CHOCOLATE: Add 1 teaspoon sifted cocoa or 1 table-spoon chocolate drink powder to the sugar.

COFFEE: Add ½–1 teaspoon instant coffee to the sugar.

The flavorings are rather delicate if using the quantities above – more may be added, if desired.

Rich shortbread

Cooking time	*40 minutes*
Oven temperature	*300°F.*

⅓ cup butter · 3–4 tablespoons granulated sugar
¾ cup all-purpose flour · ¼ cup cornstarch *or* rice flour *or* finely ground rice.

Cream the butter and half the sugar, work in the flour and cornstarch or rice flour, then the remaining sugar. Knead well. Press into a circle on the back of an ungreased layer cake pan – or into a floured shortbread mold,* score or cut in triangular shapes – or roll thinly and cut into strips. If ¼–½ inch thick, bake in a preheated 300°F. oven for 40 minutes. Cool on the pan. For thinner biscuits bake in a preheated 350°F. oven for about 20 minutes.

8 portions

* Turn onto baking pan.

PLAIN SHORTBREAD
Use the same quantity of flour as given above, but only ¼ cup butter. If the mixture is kneaded very hard it may be pressed into a circular shape on the back of an ungreased layer cake pan for a plain round of shortbread. To roll out the shortbread a little milk or egg yolk should be added.

FLAVORING SHORTBREAD

CHOCOLATE SHORTBREAD: Use ¼ cup chocolate drink powder in either recipe and omit the same amount of flour.

CHERRY SHORTBREAD: Add 2–4 tablespoons chopped candied cherries to either shortbread mixture. Grease the pan well.

FRUIT SHORTBREAD: Add ¾ cup chopped mixed candied peel or a combination of seedless white raisins, currants and chopped mixed candied peel.

CHEESE SHORTBREAD: Follow the directions for rich shortbread, but omit the sugar, add plenty of seasoning and ½ cup finely grated Cheddar cheese – bake as given.

FROSTED SHORTBREAD
Make either of the shortbread recipes, but use double the quantity. Roll out and mark into 2½-inch squares or rectangles 2 × 3 inches. Bake as the recipe. When quite cold, top with melted milk chocolate. To frost this amount you need 4 oz. chocolate. If any chocolate is left, form lines on top as in the picture, page 252, by piping with a small plain nozzle.

Cheese straws

Cooking time	*10–12 minutes*
Oven temperature	*425°F.*

2 recipes rich cheese pastry (see page 216).
TO GLAZE: little beaten egg *or* milk.

Roll out the pastry until ¼-inch thick. Cut into narrow strips 3 inches long. Lift onto a lightly greased baking sheet and brush lightly with egg or milk. Bake in a preheated 425°F. oven for approximately 10–12 minutes. Cool for 2–3 minutes on the sheet, then place on a wire rack with a spatula.

Makes 40–48

Note: if preferred, use a little of the pastry to make a ring, bake this, and put the straws through it.

Cheese and almond balls

Cooking time	*15 minutes*
Oven temperature	*325°F.*

⅓ cup butter · ½ cup finely grated Cheddar cheese
1 cup all-purpose flour
1½ teaspoons baking powder · pepper
¼ cup chopped blanched almonds.
TO DECORATE: 1 tablespoon flaked almonds.

Cream butter with the cheese, add the flour sifted together with the baking powder, plenty of seasoning and the almonds. Roll into small balls. Press a piece of flaked almond on top of each ball. Put onto well greased baking sheets and bake in a preheated 325°F. oven for approximately 15 minutes, or until pale gold. Cool on the baking sheets. *Makes 10–12*

DRINKS AND BEVERAGES

This section includes drinks that are very well known and served every day, e.g. coffee and tea; homemade fruit drinks such as lemonade or the more unusual appleade; and drinks for special occasions.

Wise choice of drinks

A punch, whether it is based upon cider or champagne, is ideal as an economical party drink and a hot punch provides a really welcoming smell. Although there is a paragraph on choosing wines, basically the right wine for each occasion is the wine that suits your own palate.

Ways to serve drinks

Serve cold drinks in tall glasses or small glass tankards or cups, as shown in the picture on page 336. Punches and fruit cups look their best if served in clear glass or silver bowls. Glasses are most attractive if the rims are frosted – to do this, dip the rim in unbeaten egg white or water and then into granulated sugar.

To use leftover drinks

Leftover coffee may be used in sauces, etc. Leftover tea is excellent for flavoring prunes in cooking for a plain fruit cake (see Boiled fruit cake, page 266). Leftover wines may be kept, unless effervescent. If not required for drinking, they are excellent in cooking.

Easy remedies when things are wrong

There is little that can go wrong with drinks.
PROBLEM – if coffee is bitter, this is probably because it is over-boiled. If it is tasteless, the coffee had become stale or an insufficient amount was used.
TO REMEDY – there is little one can do with poor coffee. If it is weak, add a little instant coffee to strengthen.
PROBLEM – if using loose tea and it is weak, it may well be that it has not had sufficient time to infuse.
TO REMEDY – stir well.

To make a chocolate drink

Before using a milk saucepan rinse out in cold water, since this helps to prevent the milk from sticking to the pan. Heat ⅔ cup milk per person and stir in 1–2 tablespoons chocolate syrup per cup.

To make cold chocolate, pour milk into a glass to within one inch of the top. Add the chocolate syrup and stir until dissolved. You can serve chocolate with straws, adding a spoonful of ice cream for special occasions, or cream and grated chocolate. Chocolate syrup is sweetened so no sugar is needed.

To make cocoa

Cocoa is the most economical and strongest way of having a chocolate flavored drink. Most people like 1 tablespoon of cocoa to approximately 1 cup milk or milk and water. Blend the cocoa with a little cold milk, heat the remaining milk and pour over the mixture, and add granulated sugar to taste.
This is the simplest way of making cocoa, but to give a slightly smoother taste the drink may be returned to the saucepan and heated for 1–2 minutes. To make

iced chocolate with cocoa: blend a little cocoa with some of the milk. Heat as before, cool, then strain over crushed ice (to remove any skin) and top with ice cold milk.

Milk shakes

There are many ways of flavoring milk:
Whisk the cold milk with 1 tablespoon of flavored ice cream – strawberry, chocolate, or coffee.
Buy a special sweetened syrup and whisk 1 tablespoon with cold milk.
Use rosehip or blackcurrant syrup and whisk 1–2 tablespoons into cold milk.
Use a little mashed fresh fruit with cold milk, e.g. whisk a small banana with 1 teaspoon granulated sugar and three-quarters of a glass of cold milk, or whisk 3 tablespoons fresh raspberries and a little sugar with three-quarters of a glass of cold milk. To obtain a fluffy milk shake, put the ingredients into a tall pitcher and whisk hard with a rotary beater. If you can use an electric blender, you will get an even better result.

To make tea

Use freshly drawn water and if there is water already in the kettle, throw it away and take the water from the cold water tap. Let the water come to a boil, but do not let it go on boiling for any length of time. When the water is nearly boiling, pour some into your teapot to make sure it is thoroughly heated. Discard it when the kettle boils and put in the tea. Your choice of tea is entirely a matter of personal taste and it is an interesting point that however good a tea may be, one is inclined to tire of it and a change of brand is advisable. The old ruling, 1 teaspoon per person and 1 for the pot, is fairly sound for small families, but in a large family you may find you need slightly less than this. Take the teapot to the kettle and pour the water onto the tea, while it is still boiling. Stir briskly, put the lid on the teapot and let it infuse for several minutes. You will then have a perfect pot of tea. To really enjoy your cup of tea, choose your cups with care. Some people only enjoy tea from a very thin cup. Remember that rather wide cups will allow the tea to cool very quickly. Real connoisseurs of tea like to warm the cups with hot water. The flavor of tea may be enhanced with milk or lemon. According to personal taste, milk may be added before or after the tea. For china tea, it is usual to serve only lemon slices.

To make coffee

Coffee loses its flavor quickly, so do not buy too much at a time unless it is stored in a tightly covered container, preferably in the refrigerator. Use the right amount of coffee – most people will like coffee made from 2 tablespoons coffee to ¾ cup water.

VACUUM COFFEE
Place the coffee in the upper bowl and water in the lower bowl. When the water boils into the upper bowl, it filters through the coffee and drains downward after it is removed from the heat.

STEEPED COFFEE
Measure the coffee into a saucepan of cold water and slowly bring to a boil. Immediately remove from the heat and add a very small amount of cold water, such as an ice cube. Steep for a few minutes, then strain.

PERCOLATOR METHOD
Place the coffee into the basket. Boiling water forces through a small tube and filters through the basket until the desired strength of coffee is obtained, about 6 minutes usually.

DRIP METHOD
Put the very finely ground coffee into the filter part, gradually pour over the boiling water, allowing the coffee to drip through.

INSTANT COFFEE
Reconstitute the soluble powder by adding boiling water. It is better to make several cups at a time and allow to steep briefly before serving.

ICED COFFEE
Make coffee in your favorite way and allow to get very cold in the refrigerator. Pour over crushed ice and top with fresh mint or lemon slices. If preferred, pour over ice cream or crushed ice and top with a little lightly whipped cream.

Irish coffee

This has become very popular in the last few years and besides not being very difficult to make gives a new flavor to after-dinner coffee. Serve in glasses rather than cups, although it may be served in an ordinary heated cup.

Irish whiskey · strong black coffee · sugar whipping cream.

Put the whiskey into the glasses, the amount depending on personal taste. Add the coffee and the sugar. Stir vigorously. Very slowly pour the cream over the back of a spoon into the coffee. It should form a thick layer of cream floating on the coffee. Sip the coffee mixture through the layer of cream.

Coffee frost

Cooking time   *None*

2½ cups milk · 1 tablespoon instant coffee blended with 3 tablespoons water and granulated sugar to taste · 1 tablespoon chocolate syrup blended with 3 tablespoons hot water · ice cubes
1 tablespoon whipping cream.

Whisk together milk, instant coffee and blended chocolate syrup. Place an ice cube in each glass, pour in coffee and top each drink with 1 teaspoon of cream.   *Serves 4*

Appleade

Cooking time   *None*

3 medium apples · peel and juice 1 lemon
2½ cups boiling water · 3–4 tablespoons granulated
sugar.

Wash the apples well, cut away any bruised parts,
but do not peel or core. Cut apples into small pieces
and put into a large pitcher with the lemon peel.
Add the *boiling* water and allow this to cool, pressing
the fruit from time to time to extract the juice. Do
this gently or the liquid will become cloudy. Strain
onto the lemon juice, add sugar to taste and serve
cold. Place in a refrigerator, if possible. Dilute with
water or soda water, see page 335.   *Serves 4*

GOOSEBERRYADE
As Appleade, using 1 lb. ripe gooseberries in place of
the apples.

Lemonade

Cooking time   *5 minutes*

2 large lemons · 2–3 tablespoons granulated sugar
3 cups boiling water.

Squeeze the juice from the lemons into a pitcher.
Put the peel, sugar, and boiling water into a second
pitcher. Allow to cool, pressing lemon halves to
extract the maximum flavor. Strain into pitcher
with the lemon juice. If desired, the lemon peel and
sugar may be boiled with the water for 5 minutes.
Then strain the lemonade again and serve, see page
335.   *Serves 4*

ORANGEADE
Use 2 large oranges, or 2 medium oranges and a
lemon, and continue as above.

Note: The juice of the fruit is never heated, as this
would destroy the vitamin C content.

HOT DRINKS

The following punches and mulled drinks are ideal
for a party. They should be very well spiced so test
the drink before serving and, if necessary, add extra
spices to flavor.

Mulled wine

Choose a claret – it may be a very cheap one. Follow
the instructions for mulled ale, adding plenty of
flavoring to the wine. This makes a most appetizing
cold weather drink. If a more potent drink is desired,
add a little more brandy.

Mulled ale

Cooking time   *10 minutes*

5 cups good ale *or* beer · 1 glass rum *or* brandy
1 tablespoon granulated sugar · dash cloves
dash ginger.

Heat all the ingredients together. Serve in heated
glasses or in a hot punch bowl.   *8–9 glasses*

Cherry and claret punch

Cooking time   *10–15 minutes*

3 lemons · 3 oranges · 1¼ cups water
½ cup granulated sugar · 2 bottles cheap claret
⅔ cup cherry brandy.
TO GARNISH: fresh *or* canned cherries
sprigs of fresh balm and mint.

Squeeze the juice from the lemons and oranges, then
put the halves into a large saucepan with the water
and simmer for 5 minutes only, pressing gently from
time to time to extract the flavor. Strain, then
return the liquid to the pan and add the sugar, the
fruit juice and 1½ bottles of claret. Heat thoroughly.
Pour into a heated bowl, add the remaining claret
and cherry brandy. Serve while hot, topped with the
cherries, balm and mint.   *18–20 glasses*

Cider punch

Cooking time   *20 minutes*
Oven temperature   *400°F.*

4 cloves · 1 large orange · 2 lemons
⅔ cup water · ¼ cup granulated sugar
5–6 cups apple cider · 1 teaspoon allspice
½–1 teaspoon ginger · dash nutmeg.

Press cloves into the orange. Bake for about 10
minutes in a preheated 400°F. oven to bring out the
flavor. Meanwhile pare the peels from the lemons
and simmer in the water for 5–10 minutes. Strain,
add sugar and return the liquid to the pan with the
lemon juice, cider, allspice, and ginger and bring to
the boil. Slice the hot orange into punch bowl, add
the boiling liquid, and sprinkle with nutmeg, see
page 336.   *10–12 glasses*

COLD DRINKS
Cherry cider cup

Cooking time   *10 minutes*

1 can tart red cherries · ⅔ cup water
¼ cup granulated sugar · peel and juice 1 lemon
peel and juice 2 oranges · 7½ cups apple cider
TO GARNISH: maraschino cherries
slices of cucumber · borage *or* mint.

Strain the juice from the can of cherries. Put into a
pan with the water and sugar and the fruit peels.
Simmer for 10 minutes in a covered pan. Strain and
cool. Add the fruit juice and the cider. Taste and add
a little extra sugar, if required. Pour over crushed
ice cubes in a large bowl – garnish with cherries,
cucumber, and borage or mint, see page 336.
     12–14 glasses

Champagne cup

Cooking time   *5 minutes*

Peel and juice 2–3 small oranges
peel and juice 2 lemons · ⅓ cup granulated sugar
1¼ cups water · 7½ cups champagne · ice cubes.

Boil orange and lemon peels with sugar and water
for 5 minutes. Strain into a large bowl. Add fruit
juices, champagne, and ice cubes.   *Makes 18 glasses*

Fruit cup

Cooking time   *None*

5 cups canned pineapple juice
juice of 2 fresh lemons
juice of 2 fresh oranges
2½ cups strained weak tea · sugar, if necessary
crushed ice. TO GARNISH: mint *or* borage
small pieces of cucumber · 1 orange
few pieces of canned *or* fresh pineapple.

Mix the pineapple juice with the fresh fruit juices
and tea. Add a little sugar, if necessary. Pour over
crushed ice in bowl and top with the mint, or borage
leaves and flowers of borage, sliced cucumber, sliced
orange, and diced pineapple.   *6–8 glasses*

CHOOSING WINES

The most important thing is to choose the wine that
you and your guests will enjoy. There is far too much
dogma about 'you *must* serve a red wine with certain
meats and game' and 'you *must* serve a white wine
with fish'. Some people only like a white wine, some
people prefer a red. On the whole, though, a lighter
wine is ideal to serve with less strong flavored food,
and a red wine complements food that has plenty of
taste.
White wine should be served cool. This does not
mean it should be iced, because too much flavor is
taken from it. You may have a very cool storage
place, but if wine is kept in a relatively warm place,
a short time in a refrigerator will improve it.
Red wine should be served at room temperature, and
the heavier the red wine, the better it is to let it
stand with the cork withdrawn so that it has time
to become warm and mature in flavor.

PRICES OF WINES
Prices of wines vary enormously. One can buy a
favorite wine, such as a Graves or a Chablis, very
cheaply but the really special Graves or Chablis will
be considerably more expensive. If you are not very
knowledgeable about wines, take time to shop and
make a friend of the assistants in the wine stores,
who usually give you really good advice.

THE APERITIF
Before guests sit down to the meal they will probably
like an aperitif. They may choose spirits, but most
people who enjoy wine with a meal appreciate that
this is inclined to spoil their taste later, and choose
a sherry or a vermouth, sweet or dry.

The first course

Often people will prefer to have another sherry or
vermouth with their soup; or you may care to begin
with a white wine.

TYPE	NAME
Bordeaux	Graves · Pouilly-Fuissé
Burgundy	Meursault · Chablis
Burgundy	Puligny-Montrachet

The above wines are also extremely suitable to serve
with veal and many people will enjoy them with
chicken. They are ideal to serve with fish, whether
as the main or the first course.

The main course

For the main course, if you still wish to serve a
white wine, any of the above are a good choice, or
try some of the Loire wines or Rhine wines given
below.

TYPE	NAME
Loire	Blanc Fumé de Pouilly
Loire	Château du Nozet
Rhine	Riesling
Rhine	Liebfraumilch
Rhine	Oppenheimer
Rhine	Niersteiner
Rhine	Deinsheimer

A sparking Rhine wine makes a pleasant change.
Some of the Australian Riesling type wines are an
excellent choice for a white wine. Or you could
choose an Italian Chianti. If you choose a red wine
with your main course, the following suit most
palates.

TYPE	NAME
Burgundy	Nuits St. George · Beaune
Burgundy	Beaujolais · Volnay
Burgundy	Pommard
Burgundy	Meursault Rouge

A sparkling Burgundy may be liked by some people,
but it is very much an acquired taste. Bordeaux is
considered the ideal drink for duck or game. There
is a great variation in price, the Château-bottled
being considerably more expensive.

TYPE	NAME
Bordeaux	Médoc · Pomerol
Bordeaux	St. Emilion · Margaux

The dessert course

To serve with the dessert course one would choose
a sweet white wine.

TYPE	NAME
Bordeaux	Sauternes · Barsac

Another suggestion would be to serve a vin rosé
throughout the meal.

NAME
Graves rosé · Tavel rosé · Mateus rosé

CANDY

Homemade candy is a challenge to make, since there is a great deal of skill necessary to produce an excellent result.

Wise choice of candy

If children are making candy, they should only be allowed to make the cooked type under the supervision of an adult, since the high temperature to which the sugar mixture is cooked can be extremely dangerous. Uncooked candy is easily and quickly made.

Ways to serve candy

Pack the candy in boxes as presents, in fancy jars – or keep in tightly covered containers to prevent their becoming sticky or hard due to exposure to the air.

To use leftover candy

Store carefully and they will be perfect.

Easy remedies when things are wrong

PROBLEM – if the recipe fails to produce the right result, this is generally due to boiling or cooking at an incorrect temperature.

TO REMEDY – if the temperature reached was below that needed for the particular recipe, reboil.

EASY UNCOOKED CANDY

These may be made with marzipan, (see recipe page 285), which may be tinted and used to stuff pitted dates or made into balls and decorated with walnuts or other nuts, see page 296 Uncooked fondant, which is the same as Royal frosting, may be tinted or flavored as peppermint creams. Similar candy to the truffles opposite may be made, or for a more economical truffle, use fine vanilla wafer or cake crumbs instead of ground almonds.

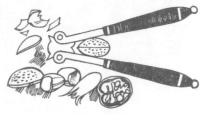

Uncooked coconut ice

¼ cup sweetened condensed milk
3 cups confectioners' sugar · 2¼ cups flaked coconut · drop red coloring.

Mix together the condensed milk and confectioners' sugar. Stir in the coconut – the mixture should be very stiff, and divide into two parts. Tint one half of the mixture pale pink. Shape the mixture into two identical bars and press firmly together. Dust a pan or plate with confectioners' sugar, and place coconut ice on this until firm.   *Yield 1 lb.*

Mixed fruit truffles

½ cup seedless white raisins
½ cup seedless raisins · ¼ cup dried figs
¼ cup dried prunes · grated peel of 1 orange
½ cup nuts · ¼ cup flaked coconut
little orange juice.
TO COAT: ¾ cup flaked coconut.

Chop the dried fruit with kitchen scissors, or put through the grinder. Add the orange peel, chopped nuts, and coconut, then press together well. Add just enough orange juice to bind – do not make these too wet. Form into balls and roll in coconut. Put either into small candy paper cups or paper muffin cups if serving for tea or coffee. Makes approximately 40 tiny truffles or 10–12 larger ones, which are excellent as an uncooked cake.

Coffee truffles

Cooking time   *few minutes*

⅔ cup semisweet chocolate pieces · ¼ cup butter
1 tablespoon instant coffee · 2 egg yolks
½ cup finely ground almonds
1½ cups sifted confectioners' sugar
cocoa or chocolate drink powder · 1 egg white
flaked coconut.

Melt chocolate and butter in a bowl over a pan of hot but not boiling water. Stir in instant coffee and egg yolks – do not heat. Remove bowl from pan, then work ground almonds and confectioners' sugar into chocolate mixture. Spread out on a flat plate, put in refrigerator for about 1½ hours until firm and set. Roll into about 30 balls and toss half of them in cocoa or chocolate drink powder. Roll remainder in lightly beaten egg white and toss in flaked coconut. Place in paper cups. *Makes 30*

Sugar boiling

Most candy is made by heating the sugar ingredients to a certain temperature. It is important to reach the recommended temperature, but not to exceed this.
There are two ways of testing the temperature:

1. With a candy thermometer. If using this, allow the mixture to boil for a minute or two after the sugar mixture has been stirred and the sugar is thoroughly dissolved. Fasten the thermometer on the side of the pan without letting the bulb touch the bottom of the pan and gently stir the mixture for a moment. This gives you an accurate reading.
2. With very cold water in a small bowl or cup. Drop a small quantity of the mixture into the cold water and watch how it reacts . . . the various stages are given below.

Whether testing with a thermometer or with cold water always remove the pan of mixture from the heat, so it does not go on cooking.

STAGES THROUGH WHICH SUGAR MIXTURES GO

Thread 230–234°F.
The syrup is so thin that it will run off the spoon into cold water when testing, but if you keep some on the spoon for a moment you can pinch it to feel a hot substance. This stage is not often used in sweet making but it does give a sticky coating on some candy.
Soft ball 234–240°F.
The sugar mixture drops into the water and can then be gathered up between your finger and thumb and formed into a soft ball which flattens. 238°F. will give you a rather soft fudge, for this is one of the main candy recipes in which this temperature is used, but as fudge tends to harden a little with keeping, many people prefer this temperature to a higher one.
Firm ball 242–248°F.
The ball is still soft and pliable when tested in your fingers, but loses its shape when pressed. It gives a firmer, harder fudge.
Hard ball 250–268°F.
The ball will hold its shape when pressed, but is still pliable.

Soft crack 270–290°F.
The hot syrup separates into hard threads which are not brittle when removed from the water, but will bend.
Hard crack 300–310°F.
The hot syrup separates into hard and brittle threads.
Caramelized sugar 310–338°F.
The syrup turns a dark brown color. At 350°F., the caramel-colored sugar becomes black, it also becomes completely unpalatable.

Coconut ice

Cooking time	20 minutes
Temperature	238°F.

⅔ cup water · 2¼ cups granulated sugar
dash cream of tartar · 1½ cups flaked coconut
2 tablespoons whipping cream · red coloring.

Put water and sugar into a heavy saucepan. Stir until sugar has dissolved, then add the cream of tartar. Boil steadily until the mixture reaches the 'soft ball' stage when tested in cold water. Add the coconut and cream. Beat until cloudy and pour half into a buttered pan. Color the remaining candy pale pink and pour on top. Cut in squares when cold.
Yield 1¼ lb

CHOCOLATE COCONUT PYRAMIDS
Make coconut ice as above, tinting a pale green color, form into pyramid shapes, and let stand to harden. Melt ¼–½ cup semisweet chocolate pieces in a bowl over hot water and dip the base of each pyramid in this. Allow to harden. Illustrated on page 296.

Chocolate coated candy

Most candies – fudge; toffee; fondants in particular – are suitable for coating in chocolate. Make the candy and allow to cool and become quite firm before trying to coat.

For 1 lb. candy you need approximately ½ lb. chocolate for coating. If you can, obtain dipping chocolate (also known as chocolate couverture), otherwise choose milk chocolate, sweet chocolate or bitter chocolate.

Put the chocolate into a bowl and melt over hot *but not boiling* water. Insert a fine skewer in the candy to be coated (if this is not sufficiently soft, hold with small tongs) and lower into the hot chocolate. Coat evenly. Remove and put onto wax paper to set. Decorate with tiny pieces of nut, candied cherry, crystallized violet leaves, etc.

TO MAKE FUDGE

Fudge is a combination of butter, sugar, and milk and it does have a tendency to stick, particularly *before the sugar has dissolved* and as it is getting thick, so stir it carefully and efficiently.

Butter fudge

Cooking time   30–35 minutes
Temperature   238°F.

2 cups sugar, granulated or loaf
5 tablespoons water · ¼ cup butter
1 cup full-cream sweetened condensed milk
flavoring.

Put the sugar, water and butter into a pan. Stir until the sugar has dissolved, then add the condensed milk and continue stirring until thoroughly blended ... continue as for the economy fudge.
Yield 1¼ lb

Extra rich fudge

Cooking time   40 minutes
Temperature   Do not exceed 238°F.

2 cups granulated sugar
1¼ cups whipping cream (evaporated milk could be used) · ¼ cup butter · ¼ cup water
⅔ cup milk · flavoring.

Put all the ingredients into a strong saucepan; this is very important because of the high cream content. Stir until sugar is thoroughly dissolved. Boil steadily, stirring quite frequently, until the mixture reaches the 'soft ball' stage. Beat until slightly cloudy. Pour into a well-oiled or buttered pan. Allow to set and cut in squares. For flavorings see below.
Yield nearly 2 lb

Economy fudge

Cooking time   25 minutes
Temperature   238°F.

2 cups sugar, granulated or loaf · 1¼ cups milk
¼ cup margarine · flavoring.*

* For flavorings see below and next column.

Put the ingredients into a strong saucepan, and stir until the sugar has dissolved. Boil steadily, stirring only occasionally, until the mixture forms a 'soft ball' when a little is dropped into a cup of cold water. Remove from the heat and beat until the mixture starts to thicken. Pour into a pan greased with butter. When nearly set cut into pieces with a sharp knife.
Yield just over 1 lb

Note: It must be remembered that you are using reasonably economical ingredients in this recipe and therefore your fudge, while very pleasant to eat, is not in any way a luxury fudge. It tends to harden with keeping and becomes almost like candy. (Illustrated on page 296).

Fudge flavorings

CHOCOLATE
Either blend ⅓–½ cup cocoa; ⅔–1 cup chocolate drink powder; or 1–1¼ cups semisweet chocolate pieces with the sugar mixture when the sugar is thoroughly dissolved.

COFFEE
Either use 1–1½ tablespoons instant coffee blended with 3–4 tablespoons water. Add this to the sugar, milk etc., or use coffee extract.

FRUIT
Add 1–1½ cups dried fruit (sultanas, raisins, chopped prunes, figs, etc.) just before the fudge reaches the 'soft ball' stage ... or use half nuts and half fruit.

GINGER
Blend 1–1½ teaspoons ginger with the sugar. Add ¼–½ cup chopped candied ginger to the fudge just before the 'soft ball' stage is reached.

NUT
Add 1 cup chopped nuts (almonds, walnuts, etc.) just before the fudge reaches the 'soft ball' stage. If using almonds, a little almond extract may be used and small pieces of nut pressed on to the fudge when nearly set in the pan.

ORANGE
Add the finely grated peel of 2–3 oranges to the sugar etc.

VANILLA
Add 1–2 teaspoons vanilla extract to the sugar etc.

FONDANTS

Fondant is the basis for many candies; the better fondant is made by the recipe below, but an uncooked fondant is made in exactly the same way as Royal frosting (see page 284). To give a softer texture a little whipping cream or condensed milk could be added to the mixture.

Cooked fondant

Cooking time   40 minutes
Temperature   238–245°F.

6 cups granulated sugar · 2 cups water
⅛ teaspoon cream of tartar.

Put the sugar and water into a pan, stir until the sugar has dissolved, boil rapidly for a few minutes, then add the cream of tartar. Cover the pan for 1–2 minutes to allow the steam to remove sugar crystals from the sides of the pan. Remove the cover and continue boiling until 'soft ball' stage ... for a fondant this may vary between 238°F. for a soft fondant to 245°F. for a firm fondant. Gently remove from the heat and pour the syrup onto a wet platter or a board. Do not scrape the pan. When cool enough to handle, blend the fondant with a folding motion from the sides of the platter to the center using a sugar scraper or a spatula. Knead well until white and firm in texture adding a little confectioners' sugar if necessary to prevent sticking.

Wrap in wax paper or foil and store in the refrigerator for at least 24 hours to ripen. When ready to use, reheat in a bowl over hot water until soft enough to knead once again.

Candy to make with fondant

FONDANT SHAPES
Roll out the cooked or uncooked fondant on a sugared board and cut into required shapes. Decorate with tiny pieces of cherry, nut, etc. or with flowers made of Royal frosting, as shown in the picture on page 296. A few drops of coloring and/or flavoring may be worked into the fondant mixture when kneading the second time.

HAZELNUT CREAMS
Either form pink colored fondant into neat shapes and top with filberts or hazelnuts or put nuts into a rubber candy mold and top with semi-set fondant. Let stand until firm.

STUFFED DATES
Stuff pitted dates with fondant and roll in granulated sugar.

PEPPERMINT CREAMS
Use either uncooked or cooked fondant. Knead a very few drops of peppermint oil or peppermint extract into the fondant. To give a 'creamy' candy, work in a little whipping cream as well. Roll out on a sugared board, cut into 1-inch circles and leave in the air to harden on the outside.

TO MAKE TOFFEE

Toffee is one of the easiest sweets to make, when the secret of testing for temperature has been mastered. Stir very thoroughly until the sugar has dissolved and make absolutely certain that the toffee reaches the right temperature. Toffee tends to become rather sticky unless it is well wrapped.

Golden toffee

Cooking time	*20–25 minutes*
Temperature	*290°F.*

6 cups sugar, preferably brown · ¼ cup plus 1 tablespoon water · 3 tablespoons butter
3 level tablespoons thin honey
1 teaspoon vinegar.

Put all the ingredients into a strong saucepan and stir over a steady heat until the sugar has dissolved. Bring to a boil and cook until the mixture reaches the 'hard crack' stage. Pour into an oiled or buttered pan and either allow to set as a slab or mark in squares as the toffee becomes partially set, then cut or break when completely set.
Yield just over 1 lb

Dark toffee

Cooking time	*20–25 minutes*
Temperature	*290°F.*

¼ cup butter · 2 cups granulated sugar
¼ cup corn syrup · ¼ cup molasses.

Put butter into a strong saucepan. When melted, stir in the sugar, molasses, and syrup. Boil steadily, without stirring, until the mixture reaches the 'hard crack' stage when tested in cold water. Pour into a pan greased with margarine or oil, and when set cut into pieces. This type of toffee is better wrapped in small pieces of waxed paper.
Yield nearly 1¼ lb

Toffee flavorings

COCONUT
Add ¾ cup flaked or shredded coconut to the toffee just before it reaches the 'hard crack' stage.

NUT
Add 1 cup chopped nuts to the toffee just before it reaches the 'hard crack' stage.

RUM
Add 1 tablespoon rum to pan when sugar has dissolved.

VANILLA
Add 1–1½ teaspoons vanilla extract when the sugar has dissolved.

Turkish delight

Cooking time	*15 minutes*

2 envelopes unflavored gelatin · 1¼ cups water
2¼ cups granulated sugar · 3–4 tablespoons lemon juice · ¼ teaspoon tartaric acid · coloring
little confectioners' sugar.

Dissolve the gelatin in the water over low heat. Add the sugar and dissolve over low heat, stirring constantly. Boil for 8 minutes, stirring constantly, then add lemon juice and tartaric acid. Pour half the mixture into a moistened pan. Color the remaining candy pink, and pour either into a second pan or cool slightly and pour on top of the white layer. When cold and firm, cut into squares with kitchen scissors and roll in sifted confectioners' sugar.
Yield just over 1 lb

Crème de menthe jelly

Cooking time	*15 minutes*

Ingredients as Turkish delight
few drops peppermint extract (or ¼ cup crème de menthe liqueur)
few drops green coloring. (See picture page 296).

Add the peppermint extract or liqueur to the water and sugar and proceed as for Turkish delight. Color *all* the mixture pale green. *Yield just over 1 lb*

PRESERVING, FREEZING AND CANNING

A well-packed storage cupboard with a good selection of jams, chutneys, and pickles, with canned fruits, etc. makes housekeeping much more interesting and if these are prepared at a time when fruit and vegetables are at their most plentiful and cheapest, then home preserving is wise economy. (See picture on page 334).

Wise choice of preserves

If you have a freezer, then this is the easiest way to preserve fruit, vegetables, etc., for later use, or you may can fruit and vegetables (the latter only in a pressure cooker). If you have no time to make jams and fruit chutneys when the fruit is available, then use the method of pulping given on this page and make the preserve with the pulped fruit when convenient.

Ways to serve preserves

Preserves may be served in so many different ways – use jam with scones, bread and butter, as a filling for tarts, in sauces, etc. Chutney and pickles give more flavor to meats and cheese, and canned fruits etc., may be used in pies and tarts.

To use leftover preserves

Leftover canned fruits etc. must be stored in a cold place and used quickly; leftover jams should be put back into jars, but use quickly as when there is a lot of air space, jam can spoil quickly.

Easy remedies when things are wrong

PROBLEM – if jams etc. ferment, this could be due to the jars being insufficiently filled, too little sugar, storing in too hot a place, overripe fruit, or insufficient cooking . . . in the case of chutney, too little vinegar and sugar.

TO REMEDY – the preserve has a wine-flavored taste, so it is not really edible.

PROBLEM – if jams etc., develop mold, this is due to some of the same reasons as above plus damp fruit, bad covering or damp storage.

TO REMEDY – remove the mold from the jam or jelly, tip the remainder into a pan and boil hard for a few minutes, use quickly.

If preserves dried, this is due to insufficient covering. (See opposite page).

PROBLEM – if jars of home canned fruits etc. do not seal, this is due to poor tops or rubber rings – renew each year; it could be that the top of the jar rim is chipped – these jars are no longer useful for canning.

TO REMEDY – there is no remedy except to use the fruit at once, unless the jar seems perfect, then resterilise.

PROBLEM – if fruit rose to the surface in jars, it was overcooked or too losely packed.

TO REMEDY – there is nothing one can do and the fruit is quite alright.

Pulping fruit

Imperfect fruit may be used for pulping if the bruised or diseased part has been cut away, leaving the rest of the fruit perfect. You must not use overripe fruit for pulping, since this could cause fermentation during storage. The following boiling water bath method of canning is suitable only for acid fruits and vegetables in a brine. Non-acid fruits should be processed only in a pressure canner.

Stew the fruit, adding little or no water, and sugar to taste. With tomatoes, add ½ teaspoon granulated sugar and ½ teaspoon salt to each lb. tomatoes; the tomatoes may be skinned, if desired. Press through a sieve if a very smooth purée is desired; if straining, bring to a boil once again. While the fruits are cooking, put tops of jars to boil for 15 minutes; drop in the rubber rings also. Sterilise jars by boiling for 15 minutes. Put boiling pulp into the very hot jars, put on the rubber rings and the tops, put on the cover according to manufacturer's directions. Stand the jars in a sterilizer or deep pan filled with BOIL-ING water. Boil for 20 minutes in the case of fruit pulp, and 45 minutes for tomato pulp. Remove and tighten the cover. Test as for all bottled fruit after 24 hours.

To make jam

Select firm, ripe, but not overripe fruit.
Follow the recipe carefully for the amount of sugar to fruit. Many people think all fruits need 1 lb. sugar to 1 lb. fruit – this is quite wrong. Where a fruit has little natural pectin (setting quality) i.e. sweet cherries – you need more fruit than sugar, and in addition it helps to add acid in the form of lemon juice, red currant juice, or commercial pectin. Where a fruit is rich in pectin, e.g. black currants, you get a better jam if you use more sugar than fruit.

Select a large pan so there is plenty of room for the jam to boil – without splashing or boiling over.

Warm the sugar slightly since this will make it dissolve more quickly.

Do stew the fruit slowly. This is very important for it: (a) extracts pectin (natural setting substance), (b) softens skins – test most carefully for the skin must be soft before you add the sugar, (c) helps to keep jam in good color.

Stir until sugar has dissolved – this is essential for it makes certain the jam or jelly does not burn, or crystallize, during cooking. You can tell if all the sugar has dissolved by tapping your wooden spoon on bottom of pan.

When the sugar has dissolved, boil the jam RAPIDLY WITHOUT STIRRING. The quicker the jam or jelly sets, the better the yield, flavor, and color. It is essential to have plenty of room in the pan or the jam will boil over.

Test early for setting. Some jams are ready within 3–5 minutes, others take 10–15 minutes, or even more. Many fruits will lose their setting qualities if boiled too long, and then the jam NEVER sets.

In the table on page 311 you will find the yield of jam you should obtain and if you have sufficiently large and strong scales, weigh the preserving pan before cooking. If you feel the jam or jelly is ready, weigh again. Deduct the weight of the pan from the total weight, and if it is more than the table, the jam needs boiling a little longer.

When you are satisfied that the jam is ready, remove the pan from the heat, and remove the scum. If there is not much scum, most of this will disappear if stirred steadily. For competitions it is wise to remove the scum with a strainer, and then stir. When making jelly, remove the scum with a strainer, and by drawing a piece of white kitchen or blotting paper quickly across the surface of the preserve.

For a jam or jelly that contains no whole fruit: pour at once into sterilized, hot, jars. Tap jar as you fill to bring air bubbles to the surface. Fill to ¼ inch from top of jar. The jam or jelly will shrink a little as it cools. This also makes certain there is less air space in the jar and, therefore, less chance of it becoming moldy. Jars filled to the brim also look more attractive. For a jam containing whole fruit: allow jam to cool in the pan until it stiffens slightly, then stir to distribute peel or whole fruit and pour into the prepared jars.

Cover the jars with hot paraffin at once unless using the type of jar with a separate metal band and lid with the rubber ring attached.
Store in a cool, dry, dark place.

To make jellies

The method of softening the fruit for jelly is similar to that in jam making opposite, also the way it should be tested and stored, also the correct yield – 1 lb. sugar should produce 1⅔ lb. jelly. Fruit for jellies should be ripe and juicy, but not overripe; do not squeeze the pulped fruit as it goes through the jelly bag since this gives a cloudy jelly.
A proper jelly bag is made of heavy duty calico or flannel. It has a very close weave so that the juice only drains and none of the pulp comes through. This is important as even a small amount of pulp will give a cloudy jelly. Jelly bags are expensive to buy, but with care they will last for a very long time. If you cannot buy a jelly bag you could make one yourself if you buy calico or flannel. Use a square 18–24 inches. Form into a triangle and machine stitch the seam, being particularly careful at the tip so that this is well joined. Attach four pieces of twill tape to the top.

Tie the pieces of tape on the four 'legs' of an up-turned chair, with a bowl underneath so that the fruit can be put into the bag and allowed to drip through gently.

You can make do without a jelly bag, by using several thicknesses of fine cheesecloth. You may also drain through cheesecloth over a fine nylon (not wire) sieve. But remember not to push the jelly through, in any way, but allow it to drip in its own time.

When using fruits such as baking apples, red currants, damson plums, gooseberries, or black currants, all of which have a high setting quality, you can produce a greater yield of liquid by boiling the fruit twice. Follow the recipe as given, and when the juice has dripped through the jelly bag, return the pulp to the preserving pan. Put only half the first amount of water over the fruit, boil again. Strain this and mix with the first amount of liquid.

By the time the juice has gone through the jelly bag it will, of course, have become quite cold. Reheat this, but do not boil for any length of time before adding the sugar, then stir until the sugar has dissolved.

Fill jam jars while the jelly is still very hot, so there is no chance of it beginning to set in the pan.

IMPORTANCE OF CAREFUL STORAGE

The introduction mentions some of the things that can go wrong with jams and jellies, and bad storage contributes to fermentation etc. Jam can become very hard and 'sugary' – although this could be due to overboiling, it may be caused by too warm storage conditions.

Apple jelly

Cooking time   *25–30 minutes*

6 medium tart baking apples *or* 2 lb. crab apples (unpeeled) · 2½ cups water · granulated sugar.

Simmer the fruit until a pulp; there is no need to either peel or core the fruit. Put the pulp through thick muslin or a jelly bag. Let stand to strain overnight. Measure the juice and allow ¾–1 cup sugar to each 1 cup juice. Stir in the sugar and boil rapidly until set.

MINT JELLY
As apple jelly (or use firm green gooseberries with the same amount of water). When the jelly is nearly at setting point, add 1½ teaspoons white vinegar to each 1 cup sugar used, plus ½–1 tablespoon finely chopped mint. Continue until the jelly is well set.

Blackberry jelly

Cooking time   *25–30 minutes*

4 cups blackberries · ⅓ cup water
1 medium baking apple* · granulated sugar.

* instead of using an apple you may use the juice of one lemon to each 4 cups blackberries. Add this with the sugar.

Put the blackberries, water, and apple into a pan. Simmer until soft, then strain the pulp through a jelly bag. Measure the juice and allow ¾–1 cup sugar to each 1 cup juice. Stir in the sugar and continue stirring until dissolved. Boil rapidly until set.

Red currant jelly

Cooking time   *25 minutes*

4 cups red currants · ⅔ cup water
granulated sugar. Use the method for apple jelly, see previous column.

OTHER FRUITS IN JELLY
If a very high setting quality, and very juicy fruit is used, follow directions for red currants. If a high setting quality, but firm fruit (like apples) use the Apple jelly recipe as a basic recipe. If low in setting quality follow directions for blackberries. You can tell the setting quality in fruits if you refer to the table on jam. Those that need the addition of lemon juice are poor in setting quality.

To make marmalade

Marmalade may be prepared from most citrus fruits. In the first method the fruit is cut up, soaked, and then cooked; in the second method the whole fruit is simmered then cut up. This produces a rather thicker type of marmalade and is usually used for the bitter Seville oranges.
Good quality oranges, lemons, etc., must be used, and the fresher they are the quicker the preserve will set. See picture on page 316.

METHOD 1

Wash and halve fruit, then squeeze out the juice. Remove the peel and slice or chop this to desired thickness. Put the white pith and seeds into a piece of cheesecloth and tie securely. These give flavor to the marmalade, but also contain the real setting quality, so must never be discarded. Place the peel and bag of seeds into a bowl with the quantity of water given in the table. Soak overnight. Next day, simmer peel and bag of seeds with the water in which they were soaked UNTIL THE PEEL IS TENDER – this is most important since once the sugar has been added the peel does not become any more tender. The simmering period may be up to 1 hour or longer because the fruit must cook slowly. Remove the bag of seeds, stir in the sugar, fruit juice and any additional lemon juice (if given in the recipe). Continue as jam, testing etc., see remarks about potting jam with whole fruit, as this also applies to marmalade peel.

METHOD 2

Wash the fruit. Put into the pan with the amount of water given in the table. Simmer steadily until the fruit is soft – test by seeing if a blunt wooden skewer or knitting needle goes easily into the peel. Remove the fruit from the liquid, cool sufficiently to handle. Halve and remove the seeds. Put these back into the liquid and simmer for 10 minutes, then strain off the liquid and return this to the pan. Meanwhile, slice or chop the fruit and add to the liquid, bring to a boil, add the amount of sugar given in the table on page 311, with any lemon juice (if given in the table) and continue as jam.

REMEMBER: The setting period for marmalade is a short one, so test early, and continue testing at very short intervals – when once the setting time is passed the marmalade becomes very liquid, and it is impossible to make that batch set.

Lemon curd or lemon butter

Cooking time   *30 minutes*

Peel 3 lemons · 3–4 tablespoons lemon juice
1¼ cups granulated sugar · ½ cup fresh butter
2 eggs.

Grate the peel carefully, removing just the yellow
'zest', but none of the white pith. Squeeze the juice
from the fruit. Put all the ingredients, except the
eggs, into a double boiler over hot water. Cook
stirring occasionally, until the butter and sugar
have melted. Add the well beaten eggs. Continue
cooking until the mixture coats the back of the
wooden spoon. Pour into sterilized jars and seal in
the usual way.

Variation
ORANGE CURD
Make as lemon curd, but use peel of 3 oranges and
juice of 2 large oranges.

PROPORTIONS FOR JAM

1 LB. FRUIT WHEN PREPARED	TO PREPARE	WATER	SUGAR	EXTRA ACID	FINAL QUANTITY OF JAM
APPLE 1 LB. BLACKBERRY 1 LB.	Peel, core, slice Wash, drain	⅓ cup	2 lb. (4½ cups)		3⅓ pints
APPLE GINGER	Cut apples into cubes, add 1 teaspoon ginger	stand for 12 hours	1 lb. (2¼ cups)		1⅔ pints
APRICOT	Halve, stone, if desired	3 tablespoons	1 lb. (2¼ cups)	juice ½ lemon or ¼ level teaspoon citric acid	1⅔ pints
DRIED APRICOT	Soak for at least 4 hours	7½ cups	3 lb. (6¾ cups)	juice 2 lemons	2½ quarts
BLACK CURRANT	Remove stems, wash, drain	1¾ cups	1¼ lb. (2¾ cups)		just over 1 quart
CHERRY-MORELLO (RED)	Wash, stem, pit	⅓ cup	1 lb. (2¼ cups)		1⅔ pints
CHERRY – BING (BLACK SWEET)	Wash, stem, pit	3–4 tablespoons	12 oz. (1½ cups)	juice 1 lemon	just over 1½ pints
DAMSON PLUM	Wash, pit during cooking of fruit or strain, return to pan	⅓ cup if fruit is ripe; ⅔ cup if fruit is under-ripe	1 lb (2¼ cups) 1¼ lb. (2¾ cups)		1⅔ pints just over 1 quart
GOOSEBERRY	Remove stems	⅓ cup if fruit is ripe; ⅔ cup if fruit is under-ripe	1 lb. (2¼ cups) 1¼ lb. (2¾ cups)		1⅔ pints just over 1 quart
LOGANBERRY (2¾ cups)	Wash, drain		1 lb. (2¼ cups)		1⅔ pints
PLUM	As apricot				
QUINCE 1 LB. APPLE 1 LB.	Peel, core, and chop	1 cup	2 lb. (4½ cups)		3⅓ pints
RASPBERRY (2¾ cups)	Wash, drain		1 lb. (2¼ cups)		1⅔ pints

1 LB. FRUIT WHEN PREPARED	TO PREPARE	WATER	SUGAR	EXTRA ACID	FINAL QUANTITY OF JAM
RASPBERRY 1 LB. (2¾ cups) RED CURRANT 1 LB. (4 cups)	Wash, drain	⅓ cup	2 lb. (4½ cups)		3⅓ pints
STRAWBERRY (4 cups)	Wash, hull, drain		1 lb. (2¼ cups)	juice 1 lemon or ⅓ cup red currant juice	1⅔ pints
RHUBARD AND GINGER	As apple ginger – use mature fruit				
ZUCCHINI AND GINGER	As apple ginger	stand for 12 hours	1 lb. (2¼ cups)	As strawberry	1⅔ pints

PROPORTIONS FOR MARMALADE

1 LB. FRUIT WHEN PREPARED	TO PREPARE	WATER	SUGAR	EXTRA ACID	FINAL QUANTITY OF JAM
LEMON MARMALADE	See page 310 method 1	5 cups	2 lb. (4½ cups)		3⅓ pints
GRAPEFRUIT MARMALADE	See page 310 method 1	6¼ cups		juice 1 lemon	just over 2 quarts
SEVILLE (BITTER) ORANGE MARMALADE, FINE OR MEDIUM, SEMI-SWEET	See page 310 method 1	7½ cups	3 lb. (6¾ cups)	juice 1½–2 lemons or 1 teaspoon citric acid	2–2½ quarts
SEVILLE (BITTER) ORANGE – VERY BITTER AND CHUNKY	See page 310 method 2	5 cups	2 lb. (4½ cups)		3⅓ pints
SWEET ORANGE	See page 310 method 1	5 cups	2 lb. (4½ cups)	juice 2 lemons	3⅓ pints

PICKLES

Always use very good quality vegetables – firm and not discolored.
Use pure malt vinegar – distilled white vinegar if preferred. Cover well – see to make chutney page 317.
Never use copper, brass, or iron pans.
You must see the vegetables are completely covered with vinegar.
It is essential to put vegetables in brine before covering with vinegar.
You should boil vinegar before using, even when allowing it to become cold afterwards – see spiced vinegar below.

Spiced vinegar

Unless stated to the contrary, this mixture of spices and vinegar gives a very good result for most pickles. Buy mixed pickling spice from the grocer, and you will find this consists of a mixture of mustard seed, celery seed, dried chili peppers, ginger root, blade mace, peppercorns, and cloves. To each 2½ cups vinegar, add 1 tablespoon mixed pickling spice. Boil together for 15 minutes, strain, then use as directed in the recipe.

Mustard pickles

Cooking time *15–20 minutes*

2 lb. mixed prepared vegetables* · brine (see page 317) · 2½ cups vinegar · 1 tablespoon mixed pickling spice · 1 tablespoon dry mustard
1½ teaspoons turmeric · ¼ cup granulated sugar
1 tablespoon all-purpose flour or 1½ teaspoons cornstarch · 1 tablespoon ginger.

* cauliflower, onions, cucumber, small green tomatoes, beans.

Cut or break the vegetables into small pieces (about 1 inch) and soak overnight in brine. Wash well under cold water and drain thoroughly. Boil the vinegar and pickling spice together for 10 minutes. Mix all the dry ingredients with a very little vinegar until a smooth paste. Pour over the strained hot vinegar, and stir well. Return to the pan, and cook until just thickened. Put in the vegetables and cook for 5 minutes. Put into sterilized jars and seal well, see page 317. *Makes 3 pints*

PICCALILLI
Use exactly the same ingredients and cooking time

Open sandwiches, pages 30 and 31

Scones, page 291; Fruit gelatin, page 243; Open fruit pie, page 218; Raspberry shortcake, page 263

Baked apple, page 237; Open fruit pie, page 218; Fruit gelatin, page 243; Apple jelly, page 310

Marmalade, page 310

for mustard pickles. Chop the vegetables into ½-inch pieces, (breaking cauliflower into flowerets) to obtain a greater blending of these in the mustard sauce.

Brine

Mention is made in pickles of using either a wet or dry brine.

WET BRINE: Dissolve 3 tablespoons salt in each 2½ cups cold water. Soak the vegetables for 24 hours – unless stated to the contrary. Rinse well under the cold tap, drain or dry.

DRY BRINE: Sprinkle enough salt over a layer of prepared vegetables to give a good covering, continue like this – vegetables – salt – then let stand for 24 hours, unless stated to the contrary. Drain liquid, rinse under cold running water, unless otherwise instructed.

Vinegar pickles

Read the directions for vinegar etc., under pickles, and for covering under chutney.

CABBAGE
Shred red cabbage, use dry brine. Drain well, do not rinse Cover with cold spiced vinegar. Use within 10 weeks as the color often fades. (See page 333).

CUCUMBER OR GHERKINS
If small leave whole, or cut into pieces, do not peel. Soak overnight only in wet or dry brine – the latter gives a more crisp result. Rinse well under cold running water, and dry. Pack into jars, pour over cold spiced vinegar.

DATES
Put the dried dates into jars, dissolve a little salt to taste in the cold spiced vinegar, pour over the dates, and seal. Excellent with cold meats – use when reasonably fresh – within a few months.

EGGS
Hard-cook eggs and shell. Cover with boiling spiced vinegar and seal. Serve with cold meats.

ONIONS OR SHALLOTS
Use either wet or dry brine; the latter gives a crisper onion. Peel with sterling silver or stainless steel knife. Soak in brine for 48 hours, proceed as given under brine, then pack into jars, cover with cold spiced vinegar.

SWEET VINEGAR PICKLES
Dissolve 3 tablespoons (or more, if desired) granulated sugar in the vinegar before using.

TO MAKE CHUTNEY

Do not attempt to cut down on the quantity of sugar or vinegar in a chutney recipe since this is the preservative. Never use copper, brass, or iron pans; aluminium is excellent.

Do not put in all the vinegar at once since this tends to take away the flavor of the ingredients – put in about one-fourth of the vinegar, then add rest gradually during the cooking period.

Cook chutney uncovered so it thickens – stir occasionally.

Pour the chutney into hot sterilized jars while still hot – filling to neck of jar.

Seal jars very well – canning jars which have glass lids are ideal but never put metal tops directly next to the chutney otherwise the vinegar in the chutney will spoil both taste and color, and will also make the lid rust and be very difficult to remove. You can buy special pickling jars, or instead put a circle of wax paper on chutney – then a thin layer of melted paraffin then the final cover, or put the wax paper then several thicknesses of brown or parchment paper over this – tying it down tightly.

Always use pure malt vinegar – distilled white vinegar may be used for light colored chutneys, if desired, and where you wish to retain bright color. Store in a cool dry place – preferably in the dark – to keep well.

Apple chutney

Cooking time   *40 minutes*

3 medium onions · 1¼ cups vinegar
6 cups chopped apples
⅓–⅔ cup currants *or* seedless white raisins (optional)
1 teaspoon mixed pickling spice · 1 teaspoon salt
1 teaspoon ginger · 1⅔ cup granulated sugar.

Put the grated or finely chopped onions into a saucepan with ⅓ cup vinegar, and simmer until nearly soft. Add the chopped apples, currants or raisins, spices (tied securely in a cheesecloth bag), salt, ginger and just enough vinegar to prevent the mixture from burning. Cook gently until the fruit is soft, stirring occasionally. Add the remaining vinegar, and thoroughly stir in the sugar. Boil steadily until the chutney is thick. Remove the spices, and pour into hot sterilized jars.

Makes 2–2½ quarts

Tomato chutney

Cooking time   *40 minutes with ripe tomatoes*
                          50–55 minutes with green tomatoes

1 teaspoon mixed pickling spice · 1 large onion
1¼ cups malt vinegar · 1½ medium apples
12 medium (2 lb.) green or red tomatoes
½ teaspoon salt · ¼ teaspoon pepper
1½ teaspoons dry mustard · ½ teaspoon ginger
1½ cups seedless white raisins
1¼ cups granulated sugar.

Put the pickling spice into a piece of cheesecloth. Put the finely chopped onion into a saucepan with 3–4 tablespoons vinegar, and simmer gently until nearly soft. Add the peeled, cored, and chopped apples, peeled sliced tomatoes, spices, salt, pepper, mustard, ginger, and raisins. Simmer gently until the mixture is quite soft, stirring occasionally. Add the remaining vinegar and the sugar. When the sugar has dissolved, boil steadily until the chutney is the consistency of jam. Remove the spices. Pour the hot chutney into hot sterilized jars and seal immediately. Illustrated on page 333.

Makes about 2 quarts

More chutneys

Most fruits and vegetables form good chutneys.

PLUM
Use apple chutney recipe and either all plums or half plums, and half apples.

MIXED DRIED FRUIT

Use apple chutney recipe with currants, seedless white raisins, and chopped mixed candied peel including some apples for sharp flavor.

RHUBARB

Use tomato chutney recipe replacing tomatoes with rhubarb.

ZUCCHINI

Use apple chutney recipe with 1½ medium apples, 9 small zucchini, 2 teaspoons ginger.

1–2 crushed garlic cloves, 1–2 chili peppers may be added to give highly spiced chutneys.

Tomato ketchup

Cooking time   *1–1¼ hours*

1¾ cups vinegar · 1 tablespoon mixed pickling spice · 16 large (4 lb.) ripe tomatoes · 1 large onion · 2 large baking apples · ¾ cup granulated sugar · 1 tablespoon salt
¼ teaspoon paprika *or* cayenne pepper.

Boil the vinegar and pickling spices together for 10 minutes. Then strain the vinegar. Cook the peeled sliced tomatoes, peeled onion, and peeled and cored apples until you have a thick pulp, stirring well to prevent the mixture from burning. Press through a sieve taking care not to leave any pulp behind, otherwise the ketchup will not thicken. Put pulp into pan with vinegar, sugar, salt, and paprika. Cook steadily until thick. Pour into hot sterilized jars while boiling and sterilize (see page 320). Seal immediately.   *Makes about 3½ pints*

FREEZING

Never attempt to freeze foods, except ice cream and ice and frozen desserts, in the freezing compartment of the refrigerator. The temperature is not sufficiently cold, and the food would not keep well for more than a few days.

GENERAL RULES FOR FREEZING

FOOD – only good quality foods should be preserved by this method. Fruits and vegetables should be frozen as soon as possible after they are picked. Meat and poultry should hang for the correct minimum length of time before freezing. When this is not possible, all foods should be put in a cool place or the refrigerator for not longer than 12–24 hours before being prepared for the freezer.

PACKAGING   –   moisture-vapor-proof   packaging materials are essential for freezing and storing produce. Food will lose moisture by evaporation unless well packed and sealed, because of the low humidity inside the freezer. The food will become dry, the texture and color deteriorate and the flavor will disappear. Badly packaged strong-smelling food may spoil other produce stored in the same freezer. Therefore, choose packaging material with care, and leave as little air as possible inside the containers before sealing.

EQUIPMENT – quality of frozen foods depend on speed, i.e. speed in preparation and quick drop in temperature when in the freezer.
For freezing, set the freezer at the coldest setting. For storing, return the freezer to the recommended temperature.
Try to freeze moderate amounts of food at one time so the freezer temperature may be kept fairly constant. There are specialist books which give greater information on home freezing, but the following are general hints.

VEGETABLES: Blanch for HALF THE TIME given in the table on canning, cool, then pack into the container, and seal carefully. Uncooked sweet peppers should be frozen on flat trays first, then packed into bags.

FRUIT: Put the fruit and cool syrup into the container and seal, or sprinkle dry fruit with the amount of sugar desired, or freeze without sugar.

MEAT, FISH, GAME, AND POULTRY: Cut into pieces or leave in large pieces, or whole. Wash and dry, put into container, and seal. Freeze. TAKE GREAT CARE THAT MEAT, ETC., IS FRESH, although it must be hung for the right time before freezing.

BREAD, PASTRY, AND CAKES: Freeze when completely cold. Decorated sponge cakes should be frozen then covered to prevent harming the frosting. Freeze pastry when mixed but not cooked, or when cooked. The crust of bread often becomes soft after freezing, crisp by heating for a short time before using.

COOKED FOODS: Stews, meat pies, puddings, may be frozen, so may cookies, and candy.

TO CAN VEGETABLES

Remember it is unsafe to can vegetables other than in a pressure cooker. Always follow the special instructions for your own make of pressure cooker. Below are the main points to remember.
Wash thoroughly to free vegetables from all traces

of soil. Pre-cook or blanch by immersing in boiling water for the time stated in the table on the opposite page, then drop into cold water. Drain well, and pack into scalded jars to within 1 inch of top. Do not pack too tightly.

Still leaving 1 inch at top, cover vegetables with a hot brine solution, made by dissolving 3–4 tablespoons salt to 5 quarts water, boiled before using. Work out air bubbles by quickly twisting the jar from side to side. Adjust rubber rings and lids.

Process jars of hot food immediately. Pour 2½ cups hot water into pressure cooker or enough to have 2–3 inches in the bottom, add 1 tablespoon vinegar. Stand jars on rack. Do not allow jars to touch each other or the sides of the cooker. Fasten cover, place on LOW heat. Do not put on pressure control; allow air to expelled through center vent for 5 minutes. Put on 10 lb. pressure control valve, still at low heat, bring to pressure. Process for the time stated in table below. See that there is always a steady flow of steam from the pressure control as pressure must not drop below 10 lb.

Turn off heat and leave pressure cooker on range to reduce pressure at room temperature. When using an electric stove, move pressure cooker gently away from heat. Do not reduce pressure with cold water as sudden cooling will crack jars. Open pressure cooker by lifting the cover away from you to prevent burning yourself, remove jars one at a time onto a cloth or wooden surface. Tighten covers and let stand until cool. Test seal after 24 hours by inverting jars. Alternatively, tap the center of the cover with

a metal spoon. If a clear ringing sound is obtained the seal is perfect. If seal is not perfect, reprocess. The loss of liquid does not interfere with the keeping quality of the food. Jars should never be opened, after processing, to replace liquid that has boiled away. When opening a jar of canned vegetables do not taste the cold food. If the contents of the jar do not smell right and the food is soft and mushy, *discard it immediately* so that it will not be eaten by either humans or animals. Canned vegetables which appear spoiled may contain the botulinus toxin which causes severe food poisoning. It is essential therefore that each step be followed precisely and that the pressure cooker is in perfect working order. As a safeguard, heat canned vegetables at boiling temperature for 10–15 minutes before tasting or using.

TIMETABLE FOR CANNING VEGETABLES

(USE 10 LB. PRESSURE CONTROL)

VEGETABLE	PREPARATION	MINUTES TO BLANCH IN BOILING WATER	MINUTES TO PROCESS QUART JARS AT 10 LB. PRESSURE
ASPARAGUS	Wash, trim off scales, cut in even lengths, tie in bundles, pack upright	2–3 minutes	40 minutes
FRESH LIMA BEANS	Shell and wash beans	5 minutes	55 minutes
GREEN BEANS	Wash, trim ends, and slice or cut into 1 inch pieces	5 minutes	25 minutes
BEETS	Cut off top. Blanch before peeling, then slice or dice	15–20 minutes	40 minutes
CARROTS	Wash, scrape, slice or dice Young new – leave whole	10 minutes	45 minutes
CELERY	Wash, cut in even lengths	6 minutes	40 minutes
CORN	Husk, remove silk, wash, cut from cob	2–3 minutes	85 minutes in pint jars only
PEAS	Wash, shell and grade	2–3 minutes	50 minutes
POTATOES, NEW	Wash, scrape carefully or peel thinly	5 minutes	50 minutes

To make a syrup

Obviously the strength of syrup you use will depend very much on personal taste and also on the fruit to be canned. Peaches, for example, are best in a heavy to very heavy syrup. Plums, on the other hand, are best in a light to medium-heavy syrup.

LIGHT SYRUP – $\frac{1}{2}$ cup granulated sugar to $2\frac{1}{2}$ cups water

HEAVY SYRUP – $1\frac{1}{4}$–$1\frac{1}{3}$ cups granulated sugar to $2\frac{1}{2}$ cups water

VERY HEAVY SYRUP – $1\frac{1}{2}$–$2\frac{1}{4}$ cups granulated sugar to $2\frac{1}{2}$ cups water.

The lighter the syrup, the better the appearance of the fruit, so for show purposes can fruit in a really light syrup.
To make the syrup, boil the sugar and water together until the sugar has dissolved. If the syrup is slightly cloudy, strain through very fine cheesecloth.

To can acid fruit in a boiling water bath

Cooking time   *See method*

Ideally, one should have a deep canner so the jars can be completely covered with 1 inch of water. If you do not have a canner, a large kettle or very deep saucepan may be used.

TO PREPARE SOFT FRUIT
If this requires washing, place the soft fruit in a sieve and run cold water very gently over the fruit. Let stand to drain.

TO PREPARE HARD FRUIT
If possible, try to wipe rather than wash the fruit, as using too much water will tend to spoil the flavor.

APPLES: Peel, core, and slice and immediately drop into a bowl of salted water, i.e. 1 tablespoon salt to each 5 cups cold water. Leave the apples for 10 minutes, with a plate on top of them if desired, though this is not really necessary. This will prevent the apples from becoming brown. Boil 1 minute in light syrup, pack in jars, cover with boiling syrup, and process for 20 minutes.

PEACHES: Lower the peaches into boiling water and leave for $\frac{1}{2}$–1 minute. Remove, and put into cold water, then peel them. Leave them in the water until ready to pack the jars. This prevents their

discoloration. Pack peach halves in jars, cover with boiling heavy syrup, and process for 20 minutes.

PEARS: Preparation is similar to apples. If using hard cooking pears, simmer these until soft. If pears are ripe, then remove from the salt water and put for 1 minute only in boiling water or boiling syrup. Pears treated in this way should remain absolutely white in color. Boil quarters or slices for 3–5 minutes in heavy syrup, pack in jars, cover with boiling syrup, and process for 20 minutes.

TOMATOES: If you wish to peel the tomatoes, then drop them into boiling water for 30 seconds, then put into cold water. The skins will then come off. Pack quarters, halves or whole loosely in jars, fill with boiling water or tomato juice, and process for 45 minutes.

Pack the fruit into quart jars, packing as tightly as possible. Fill the jars to the very top with COLD water or COLD sugar syrup. Put on the boiled rubber rings and the covers. Put a wire rack in the bottom of the canner to prevent the jars from having direct contact with the metal when they might crack. Fill the canner half full with water and bring to a boil. Stand the jars on the rack with about 2 inches between them, being careful they do not touch the sides of the pan, or each other. Cover the tops of the jars with 1 inch of boiling water. Continue to add boiling water when necessary. Count the time after the water returns to a boil when the jars are added. Remove the jars with tongs or a special jar lifter which will not disturb the seal. Stand the jars on a wooden surface with several inches between each jar away from any drafts which may cause the jars to crack.

TO TEST IF JARS HAVE SEALED:
Tap the lids lightly with a metal spoon. If the sound rings, then the seal is perfect. If the sound is dull it may be due to food touching the lid. If the sound is both dull and hollow, reprocess the jar, or use the contents immediately.

ENTERTAINING AND SPECIAL OCCASIONS

Throughout this book there are recipes suitable for many different occasions and a wide range of tastes.

This last chapter is full of suggestions and hints on food for special people – the elderly, weight watchers, vegetarians – and for certain times of day – breakfast, children's snacks, and suppers. Finally, to help with menu planning, there are ideas for buffet meals, hot and cold weather fare, and food for guests.

BREAKFAST TIME

Planning

At this hour in the morning there is generally a great deal to do, so plan as many preparations the night before as possible. Set the table; assemble equipment and ingredients for cooked dishes.

DISHES TO CHOOSE:

FIRST COURSE: Porridge or dry cereals – the former may be made with quick cooking oats following the manufacturer's directions on the box.
Fresh or canned fruit juice (or tomato juice); hot or cold grapefruit may be served instead of a cereal or precede this. The picture on page 197 shows hot grapefruit – halve the fruit, top with a little butter and brown sugar, and heat for a few minutes under the broiler or in the oven.

MAIN COURSE: Choose egg dishes – bacon, etc. – fish. A bacon 'mixed grill' of cooked bacon, sausages, kidney, etc., is shown in the picture page 132 and another way of serving bacon is given on this page; as the picture shows the bacon is cooked and put between pancakes (see recipe). Growing children and active adults need a satisfying breakfast so serve bread or toast or cooked potatoes for breakfast. The picture on page 156 gives an interesting way of serving scrambled eggs, i.e. on a round potato cake and topped with a ring of potato cake.

COMPLETE BREAKFAST WITH: Piping hot toast straight from the toaster. Serve good coffee or tea.

Bacon pancakes

Make up the pancake batter as the recipe page 208. This may be done the night before. To have a rather more solid pancake than usual, as shown in the the picture on page 197, use only ¾ cup milk to 1 cup flour. Cook the pancakes in the usual way. Meanwhile fry or broil bacon – place several slices of crisp bacon between the pancakes.
Fried sliced tomatoes; fried mushrooms; scrambled eggs may be added to the bacon, if desired.

Waffles

As an alternative to pancakes, make waffles and fill with bacon, fish, or eggs. You will need a waffle iron.
Season a new waffle iron according to the manufacturer's directions. Thereafter, wipe the outside with a damp cloth, and brush away any crumbs from the grid. Never grease or wash the iron.

Cooking time   *few minutes*

1 cup all-purpose flour · dash salt · 1 egg
¾ cup milk · 2 tablespoons melted margarine
3 tablespoons granulated sugar.

Sift the flour and salt together. Make a well in the center, and drop in the egg. Beat the batter thoroughly, then gradually add the milk, beating constantly, until a smooth, thick batter. Put in the melted margarine and sugar. Heat the waffle iron, and pour in just enough of the batter to cover this. Cook quickly until crisp and brown. For a richer waffle batter increase the amount of fat to ¼ cup.

AUTOMATIC RANGES – AND THEIR USE FOR BREAKFAST

An automatic electric range is invaluable in most homes – for food may be put into the cold oven – the timing device set – the oven temperature set – the automatic setting adjusted, and then the range will light, in the case of gas, or switch on with electricity, at the pre-determined time and turn off or switch off at the end of the cooking time. Many breakfast menus may be cooked or warmed in this way. Generally, the food may be put into the oven the night before if it will not deteriorate upon standing at room temperature for overnight.

Porridge: if using rolled oats then bring this to a boil in water, cook for a few minutes, put into a casserole, and cover tightly. If using quick cooking rolled oats, then pour boiling water over these, stir and let stand. Put into the oven.

Breads and rolls: Place in the oven the night before for tempting hot bread with your meal.

Bacon, sausages: Put into greased open dishes and put into the refrigerator, ready to put into the oven the next morning. Tomatoes and mushrooms may be included – cover these with plenty of fat to prevent drying.

Cook *fish* in covered containers to prevent the smell affecting other food cooked at the same time.

COOKING FOR VEGETARIANS

Planning

Since vegetarians do not eat meat, fish, and poultry, make sure that plenty of alternative protein foods are served in the form of cheese, eggs, and vegetable proteins – nuts, lentils, peas, and beans. Include milk wherever possible in the diet. There are many recipes suitable for vegetarians throughout this book. Of course some vegetarians do not include cheese, milk, or eggs in their meals, so extra care must be taken in their case to replace these foods with extra amounts of vegetables which can provide the necessary proteins.

One of the easiest dishes to make is a Vegetable Mornay. Make a Béchamel sauce as recipe page 183. Add 1 cup grated Cheddar cheese to each 1¼ cups sauce. Stir until the cheese has melted. Arrange the vegetables – asparagus, artichokes, carrots, mixed vegetables, etc., in a dish and top with the sauce. If desired, they may be covered with more cheese and bread crumbs, or a little butter or vegetarian fat and browned under the broiler to give vegetables au gratin.

Creamed vegetables

Make a thick white sauce with 2 tablespoons vegetarian margarine, ¼ cup all-purpose flour, 1¼ cups milk, and seasoning. Cook 5–6 cups diced fresh mixed vegetables in a very little salted water, strain, and add the vegetable stock to the sauce. Reheat the sauce, and blend with the vegetables.

Creamed vegetables are shown in the picture on page 84, in this case as an accompaniment to meat, but they are excellent with any meal.

Cheese tomato cases

Cooking time	15 minutes
Oven temperature	425°F.

2 recipes Cheese pastry (see page 215)
2 (3 oz.) packages cream cheese · 2 eggs
2–3 tomatoes · parsley.

Roll out the pastry and line small patty pans or muffin pans. Blend the cream cheese and the eggs, and spread over the pastry. Bake in a preheated

425°F. oven for approximately 12–15 minutes, or until crisp and golden brown. Let stand until cool. Top with slices of tomato and parsley. See picture on page 200. *Makes 12–15*

Sauerkraut

While this vegetable dish is not necessarily one served a great deal in vegetarian diets, it is an excellent choice, since the sharp interesting flavor gives a 'bite' to dishes such as lentil roast or nut cutlets in this section.

Sauerkraut is easily obtained in cans or jars. Canned sauerkraut just needs reheating, by straining and tossing in butter, but an uncooked sauerkraut should be cooked in fresh unsalted water until nearly tender, seasoned well (the reason for adding seasoning fairly late in cooking is that one can judge the amount required better). The vegetable needs cooking for about 45 minutes. When tender, strain and toss in butter or vegetarian fat.

Cooked sauerkraut may be served with cooked noodles blended with a few caraway seeds and topped with cheese. In non-vegetarian diets it is excellent with very savory meats – sausages of all kinds – duck – pork.

Lentil roast

Cooking time	1 hour 45 minutes–2 hours
Oven temperature	375°F.

1 cup lentils · ¼ cup vegetarian fat *or* oil
2 chopped onions · 2 large tomatoes
1 small peeled, cored, and chopped apple
⅔ cup fine fresh bread crumbs · 1 teaspoon sage
seasoning · 1 egg.

Soak the lentils overnight in cold water. Cook in the same water until they are soft and the water absorbed. Beat until smooth. Heat the fat, and sauté the onions, peeled tomatoes, and apple until quite soft. Add to the lentils, with the bread crumbs, sage, and seasoning. Bind with the egg, and press into a greased 9-inch by 5-inch loaf pan, and cover with greased wax paper. Bake in a preheated 375°F. oven for 45–60 minutes. Serve with brown gravy and vegetables. *Serves 4*

Nut cutlets

Cooking time	Approximately 15 minutes
Oven temperature	400°F.

1 cup peanuts · ¼ cup vegetarian fat
2 onions · 2 large tomatoes
1 small peeled, cored, and chopped apple
⅓ cup finely ground rolled oats *or* fine fresh bread crumbs · 1 teaspoon sage · seasoning
1 beaten egg · little milk.
TO COAT: 1 egg · toasted bread crumbs.

Chop or grind the peanuts. Heat the fat, and sauté the onions, peeled tomatoes, and apple until soft. Add the peanuts, rolled oats or bread crumbs, sage, and seasoning. Bind with the egg and enough milk to give a fairly moist consistency. Form into cutlets, brush with beaten egg and bread crumbs and fry, or bake in a preheated 400°F. oven for approximately 15 minutes, or until crisp and brown.
Serves 4

COOKING FOR CHILDREN

Planning

It is important that children have a well balanced diet – see notes on page 13 about food values; and also that they develop a liking for as many different foods as possible.

Try to make meal times enjoyable and avoid 'fuss and bother' about eating food by making this look as interesting and appetizing as you can. The picture on page 174 illustrates this point, for mashed potato or potato cake mixture is formed into animal shapes and fried. Give children generous amounts of protein foods at all main meals, e.g. if grated cheese is added to the potato mixture mentioned above, it becomes an ideal food for children. Frequently a child becomes 'bored' with a very essential food, e.g. green vegetables – so try them in a different way; e.g. as a cole slaw page 169, instead of cooked. Milk often has to be 'disguised' in a dessert to encourage a child to have the necessary amount. Evaporated milk may be used and most children like the flavor.

Pasta dishes

Most older children enjoy pasta dishes, so the recipes on page 191 to 195 are ideal for supper, or lunch.

In order to save time, both pasta and rice may be cooked and used on one day with a particular sauce and the remaining plain pasta or rice kept in the refrigerator and reheated. Cover the pasta or rice with foil to prevent hardening on the outside. To reheat: Put into cold water with a little seasoning and a knob of butter or margarine, and bring the water to a boil, then strain and use the pasta or rice in the recipe as indicated.

Macaroni and cheese, a favorite dish with many children, is given on page 213 but an even quicker way to make this is to blend cooked pasta with plenty of grated cheese. Put onto the serving dish or plates, top with cheese, bread crumbs and butter, and put under the broiler for 2–3 minutes. Make certain the dish or plates are strong enough to be put under the heat in this way.

Cheese kebabs

Cooking time   *Approximately 3 minutes*
Cheddar cheese · pieces of tomato
small squares of buttered bread · bacon
pickled onions (optional).

Put cubes of cheese, pieces of tomato, buttered bread, bacon, and pickled onions alternately onto skewers. Cover wire rack on broiler with foil and place kebabs on foil. Broil for approximately 3 minutes, turning once.

Many older children have a taste for very savory foods so would enjoy the recipe above, but this same idea for cooking cheese may be used with cheese and fruit.

CHEESE FRUIT KEBABS
Put cubes of cheese onto skewers alternated with thick slices of banana and cubes of apple. Brush with melted butter, and cook the kebabs as above.

MAIN DISHES FOR CHILDREN

Fortunately few children have a genuine dislike for a basic food such as meat, fish, etc. Sometimes they will not eat these foods – it may well be they are tired of them or dislike the particular method of cooking the food. In this case it is better to give them another protein food instead at further meals – choose eggs or cheese instead of the meat or fish. Let a reasonable period elapse then present the dish again, and it may well be eaten and enjoyed. If on the other hand the child still refuses to eat the food accept their decision and continue with other dishes. Nutritionally, one meat that it is important for children to eat is liver, so take particular care in cooking and serving this so it will be enjoyed.

PUDDING, CAKES, ETC. FOR CHILDREN

Naturally these should contain essential nutrients milk, eggs, etc., but try and make them 'fun' to look at as well as good to eat.

Marble cream

Cooking time   *8–10 minutes*

Vanilla cream (see page 325)
1 tablespoon chocolate drink powder.
TO DECORATE: semisweet chocolate pieces.

Make the vanilla cream. Divide in half, and mix chocolate drink powder with one portion. Lightly stir in the other portion. Pour into a 2½ cup mold and let stand until set. Unmold and decorate with chocolate pieces, see picture on page 225.   *Serves 4*

Raspberry whip

Cooking time   *10–12 minutes*

Vanilla cream (see page 325)
½ package raspberry gelatin.

Make vanilla cream. Dissolve gelatin in a little boiling water and make up to 1 cup with cold water. When almost setting, put spoonfuls of gelatin and vanilla cream alternately into glasses, reserving some gelatin to be chopped when set for decoration. See picture on page 225.   *Serves 4*

Melting moments

Cooking time   *15–20 minutes*
Oven temperature   *350°F.*

¾ cup all-purpose flour · ¼ cup cornstarch
dash salt · ¼ cup butter
3 tablespoons granulated sugar
3 tablespoons milk · ¼ teaspoon vanilla extract.
FILLING: Butter frosting with 2 tablespoons butter
½ cup confectioners' sugar · little coloring.

Sift together the dry ingredients; cream the butter, sugar, until very light and add the milk and vanilla extract. Add the dry ingredients gradually, beating hard. Using a teaspoon, drop onto a buttered baking sheet, allowing room to spread. Bake in a preheated 350°F. oven for 15–20 minutes. Cool slightly before removing from the pan with a spatula. Sandwich together when quite cold with the butter frosting made as page 283. Color half the frosting with a few drops red coloring (see picture page 252).
Makes 13–14 completed biscuits

COOKING FOR THE ELDERLY

Planning

In many ways cooking for the elderly is not unlike cooking for a small child, since their appetite is smaller than that of a school child or active adult. It is very important that older people include ample proteins, vitamins, and calcium in their diets and that the food chosen is interesting and easily digested.

Where old people live by themselves and have to cook for one person only, there is also the problem of 'not caring', so wherever possible encourage them to get out, to meet people and to develop an interest in the community around.

CHOICE OF FOOD FOR THE ELDERLY

Do not make the mistake of having flavorless foods for older people, for many retain their liking for savory and well-seasoned foods.

SOUPS: Many of these are ideal and are an easy way to have a light meal. Choose soups containing protein foods where possible, i.e. fish soup, etc. If using dehydrated or canned soups blend with a little milk to give extra food value.

FISH: The cheaper fish dishes, herrings (make sure this is well boned before serving), cod, etc., are ideally suited for limited budgets and the maximum of food value. Broil, fry, or bake. Try serving Fish in savory custard as on page 325.

MEAT DISHES: It may be necessary to grind many kinds of meat or dice them finely. Choose easily digested meats or cook in a way that is not too rich. Lamb, beef, and of course chicken, are better than veal or pork. Tripe and sweetbreads are excellent.

CHEESE DISHES: Cheese is an admirable food since it is rich in calcium, but some elderly people find it difficult to digest when cooked. Serve at lunch or at least 2 hours before going to bed. Uncooked cheese is easier to digest.

VEGETABLE DISHES: Strain if necessary, but try to include a reasonable amount of green vegetables in the diet.

PUDDINGS AND DESSERTS: Most light desserts are ideal and are often a good way of introducing milk into the daily diet. Packaged puddings, while costing more than homemade puddings save time, fuel, etc., so a wise choice when older people have to cook for themselves.

MILK: In many cases older people enjoy milk to drink, but where they do not, add it to soups, gravies, stews, or coffee flavoring, etc., for drinks.

Creamed tripe

Cooking time   *1¼ hours*

1 lb. tripe · water · little lemon juice
1–2 onions · seasoning · ¼ cup all-purpose flour
1¼ cups milk · little cream (optional)
2 tablespoons butter.
TO GARNISH: Chopped parsley, or paprika.

Cut the tripe into neat strips, and soak in cold water for 1 hour. Blanch by putting in a saucepan, barely cover with cold water, and then bring the water to a boil and simmer for 1 minute. Discard the water. Blanching both whitens the tripe and gives it a better flavor. Add just enough water to cover the tripe, a little lemon juice, and the onions. Season well, and simmer gently for 1 hour. By this time the liquid will only be half covering the tripe. Blend the flour with the milk, add to the tripe, bring to a boil, and simmer until thickened. Stir in the cream and butter. The tripe may be placed on a heated dish and the sauce cooked until it has thickened more. The onion may be strained and added to the sauce, if desired. Sprinkle with the parsley or paprika.
Serves 4

Tripe Mornay

The previous recipe for cooking tripe is the usual one and a well flavored dish. Unfortunately it has a rather colorless appearance. The recipe below, however, not only looks more interesting since the sauce is golden in color, but has additional food value and flavor.

Cook the tripe as previous recipe, then remove the meat onto a heated serving dish. Blend ¾ cup finely grated Cheddar cheese with the sauce, and cook for a few minutes only. Pour over the tripe and serve. If desired, the dish may be topped with more cheese and with bread crumbs and browned under a hot broiler for a few minutes. *Serves 4*

Coffee and chocolate creams

Cooking time   *10 minutes*

1 package chocolate pudding
1 cup strong coffee · ½ cup milk
½ cup coffee cream *or* evaporated milk.
TO DECORATE: little whipped cream
flaked almonds · grated chocolate.

Make the pudding according to the directions, but mix with coffee, and milk. Add cream or evaporated milk when thickened in pan. When cold, decorate with whipped cream, flaked almonds (which may be browned under the broiler) and grated chocolate.
Serves 4

Vanilla cream

Cooking time   *8–10 minutes*

¾ cup evaporated milk · 1¼ cups water
¼ cup cornstarch · ¼ cup granulated sugar
vanilla extract.

Place the evaporated milk and the water in a saucepan. Blend the cornstarch and sugar with a little of the milk in a bowl. Bring the milk mixture in the saucepan to a boil. Pour onto the cornstarch mixture, and stir well. Return to the saucepan, and bring to a boil again. Continue cooking, stirring constantly, until thick. Add ¼ to ½ teaspoon of vanilla extract. Illustrated on page 225. *Serves 4*

COOKING FOR INVALIDS

Planning

The type of food served to an invalid very much depends on the particular illness or complaint. Where people are diabetic, they must follow the prescribed diet given by their doctor or hospital. In the case of gastric disorders or stomach ulcers, it is important to have light, easily digested foods with little, if any, roughage (this means vegetables and fruits must be strained), no twice-cooked or highly spiced or fried foods and generally something to eat at regular 2-hourly intervals. When cooking for people who are recovering from an illness, make the tray of food look attractive, and do not serve too much food at one time. Many of the fish and chicken dishes in the book are ideal for invalids.

FISH DISHES FOR INVALIDS

Many invalids, particularly when on a strict gastric diet, have to eat fish far more often than normal. There is the added disadvantage that in many cases it must be steamed or poached and served without sauces. In this case try and make it look attractive with colorful garnishes of lemon, tomato, etc. (even if these may not be eaten). Fortunately in many invalid diets more imaginative fish dishes may be served. Flounder and halibut are ideal fish for invalids since they are particularly fine textured and easy to digest. They are fairly expensive though so substitute cod, whiting or fresh haddock from time to time. Cod is particularly suitable to serve with well flavored stuffings.

Fish in savoury custard

Cooking time   *45 minutes*
Oven temperature   *325°F.*

4 small pieces cod *or* flounder · seasoning
1 egg · 1¼ cups milk
1 teaspoon chopped parsley.

Skin the fish, and remove any bones. Put into an ovenproof dish, and season lightly. Beat the egg with seasoned milk, and add the parsley. Pour over the fish, and bake in a preheated 325°F. oven for approximately 45 minutes or, until the fish is tender and the custard just set. This may be baked for a slightly shorter time at 350°F. and then the fish will be cooked and the custard set so lightly that it is almost a pouring sauce. *Serves 4*

Steamed sole in white wine sauce

Cooking time   *15 minutes*

4 small skinned soles · little butter
seasoning · milk *or* cream.
FOR THE SAUCE: 2 tablespoons butter
¼ cup all-purpose flour · 1¼ cups dry white wine.

Put the soles onto buttered plates, adding the seasoning and just a very little milk or cream (this could be coffee or whipping cream – but only give whipping cream to invalids who have no gastric disorders). Cover and steam as page 13. Blend the butter and flour as in a white sauce, then gradually blend in the white wine. Bring to a boil, and cook until thickened and smooth. Lift the sole onto heated serving plates and top with the sauce. Sometimes a white wine sauce has a slightly 'grey' color, so blend in a very little cream to prevent this.

Serves 4

Baked cod with parsley stuffing

Cooking time	*See method*
Oven temperature	*See method*

1 small codling or 4 cod steaks
Veal (parsley) stuffing (see page 189)
1 tablespoon chopped parsley extra.

Prepare and bake the fish as given on page 55. putting in the stuffing. The parsley stuffing is made by using more parsley than usual in the veal stuffing. If serving a whole fish, make sure to cut this into appetizing portions, and arrange these attractively on a dish. *Serves 4*

Milk gelatin

Cooking time	*None*

1 package fruit flavored gelatin · ⅔ cup water
2 cups milk.

Dissolve gelatin in boiling water. Allow the gelatin to cool and add the cold milk. *Serves 4*

Individual vanilla creams

Cooking times	*8–10 minutes*

Vanilla cream (see page 325)
small can apricots *or* cooked apricots.

Make the vanilla cream, and pour into 4 individual molds, rinsed in cold water. Let stand until set. Turn out and top with the fruit, press through a sieve to give a smooth purée. See picture on page 225.

Serves 4

COOKING FOR WEIGHT WATCHERS
Planning

It is generally recognized today that to be overweight is a danger to health, so people who are considerably above their ideal weight should try to lose some weight. Any strict diet should be followed only under doctor's orders. Reducing diets vary to a great degree – some restrict foods according to a set number of calories per day – and it is important to select these wisely so you have the most important protein foods.
Other diets allow a person to eat fairly generous amounts of protein foods, but restrict carbohydrates; i.e. starches and sugars (this may even mean counting the natural sugar in many fruits).

Salads are normally allowed and the following low calorie dressing makes any salad more interesting.

Low calorie salad dressing

Cooking time	*None*

3 tablespoons milk
3 tablespoons lemon juice *or* vinegar
seasoning · dry mustard
1 tablet saccharine, crushed *or* liquid saccharine to taste.

Mix milk with lemon juice or vinegar. Add seasoning, mustard, and saccharine and blend thoroughly. This gives flavor and moisture to rather dry salads.

CALORIE VALUES OF SOME EVERYDAY FOODS

Food	Amount	Calories
MILK GROUP		
Cheese		
AMERICAN	1 oz.	105
CHEDDAR	1 oz.	90
GRATED	½ cup	225
COTTAGE	½ cup	100
CREAM	2 tablespoons	105
GOUDA	1 oz.	110
PARMESAN, GRATED	2 tablespoons	40
SWISS	1 oz.	95
Cream		
COFFEE	1 tablespoon	35
HALF AND HALF	1 tablespoon	20
WHIPPING	1 tablespoon	50
Custard, baked	½ cup	280
Eggnog	1 cup	250
Ice cream, vanilla	½ cup	175
Ice milk	½ cup	140
Milk		
BUTTERMILK	1 cup	85

Food	Amount	Calories
CHOCOLATE MILK	1 cup	210
CONDENSED, SWEETENED	½ cup	375
DRIED, NON FAT	1 tablespoon	30
EVAPORATED	½ cup	170
MALTED MILK	1 cup	280
SKIM	1 cup	90
WHOLE	1 cup	165
Yogurt		
PARTIALLY SKIM MILK	1 cup	120
WHOLE MILK	1 cup	155
BREAD-CEREAL GROUP		
Biscuits		
BAKING POWDER	1 medium	140
Bread 1 (1 lb.) loaf with 16 slices		
CRACKED WHEAT	1 slice	60
FRENCH	1 slice	65
RAISIN	1 slice	75
RYE	1 slice	55

Food	Amount	Calories
WHITE	1 slice	70
WHOLE WHEAT	1 slice	65
Cereals, breakfast		
CORN FLAKES	1 cup	75
OATMEAL	1 cup	150
RICE, PUFFED	1 cup	56
WHEAT, SHREDDED	2 biscuits	140
Coffee cake, frosted	1 (4½-inch) piece	200
Crackers		
GRAHAM	2 medium	55
MELBA TOAST	1 piece	20
SALTINES	2 (2-inch) crackers	35
Doughnuts		
CAKE	1 medium	135
YEAST	1 medium	120
French toast	1 slice	185
Macaroni		
PLAIN, COOKED	1 cup	155
WITH CHEESE	1 cup	475
Muffins		
BRAN	1 medium	130
CORN	1 medium	155
PLAIN	1 medium	140
Pancake	1 medium	60
Popover	1 medium	90
Pretzles	4 (3-inch) sticks	35
Rice, white	½ cup, cooked	100
Rolls		
DANISH PASTRY	1 small	140
HARD, ROUND	1 medium	95
PLAIN	1 medium	120
SWEET	1 medium	200
Spaghetti		
PLAIN	¾ cup	100
WITH MEATBALLS	¾ cup	250
Tortillas	1 medium	50
Waffle	1 medium	200
FRUIT-VEGETABLE GROUP		
Apples, raw	1 medium	70
Apple sauce		
SWEETENED	½ cup	115
UNSWEETENED	½ cup	50
Apricots, raw	3	55
CANNED IN WATER	½ cup	45
CANNED IN SYRUP	½ cup	110
Asparagus, cooked	½ cup	40
Banana, raw	1 (6-inch)	80
Beans, green, wax, cooked	½ cup	35
Beets, cooked	½ cup, diced	30
Berries		
BLUEBERRIES	½ cup	45
CANNED IN WATER	½ cup	50
FROZEN, SWEETENED	½ cup	120
RASPBERRIES	½ cup	35
FROZEN, SWEETENED	½ cup	120
STRAWBERRIES	½ cup	30
FROZEN, SWEETENED	½ cup	140
Broccoli, cooked	½ cup	40
Brussels sprouts, cooked	½ cup	30
Cabbage, raw, shredded	½ cup	10
COOKED	½ cup	25
Cantaloup, raw	½ small	50
Carrots, raw	½ cup, grated	20
COOKED, DICED	½ cup	25
Cauliflower, cooked	½ cup	30
Celery, raw	2 (8-inch) stalks	10
Cherries, raw, sweet	½ cup	40
Corn	½ cup	70
Cranberry juice	½ cup	75
Cucumber, pared	¾-inch slice	5
Fruit cocktail		
CANNED IN SYRUP	½ cup	100
Grapefruit, raw	½ medium	50
JUICE, CANNED, SWEETENED	½ cup	65
JUICE, CANNED, UNSWEETENED	½ cup	45
Grapes		
CONCORD	½ cup	30
THOMPSON	½ cup	50
Lemon, juice	1 tablespoon	5
Lettuce, raw	2 large leaves	10
Mushrooms, sautéed	½ cup	120
Onions	½ cup	30
Oranges, raw	1 medium	70
JUICE, CANNED, UNSWEETENED	½ cup	60
JUICE, FRESH	½ cup	55
Peaches, raw	1 medium	35
CANNED IN WATER	½ cup	40
CANNED IN SYRUP	½ cup	100
FROZEN, SWEETENED	½ cup	105
Pears, raw	1 medium	100
CANNED IN SYRUP	½ cup	100
Peas, cooked	½ cup	75
Pineapple, raw	½ cup, diced	40
SLICES IN SYRUP	2 medium	90
JUICE	½ cup	75
Plums, raw	1 medium	25
Potatoes		
BAKED	1 medium	85
BOILED	½ cup, diced	40
CHIPS	10 medium	120
FRENCH FRIES	10 medium	150
MASHED, MILK, BUTTER	½ cup	120
Prune, juice	½ cup	50
Raisins	½ cup	230
Rhubarb, cooked sweetened	½ cup	200
Spinach, cooked	½ cup	40
Squash		
SUMMER, COOKED	½ cup	15
WINTER, BAKED	½ cup	95
Tomatoes, raw	1 medium	30
CANNED	½ cup	20
JUICE, CANNED	½ cup	25
Watermelon	4 × 8-inch wedge	120
MEAT GROUP		
Beans, dry		
BAKED, PORK, MOLASSES	½ cup	200
LIMA, COOKED	½ cup	130
RED KIDNEY, CANNED	½ cup	115
Beef		
BRISKET, BRAISE	4 oz.	470
CHEESEBURGER	1 (3 × 1-inch)	370
CHIPPED BEEF	2 oz.	115
CHUCK, POT-ROASTED	4 oz.	400
CLUB STEAK, LEAN	4 oz.	280
CORNED BEEF, CANNED, LEAN	3 oz.	180
CUBE STEAK	3 oz.	220
FLANK STEAK, POT-ROASTED, LEAN	4 oz.	225
GROUND BEEF, BROILED	4 oz.	325
HAMBURGER	1 (3 × 1-inch)	265
LIVER, FRIED	4 oz.	230
MEAT LOAF	3 oz.	170
PORTERHOUSE STEAK, BROILED	4 oz.	255
POT PIE	1 (4½-inch)	460
RIBS, ROASTED, LEAN	4 oz.	300
SIRLOIN, BROILED, LEAN	4 oz.	240
STEW WITH VEGETABLES	1 cup	185
T-BONE STEAK, BROILED, LEAN	4 oz.	250
TONGUE	3 oz.	200
Eggs		
CREAMED ON TOAST	¾ cup, 1 slice	335
FRIED	1 large	110
HARD-COOKED	1 large	80
SCRAMBLED	1 large, milk	110
YOLK	1 medium	60
Fish and shellfish		
ANCHOVY, CANNED	4 fillets	30
CLAMS, CANNED	3 medium	45
COD, RAW	3 oz.	65
CRAB MEAT, CANNED	½ cup	90

Food	*Amount*	*Calories*
FISH STICKS	5 sticks	200
FLOUNDER, RAW	3 oz.	60
HADDOCK, DEEP-FRIED	3 oz.	150
LOBSTER, CANNED	3 oz.	75
MACKEREL		
BROILED	3 oz.	200
CANNED	3 oz.	155
OYSTERS	1 cup	160
PERCH, BREADED, FRIED	3 oz.	195
SALMON, BROILED	3 oz.	175
SARDINES, DRAINED	3 oz.	185
SHRIMP		
CANNED, DRAINED	3 oz.	110
FRENCH FRIED	5 shrimp	225
SWORDFISH, BROILED	3 oz.	155
TUNA, CANNED, DRAINED	3 oz.	170
Lamb		
LEG, ROASTED	4 oz.	320
LOIN CHOP, BROILED	4 oz.	240
RIB CHOP, BROILED	4 oz.	140
SHOULDER, ROASTED	4 oz.	400
Miscellaneous		
BOLOGNA	1 slice	65
FRANKFURTER, BOILED	1 medium	155
LIVER SAUSAGE	2 oz.	120
LUNCHEON MEAT	1 slice	80
SWEETBREADS	½ pair	185
Nuts		
ALMONDS	13 whole	105
BRAZIL	½ cup, chopped	500
CASHEWS	8 medium	60
MIXED	½ cup	200
PEANUT BUTTER	1 tablespoon	95
PEANUTS	2 tablespoons	100
PECANS	2 tablespoons chopped	100
WALNUTS	6 halves	90
Pork		
BACON	2 slices	95
CANADIAN-STYLE	1 slice	70
HAM		
CANNED, DEVILED	4 oz.	400
CREAMED	1 cup	400
FRESH, BOILED	4 oz.	440
SMOKED, BOILED	4 oz.	360
LOIN CHOP	4 oz.	460
SAUSAGE	1 link	85
SAUSAGE MEAT	2 oz.	270
SPARERIBS, ROASTED	6 medium	245
Poultry		
CHICKEN		
CREAMED	½ cup	205
BROILED	¼ small chicken	185
FRIED	½ breast	200
	1 drumstick	100
LIVER, SIMMERED	4 oz.	180
SALAD	¾ cup	340
DUCK, COOKED	4 oz.	190
GOOSE, COOKED	4 oz.	355
POT PIE, CHICKEN OR TURKEY	1 (4½-inch)	485
TURKEY, ROASTED		
DARK MEAT	4 oz.	185
LIGHT MEAT	4 oz.	170
Veal		
CHUCK, ROASTED	3 oz.	210
LOIN CHOP, LEAN	4 oz.	250
STEW	½ cup	120

OTHER FOODS

Food	*Amount*	*Calories*
Beverages		
ALCOHOLIC		
BEER 3·6% ALCOHOL	12 oz.	150
WHISKY, VODKA, GIN, RUM		
70 PROOF	1½ oz.	85
80 PROOF	1½ oz.	95
90 PROOF	1½ oz.	110
100 PROOF	1½ oz.	125
WINES		
DRY	3 oz.	75
MEDIUM	3 oz.	125
SWEET	3 oz.	165
CARBONATED		
COLA	12 oz.	150
GINGER ALE	12 oz.	120
LOW CALORIE	12 oz.	approx. 10
ROOT BEER	12 oz.	150
COFFEE AND TEA		
WITHOUT SUGAR	1 cup	0
1TEASPOON SUGAR	1 cup	15
1 TABLESPOON CREAM	1 cup	35
1 TABLESPOON WHOLE MILK	1 cup	10
1 TABLESPOON LEMON JUICE	1 cup	5
Candy		
CHOCOLATE CREAM	1 oz.	110
FUDGE	1 oz.	115
HARD CANDY	1 oz.	110
MILK CHOCOLATE	1 oz.	145
PEANUT BRITTLE	1 oz.	125
Desserts		
APPLE, BAKED	1 medium	195
BREAD PUDDING, RAISINS	½ cup	250
CAKES		
FRUIT	2 × 2 × ½-inch slice	140
PLAIN	1 cup cake	120
SPONGE	1/12 of 8-inch diameter	115
COOKIES		
CHOCOLATE CHIP	1 large	50
FIG	1 large	85
OATMEAL	1 large	115
PLAIN	1 large	120
VANILLA WAFER	1 medium	14
GELATIN		
PLAIN	½ cup	80
WITH FRUIT	¾ cup	85
PIES		
APPLE	⅙ of medium	375
CUSTARD	⅙ of medium	260
SHERBET	½ cup	120
Fats and oils		
BUTTER OR MARGARINE	1 pat	50
	1 tablespoon	100
LARD	1 tablespoon	135
SALAD OIL	1 tablespoon	125
Honey	2 tablespoons	120
Jam, jelly	2 tablespoons	100
Olives		
GREEN	10 medium	75
RIPE	10 medium	100
Pickles		
BREAD AND BUTTER	6 slices	30
DILL	1 large	15
SOUR	1 large	15
SWEET	1 medium	20
Salad dressings		
BLUE CHEESE	1 tablespoon	75
FRENCH	1 tablespoon	60
ITALIAN	1 tablespoon	80
LOW CALORIE	1 tablespoon	15
MAYONNAISE	1 tablespoon	95
RUSSIAN	1 tablespoon	75
Soups		
BOUILLON CUBE	1	10
CELERY, CREAM OF	1 cup	200
CHICKEN BROTH	1 cup	10
CONSOMMÉ	1 cup	10
TOMATO, CREAM OF	1 cup	90
VEGETABLE	1 cup	80
Sugar		
CONFECTIONERS	1 tablespoon	30
GRANULATED OR BROWN	1 tablespoon	50
Syrup		
CHOCOLATE	1 tablespoon	40
CORN	1 tablespoon	60
MAPLE	1 tablespoon	65

COOKING IN COLD WEATHER

Planning

In cold weather the family needs warming and sustaining foods and even if they rarely eat puddings and pastry during warmer weather, these provide carbohydrates in the form of starch and sugar, so are a wise choice.

A really warming soup at the end of a busy day and possibly after a tiring and cold journey will be much appreciated.

There are many recipes in this book which are ideal for cold weather, but the following are real 'cold weather fare'.

Cream of onion soup

Cooking time   *30 minutes*

1 large onion · 2 tablespoons butter
3 tablespoons cornstarch · 5 cups milk
2 egg yolks · ¼ cup whipping cream · seasoning.

Chop and gently sauté the onions in the hot butter until soft, but do not brown. Add the cornstarch and mix in well, then cook for a further minute. Add the milk, and cook gently for about 20 minutes. Mix egg yolks and cream together, add a little soup, then return all to the saucepan and reheat without boiling. Season to taste.   *Serves 4*

Fish and corn casserole

Cooking time   *45 minutes*
Oven temperature   *375°F.*

1¼–1½ lb. cod *or* flounder · 3 large ripe tomatoes
1 small onion · ¼ cup butter *or* margarine
¼ cup all-purpose flour
1¼ cups fish stock *or* water · seasoning.
TO GARNISH: 1 (12 oz.) can sweet corn *or* cooked corn removed from the cob · lemon slices.

Skin the fish and cut into 4 portions. Peel the tomatoes and onion, and slice or chop, then sauté in the hot butter or margarine for several minutes. Stir in the flour, cook for 2–3 minutes, then blend in the stock or water. Bring to a boil, and cook for 5 minutes, season well. Put the fish into an ovenproof casserole, top with the sauce, cover, and cook for 30–35 minutes in a preheated 375°F. oven. Remove the dish from the oven about 10 minutes before serving, add the corn, and replace in the oven. Garnish with lemon slices. (See picture on page 82).   *Serves 4*

Bacon crumb pie

Cooking time   *20 minutes*
Oven temperature   *400°F.*

8–12 slices Canadian-style bacon
¼ cup butter *or* margarine
1 cup fine fresh bread crumbs
1 (8 oz.) can sliced carrots *or* 1 cup sliced carrots
2 hard-cooked eggs · seasoning
⅔ cup chicken stock · 2–3 tomatoes.
TO GARNISH: parsley.

Remove rinds from bacon and cut into fairly small pieces. Fry lightly and remove from pan. Melt margarine in pan and toss the bread crumbs in it. Place layers of bacon, carrots and sliced eggs in a pie dish, pour over well-seasoned stock and cover with bread crumbs. Bake in a moderately hot oven for 20 minutes. For the last 5 minutes lay sliced, peeled tomatoes on top. Garnish with chopped parsley and serve with baked mushrooms and scalloped potatoes (see page 167).   *Serves 4*

Jam suet pudding

Cooking time   *1½ hours*

1 cup all-purpose flour
1½ teaspoons baking powder · ¼ teaspoon salt
¼ cup granulated sugar · ⅓ cup chopped beef suet
approximately 3 tablespoons milk
3 tablespoons jam.

Sift together the flour, baking powder and salt, add the sugar and the suet. Gradually stir in the milk, binding together. This should be a stiff consistency but since flour varies somewhat you may need a little extra milk. Put the jam at the bottom of a greased ovenproof bowl and put in the mixture. Cover with greased foil or greased wax paper, and steam over boiling water for 1½ hours. Turn out onto a heated dish. Heat more jam as a sauce. (See picture on page 227.)   *Serves 4*

Sauces to serve with steamed puddings

The steamed pudding recipe above, may be cooked without jam at the bottom and then served with various sauces. More than one may be made.

Lemon sauce

Cooking time   *8 minutes*

juice of 2 lemons · water · 1 tablespoon arrowroot *or* cornstarch · ¼ cup granulated sugar
finely grated peel 1 lemon.

Measure the juice from the lemons and make up to 1¼ cups with water. Mix arrowroot to a smooth paste with a little of the liquid. Heat remaining lemon mixture in a saucepan, add sugar, and stir until dissolved. Pour over the paste, and return to pan. Cook until sauce thickens and becomes clear, stirring constantly. Stir in the finely grated lemon peel, and pour into a sauceboat.

ORANGE SAUCE
Use either 2 large oranges, or you have a better flavored sauce if you use 1 large orange and 1 small lemon. Continue as above.

Sweet syrup sauce

Cooking time   *few minutes*

¼ cup corn syrup · 1 lemon
⅔ cup water.

Put the corn syrup into a saucepan with the grated peel and juice of the lemon. Add the water and heat gently for a few minutes.

COOKING IN HOT WEATHER

Planning

Most people enjoy the sun and warmth, but it does pose certain problems in preparing nourishing food, for cooking is tiring in the heat and many people lose their appetites.
Try to eat out of doors as much as possible – for picnics or outdoor meals you will find many interesting patties, flans, sandwiches, etc. in this book.
Plan an outdoor barbeque – make kebabs with meat and vegetables as in the picture on page 177 or recipe below; or cook the whole meal – chops, tomatoes, onion rings – in one pan over a barbeque fire – see picture page 101.
Cook baked potatoes, and blend the pulp with butter and ground or chopped cooked ham as the picture, page 155.
Prepare interesting sauces for salads and desserts, and include as much fresh fruit as possible.

Pepper cocktail sauce

Cooking time   *None*

½ cup mayonnaise
1 tablespoon lemon juice · 1 teaspoon chili sauce
1 tablespoon tomato ketchup *or* tomato paste
seasoning · 3 tablespoons whipping cream
1 tablespoon finely chopped green sweet pepper
1 tablespoon finely chopped red sweet pepper
2 teaspoons sliced stuffed olives.

Blend all the ingredients together. This sauce is excellent to serve with fish salads or in a fish cocktail. When red peppers are not available use all green.   *Serves 4*

Cheese and shrimp flan

Cooking time   *25 minutes*
Oven temperature   *400°F.*

1 recipe cheese pastry (see page 215)
TO FILL: 2 tablespoons butter
¼ cup all-purpose flour · 1 cup milk
1½ cups grated Cheddar cheese
½ cup fresh or frozen shrimp, cleaned and cooked
4 slices Canadian-style bacon, diced and cooked
seasoning.
TO GARNISH: few shrimp · 8 bacon rolls.

Roll out the pastry and line an 8-inch flan ring or 8-inch layer cake pan with this. Bake in a preheated 400°F. oven for about 10 minutes, or until crisp and golden brown. Melt the butter, add the flour, and

cook for 2–3 minutes. Remove from the heat and stir in the milk. Return to the heat, and bring to a boil, stirring well. Cook until smooth and thick, add the grated cheese, shrimp, bacon, and seasoning. Pour into the prepared flan case. Garnish with shrimp and bacon rolls. Illustrated on page 150.
         Serves 6

TO MAKE BACON ROLLS
Remove any rind from slices of bacon. Cut each slice in half and roll, put onto skewers and broil or fry for 5 minutes or cook for 10–20 minutes (depending on the heat) in the oven. Allow 1–2 rolls per person. Illustrated on page 108.

Mixed meat kebabs

Cooking time   *10–15 minutes*

½ lb. boneless sirloin *or* tenderloin steak
½ lb. lamb leg steak *or* veal
few tiny mushrooms · butter.

Cut the meat into small cubes and thread with the mushrooms onto four or more metal skewers. Brush with melted butter and cook under a hot broiler until the meat is tender. Serve with Tangy barbeque sauce (see page 185).   *Serves 4–6*

The best accompaniment to meat or sausages and the barbeque sauce are baked potatoes topped with plenty of butter and a really crisp green salad. Instead of the meat kebabs above, serve broiled or fried sausages to dip into the sauce.

SAFFRON RICE
Cook rice as page 194, but add a little saffron to flavor and color. Serve as picture on page 177.

Pineapple fruit salad

Cooking time   *None*

1 fresh ripe pineapple · 1 lb. mixed fresh fruit
little sugar · kirsch or sherry, optional.

Cut the top off the pineapple and cut out the center pulp. Dice this neatly, discarding the hard central core. Prepare the rest of the fruit salad as page 253. Mix with the pineapple, sweeten, and sprinkle with kirsch or sherry, if desired – do not use too much as the fruit makes its own juice. Pile back into pineapple case and serve very cold. Illustrated on page 154.   *Serves 6–8*

ORANGE FRUIT SALAD
A more economical dessert can be made by blending the fruit salad with the pulp from 6–8 large oranges, then piling this back into the orange cases.
         Serves 6–8

COOKING FOR ECONOMY

Planning

While it is wise to spend a reasonable amount of money on good, nourishing food for the family, there are many ways in which housekeeping money may be saved.

Buy wisely – choose foods which are in season so they are plentiful, or good quality and cheap. Do not waste food – there are many hints throughout this book on using leftover food, and most of the recipes on this page do this too.

Plan cooking to use one part of the range only.

Sausage salad

Cooking time   *None*

1 lb. cooked sausages
1 lb. cooked fresh *or* frozen beans
2–3 tomatoes · lettuce · French dressing (see page 186).

Cut the sausages lengthwise. Cut the beans into neat pieces and the tomatoes also. Shred the lettuce. Toss the lettuce, beans and tomatoes in French dressing. Put the lettuce at the bottom of a bowl. Arrange the sausages around, and top with the beans and tomatoes. (See picture page 152).   *Serves 4–6*

Sausage and bean pie

Cooking time   *1¼ hours*
Oven temperature   *375°F.*

RAISED PIE PASTRY OR HOT WATER PASTRY:
3 cups all-purpose flour · ¼ teaspoon salt
⅔ cup water · ½–⅔ cup lard *or* fat.
FILLING: 1½ lb. sausage meat
1 tablespoon chopped parsley · 1 egg
1 (14 oz.) can baked beans in tomato sauce.
TO GLAZE: either milk of 1 egg and little milk.

To make the pastry, sift the flour and salt into a mixing bowl. Heat the water and lard or fat until this has melted. Pour over the flour, and knead gently but firmly. Use part of the pastry to line an 8-inch pie pan or mold into the required shape. Blend all the ingredients for the filling, put into the pie shell, top with the remaining circle of pastry. Seal the edges well, and make a slit on top for the steam to escape. Glaze with milk or beaten egg and milk, and bake in a preheated 375°F. oven for 1¼ hours.   *Serves 5–6*

Haslet

Cooking time   *1 hour*
Oven temperature   *375°F.*

1 lb. bread · 1 lb. ground pork
1–2 tablespoons chopped fresh sage · seasoning.

Soak the bread in water until soft, squeeze to remove the excess water, beat into crumbs, and add to the ground pork. Mix with the sage and seasoning, and stuff into a sausage casing, or wrap in greased foil. Bake in a preheated 375°F. oven for about 1 hour. Serve hot with a good gravy or cold.   *Serves 4*

Ground rice tarts

Cooking time   *25 minutes*
Oven temperature   *425°F.*

1 recipe short crust pastry (see page 215)
1¼ cups milk · 1 bay leaf · 1 small lemon
3 cups finely ground rice · 2 tablespoons butter
2 egg yolks · 1 egg white · dash mixed spice (cinnamon, nutmeg, and allspice)
¼ cup granulated sugar
¼ cup chopped mixed candied peel
3 tablespoons currants.

Prepare and roll out the pastry thinly and line small patty tins or muffin pans with this. Keep in a cool place while the filling is prepared. Put the milk, bay leaf, and thinly pared lemon peel into a saucepan, and bring very slowly to a boil, then stand pan in a warm place until lukewarm. Put ground rice into a second pan, stir in the strained cooled milk, add butter, and bring slowly to a boil, stirring constantly. Beat egg yolks and white. Remove rice mixture from the heat, and stir in eggs; add spice and sugar, then cool. Divide filling between pastry-lined pans, put a thin slice of peel and a few currants on top of filling, and bake immediately in a preheated 425°F. oven for 12–15 minutes, or until the filling has risen and pastry is cooked. (See picture on page 245).   *Makes 12–14*

COCONUT CHEESE CAKE
Use ingredients as ground rice tarts above, but add 1½ cups flaked coconut. Either bake in small tarts as given above, then top with jam and coconut or bake in one large tart as picture page 201 and decorate with candied cherries and sifted confectioners' sugar. Omit the peel and currants, if desired.

ENTERTAINING

Planning

Most people enjoy entertaining their friends, but all too often the occasion is marred by the fact that the preparation can seem very hard work. Do not let this happen – plan your entertaining so it is NOT too difficult or too much hard work.

FOR COCKTAILS:
Choose savories where much of the preparation may be done well ahead of time of dispense with small hors d'oeuvres and offer your guests dips instead.

Dips

The recipes on this page are ideal for an informal hors-d'oeuvre or an evening party.

When the dip is made, it should be the consistency of a rather thick cream, so pieces of food may be put in without the possibility of the dip dripping off the potato chips, crackers, etc.

Arrange the dips in attractive shallow bowls, garnish on top with fresh chives if available, parsley, nuts, paprika, etc., and try to have a good variety of color as well as flavor. The small pieces of food to go in the dip are very important. Choose tiny cheese crackers; potato chips; crispbread; raw strips of carrot or celery; segments of apple (sprinkled with lemon juice), and tiny cauliflowerets. Put on small plates on the tray around the bowl or bowls of dip.

Corn dip

Cooking time None

1 (8 oz.) can corn *or* about ¾ cup cooked frozen *or* fresh corn on the cob
⅔ cup whipping cream
2 cups finely grated Cheddar cheese
¼ cup finely grated Parmesan cheese
3 tablespoons mayonnaise · 1 tablespoon finely chopped chives *or* shallot *or* onion.

Drain the corn well, whip the cream lightly, and blend with the corn, cheeses, mayonnaise, and chives or onion. *Serves 4–6*

Fruity dip

Cooking time None

4 (3 oz.) packages cream cheese *or* 3 cups finely grated Cheddar cheese blended with 1 tablespoon whipping cream · 1 small can pineapple rings
¼ cup dates · ½ cup walnuts · seasoning
lettuce.
TO GARNISH: chives or parsley.

Blend the cream cheese with the chopped drained pineapple, chopped dates, and chopped walnuts. Season well, and arrange on a bed of lettuce in a shallow dish. Garnish with chives or parsley.
Serves 4–6

Ham and mayonnaise dip

Cooking time None

1¼ cups mayonnaise
2–3 tablespoons tomato ketchup
1 teaspoon prepared mustard
2 teaspoons horseradish relish
½–¾ cup chopped nuts.
TO SERVE: ½–¾ cup diced cooked ham.

Blend the ingredients. Put in a bowl. Have cubes of ham and the usual accompaniments. *Serves 4–6*

Cheese croutons

Cooking time About 15–20 minutes
Oven temperature 375°F.

½-inch thick slices of day-old white or brown bread
melted butter · grated Cheddar cheese.

Remove the crusts, and cut the bread into ½-inch cubes. Dip in melted butter, then toss in grated Cheddar cheese to coat thoroughly. Place on a baking sheet, and put in a preheated 375°F. oven to crisp and brown, about 15–20 minutes. The croutons are delicious with many soups.

Aspic canapés

These are among the best appetizers to serve at cocktail parties since the aspic covering protects the food and prevents it from becoming dry.
For the base: use pieces of toast; fried bread; bread or crackers.
For the topping: use tiny pieces of cooked fish; chicken; meat; canned fish; shellfish; hard-cooked egg.
To coat: use 1 package unflavored gelatin to 2 × 10 oz. cans consommé, this will cover approximately 100 'bite-sized' canapés.

Make the toast, etc., and arrange the portions of food on this. Do not cut up the pieces to begin with. Put onto a wire rack or the rack from the broiler with a large tray or plate underneath. When arranging the pieces of food use contrasting colors, e.g. ham with a ring of cooked peas; smoked salmon with tiny pieces of tomato and gherkin; a slice of hard-cooked egg with very tiny pieces of anchovy fillet. Make the gelatin according to the directions on the package. Allow this to cool and become slightly stiffened; if too runny it will soak into the base, if too stiff it will be difficult to spread. Spread or brush the gelatin over the food very carefully so you do not dislodge the arrangement. Let stand until set, gather up any gelatin that has dropped into the tray beneath and use again. When quite firm, cut toast into portions with a knife dipped in hot water.

Vol-au-vent cases

Cooking time few minutes
Oven temperature 425°F.

These are ideal for so many occasions.

Choose puff, rough puff, *or* flaky pastry. Roll out until about ⅓–½ inch thick for tiny cases but up to 1 inch thick for large ones. Cut into circles – about 1½ inches in diameter for cocktail vol-au-vent cases. Take a cutter about ¾ inch in diameter and mark the pastry on top to a depth of approximately ¼ inch. Brush the pastry with beaten egg mixed with water, and bake in a preheated 425°F. oven, or until crisp and golden brown. Remove the 'lid' and return the case to the oven for a few minutes to 'dry out'. Fill with flaked cooked fish or shellfish, chicken, vegetables, etc., in creamy sauces (see page 183) or with fruit and cream.

Tomato chutney, page 317; Mustard pickles, page 312; Pickled red cabbage, page 317; Sweet vinegar pickles, page 317

Cider punch, page 302; Cherry cider cup, page 302

Buffet parties

There is a very wide choice of food for this type of entertaining. Have plates of sliced cold meats, and/or poultry with interesting salads. Have hot dishes such as risotto, blanquette of chicken, etc. (making pieces of chicken small enough to eat with a fork alone), make larger sized vol-au-vent cases (see cocktails and the picture page 200). If entertaining younger guests, pasta dishes are an excellent choice.

Choose a selection of cold desserts, interesting pies and pastries and always have a plentiful selection of cheeses.

Chaudfroid dishes

Cold meat, poultry, or fish keep more moist if coated with aspic, (see page 332) or with a chaudfroid sauce (see page 186).

Make the chaudfroid sauce, see recipe page 186. Allow this to stiffen very slightly. Put the portions of food on a wire rack, then pour over the sauce or spread with a knife dipped in hot water. Let stand until set, then garnish with tiny pieces of gherkin, tomato, etc. For a very professional result make up a small quantity of unflavored gelatin and give a clear coating on top.

Pressed ox tongue

Cooking time   *See below*

1 tongue, preferably salted · 1 onion · 1 carrot
1 bay leaf · 1 teaspoon unflavored gelatin.

Ask for a salted tongue and soak for several hours, or overnight, in cold water. If it is not possible to obtain a salted tongue then cook at once, adding salt to taste. The color is never as good, though, as when salted. Put into cold water, bring to a boil, and add the onion, carrot, and bay leaf. Simmer very gently in a covered pan. Allow 40 minutes per lb. At the end of this time, remove the tongue from the stock, and allow to cool until you can handle it. Meanwhile, boil the stock uncovered until only about ⅔ cup is left. Remove skin from the tongue and the tiny bones at the root. Lift into a round layer cake pan or saucepan, curling it around to give a good shape. It needs to be a fairly tight fit. Dissolve the gelatin in the stock and strain over the tongue. Put a plate with a weight on top to press into shape, and let stand until cold. Remove weight, etc., dip base of pan or saucepan into hot water for 30 seconds to loosen the jelly around the meat, and turn out. Illustrated on page 129.

Serves up to 20 depending on size

Chicken and ham galantine

Cooking time   *1¼ hours*
Oven temperature   *375°F.*

1½ lb. uncooked chicken · 1½ cups (¾ lb.) ground cooked ham · 1⅓ cups fine fresh bread crumbs 2 eggs · ⅔ cup whipping cream · seasoning 6–8 slices bacon.

Grind the chicken and ham, add the bread crumbs, eggs, cream, and seasoning. Line a 9-inch by 5-inch loaf pan with the bacon, put in the chicken mixture, and cover with greased foil. Bake in a preheated 375°F. oven for 1¼ hours, serve hot or cold.

Serves 6–8

This method of lining a pan may be used for the liver pâtés on page 25.

The picture on page 60 shows a similar galantine to the recipe above, but in this recipe 1 lb. chicken and 1 lb. ham is used, the chicken is ground finely, but the ham chopped to give a slightly more definite texture.

Picture frame flan

This is an excellent way to make a flan for a special occasion.

Cooking time   *25–30 minutes*
Oven temperature   *See page 220*

3 recipes flan (fleur) pastry (see page 216)
1 (16 oz.) can Bing cherries
1 (16 oz.) can pitted red tart cherries
2 (11 oz.) cans mandarin oranges
1 tablespoon arrowroot *or* cornstarch.

Roll out the pastry and use most of this to make a rectangle shape. Put onto the back of a baking sheet; this makes it easier to remove. Roll out the remaining pastry and make long strips to go round the edge of the oblong of pastry; this makes the 'picture frame'. Prick the bottom, and bake in a preheated 425°F. oven for 10–12 minutes, or until golden brown. Drain the cans of fruit and arrange the fruit in neat lines, as shown in the picture on page 200. Blend the arrowroot with 1¾ cups of the mixed fruit syrup, then boil, stirring constantly, until smooth and thick. Let stand until slightly cooled, then brush over the fruit to glaze. The syrup may be tinted with a very few drops of red or yellow coloring, if desired.   *Serves 12*

Cherry flan

Cooking time   *20–25 minutes*
Oven temperature   *400°F.*

1 recipe (fleur) pastry (see page 216)
1 vanilla cream recipe (see page 325)
1 (16 oz.) can pitted red tart cherries *or* cherry pie filling.

Roll out the pastry and line an 8-inch flan ring or layer cake pan. Prick the bottom, and bake in a preheated 425°F. oven for 10–12 minutes, or until golden brown. Make and cool the vanilla cream. Spread half the well-drained cherries or the cherry pie filling into the flan ring, top with the vanilla cream and decorate with well-drained cherries or cherry pie filling (see picture on page 225).

Serves 6

Raisin apple meringue

Cooking time *2 hours*
Oven temperature *300°F.*

4 medium peeled and cored baking apples
⅔ cup seedless raisins · ¼ cup granulated sugar
juice 1 orange · 1 tablespoon rum *or* extra orange juice · 2 egg whites
¼–½ cup granulated sugar*.
TO SERVE: whipped cream.

* use the larger amount of sugar for a cold dessert.

Slice the apples, put into a shallow 2½-pint ovenproof dish with the raisins, sugar, orange juice, and rum or extra orange juice. Cover tightly or use foil, and bake in a preheated 300°F. oven for about 40 minutes, or until the apples are just tender. Remove from the oven. Whisk the egg whites until stiff. Gradually whisk in half the sugar, then fold in the remaining sugar. Pile or pipe the meringue over the apples. To serve hot, return to the oven for about 35 minutes until the meringue is set and a light golden color. To serve cold, bake the meringue in a preheated 200°F. oven for about 1 hour. (See picture on page 248). Serve hot or cold with whipped cream.

Serves 4–5

Ways to decorate pastry

The tarts shown in the picture on page 201 owe much of their attractive appearance to the way they are decorated.
1. Coconut cheesecake, page 331. The edges of this were made by cutting the pastry at regular intervals, then folding alternate pieces back to give a 'turreted' effect. The top of the cheesecake is decorated with sifted confectioners' sugar and candied cherries.
2. A fruit tart. The pastry edge is covered with tiny circles to form a pattern.
3. Honey tart, page 219. Here the pastry edge gives a 'sunflower' effect. Cut the edge at regular intervals, then fold the pastry diagonally.
4. The jam tart, page 219, is given a much more effective appearance by its pointed edging and strips of pastry.
5. The blackcurrant tart, similar to jam tart, page 219, had a fluted edge made by pinching the pastry with the forefinger and thumb. The top of the tart was decorated with shapes in pastry – these may be baked on top of the filling or separately and then put on top.
6. A marmalade tart is decorated with strips of pastry cut with a pastry wheel, arranged in the center of the tart like the spokes of a wheel. The pattern round the edge is cut with a melon baller.

Mincemeat

Cooking time *None*

½ cup chopped beef suet *or* melted margarine
1 small grated apple · 1 cup currants, 2 cups chopped mixed candied peel, 1 cup seedless white raisins · ½ cup brown sugar
1 cup blanched almonds
finely grated peel and juice 1 large lemon
1 teaspoon cinnamon · ¾ teaspoon nutmeg
¼ teaspoon allspice
⅓ cup brandy, whisky *or* rum.

Mix all the ingredients thoroughly. Place in sterilized dry jars and seal. Keep in a cool dry place. Use these quantities of sugar, fat, and alcohol if you wish mincemeat to keep well. Make certain fruit is dry. If it has been washed, let it dry for at least 24 hours before making mincemeat.

More formal occasions

There are many pictures in this book depicting dishes or complete menus which would be suitable for entertaining – the recipes are in the earlier part of the book or included with those below. Choose a well balanced menu, many of the dishes in the various chapters would be ideal for a special dinner party, especially those at the end of the sections 'to impress'. A good meal need not be an expensive one, just consider the tastes of your guests – the time you have to prepare and serve the meal and plan accordingly. It is a good idea to have at least one cold dish, or even two, i.e. the hors d'oeuvre and the dessert.
In many of the pictures in this book are complete meals that are suitable for parties, for example: Smoked salmon, chicken chasseur (see opposite), and meringues.
Roast pork with stuffed tomatoes, coconut stuffed peaches, (see opposite) and jam sauce. This could be followed by cheese, or the meal start with an interesting soup or light hors d'oeuvre.
A typical Christmas menu page 108. Ignite the pudding by pouring over warm brandy, then lighting.
Anchovy eggs, chicken and ham galantine, and pineapple fruit salad.
Give the main dish an original touch either by a clever garnish or a new stuffing or flavoring. Try flavoring leg of spring lamb with fresh rosemary – put the herbs on the meat before roasting. Slit the skin of a leg of veal before roasting and insert tiny pieces of a clove of garlic (whole cloves are too strong) and very narrow strips of canned anchovy.
Casserole dishes of meat, poultry, or fish are ideal for parties and there are many in this book.
Make your desserts 'fit the season', have either luscious fruit pies, tarts, cold desserts or mince pies for Christmas season parties or the unusual Pashka for Easter.
Always have a good selection of cheese to complete the meal and a cup of perfect coffee.

Stuffed eggplant

Cooking time *30–35 minutes*
Oven temperature *425°F.*

2 large eggplants · ¼ cup butter *or* fat
1 onion · 2 tomatoes
½ lb. ground lamb *or* beef · ½ teaspoon salt

¼ teaspoon cayenne pepper (optional)
⅔ cup fine fresh bread crumbs.
FOR THE TOPPING: ¼ cup toasted bread crumbs
2 tablespoons butter.

Wash the eggplants and halve them. Scoop out the pulp, leaving four thin shells. Dice the eggplant pulp and cook in the butter or fat in a covered pan with the chopped onion over a low heat until soft. Skin and chop the tomatoes. Mix all the ingredients (except the toasted bread crumbs) together, and fill the shells with the mixture. Sprinkle with the toasted bread crumbs and dab with butter. Bake in a preheated 425°F. oven for 20 minutes. *Serves 4*

Chicken chasseur

Cooking time *2–3 hours*

2½ cups *chasseur* sauce made with:
2 tablespoons fat · ¼ cup all-purpose flour
2 large tomatoes · 2–3 mushrooms *or* mushroom stems · 1 onion · 1 carrot · 2½ cups brown stock · 3–4 tablespoons sherry, (optional)
seasoning · 1 small roasting *or* stewing chicken
1 (6 oz.) can tomato paste.

Make the chasseur sauce by heating the fat and stirring in the flour. Cook for several minutes until brown, but not burned. Stir well during cooking. Chop tomatoes, mushrooms, onion, and carrot. Add to the brown fat mixture with the stock, sherry and seasoning. Simmer covered tightly for about 45 minutes until the sauce has thickened and the vegetables are very tender. Cut the chicken into pieces, and put into the sauce. Cook for 1 hour in the case of a young roasting chicken, 2 hours in the case of a stewing fowl. The picture on page 60 shows a chicken cooked in this way and in order to give additional flavor and color it is topped with concentrated, well-seasoned tomato paste.
You may also add a few small onions and green beans to the pan for the last 10–15 minutes.
Serves 4

Pashka

Cooking time *30 minutes*

1 lb. cream cheese · 1 lb. cottage cheese
1 cup butter · 4 egg yolks
1 cup cultured soured cream *or* coffee cream plus 2 tablespoons lemon juice
1½ cups granulated sugar
1–1½ teaspoons vanilla extract
1½ cups blanched chopped almonds
⅔ cup seedless raisins
¾ cup chopped mixed candied peel.

Mix cream and cottage cheese together and put into several thicknesses of cheesecloth. Let stand in a cold place (not the refrigerator) to drip overnight to make sure that the cheese is really dry. Next day, press through a nylon (not metal) sieve. Melt the butter, and let stand until cool but not set. Mix egg yolks and soured cream, add sugar and vanilla extract, and beat all together for about 10 minutes, or until the sugar has dissolved.
Stir in the melted butter and beat again until the mixture is like whipped cream. Stir into the cheese mixture, add almonds, whole raisins, and candied peel then turn into a heavy saucepan. Put the pan on a very low heat and cook, stirring constantly. When the mixture shows signs of boiling (in about 30 minutes), remove it from the heat at once and stir until it is almost cold. Take a sterilized earthenware flower pot (nearest approximation to a pashka mold) or a similar shaped vessel (not metal) of about 3½-pint capacity with draining hole or holes, line it with cheesecloth and turn in the prepared mixture. Set the pot on a rack over a plate, lay a piece of wax paper over the mixture, set a saucer on top, and weigh down with about a 2 lb. weight to press. Place in the refrigerator overnight. To serve, remove weight, etc., cheesecloth and contents from flower pot and invert onto a plate. Remove cheesecloth, smooth over cheesecloth marks with a knife or spoon, decorate with an artificial flower and serve. Pashka should be cut horizontally from the top and can be served with a rich yeast dough bun, a rich fruity yeast cake or a roll resembling brioche. Any of this dessert not eaten immediately, may be covered with wax paper, then with foil or a bowl and kept for a few days in the refrigerator until wanted again. (See picture page 245.) *16–32 portions*

Coconut stuffed peaches

Cooking time *few minutes*

8 halved drained canned peaches
¼ cup butter · ¼ cup granulated sugar
¾ cup flaked coconut
Jam sauce (see page 187).

Put the drained peaches into a dish. Blend the butter, sugar, and coconut together. Put a little of the butter mixture into each halved peach, and heat under the broiler. Serve with hot or cold jam sauce. Illustrated on page 77. *Serves 4*

Ice cream sodas

Cooking time *few minutes*

1–2 cups (½ lb.) ripe fruit (cherries, strawberries, raspberries, etc.) · ⅔ cup water
⅓ cup granulated sugar
4–5 scoops ice cream
approximately 2½ cups cold milk
approximately 2½–3½ cups soda water. (See page 335).

Prepare the fruit; make a syrup of the water and sugar, and poach the fruit in this for a few minutes, then cool. Put in the bottom of four or five tall glasses, top with the ice cream, cold milk, and fill with soda water.

INDEX